Textbook of Human Genetics

An illustration of the varied approaches that are often necessary to determine the hereditary nature of a human trait.

"Invitation to a Glass of Milk" by Henri de Toulouse-Lautrec, drawn for an invitation to a party. The self-caricature illustrates some of the evidence, supported by the fact that his parents were first cousins, that the painter suffered from pycnodysostosis, mediated by an autosomal recessive gene. Note the short stature and the narrow lower jaw (micrognathia), which he hid to some extent by growing a beard. The sketch shows also his tendency to wear a hat, especially in photographs, apparently to protect—and hide—incomplete ossification of the skull, including a persistent anterior fontanelle. (Maroteaux and Lamy, 1965.) Courtesy of P. Maroteaux, the *Journal of the American Medical Association,* and the Musée Toulouse-Lautrec Albi, Paris.

Textbook of
Human Genetics

THIRD EDITION

MAX LEVITAN

Mount Sinai School of Medicine
of the City University of New York

New York   Oxford
OXFORD UNIVERSITY PRESS
1988

Oxford University Press

Oxford   New York   Toronto
Delhi   Bombay   Calcutta   Madras   Karachi
Petaling Jaya   Singapore   Hong Kong   Tokyo
Nairobi   Dar es Salaam   Cape Town
Melbourne   Auckland

and associated companies in
Beirut   Berlin   Ibadan   Nicosia

Published by Oxford University Press, Inc.,
200 Madison Avenue, New York, New York 10016

Oxford is a registered trademark of Oxford University Press

Library of Congress Cataloging-in-Publication Data
Levitan, Max.
Textbook of human genetics.
Bibliography: p.   Includes index.
1. Human genetics.   2. Human chromosome abnormalities.
3. Medical genetics.   I. Title.
[DNLM: 1. Genetics, Medical.   QH 431 L667t]
QH431.L41785   1988   573.2'1   86-33130
ISBN 0-19-504935-7

1 2 3 4 5 6 7 8 9

Printed in the United States of America
on acid-free paper

To
Myron M. Kaplan
and
Chana Levitan Gerber

A friend may well be reckoned
the masterpiece of Nature
—EMERSON

Preface to the Third Edition

The preface to the second edition noted "the increasing influence of molecular biology on human genetics." It also stated that developments in immunogenetics "are coming so thick and fast that the subject will undoubtedly demand a chapter all to itself in the next edition." Both predictions have been borne out to an extent undreamed of even five years ago. As a result, it has become necessary not only to have the indicated "chapter all to itself" for immunogenetics but also to have a chapter devoted entirely to the molecular biology of human genes. Indeed, the new molecular methods have caused major revisions in the discussion of such topics as linkage and thalassemia, and they are responsible for the many recent advances that necessitated a separate chapter on the genetics of tumors and cancers.

The major problem in preparing this new edition was how to incorporate all this new material and not have the book become so cumbersome that it would discourage the typical college student, undergraduate or graduate, from even beginning to read it. It was decided to follow two main approaches: (1) to condense, wherever possible, the classical aspects of the field; and (2) to modify the reviewlike pattern of the first two editions by removing direct references unless they were needed to identify data in figures, tables, or exercises. The first of these approaches had the effect of combining into single chapters such topics as the effects of chance and the correction of truncate methods of collecting progeny data, which were treated in separate chapters in earlier editions. It was hoped that the second approach would not only make the material more accessible—especially for the student dipping into human genetics for the first time—but would also cut publishing costs enough to keep the price within the reach of such students.

One exception to the basic tendency to reduce and shorten is the new chapter on polygenic inheritance. In response to many requests and comments from teachers of human genetics, it was decided that this topic should be expanded, especially since it was felt that future advances in clinical genetics will necessitate a more fundamental understanding of this area.

Another significant change from the previous edition—following the example of Drs. Kurt Hirschhorn, Robert Desnick, and other leading teachers of human genetics—has been to begin the book by introducing the basic features of Mendelian inheritance in humans, including the study of pedigrees. This is followed, as in previous editions, by a discussion of the chromosomal background and the known chromosomal abnormalities (with aberrations of number and aberrations of structure discussed in separate chapters). A chapter on the relation between gene and phenotype is followed by the basic chapter on molecular biology. This, in turn, is succeeded by a chapter devoted to modifications related to sex, especially X-linkage. A series of chapters then emphasize the classic, mathematically related aspects of the field, with discussion first centering on problems of the single locus and then on multiple loci. Related to the latter are a chapter on gene interactions, including a detailed look into our new understanding of thalassemia, and the afore-mentioned chapter on polygenic inheritance. Finally, three specialized chapters deal with immunogenetics, the genetics of tumors, and genetic counseling.

As in the case of the previous two editions, this work would have been impos-sible without the splendid cooperation and assistance of so many persons that it is impossible to give proper credit to all of them. I am particularly grateful to the many colleagues named in the figure legends who have taken the time from already busy schedules to provide me with illustrative material drawn from their research. Drs. Tibor Barka, Fred Gilbert, and Sara Anne Levitan have been especially helpful in reading and criticizing selected portions of the manuscript. I am also deeply grateful to Dr. Ashley Montagu, not only for the sections of the first edition, written with so much style, that have been carried over into the next two, but also because his instigation and encouragement in the first place enabled this enterprise to become a reality. Finally, the personnel of Oxford University Press, especially Wil-liam Curtis, Jeffrey House, and Henry Krawitz, have my gratitude for their splen-did work and encouragement.

February 1987   M.L.
New York

Contents

Textbook of Human Genetics

Simple Mendelian Inheritance

All branches of genetics owe their standing as a science primarily to the rediscov-ery—and full appreciation—in 1900 of experiments performed some 35 to 40 years earlier by the Bohemian monk Gregor Mendel.

Mendel studied 14 varieties of the common garden pea which differed in the seven characteristics shown in the left-hand column of Table 1–1. When one of two forms acts as the male plant and the other as the female, he obtained the data shown in the other columns of Table 1–1. The offspring of the original crosses, termed the F_1 ("F-one," meaning "first filial") generation, all showed only one form of each trait. Crossing the F_1 (or allowing them to self-pollinate, as is more natural for peas) produced the second filial (F_2) generation. Here in each case, both original forms, the so-called P_1 or parental traits, reappeared. Regularly, however, the form which had appeared exclusively in the F_1 was the more frequent of the two forms in the F_2. Mendel noted that in fact there was a regular tendency for the F_1 form to be three times as frequent as the other in the F_2. Thus was born the classical 3:1 ratio of genetics.

Mendel was so impressed that these results came out in a similar way in all seven sets of experiments that he coined terms for the alternate forms of each trait. He dubbed the P_1 form that appeared exclusively in the F_1 and in three-fourths of the F_2 as *dominant*. The behavior of the other P_1 form, which did not appear in the F_1 but reappeared in one-fourth of the F_2, suggested to him that it was somehow "hiding" in the F_1; he therefore called it *recessive*.

It is to Gregor Mendel's eternal credit that, as exciting as were these regular results, he did not stop there. Instead, he asked a further question: What are the breeding characteristics of the F_2 of the dominant type? If self-pollinated, are they (a) like the F_1, producing both types of progeny, (b) like the P_1, which when self-pollinated produce only plants like themselves ("true breeding"), or (c) different in breeding behavior from either P_1 or F_1? Similarly, did the F_2 of the recessive form breed true, like their grandparental counterparts, or did they, once they had now reappeared, act differently, just as the F_1 dominants had bred differently from *their* counterparts of an earlier generation?

The results of these further experiments are summarized in Table 1–2. Again the data for each of the seven characteristics were very similar. In every case all the "recessive" F_2 bred true. The dominant F_2, however, were of two kinds. Some bred

Table 1-1 The appearance of the F_1 and F_2 in Mendel's classic experiments with the garden pea (from Mendel, 1865)

Trait	F_1	F_2		Ratio
Seed form	round	5474 round	:1850 wrinkled	2.96:1
Cotyledon color	yellow	6022 yellow	:2001 green	3.01:1
Seed coat color	gray-brown	705 gray-brown	:224 white	3.15:1
Pod form	inflated	882 inflated	:299 constricted	2.95:1
Unripe pod color	green	428 green	:152 yellow	2.82:1
Flower position	axial	651 axial	:207 terminal	3.14:1
Plant height	tall	787 tall	:277 dwarf	2.84:1
All Traits	dominant	14,949 dominant	:5010 recessive	2:98:1

Table 1-2 The data in Mendel's tests of the breeding characteristics of the F_2 "dominant" plants as shown in Table 1-1 (from Mendel, 1865)

Trait	Produced Only "Dominant" Progeny (Parental Form)	Produced Both Types ("Hybrid" Form)	Total
Seed form	193	372	565
Cotyledon color	166	353	519
Seed coat color	36	64	100
Pod form	29	71	100
Color of unripe pod	40	60	100
(repeated experiment)	35	65	100
Flower position	33	67	100
Plant height	28	72	100
Total	560	1124	1684
Ratio	1 :	2.007	
Indicated proportion of F_2[a]	1/4	1/2	

[a]Plus 1/4 recessive, all found to be true-breeding (like parental type).

true, resembling the P_1, while others resembled the F_1 in producing both dominant and recessive progeny. Although Mendel may not have analyzed some of the traits correctly, in every experiment there appeared to be approximately twice as many of the nontrue-breeders as of the true-breeders.

Mendel was now able to enumerate a new ratio. He saw that the 3:1 of the F_2 could be restated as 1:2:1 in terms of both appearances and breeding characteristics.

THE LAW OF SEGREGATION

The second ratio provided the clue to his major hypothesis, a hypothesis that has been enshrined as the First Law of Genetics. The data could be explained, he reasoned, if the "hybrids," as he termed the F_1, received factors for the dominant and recessive traits from the respective P_1, and, despite the nonappearance of the recessive trait, would pass on these factors equally. Half the eggs and pollen of the F_1, in other words, contained a factor for the dominant parental form and half a factor for the recessive parental form.

Hence, 1/4 of the fertilizations needed to produce the F_2, that is, 1/2 times 1/2, would receive a factor for the dominant trait from both eggs and pollen; having only dominant factors, they would be dominants that are true-breeding. Moreover, 1/2 of the F_2 would be dominants, which are not true-breeding, resembling the F_1, because 1/4 of the fertilizations would receive the dominant factor in the egg and the recessive factor in the pollen, and 1/4 of the dominant in the pollen and the recessive in the egg. Furthermore, 1/4 of the fertilizations would receive a factor for the recessive trait from both eggs and pollen; they would be true-breeding recessives.

The critical point is that the hybrids produced as many gametes containing the recessive factor as those containing the dominant one. Hence, the factors of the parents did not blend in the hybrids. Instead, these factors remained intact and were then *segregated* by the hybrids when they produced seed for the next generation.

A more formal statement of this First Law of Mendel is:

> When an individual is formed by a union of egg and pollen (or sperm), he receives corresponding genetic materials from both parents. These parental contributions separate when he in turn produces gametes; so that, for any specified piece of the genetic material, each gamete he produces contains either the maternal or the paternal contribution.

Since 1900 some traits have been found in which the F_1 from a cross such as Mendel made are intermediate in appearance between the characteristics of the P_1. These characteristics are therefore said to be incompletely dominant or incompletely recessive. In still other traits we have quantitative evidence that both P_1 traits are equally evident in the F_1. These are called codominant traits. We shall have more to say about them in Chapter 3.

THE PHYSICAL BASIS OF THE FIRST LAW

Why was Mendel's work accepted so readily after its rediscovery in the early years of this century? A major cause was the demonstration by Sutton, Boveri, and others that the First Law fitted so well what had by that time become known about meiosis, the form of cell division that results in the formation of male and female gametes.

As illustrated in Fig. 1–1 for spermatogenesis, meiosis consists of two divisions. In the first of these the typical chromosome is seen to find and pair with another in the cell (top line, zygotene portion of Prophase I). The chromosomes that pair are not only morphologically similar (the same length, staining properties, and so forth), but we know they contain corresponding genetic materials. One had been contributed by each of the two parents, so we can refer to one as the maternal member of the pair and one as the paternal member. Although the material had been replicated earlier, it is not until after they pair that each of the meiotic chromosomes takes on the typical double-stranded (two-chromatid) form in which chromosomes are usually seen. The pair with its four chromatids is now called a *tetrad*.

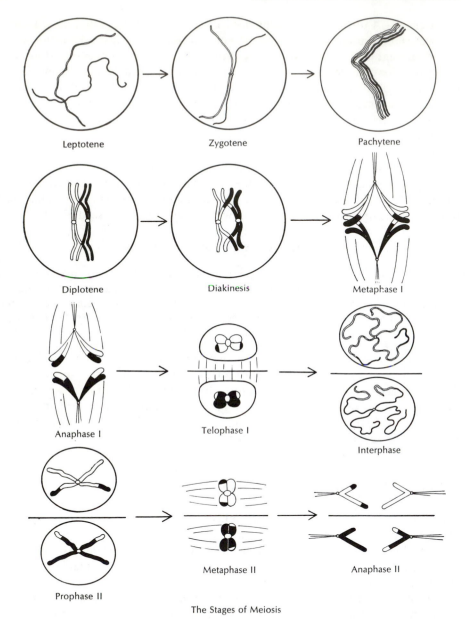

The Stages of Meiosis

Fig. 1-1 Highly schematized diagram of stages of meiosis in which a single pair of chromosomes is followed. (Slightly modified from Rhoades, 1950). This author uses alternative frequently used names for the stages of Prophase 1 based on the Greek root *nema*, meaning "thread." (Courtesy of M. M. Rhoades and the *Journal of Heredity*.)

Figure 1–1 shows that the effect of meiosis is to *segregate* the maternal and paternal chromosomes that had paired in zygotene, so that each of the resulting gametes—indicated by the single chromosomes going to the poles in Anaphase II—receives only one member of each pair. This is exactly the result predicted by Mendel's First Law.

Figure 1–1 shows that in pairing the chromosomes do not fuse. They retain separate identities. Even when four strands (the tetrad) are seen (e.g., in pachytene), these are in *two* distinct chromosomes, each consisting of two chromatids closely associated at their centromeres.

The degree of association of the centromeres in effect determines the number of chromosome units present. In Anaphase I the association of the chromatids of each chromosome remains tight; thus the number of chromosomes in the cell remains unchanged. Half go to one pole and the resultant secondary spermatocyte, and half to the other pole. In Anaphase II (and a typical anaphase of mitotis) the chromatid centromeres dissociate, and each chromatid becomes a unit chromosome.

One may now ask: If meiosis accomplishes its purpose by segregating the originally maternal and paternal chromosomes, why are two divisions necessary in meiosis? Has not the segregation been effected at the end of the first division (Anaphase I and Telophase I)?

The answer is that sometimes paired genetic materials remain together after

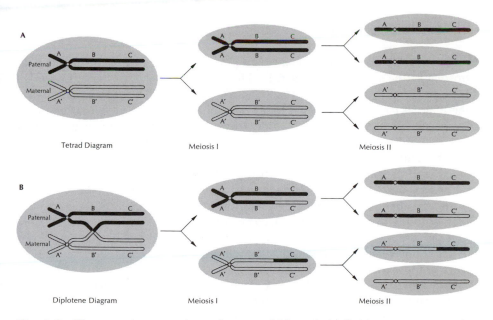

Fig. 1–2 How crossing over determines at which meiotic division gene segregation takes place. **A.** Without crossing over. Note that all the paternal and maternal factors were separated at meiosis I. Meiosis II merely serves as a haploid mitosis. **B.** With crossing over. For some genes, the paternal and maternal contribution (A and A', B and B') are separated at meiosis I; others, such as C and C', are not segregated, however, until meiosis II.

the first meiotic division. This happens because the maternal and paternal chromosomes may exchange pieces during the first meiotic division: the phenomenon of *crossing over.* These exchanges, which had occurred earlier, become cytologically evident in diplotene. At that time the members of the pair are already starting to separate even though the tetrad has not yet reached the metaphase plate. The genetic materials exchanged in most crossovers do not segregate until the second meiotic division.

The point is illustrated in Fig. 1–2. In part 1 there is no crossing over, so all the corresponding genetic materials, indicated by A and A′ and so on, have been segregated in Meiosis I. In part 2, however, crossing over causes C and C′ to remain together after Meiosis I. These maternal and paternal materials are not segregated until the second division.

Genetic materials on the same chromosome are *syntenic* (noun form: synteny, from syn = same, tainia = ribbon). If they are close together, they are also said to be *linked* (noun form: linkage). These terms will be discussed more in later chapters.

Similar considerations apply to meiosis in the female. The basic processes are the same although usually only one product of the second division becomes a functional ovum. When it is recalled that each fertilization also uses only one sperm, that is, only one functional product of a male meiosis, it is clear that in either case the gametes of a *series* of meioses give rise to the conclusions of the First Law.

THE GENE CONCEPT

We owe a great deal of our understanding of crossing over to experiments with Drosophila, the so-called fruit flies, by Thomas Hunt Morgan, who was awarded the Nobel Prize in Medicine in 1933, and his colleagues. They concluded that (1) inheritance is particulate, which is to say that only a small piece of the chromosome is responsible for each trait, and (2) ordinarily this "particle" is in the same position on both of the chromosomes that first pair and are then segregated in meiosis.

This unit of genetics is now universally known as the *gene,* a term that was coined in 1908 by Johannsen, a Danish plant geneticist. The chromosomes that pair and segregate at meiosis are referred to as *homologous chromosomes,* and the position on them of corresponding genes for a trait is the *locus* of the gene. The different forms that the genes of a locus can take are referred to as *alleles.* Quite often the terms gene, allele, and locus are used interchangeably. Another major advance came when it was established that the alleles of a locus could take multiple forms, not just two, in the populations.

The pioneer geneticists who worked with *Drosophila,* corn, mice, poultry, and other organisms defined the gene as the smallest amount of genetic material that could be separated from adjacent chromosomal material by crossing over without disrupting its activity. This concept came under fire when the genetics of microorganisms showed that crossing over can take place within the confines of the traditional gene, that is, that the unit of recombination may be different from the unit of action. It was rescued, so to speak, by the emergence of molecular genetics. One of its fundamental findings is that the unit gene is a valid entity, with a definite beginning and end.

The genes at a given locus may be the same on both members of a pair of homologous chromosomes. This would usually be the case, for example, in any member of a true-breeding line. This individual is said to be a *homozygote* (adjective, homozygous) for this locus. If the genes at homologous loci in one individual are different, such, for example, that one is responsible for green seed color in peas and one for yellow seed color, the individual is *heterozygous* and is referred to as a *heterozygote* for that locus.

The description of the genes carried by an individual is the *genotype,* as contrasted to the description of the traits shown, the *phenotype.* These terms, too, were coined by Johannsen. They are especially useful because of the phenomenon of dominance. Thus the genotypic ratio of Mendel's F_2 was 1:2:1, but, because of dominance, their phenotypic ratio was 3:1.

SEGREGATION IN HUMANS

In humans and other animals the validity of the law of segregation is best shown by the offspring when one parent is a heterozygote for a dominant trait and the other parent exhibits its recessive counterpart. This is sometimes called a "backcross" because it resembles the mating of an F_1 from an experimental cross (such as Mendel's) "back" to a homozygote from one of the P_1 types. When the mating involves an individual of the dominant phenotype whose genotype is unknown, it is called a "testcross," since the progeny from the mating to the recessive type can test whether the individual with dominant phenotype is homozygous or heterozygous. If the individual is heterozygous, progeny of the recessive type are expected, but none are expected if the individual is homozygous.

The special value of the backcross and testcross is that the gametes of the recessive parent cannot by themselves determine the phenotypes of the progeny. Hence the ratio of phenotypes in the progeny reflects exactly the ratio of gamete types in the dominant parent.

Table 1–3 Progeny from testcrosses for several dominant traits (For references see Table 5–1 of Levitan and Montagu, 1977)

Trait	Number of Test Cross Sibships	Normal	Affected	Total
Anonychia with ectrodactyly (Fig. 1–9)	39	57	66	123
Elliptocytosis (ovalocytosis), both loci (Fig. 13–2)	65	113	99	212
Epidermolysis bullosa, all dominant forms (Fig. 1–3)	50	80	62	142
Nail-patella syndrome (Fig. 1–4)	157	268	288	556
Total	311	518	515	1 033
Ratio		1.006 :	1	

Persons exhibiting rare dominant abnormal traits are almost always hetero-zygotes since one of their parents almost always has the more common recessive normal trait. Hence the matings of persons with these dominants with normal indi-viduals are almost always crosses that test the law of segregation. Table 1–3 shows the results of a number of such matings; some of the traits involved are illustrated in Figs. 1–3, 1–4, and 1–9. The data establish that heterozygotes for dominant traits produce gametes containing the dominant and recessive alleles in 1:1 ratio, as pre-dicted by Mendel's First Law.

Similar results are found among the progeny of heterozygotes for codominant genes. In Table 1–4, for example, the matings of persons with blood type MN (dis-cussed further in Chapter 16) to type M and type N individuals are testcrosses. Note also that when both parents are type MN the progeny fit closely the Mende-lian 1:2:1 ratio.

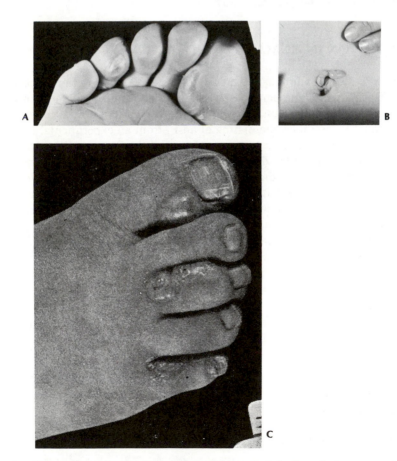

Fig. 1–3 Characteristic lesions in types of epidermolysis bullosa that appear to be dom-inant. **A.** Epidermolysis bullosa simplex, Weber–Cockayne type (localized to hands and feet). **B** and **C.** Epidermolysis bullosa simplex, Koebner type (generalized). The progeny counts in Table 1–3 include these disorders. (From Gedde–Dahl, 1969. Courtesy of T. Gedde–Dahl, Jr.)

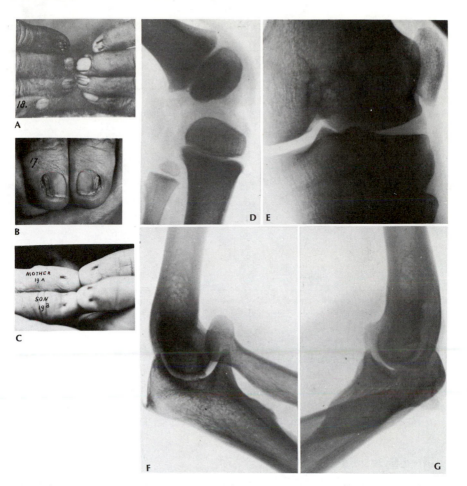

Fig. 1-4 A–C   Nail defects in the nail-patella syndrome (anonycho-osteo-dysplasia). In **A** they are most severe on the index fingers and (not shown) the thumbs. The little fingers appear normal. **B.** Dystrophy of thumbnails in an affected brother. The lunulae are abnormally large. **C.** Complete absence of thumbnails in a daughter of the patient in **A** and in her eight-year old son. **D–G.** Some of the bone defects encountered in the nail-patella syndrome. **D.** Absence of the patella in the eight-year old boy whose nail defects are shown in **C.** (The epiphyseal centers of his femur and tibia have not yet fused to the shafts.) The boy's mother has a patella (**E**) but suffers greater difficulties in walking because the patella—and the associated extensor tendon—is displaced laterally. In other affected the patella may be in normal position but hypoplastic. **F** and **G**: Typical elbow defects. In **F** the head of the right radius, somewhat abnormally shaped, is displaced forward; in **G** the left radius, similarly abnormal, is displaced backward. In other cases the capitulum of the humerus is poorly developed, compounding the problem. Note also, in **F,** the exostosis of the coronoid process of the ulna. (**A–D** courtesy of L. S. Wildervanck. **E–G** from Wildervanck, 1950b; courtesy of L. S. Wildervanck and *Acta Radiologica.*)

Table 1-4 Offspring in 416 marriages between various M-N blood types. Data from Wiener et al. (1963).

Father	Mother	Progeny M	Progeny MN	Progeny N	Total Offspring	Number of Families
M	M	71	1[a]	0	72	42
N	N	0	0	29	29	20
M	N	0	43	0	43	23
N	M	0	24	0	24	13
All M × N		0	67	0	67	36
M	MN	67	46	0	113	63
MN	M	60	55	0	115	59
All M × MN		127	101	0	228	122
N	MN	0	31	44	75	39
MN	N	0	40	27	67	35
All N × MN		0	71	71	142	74
MN	MN	61	118	53	232	122
Totals		259	358	153	770	416

[a]This apparent contradiction to the laws of heredity is believed to be owing to illegitimacy, but it may represent a new mutation, a change in the genetic material of one of the parents.

GENETIC INFERENCE IN HUMANS

Despite the good fit of these data, such tables have not been the way the heredity of most human traits has been inferred. Instead the first clue to their inheritance has usually come from the study of pedigrees.

Pedigree Symbols

As with genetic nomenclature, no universal agreement on pedigree symbols exists among human geneticists. The result is that superficially most of the pedigrees in this book and those in American and most continental journals look very different from many of the pedigrees published in their British counterparts (e.g., Fig. 1–5). In the former, squares represent males and circles females, whereas the British in their pedigrees favor the standard sex symbols: a ♂ for the male (the mythological sign of Ares (Mars; shield and spear)) and ♀ (the mirror of Venus) for the female. In the square-circle system, unknown sex is usually shown by a diamond; in the British system by a circle.

Almost all published pedigrees, however, contain many elements in common. In order to refer more easily to pedigree individuals in the text of a paper or book, they are numbered almost invariably by generation, in Roman numerals which increase from top to bottom placed in the left-hand margin, and by Arabic numerals which increase from left to right within each generation. Thus the three persons in the second generation of pedigree A of Fig. 1–5 would be referred to, reading from left to right, as II-1, II-2, and II-3. Only rarely are numbers out of order, as are V-51 and V-52 in Fig. 1–5**B**.

Since all the persons on a line are numbered consecutively, irrespective of relationship, one must be very careful in distinguishing siblings from spouses and from the others of the same generation who are not related genetically to the carriers of the trait under study. In Fig. 1–5**A,** for example, the only sib of II-1 is II-3.

This numbering system, incidentally, is the nearest thing to a universal convention among human geneticists, so much so that many authors assume implicitly that the reader understands it and leave most or all of the numbers off the chart. Some of pedigrees nevertheless number all individuals consecutively irrespective of generation, but moving in each line from left to right as usual. Under such a scheme, II-1 in Fig. 1–5A would be number 3, II-3 number 5, III-2 number 7, etc.

To save space, uninformative progeny are often not shown individually; instead they are represented by a number inside a sex symbol: ⑨. Generation V of Fig. 1–5**B,** for example, contains 17 persons of unknown sex and 2 males who are not shown individually. Note, however, that they are assigned numbers, the 2 males being V-26 and V-27. In Fig. 17–2 normal individuals are not numbered at all.

Husband and wife are joined by a horizontal line, directly: □————○ ♂————♀ or less desirably, one connecting small dropped lines: ♂————♀ . Dice has suggested that the symbols be connected directly through their tops, □————◌◻ except when the same person marries twice. □————○————◻ but this has not found wide acceptance. Generally the male partner is shown on the left and the female on the right (as in all "large animal" genetics) unless a special exigency, e.g. a female with two husbands (III-5, -6, and -7 in Fig. 1–5A), deems otherwise. An illegitimate union is indicated by a dotted horizontal: □----○ . Consanguineous unions of whatever degree are shown usually by a double line: □═══○ . Uninformative spouses and those who were undoubtedly normal often are omitted entirely from the chart, e.g., the husbands of IV-4 in Fig. 1–5**A.**

A line dropped from the marriage horizontal leads to a second horizontal which we may term the "fraternity" or "progeny" line. Short perpendiculars attach the progeny to this line in the order of birth, from eldest on the left to youngest on the right. A broken horizontal progeny line, such as the one to which generation II in Fig. 1–5**B** is attached, indicates that the birth order is uncertain, and a broken vertical from it to one of the progeny indicates usually an adoption or doubtful legitimacy of the child. Note, however, that the authors of Figure 1–5A did not use this device to denote the likelihood that IV-7 and IV-8 are probably not the legitimate children of III-7; instead they mention the point in the legend.

General unanimity prevails also in the manner of designating affected persons. Those exhibiting the trait under study are indicated by an inked-in sex symbol, normals by an empty symbol. Normals who probably have a gene in question but do not express it, due to dominance or incompete penetrance, are often partially inked in, thus: ▣. The major difficulties arise when there is variable expressivity and when two or more traits are being followed simultaneously. In these cases most authors subdivide the sex symbol and ink in the parts according to the number of variables present (Figs. 1–10 and 14–8). When many normal traits, such as blood groups and serum types, are known for each person in addition to the major trait under study (see Fig. 1–5), they are generally printed adjacent to or below the sex symbol to avoid cluttering it up further. Note that both techniques may be employed, as in Fig. 1–5. In such cases, close study of the "key" to the pedigree is indispensable. When several traits are present in a family, it is often better to draw separate pedigree charts for each trait than to confuse matters by too much subdivision of the symbols. In Fig. 14–8, all of the complexities relate to the hemoglobin picture.

A *sine qua non* of every published pedigree is an arrow pointing to the *propositus* or *proband* (or index case), the first person in the pedigree examined by the investigator(s). The propositus (proband) is in effect the person responsible for our detection of the family study. An occasional pedigree will have more than one propositus. We will see later that the propositus is very important in evaluating possible ascertainment biases in pooled data. In the British style pedigrees, the arrow should point to the left in order to avoid confusion with the male sex symbol. Note III-7 and III-42 in Figs. 1–5A and **B,** respectively.

On the subject of ascertainment, it is very useful to differentiate in some way the persons seen personally by the investigator or by a professionally reliable col-

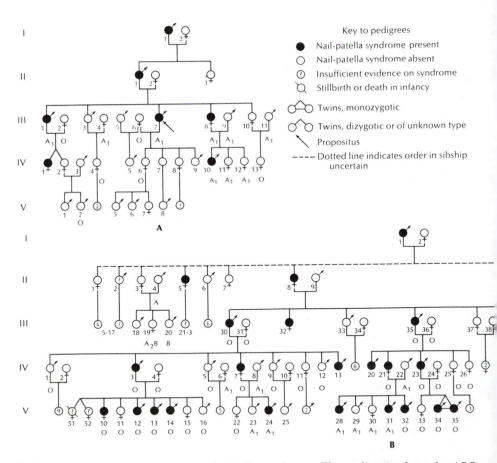

Fig. 1–5 Two kindreds with the nail-patella syndrome. The pedigrees show the ABO blood types of some members, because these families demonstrate that the ABO and nail-patella loci are on the same chromosome (Chapter 13). Other blood types indicate that, assuming III-6 is their mother, IV-7 and IV-8 of A are probably not children of III-

league and those adjudged affected or normal merely on the basis of hearsay. It is also helpful to indicate which members of a pedigree were dead when the family was examined, especially if the trait has a variable age of onset; generally this is done by means of a plus sign within or immediately adjacent to the symbol (e.g. Fig. 1–10). Abortions, stillbirths, or deaths in early infancy are designated in a special way, often by minute sex symbols at the appropriate place on the progeny line (III-2, -3, and -4 in Fig. 1–15) or by a complete or incomplete diagonal bar through the progeny symbol (V-51 near the left end of Fig. 1–5B). Generally, the minute symbols are shaded without any implication that the infant or fetus was affected with the trait under study.

Multiple births should be connected to the same point of the progeny line. In addition, monozygotic twins are joined by a horizontal line. Compare, for example, V-34 and v-35, concordant monozygotic twins of Fig. 1–5B, with IV-1 and IV-2, discordant dizygotic twins of Fig. 1–5A. If zygosity is unknown, a question mark should be placed between the sex symbols: ⌒?⌒ . In some of the older literature, monozygotic twins were attached to a short vertical from the progeny line, thus, ⌒ whereas dizygotics were attached directly to the progeny line in the same way as they are in Fig. 1–5A. This was probably done to underscore the fact that monozygotic twins count as one individual in the progeny count, dizygotics as two. However, monozygotics are almost always assigned separate numbers on the pedigree chart.

A typical pedigree of a simple (single locus) dominant trait is shown in Fig. 1–5. This form of inheritance lends itself to the most straightforward pedigree analysis. The usual pattern calls for appearance of the trait in successive generations. Whether the trait is rare or common, each individual manifesting it generally has at least one parent with the trait.

As indicated by Fig. 1–6, pedigrees of simple recessive traits typically contain only a single sibship or a single generation in which the trait appears. Neither the parents nor the children of the affected manifest the trait.

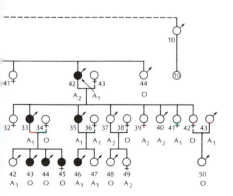

7, and they should not be included in a progeny count from this pedigree. (From Lawler et al., 1957, **B** after Wildervanck, 1950a. Courtesy of S. D. Lawler and the *Annals of Human Genetics*.)

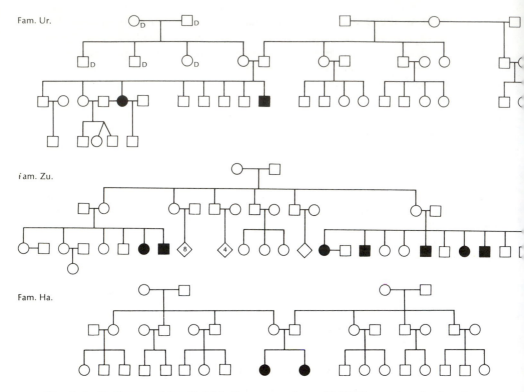

Fig. 1-6 Pedigrees of familial Mediterranean fever (FMF) illustrating the fact that typical pedigrees for a recessive trait contain only a few (Zu.), and very often single (Ha.) sibships with affected individuals. (From Sohar et al., 1961. Courtesy of J. Gafni and the *Archives of Internal Medicine.*)

Complications come in when a recessive trait is quite common in the population. This is true, for example, for blood type O in most of the world. In Fig. 1–5, which is typical, note that blood type O is manifested in every generation for which blood group data are available. The pedigree of this recessive trait therefore mimics the pedigree pattern of typical dominants.

The same problem is encoutered when a usually rare recessive trait becomes common in one ethnic group or country. This is illustrated by familial Mediterranean fever in Sephardic or Oriental Jews (Fig. 1–7). The same considerations would apply to such traits as red hair in Scotland or blond hair in Scandinavian countries.

A similar complication can occur when there is a great deal of consanguinity—marriage of close relatives—in a pedigree. The point is well illustrated by Fig. 1–8 concerning the rare recessive disease alkaptonuria. Were part **A** the only available pedigree, one would be convinced that the trait is inherited as a dominant. When the correct relationships among the parents of affected are established, however (Fig. 1–8**B**), the pattern is compatible with recessive inheritance, since it now becomes easy to understand why the nonaffected parents of Fig. 1–8**A** are probably heterozygous.

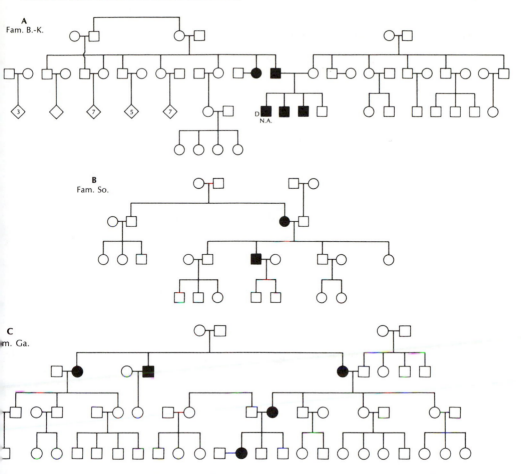

Fig. 1-7 Sephardic and Iraqi Jewish families with two or more generations affected by familial Mediterranean fever. (From Sohar et al., 1961. Courtesy of J. Gafni and the *Archives of Internal Medicine.*)

In case of doubt in interpreting a pedigree, one should seek so-called critical matings. One occurs when the mates lack the trait but have an affected child. Usually, this indicates that the trait is recessive. If, on the other hand, both parents manifest the trait but have a child who lacks it, this suggests dominant inheritance.

Unfortunately, there exist genetically valid reasons why these interpretations of critical matings can be wrong. One is the fact that genes can change: the phenomenon of mutation, to be discussed in Chapter 5. Another reason derives from the phenomenon of *variable expressivity* and its extreme form, *incomplete penetrance.* Both are illustrated in Fig. 1-9.

Variable expressivity means that not everyone with a given genotype manifests the trait in question to the same degree or in the same way. Thus, several individuals in Fig. 1-9 show the trait, ectrodactyly, in only one hand, but one person has it in both. Others may manifest it only in a foot, the trait being normally hidden

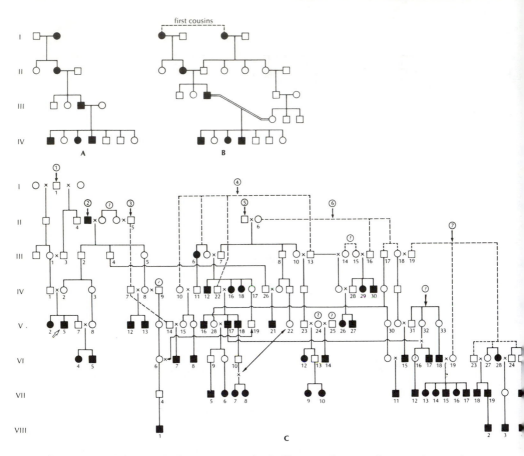

Fig. 1-8 Pedigrees of alkaptonuria, which illustrate how pedigrees of recessives can mimic those of dominants. **A** and **B**: A Lebanese family studied by Khachadurian and Abu Feisal (1958). **A** shows an incomplete analysis of this family. Since the trait is quite rare, the responsible gene seems to be dominant. **B** is a fuller analysis of the same family revealing the consanguinity responsible for the appearance of the trait in successive generations. **C**. Pedigree of an inbred group in the Dominican Republic in which the trait has appeared in six successive generations. (From McKusick, *Heritable Disorders of Connective Tissue*, 4th ed., 1972. Courtesy of V. A. McKusick and the C. V. Mosby Co., St. Louis. **C** is based on the work of R. A. Milch.)

from view. Variation in another dominant trait, the Marfan syndrome, is described in Chapter 5 (note especially Table 5–4). There the symptoms quite often occur to such a minor degree that they would not have been noted at all if the person in question were not the parent, child, or sibling of someone more obviously affected.

Incomplete penetrance carries this one step farther: the trait is absent entirely even though there is good reason to believe that the person has the same genotype at a given locus as those who manifest it. This is the case of the two brothers in generation 1 of Fig. 1–9 who have children and grandchildren with ectrodactyly. Clearly this phenomenon, unless recognized, could wreck havoc on pedigree analysis, particularly on the analysis of critical matings. Fortunately, an impressive body of data has been accumulated to indicate which traits commonly show variable expressivity or incomplete penetrance, or both. Often a definitive statement can be made, such as "70 percent penetrant." This means that the phenotype is expressed in 70 percent of the individuals with the particular genotype.

Another factor that can disturb the analysis of critical matings is *X-linkage.* X-linkage (also referred to as sex linkage, especially in the older literature) means that the locus in question is on the X-chromosome. This chromosome is normally present doubly in the female but singly in the male. (Contrariwise, the chromosomes—and the loci on them—that are usually present doubly in *both* sexes are referred to as *autosomal.*) X-linkage will be discussed at greater length in Chapter 7. For present purposes it may be noted from a glance at the pedigrees in that chapter that this form of inheritance at times resembles autosomal dominance when in fact the trait behaves in the heterozygote as though it were recessive. We shall see that one cannot distinguish X-linkage from autosomal inheritance by the fact that the trait appears to occur mostly in one sex or the other. Instead one must always fall back on the primary characteristic of X-linkage: that males can obtain X-linked genes only from their mothers. If there is male-to-male transmission, chances are very high that the trait is autosomal.

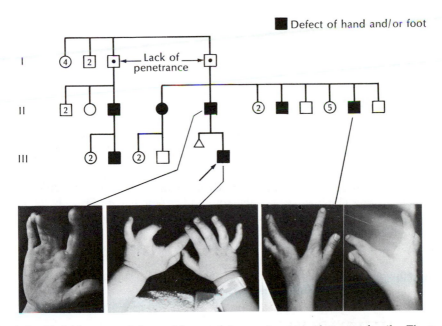

Fig. 1–9 Variable expressivity and incomplete penetrance in the same family. The trait in question, ectrodactyly, congenital complete or partial absence of fingers or toes, appears to be dominant. However, the two brothers in generation I with affected children have normal digits. To avoid a conclusion of incomplete penetrance, one would have to postulate that mutation affecting this trait occurred in both brothers—a very unlikely coincidence. (From Smith, 1966. Courtesy of D. W. Smith, and the C. V. Mosby Co., publishers of the *Journal of Pediatrics.* The picture was originally furnished by Dr. J. Frias.)

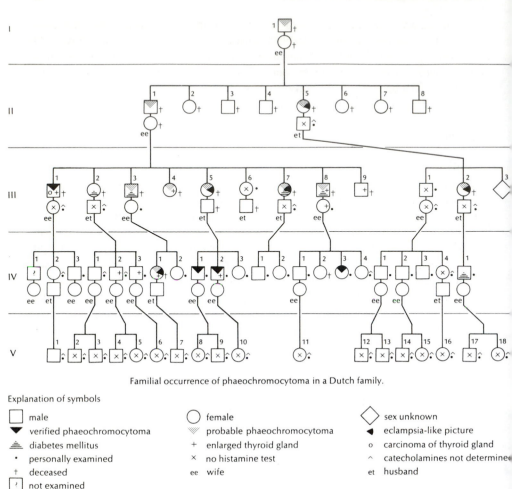

Familial occurrence of phaeochromocytoma in a Dutch family.

Explanation of symbols

	male		female		sex unknown
▼	verified phaeochromocytoma	⬚	probable phaeochromocytoma	◄	eclampsia-like picture
≜	diabetes mellitus	+	enlarged thyroid gland	o	carcinoma of thyroid gland
·	personally examined	×	no histamine test	^	catecholamines not determined
†	deceased	ee	wife	et	husband
?	not examined				

Fig. 1–10 An unusual pedigree chart in which spouses are shown at a different level than siblings, thus eliminating a possible source of error in making progeny counts from pedigrees. The figure also demonstrates methods of showing several traits in one chart. The trait in question, phaeochromocytoma (also written "pheochromocytoma"), is a rare chromaffin cell tumor of the sympathetic nervous system, found most often in the adrenal medulla. Note that individuals are numbered by sibship instead of by the customary method by generation. (From Smits and Huizinga, 1961. Courtesy of M. Smits and S. Karger Basel/New York, publishers of *Acta Genetica et Statistica Medica*.)

SUGGESTED EXERCISES

All questions asking for expected progeny should be answered not only in terms of genes and characters but also by indicating relative proportions, if there is more than one possibility. Stating the results without proportions implies that all types of progeny are produced equally, and this may not be true.

   Exercises 1–1 through 1–3 are designed to review and to point up the major differences in the normal forms of cell division.

1-1. Sketch the details of mitosis of an animal cell with 12 chromosomes composed of two large metacentrics (centromere at or very close to the middle), two small metacentrics, two very small metacentrics, two submetacentrics (centromeres about halfway between the middle and the right end), two large acrocentrics (centromere very close to one end), and two small acrocentrics. Use large figures for clarity, and pay particular attention to the correct positions of the centromeres at each stage of division.

1-2. Sketch the details of spermatogenesis in the same animal that was used for the previous exercise, assuming, however, that one of the large submetacentrics is larger than the other in the male. Include all the subdivisions of Prophase I and show crossing over for all except the large metacentrics.

1-3. Sketch oogenesis in this organism. Assume that the chromosome description in exercise 1-1 represents that of the female of the species.

1-4. In some species of birds males produce gametes with an even number of chromosomes, whereas females produce two kinds of eggs, about half with the same number as the sperm and half with an odd number, one less than the number in the sperm. How would you account for this?

1-5. Consider the chromosomes of the organism referred to in exercises 1-1 and 1-2. One of each type, which was obtained from its female parent, may be referred to as maternal and the other member of the pair as paternal. If there were no exchanges of material between chromosomes, what proportion of the gametes produced in exercise 1-2 are expected to contain the paternal large acrocentric?

1-6. Anonycho-osteo-dysplasia, better known as the nail-patella syndrome (Fig. 1-4), is one of the traits listed in Table 1-3. Call it the *np* locus. A man and his sister both have the trait, and both marry persons who lack it. The man's son, who lacks it, marries the sister's daughter, his cousin, who does have it. (a) What is the outlook for their children? (b) If their first child is normal with respect to this trait, what is the outlook for their next child?

1-7. Suppose you examine the widowed mother of the man and his sister of exercise 1-6 and you find that she lacks the nail-patella syndrome. What would you conclude about the phenotype and genotype of her late husband (their father)? If more than one answer is possible, which is the more likely, and why?

1-8. Hsu (1948) reported that the ability to fold the tip of the extruded tongue upward appears to be a recessive trait. Call this the *up* locus. Two of the children in a family are capable of upfolding and two are not. Neither of the parents is capable of it. (a) What are the probable genotypes of the parents? (b) If they were to have four more children, what would you expect them to be with respect to this trait?

1-9. If you were told the trait in Fig. 1-11 is recessive, would you suspect that it is common or that it is rare? Explain showing the critical matings(s), if present.

1-10. If you were told the trait in Fig. 1-12 is rare, would you conclude that it is probably a simple dominant or that it is recessive? Explain showing critical mating(s), if present.

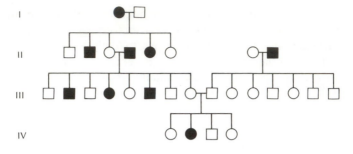

Fig. 1-11   Pedigree of a recessive trait.

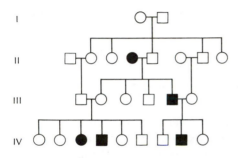

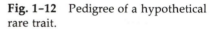

Fig. 1-12   Pedigree of a hypothetical rare trait.

1-11. Although the trait is generally rare and it appeared in several consecutive generations in the pedigrees of Fig. 1–7, what two arguments, one from the pedigrees and the other outside them, argue that the trait is recessive?

1-12. Assuming the trait referred to in the previous exercise *is* recessive, (a) What are the probable genotypes of I-2 and I-4 in the uppermost pedigree of Fig. 1–7? (Call this the *fm* locus.) (b) Note that II-6 was married to a cousin. If she lost this husband and were to marry her affected nephew, III-27, what can one predict about their children with respect to this trait? (c) Would the answer to (b) be different if the aunt in question were II-4? If so, how?

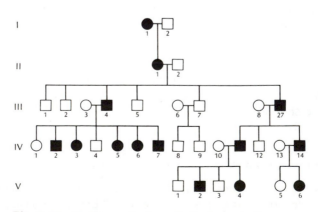

Fig. 1-13   Pedigree of a hypothetical rare trait.

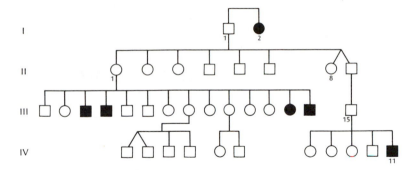

Fig. 1-14 Pedigree of a relatively rare disorder. Assume that mates who are not shown do not have the disorder. (From Fogh–Anderson, 1942. Courtesy of *Opera ex Domo Biologiae Hereditariae Humanae Universitatis Hafniensis.*)

1-13. Refer to Fig. 1–13. (a) What progeny would be expected for this trait from a marriage of III-1 to his niece, IV-1? (b) What would be the expected progeny for this trait if IV-2 were to marry his first cousin once removed, V-4? (c) What would be the answer to (b) if he were to marry his cousin of similar degree, V-5?

1-14. Refer to Fig. 1–14. (a) Does the pedigree of this relatively rare disorder suggest dominance or does it suggest recessiveness? Why? (b) Indicate contradictions to the alternative chosen in (a). (c) What genetic phenomenon studied thus far could explain the "aberrant" data in Fig. 1–14?

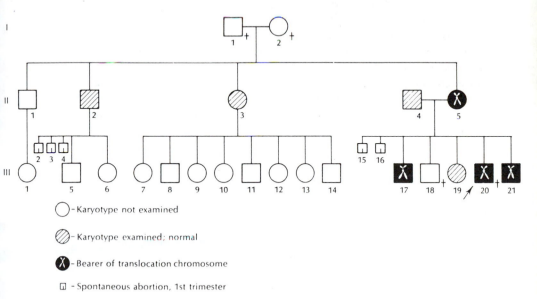

○ - Karyotype not examined

⊘ - Karyotype examined; normal

Ⓧ - Bearer of translocation chromosome

▫ - Spontaneous abortion, 1st trimester

Fig. 1-15 Transmission of a chromosomal aberration. The karyotypes of several persons with a similar aberration are shown in Fig. 4–9. Unlike most pedigrees, this one uses some shaded symbols for persons with normal karyotypes. "+" means the person is deceased. (From German et al., 1962. Courtesy of J. L. German III and the *American Journal of Human Genetics.*)

2

Human Chromosomes

Before delving deeper into the nature and behavior of the genes, it behooves us to know more about the structure and identification of the chromosomes on which they reside. We shall emphasize here the normal situation, devoting several later chapters to abnormalities of number and structure.

GENERAL FEATURES

Chromosomes can generally be differentiated in three ways by (1) lengths, (2) position of the centromere, and (3) staining characteristics.

The parts of a chromosome on each side of the centromere are called arms. A chromosome whose centromere is near the middle, so that it has two nearly equal arms, is said to be *metacentric* (Fig. 2–1**A**). When the centromere is between the center and one end, it is *acrocentric,* but human cytologists restrict this term to chromosomes in which the centromere is very near to one end. A truly acrocentric chromosome of man, therefore, has arms of very disparate size, referred to as the long arm and the short arm (Fig. 2–1**C**). Sometimes chromosomes with centromeres intermediate between metacentrics and acrocentrics are called *submetacentrics* (Fig. 2–1**B**). The centromere of a submetacentric is submedian, that of an acrocentric is subterminal. Chromosomes exist that have short arms so small as to be nearly imperceptible, in which case the chromosome is termed *telecentric* (Fig. 2–1**D**), but none of the human chromosomes appear to be of this type. There is evidence that the centromere is never at the very end, which is to say that no truly unibrachial (one arm) or perfectly telocentric chromosomes exist.

The shorter of the two arms of a chromosome is designated "p" (from the French "petite") and the longer arm "q." Thus chromosome 1 consists of 1p and 1q, chromosome 2 of 2p and 2q, and so forth.

Usually each chromosome consists of two strands, which are apparently identical in every respect. They are called *sister chromatids,* or simply *chromatids.* The two chromatids of a chromosome are closely associated by means of their respective centromeres; indeed, the two centromeres are commonly spoken of and drawn as a single unit, as in Figs. 1–1 and 2–2. It is when this close association is broken, at the beginning of anaphase in mitosis and of anaphase II in meiosis, that each

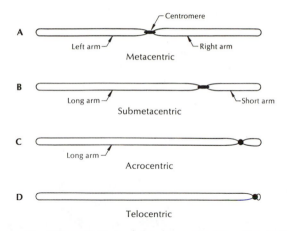

Fig. 2-1 Diagrammatic differentiation of chromosomes according to the position of the centromere. None of the normal human chromosomes is considered telocentric, but even such telocentric chromosomes as the X-chromosomes of *Drosophila melanogaster* have some short arms. No chromosomes are known for certainty to have centromeres at the very ends.

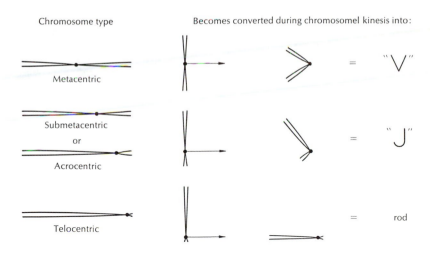

Fig. 2-2 Transformation of chromosomes into V, J, or "rod" shapes during their movements in the spindle apparatus.

chromatid becomes an independent chromosome; it is not suitable for another division, however, until it becomes double-stranded again (after interphase). (The chromatids are not to be confused with the double strands of the DNA helices in each one).

When the chromosomes move toward the poles in cell division, the centromeres, which are attached to spindle fibers, lead the movement, and the arms of the chromosome follow. As a result a metacentric or mildly submetacentric comes to resemble the letter "V" (and is often so termed), an acrocentric becomes a "J," and a nearly telocentric is termed a "rod," as illustrated in Fig. 2-2.

CHROMOSOME NUMBER

For many years textbooks of biology and genetics stated positively that the normal *diploid* number of chromosomes in the zygote and body cells of humans was 48. In 1956, however, a historic paper published by J. H. Tjio and A. Levan (Fig. 2–3) demonstrated that the correct number is 46.

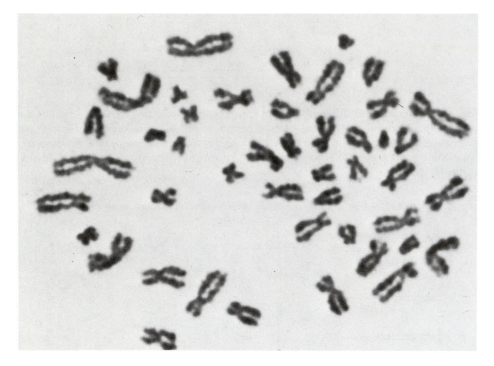

Fig. 2–3   Polar view of a lung fibroblast culture metaphase that demonstrated conclusively that the diploid number in man is 46. (From Tjio and Levan, 1956. Courtesy of J. H. Tjio and *Hereditas*.)

Fig. 2–4A   Polar view of the metaphase plate in a cultured human lymphocyte. The 46 chromosomes are more spread out than usual as a result of immersion of the cell in a hypotonic solution. Note that each chromosome consists of two identical sister chromatids joined together at a centromere and that the chromosome is markedly narrowed (primary constriction) at this point. The apparent four-strand unit at the left is formed by two chromosomes that happen to be superposed. (Courtesy of W. R. Breg.)

Fig. 2–4B   Line up of cut-out metaphase chromosomes to form a "karyotype" chart. In this instance two chromosomes, a number 5 and a number 6, happened to overlap, hence, the extra bits of chromosome attached to each. Note the deficient short arms of the other number 5 (upper arrow) and the subdivision (lower arrow) of the short arms of both chromatids of one X-chromosome (an "isochromatid break"). (Courtesy of O. J. Miller.)

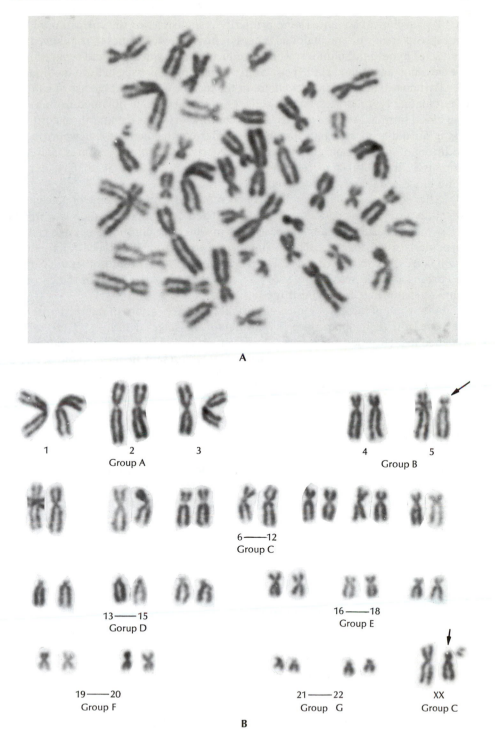

A

1	2	3		4	5
	Group A				Group B

6——12
Group C

| 13——15 | | | | 16——18 | |
| Gorup D | | | | Group E | |

| 19——20 | | 21——22 | | XX |
| Group F | | Group   G | | Group C |

B

Two technical advances were primarily responsible for the correction of this widespread error and the major advances in human cytogenetics that followed: (1) the use of hypotonic solutions, which produced better spreading and separation of the chromosomes, and (2) the perfection of mammalian tissue culture methods.

Particularly notable improvement in the technique enabled the use of cultures of circulating lymphocytes, so that cells for culture could be obtained from a routine blood sample. As little as a few cubic centimeters from the umbilical cord vessels is adequate to ascertain the chromosomal complement of a newborn baby. Addition of phytohemagglutinin, a plant derivative, to the cultures increases immensely the number of cells undergoing division; without it, in fact, normal white blood cells rarely divide in culture.

After some tissue culture cells have been treated with colchicine or colcemide, placed in a hypotonic solution, stained, and fixed on a slide, the slide is searched at low magnifications for a metaphase plate in which the chromosomes of a cell are particularly well separated. This is photographed and the developed microphotograph is greatly enlarged (e.g., Fig. 2–4A). The individual chromosomes are cut out and arranged in decreasing order of size, and the complete lineup of the chromosome set, as in Fig. 2–4B, constitutes a *karyotype*.

As a result of these techniques almost all characterizations of the chromosomes are based on their appearance in the metaphase stage of mitosis. The *number* assigned to a chromosome is based, however, on the 23 in the meiotic product, the haploid set. The set of genes and chromosomes present in the haploid set of a gamete is commonly referred to as the *genome*.

DISTINGUISHING THE CHROMOSOMES

In the early uses of these techniques cytogeneticists found it difficult to agree on the identity and relationships of the individual chromosomes. They did agree that the autosomes should be numbered from 1 to 22 in decreasing order of length, but there were often disputes about specific numbers. A conference at Denver in 1960 decided that the chromosomes could be divided into seven groups based on length and, where there is any overlap of lengths, by position of the centromere:

Group A: Large chromosomes with approximately median centromeres (chromosomes 1–3).

Group B: Large chromosomes with submedian centromeres (4–5).

Group C: Medium-sized chromosomes with submedian centromeres (6–12). The X-chromosome was often included in this group, especially resembling number 6.

Group D: Medium-sized acrocentric chromosomes (13–15).

Group E: Rather short chromosomes (16–18) with approximately median (number 16) or submedian centromeres.

Group F: Short essentially metacentric chromosomes (19–20).

Group G: Very short, acrocentric chromosomes (21–22 and the Y-chromosome).

In group G, many felt they could distinguish the Y-chromosome from numbers 21 and 22. Moreover, we know now that the chromosome designated number 21 should have been called number 22, and vice versa.

A few investigators used Roman numerals I to VII instead of A to G to designate the groups.

It was noted that on many chromosomes there are regions besides the centromere area that appear narrowed or constricted. If the centromere is thought of as the *primary constriction* of a chromosome, the points demarcating other narrowings are referred to collectively as *secondary constrictions* (Fig. 2–5).

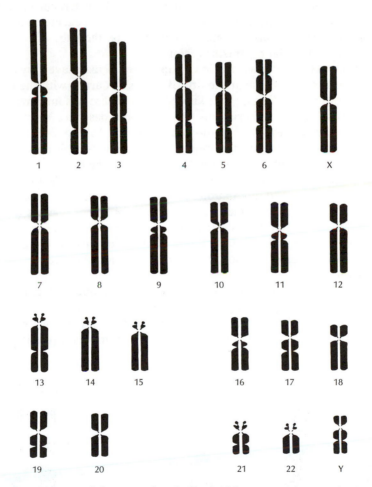

Fig. 2-5 An idiogram of the normal male haploid karytope, showing both X- and Y-chromosomes. (From Ferguson-Smith et al., 1962.) These investigators consider chromosome 6 to belong to the same group as numbers 4 and 5 and to be consistently larger than both the X- and number 5 chromosomes. Many workers also do not agree with the indicated distribution of secondary constrictions; most do agree on the reality of those on chromosomes 1,9, and 16. Note the separation of the distal-most portions from the rest of the short arms of the acrocentric chromosomes; these distal-most bits are called "satellites." (Courtesy of M. A. Ferguson-Smith and *Cytogenetics*.)

The materials at the primary and secondary constrictions have usually exhibited different staining properties than the rest of the chromosomes. Cytologists have called this material *heterochromatin,* as opposed to the *euchromatin* of the rest of the chromosome. Heterochromatin may not be completely confined to the constrictions, however. In many organisms small intercalations of it may be discerned in the euchromatic portion; this is often referred to as *interstitial* heterochromatin, and the larger masses at the constrictions are called *constitutive* or centromeric heterochromatin. Sometimes whole chromosomes are heterochromatic as well.

Though the matter has not been clarified completely, heterochromatin apparently has a different structure and physiological activity than euchromatin. In addition, secondary constrictions commonly appear to be the sites of formation of nucleoli, that is, "nucleolar organizing regions."

Some or all of the chromosomes in Groups D and G may have very prominent secondary constrictions very near the tips of their short arms, with the result that the tips appear to be *satellites,* or little knoblike bits of chromosomal material (Fig. 2–5). Constant secondary constrictions have also been described not far from the centromere on the long arms of chromosomes 1, 9, and 16 (Fig. 2–5).

A number of secondary constrictions which are demonstrable only with special staining methods are referred to as *fragile sites.* One of the most frequent of these is at Xq27-28 (Fig. 2–6), and its carriers are said to have a *fragile X chromosome.* It is associated with mental retardation in most of the males that have it and, to a lesser degree, in some of the females heterozygous for it. For reasons that will be clarified in Chapters 7 and 9, this is thought to be one of the main reasons for the higher frequency of mental retardation in males than in females. The exact nature of the chromosomal defect and how it is involved in mental retardation are at this writing unknown.

Several chromosomes can be identified by means of autoradiography. In this technique, thymidine containing tritium (^{3}H)—thereby made radioactive—is placed in the culture of cells to be karyotyped, and these are harvested at various times and stained as usual. By appropriate photographic techniques it is possible

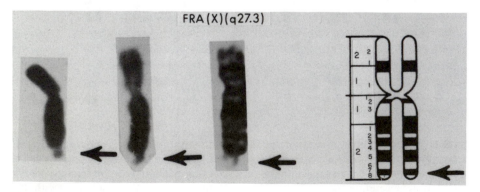

Fig. 2–6 Fragile-X chromosomes from a mentally retarded male. Shown are two unbanded examples (on the left), a G-banded one, and a schematic of a normal G-banded X-chromosome indicating the q27.3 fragile site. Note how the end of the abnormal Xq resembles a satellite. (Courtesy of L. R. Shapiro, M.D., Valhalla, N.Y.)

to determine whether they have incorporated the radioactive (tritiated) thymidine in synthesizing new chromatids. If a chromosome contains the ^{3}H-thymidine, it is said to be *labeled*.

Identifications stem from the fact that the chromosomes, or parts of chromosomes of the diploid set, do not synthesize chromatids synchronously. The parts completing their synthesis before the radioactive material is introduced remain unlabeled; the parts that synthesize later become labeled.

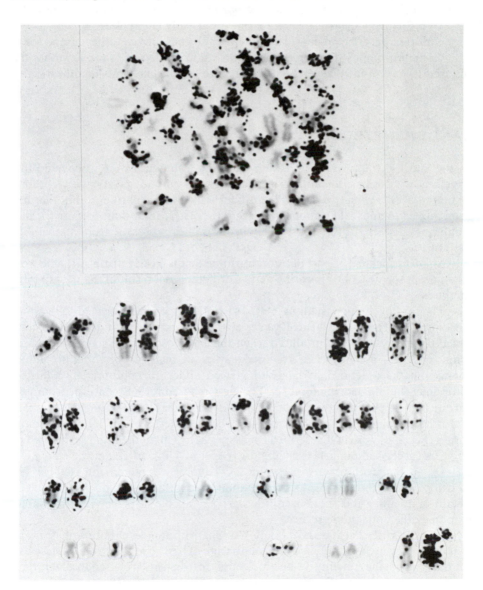

Fig. 2–7 Radioautograph of the chromosomes in Fig. 2–4. Note how heavily labeled one X-chromosome is as compared with the other and the rest of the group C chromosomes. Other label differences are discussed in the text (p. 32). (Courtesy of W. R. Breg.)

By these means it was possible to distinguish between chromosomes 4 and 5 in group B, between the members of the D group, and between numbers 17 and 18 of group E (Fig. 2–7).

More significantly, it was noted that in the normal female the two X-chromosomes do not behave the same way autoradiographically. One of them consistently labels, that is, it replicates much later than the other, in all body cells and in the follicle cells—but not in the oogonia or oocytes—of the ovary (Fig. 2–7). Similarly, in persons having more than the normal number of X-chromosomes (discussed in Chapters 3 and 7), all except one are usually late replicating.

Unfortunately, the process of autoradiography has proven rather cumbersome. The "strictures imposed by time, resolution, and sample size" (as one author has phrased it) have limited severely its routine use for chromosome identification.

BANDING METHODS

In the late 1960s and early 1970s new staining techniques were discovered that have made it possible for human cytogenetics not only to specify every chromosome but even, in many cases, to identify exactly parts of chromosomes that had been moved to unusual locations in the genome. This came about because the new techniques disclosed that each of the chromosomes possesses a unique banding pattern.

A *band* is defined as part of a chromosome that is clearly distinguishable from its adjacent segments by appearing darker or lighter as a result of the new staining methods.

The first of the new staining methods to be discovered is called Q-banding. Torbjorn Caspersson and his colleagues at the Karolinska Institute in Stockholm noted that such bands are produced when the chromosomes are stained by quinacrine mustard—a fluorescent dye used earlier in many laboratories to induce changes in the genetic material—and viewed under an appropriately adjusted, ultraviolet-illuminated microscope. The first report in 1968 concerned hamster chromosomes, but subsequent papers quickly extended these findings to humans and other organisms. The 24 definitive Q-band patterns of the human chromosomes (Fig. 2–8) were first described by Caspersson et al. in the same journal which 15 years earlier had published the historic paper of Tjio and Levan.

Despite its revolutionary importance, Q-banding was not an unmixed blessing to cytogenetics laboratories, for it demanded a dye that is relatively difficult to obtain in quantity and specialized microscopes capable of perceiving and photographing differential fluorescence.

In 1970 M. L. Pardue and J. Gall, working with mouse chromosomes, found that when they used the Giemsa stain, a mixture of basic dyes known to histologists for many years, the constitutive heterochromatin (often also referred to as *repetitive* heterochromatin) area of each chromosome stained much more deeply than the rest. Other workers modified the technique slightly and extended it to humans and other mammals, where it has come to be known as C-banding (Fig. 2–9). The C-bands are particularly large on chromosomes 1, 9, and 16.

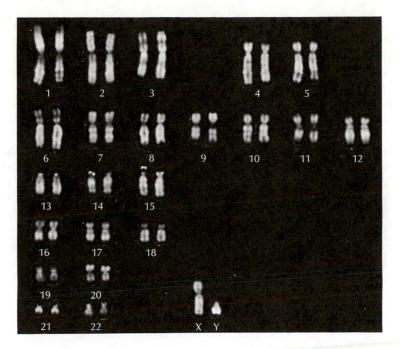

Fig. 2-8 Q-banding karyotype of an XY male. Note especially the brilliant fluorescence of most of the long arm of the Y-chromosome. (Courtesy of T. Caspersson.)

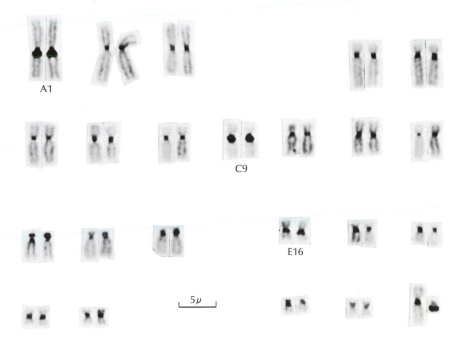

Fig. 2-9 C-banding karyotype. Note the particularly prominent bands in the centromeric areas of chromosomes 1, 9, and 16. (Courtesy of T. -R. Chen and F. H. Ruddle.)

The next major advance followed the observation of Arrighi and Hsu that C-bands are prominent in chromosome areas, such as distal Yq, which exhibit intense Q-bands. This correspondence between some aspects of Q- and C-banding excited cytogeneticists because Giemsa staining could be detected with ordinary light microscopes. They found that after pretreating the chromosomes with proteolytic enzymes staining with Giemsa produced results that generally duplicated the Q-band specificities. These techniques became known as G-banding (Fig. 2–10).

In 1971, Dutrillaux and Lejeune developed an additional technique that produces bands in reverse contrast to the Q- and G-bands, that is, the chromosomes are dark where Q- and G-staining leaves them light and light where the dark Q- and G-bands would be. This is known as R- (for "reverse Giemsa") banding (Fig. 2–11). It is particularly useful for studying the ends of the chromosomes, most of which stain vividly with this technique.

Several modifications of the basic Giemsa method are now in use, depending primarily on the protease used. Additional advances are being made in increasing the number of detectable bands by studying prophase chromosomes (Fig. 2–12).

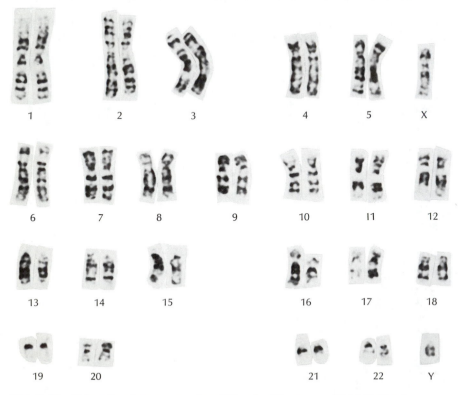

Fig. 2–10 G-banding karyotype of an XY male. (Courtesy of L.Y.-F. Hsu.)

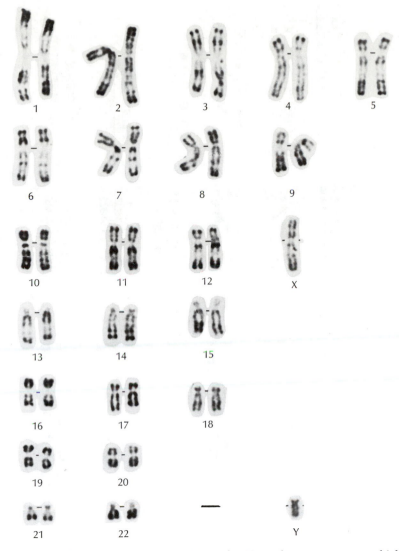

Fig. 2-11 R-banding karyotype of an XY male. Note that many areas which stain poorly in Q-and G-banding become very prominent in this technique. (Courtesy of B. Dutrillaux.)

SUBDIVIDING THE CHROMOSOMES

The Q- and G-banding patterns are so consistent that they can be used to assign numbers to subdivisions of the chromosome arms for ready reference. Figure 2-13 details the system established at the Paris Conference (1971).

The first step was to choose chromosomal landmarks, defined as consistent and distinct morphologic features that can be important diagnostic aids in identi-

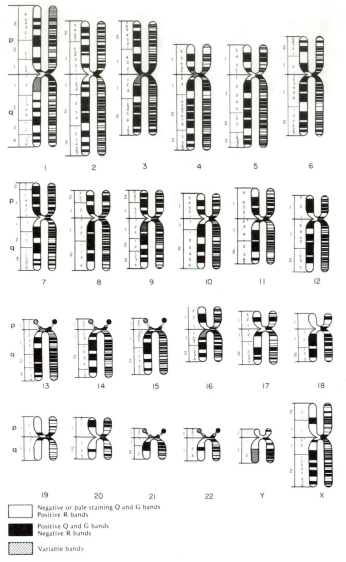

Negative or pale staining Q and G bands
Positive R bands

Positive Q and G bands
Negative R bands

Variable bands

Fig. 2–12 Diagrammatic representation of the 24 kinds of human chromosomes. The left-hand portion of each chromosome shows the numbering system adopted at the Paris Conference (1971) for the bands and regions observed in metaphase spreads with Q-, G-, and R-staining methods. Each right-hand portion indicates additional subdivisions of these bands and regions that may be perceived by G-staining of *prophase* chromosomes. (From Yunis, 1976. Courtesy of J. J. Yunis and *Science,* copyright 1976 by the American Association for the Advancement of Science.)

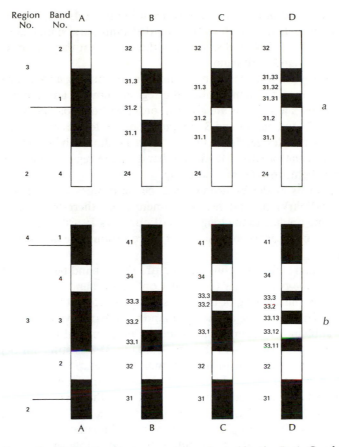

Region   Band   A   B   C   D
No.   No.

Fig. 2-13 Examples illustrating the convention adopted by the Paris Conference (1971) for subdividing a landmark band (a) and a band within a region (b). In part a, A shows the original landmark (band 31); B the subdivision of band 31 into three equal bands, 31.1, 31.2, and 31.3; C the subdivision of 31 into three unequal bands; and D the further subdivision of band 31.3 from C into three equal bands 31.31, 31.32, and 31.33. Part b shows corresponding diagrams for band 33 and band 33.1. (Courtesy of The National Foundation.)

fying a chromosome. These include the ends of the arms, the centromere, and certain prominent bands. The area of a chromosome lying between two adjacent landmarks is designated a *region.*

Regions and bands are numbered consecutively from the centromere outward along each arm. A band bisected by the centromere is considered two bands, each labeled as band 1, in region 1, of its arm. Thus each chromosome has a p11 band and a q11 band adjoining the centromere. More distal bands used as landmarks are considered to belong entirely to the region distal to the landmark; therefore, each is band number 1 of that region. This point needs to be emphasized because the boundary line between regions on the map is drawn through the middle of the band, a fact that would at first glance cause one to think that half of the band belonged to the region proximal to it. Less prominent bands of a region, if they are prominent or consistent enough to be accorded landmark status, are then numbered consecutively, 2, 3, 4, and so forth, in the order that they occur, in the distal direction from the landmark band.

Under this system four items are required in designating a particular band: the chromosome number, the arm symbol, the region number, and the band number within that region. These items are given in order without spacing or punctuation. For example, 6q23 indicates band 3 in region 2 of the long arm of chromosome 6. Note that when the designation ends in "1" a landmark band is indicated; for example, 6q21 is the proximal landmark band of the region containing 6q23. It may be dark or light from Q- or G-staining.

The short arms of the Y-chromosome, chromosomes 4 and 5, and 10 to 22 contain no landmarks beyond the centromere area; therefore, each is a single region. The same applies to the long arms of numbers 19, 20, 22, and the Y-chromosome. All the other arms contain two or more regions, the largest number, four, occurring on 1q.

If more refined staining techniques require that a band be subdivided, a decimal point would be placed after the Paris Conference band designation cf Figure 2–13, followed by numbering of the new subbands sequentially from the centromere outward. The same rule applies to a landmark band even though this causes one or more subbands to seem to lie in the region proximal to the original band. Thus in the example of Fig. 2–13 the new subband 31.1 is still considered part of region 3 even though it seems to lie proximal to the map line between regions 2 and 3. Where the designation of the original band is in doubt, the decimal point should be followed by a question mark (?) and then the proposed subband number—for example, 1p33.?1. No other spacing or punctuation is to be used in further subdividing bands. For example, if 1p.33 were to be subdivided into three subbands, 1p33.1 to 1p33.3, and the second of these were now subdivisible into four additional bandings, these would be designated 1p33.21, 1p33.22, and so forth.

SUGGESTED EXERCISES

2–1. Without referring to the text, state the number of chromosomes normally found in each group, A to G, in the diploid set of: (1) the human male; (b) the human female.

2–2. Perform an exercise similar to 2–1 for the gametes of (a) the female and (b) the male.

2–3. What are the special advantages and disadvantages, if any, of (a) Q-banding; (b) G-banding; (c) C-banding; and (d) R-banding?

2–4. What do Q, G, C, and R stand for in the names of the banding methods?

2–5. What is the correspondence between Q-, G-, and R-banding patterns?

2–6. What are the accepted designations for "long arm" and "short arm" of a chromosome? What is the basis for these designations?

2–7. What is a "fragile site?"

2–8. How has the term *chromosome region* been defined since the Paris Conference (1971)?

2–9. Criticize the following statement: "A band is a dark-staining region of a chromosome."

2–10. What is a "landmark band"? How is it designated?

2–11. If the landmark band of region 2 on the long arm of chromosome 2 were to be subdivided into five parts, and the fourth of these further subdivided into four parts, how would the latter four be numbered?

3

Disorders of Chromosome Number

The processes of cell division usually ensure the orderly distribution of chromosomes from one generation to another. Errors in division and changes in the structure of the chromosomes do occur, however, resulting in cells and individuals with abnormal numbers of chromosomes or with modified chromosomes.

Such chromosomal deviations from normal development occur much more frequently than had once been suspected. It is estimated that a visible chromosomal abnormality is present in between six and seven of every 1000 live births. The incidence is about 70 to 80 times greater in spontaneously aborted pregnancies, gross chromosomal anomalies being present in about half of spontaneous abortions. Since about one out of seven recognized fertilizations ends in a recovered spontaneous abortion, at least 76 out of every 1000 recognized conceptions (7.6 percent) contain deleterious chromosomal abnormalities. This estimate is quite conservative since it does not take into account the high frequency in stillbirths and the possible high frequency in resorbed fetuses. It also does not include abnormalities that were not demonstrable by the then available methods. Many additional cases of abnormalities are coming to light, for example, with the molecular techniques to be discussed in Chapter 6. In another study it was estimated that 25 percent of women with primary amenorrhea, 11.0 percent of men with high-grade subfertility, and about 6 percent of people institutionalized as mental defectives have chromosomal abnormalities. It is clear that chromosomal abnormalities must be reckoned among the most significant of the causes of developmental disorders.

Chromosomal abnormalities may be divided into two major groups: (1) changes in the *amount* of chromosomal material—usually a change in chromosome number, the subject of this chapter, and (2) changes in the *arrangement* of the chromosomal material, to be considered in Chapter 4. Distinction between the two is largely a matter of convenience, as rearrangement of the chromosomal material has rarely been implicated in any abnormality unless it causes a change in the *amount* of a chromosome in this or a later generation.

An abnormal quantity of chromosomal material can involve either a loss or an excess. Both types occur, but a pathological outcome from the latter is the more difficult to explain. It is easy to understand why the lack of some chromosomal material can lead to abnormal structures or functions, but it is less easy to comprehend how it comes about that having extra genetic material can also be deleterious. Normal structure and function seem to depend not only on the action of the individual units of chromosomal material but also on a normal "balance" between the genetic material on the different chromosomes and a normal "balance" between the product of the genetic material in the cell. Such a balance, which obtains in normal haploid or diploid sets, has been dubbed *euploidy* by plant and animal geneticists. Any cell carrying a chromosome complement that is an exact multiple of the haploid sets basic to the species is said to be *euploid*.

The presence of an irregular number of chromosomes—variously referred to as *aneuploidy* or *aneusomy*—usually results in an unablanced condition. A euploid set can also be unbalanced. This would be the case if the dosage of particular bits of genetic material in the chromosomes is incorrect. A gamete is unbalanced, for example, if any genetic material of its chromosomes is present in other than single dose, as is a diploid cell if any autosomal material is present in other than double dose.

NONDISJUNCTION

Changes in the total number of chromosomes most frequently result from the occasional failure of chromosomes to move to opposite poles or *disjoin* during anaphase of cell division. Such a failure is called *nondisjunction*. Many authors distinguish between (1) nondisjunction in the narrow sense, which is a failure of the two chromosomes involved to separate properly at the end of metaphase, and (2) *anaphase* or chromosomal *lag,* which is a failure of one of the chromosomes to move (or move rapidly enough) toward the proper pole during anaphase to be included with its set once the nuclear membrane becomes reestablished; this is sometimes also referred to as *maldisjunction*. Generally it is difficult to establish which process is reponsible, so we shall refer to both as nondisjunction. When used here "nondisjunction" is meant in *sensu lata,* the broad sense, unless otherwise noted.

Figure 3–1 illustrates some of the different consequences of nondisjunction depending on whether it occurs in the first meiotic division, in the second meiotic division, or in a mitotic division of the zygote. In the male, a first meiotic nondisjunction for one pair of homologous chromosomes results in two sperm each of which has one extra chromosome, and two sperm each of which lacks one chromosome. If the nondisjunction occurs in one of the second meiotic divisions, one sperm is formed with 24 chromosomes, one sperm with 22, and two sperm with the normal 23 chromosomes. In the female, however, the results of nondisjunction are the same whether it occurs in the first meiotic division or the second: the egg either has an extra chromosome or it lacks one chromosome.

Meiotic nondisjunction that occurs in a cell with a normal chromosome complement is called "primary nondisjunction." If, however, the cell already contains an abnormal chromosome set as the result of a prior nondisjunction, nondisjunction in its division is referred to as "secondary nondisjunction."

MOSAICISM

If nondisjunction occurs during the first cleavage of a normal embryo, two kinds of abnormal cells result: some with fewer chromosomes than normal and the rest

A. Nondisjunction in First Meiotic Division   B. Nondisjunction in Second Meiotic Division

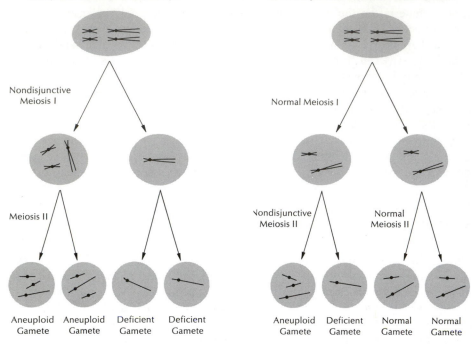

Fig. 3–1 Consequences of nondisjunction of one chromosome if it occurs **(A)** in meiosis I, **(B)** in meiosis II, or **(C)** after fertilization. If the postfertilization nondisjunction

with more chromosomes than the normal diploid number. Nondisjunction subsequent to the first cleavage (Fig. 3–1C) leads to these two kinds of abnormal cells from that particular division, but at the same time normal cells are being produced in other cell divisions of the embryo. In either case, then, mitotic nondisjunction produces cells with at least two different chromosome numbers. If these cells are viable, the resulting individual is a *mosaic.* Hence, mosaicism for chromosome number is diagnostic of *mitotic* nondisjunction.

Mosaics of number are sometimes referred to as *mixoploids. Developmental mosaicism* results from abnormal mechanics occurring during an early cleavage of the zygote. *Proliferative mosaicism* may occur from mitoses after the completion of embryogenesis. Mosaicism can also occur if chromosome *structure* differs in different cells of an organism.

A constant abnormal chromosome number does not rule out a mitotic basis, however, since one first cleavage product, usually the deficient one, could die, leaving all the cells of the embryo to descend from the other daughter cell, usually the one with extra chromosomes. Mitotic nondisjunction in the spermatogonial or oogonial stage preceding meiosis could also lead to a constant chromosome number in the zygote.

In the mosaic state some abnormal chromosome complements are capable of

C. Nondisjunction During Mitotic Divisions of Zygote

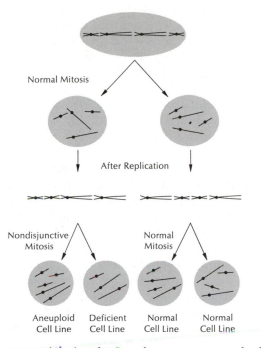

Normal Mitosis

After Replication

Nondisjunctive Mitosis

Normal Mitosis

Aneuploid Cell Line

Deficient Cell Line

Normal Cell Line

Normal Cell Line

occurred during the first cleavage, no normal cells would be present, unless there was a reverse secondary nondisjunction in a later division.

survival which in the nonmosaic state would usually result in early embryonic death.

Strictly speaking, the cells of a mosaic must be derived from a single zygote based on a single fertilization. Such a mosaic cannot be differentiated easily, however, from a case with two or more cell lines resulting from a union of cells following double fertilization or from an implantation of cells from one individual in another. Hence, the latter, which should properly be referred to as a *chimera*, is also generally spoken of as a mosaic. The several XX/XY mosaics that have been identified are probably chimeras. In some instances they are attributed to independent fertilization of a single egg by both a Y-bearing sperm and an X-bearing sperm. In other XX/XY it has been assumed that an ovum (ootid) and its polar body (PB II) were separately fertilized, with the fertilized polar body and its cleavage clone becoming amalgamated into the cleavage clone of the fertilized ovum. Blood type chimeras can have a similar basis, or they can result from exchanges of hemapoeitic tissues between twins *in utero*.

Cells of a mosaic usually contain the normal *(modal)* number of chromosomes and one or two more than the normal numbers (*hypermodal* or *hyperdiploid*) or one or two less than the normal number (*hypomodal* or *hypodiploid*).

As mentioned earlier, mitotic nondisjunction appears to be the principal mechanism by which mosaicism is produced. In the type of nondisjunction referred to as *anaphase lag,* the lagging chromosome may be included in the wrong daughter cell or be altogether excluded and lost. In wrong-cell inclusion two *cell lines* will be produced, one trisomic and the other monosomic for the particular chromosome, with 47 and 45 chromosomes, respectively. The end result will in no way be distinguishable from nondisjunction due to failure of the centromere to break or of the separated chromatids to move away from one another. Where, however, a chromosome has been lost, there will be one cell line with the normal number of chromosomes 46, and another cell line with 45 chromosomes. XY/XXY and XX/XXY mosaics could arise in this way from XXY zygotes, or XO/XX and XO/XY mosaics from normal zygotes.

Mosaicism is often difficult to diagnose correctly (a) because the abnormal cells are in the minority, (b) because culture conditions may alter the proportions of cells, or (c) because the mosaicism may be confined to certain tissues.

When a mitotic error occurs in some division soon after conception, an equal number of deviant and ancestral cells may result. But when many hundreds of normal divisions have occurred before a mitotic error occurs in a cell leading to the proliferation of an abnormal stem line, the number of normal cells will outnumber the aneuploids. An early error followed by differential survival favoring the normal cells could also result in the aneuploid cells being in the minority. In either case the rarity of the abnormal cells may render the error inapparent or render it difficult to determine whether mosaicism in fact exists. It may well be that to some extent every individual is a mosaic.

The determination of the karyotype depends upon obtaining samples of one or more tissues such as peripheral blood, bone marrow, or skin from an individual from whom it may not be possible to obtain further samples of such tissues. Also, under conditions of *culture* the cell lines may have differential survival rates. Hence, it may not be possible to arrive at an accurate estimate of the actual proportions maintained by the different cell lines in the living individual.

Finally, different tissues of the same body may contain different proportions of modal, hypomodal, and hypermodal cells. Although the proportions of these types of cells tend to remain fairly constant for any one tissue, it is sometimes necessary to examine several tissues before one can arrive at a diagnosis of mosaicism. Cells from one tissue may show modal karyotypes, while from another they may show modal, hypomodal, and hypermodal stem lines. Often only one or two of the useful tissues may be available for study.

Since sex chromosome mosaicism generally results from mitotic nondisjunction or anaphase lag during an early mitotic division of the zygote, the possible alternative mechanisms responsible for a particular mosaic can seldom be determined with certainty. However, those possible mecahnisms can often be inferred. The equivocal nature of such inferences is illustrated by the apparently simple case of XX/XO mosaicism. Does this condition originate with a normal XX zygote in which one of the X-chromosomes is lost by anaphase lag, or with an abnormal XO zygote? Though it is not at present possible to return an answer to this question, it is quite possible that both types of zygote may be the starting points in different cases. Of course, the first-named possibility is the more likely one by far.

NONDISJUNCTION AND AGING

Several studies have documented a statistically significant increase in hypodiploid cells in older persons, particularly females. This has generally been interpreted as a concomitant of, rather than a causative factor in, the aging process. Quite possibly a pattern of feedback is involved, with somatic aging representing the effect of the reciprocal interaction between the decreasing efficiency of the cellular tissues due to age, and the effect of these inefficient cellular tissues, in turn, upon the organism itself.

DERMATOGLYPHICS

As the various chromosomal aberrations are described below, it will be noticed that very often they are accompanied by the same symptoms and malformations. Cyto-geneticists have found that dermatoglyphics, the analysis of patterns of epidermal ridges on the volar (palmar or plantar) surfaces of the hands and feet, sometimes provide a unique diagnostic tool. Particular attention is paid to possible predominance of certain finger patterns (Fig. 3–2 I,II) and to the characteristics of palmar landmarks, especially the *a t d angle,* the measure of the angle formed by connecting the triradii *a, t,* and *d,* as shown in Fig. 3–2 III,IV. The nature of the flexion creases of the palm is also considered, though these are not related to the epidermal ridges; an abnormal flexion crease pattern is illustrated in Fig. 3–6.

PLOIDY

Presence of extra complete sets of chromosomes is referred to as polyploidy, with an appropriate prefix to indicate the number of sets. A $3n$ zygote is *triploid,* and one that is $4n$ is *tetraploid.* In humans even an apparently balanced polyploidy seems to be poorly compatible with life, though some body cells, for example, liver cells, are polyploid. As a result polyploid individuals are often spoken of as *heteroploid* even when their condition is essentially euploid.

One possible basis for heteroploidy is nondisjunctional error that involves *all* 23 pairs of chromosomes. If it occurred in meiosis, a gamete with $2n$ chromosomes would be formed. If such a diplolid gamete were fertilized by a normal haploid one, the resulting zygote would be triploid. This is *diandry* if the sperm was $2n$, *digyny* if it was the egg. Triploid or tetraploid cells could also be produced by mitotic nondisjunction or by fertilization of an egg by more than one sperm *(dispermy).*

Triploids, $3n = 69$, form an appreciable segment of human abortus material with chromosomal abnormalities (Fig. 3–3). Several tetraploids, $4n = 92$, have also been reported in this material. Most appear due to dispermy or digyny, though diandry cannot always be ruled out in the cases suspected to result from dispermy.

Term or live births with triploidy have generally proved to be mosaics, with diploid as well as triploid cells. In the apparent exceptions, probably not enough tissues were studied. Similarly, a child with apparent tetraploidy was shown to be a mosaic with diploid cells (Fig. 3–4).

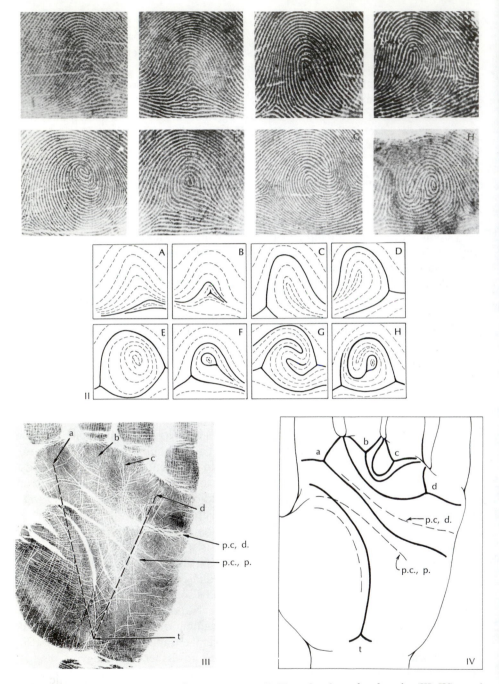

Fig. 3-2 The most common finger patterns (I, II) and palmar landmarks (III, IV) used in dermatoglyphic analysis. In I and II, A = simple arch; B = tented arch; C = ulnar loop; D = radial loop; E = simple whorl; F = central pocket whorl; G = double loop whorl; H = accidental whorl. In III and IV, a, b, c, d = digital triradii; t = axial triradius; p.c., d. = palmar crease, distal; p.c., p. = palmar crease, proximal. An important item is the a-t-d angle indicated in III. (From Alter, 1966; courtesy of M. Alter and *Medicine*.)

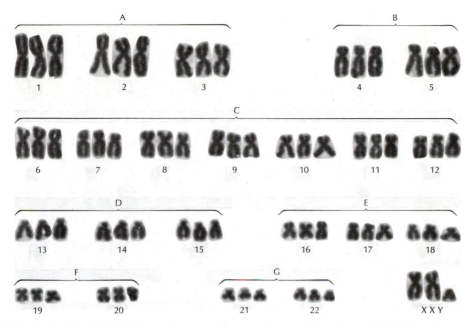

Fig. 3-3 Triploid, XXY karyotype in a human abortus. (Courtesy of D. H. Carr.)

SOMY

Usually, nondisjunctional errors, at least the kinds of nondisjunctional errors that can result in viable offspring or in observable fetuses, involve only one pair, or at most a few pairs, of chromosomes. The resultant modification in chromosome number is called a *somy* with an appropriate prefix. Thus a chromosome set containing an extra homologue of one chromosome type, all the other types being present in normal numbers, is a *trisomy* (a zygote with $2n + 1$). The $2n + 2$ condition in a zygote would be a *tetrasomy* if the two extra chromosomes were homologues, or a *double trisomy* if they were not; in the latter case there would be one extra homologue of each of *two* types of chromosomes. Conversely, if one chromosome is *absent*, the condition is referred to as *monosomy*, the number being $2n - 1$. When there are two less than the normal number of chromosomes, either both members of a pair are absent, a *nullosomy*, $2(n - 1)$, or two types lack one member each, a *double monosomy* $[2n - 2 = 2(n - 2) + 1(2)]$.

AUTOSOMAL TRISOMIES

The first proof that a chromosomal abnormality could be associated with a clinical entity was provided by Lejeune, Gautier, and Turpin in 1959 when they showed that children with the syndrome commonly known as mongolism or mongolian idiocy, but more properly named Down syndrome, for its first clear describer, Dr. J. Langdon–Down, were trisomic for one of the small acrocentrics of the G-group

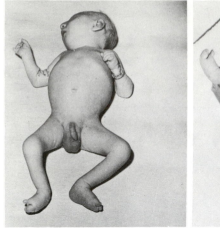
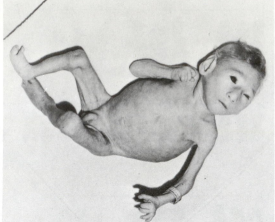

A   B

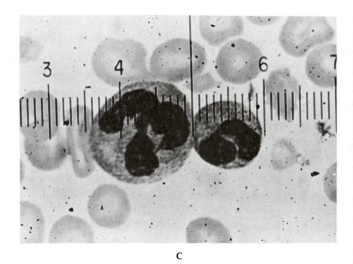

C

Fig. 3-4A Child with tetraploid/XXYY-diploid/XY mosaicism at six weeks. **B.** The same child at eight months, about a month before he died. Defects apparent are failure to thrive, microcephaly, micrognathia, small mouth, short fingers (each with only two phalanges), and malformed feet. **C.** Comparative size of an apparent tetraploid neutrophilic granulocyte (left) and a diploid one in a peripheral blood smear of this child. Apart from size, however, the larger cell appears morphologically normal. (From Kohn et al.,1967. Courtesy of W. J. Mellman and *Pediatric Research*.)

(Fig. 3–5). When this fundamental discovery was made there was general agreement that the trisomic chromosome is number 21, so that the preferred designation for the syndrome is "trisomy-21." We shall see in Chapter 4 that the abnormality may also occur in a context of 46 chromosomes instead of 47, but those account for less than five percent of the cases.

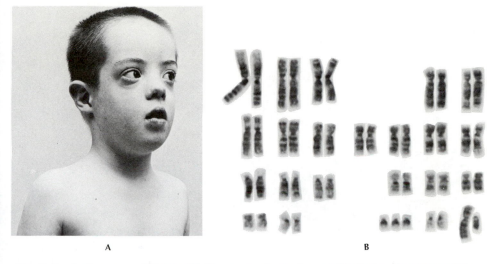

A   B

Fig. 3–5 A nine-year-old boy with Down syndrome (mongolism) showing some of the characteristic stigmata of the disorder: rounded face and broad head; small but perceptible medial epicanthic folds; narrowed and slightly slanted palpebral fissures; and flattened bridge of the nose, which is generally smaller than normal (as are the ears). The open mouth is suggestive of the usual protruding tongue, typically furrowed. The Brushfield spots (of the iris) commonly encountered in this syndrome are not visible. **B.** Giemsa karyotype of a Down syndrome male. Note the extra chromosome 21. (Courtesy of W. R. Breg.)

Some of the diagnostic characteristics of trisomy-21 that contribute to the typical facies are shown in Fig. 3–5. Other quite regular features are short, broad hands, with a single simian type of palmar crease (Fig. 3–6); short crooked (incurved) little finger; narrow high palate, small, irregular teeth; flat occiput; short stature; hyperflexibility of joints; and mental retardation. The IQ ranges from under 25 to 74, with a mode of 40–44. The Moro embrace reflex of the infant is characteristically absent.

Congenital heart disease, mostly septal defect, is very frequent. This and an increased susceptibility to respiratory infection are major causes of death in infancy. Those that survive often exhibit retarded motor development, but most can walk by three to four years of age and almost all develop simple speech by age five.

In the male, testicular degeneration and infertility seem to be the rule, with undescended testes and a small penis common. In females the labia minora are frequently small or absent. In a tabulation of 15 known Down females with offspring, four, possibly five, of the children were affected. Two stillborn cases were still under query. Of those definitely without Down syndrome, one was mentally retarded, two were stillborn twins, and six were normal.

The female with Down syndrome produces two types of eggs. One will have 24 chromosomes, and when fertilized by a normal sperm will develop Down syn-

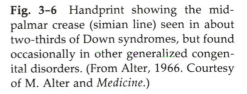

Fig. 3-6 Handprint showing the mid-palmar crease (simian line) seen in about two-thirds of Down syndromes, but found occasionally in other generalized congenital disorders. (From Alter, 1966. Courtesy of M. Alter and *Medicine*.)

drome. The other type of gamete will contain the normal haploid number of 23, and when fertilized by a normal sperm will develop as a normal zygote.

Down syndrome occurs in all population groups that have been studied. (Indeed, a very similar syndrome has been found in chimpanzees trisomic for a very small chromosome presumably homologous to number 21 of man.) Its incidence in newborns is usually given as about 1.5 per 1000 births, or about 1 in 700, but several recent studies in the United States and Canada have found lower numbers, 1 per 1000 or less. The difference is probably due to a lower frequency of older mothers in the American populations.

It was the British human genetics pioneer Lionel S. Penrose who first demonstrated conclusively in 1933 the significance of maternal age in the etiology of Down syndrome. The mean maternal age in Downs is about 35 years, compared with 28 years in a control population (Tables 3–1 and 3–2; see also Fig. 3–7). In one very large sample, a mother between 30 and 34 had less than three times as much likelihood of bearing a Down child as a 15- to 19-year-old mother, but this relative risk factor rose to more than seven times for the 35- to 39-year-old and more than twenty times for the 40- to 44-year-old, the mother who was 45 years of age or older having 50 times as much chance of such a child as the 15- to 19-year-old.

Another way of looking at the data is that until very recently women over 35 years of age had only 13 percent of all pregnancies but gave birth to over 50 percent of infants with Down syndrome. As the proportion of older mothers has been decreasing, so, too, has the proportion of Down syndromes born to them. Thus in one Massachusetts hospital between 1972 and 1975 women over 35 accounted for 7 percent of the pregnancies and 35 percent of the infants with Down syndrome.

Table 3-1 Average age of mothers bearing children with Down's syndrome in various countries (From Penrose and Smith, 1966, which should be consulted for the original references)

Country	Number of Cases	Mean Maternal Age Downs	Controls
Australia	1119	33.7	28.0
Canada	312	34.9	27.8
Denmark	518	34.6	28.3
England	2605	35.1	28.4
Finland	946	34.9	28.2
Formosa	20	36.6	28.3
Germany	225	34.2	27.1
Japan	321	33.2	28.2
Sweden	1242	35.4	28.7
United States	1788	33.3	27.7
USSR	345	33.7	27.9
All	9441[a]	34.43	28.17

[a]An earlier tabulation by Penrose (1965) had a mean maternal age of 34.44 for the mongols and 28.21 for the controls, showing how little effect the addition of 3635 cases, including material from two additional countries, had on the results.

Table 3-2 Maternal age distribution of the cases of Down's syndrome and controls in Table 3-1 (for references see Table 3-1)

Mother's Age	Downs	Controls[a]	Index[b]
≤19	184	462.4	0.398
20-24	988	2465.1	0.401
25-29	1364	2920.7	0.467
30-34	1569	2082.9	0.753
35-39	2547	1128.5	2.257
40-44	2383	353.7	6.737
≥45	406	27.7	14.657
Total	9441	9441.0	1.000

[a]The control totals for each age were scaled down so that the total agrees with the observed total number of Down's cases, thus permitting calculation of the index.
[b]Downs/control.

The risk for the woman over 35 is still very high, but an ever increasing percentage of the Down syndrome cases are being born to younger mothers.

There are conflicting reports on a possible paternal age factor as well. Where the source of the extra chromosome can be traced, it is derived from the father about 25 percent of the time.

The prevalence in the population is less than half the incidence at birth, because of the high rate of infant mortality of the syndrome, about one in six dying in the first year. Average expectation of life is about 16.2 years.

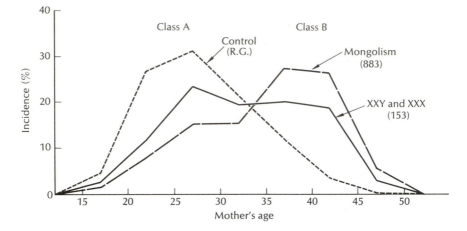

Fig. 3-7 Frequency of normal (control), gonosomal trisomy (XXY and XXX), and tri-somy-21 (Down syndrome or mongolism) births to mothers in various age brackets. The trisomy groups are seen to have bimodal distributions, one (Class A) very similar to the control group and therefore independent of maternal age and one (Class B) which is very different from the control distribution and therefore maternal age-dependent. The Class A fraction is much smaller in Down syndrome than in XXY and XXX. (From Penrose, 1965. Courtesy of L. S. Penrose and the publishers.)

The very next year after Lejeune and his group noted the association of tri-somy-21 and Down syndrome, two other trisomies involving moderately small autosomes and showing rather consistent symptomatology were described in successive articles in *The Lancet*. These are the Edwards and Patau syndromes. The former is a trisomy for E group chromosome 18 (Fig. 3–8). The latter was referred to by the vague term "D_1 trisomy" (Fig. 3–9) until radiographic and banding studies established that the chromosome in triplicate is number 13.

Trisomy-18, the Edwards Syndrome

Trisomy-18 is a syndrome characterized by multiple congenital malformations in which virtually every organ system is affected. Common features are elongated skull, micrognathia, low-set malformed ears, epicanthal folds and other eyelid abnormalities, hypertonicity, clenched fingers with second digit overlapping the third, short dorsiflexed big toe, hypoplasia of nails, skin redundancy, webbed neck (in about 30 percent), short sternum, ventricular septal defect and patent ductus arteriosus, horseshoe kidney, double ureter, male cryptorchidism, eventration of the diaphragm, and failure to thrive. The fingerprints (dermatoglyphics) show a characteristic pattern, consisting almost exclusively of simple arches on all fingers. The few that survive the first few weeks are severely retarded, mentally and developmentally.

Incidence is about 1 per 7500 live births, though here, as in trisomy-21, the

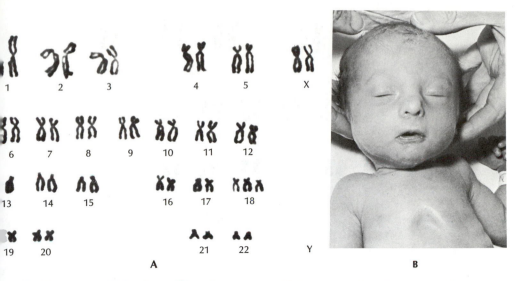

Fig. 3–8 Typical karyotype (**A**) and appearance (**B**) in trisomy-18. Note especially the elongated skull, unusually short sternum, webbed neck, and hypoplastic nails. The shortness of the neck and low-set malformed ears are also found frequently in trisomy-13. (**A.** Courtesy of S. Verbo and K. Hirschhorn; **B.** Courtesy of A. I. Taylor.)

presence of a maternal age effect causes some variation in the incidence in different populations. In one study 52.5 percent of the mothers of such offspring were 35 years or older at the birth of the affected child. Like the trisomy-21 curve in Fig. 3–7, the maternal age curve is bimodal.

The sex ratio at birth is very striking: nearly four females to one male. This difference in sex ratio has been attributed to the survival advantages of the genetically more balanced XX females in utero. If so, 18-trisomic males should predominate in fetal wastage studies. Although trisomy E accounts for one-third of all trisomic abortuses, very few are trisomy-18. Similarly this trisomy was the most frequent chromosomal abnormality in an analysis of 500 perinatal deaths, but only one of the five 18-trisomic males and two of the three females were stillbirths; the rest were "neonatal deaths," that is, live born. This means that either more males die in preimplantation stages or there is selection against Y-bearing unbalanced gametes prior to or during fertilization. Both possibilities are difficult to test, but the latter is supported by the more aberrant segregation ratios encountered in male carriers of some abnormalities of arrangement to be discussed later.

In view of the typical symptoms it is not surprising that in 90 percent of cases death occurs within the first six months. The mean survival time again favors females, 294 days versus 96.3 days for males. There are reports of severely retarded females alive at age 10 and 15, but the possibility of mosaicism cannot be ruled out. In one small sample of known mosaics the mean survival was close to four years.

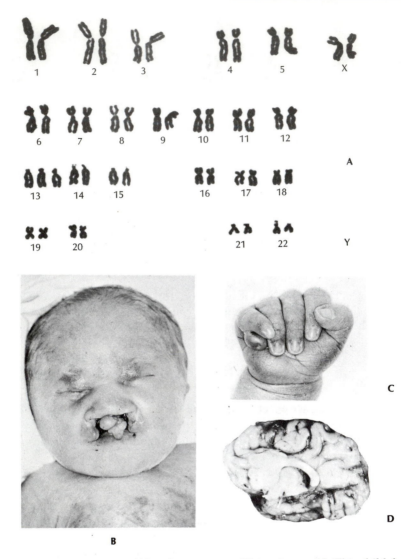

Fig. 3–9 Typical karyotype (**A**) and appearance (**B**) in trisomy-13. This child, born prematurely after 7 months' gestation and dead following an operation to reduce an omphalocele shortly after birth, exhibits many of the characteristics of the syndrome: microcephaly, microphthalmia, low-set malformed ears, bilateral hare-lip and cleft palate; postaxial polydactyly (**C**) and a flexion deformity of the fingers (**C**), the latter so strong that the dermatoglyphics could not be studied; and agenesis of the olfactory bulb of the brain and atrophy of the optic chiasma (**D**). There were also congenital heart and other defects. Unlike most infants with the syndrome, who have 47 chromosomes, this child had only 46 chromosomes, 2 of the 3 D chromosomes involved being fused into a single one (a homologous translocation or isochromosome as described on p. 87 and shown in Fig. 4–12. (**A.** Courtesy of K. Hirschorn. **B.** Courtesy of J. Hemet and *Annales d'Anatomie Pathologique*.)

Trisomy-13 (D₁), Patau's Syndrome

This is about half as frequent as trisomy-18, the incidence being about 1 per 15,000 births. The maternal age effect is similar to that in the other trisomies described. Unlike trisomy-18, there is only a slight excess of females, and survival time is quite similar in the two sexes. Most die before the age of three months.

Although trisomy-13 and trisomy-18 present many of the same symptoms—such as mental and developmental retardation, cardiac anomalies, epicanthal folds, hypertonicity, and low-set ears in most cases—those that appear more frequently in trisomy-13 (Fig. 3–9) and serve to characterize it are: presumptive deafness, minor motor seizures, agenesis of the olfactory bulbs, sloping forehead or microcephaly, microphthalmia and/or colobomata of the iris, cleft lip and/or palate, capillary hemangiomata, polydactyly, posterior heel prominence, necrotic ulcers of the scalp, incomplete rotation of the colon, and partially bicornuate uterus in the female.

Other Autosomal Trisomies

Although many of them have been found in abortuses, pure trisomies for other autosomal chromosomes probably do not occur in live births. Some workers recognize live-born trisomy-8 and trisomy-22 syndromes, but most, if not all, of the reported cases involve mosaicism with euploid cell lines. Partial trisomies, in which extra *pieces* of chromosome are present, are better established entities. They will be discussed in the Chapter 4, in the section on "Duplications."

GONOSOMAL ABNORMALITIES OF NUMBER

Well over 70 anomalies of the sex chromosomes have been described, the best known of these having been given different names by different workers. At this stage we are concerned only with those involving monosomy and polysomy.

Diagnosis of X-chromosome anomalies of number was given a tremendous boost by the earlier discovery of the sex chromatin often referred to as the "Barr body" (also discussed in Chapter 7). This is often referred to as "nuclear sex." Persons with only a single X lack sex chromatin and therefore are often referred to as "chromatin negative" (Fig. 7–9). Those with more than one X are "chromatin positive," the number of chromatin (or Barr) bodies being always one less than the number of X-chromosomes present (Figs. 7–9, 7–10, 3–13, and 3–15).

Since sex chromatin can now be determined with considerable good reliability by such relatively simple techniques as a smear of the easily sloughed-off cells of the buccal or vaginal mucosa, this method has proven to be extremely useful. It should be kept in mind, however, that the Barr body may be visible in as few as one-fifth of the buccal cells of a normal female (somewhat higher in vaginal material) and that often a few cells of a normal male will appear to be chromatin positive. (100 "good" cells are usually counted for each test.) Hence the buccal chromatin technique is mainly a spot-checking device to determine which person would be worth testing by means of the more laborious tissue-culture karyotype methods. It is particularly useful for cells obtained via amniocentesis (Chapter 18).

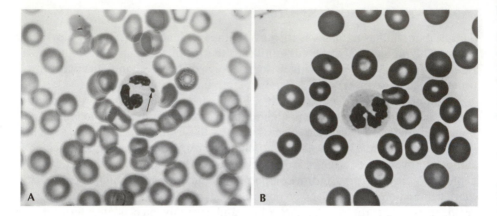

Fig. 3–10 Blood smears showing neutrophil polymorphonuclear leukocytes **A.** Female **B.** Male. Note the "drumstick" (arrow) attached to the nucleus in **A** but absent in **B**. (From Barr, 1957. Courtesy of M. L. Barr and Grune and Stratton, Inc., publishers of *Progress in Gynecology.*)

A less reliable, but sometimes interesting, guide to nuclear sex is the "drumstick" (Fig. 3–10**A**), first noted in 1954 in a small percentage of polymorphonuclear leukocytes of a normal female, but almost always missing from the corresponding cells of the normal male (Fig. 3–10**B**). The number of drumsticks present may correspond to the number of Barr bodies (Fig. 3–15**D**), but it is not consistent. The technique is much more laborious than the chromatin test since at least 500 cells must be counted each time to reach a conclusion.

The Y-chromosome stains intensely in Q-banding. This led to the demonstration that interphase cells, such as buccal smears and amnion cultures, and gametes could be sexed according to whether or not they contain a small, brightly fluorescent spot, the "Y body," in their nuclei (Fig. 3–11). Thus nuclear sex can be diagnosed for both X- and Y-chromosomes, so many are referring to the Barr body as "*X*-chromatin."

Disorders Due to the Absence of the Second Sex Chromosome: XO Turner Syndrome (Gonadal Dysgenesis, Ovarian Agenesis, Bonnevie–Ullrich Syndrome)

The clinical condition was first described by Turner in 1938. While the term "Turner syndrome" is commonly used to describe the monosomic XO phenotype, other aberrations of the sex chromosomes may present with phenotypic traits scarcely if at all distinguishable from pure Turner syndrome. Hence, the nomenclature preferred by many authorities to cover all these phenotypically similar cases is *gonadal dysgenesis,* for the principal trait common to all of them is maldevelopment of the gonads. Figure 3–12 shows a typical phenotype and karyotype in this condition, the latter from the first authors to associate the two.

The major traits of gonadal dysgenesis or XO Turner syndrome are: female phenotype; short stature, usually less than five feet in height; streak gonads, hence

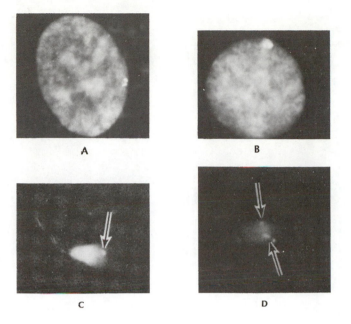

Fig. 3-11 Y bodies observed with quinacrine fluorescence. **A.** Lymphocyte from peripheral blood of a male. **B.** Cultured amniotic fluid cell showing a fluorescent single bifid Y. It is probably bifid because of slight separation of the distal portions of the two chromatids of Yq. **C.** Haploid sperm with a single Y body. **D.** Haploid sperm with 2 Y bodies, presumably because of the presence of two Y chromosomes. This is found in about 2 percent of otherwise normal spermatozoa. (**A** and **B** courtesy of W. R. Breg; **C** and **D** from Pearson, 1972, courtesy of R. B. Bressler, P. Pearson, and the *Journal of Medical Genetics.*)

primary amenorrhea, hypoestrinism, and sterility; short, broad neck with webbing or looseness and redundancy of the skin. The chest is usually also broad ("shield-like"), and nipples tend to be widely spaced. Secondary sex characteristics fail to develop spontaneously, except that pubic hair is often present.

Excretion of urinary gonadotrophins is high after puberty, sometimes also in childhood. In about one-fourth of the cases there are cardiovascular abnormalities, and sometimes there are pigmented nevi and predisposition to keloid formation. If present, congenital lymphedema of the extremities is almost diagnostic. There may be a variety of kidney, ear, and eye abnormalities. Shortening of a metacarpal or metatarsal and cubitus valgus are not uncommon. Rarefaction of the bones, particularly of the hands and feet, occurs with some frequency in affected children, and postmenopausal type of osteoporosis in young adults. There is a tendency also to precocious senility. The intelligence quotient tends to be normal.

The symptomatology here described for Turner syndrome may, in any one or more of the traits listed, show every kind of variability from complete absence to complete expression. Menstruation for some years may occur in some cases, and the birth of a normal child has been recorded in at least one apparent XO woman, but occult mosaicism cannot be ruled out.

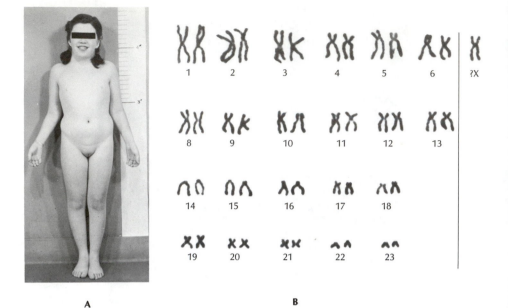

A   B

Fig. 3–12A A 16-year-old patient with gonadal dysgenesis (Turner syndrome). Note the small stature, broad neck, wide-spaced nipples, and the absence of secondary sex characteristics. The gonads consisted of streaks of connective tissue. (From Barr, 1960. Courtesy of J. C. Rathbun, M. L. Barr, and the *American Journal of Human Genetics*.) **B.** An example of the karyotype found in most cases of Turner syndrome. There is only one sex chromosome, an X. This karyotype, from Ford et al. (1959b), is characterized somewhat differently than most in that the X is considered chromosome number 7 (where it belongs on the basis of size); as a result each chromosome smaller than X is given a number which is larger by one than in most current reports. (Courtesy of C. E. Ford and *Lancet*.)

In monosomic 45,X Turner syndrome, since these have no second sex chromosome, the cells are chromatin negative. About 80 percent of all varieties of Turner syndrome are associated with this particular karyotype. The frequency is about one in 2000 newborn females, with a much higher frequency of about 7 percent of all abortuses, and 20 percent of abortuses with a chromosomal abnormality. About 1 percent of all fertilizations are estimated to be XO, of whom less than 5 percent survive to be born alive.

The most probable explanation of the loss of the second sex chromosome is that it occurs after the establishment of an XX or XY zygote. This interpretation is supported by the high frequency of mosaicism, always a postzygotic event, in Turner syndrome. Thus a composite of six surveys with over 16,000 liveborn females included 7 with 45,X cells; at least 5 of the 7 were mosaics. The fact that maternal age is not a significant factor in these cases, as it is in chromosomal aberrations that probably have a meiotic basis, and that there is a high frequency of a monozygotic twinning in the sibships of Turner individuals is further suggestive of some abnormality of mitosis leading to the loss of a sex chromosome during post-zygotic cleavage.

The high frequency of nonmosaic XOs in early abortus material also supports the suspicion that those XOs that do survive the early gestation period have a normal cell line for at least part of their embryonic existence.

Live-born XO/XX mosaics exhibit Turner syndrome, but are generally taller than 45,X individuals, show fewer anomalies, more feminization, and, in many cases, ovulate and menstruate spontaneously.

Karyotypically normal 46,XX and 46,XY cases have been described showing many features of Turner syndrome, all of female phenotype. In the 46,XY cases pure gonadal dysgenesis was present, as was tallness, primary amenorrhea, and increased urinary gonadotrophic excretion. Gonadal neoplasms, such as seminoma and gonadoblastoma, are usually common. It may be conjectured that one of the sex chromosomes—albeit normal in appearance—is deficient in these cases. In XY pure gonadal dysgenesis with female phenotype it is clearly failure or suppression of the Y-chromosome in the presence of an X-chromosome that is responsible for the condition. In several cases banding methods have demonstrated that the Y-chromosomal material present is confined to the long arm (sometimes double), evidence that the genetic material for maleness is on the short arm.

Phenotypic males with short stature, webbed neck, small and frequently undescended testes, and some of the other symptoms described above for XO females have the Noonan syndrome. This has sometimes been referred to as "male Turner syndrome," but this is a misnomer, since recognizable gonads are present; hence the basis, while unknown, is probably very different from that of the true Turner syndrome. A female counterpart of this condition also exists.

Several additional forms of Turner syndrome will be mentioned in Chapter 4, one of them familial.

Klinefelter Syndrome (Seminiferous Tubule Dysgenesis, Testicular Dysgenesis, Medullary Gonadal Dysgenesis, Chromatin Positive Micro-orchidism)

In 1942 Klinefelter, Reifenstein, and Albright described nine men with small testes, aspermia, gynecomastia, and elevated urinary gonadotrophins. This combination of symptoms has since come to be known as Klinefelter syndrome (Fig. 3–13A). Later studies showed that Klinefelter individuals are chromatin positive, thus indicating the presence of at least two X-chromosomes. In 1959 this indication was confirmed by the demonstration of the presence of two X-chromosomes in addition to a single Y in such Klinefelter cases by Jacobs and Strong. The most usual karyotype in Klinefelter syndrome, in more than three-fourths of the cases is 47,XXY (Fig. 3–13B), but Klinefelter syndrome will usually be the result whenever more than one X occurs in the presence of a Y (Fig. 3–13C–F).

Klinefelter syndrome occurs with surprisingly similar frequency in all surveys of liveborn males: about one in 1000 (0.1 percent). Though not invariably retarded, Klinefelters account for about 1 percent of institutionalized mentally defective males. They also account for close to 5 percent of male subfertility cases seen in fertility clinics.

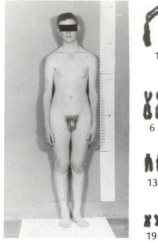

A

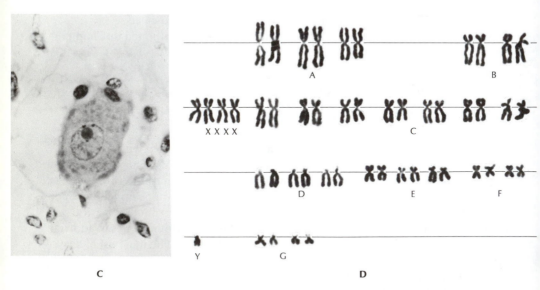

Fig. 3–13 Some varieties of the Klinefelter syndrome. **A.** A 15-year-old patient with seminiferous tubule dysgenesis and a positive chromatin pattern. Note the long limbs, gynecomastia, broad pelvis, and horizontal limit of pubic hair. **B.** The usual karyotype in this condition. **C.** Chromatin picture (sympathetic ganglion cell) in a 48,XXXY Klinefelter. There are two chromatin bodies at the nuclear periphery. The internal smaller spot is not a chromatin body; it is a perinucleolar chromocentre central dot normally

The phenotypic expression of the disorder runs the full gamut of variability from almost no phenotypic evidences of the condition with spermatogenesis and probable fertility in some cases, to severe degeneration and hyalinization of the seminiferous tubules (after puberty), complete aspermia, well-developed breasts, broad pelvis, knock knees, horizontal limit of pubic hair, and feminine-pitched voice. The limbs tend to be long, the hands and feet large. Gynecomastia occurs in about 80 percent of cases. The rule governing the degree of mental retardation is: the greater the number of X-chromosomes present the severer the mental defect. The internal and external genitalia are of normal appearance grossly, except for the testes, which are usually small, and although libido is normally reduced the Klinefelter male is usually capable of erection and intercourse.

A number of other disorders are quite frequent in association with Klinefelter's syndrome. Depressed thyroid function is usual, as are chronic pulmonary conditions such as asthma, bronchiectasis, emphysema, alone or in combination, varicose veins, and diabetes mellitus. The frequency with which thyroid dysfunction and also diabetes mellitus occur in the various chromosomal disorders of gonadal development and in the normal relatives of such individuals has suggested some causal connection between these conditions and the nondisjunction resulting in the disordered gonadal development.

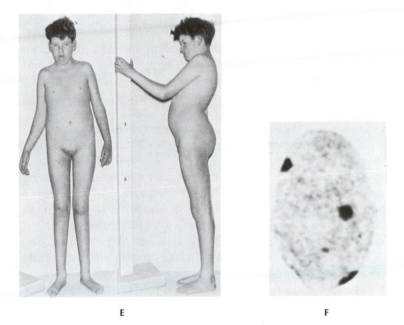

E   F

present in human nerve cells of both sexes. D. Karyotype, E, appearance, and F, chromatin picture, of a 12-year-old mentally retarded 49,XXXXY studied by Fraccaro et al. (1962). He is 4 ft. 10 in. tall and has an arm span of 4 ft. 7 in. (A. From Barr, 1960. Courtesy of M. L. Barr and the *American Journal of Human Genetics*. B. Courtesy of S. Verbo and K. Hirschhorn. C. Courtesy of M. L. Barr. D–E. Courtesy of M. Fraccaro and *Cytogenetics*.)

The average maternal age in 47,XXY Klinefelter syndrome is about 32.3 years. While not as marked as in Down syndrome (Fig. 3–8), this maternal age effect probably has much the same basis: aging of the ovum, especially the prolonged diakinesis.

The finding that polysomy-X in the presence of a Y produces males whereas the XO condition results in females in man (and other mammals) was surprising at first, because the XXY is a female and the XO a male in flies, the organisms whose cytogenetics had been studied most. These data indicated therefore that the Y-chromosome in man contains factors for maleness. As noted earlier, they are probably on the short arm.

Other Karyotypic Varieties of Klinefelter Syndrome

Some seven different single stem-line karyotypes have been established in Klinefelter syndrome. Five of these are listed in Table 3–3, part A. A sixth karyotype associated with Klinefelter syndrome has been described in half a dozen cases. These have a 46,XX karyotype without apparent mosaicism, are of average intelligence, and are otherwise unremarkable. The presence of hyalinized testes suggests that these cases may be occult XXYs, that is, a Y-chromosome is or may have been present at one time in some, at least, of the cells of the individual. In some such cases it can be demonstrated that the Y-chromosome is in fact present but translocated to another chromosome.

The occurrence of 46,XX Klinefelter cases would of itself suggest that similar cases are possible with the karyotype 46,XY, and such cases, indeed, have been reported. Four of the original nine cases of Klinefelter syndrome were traced and reexamined, and two of these were found to be chromatin negative. Phenotypically, such individuals are indistinguishable from chromatin positive 47,XXY Klinefelter syndrome.

Can it be that in these 46,XY cases an occult X is or was at one time present? How otherwise can the abnormal developments be explained? Future research will, no doubt, provide the answer.

Mosaicism is a frequent cause of Klinefelter syndrome (Table 3–3B), and its most frequent occurrence is in the form of XY/XXY. Individuals of this karyotype differ from the typical XXY Klinefelter in a number of important respects. Small testes are present in only about 80 percent as compared with 100 percent in XXYs; aspermia occurs in about 60 percent instead of 90 percent; and 30 percent are presumptive fathers as compared with only 3 percent in the other group. Subnormal intelligence is significantly less frequent.

The XX/XXY karyotype appears to be less common than the XY/XXY. This group is not in any way distinguishable from the typical 47,XXY individual, except possibly in a lower frequency of mental subnormality. It is not surprising that the cytogenetically more normal (for males) XY/XXY should present a clinically more normal phenotype than the XX/XXY.

Other forms of mosaicism in Klinefelter syndrome are not otherwise remarkable, except when they take such a bizarre form as in the case of a boy with multiple malformations, idiocy, cryptorchidism, and germinal cell aplasia, who had no less than six different cell ines: XXXY/XXX/XXXXY/XXXX/XXXXXY/XXXXX.

Table 3-3 Chromosomal aberrations in Klinefelter or Klinefelter-like syndromes. Some forms, especially the mosaics, show considerable variability in degree of abnormality (Adapted, with modification, from Reitalu, 1968

		Sex Chromosomal Constitution		
A. Only one karyotype observed		XXY XXYY XXXY XXXYY XXXXY		
B. Numeric mosaics	Double	XX XY XY XXY XXY XXXY XXXX	XXY XXY XXXY XXXY XXYY XXXXY XXXXY	
	Triple	XY XX XY XY XO XX XXXY XXXY	XXY XXY XXY XYY XY XY XXY XXXXY XXXXY	XXYY XXXY XXXY XXYY XXY XXY XXYYY XXXXYY XXXXX
	Quad-ruple	XXY XY XX XO		
	Sex-tuple	XXX, XXXY, XXXX, XXXXY, XXXXX, XXXXXX		
Numeric and structural mosaics	Double	XXY XXxY		
	Triple	XY XXY XXxY XxY Xx XY		

Klinefelter syndrome occurs also in conjunction with autosomal chromosome anomalies. In the first instance of this type reported the child had 48 chromosomes with both Down syndrome and XXY Klinefelter (Fig. 3–14). As might be expected from the maternal age effects mentioned previously, as maternal age advances the chances increase not alone for Down or Klinefelter syndrome but for the combination of the two. Similar considerations apply to XXY,E and XXY,D double trisomies.

Polysomy of X: Triple 47,XXX, Tetra 48,XXXX, and Penta 49,XXXXX

Figure 3–15 shows the first triple-X case. The patient, a Scotswoman, presented at age 22 with secondary amenorrhea. Menstruation had commenced at 14 years but was always irregular and ceased completely at 19. Laparotomy performed when she

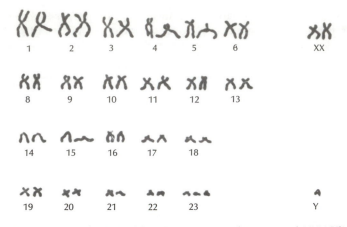

Fig. 3-14 The first reported double trisomy, a combination of XXY-Klinefelter and Down syndromes. Note the karyotype enumeration similar to that in Figure 3–12**B** (from the same laboratory). The extra G chromosome was placed with number 23 (22). The designation as the smallest autosome happens to be correct, but it is number 21 in the currently accepted terminology. (From Ford et al., 1959a. Courtesy of C. E. Ford and *Lancet.*)

was 28 showed menopausal ovaries, and an ovarian biopsy revealed a marked follicle deficiency. The breasts and internal genitalia were underdeveloped and external genitalia were infantile, though there was some response in these characters after estrogen therapy (Fig. 3–15**B**). Urinary gonadotrophin secretion was high. Intelligence was below average.

Since this original case, the numerous others that have been described have shown that 47,XXX cases cannot all be resumed easily under a single clinical syndrome, but that the variation in these cases runs all the way from normal to the kind of symptoms exhibited by the woman in the first case described (above). Although they are as frequent as XXY and XYY males and much more frequent than live-born XO females, most triple-X individuals are likely to go unnoticed because they show no major abnormalities, and will only be detected on a buccal smear or karyotype analysis. When any abnormalities do occur, they are of two kinds: (1) those affecting the developing of the sexual traits and (2) those affecting intelligence and behavioral development. Intelligence in some cases is reduced and personality problems are reported with some frequency. The symptoms tend to be more severe in the 48,XXXX (Fig. 3–16) and 49,XXXXX that have been described.

In some of the early reports the human 47,XXX was dubbed "superfemale," the term often applied to the XXX karyotype in *Drosophila melanogaster*. This practice has been discontinued in view of the poor analogy between the two. The *Drosophila* XXX tends to be larger than the normal female, and exhibits considerable secondary nondisjunction at meiosis.

Although several of these children have been born to older mothers (Fig. 3–7), the overall average age of the mother at birth of XXX females is about 23 years.

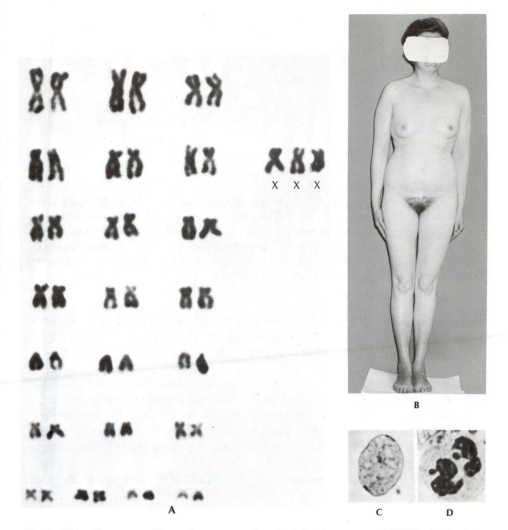

X X X

B

A

C D

Fig. 3–15A Karyotype (Sternal marrow culture) of the first reported XXX individual. **B.** The patient at age 35 after estrogen therapy. **C.** A buccal mucosa cell showing two chromatin bodies. **D.** An unusual polymorphonuclear cell with double drumsticks; the other drumsticks observed were more typical. (From Jacobs et al., 1959a. Courtesy of P. A. Jacobs and *Lancet*.)

THE XYY ANOMALY AND BEHAVIOR

In December, 1965 Patricia Jacobs and her colleagues published their findings on a population of 197 mentally subnormal male patients with dangerous, violent, or criminal propensities undergoing treatment in a special security institution in Scotland. Seven of these males were found to be of XYY chromosome constitution, one was an XXYY, and another an XY/XXY mosaic. Since, as expected on the-

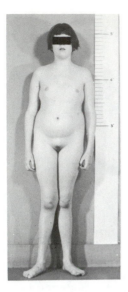

Fig. 3–16 A 48,XXXX female, age 12 years and 4 months at the time the picture was taken, reported by Carr et al. (1961). In contrast to the average 47,XXX, this patient and other poly-X cases that have been described have been severely mentally defective. (Courtesy D. H. Carr, M. L. Barr and the *Canadian Medical Association Journal.*)

oretical grounds, the XYY chromosome constitution is about as frequent at birth as the XXY constitution, about one out of every 1000 liveborn males, the 3.5 per 100 occurrence of XYY males in this security population consituted a highly significant finding.

First reported by Sandberg, Koepf, Ishihara, and Hauschka in 1961, the XYY complement most probably comes about as a consequence of nondisjunction at the second meiotic division of the paternal germ cells. Such a chromosomal complement could also be produced in a mitotic nondisjunction in the early zygotic cleavages, but in such an event XO/XYY or XO/XY/XYY mosaicism is more likely to occur.

Since the publication of the paper by Jacobs and her colleagues many other reports have been published on XYY individuals, some of which lead to very different conclusions from those drawn by the early investigators. A sample of these reports is set out in Table 3–4.

Since most early investigations on the XYY anomaly were carried out in security institutions, the findings of an excessive number of incarcerated individuals with the XYY anomaly led most investigators to conclude that the extra Y-chromosome was the cause of these conditions. Subsequent investigation has revealed that many XYYs are perfectly normal adults. Indeed, while aggressive behavior may occur in some XYY incarcerates, most of them have committed offences against property rather than against the person and often tend to be very mild individuals.

On the other hand, a number of recent surveys and studies continue to suggest statistically significant psychological differences between the XYY group and other males. The idea also finds some support from studies in mice. Unfortunately, the problem has in some places become a matter of public controversy, and this may further impede a scientific solution.

Major physical abnormalities do not occur regularly in XYY individuals,

Table 3-4 Selected male population surveys containing apparent cases of the XYY anomaly

Population	Status	Number	Abnormal Gonosomal Karyotypes
Security	Criminal	315	9 XYY, 1 XXYY, 1 XXY, 1 XY/XXY/XXXY
Detention center	"Antisocial acts"	50	4 XYY
Institutional	Criminal	24	2 XYY
Security	Criminal	315	9 XYY
Detention center	Apparently criminal	19	1 XYY
Institutional	Criminal	129	5 XYY, 7 XXY
Prison	Criminal	40	4 XYY, 1 XYY/XYYY
Institutional		200	9 XYY
Security	Criminal	155	2 XYY
Security	Criminal	204	2 XYY, 2 XXY, 1 XY/XXY
Institution		23	3 XYY
Prison		86	2 XYY
Newborn Males	("Control")	1,066	4 XYY, 1 XXY
Newborn Males	("Control")	266	(No XYY)
Adult males	("Control")	2,094	1 XYY
Summary			
Institutional		1560	52 XYY (3.3 percent)
"Control"		3426	5 XYY (0.1 percent)

Note: For references see Levitan and Montagu (1977).

probably because the Y-chromosome carries relatively little genetic material of the usual trait-determining type that will be discussed in later chapters. The physical abnormalities that do occur are interesting though none are unique to this condition. As in most cases in which an extra sex chromosome is present, whether X or Y, there is a high incidence of developmental anomalies affecting the internal and external genitalia. Undescended testes, hypogonadism with seminiferous tubule dysgenesis, and various other genital anomalies have been described in many cases. Urinary gonadotrophins tend to be elevated. Facial acne appears to be frequent in adolescence, probably a high gonadotrophin effect. These individuals are usually dull mentally, with IQs ranging between 80 and 95. Abnormal electroencephalographic recordings and a relatively high incidence of epileptiform conditions suggest a wide spectrum of brain dysfunction. Disorders of the teeth, such as hypoplastic or discolored enamel and/or malocclusion, have also been noted.

Does the XYY male transmit the abnormality to his offspring? The answer seems to be that he usually does not, that somehow during gametogenesis the extra Y is weeded out, but several exceptions have been reported.

OTHER DISORDERS OF SEXUAL DEVELOPMENT

In addition to the Turner, Klinefelter, and other syndromes described above, there are a number of other disorders of sexual development that appear to have some genetic or chromosomal basis. These include mixed gonadal dysgenesis pure gonadal dysgenesis, true hermaphroditism, and several forms of male and female pseudohermaphroditism. Some of the last named, such as testicular feminization, which are XY, are taken up in Chapter 7. Of the others, in some patients normal karyotypes are presented and in others, complex mosaicism. Several were discussed above in connection with Turner's syndrome. Since their etiology—or even their identity—is so poorly understood at present, we shall not discuss them further here, but suggest that the interested reader pursue them in the literature.

Exercises concerning the material of this chapter will be incorporated into the exercises for Chapter 4.

4

Disorders of Chromosome Structure

Aberrations of structure refer to changes in the arrangement of the chromosomal material. They generally stem directly or indirectly from breaks in the chromosomes. The causes of chromosome breaks are not completely understood, though they are known to include viruses, radiation, and many of the chemicals and other agents that cause structural changes in the gene (Chapter 5). Suffice it to say, evidence exists that chromosomal breaks occur more frequently than chromosomal aberrations. This means that broken chromosomes often reunite in the original form, leaving no trace of the breakage.

TRANSLOCATIONS

If two chromosome breaks are on different chromosomes, usually heterologous (nonhomologous), the chromosomes may exchange pieces, forming a *reciprocal translocation* (Fig. 4–1). As the diagram indicates, there are two alternative new unions of the four pieces resulting from the two breaks: (1) the union may be aneucentric, forming a dicentric and an acentric fragment, or (2) the union may be eucentric, forming two new chromosomes, each with a single centromere. Aneucentric translocations almost never survive the next cell division, whereas eucentric ones commonly survive at least one generation. Thus almost all of the translocations usually encountered are of the eucentric variety, and this is the type that will be discussed at greater length below. Figure 4–2 shows, however, a dicentric chromosome encountered in an experiment in which the simian virus, SV-40, apparently induced chromosome breakage and neoplasticlike growth in human tissue culture cells.*

Reciprocal translocations are the most frequent changes in arrangement encountered in radiation experiments and in the occasional eruption of spontaneous aberrations in well-studied organisms with more than one chromosome pair (e.g., Levitan, 1964). Since breakages are usually random in these cases, the chances are greater that two breaks will be on different chromosomes rather than on the

*These cells are then said to be "transformed," but this is not the same as genetic transformation in bacteria.

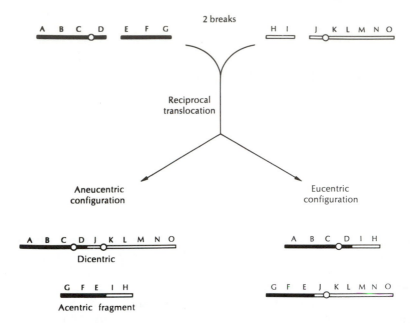

Fig. 4-1 Interchromosomal exchanges that may result from single breaks on each of two chromosomes. (Modified from King, 1965.)

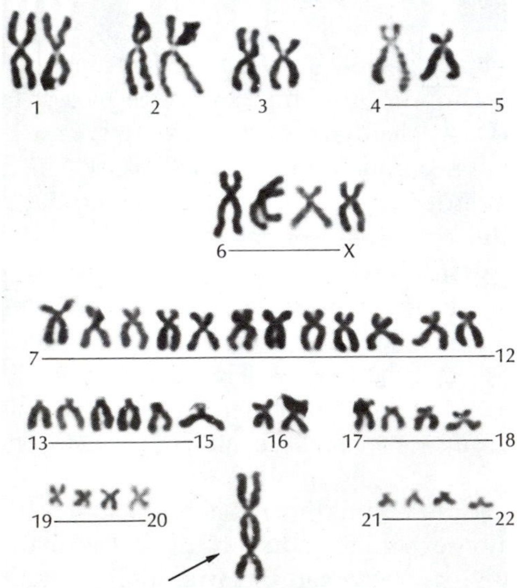

Fig. 4-2 Karyotype of a cell from a human fibroblast tissue culture infected with the simian kidney virus, SV-40, showing a large dicentric (arrow). Presumably, this represents the bulk of an aneucentric translocation between a number 4 and a number 5, the acentric fragment having been lost. (Courtesy of P. S. Moorhead. Similar figures have been published by Moorhead and Saksela, 1963 and others.)

same chromosome. The more chromosomes there are in the diploid set the greater becomes the likelihood that two breaks occurring about the same time will affect different chromosomes. It is not surprising, therefore, that two-break reciprocal translocations are also the most frequent structural rearrangements to be encountered thus far in human chromosomal analyses.

A reciprocal translocation does not change the amount of chromosomal material. Only the arrangement or position of the genetic material is changed. As a matter of fact, the exchanged pieces may even be the same size, in which case even the gross appearance of the chromosomes may not be altered. In some organisms merely the change in position, or *position effect,* is enough to produce abnormalities in visible characters or disturbances of viability and fertility. These effects are especially likely if both chromosomes of the affected pair carry the translocation (in which case the individual is said to be *homozygous* or *homokaryous* for it). The observed morphological or physiological abnormalities may stem from actual damage to the genetic material at the point of breakage and not merely because it has "new neighbors" on the chromosomes. Be that as it may, many carriers of reciprocal translocations in man appear to be normal, possibly because to date no human translocation homozygote has been found. Instead, all human carriers of reciprocal translocations have proved to be *heterozygous* or *heterokaryous* for the aberration. As in Fig. 4–1, one member of each pair maintains the normal arrangement and one member of the pair is involved in the translocation. Since the genetic material is present in normal amount such a translocation heterozygote is said to be *balanced.*

Even though translocation heterozygotes often appear to be normal, they tend to be characterized by lower fertility. This is probably less obvious in man than in other animals. Sometimes a translocation heterozygote will produce a normal number of viable offspring, but usually also a number of miscarriages or stillbirths. The lowered fertility of translocation heterozygotes stems from the fact that the tetrads including the translocation, which exhibit a characteristic quadriradial ("cross") figure, may reach the equator of the spindle during the first meiotic division oriented in different ways in relation to the poles. Figure 4–3 represents the synaptic pairing of the eucentric reciprocal translocation and its normal homologues of Fig. 4–1. The normal arrangements *abc.defg* and *hij.klmno* are designated I and II, and translocation chromosomes *ABC.DIH* and *GFEJ.KLMNO* III and IV, respectively (Fig. 4–3).

The cross-shaped quadriradial at the top of Fig. 4–3 is diagnostic for a reciprocal translocation. It can also be observed in mitotic prophase or metaphase (1) in organisms with somatic pairing of homologues, or (2) if the translocation involves chromatid rather than whole chromosome breaks (Fig. 4–4).

If during the metaphase of meiosis I, arrangements I and IV are turned toward one pole, with II and III toward the other (Fig. 4–3), this is referred to as *adjacent-1 segregation.* Some of the resultant gametes will lack any representation of the HI area (but have extra EFG) while the others will lack EFG (and have extra HI). These gametes and any zygote resulting from fertilization with one of them are unbalanced. Similarly, if I and III are turned toward the same pole, with II and IV toward the other, this is called *adjacent-2 segregation,* and unbalanced gametes result. They have either a deficiency or duplication for A–D and J–O. The only

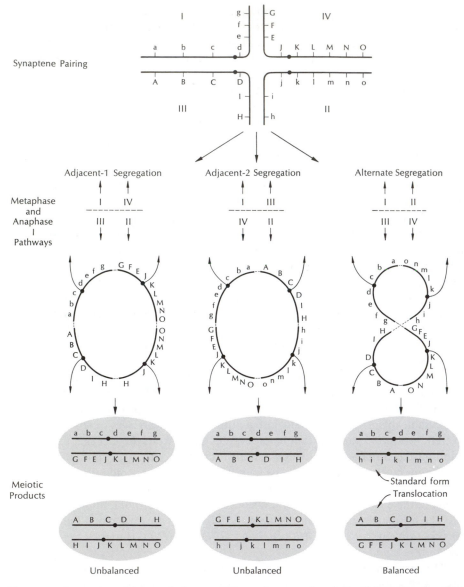

Fig. 4-3 Synaptic pairing and the possible pathways of meiotic disjunction in a heterozygote for the eucentric translocation of Fig. 4–1. For diagrammatic purposes, only one chromatid is shown per chromosome.

way balanced gametes could be produced would be to have *alternate segregation*, in which I and II move toward the same pole, III and IV toward the other (right side of Fig. 4–3). These alternatives are best visualized in early anaphase, when the centromeres have just begun to lead the way toward the poles.

The segregations can also be referred to as *nonhomologous adjacent, homologous adjacent,* and *alternate,* with the term "homologous" referring to the centro-

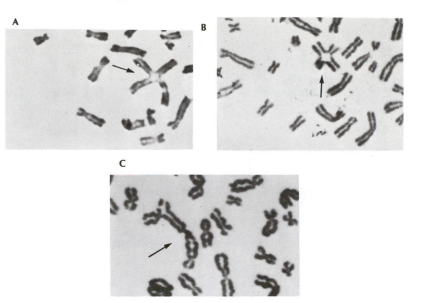

Fig. 4-4 A and **B.** Quadiradials indicative of interchromatid translocations in mitotic metaphases from the mother (**A**) and maternal uncle (**B**) of a boy with both Down syndrome and leukemia. Mongolism in this case was attributable to still another translocation inherited by the boy from his mother, this one involving whole chromosome breaks; it would show a quadriradial only in meiosis. **C.** Complex breakage figure from the SV-40 work referred to in Fig. 4–2. Visibly there has been an interchromatid translocation (denoted by the quadriradial), a chromatid break (denoted by the gap in one arm of the cross), and an aneucentric whole-chromosome translocation (denoted by the di(tri?)centric condition of the chromosome). (**A** and **B.** From German et al., 1962. Courtesy of J. L. German and the *American Journal of Human Genetics.* **C.** Courtesy of P. S. Moorhead.)

meres. In these segregations two centromeres are oriented toward each pole. This is *concordant* orientation.

It is also possible for the quadrivalent to be so oriented that one centromere is pointed toward each pole, the other two centromeres being in the metaphase plate and pointing toward the periphery of the spindle equator rather than toward the poles. This is called *discordant* orientation of the quadrivalent. If at anaphase each pole-directed centromere moves toward the pole along with one of the adjacent plate-oriented centromeres, the result will be the same as an adjacent-1 or an adjacent-2 segregation of a concordantly oriented quadrivalent. For example, were the quadrivalent in Fig. 4–3 rotated 45° in a clockwise direction, the centromeres of I and II would point toward the poles, and those of III and IV would be in the plate. If, now, III followed the lead of I toward its pole, and IV followed II to the opposite pole, gamete production would be exactly the same as in adjacent-2 concordant segregation. Discordant segregation lends itself, however, to a result that would be very unlikely from concordant segregation: *Both* of the plate-oriented centromeres may follow one of the pole-directed centromeres to its pole, leaving only the other pole-directed member of the quadrivalent to go to the other pole. Such a 3:1 seg-

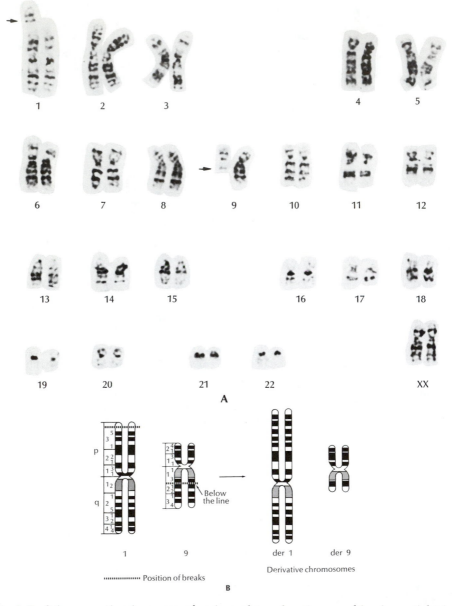

Fig. 4-5 3:1 segregation in a case of reciprocal translocation, resulting in partial tri-somy 9. **A.** Giemsa banding pattern of the mother of the affected child. Note the bal-anced 1,9 reciprocal translocation which is diagrammed in **B. C.** Giemsa banding of the proposita. The arrow points to 9, containing extra: 9p, part of 9q, and presumably also a small part of 1p. If I in Fig. 4–3 represents chromosome 1, this karyotype is probably the result of I, II, and IV going to the same pole in meiosis. **D** and **E.** The proposita, with partial trisomy, showing her absent secondary sex characteristics **(D)** and her facies **(E).** (From Mason et al., 1975; courtesy of M. K. Mason and the *Journal of Medical Genetics.*)

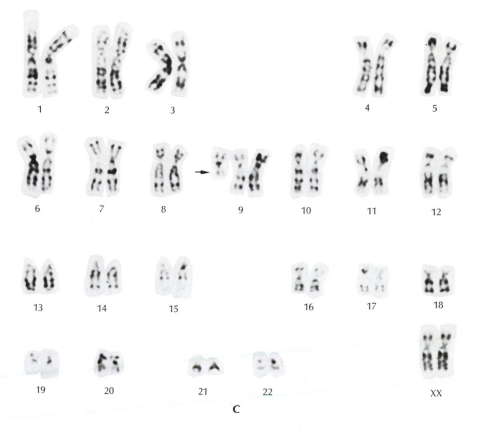

1   2   3   4   5

6   7   8 → 9   10   11   12

13   14   15   16   17   18

19   20   21   22   XX

C

D   E

regation would be, in effect, a form of nondisjunction, and it would always lead to aneusomy if the resultant gametes were used in fertilization.

The young woman in Fig. 4–5 is almost certainly attributable to such 3:1 discordant segregation. In a 1975 review of 68 additional cases, 90 percent of the unbalanced gametes were maternal in origin, suggesting that male gametes resulting from 3:1 segregations are selectively eliminated during spermiogenesis or sperm transport.

A further complication is introduced by crossing over in the so-called *interstitial* region of a quadrivalent, that is, between the centromere and a breakpoint of the translocation. In Fig. 4–3 a crossover just to the left of J, or just to the right of it (between J and the centromere), for example, would be in the interstitial region. For the chromatids involved in the exchange, the crossover chromatids, an adjacent-1 segregation thereby becomes, in effect, an alternate segregation, producing balanced gametes. It must be recalled, however, that crossing over takes place after the tetrad has been formed. The noncrossover chromatids of this quadrivalent would still undergo adjacent-1 segregation. The net result of a single crossover in the interstitial region followed by adjacent-1 segregation of the centromeres would be 50 percent balanced and 50 percent unbalanced gametes. The same result would be expected if such a crossover were followed by alternate segregation, except that in this instance it is the noncrossover chromatids that would be balanced. Crossing over does not change the results of adjacent-2 segregation, but McClintock has found that in some organisms no adjacent-2 segregations follow such crossing over; whether this is true in man is unknown.

It is clear that if the distribution of segregations is random, at least two-thirds of the gametes of the carriers of a reciprocal translocation would have an unbalanced chromosomal complement.

The fate of the abnormal gametes produced by a translocation heterozygote depends on the extent of the aneuploidy or imbalance in the resultant zygote; and this in turn depends on the location of the original breaks and the nature of the genetic material interchanged. In the diagram (Fig. 4–3), for example, all the gametes derived from the adjacent-2 segregation are unbalanced, but the chromosomes at the "south" pole are deficient for only the short region represented by ABCD, whereas those at the "north" pole are deficient for the longer region represented by JKLMNO. Ordinarily the resultant zygote with the longer deficiency is the more likely to be lethal. This would not be true, however, if A–D controlled vital functions but segment J–O did not. Furthermore, the gametes deficient for a short segment of one chromosome may have a large amount of the other chromosome in excess, and this could be as detrimental to the organism as a complete trisomy, as will be illustrated below by one of the best-studied translocations in man.

Two-break translocations have been found involving nearly all possible combinations of the human chromosomes. In surveys of consecutive live-born babies, the frequency of such translocations is consistently about 2 per 1000 births, equally divided into two major classes to be discussed below. The vast majority of these translocations have been balanced. Aside from such surveys, most translocations have been detected because of multiple malformations in a family member with an unbalanced chromosomal set attributable to one of the segregations in meiosis described above. In one list of 76 translocations culled from the literature, for example, only 19 were first noticed in a person with an apparently balanced chromosomal complement—and almost all of these were reported prior to the development of banding techniques, which allow finer determination of duplications and deficiencies than was possible previously. The more typical, unbalanced, findings will be discussed later in this section and in a later section of this chapter concerned with partial trisomies.

The remainder of this section on translocations will describe in more detail three special forms of this aberration: (1) the Philadelphia chromosome, (2) Robertsonian translocations, and (3) isochromosomes. The first has usually been classed as a deficiency; the second is commonly in an aneusomic—albeit "balanced"—chromosome set; and the third may not involve two breaks or two chromosomes and so may not be a translocation in all cases. Two other forms, insertional and tandem translocations, will be taken up under *complex aberrations,* those involving more than two breaks.

The Philadelphia Chromosome—Ph[1]

In 1960 Nowell and Hungerford found that patients with chronic granulocytic leukemia, commonly referred to also as chronic myelogenous, or myelocytic, leukemia (CML), almost invariably carry a G chromosome whose long arm is shorter than in the usual chromosome (Fig. 4–6). This chromosome was later named the Ph[1] (Philadelphia) chromosome after the city where it was discovered. Although interference with normal chromosome functioning has often been postulated as a factor in carcinogenesis, this finding aroused a great deal of interest because it represents the first specific association between a chromosomal aberration and cancer.

It was generally assumed that Ph[1] was a deletion in the same chromosome that was trisomic in Down syndrome. In 1970, however, Q-banding demonstrated that the CML deficiency is in the *other* G chromosome, number 22.

In 1973 Rowley announced that nine consecutive CML patients who were Ph[1] positive had extra material, approximately equivalent to the deletion in amount and degree of fluorescence, near the tip of the long arm of a number 9 chromosome (Fig. 4–7). This indicated that in these patients at least Ph[1] is not a deletion but a translocation involving 9q and 22q. One could not be certain whether the translocation is reciprocal or insertional (p. 100), though the law of economy favors the two-break (reciprocal) over the three-break (insertional) hypothesis. The association between the missing piece of 22q and the extra piece of 9q was further strengthened by the author's finding that CML patients lacking the G deletion invariably lack the extra material on 9q as well.

In about 5 percent of Ph[1] positive cases the extra material is on a chromosome other than number 9 and, in a still smaller minority (about 1 percent) of Ph[1] positive cases, no extra material can be detected elsewhere. The failure to find the deleted 22q matter in a few cases may again be attributable to the imperfection of the available techniques, but it may indicate that the deletion alone is responsible for the relationship between the chromosomal aberration and CML.

A number of other puzzles remain in the relationship between Ph[1] and CML. It was determined very early that about 85 percent of those diagnosed as having

CML are Ph^1 positive. Why not the other 15 percent? Many believe that Ph^1+ and Ph^1− CML are two different diseases. The Ph^1 positive form has an earlier median age of onset, responds better to therapy, and exhibits longer median survival after diagnosis, 31 to 40 months as compared to 8 to 15 months, depending on the study. Perhaps they also have different etiologies.

Ph^1 positive leukemics are mosaics for it, as only the bone marrow stem cells of the granulocyte, thrombocyte (platelet), and erythrocyte series show the aberration. Fibroblasts, for example, are normal, as are lymphocytes. Apparently the chromosomal anomaly is not present at conception, but is acquired later in specific hemopoietic tissue; and this conclusion is supported by genetic evidence. Using heterozygotes for the X-linked G6PD locus (to be discussed in Chapter 7), Fialkow and his co-workers have demonstrated that all the cells containing Ph^1 in a given leukemic belong to the same clone, indicating that the aberration—and probably the malignancy—can be traced to a single cell. This, too, is supported by other evidence, notably the distribution of satellite-marked chromosomes 22 with Ph^1. If so, which came first, the aberration or the disease? Is one the cause of the other, or do they have a common etiology, selectively associated perhaps to one of the breakpoints of the chromosomal aberration? These problems remain to be solved.

Chapter 17 will note another translocation quite consistently associated with

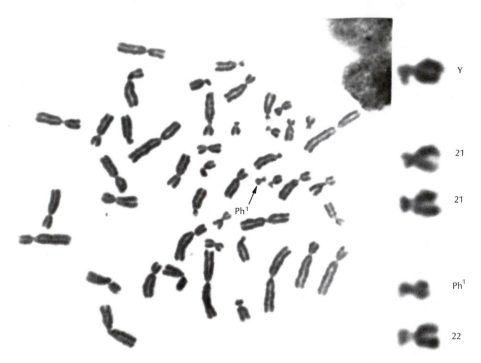

Fig. 4-6 Metaphase from one of the first cases of chronic granulocytic leukemia in which the Ph^1 chromosome (arrow) was found. The G chromosomes are enlarged further on the right. The Ph^1 chromosome appeared to be a 22 that has lost approximately one-half of its long arm. (From Nowell and Hungerford, 1961. Courtesy of P. Nowell and D. A. Hungerford and the *Journal of the National Cancer Institute*.)

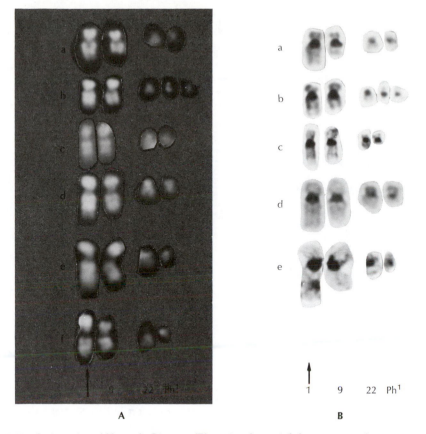

A   B

Fig. 4-7 Quinacrine (A) and Giemsa (B) stained partial karyotypes from cases of chronic granulocytic leukemia showing the Philadelphia chromosomes and the extra material near terminal end of 9q. (From Rowley, 1973; courtesy of J. Rowley; reprinted by permission from *Nature* © 1973, Macmillan Journals Ltd.)

malignancy: between 8q and 14q—though sometimes between 8q and 2p or 22q— and Burkitt-type lymphomas.

Robertsonian Translocations

Robertsonian translocations are unequal interchanges between acrocentric chromosomes, produced by breaks near the centromeres, with resultant formation of a new V-shaped chromosome and subsequent loss of the very short chromosome formed from their short arms (Fig. 4-8). Named in honor of the pioneering work of W.R.B. Robertson on this phenomenon in grasshoppers, they are encountered in many animals. They are often referred to as "centric fusions," a somewhat unfortunate term since it implies, incorrectly, that centromeres fuse. Centric fusions, or *whole arm transfers,* a better, more general term coined by H. J. Muller, have frequently served during evolution to produce differences in chromosome number and morphology.

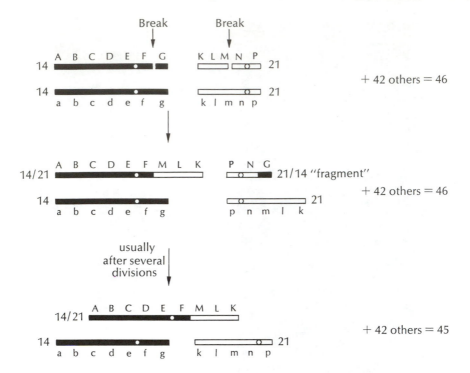

Fig. 4-8 Formation of a Robertsonian translocation. An unequal exchange of pieces between acrocentric chromosomes leads to a new metacentric or submetacentric chromosome containing the bulk of the genetic material of two normal chromosomes and, by loss of the smaller part of the translocation, a reduced but nevertheless relatively balanced chromosome set. In the example the translocation is between number 14 of the D group, which contributes the centromere, and the number 21 of the G group; this is the aberration most frequently productive of translocation Down syndrome.

The "fragment" produced by fusion of the short arms consists almost entirely of heterochromatin. The fact that this material tends to be genetically relatively inert and to replicate later than the euchromatin probably explains why this "fragment" is frequently lost and why it is so little missed by the organism when it is gone.

Robertsonian translocations should, in theory, constitute a small minority of the translocations in man, since only D, G, and Y chromosomes could be involved. Counting X and Y as separate chromosomes, there are 276 possible combinations of the 24 kinds of chromosomes two at a time (neglecting combinations of homologues), hence 276 kinds of reciprocal translocations. Interchanges between the six kinds of acrocentric chromosomes account for only 15 of these. The relatively small size of these chromosomes, plus the restrictions inherent in the definition as to where the breaks take place, should further diminish their relative frequency. It is noteworthy, therefore, that in surveys of newborns the incidence of Robertsonian translocations, about one per 1000 births, is consistently at least equal to, and often greater than, the incidence of all other reciprocal translocations combined. One form, D/D, has the highest incidence of any euploid aberration. It is interesting that almost all of these involve chromosome 14, the majority being interchanges between 13 and 14. A preponderance of aberrations involving chromosome 14 will be noted again later, in the discussion of ataxia telangiectasia and Burkitt's lymphoma.

Particularly significant are the cases of Down syndrome due to translocation of chromosome 21. About 2 percent of all unselected cases of Down syndrome have translocations, most of them Robertsonian. Several features differentiate the Robertsonian translocation Down syndrome from typical trisomy-21 cases:

(a) Most of the mothers are in the usual childbearing ages. (This should not be misinterpreted, however; most of the Down children born to younger mothers are still the typical 21-trisomies.)

(b) The cases are often familial, Down syndrome sometimes appearing in three or more successive generations in a pedigree. In addition, although most instances of mongolism in siblings are typical 21-trisomies, in translocation Down's the risk of recurrence in the same sibship is much higher than in typical trisomy-21.

(c) The propositus (individual with Down syndrome) has 46 chromosomes.

(d) If this is a familial condition one of the parents (almost always the mother), apparently normal, has 45 chromosomes; often some of the normal siblings also have only 45 chromosomes.

A typical pedigree of translocation Down syndrome is shown in Fig. 1–15, and Fig. 4–9 shows the karyotypes of one of the affected persons and of a normal carrier. The 46 chromosomes of the affected person apparently lack one chromosome in group D but include an extra metacentric resembling those of group C. The carrier's karyotype also contains such a pseudo-C chromosome, but his karyotype is not only minus one chromosome in group D but is also lacking one from group G. Apparently the extra chromosome is a translocation chromosome formed by breaks near the centromeres of a group D chromosome, number 14 in most cases, and a number 21 (Fig. 4–9), followed by a union of their long arms. Probably the short arms also fused, the 21/14 shown in the diagram, but this "fragment" is almost always lost, even though it possessed a centromere. The carrier of Fig. 4–9 is apparently normal because the translocation chromosome contains nearly all the genetic material of his missing chromosomes of group D and group G. He is said to carry the translocation in *balanced* condition, inasmuch as he shows no effect of his minor aneuploidy.

Apparently the loss of the fragment often occurs by nondisjunction very soon after the reciprocal interchange. However, several reported karyotypes appear to contain a fragment that did persist.

During meiosis the translocation chromosome pairs with a group D chromosome and a group G chromosome, forming the modified, trivalent or triradial, cross diagrammed in Fig. 4–10.

As in the more orthodox translocation heterozygote, there are mainly three alternative disjunctions (or segregations). One results in normal progeny (Fig. 4–10 alternate segregation C), though half resemble the mother in being "balanced" translocation carriers. Fertilizations receiving gametes from disjunction B are probably lethal, because they are either monosomic-14 or trisomic-14. Presumably,

A

B

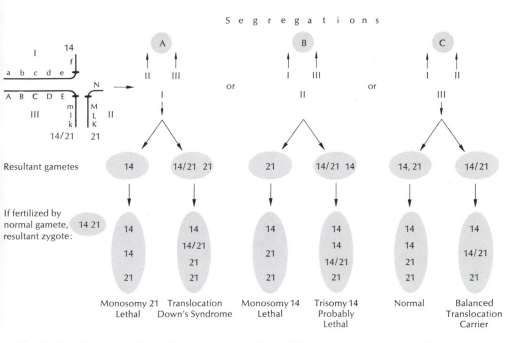

Fig. 4-10 Diagram of meiotic segregation of a 14/21 translocation in a female hetero-zygous for it, and the resultant zygotes. For some reason this pattern is more closely approximated in female heterozygotes for the D/G translocation than in males carrying it; in the latter the progeny are almost exclusively those expected on the basis of segregation C.

these account for many of the stillbirths and abortions from female balanced trans-location carriers; none, however, have been identified with certainty. Disjunction A resembles adjacent-2 segregation. Zygotes receiving only a chromosome 14 from this segregation are also probably lethal, because they are monosomic-21. However, the gametes containing one 21 and the 14/21 translocation usually form viable off-spring with 46 chromosomes. These zygotes contain excess chromosome 21, being nearly as trisomic for this chromosome as the Down's syndrome cases with 47 chromosomes, and therefore they also show most of the features of the syndrome. Since the G chromosome will not be broken in the same spot in different translo-cations, the pattern of defects is even more variable for translocation Down's syn-dromes than in the more frequent typical G-trisomies. In the meiosis, it is possible also for all three parts of the trivalent (14, 21, and 14/21) to go to the same pole, nothing to the other; but this must be very rare.

←

Fig. 4-9A Karyotype of one form of translocation Down syndrome. **B.** An apparent carrier of the translocation. Note that the carrier has only 45 chromosomes, and the affected child has 46, the normal number in man. The translocation (or centric fusion) chromosome (arrow), which resembles the ones in Group **C,** involves number 14 in this case, as determined by autoradiography. (Courtesy of J. L. German.)

Although most often the long arm of 21 appears to be translocated to a member of the D(13–15) group, Down's syndrome has also been observed with translocations between the members of groups E and G and with translocations between the several members of group G(21–22). Most G/G translocations are presumably 21/22 or 22/21. The 21/21 centric fusions are (or resemble) *isochromosomes,* with the attendant serious consequences as described below (pp. 84–89).

Mean maternal age in translocation Down's offspring is 27.3 years. When the mother is less than 30 years of age, about 8 to 10 percent of Down syndromes are translocation "trisomies," but the figure is only slightly more than 1 percent for older mothers.

A priori, one would expect the same distribution of normal, Down, carrier, and aborted progeny whether the translocation carrier were the mother or the father. It turns out, however, that this is not the case. When a male has the balanced translocation, only about 2 percent of the live children are Down's, whereas about 11 percent are affected when the female brings in the abnormal chromosome. Presumably the sperm derived from adjacent segregations are less capable of fertilizing than the euploid sperm derived from the alternate segregation. In effect, then, there is a form of gametic selection or "meiotic drive" among the active male gametes that does not obtain among the relatively inactive eggs.

Simple Translocations?

Thus far we have discussed the consequences of *two* breaks on different chromosomes. The reader may wonder what happens if only one chromosome breaks. Could not a piece of one chromosome stick to the unbroken end of another and thus produce a *simple,* that is, nonreciprocal, *translocation?* The evidence is strong that this is an extremely rare event, if it occurs at all. As a matter of fact the very rarity of suspected cases is an argument against its occurring at all. If it could happen, it would be expected to be the most *frequent* type of translocation, for only one break is needed, whereas reciprocal interchanges need at least two. Muller and others have postulated that simple translocations do not occur because the ends of eukaryote chromosomes, which are called *telomeres,* have special properties, especially the inability to stick to other chromosome material.

The development of the telomere in organisms with more than one chromosome is probably very useful to the organism because it helps maintain the unicentric nature of the chromosome. (A few organisms have polycentric chromosomes, but the vast majority do not.) Were ends sticky, the centric piece of a broken chromosome, the part containing the centromere, could become stuck to the end of another chromosome as easily as the acentric piece. The result would be a dicentric chromosome whose centromeres might pull toward opposite poles of the spindle during cell division. Whether the dicentric breaks in the process or all of the dicentric passes to one pole, some of the daughter cells are apt to lack vital genetic material.

Isochromosomes

Some investigators believe that the aberration known as an *isochromosome* involves only a single break, through the centromere. As shown in Fig. 4–11**B**, this

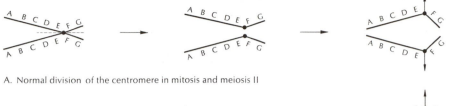

A. Normal division of the centromere in mitosis and meiosis II

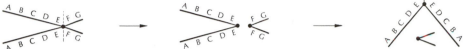

B. "Misdivision of the centromere" sometimes postulated as cause of an isochromosome (and a centric fragment)

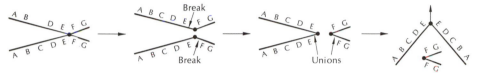

C. Isochromosome produced by "centric fusion" of daughter chromatids

Fig. 4–11 Isochromosome production. **A** and **B** contrast the normal and abnormal divisions of the centromere according to one theory of isochromosome production; **C** shows a more likely method: by whole arm transfer akin to "centric fusion." Several additional, but probably less likely, possibilities exist.

could result if the centromere were to break transversely, instead of longitudinally, in mitosis, or in the second meiotic division. As a result the long arms of sister chromatids become stuck together to form one chromosome, and the short arms form another. The chromosome resulting from fusion of the short arms is commonly lost, similar to the fate of the "fragment" after a Robertsonian translocation. The misdivided chromosome is now represented in the karyotype by a relatively large metacentric chromosome whose two arms are mirror images of one another genetically. The well-known attached-X chromosomes of *Drosophila melanogaster* are isochromosomes.

Figure 4–11C shows how isochromosomes could also result from a Robertsonian translocation, for example, in early anaphase, between the strands that were sister chromatids until that stage. Although this requires two breaks instead of one, it is, in our opinion, the more likely cause. Otherwise true unibrachial (one-arm) chromosomes, produced by a combination of longitudinal and transverse breaks, would be produced. Furthermore, as Darlington has shown, in plants at least, chromosomes resulting from transverse breaks through the centromere are always unstable.

A number of presumptive isochromosomes have been found in man. Those that involve the X-chromosome are of two distinct types, according to whether the long or the short arm of the X is duplicated (and the opposite arm lost). Isochromosome for the long arm, 46,X,i(Xq), implies absence of all or most of the short arm(s), and its carriers resemble Turner syndrome (Figs. 4–12C,D), except that, as one might expect, the chromatin body tends to be larger than normal and there is a somewhat lower frequency of webbing and cardiovascular defects. An additional significant difference is that these individuals exhibit a tendency to develop chronic lymphocytic inflammation of the thyroid or Hashimoto's thyroiditis.

Persons with an isochromosome for the short arm of the X-chromosome, 46,X,i(Xp), usually have streak gonads, but short stature and other anomalies characteristic of Turner syndrome are not found.

Isochromosomes of the long arm of the X exhibit a curious paternal age effect, the mean age of the father, 34.6 years, being 6.7 years greater than that of the mother. This suggests that this type of chromosomal error is more likely to occur

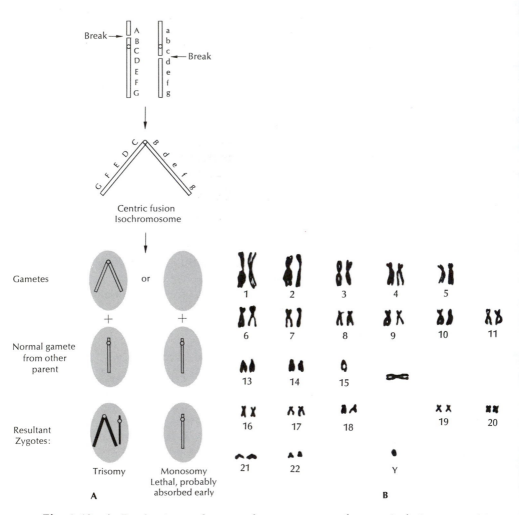

Fig. 4-12   A. Production and expected consequences of a centric fusion type of isochromosome between homologous acrocentric autosomes. B. Karyotype with the apparent homologous translocation isochromosome responsible for the case of trisomy-D₁ shown in Fig. 3–9B. C. Karyotype with an isochromosome (arrow) of the long arm of the X-chromosome (46X/iso-X). D. Appearance of carrier of the karyotype shown in C,

in spermatogenesis than in oogenesis. The point is also supported by blood group data.

Isochromosomes of the autosomes appear to be most numerous for the acrocentric or nearly acrocentric chromosomes. Many are really Robertsonian translocations between homologous chromosomes. Unlike heterologous centric fusions, however, *the chances of having a normal child is quite remote* (Fig. 4–12A). If the isochromosome develops early in the germ line, all the offspring would be trisomic or monosomic.

The results would depend on which chromosome was involved. Most of the autosomes are lethal in both monosomic and trisomic condition, so the net effect of a homologous centric fusion involving one of these would be complete absence of liveborn children. In the case of autosomes that come to term in trisomic form, a high frequency of trisomic siblings are expected in the progeny of a carrier of such an aberration. Thus, one mother who probably had an isochromosome 21 is known to have had five pregnancies, four of them Down's and the fifth aborted. Similarly, a familial E/E translocation has been described in an infant with stigmata of trisomy-18. An earlier affected sibling was dead, and the mother had also noted three "late heavy periods" with cramps, suggestive of early abortion. The child with trisomy-D, shown in Fig. 3–9B, probably also had such an isochromosome (Fig. 4–12B). Fortunately, balanced carriers of homologous translocation isochromosomes are extremely rare. In fact, such a balanced condition would usually exist only in the germ line of the person in whom the aberration rose. If a person inherited, for example, a 21,21 isochromosome from one parent, he could not attain a balanced

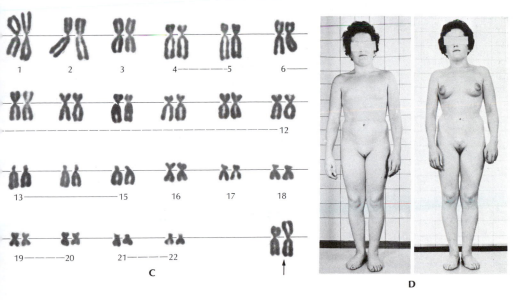

before (left) and after (right) estrogen therapy. Note the many similarities of the left figure to typical Turner's syndrome (Fig. 3–12). (**B.** From Hemet et al., 1967, courtesy of J. Hemet and *Annales d'Anatomie Pathologique;* **C** and **D.** From Lindsten et al., 1963, courtesy of J. Lindsten and the *Annals of Human Genetics.*)

condition unless the other parent's gamete lacked a 21 (from nondisjunction). Had he received a normal gamete from the other parent he would be trisomic and exhibit Down syndrome.

INTRACHROMOSOMAL TWO-BREAK ABERRATIONS

To return to aberrations involving two chromosomal breaks, if they occur on the same chromosome and the chromosome does not reheal in the old pattern, four alternative aberrations may result (Fig. 4–13). If both breaks are on the same arm and the piece between drops out, and, being acentric, is lost, a shortened chromosome called a *deficiency* or *deletion* is produced. If the segment between the breaks reheals after rotating 180°, an *inversion* is formed. This may take two forms: (1) *paracentric* inversion if both breaks were in the same arm; (2) *pericentric* inversion if they were in different arms. Finally, if the two breaks are in different arms and

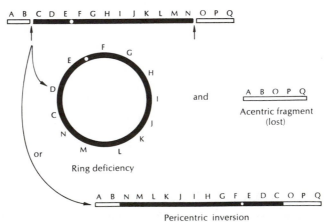

Fig. 4–13 Four alternative results from two breaks on the same chromosome.

the two terminal pieces drop off, the broken ends of the remaining chromosome will fuse to form a *ring* chromosome. Thus, two of the aberrations, the deficiency and the ring, result in immediate loss of some genetic material. They qualify as rearrangements because parts of the chromosome are brought into closer proximity than before. The other two, the inversions, merely rearrange chromosomal material, but we shall see that these, too, may cause changes in amount (in later generations).

DEFICIENCIES (DELETIONS)

We encountered deficiencies earlier, in our discussion of segregation in a translocation heterozygote. We noted there that the consequences of a deficiency depended on its length and the role of the genetic material involved. In *Drosophila,* where minute deficiencies may be detected and measured accurately, deletion in some areas of even a single chromomere* may be lethal. There are areas, on the other hand, where loss of as many as 50 chromomeres may be viable as long as the organism is heterozygous for the deficiency. Many deletions in humans are so small that they are not detectable in ordinary cytological preparations (Chapters 5, 6, 14). Here we discuss relatively large deletions.

Deletion of part of a chromosome is often referred to as *partial monosomy.* As in the case of trisomies and partial trisomies, affected individuals generally exhibit a number of symptoms and malformations, most of which are not specific or diagnostic. Often the diagnosis can only be made from the karyotype. Furthermore, since the breakpoints of any two deficiencies are rarely, if ever, identical, the spectrum of features varies even for those with the same karyotypic designation.

Since the Chicago Conference (1966) deletions have been indicated by placing a minus sign $(-)$ after the arm involved. Xq$-$, for example, means that the long arm of the X is shorter than usual. The Paris Conference (1971) suggested adding "del" before the chromosome number to distinguish a simple deletion from instances where the shortening was part of other aberrations, such as the translocations or pericentric inversions. The full karyotype of the example above may then be stated as 46,X,del(Xq) without need to use the minus sign. If the breakpoint bands are known, they are added in another parentheses; thus, 46,X,del(X) (q13q25), indicates that part of q13, part of q25, and the bands in between, are deleted.

As may be surmised from the sometime viability of the XO condition, which is, in effect, a whole chromosome deletion, the largest and most frequent deficiencies in man compatible with life have been described on the X-chromosome. We have already mentioned the presumed X-isochromosome in which the major portion, if not the entire length, of one arm is lost. Smaller deficiencies have also been observed. These X-chromosome deficiencies (including the isochromosomes) are mainly significant because they frequently give rise to a Turner syndrome which is *chromatin positive.*

---

*Represented by a band of the salivary gland chromosomes, probably a single gene, in these organisms.

Deletion of part of one of the short arms (Xp−) is associated with the full expression of Turner syndrome. In several families this occurred as unbalanced consequences of transmitted X-autosome translocations, giving rise to a familial Turner syndrome, even though those with the syndrome are, of course, sterile. On the other hand, a deletion of part of one of the long arms (Xq−) is associated with an attenuated expression of the syndrome, for while the affected individuals are characterized by primary amenorrhea and streak gonads, they usually have few or no other anomalies and are of normal height. It is interesting to note that in several of these cases the chromatin body has been found to be smaller than usual.

Well-defined autosomal deficiency syndromes will be discussed below. They are of particular interest when the deletion presumably makes significant autosomal loci hemizygous, allowing the expression of recessive mutant alleles on the homologous chromosome.

The Wolf−Hirschhorn (4p−) Syndrome

This partial deletion of 4p is often also referred to as the "defect of midline fusion" syndrome. Commonly affected are the scalp, nose, lips, palate, and in the males the penis. Some involve ring chromosomes. 4p deletions may, however, lack the midline fusion defects.

Cri-du-Chat (Cat's Cry) Syndrome (Fig. 4-14)

Babies exhibiting this syndrome have a peculiar plaintive mewing catlike cry. It is associated with a 5p deletion, particularly 5p15.

Other symptoms associated with the cat-cry syndrome are mental, motor, and growth retardation, broadheaded microcephaly, epicanthic folds, ocular hypertelorism, downward and outwardly sloping palpebral fissures, broad face, and saddle nose; micrognathia and strabismus occur frequently. A simian crease is generally present on both hands, and other dermatoglyphic features may be unusual. As in trisomy-E, there is a significant preponderance of females.

That the chromosomal aberration may be transmitted from parent to child was first shown in a case in which a phenotypically normal mother was a balanced translocation carrier involving B4–5 and D13–15 groups. The affected child received the deleted B5 chromosome but not the chromosome of the D13–15 group to which the deleted portion of the B5 had been translocated. In one series of cases, 88.4 percent resulted from a del(5p) without other aberrations involved, 4.7 percent from a translocation in one parent, 2.9 percent from a ring deficiency, and the rest (4.0 percent) with no detectable aberration.

The Refractory Anemia (5q−) Syndrome

Deletion of bands 5q13 to q33 is a consistent finding in older patients, especially females, with refractory macrocytic anemia and abnormal megakaryocytes, often also elevated platelet counts. Clinical course is usually mild, but some patients progress to acute nonlymphocytic leukemia (ANLL), especially if they have additional chromosomal abnormalities. It is suspected that the deletion allows the

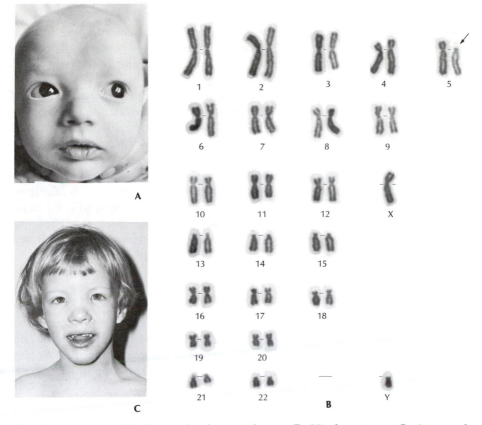

Fig. 4–14A Boy with the cri-du-chat syndrome. **B.** His karyotype. **C.** A severely retarded 6-year-old girl with the same syndrome; such children usually lose the "cat cry" characteristic of infants with the condition. Both illustrate many of the characteristic stigmata, especially hypertelorism, epicanthic fold, and saddle nose; **C** also has some micrognathia, while **A** exhibits the more typical broad head and rounded facies. (**A** and **B.** Courtesy of J. Lejeune. **C.** Courtesy of W. R. Breg.)

expression of recessive mutant alleles at least one of two hematological malignancy-related loci in this region: (a) GM-CSF: granulocyte/macrophage colony stimulating factor and (b) FMS, a proto-oncogene (Chapter 17), which encodes for a protein related to the receptor for CSF-1, a macrophage colony stimulating factor.

Wilms Tumor, Aniridia, and 11p—

Deletion of all or part of the short arm of chromosome 11 is often associated with the AGR triad: aniridia, ambiguous genitalia, and mental retardation. If the deficiency includes 11p13, these are accompanied in many families by an apparently recessive form of Wilms tumor, a kidney malignancy, that accounts for about 6 percent of childhood tumors.

13q— Syndromes

At least two syndromes due to deletions in the long arm of chromosome 13 have been described. One is characterized mainly by severe malformations of the face and head: microcephaly, trigonocephaly (a fusion defect of the frontal bones with resultant compression of the front of the head), protruding upper incisors, micrognathia, large malformed ears, broad prominent nasal bridge, hypertelorism, and, less constantly, microphthalmia, coloboma of the iris, imperforate anus, hypoplastic or absent thumbs, and genital malformations. It involves deletion of portions of the distalmost segment of the arm. Some writers believe that it can be subdivided into two syndromes depending on whether the deficient segments are q31–32 or q33–34.

Deletions involving 13q14 often are characterized by the presence of retinoblastoma, the most common intraocular tumor of childhood, responsible for about 1 percent of all deaths caused by childhood cancer and about 5 percent of blindness in children. Molecular studies (Chapter 6) indicate that in contrast to cases inherited as simple dominants, deletion forms are associated with a recessive gene.

Chromosome 18 Deletion Syndromes (18q— and 18p—)

A syndrome associated with partial deletion of the long arm of chromosome 18 has been known since 1964. The most typical features seem to be retarded mental and motor development, microcephaly, a certain recess or retraction of the middle part of the face, abnormal ears, spindle-shaped fingers, and hypotrophy of external genitalia.

Partial deletion of the short arm of the same chromosome, 18p—, has been reported as frequently as 18q—, but the features are more variable. Some of the subjects resemble Turner's syndrome—there is a preponderance of affected females—but lack its gonadal anomaly and have a greater incidence of mental retardation.

Chances of survival with chromosome 18 deletions appear to be good; one 18q— is known to be 15 years old and one 18p— to be 33. As expected, persons with ring chromosome 18's present features that overlap both arm deletion syndromes.

G Chromosome Deletions

The congenital defects of infants with partial deficiencies of a G chromosome were early characterized as the opposite of Down syndrome, or as some have dubbed it, *antimongolism.* At that time it was difficult to distinguish chromosomes 21 and 22. The term *antimongolism,* even if correct, would be apt only with respect to number 21. Since the development of the banding techniques, the loss of chromosome 21 material has been called G deletion syndrome I, that of 22, G deletion syndrome II.

G deletion syndrome I appears to be the better characterized of the two, primarily because more cases are known. It is still often referred to as antimongolism, based mainly on the fact that affected individuals generally have large ears, a prominent nasal bridge, and antimongoloid slant of the eyelids, and long fingers and toes, are microcephalic or dolichocephalic (long-headed) instead of broadheaded, and have hypogammaglobulinemia (instead of hyper-, typical of Down). Confusing the picture, however, is the frequency of symptoms that are also seen often in trisomy 21, such as retarded growth, simian crease, congenital cardiac and renal anomalies, and microretrognathia (small jaws set behind the plane of the forehead).

G deletion syndrome II shares with I a tendency to be characterized by low-set ears, mental and physical retardation, microcephaly, and musculoskeletal abnormalities. It also features a flat nasal bridge, ptosis, epicanthal folds, and cutaneous syndactyly.

Many of the deletions have involved ring chromosomes, and some were derived from translocations.

Deletions of chromosome 22 seem to characterize the cells of the meningioma, a rare tumor.

RINGS

Ring chromosomes are basically deficiencies and therefore render the carrier liable to the usual consequences of missing genetic material. They are, however, rarer than other deletions, probably because they are subject to fertility and division problems not encountered by the others. As shown in Fig. 4–15, for example, interchange between a ring and its homologue produces a dicentric chromosome. In addition, mitoses of rings often result in interlocking rings or in a dicentric double-sized ring and bridge formation in anaphase instead of free rings with one centromere each. These result, perhaps, from sister-strand interchanges during replication. Unless special techniques are used such interchanges would be imperceptible in normal chromosomes. They may be more frequent in rings because the chromosomes probably need to "break open" somewhere during replication.

Several instances of the deletion syndromes described in the preceding section have involved ring chromosomes. They have been particularly frequent among the reported cases of 13q− with multiple malformations and of G deletion syndromes. In the latter a common finding is a cell line with 46 chromosomes including the ring, and a line with 45 chromosomes apparently monosomic for 21 or 22. This is entirely consistent with the known tendency of tissues to lose their ring chromosomes during mitosis (Fig. 4–16C), and this may account for the reports of live individuals with apparently pure monosomy G. The hypothesis is supported by the rarity of autosomal monosomy in abortuses.

Ring chromosomes have now been found in every chromosome group. Several examples are shown in Fig. 14–14. Many have not been associated with any consistent syndrome, except that mental retardation seems to be a regular finding. Ring X-chromosomes have also been described. Analogous to other X-chromosome deficiencies, they usually come to our attention because the carriers are Turners, and quite often chromatin positive.

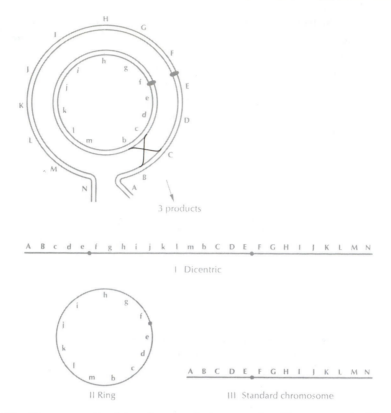

3 products

A B c d e f g h i j k l m b C D E F G H I J K L M N

I Dicentric

II Ring

A B C D E F G H I J K L M N

III Standard chromosome

Fig. 4–15 Consequences of crossing over between a ring chromosome and its normal homologue. The dicentric would be pulled to both poles and probably not be able to enter a gamete; zygotes not receiving the ring (II) or standard (III) chromatids would be monosomic (lethal). If, on the other hand, the dicentric broke during first meiotic anaphase, some of the resultant zygotes would be unbalanced (since it is unlikely that the break would always be between *b* and *C*).

INVERSIONS

Paracentric inversions were difficult to identify in human material because they cause no change in chromosome morphology in karyotypes. Large ones do, however, produce noticeable modification of banding pattern. Even these methods understate their numbers because they do not detect intraband changes—a typical band includes many hundreds of genes—and shifts of some of the less distinct bands can be easily missed. When the techniques of preparing meiotic materials are improved, it should become easier to find them, because a single (or triple) crossover between a paracentric inversion and the corresponding region of its normal homologue would produce a dicentric bridge and an acentric fragment at anaphase I. Crossovers between the centromere and the inversion (in the interstitial region) may lead to additional aneuploid gametes. As a result heterozygous carriers of paracentric inversions are apt to be reproductively inferior, unless some mechanism exists to reduce crossing over in such cases.

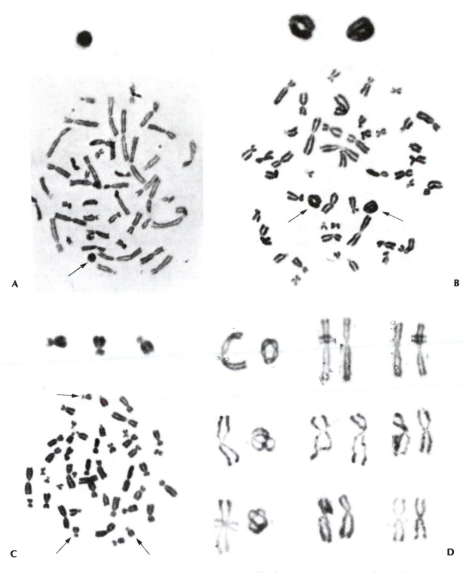

Fig. 4-16 Ring chromosomes. **A–C.** Three cells from a patient with an E17–18 ring reported by Gripenberg (1967). In **A** there is a single monocentric ring, in **B** two (dicentric?) rings, but in **C** the ring has been lost. The chromosomes above **C** are magnifications of the three E17–18 chromosomes present. **D.** Group A chromosomes from a severely retarded girl reported by Wolf et al. (1967) showing clearly the double chromatids of a chromosome 1 ring. (**A–C.** Courtesy of U. Gripenberg and *Chromosoma*; **D.** Courtesy of C. B. Wolf and the C. V. Mosby Co., publishers of the *Journal of Pediatrics*.)

A recent survey of 50 known paracentric inversions found 14 different chromosomes involved, with chromosomes 3 (8 cases), 7 (10 cases), and 11 (7 cases) the most often represented. 34 of the 50 appeared to be familial, and two were found in several apparently unrelated individuals. There was no evidence that any had harmful effects, the numbers with possible fertility problems and coincident additional aberrations being too small to draw meaningful conclusions.

Pericentric inversions are also likely to be reproductively inferior. Crossing over between a pericentric inversion and the corresponding region of its normal homologue (Fig. 4–17) could result in some unbalanced gametes. Some of the chromatids may be deficient for a portion of the chromosome and retain an excessive amount of another portion.

Since they often move the centromere to a new location on the chromosome, pericentric inversions are easier to identify. Thus an acrocentric can be converted into a metacentric and vice versa, by an appropriate pericentric inversion (Fig. 4–18A II and Fig. 4–18B). However, pericentrics do not always produce obvious alterations in morphology; a metacentric may remain a metacentric or submetacentric, for example, even after a pericentric inversion (Fig. 4–18A IV and V). Hence detection of pericentric inversions has also been greatly assisted by the development of the banding techniques.

Surveys of consecutive births have found pericentric inversions at the rate of about one per 7500 births, about one-fifteenth the incidence of translocations of all types. As expected on theoretical grounds, the relative proportion of translocations

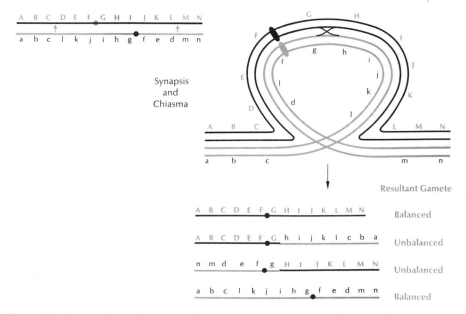

Fig. 4–17 Expected results of crossing over between a pericentric inversion and its normal homologue. Half the resultant gametes (and zygotes) are expected to be unbalanced because of duplications and deficiencies. This constitutes an intrinsic selectional disadvantage for pericentric inversions.

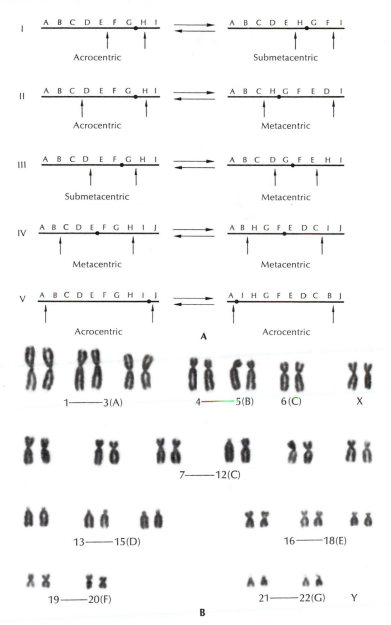

Fig. 4-18A Diagram of some possible effects of pericentric inversions on chromosome morphology. InI–III the morphology is altered, but in IV and V it is unchanged. **B.** Karyotype of a female with an apparent pericentric inversion in Group C chromosome 10. If so, a metacentric has been converted to an acrocentric. The same aberration was found in her mother and a maternal aunt and was apparently responsible for five births with multiple congenital abnormalities as predicted by Fig. 4–17. (**B.** From Ferguson-Smith, 1967. Courtesy of M. A. Ferguson-Smith and the Johns Hopkins Press.)

to pericentric inversions among *newly formed,* as opposed to familial, aberrations is probably even greater. Some measure of this is obtained when the parents of a child born with an aberration are also studied. In one report all five pericentric inversions detected in a child were present in one of the parents. Ten of the 47 translocations, on the other hand, were *not* present in the parents (8 of the 24 reciprocal, and 2 of the 23 Robertsonian).

It is not surprising, therefore, that the vast majority of reported inversions have been found in several generations. One group traced a pericentric inversion of chromosome 3 through six generations of a widespread kindred in the United States and Canada. The 20 infants with multiple malformations in this family suggested a specific chromosome-3 duplication-deficiency syndrome resuting from crossing over in inversion heterozygotes, both male and female. It would not be surprising if in such a group many members were not aware that they were related, leading to the possibility that the same inversion could be reported as being present in different families in different areas. Experience with *Drosophila* and other organisms in which inversions are quite common—albeit not *pericentric* inversions—indicates that inversions are probably unique events, no two having exactly the same break points.

DUPLICATIONS (PARTIAL TRISOMIES)

The unbalanced condition in which a portion of a chromosome is represented more than once in a gamete or more than twice in a zygote is often called a duplication.

Several kinds of duplications may be distinguished. In one form a relatively large amount of extra chromosomal material lies far from its usual position as a result of another chromosomal aberration. This is called a *partial trisomy.* We have seen that duplications in this sense are produced by certain segregations in a translocation heterozygote or by crossing over in a heterozygote for a pericentric inversion. They may also arise from crossing over in more complex aberrations to be described below. The French workers have established the term "aneusomie de recombination" to account for such consequences of crossing over, and the term has persisted even in the reports written in other languages. These duplications do not usually have as drastic effects as deficiencies of comparable size. Thus, a small duplication is rarely lethal, even when homozygous, whereas small deficiencies may be lethal even in heterozygous condition. Duplications can be pathological however. We have seen, for example, that duplication of most of the long arm of a group-G chromosome (as a result of a translocation) may be indistinguishable from a complete G-trisomy.

As partial trisomies have accumulated, particularly from the large number of reciprocal and Robertsonian translocations discovered in recent years, attempts have been made to discern patterns of congenital effects associated with them similar to the deletion syndromes described earlier. Consistent features have been claimed, for example, for partial trisomies of 2p, 3p, 4p, 5p, 7q, 10p, 10q, 11p, 11q, 13q, 14q, and 15q. Although these exhibit considerable variability, the rate of discovery promises that soon partial trisomy syndromes will be established for each substantial chromosome arm. Indeed, some arms will undoubtedly have several

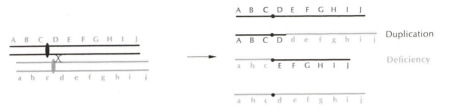

Fig. 4-19 Production of a duplication chromosome (and a deficiency) by "unequal crossing over."

trisomies, each associated with duplication of particular bands. Most features of Down syndrome appear, for instance, whenever the terminal portion of 21q22 is trisomic.

A second form of duplication is often referred to as a *repeat* or *tandem duplication*. Muller and others have called attention to the special evolutionary interest of this type of duplication. It arises from "unequal crossing over," a result of the rare accident that the two homologues do not pair exactly before crossing over takes place. As shown in Fig. 4–19, the result is a small deficiency on one homologue and a small duplication on the other. Being small, the duplication is unlikely to be deleterious, but it opens up new evolutionary possibilities. With the normal genetic material present adjacent to it, the duplicated area is dispensable. It may mutate to produce a new substance without the danger of the cells being deprived thereby of their normal product. Thus the organism may experiment with new biological "ideas" in relative safety. Adding to the plausibility of this thesis are the considerable number of instances, most notably the globin and immunoglobulin genes (Chapters 14 and 16), where adjacent areas of the chromosome have similar fine structure and control similar cell structures and functions.

Most cytogeneticists favor the hypothesis that the so-called normal marker* chromosomes 1qh+ (Fig. 6–6), 9qh+, and 16qh+ owe their abnormal length to duplication of heterochromatin of the long arms of these chromosomes in the vicinity of their secondary constrictions, hence their usual designation. Alternative explanations for their origin have been advanced, however. They are almost always familial and seem to cause no pathology, but one study found that mothers carrying 9qh+ have an increased risk of new chromosome aberrations in their offspring.

COMPLEX ABERRATIONS: MORE THAN TWO BREAKS

Yet another way in which duplications and deficiencies can be produced is by three-break aberrations (Fig. 4–20) in which a chromosome segment drops out, as a result of two breaks, but becomes inserted at a single break elsewhere in the chromosome

---

*Any variant chromosome detected in a karyotype may be termed a "marker" chromosome. Usually, however, the designation is restricted to variant chromosomes that defy identification and analysis, remaining ambiguous. The Chicago Conference (1966) suggested the symbol "mar." Thus, the karyotype of a normal female that contained two unidentified, apparently centric chromosome fragments would be 48,XX,mar1+,mar2+.

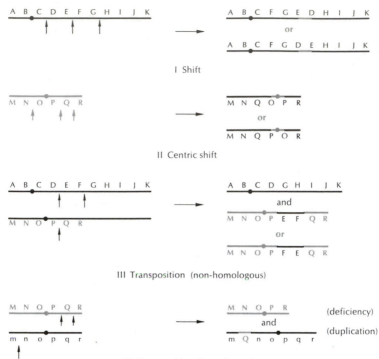

Fig. 4-20 Production of insertions, shifts, and transpositions ("insertional transloca-tions") by three breaks and rearrangement. Shifts may be produced also by more complex methods such as successive inversions or successive but differently spaced unequal crossovers.

set. This aberration has been called a *shift,* a *transposition,* or an *insertional trans-location* by various authors. The Paris Conference (1971) has proposed the blanket term *insertion,* a *direct insertion* being one in which the parts of the inserted piece maintain their previous relations to the centromere, as opposed to an *inverted insertion,* in which those relations are reversed.

The term *shift* should be restricted to insertions into the same chromosome from which the "deletion" occurred (Fig. 4-20 I). A centric shift (Fig. 4-20 II) is the special case in which the centromere is thereby moved (because each of the "deletion" breaks was in a different arm). Shifts merely change the order of the genetic material. They do not cause any duplications or deficiencies unless crossing over occurs in the shifted area in a heterozygote (in which case the consequences resemble crossing over in pericentric inversions).

If the insertion occurs on a different chromosome, whether homologous (hom-osomal) or nonhomologous (heterologous), the term *transposition* is most apt.*
Clearly a transposition involving *homologues* resembles unequal crossing over: it automatically produces duplication and deficiency chromosomes (Fig. 4-20 IV).

---

*Insertional translocation, while descriptive, is not only too long but also implies that the chro-mosomes involved are always nonhomologous, as in reciprocal translocations.

After meiosis all gametes, and the resultant zygotes, will be unbalanced in one way or the other; the effects will depend on the size of the transposed block. A *heterologous* transposition (Fig. 4–20 III, 4–21) is balanced, but it may resemble a reciprocal translocation in forming gametes: the pattern of segregation will determine whether it will lead to a balanced condition (e.g., Fig. 4–21*a*), a deficiency (Fig. 4–21*b*), or a duplication (Fig. 4–21*c*) in the next generation. Crossing over in a heterosomal transposition can further complicate the picture by producing complex translocations, duplications, and deficiencies.

Many three-break insertions, almost all of them heterologous, have been

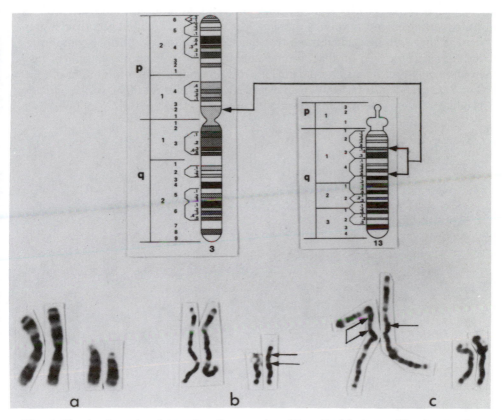

Fig. 4–21 An insertional translocation causing 13q-retinoblastoma. The top portion shows diagrams of normal G-banded chromosomes 3 and 13, indicating the derivation of the transposition found in a family with 10 cases of retinoblastoma over four generations. The segment of chromosome 13 in brackets is inserted into chromosome 3 at the site of the arrow. Note that it includes band 13q14. On the bottom, *a* shows a partial karyotype (G-banded) of these chromosomes in a balanced (unaffected) carrier; *b* a partial prometaphase karyotype of the unbalanced deletion of 13q in a family member with retinoblastoma, the arrows indicating break points on the normal 13q; and *c* a partial prometaphase karyotype of an apparently normal individual with a partial trisomy of a portion of chromosome 13, one copy inserted in chromosome 3 in addition to two on normal chromosome 13's. (From Strong et al., 1981; courtesy of L. C. Strong and the American Association for the Advancement of Science, publishers of *Science*.)

reported, usually because abnormal children, as in Fig. 4–21, contain unbalanced crossover products of the original aberration. An even more bizarre transposition, involving four breaks in two C chromosomes, was transmitted in balanced fashion from a carrier to her daughter. It came to attention when the daughter had four successive miscarriages, apparently because of unbalanced crossovers.

Many reports have also appeared of reciprocal translocations that involve three or more chromosomes, for example, if a piece of chromosome A becomes attached to B, a piece of B to C, and the broken-off piece of C to A. In one review of 187 Ph[1] translocations, for example, five involved breaks on number 22, number 9, and a third chromosome.

Tandem translocations are complex aberrations produced by at least two separate rearrangements involving the same chromosome and often occurring in tandem in the same individual, such that the second of the two further complicates the changes produced on that chromosome by the first. Each rearrangement may involve only two breaks, but the final aberration results from a minimum of four. The 21/21 tandem translocation shown in Fig. 4–22, for example, was apparently produced by a pericentric inversion with breaks in 21p11 and q22, followed by a

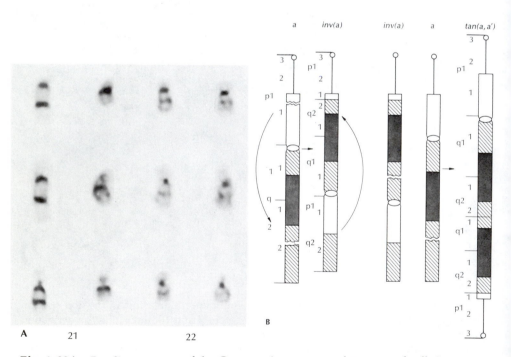

Fig. 4–22A Banding patterns of the G group chromosomes from several cells in a case of tandem translocations. Note the satellites on both ends of the abnormal chromosome 21 (left-hand column). **B.** Suggested mode of formation of the tandem translocation. The first step (shown on the left) is formation of a pericentric inversion following breaks in 21q2 and 21p1. This is followed by a reciprocal translocation between the inverted chromosome and the normal chromosome 21, resulting in the doubly satellited chromosome on the extreme right. (**A** from Schuh et al., 1974; courtesy of B. E. Schuh, M. J. Salwen, and the *Journal of Medical Genetics*. **B.** modified from Schuh et al., 1974.)

reciprocal translocation between the inversion chromosome and its homologue so as to produce a duplication 21 chromosome with satellites at both ends.

Several tandem translocations have been interpreted as dicentrics. The implication is that one centromere becomes inactive in such cases, for the chromosomes have persisted through many mitoses. An alternative possibility is that the centromeres are so close together that they are always pulled toward the same pole.

NOMENCLATURE

The Chicago Conference (1966) suggested that karyotypes be summarized by indicating (1) the number of chromosomes; (2) the status of the gonosomes; (3) the presence or absence of whole or parts of chromosomes (by the number of the chromosome (and arm) and the symbol + or −, respectively, placed before the chromosome symbol if the whole chromosome is extra or missing, after it (or the arm) if it is larger or smaller than normal); and (4) the presence of any diagnosed interchange by an appropriate symbol such as:

"inv" for inversion (placed before the chromosome symbol)

"t" for translocation (placed before the chromosome symbols)

"i" for isochromosome (placed *after* the chromosome symbol)

"r" for ring (placed *after* the chromosome symbol)

The symbol **p** stands for short arm, **q** for long arm; / separates cell lines in mosaicism; and a question mark indicates questionable identification of *chromosome* if placed before the number or letter, questionable *arm* if placed after the chromosome symbol. A semicolon separates the two chromosomes in a reciprocal translocation; it is omitted for a centric fusion when the "fragment" is absesnt.

The Paris Conference (1971) modified and expanded the Chicago Conference (1966) nomenclature to provide for the more precise identifications now possible. In addition to new abbreviations,

"del" for deletion

"dup" for duplication

"ins" for insertion

"inv ins" for inverted insertion

"ter" for teriminal or end

including optional ones, rcp, rob, and tan, to designate reciprocal, Robertsonian, and tandem translocations, respectively ("rec" being reserved for recombinant chromosomes), it made changes in order and punctuation. All rearrangement symbols are now to be placed before the chromosomes, as are plus and minus signs where needed. (They are no longer to be used for structural rearrangements such as deletions, inversions, or translocations.) Chromosomes involved are placed in parentheses, spearated by a semicolon if more than one is involved and in numerical order with X and Y listed first if they are involved, except that for an insertion the *receptor* chromosome is specified ahead of the donor chromosome. A colon signifies a break with no reunion (as in an apparent terminal deletion), a double colon (::) indicates breakage and union, and an arrow, directed from left to right, means "from → to." 46,XX,del(1)(pter → q21 :: q31 → qter), for example, would be the detailed designation of a female karyotype containing a deletion of chromosome 1 (that is, with breaks in) between bands q21 and q31, so that the remaining chromosome 1 consists of the portion from the end of the short arm to the breakage-union point, where the remainder of q21 and the remainder of q31 are now joined, and the portion from q31 to the end of the long arm. A suggested shorter notation for the same karyotype would be 46,XX,del(1)(q21q31). A new symbol, "der" is suggested to indicate new "derivative" chromosomes formed from production, segregation, or crossing over in rearrangements (see Fig. 4–5B).

SUGGESTED EXERCISES

4–1. What would be the interpretation in words of the following sets of symbols in the Chicago notation:
    (a)   47,XY,+G;
    (b)   46,XX/47,XXX;
    (c)   46,X,t(Yp+; 16q−);
    (d)   46,XX,inv(Dp+ q−); what is the alternative way of writing this if no meiotic cells are available?;
    (e)   45,XY,−D,−G,t(DqGq)+;
    (f)   46,XXX,?3+;
    (g)   46,XY,18q−.

4–2. Use Chicago notation to designate the karyotype of the following:
    (a)   usual Klinefelter;
    (b)   usual cri-du-chat;
    (c)   a female with a reciprocal translocation between the long arm of an X and the short arm of chromosome 5;
    (d)   a male with a pericentric inversion in chromosome 1;
    (e)   a female with an E ring;
    (f)   a male with the most common aberration involving the Ph^1 chromosome;
    (g)   a mosaic Down's female having some normal cells and some standard trisomic cells.

4–3. Restate the karyotypes of exercises 4–1 and 4–2 in the shorter form of the Paris Conference notation, assuming that all breaks, where pertinent, are in region 11 of the indicated arm(s). For 4–1(g) and 4–2(b) assume an additional break in band 12.

4–4. It has been estimated that the most frequent detectable aberration in normal human populations is for a centric fusion translocation between two D chromosomes. About 0.1 percent of people are estimated to be heterozygous, 45,XY, −D, −D, t(DqDq)+ or 45,XX, −D, −D,t(DqDq)+ according to the Chicago conference notation.

What are the theoretically expected consequences of meiosis in such individuals (a) if the D chromosomes involved are nonhomologous? (b) if the D chromosomes involved are homologous?

4-5. Figure 4-12**B** shows that quite typical trisomy-D may be the result of translocation. Give several possible reasons why trisomy-D occurs so rarely in the offspring of heterozygotes for D/G centric fusions.

4-6. Suppose a small duplication is produced by unequal crossing over. What might be the results of an identical amount of unequal crossing over in a heterozygote for the duplication, that is, an individual having this duplication and a normal chromosome of this type?

4-7. Figure 4-13 shows the production of a ring as a result of certain chromosome breaks. Note that this is a centric ring. Some investigators have reported finding *acentric* rings as a result of irradiation and radiomimetic agents.

  (a)   Diagram a possible method of producing acentric rings.

  (b)   A priori, which type of ring, centric or acentric, would be expected to be *produced* most often?

  (c)   Which type of ring would be *found* most often? Why?

4-8. By means of a diagram analogous to Fig. 4-17 demonstrate the consequences of crossing over within a paracentric inversion predicted on p. 94.

4-9. Demonstrate that the results of crossing over in a heterozygote for a shift resemble crossing over in a heterozygote for a pericentric inversion.

4-10. Demonstrate the difference between crossing over in heterozygotes for a two-chromosome reciprocal translocation and in heterozygotes for a heterologous transposition. In which situation is "aneusomie de recombination" most likely to be a factor?

4-11. Hongell (1974) studied 480 inmates of a mental institution who had multiple congenital anomalies, and were therefore suspected of having a chromosomal abnormality. Nearly one-third, 156, were in fact found to possess some chromosomal anomaly, and 145 of these, distributed nearly equally among the two sexes, had the same basic abnormality.

  (a)   Would you suspect the predominant anomaly to be autosomal or gonosomal or a mixture of the two?

  (b)   What chromosome or chromosomes are probably involved?

  (c)   How would you describe it (them)?

In addition to difference in quantitative effect—number of aberrations induced per unit agent employed, chromosome breakers seem to fall into two major qualitative categories. Some agents produce mostly breakages that lead to positional rearrangement, most often observed as quadriradials (eucentric translocations), dicentrics, fragments, and rings; others cause chromatid and isochromatid gaps (Fig. 4-4C) or similar evidence of breakage *without* interchanges or new adhesions of broken surfaces. Those that do produce new adhesions or interchanges are said to be *radiomimetic* because their effects are similar to those produced by X-rays and other radiations. Many drugs and chemicals, for example, chlorpromazine, cause only breaks without rearrangement, whereas the oncogenic viruses (Fig. 4–4) and such drugs as lysergic acid diethylamide (LSD) appear to be radiomimetic.

Most of the controversy in this field centers on the suitability of controls and the relative meaning of negative and positive results reported by different groups of investigators. These problems pose particular difficulties with respect to the non-radiomimetic group, for gaps and similar breaks are quite frequent in many control situations—especially in tissue cultures, where the extent of cell division is an important factor and where the results often depend on the age of the culture. Furthermore, nonrearrangement breaks tend to restitute (heal back to the old unions) quite readily, an obvious source of controversy in comparing experiment and control. Aberrations induced by radiomimetic agents can often be found several years after the treatment has stopped.

4–12. In a 1965–1966 cytogenetic study of 94 atomic bomb survivors in Hiroshima and Nagasaki and 94 suitably chosen controls, Bloom et al. (1967) obtained the following results:

Number of Cells Examined	Controls	Exposed
Single chromatid breaks and gaps	223	232
Isochromatid breaks and gaps	18	21
Rings	0	2
Dicentrics	0	7
Fragments	1	31
Translocations	0	10

(a)   Compare the results for the two groups.

(b)   Do these results help you to understand some of the controversy concerning "nonradiomimetic aberration inducers"? Explain.

4–13. Figure 1–15 shows the transmission of a chromosomal aberration through several generations.

(a)   What type of gene inheritance does this resemble?

(b)   If the G part of the translocation includes most of 21q, how likely is it that III-21's marriage to a cousin, say, III-7, would result in a child with Down syndrome? Note that there may be a difference between theoretical and empiric probabilities here.

5

Gene Structure, Gene Action, and the Phenotype

The idea that the genetic material consists of discrete particles on the chromosomes—the gene theory of inheritance—has been generally accepted since about 1915. It was not until 1953, however, that DNA as the basic structure of the gene was described, in the classic paper in *Nature* by James D. Watson and Francis H. C. Crick. Very soon this led to elegant explanations by Arthur Kornberg, Marshall W. Nirenberg, Severo Ochoa, and others of how genes are reproduced and how they act in the cell.

Although much of our understanding of gene structure and gene action has been derived from the study of prokaryotes, microorganisms that lack nuclei and usually have a single, relatively simple chromosome, many of the basic features apply as well to organisms whose cells contain nuclei, the eukaryotes, including humans.

The basic structure of DNA and most RNAs contain the same elements except that (1) the sugar in RNA is ribose instead of deoxyribose and (2) the common nitrogenous bases in RNA are A, C, G, and U (uracil) instead of A, C, G, and T. Some RNAs may contain other nitrogenous bases as well, such as inosine (I), the riboside of hypoxanthine (which can substitute for guanine), and pseudouridine (ψ), the riboside of pseudouracil (and like U relates to A).

Genes usually function by acting as templates, or indirect patterns, for the production of (a) polypeptides, chains of amino aids that are the major, if not the sole, constituents of the proteins, or (b) other nucleotide chains that, as various forms of RNA, are involved in the assembly of the polypeptide chains. Thus the ultimate function of the gene is, in either case, to govern the synthesis of proteins.

Proteins fall into three general classes: (1) structural proteins; (2) enzymes; and (3) regulators of gene activity.

The term "structural protein" includes (a) the essential intracellular molecules, such as hemoglobin, collagen, and myosin, that determine the nature of cells, (b) proteins, such as the serum albumins and globulins, which are largely extracellular, and (c) the proteins that play similar roles in many different cells in providing the framework of their organelles. The antigens that we detect in demonstrating blood types or histocompatibility variants to be discussed in later chapters are probably also complex structural proteins of blood cells; in this case, however, the detected specificities may not reside on the polypeptide part of the protein, but on carbohydrate or lipid moieties (haptens) attached to it; but they are themselves incapable of inducing antibody formation.

Enzymes are responsible for the synthesis of carbohydrates, fats, and combinations of these with protein, as well as of almost all of the other complex chemicals that the cells produce to govern all the myriad metabolic and energy transport mechanisms of the cell. Enzymes, which are organic catalysts, may be pure proteins (polypeptide chains), or they, too, may have nonproteins attached to them. Generally, the latter are called coenzymes and often contain a critical metal such as zinc or magnesium. The regulator substances are not as fully understood, but many of these, too, are proteins.

The two main steps in protein synthesis are *transcription* and *translation.* Transcription is the production of messenger (m) RNA, as the complement of one of the strands, the *sense* strand, of DNA. Translation is the production of a chain of amino aids from an mRNA template.

Tables 5–1 and 5–2 review the correspondence between the codons of mRNA and the amino acids that transfer (t) RNA brings in to form the polypeptide chain during translation. Note that two codons, UAA and UAG, termed "ochre" and "amber," respectively, relate to no amino acids. They are often referred to as *terminator* codons because their presence ends the production of a given polypeptide. At the place of synthesis there are additional RNA particles of various sizes known as ribosomal (r) RNA.

A special feature of the gene templates for rRNA and tRNA is that they exist in multiple copies, as do the genes encoding for the histone proteins that make up a large part of eukaryote chromosome structure. Many of these repetitive genes cluster in the constitutive heterochromatin near the centromeres, whereas the usual polypeptide genes are mainly in the euchromatin. Other clusters of repetitive genes are near the tips of the short arms of the acrocentric chromosomes.

DISCONTINUITY IN THE GENE AND THE CHROMOSOME

Many, perhaps all, eukaryote genes differ in a very interesting way from the basic structure, which has been inferred largely from the study of prokaryotes: Instead of a continuous chain of sense nucleotides, the information that patterns the eukaryote polypeptide chain is encoded in several separate pieces. Between these pieces are nucleotide chains called *intervening sequences* that apparently do not contribute to protein synthesis. Each sense portion is now called an *exon,* each intervening sequence an *intron.*

The number of exons and introns varies. The functional part of the gene for the enzyme deficient in Lesch–Nyhan disease, hypoxanthine-guanine phosphoribosyl transferase (HGPRT), for example, is divided into nine segments by eight introns. The genes for human globins to be discussed below are simpler. Each consists of 3 exons and 2 introns (Fig. 5–1). In the case of the β-like genes, for example, the 5′ end is a segment with 30 codons for the N-terminal end of the globin, followed by a short intron, then a functional segment of 74 codons, a long intron (950–

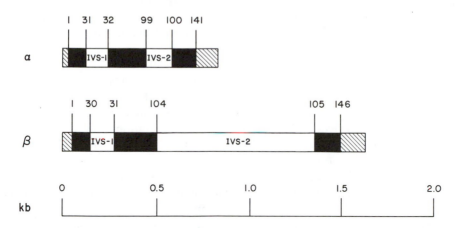

Fig. 5-1 Diagrammatic representation of α-like and β-like globin genes. Filled blocks represent coding regions (exons) of the gene; hatched blocks represent adjacent untranslated sequences; and IVS-1 and IVS-2 are the intervening sequences (introns). Numbers above the diagrams indicate amino acid codon positions of the exons; the numbers below indicate the number of kilobases (kb) involved. Note that the rightward intron in the β-like genes is much longer than in the α group. (From Spritz and Forget, 1983, after Forget, 1983; courtesy of B. G. Forget and *American Journal of Human Genetics*.)

1000 nucleotides), then the C-terminal exon, with 42 structural codons and a terminator on the 3' side.

This complicates transcription in the eukaryote. Instead of one step there must be three: (1) fully transcribing the gene to produce a *precursor-mRNA;* (2) snipping out the nucleotides complementary to the intron(s) by special enzymes (endonucleases); and (3) splicing the sense pieces together, via "joining" enzymes (ligases), to produce an mRNA that can be translated without interruption.

Although the function of the introns is at this writing unknown, some of the gene changes discussed below occur in them as well as in the sense areas. This has become useful, we shall note, for several aspects of gene analysis and prenatal diagnosis.

The chromosome contains interesting interspersions of DNA sequences in relation to its other major constituent, the basic histones. The DNA appears usually bunched into spherical units (nucleosomes, beads, or *nu* particles), each about 200 base pairs coiled around regular groupings of histones H2a, H2b, H3, and H4. These units are interconnected by the H1 histone. This finding accounts for some of the "packing" of the DNA, which is much longer than the chromosome.

HOW GENES CHANGE: MUTATION

The development of genetics as a science—and all organic evolution—has depended not only on the ability of genes to replicate (hence, mitosis and meiosis) but also on the fact that they and, therefore, their carriers, vary. Genetic variation occurs because the gene can occasionally change its structure without losing the ability to duplicate itself. Most changes in the structure of the genes are thereupon reflected in changes in their action. These changed actions result in different phenotypes.

New phenotypes may be produced in other ways than by changes in the gene. Gene changes may be mimicked, on the one hand, by environmental factors that modify the development of the organism and, on the other, by chromosomal deletions. A new combination of genes or even a rearrangement of the position of the genes, from crossing over or from a chromosomal aberration, may also produce a new phenotype. Nonetheless, many new phenotypes result from new genes produced by structural changes of existing genes.

Structural changes in the genetic material are called mutations. In its broadest sense, mutation also includes the gross chromosomal changes discussed in previous chapters. In common usage, however, the term is restricted to changes within the confines of a single gene or cistron. Some indicate the restriction by referring to these as "point mutations." In a negative way, (point) mutations are said to comprise all genetic changes for which no other explanation (gross chromosomal change or exchange) can be found. The new gene is called a *mutant,* but this word is applied as well to the individual showing the new phenotype.

Geneticists have found that mutations may be caused ("induced") by a number of external agents, as will be discussed later. Many mutations appear, however, without any evidence that any external agent was responsible. These are known as *spontaneous mutations.*

According to current theory, most mutations represent substitutions of one or more nucleotides of a DNA molecule or of its RNA counterpart, particularly during replication. Thus, the *muton*—the amount of a gene that must be changed to effect a mutation—may be as little as a single purine or pyrimidine base.

Some of the best evidence for such mutations has come from the study of abnormal hemoglobins.

Human hemoglobin exists in a number of forms at various stages of development (Fig. 5–2). These differ according to which of the six kinds of globin chains, termed alpha, beta, gamma, delta, epsilon, and zeta, are present. Most forms consist of two molecules of alpha chains, with 141 amino acids in each chain, and two molecules of one of the β-like globins, β, γ, δ, or ϵ, each containing 146 amino acids. (In some of the earliest hemoglobins an α-like globin, zeta, is present instead of alpha, usually along with ϵ or γ.) Every hemoglobin molecule also contains four molecules of heme, an iron-protoporphyrin complex, one attached to each of the globin chains. (Protoporphyrin is a complicated ring compound; disorders of its metabolism are called porphyrias.)

About 97.5 percent of normal adult hemoglobin has the formula $\alpha_2\beta_2$. It is called hemoglobin A (Hb A). About 2.5 percent, called hemoglobin A_2, has delta chains instead of betas. Fetal hemoglobin (Hb F) has the formula $\alpha_2\gamma_2$. It may also be a minor fraction—less than one percent—of normal adult hemoglobin. Early embryonic hemoglobin apparently takes two forms, Gower I, which seems to be a tetramer of epsilon chains (ϵ_4) and Gower II, which is $\alpha_2\epsilon_2$.

With the development of techniques to determine the amino acid composition

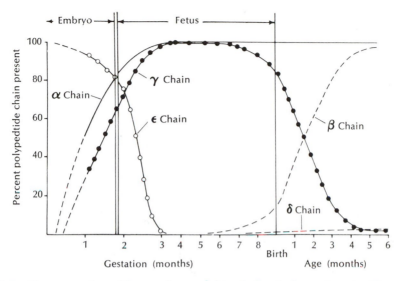

Fig. 5-2   The succession of human hemoglobin chains during ontogeny. (From Huisman, 1972; courtesy of T. H. Huisman and Academic Press, Inc., publishers of *Advances in Clinical Chemistry*.)

of proteins, one of the first to come under intensive study was hemoglobin S, an abnormal hemoglobin found in persons suffering from sickle-cell anemia. The disease derives its name from the oddly shaped red blood cells (Fig. 5–3) frequently encountered in affected individuals, who are usually Africans or of African descent. Their parents (and some siblings) generally have normal-appearing red blood cells; under conditions involving a sharp drop in oxygen tension (such as might occur on a ride in an unpressurized airplane), however, they, too, may have sickled eryth-

Fig. 5-3   The blood picture in sickle-cell anemia. Note the bizarre shape of the red blood cells, all of which contain hemoglobin S instead of hemoglobin A. A similar picture is obtained in sickle-cell trait when the red blood cells are deoxygenated. (Courtesy of J. V. Neel.)

HbA . . . . Val—His—Leu—Thr—Pro—Glu—Glu—Lys. . . .

HbS . . . . Val—His—Leu—Thr—Pro—Val—Glu—Lys. . . .

HbC . . . . Val—His—Leu—Thr—Pro—Lys—Glu—Lys. . . .

HbG$_{San José}$ . . . Val—His—Leu—Thr—Pro—Glu—Gly—Lys. . . .

Fig. 5–4   Amino acid sequence of the N-terminal end of the beta chain in four of the first hemoglobins studied by Ingram and his co-workers. The underlined amino acids indicate the substitutions in S, C, and G-San Jose as compared with A. (Based on Ingram, 1963. Courtesy of V. Ingram and Columbia University Press.)

rocytes and some of the symptoms associated with more severe anemia. These persons are said to have "sickle-cell trait."

Sickle-cell trait represents the heterozygote, carrying one dose of the abnormal gene producing Hb S, and sickle-cell anemia the homozygote, for that gene. In the homozygote almost all the hemoglobin is S; in the heterozygote about 60 percent

Table 5–1   The 20 amino acids commonly used in protein synthesis and their functional mRNA codons in *E. coli*. Most, possibly all, of these codons are also valid for higher organisms. Codons UAA and UAG, called "ochre" and "amber," respectively, and UGA have not been associated with amino acids in any organism and act apparently as terminal or "nonsense" codons

Amino Acid	Symbol	mRNA Code Words[a]			
Alanine	Ala	GCA	GCC	GCG	GCU
Arginine[b]	Arg	CGA	CGC	CGG	CGU
		AGA		AGG	
Asparagine	Asn		AAC		AAU
Aspartic Acid	Asp		GAC		GAU
Cysteine	Cys		UGC		UGU
Glutamic Acid	Glu	GAA		GAG	
Glutamine	Gln	CAA		CAG	
Glycine	Gly	GGA	GGC	GGG	GGU
Histidine[b]	His		CAC		CAU
Isoleucine[b]	Ile	AUA	AUC		AUU
Leucine[b]	Leu	CUA	CUC	CUG	CUU
		UUA		UUG	
Lysine[b]	Lys	AAA		AAG	
Methionine[b]	Met			AUG	
Phenylalanine[b]	Phe		UUC		UUU
Proline	Pro	CCA	CCC	CCG	CCU
Serine	Ser	UCA	UCC	UCG	UCU
		AGC			AGU
Threonine	Thr	ACA	ACC	ACG	ACU
Tryptophane[b]	Trp			UGG	
Tyrosine	Tyr		UAC		UAU
Valine[b]	Val	GUA	GUC	GUG	GUU

[a]The corresponding tRNA carry the complements (anti-codons) of these codons.

[b]Considered an irreplaceable essential amino acid in man.

Table 5-2 An alternative method of showing the correspondence between amino acids and the mRNA codons in *E. coli*. This method relates each codon to the amino acid it can recognize and bring to polypeptide synthesis. The functional codon of the tRNA in each case is the complement of the one shown and is referred to as an "anticodon" (Based essentially on Marshall et al., 1967)

1st Base	U	C	A	G	3rd Base
U	PHE	SER	TYR	CYS	U
	PHE	SER	TYR	CYS	C
	LEU	SER	Ochre	Term.	A
	LEU	SER	Amber	TRP	G
C	LEU	PRO	HIS	ARG	U
	LEU	PRO	HIS	ARG	C
	LEU	PRO	GLN	ARG	A
	LEU	PRO	GLN	ARG	G
A	ILE	THR	ASN	SER	U
	ILE	THR	ASN	SER	C
	ILE	THR	LYS	ARG	A
	MET	THR	LYS	ARG	G
G	VAL	ALA	ASP	GLY	U
	VAL	ALA	ASP	GLY	C
	VAL	ALA	GLU	GLY	A
	VAL	ALA	GLU	GLY	G

is A, about 40 percent S. (There are at least seven other abnormalities of human hemoglobin in which sickling can occur, but these are much rarer than the condition being discussed here).

The new techniques disclosed that Hb S differs from Hb A only in the beta chain and only in a single fragment of that chain. Moreover, S and A differ in only one amino acid among the eight in the fragment: substitution of a valine for the glutamic acid normally found in position number 6 (Fig. 5-4). Now, according to Tables 5-1 and 5-2, the messenger RNA code words for glutamic acid are

GAA or GAG

Valine, on the other hand, is brought into a polypeptide by the mRNA sequences

GUA, GUC, GUG, or GUU,

which correspond to the DNA sequences CAT, CAG, CAC, and CAA, respectively. All it takes, then, to change from glutamic acid to valine is for the change of

GAA to GUA,

or, in the DNA, for the change of

CTT to CAT.

So, only one nucleotide difference causes the gene to produce S instead of A hemo-globin. A change of this type, whereby a pyrimidine is substituted for a purine, or vice versa, is called a *transversion*.

Another abnormal hemoglobin, C, involves a different change, from glutamic acid to lysine, at this position (Fig. 5–4). Homozygotes for C also suffer from a clinical, but somewhat less severe, anemia. Their hemoglobin formula is $\alpha_2^A\beta_2^C$. AC heterozygotes produce both $\alpha_2^A\beta_2^A$ and $\alpha_2^A\beta_2^C$,* and thus exhibit the Hb C trait. Per-sons with both Hb C and Hb S exist, and they manifest a rather severe condition termed S-C disease.

Since lysine is coded in mRNA by

AAA or AAG,

a single change, this time in the first code letter for glutamic acid,

from GAA to AAA, or from GAG to AAG,

is all that is required to transform a normal beta chain into a C chain, with lysine instead of glutamic acid at position 6. Substitution of a purine for another purine, or a pyrimidine for another pyrimidine, is called a *transition*.

Although they do not shed light on many other properties, these findings help explain differences in electrophoretic mobilities of various hemoglobins. The nor-mal occupant of position 6, Glu, is negatively charged, whereas its occupant in Hb S, Val, is neutral, and that of Hb C, Lys, is positively charged. Since each molecule of hemoglobin contains two beta chains, Hb S differs from Hb A by two charges, Hb S from Hb C by two, and Hb C from Hb A by four.

The possible transformations may be indicated thus in terms of charge:

$$
\begin{aligned}
\text{Hb A} \rightarrow \text{Hb S} &= 2\,(\text{Glu}^- \rightarrow \text{Val}) &&= 2+ \\
\text{Hb S} \rightarrow \text{Hb A} &= 2\,(\text{Val} \rightarrow \text{Glu}^-) &&= 2- \\
\text{Hb A} \rightarrow \text{Hb C} &= 2\,(\text{Glu}^- \rightarrow \text{Lys}^+) &&= 4+ \\
\text{Hb C} \rightarrow \text{Hb A} &= 2\,(\text{Lys}^+ \rightarrow \text{Glu}^-) &&= 4- \\
\text{Hb S} \rightarrow \text{Hb C} &= 2\,(\text{Val}^+ \rightarrow \text{Lys}) &&= 2+ \\
\text{Hb C} \rightarrow \text{Hb S} &= 2\,(\text{Lys} \rightarrow \text{Val}^+) &&= 2-
\end{aligned}
$$

Of the amino acids commonly found in proteins, glutamic and aspartic acids are the only two that are acid (and therefore bear a negative charge). Four are basic (positive charge): lysine, hydroxylysine, arginine, and histidine, though histidine is neutral above pH 6. All the other common ones are neutral.

Similar determinations have since been made for many other hemoglobins, and more are being added every year. At first the new variants were given alpha-betical names similar to S and C, but recently they have been named for the city or region where they were discovered: for example, Norfolk, Stanleyville, Lepore, Hopkins (referring to John Hopkins University). Since some amino acid substitu-tions involve no net change in charge, the electrophorectic mobilities of several hemoglobins have been identical. In such cases combination or modified names

---

*Note that they do not produce $\alpha_2^A\beta^A\beta^C$ molecules; this suggests that the β^A and β^C chains are syn-thesized at different organelles (different ribosomes) of the cell and immediately joined. β^A and β^S follow a similar pattern.

are used that show both the old relationship and the distinction: thus, Hopkins-1 and Hopkins-2, D-α and D-β, M-Boston, M-Emory, and M-Milwaukee.

Six other hemoglobins resemble C in substituting lysine for glutamic acid on the beta chain, namely:

Hemoglobin	Position
Siriraj	7
E-Saskatoon	22
E	26
Agenogi	90
British Columbia	101
O-Arabia	121

The differences between these hemoglobins demonstrate that the position as well as the nature of the amino acids present is significant in determining the properties of a hemoglobin. The same substitution has occurred also at least three times each on the α and the γ chains and once on the δ chain, for a total of 14. Indeed, F-Texas II mimics C exactly in the substitution's being at position 6, and F-Hull mimics O-Arabia in the same way at position 121.

On this model, some more complicated differences represent accumulations of single-step modifications. Thus, the gene for the beta chain of Hb C-Harlem, which has valine instead of glutamic acid at position 6 and asparagine instead of aspartic acid at position 73, could be visualized as a single nucleotide mutation of an S gene. This could happen by an mRNA change from GAU or GAC, for aspartic acid, to AAU or AAC, respectively, for asparagine. In effect, a phylogenetic sequence can then be visualized:

$$Hb\ A \rightleftarrows Hb\ S \rightleftarrows Hb\text{-Harlem}$$

We do not know in which direction the evolution occurred, but the longer arrows indicate the most probable sequence. Of the double substitutions known to date, three (possibly four) are in the beta chain, all involving position 6, one in the alpha chain.

At this writing one or more substitutions have been found in at least 70 of the 141 amino acid positions of alpha globin and, in the chains with 146 positions, at 122 beta, 10 delta, and 18 gamma.

One double-step substitutional change at the same position has been identified: from threonine in the normal beta chain to glutamine in the normal delta chain at position 87. Delta apparently originated as a duplication of beta (in the manner of Fig. 4–19), and there are normally only nine other differences between the two chains.

In 12 abnormal hemoglobins one or more amino acids are absent, either by *deletion* of whole codons or by transformation of a subterminal codon to a terminator. Eleven of these involve beta chains, one an alpha.

Another form of genetic change is the *frameshift* mutation, an extensive misreading of the genetic code during protein synthesis. Three ways that this can happen have been found in abnormal hemoglobins:

(a) Deletion of less than a whole codon.
(b) Ectopic insertion of less than a whole codon.

(c) Transformation of a terminator codon to a sense (amino acid attracting) one, with the result that the translation continues beyond the usual stop (into intergenic DNA?).

Because the changes usually involve combinations of one of the first two (*a* or *b*) and the third, all of the frameshift globins are unusually long.

To understand the first discovered, Hb Wayne, note that normally the last four codons, 139–141 and terminator, of alpha globin mRNA are:

AAG UAC CGU UAA,

which is translated

140
-Lys-Tyr-Arg-COOH.

In Hb Wayne this final sequence is missing, replaced by

140   145
Asn-Thr-Val-Lys-Leu-Glu-Pro-Arg-COOH.

This can be readily understood if, at position 139, the third nucleotide of the normal Lys codon (G) were deleted, so that the new codon sequence would be

AAU ACC GUU AAG CUG GAG . . . etc.

Three abnormally long alpha variants are attributable to mutations of the terminator codon, UAA. In Hb Constant Spring, named for a locality in Jamaica where the index case, a Chinese, resided, the change was in the first nucleotide: to CAA, for glutamine. The resultant CS α-globin has 31 extra amino acids. Hb Icaria, named for an Aegean Island, is also 172 residues in length, but the change in the terminator codon was probably to AAA, for lysine. In Hb Koya Dora, found in high frequency in the Koya Dora population in India, the second nucleotide of UAA was apparently modified to UCA, for serine; it has at least 16 extra residues. These three hemoglobins are medically significant because they cause disorders resembling α-thalassemia (Chapter 14) or they can increase the severity of that disease.

The two known frameshifts of *beta* globin, Hb Cranston and Hb Tak, were apparently caused by the insertion of two nucleotides in each case as a result of unequal crossing over between normal beta genes. Unequal (or nonhomologous) crossing over may occur between genes (Fig. 4–19) or within genes (Fig. 5–5). The case diagrammed in Fig. 5–5 is a rather extreme one, involving an interchange between an area near the N-terminal end of one gene and an area near the C-terminal end of the other; the inequality needed to produce the beta frameshifts would be much smaller.

Hb Cranston probably resulted from an interchange involving position 144, thus:

145
AAG UAU CAC UAA GCU · · ·
X
AAG UAU CAC UAA GCU · · ·

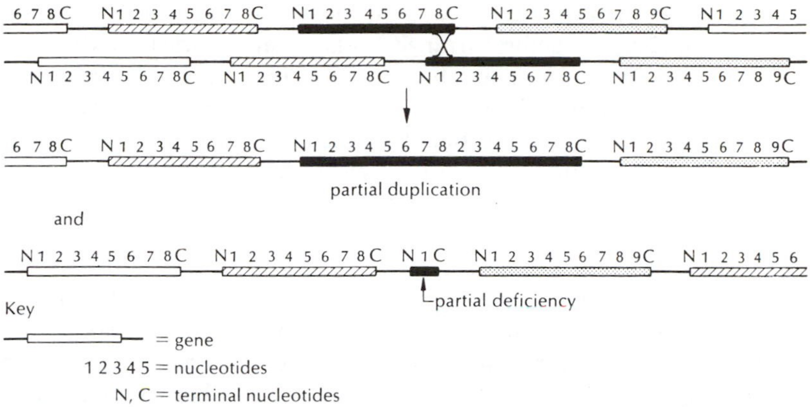

Fig. 5-5 Diagram of possible production of a partially duplicated gene by intragenic unequal crossing over. Compare with the production of complete duplications in Figure 4–19. Comparable result could be obtained by intragenic breakages and selective refusion independent of chiasma formation. The duplicate portion is shown very large, nearly doubling the gene size, but the same mechanism could account for the doubling of much smaller amounts, as little as a single nucleotide. Similar crossovers involving nearby, but nonallelic, genes could be responsible for such "hybrid" molecules as hemoglobin Lepore (p. 330, Figs. 14–12 and 14–13).

to produce the new sequence

145
AAG AGU AUC ACU AAG CUX · · ·

translated

145
Lys-Ser-Ile-Thr-Lys-Leu . . . ,

with 11 extra amino acids. For Hb Tak, which has 10 extra residues, a similar abnormal crossover inserting AG appears to have occurred at position 146.

All the known abnormally long globins involve the carboxyl (3') end of the chain. Presumably frameshifts in other parts of the chain are inviable or undetectable, unless they result in complete or nearly complete gene duplications. Whole gene duplications as illustrated in Fig. 4–19 probably account, incidentally, for the production of beta, gamma, and delta globins from a primordial form with 146 amino acids, also for the existence of two separate alpha chain loci in most individuals (Chapter 14). A variation on this process, involving adjacent loci, results in the Lepore, Miyada, and Kenya hemoglobins to be discussed in Chapter 14. (See also the discussion of haptoglobin alleles below.)

THE MECHANISM OF MUTATION

Considerable light on the way mutations occur has been shed by experiments with mutagenic agents. These have underscored, for example, that the structures of the nitrogenous bases is not as fixed as was intimated earlier. Each of the bases can assume several different structural arrangements, or tautomeric forms. Some examples are shown in Fig. 5–6A. The left-hand form in each case is the most likely tautomer, its keto or amino form, the one usually shown in figures of DNA or RNA. The others differ in the positions at which one hydrogen atom is attached. This change is accompanied by a shift of electrons so that some double bonds become single bonds, and vice versa. These less likely tautomers are said to be an enol (=C−OH) or imino (=NH) form. The relative frequencies of tautomers depend on several factors, including the pH.

The tautomeric shifts can be important for mutation, both spontaneous and induced, because they often cause changes in base-pairing. The usual (amino) tautomer of adenine, for example, pairs with thymine, but one of its less common imino tautomers can base-pair with cytosine (Fig. 5–6B). Reciprocally, a rare imino tautomer of cytosine can pair with adenine. In like manner, T and G can pair by forming three H bonds between G and an enol tautomer of T, or between T and a tautomer of G.

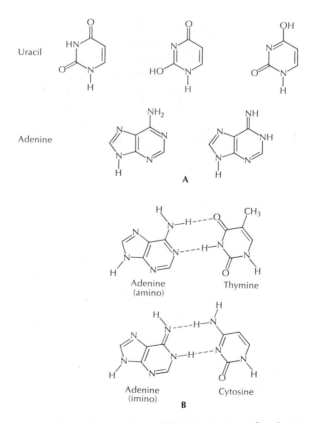

Fig. 5–6A   Tautomers of adenine and uracil. **B.** Illustration of a change is base-pairing as a result of a tautomeric shift. In this case adenine comes to pair with cytosine instead of its usual partner, thymine. (From Herskowitz, 1973, **B** after Watson and Crick, 1953; courtesy of I. H. Herskowitz and the Macmillan Co.)

The existence of tautomers explains the mutagenic action of such chemicals as 5-bromouridine (BU) or 2-aminopurine. These are often referred to as "base analogues" because they act by substituting for existing bases, "errors of incorporation," as they are called. If bromouracil, for example, is incorporated by mistake into DNA, it would usually be in its keto tautomer, which base-pairs with adenine and causes no problem. The rare enol tautomer of bromouracil, like that of thymine, can pair with guanine, however, producing eventually the transitional replacement of adenine by guanine. If BU reverts to its keto form, as commonly happens, it will accept adenine in the next replication to effect the reverse, G to A, transition. Similarly, 2-aminopurine, if mistakenly incorporated, can pair with thymine or cytosine in its normal tautomeric form, or, as a less common tautomer, it can pair with cytosine. As a consequence pyrimidine transitions (T—C) are possible. BU may also cause normal bases that are adjacent to it in the same strand to commit errors of replication.

A number of mutagenic agents cause abnormal joining of adjacent nitrogenous bases of the same DNA or RNA strand *(dimerization)* or different strands *(cross-linking)*. Ultraviolet light, for example, induces pyrimidines to form dimers by converting their normal $C4=C5$ double bonds to junctions of C4 and C5's of adjacent thymines, cytosines, or uracils (Fig. 5–7). The same agent may also cause abnormal hydration of pyrimidines, by adding an OH at, say, C4 and an H at C5. Nitrogen mustard may cause cross-linking of guanines, and mitomycin C, a mutagenic antibiotic, is known to cause interchain cross-linking of all purines. Dimerization, cross-linking, and abnormal hydration interfere with nucleic acid synthesis; in the case of mRNA they may also cause mistranslation.

Some chemicals and other mutagens can cause breaks of the backbone of the DNA strand at two or more places, obtaining deletions or other rearrangements of one or more nucleotides. Mustard compounds may specifically delete guanine; its replacement by any of the other bases could produce a transition or transversion. Acridine compounds, on the other hand, by inserting themselves into the double helix between nucleotides, may lead to insertion of an extra nucleotide or to loss of one.

How ionizing radiations induce mutations is less well understood. This is true even though these agents have been studied intensively for a much longer period and some of them are in common use in medical procedures.

Ionizing radiations exist in two forms, those, such as light, gamma rays, X-rays, and radio waves, which are "electromagnetic" in nature and those, such as alpha particles and neutrons, which consist of particles of finite mass. The latter vary according to the mass of the particles and the speed with which they move, the former according to wave frequency. Both types can cause "ionizations" when they pass through matter, including living matter, and their mutagenic and other damaging effects probably stem from this property. Generally they contain considerable energy; in fact, they are often referred to as "high-energy radiations." When they affect one of the electrons of an atom, they often knock it out of the atom. As a result, the atom is no longer neutral; it is now positively charged, since it has more positive charges (in the nucleus) than it has negative charges outside the nucleus. It may be recalled that such a positively charged atom is an ion.

Ionized atoms and the molecules containing them are much more chemically

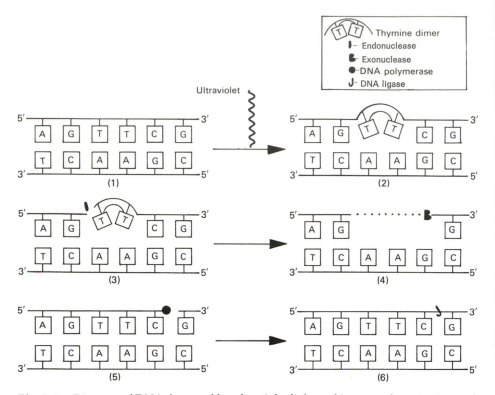

Fig. 5-7 Diagram of DNA damaged by ultraviolet light and its normal repair. A stretch of DNA (1) is exposed to ultraviolet light, and a thymine dimer forms, distorting the DNA (2). An enzyme, a nuclease, recognizes the region and produces a nick in the vicinity of the damage (3). A second enzyme, another nuclease, recognizes the free end and digests away a segment of the DNA strand, which includes the damage (4). DNA polymerase synthesizes the portion that has been eliminated (5). Finally, a joining enzyme (ligase) links the newly formed segment to the original strand (6), and the DNA is restored to normal. (From Rothwell, 1976; courtesy of N. V. Rothwell and Williams and Wilkins Co.)

active than are neutral ones. Presumably this applies to a gene containing an atom ionized by radiation as well as to other molecules and is responsible for its ensuing change to become a mutant allele.

When radiation causes the loss of an electron, it loses some of its energy. When it thereupon "hits" another electron, it will again dissipate some of its energy. It may still have had enough energy to knock it out of its orbit, too, but more than likely its main effect will be to increase the "thermal agitation" of the second electron. In fact, this is all that the radiation may have done to the very first electron. Such "thermal agitation" or "excitation" also makes a molecule containing it more susceptible to chemical change, and probably also contributes to the likelihood of mutagenesis or other damage to tissues by these radiations.

Ionizing radiations may cause some gene mutations indirectly. Instead of hitting the gene, other substances in the cell, such as amino acids or proteins, are hit and modified, and these in turn act as chemical mutagens. Evidence exists that the treatment produces chemical changes to hydrogen peroxide and organic peroxides, which are known to be able to oxidize deoxyribose, to deaminate and dehydroxylate nitrogenous bases, and to form peroxides in DNA. These changes may increase the chance of strand breakage, probably the major effect of high-energy electromagnetic radiation in bacterial studies. Double-strand breaks of the sugar-phosphate backbone are particularly serious because they cannot be repaired.

DNA REPAIR

Mutagenic activities of the type outlined above are apparently occurring all the time, in part under the influence of substances produced in normal metabolism. The strand abnormalities do not usually persist long enough to be considered mutations, however, because cells contain repair mechanisms to restore the strands to their normal condition. A particularly critical part is played by endonucleases, enzymes that are capable of excising defective segments, and by polynucleotide ligases, which effect new junctions of strands interrupted during the excisions (Fig. 5–7).

Some mutations may occur because of failure of the repair mechanisms. Mutations may also persist if the changes in the nucleic acids are not sufficiently drastic enough to be recognized and excised by a repair mechanism but are sufficiently different to cause mistakes in replication. Sometimes there may even be errors in the repair process, akin to iatrogenic diseases.

Genetic disorders, such as Xeroderma Pigmentosum, which are due to defects in these repair mechanisms, are discussed further in Chapter 17.

MUTATION AND THE PHENOTYPE

Our discussion of gene change implies three kinds of new alleles:

1. *Sense:* Mutation leads to translation into the same amino acid and, therefore, to no change in the resultant protein, for example, a DNA change from AAC to AAT results in a change in mRNA from UUG to UUA but still leads to leucine at that point. The new gene is an "isoallele." The term is also used at a nonmolecular level for homologous genes with apparently similar effects.
2. *Missense:* Mutation leads to translation to a modified polypeptide. Most "mutant" or "variant" genes are missense alleles.
3. *Nonsense:* Mutation leads to premature termination of translation, producing a shortened polypeptide or no product at all; for example, a DNA change from AAC to ATC would result is an mRNA change from UUG to UAG, a terminal codon. This results in a "null" allele or "amorph." A missense allele that has lost all function is also sometimes called an amorph.

Nonsense alleles would appear to be the ideal personification of Mendelian recessiveness. If, for example, *a* is an amorphic gene, both *A/A* and *A/a* would produce only polypeptide A; yet the former would produce all A gametes and the latter $0.50\ A$ gametes, $0.50\ a$ gametes. However, nonsense alleles may be mimicked by the effect of suppressor or inhibitor genes; see, for instance, the comment about S-Thal in Fig. 5–10. Also, their recessiveness is blurred if a quantitative test is possible; thus, the A/A of the earlier example produce twice as much A substance as do the A/a. This point is especially significant in devising a means of heterozygote detection.

Whether the responsible genes are truly amorphs or are instead missense alleles whose product has little or no activity, enzyme deficiency disorders are almost invariably Mendelian recessives, since the heterozygote, which has a normal allele, usually produces sufficient amounts of the normal enzyme to appear clinically normal.

Nevertheless, methods to differentiate "carriers" from normal homozygotes are commonly based on the expectation that the heterozygotes will have some measureable effect, as illustrated in Table 5–3. Unfortunately, these expectations are not always realized (Fig. 5–8). Note also the ranges in Table 5–3 for the enzyme deficient in galactosemia. Such overlapping distributions compromise clear-cut distinctions between the clinically normal genotypes. In some cases it has been possible to get around this difficulty by methods that detect directly an abnormal product produced by the heterozygotes but not by the homozygous normals.

In a recent compilation of well-established enzymopathies, disorders due to an enzyme defect, 5.3 percent were autosomal dominants, 6.4 percent X-linked, and 88.3 percent autosomal recessives.

So pervasive is the association between enzymopathy and recessiveness that many geneticists accept it as a rule-of-thumb that if a trait is recessive its basis will be found to lie in a defective enzyme. Conversely, dominant hereditary diseases are generally assumed to be due to abnormalities of structural proteins, such as those localized in cell membranes and in bone matrix or other connective tissues. The implication is that a heterozygote with 50 percent abnormal structural protein cannot compensate by means of the 50 percent normal protein produced by his normal allele.

Table 5–3 RBC enzyme activity measurements of normals (homozygous dominants), presumed heterozygotes, and affected (homozygous recessives) for several loci (Data on diaphorase from Harris, 1963b, after Scott, 1960; pyruvate kinase from Tanaka et al., 1962; TPI, triose-phosphate isomerase, from Valentine et al., 1966; and galactose-1-P-uridyl transferase from Hsia et al., 1958)

| | Enzymes Studied | | | | | | | |
| | Diaphorase | | Pyruvate Kinase | | | TPI Reported Value | Galactose-1-P-Uridyl Transferase | | |
	Number	Mean	Number	Mean	Range		Number	Mean	Range
Normals	88	45.5	40	2.65	2.00–3.40	95	11	4.5	2.8–7.0
Heterozygotes[a]	13	21.8	34	1.19	0.35–1.73[b]	84–125	12	3.3	1.7–5.5
Affected	14	0.9	7	0.38	0.00–0.83	15	8	0.5	0–1.1

[a]Parents of affected and certain sibs and other close relatives.
[b]Excluding one individual, the range was 0.65–1.73.

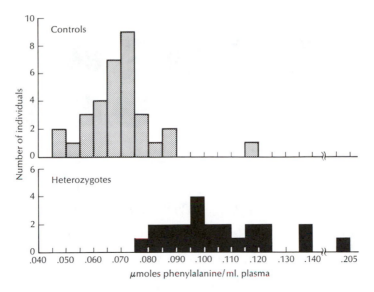

Fig. 5-8   Distribution of plasma phenylalanine in 33 controls and 23 individuals heterozygous for the phenylketonuria gene. Note the overlap of the heterozygotes and the probable homozygotes for the normal allele (controls). (From Knox and Messinger, 1958; courtesy of W. E. Knox and *The American Journal of Human Genetics*.)

While the rule-of-thumb for enzymopathies being recessive holds better than the one for structural protein defects being dominant, none of these generalizations can be considered rigid rules. For one thing, 6 percent of the aforementioned enzymopathies are autosomal dominants. Although some may not be true enzyme defects, being perhaps structural defects in other (regulatory) loci that affect the enzyme action, a recent review of the five dominant forms of porphyria, for example, has established that they are indeed due to true enzyme deficiencies.

Contrariwise, many autosomal recessives are known that involve a deficiency or other defect in structural proteins. These include the rarer bleeder diseases ("coagulopathies") in Table 14–1, four deficiencies of components of complement, a number of hormone deficiencies, and deficiencies of such serum proteins as albumin, transferrin, and several lipoproteins. One of the best known in this category is Wilson's disease, characterized by low serum concentrations of ceruloplasmin, a factor important in copper metabolism. Its deficiency leads in turn to reduced levels of activity of copper-containing enzymes, such as cytochrome oxidase.

Some true Mendelian recessives are also found in the blood groups, determined in most instances by antigenic proteins on red blood cell surfaces. Although the critical factor in some of these conditions may be the absence or inactivity of an enzyme needed in the manufacture of the structural protein or in its proper use by the body, many are traceable, as with the enzyme deficiencies, to an amorph allele.

A clear distinction exists between enzyme deficiency disorders and enzyme variants caused by missense mutations. Mutational variants of many enzymes can be detected by the same methods, chiefly electrophoresis, that detect the variants

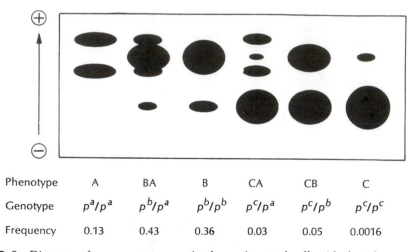

Phenotype	A	BA	B	CA	CB	C
Genotype	p^a/p^a	p^b/p^a	p^b/p^b	p^c/p^a	p^c/p^b	p^c/p^c
Frequency	0.13	0.43	0.36	0.03	0.05	0.0016

Fig. 5–9 Diagram of components seen in the various red-cell acid phosphatase phenotypes after electrophoresis at pH 6.0. Note the clear distinction between the single-letter base *(p)* for the gene symbols and the double letters for the phenotypes. (Modified from Harris, 1966; courtesy of H. Harris and *The Proceedings of the Royal Society of London.*)

of hemoglobin mentioned earlier in this chapter. Figure 5–9 shows, for example, three variants, termed A, B, and C, or erythrocyte acid phosphatase. These result, respectively, from three alleles of the enzyme locus, p^a, p^b, p^c. In some cases, as is true in Fig. 5–9, a single variant may be responsible for several electrophoretic spots, and some of these may coalesce in certain genotypes, but one can, nevertheless, determine how many variants are present and which ones they are.

It turns out that there are two different kinds of enzyme variants. Some represent allelic mutation of a typical polypeptide (or polypeptides, if the enzyme involves two or more chains). Others, being multimeric, are merely different combinations of the polypeptides that make up the enzyme (Figs. 14–2, 14–3). The enzyme may consist of four parts, for example, which are mixtures of two chains, A and B. In one tissue there is a form with three parts of chain A and one part of chain B, as opposed to a form in another tissue with two parts chain A and two parts chain B, the A chains in the two forms being completely identical, as are the B chains. Although some authors would like to restrict the term to the second (component mixture) type, the prevailing tendency is to refer to both types of enzyme variants as "allozymes" or "isozymes." Of course, our greatest interest at this point is in the mutational variety, and this is the type shown in Fig. 5–9. The component mixture isozymes, incidentally, may also have allelic variant isozymes.

As indicated in Fig. 5–9, each homozygote produces only a single form of the enzyme, whereas each heterozygote produces two forms. Since each gene is expressed in the heterozygote, the variants would appear in consecutive generations of a pedigree. Many human geneticists therefore think of enzyme variants as dominants.

It seems a bit odd, however, to say that the heterozygote in such cases contains two dominant alleles. Clearly neither is dominant in the phenotype in the same

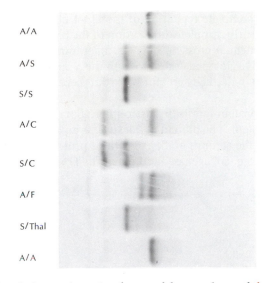

A/A

A/S

S/S

A/C

S/C

A/F

S/Thal

A/A

Fig. 5-10 Starch gel electrophoresis of several human hemoglobins. The origin is at the left, the anode at the right. Note that the structural gene homozygotes (AA and SS) show only one band each, the heterozygotes (AS, AC, and SC) two each. The S Thal individual is probably AS at the beta structural locus but carries an abnormal allele at an associated locus that suppresses production of β globin chains of A Hb. (Courtesy of D. L. Rucknagel, Department of Human Genetics, University of Michigan.)

sense that the normal allele of galactosemia, say, is dominant in the parents or heterozygous siblings of a child affected by that recessive disorder. True Mendelian dominance implies that only one of the two alleles of a heterozygote is expressed in the phenotype. The enzyme variants are therefore more properly referred to as "codominant."

They share this property with many variants of structural protein loci, such as those responsible for the globin chains discussed earlier in this chapter. Thus the homozygotes, A/A and S/S, of Fig. 5–10 each show a single electrophoretic band, whereas each of the heterozygotes, A/S, A/C, and S/C, manifest two globin bands.*

Similar considerations apply to the variants of various serum proteins. Some of the better studied (because several alleles are common in most populations) are the mutational forms of serum albumin, of the group specific (Gc) component, an α_2-globulin, of haptoglobin (Hp), another α_2-globulin, and of transferrin (Tf), a β-globulin.

In the case of haptoglobin there are two common variants, Hp-1 and Hp-2. The latter is interesting because it is not a typical missense allele caused by nucleotide substitition. Like hemoglobin, haptoglobin contains two different polypeptide chains, also unfortunately referred to as α and β. In Hp-2 the alpha chain is nearly twice as long as the corresponding chain of Hp-1. Furthermore, its amino acid

*The A, F of Fig. 5–10 also show two bands, but these are not due to allelic variants; they represent the presence of both A and F hemoglobins. Each band represents homozygosity at its locus.

sequence is a nearly complete repetition of the Hp-1 chain. The variant is apparently the result of a nearly complete duplication of the basic alpha chain gene, probably by intragenic unequal crossing over as diagrammed in Fig. 5–5. Evidence exists that the primitive globin ancestral to both the α- and β-globins of hemoglobin was originally about half their present size but became doubled by a similar process.

Another serum protein merits discussion here because of its significant effects on the respiratory system. The protein in question is an α_1-globulin which possesses about 90 per cent of the serum's ability to inhibit proteolytic enzymes (proteases) such as trypsin, elastase, collagenase, and plasmin. Trypsin being the best known,

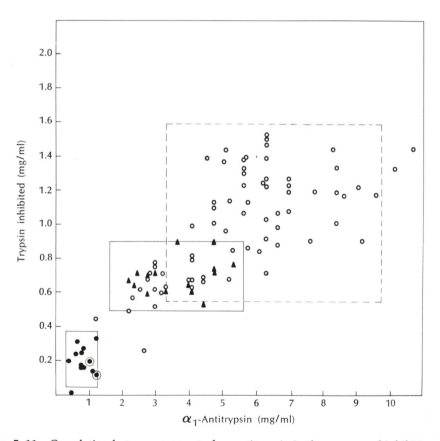

Fig. 5–11 Correlation between amount of α_1-antitrypsin in the serum and inhibition of trypsin activity. The calculated correlation coefficient, 0.84, is very close to the maximum, 1, which would be the case if there was a perfectly straight line, direct relationship between points on the abscissa and the ordinate. (The minimum, -1, would occur if the relation was a completely inverse one.) The inked-in circles represent persons in the families being reported who are considered to have α_1-antitrypsin deficiency, and the triangles their parents. The open circles are members of the population, including some relatives of the affected, considered normal in this regard. The encircled inked-in circles are reference individuals previously known to be affected. (From Talamo et al., 1968; courtesy of R. C. Talamo and the *New England Journal of Medicine*.)

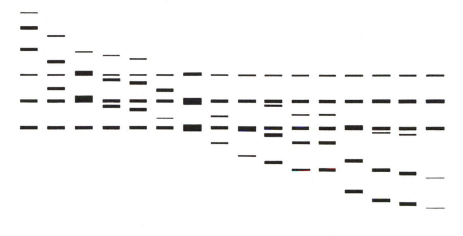

BM DM EM FM GM IM MM MP MS MV MW MW^2 MX MY MY^2 MZ

A

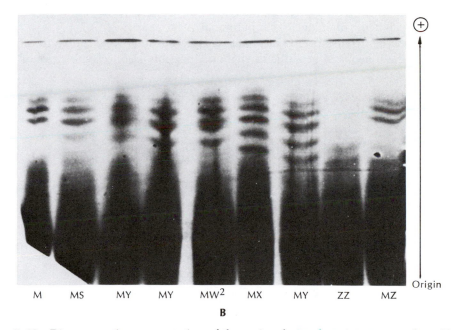

M MS MY MY MW^2 MX MY ZZ MZ

B

Fig. 5–12 Diagrammatic representation of the major electrophoretic patterns when 15 variant *Pi* alleles are combined with *Pi*^{M}. For simplicity only three bands are shown for each allele. Some heterozygotes evidence fewer than six bands, probably because some are so close together that they coalesce. **B.** Starch gels of some slow variants. Compare especially the M (almost always MM) and ZZ with the heterozygous forms. (From Cook, 1975; courtesy of P.J.L. Cook and the *Annals of Human Genetics*.)

the inhibitor has been named α_1-antitrypsin (Fig. 5–11). The locus governing its production is commonly designated *Pi* (protease inhibitor).

Many inherited normal variants of α_1-antitrypsin are detectable by differences in electrophoretic mobility, and the heterozygote typically shows bands characteristic of both alleles present (Fig. 5–12), indicative of co-dominance. The number of bands per allele is often multiple even though there is evidence that the underlying protein consists of a single chain (monomere): they are thought to result from splitting of the molecule during preparation for electrophoretic study.

When the trypsin inhibitory capacity (TIC) of a large population is plotted, as in Fig. 5–13, a fairly continuous distribution is obtained. Those at the lowest end of the spectrum, with antitrypsin activity about 25 percent of the mean or less are considered to have "α_1-antitrypsin deficiency" (Figs. 5–11, 5–13). Their frequency varies from 1 in 2500 to a figure ten times as great in various studies.

A striking association exists between α_1-antitrypsin deficiency and some pulmonary diseases, especially emphysema of the "familial panacinar" type. It usually begins with exertional dyspnea in the third or fourth decade of life, relatively early for this disease. Chest X-rays and radioisotope scans show diffuse loss of parenchyma and vasculature, with a preference for the lower zones. The prognosis is poor, death being often due to cor pulmonale.

Alpha$_1$-antitrypsin individuals may also be unusually susceptible to infantile liver disease, neonatal hepatitis or cirrhosis, possibly also to some types of adult

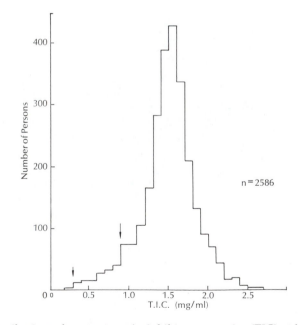

Fig. 5–13 Distribution of serum trypsin inhibitory capacity (TIC) values in a random sample of 2586 Tucson, Arizona white people over 5 years of age. Arrows indicate the apparent upper levels of "deficiency" and "intermediate deficiency" conditions, respectively. (Modified from Morse et al., 1975; courtesy of J. O. Morse and the *New England Journal of Medicine*.)

cirrhosis. The prevailing theory is that α_1-antitrypsin normally inhibits lysosomal proteases released during inflammation, thus preventing breakdown of tissue proteins; this protection is absent when there is a deficiency of the inhibitor.

α_1-antitrypsin deficiency is usually referred to as a recessive condition because most individuals with this phenotype are homozygotes for Pi^Z, the allele producing the slowest-moving variant, Z, or for a null allele, Pi^-. The category also includes, however, the heterozygotes for these genes, the Pi^Z/Pi^-. Some SZ heterozygotes may also exhibit the full deficiency phenotype. Pi^S attains a frequency of 5 percent or more in many populations.

Further complicating matters is evidence that persons with intermediate deficiency may share some of the increased risk of disease. These are individuals with trypsin inhibitory capacity between 25 and 60 percent of the overall means, the ones with TIC between 30 and 90 mg/100 ml in Fig. 5–13, about 6 percent of the population. They include homozygotes for the S allele, but most are probably heterozytes (including Pi^M/Pi^Z, M being the most common normal variant).

HETEROGENEITY

The basically simple scheme of gene action, gene to messenger to polypeptide, often obscures a world of complexities in the development of the phenotype. One that causes considerable problems in human genetics is *heterogeneity:* similar or even apparently identical phenotypes with different genetic bases. We noted, for instance, that sickling is a major phenotypic observation in a number of hemoglobinopathies, although several of these can be differentiated on the basis of other clinical data before investigating the globin abnormality involved.

Such differential diagnoses are often more difficult in the enzymopathies that affect the nervous system. A brilliant series of discoveries in the 1960s by J. S. O'Brien and R. O. Brady and their co-workers demonstrated the enzyme deficiencies in the gangliosidoses, such as Tay–Sachs disease, the sphingomyelin lipidoses (Niemann–Pick diseases), and the glycosphingolipidoses. The last-named group includes Gaucher, Fabry, and Krabbe diseases, lactosylceramidosis, and metachromatic leukodystrophy. In each instance the neuropathology can be traced to the accumulation in nerve cells, and, in some cases, in other tissues as well, of substances whose further metabolism is blocked because of the missing enzyme.

It turns out that many of these diseases are much more heterogeneous than had been suspected. At least three forms of Gaucher disease are now known, for example. Surprisingly, in many instances the same enzyme deficiency appears to be involved in recognizably different clinical entities. So the question arises: why does the disease in some families follow a different course than in others?

Some clue is provided by studies of metachromatic leukodystrophy (MLD). Although it received only one "starred" entry in Mckusick's catalog, some authors distinguish as many as seven inherited forms, each consistent in any given pedigree. Three that differ by age of onset (late infantile, juvenile, and adult) appear to have the same biochemical basis: accumulation of cerebroside sulfate (hence, the metachromasia or tissue stains) due to deficiency or dysfunction of cerebroside sulfatase. The enzyme is also often called arylsulfatase A (ARS A). The differences in age of onset may result from modifications in the structural gene that produce functionally different enzymes. That is, ostensible amorphs may not be equally nonfunctional, even though an assay may indicate the absence of a normal enzyme in each case. In other cases, (a) the enzyme is present in a modified form that hydrolyzes sulfatide at functional levels but overlaps ARS A deficiency in other tests ("pseudo ARS A deficiency"); (b) normal enzyme is present but typical MLD symptoms are present because an enzyme-activating factor is absent ("cerebroside sulfatase activator deficiency"); (c) normal enzyme is present but the patient exhibits the disease, albeit in a milder form, presumably because of a modified substrate binding site ("partial cerebroside sulfatase defect"); or (d) the ARS A defect is part of a generalized sulfatase deficiency ("multiple sulfatase deficiency disorder"), probably due to a mutation in a substrate binding site that affects the function of all such enzymes.

If this situation is at all typical, it appears that heterogeneity in an enzyme deficiency may result from several sources. Often these are grouped under two broad headings: (a) *allelic,* due to variation at the structural locus, and (b) *nonallelic,* due to variation at other loci that can affect an enzyme's activity.

Another interesting case of heterogeneity, this time for a structural protein, has recently been uncovered in familial hypercholesterolemia (FH), a simple dominant. FH heterozygosity with one normal allele and one abnormal one has a frequency of about 1 in 500, making it perhaps the most common of all Mendelian disorders. It accounts for about 1 in every 20 myocardial infarctions (the usual pathology of heart attacks in patients under the age of 60). Homozygosity, while much rarer, almost invariably has fatal cardiac effects at an early age.

Michael S. Brown and Joseph L. Goldstein, the Nobel laureates in Medicine in 1985, and others have demonstrated that this disorder results from mutations at a locus on chromosome 19 for the cells' low density lipoprotein (LDL) receptors. Since it is insoluble in serum, cholesterol is bound to LDL when it is transported by the blood to the cells that use it to build cell membranes, secrete steroid hormones, or produce bile salts. Malfunction of the cells' ability to capture cholesterol from the blood results in abnormal accumulations of this fatty substance and its deposition in the linings of critical vessels, such as the coronary arteries, with the aforementioned serious sequelae.

In their Nobel address Brown and Goldstein noted that at least 10 different FH mutations exist, and they fall into four broad classes in the way they affect the phenotype. The most common group produce no LDL receptor protein or only trace amounts. Another group is able to synthesize receptors, but in a form that cannot be transported from the endoplasmic reticulum to the surface of the cell. Yet a third group produces receptors that reach the surface, but these are unable to bind LDL normally. Finally, a fourth group produces receptors that can bind LDL but are unable to cluster in the "coated pits" of the cell (because the mutations result in alterations of the receptor protein near its carboxyl end, its so-called "cytoplasmic tail").

A further interesting sidelight is that many apparent FH homozygotes are really heterozygotes for two different FH mutations.

These forms of heterogeneity would help explain anomalously high incidences of some inherited diseases in the face of strong selection (Chapter 11) against them.

It has not been found in Tay Sachs disease (hexosaminidase A deficiency), however, and therefore is of no assistance concerning the puzzling frequency of this disease among Aschkenazic Jews.

At another level, heterogeneity is probably a major factor in the confusion surrounding possible genetic influences in the affective mental disorders, such as schizophrenia. In the so-called cyclical conditions, for example, there is much debate as to whether the unipolar form (depression only) and the bipolar form (depressive alternated with manic phases) are parts of the same disease or are different diseases. Some also distinguish between early onset and late onset types within each of these forms. Thus, there may be as few as one or as many as four cyclic psychoses.

Closely intertwined with heterogeneity are two phenomena encountered in Chapter 1, variable expressivity, differences in the phenotype of individuals having the same genotype, and incomplete penetrance, the failure of some individuals to express a phenotype that others of the same genotype do, and a third, pleiotropism, the multiple effects that many genes seem to have on the phenotype.

Figure 5–14 diagrams these three phenomena in the recessive trait of Fig. 1–4 and 1–5, familial Mediterranean fever, and Table 5–4 demonstrates the pleiotropism and variable expressivity in a typical series of cases of the dominant Marfan syndrome alluded to in Chapter 1 (Fig. 5–15). Note in the table that some of the effects were expressed more consistently than others. Also, even though some musculoskeletal manifestation occurred in every case in this series, no particular form

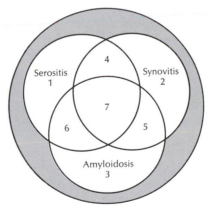

Fig. 5-14 A Venn diagram, which demonstrates schematically the spectrum of variable expressivity in familial Mediterranean fever (FMF). Affected individuals are homozygotes for a recessive gene that appears to be most frequent in Sephardic Jews, Armenians, and certain Arab groups. (1) Pleuritis or perotonitis only; (2) arthritic attacks only; (3) amyloidosis (and, eventually, nephropathy) only; (4) serosal and synovial attacks; (5) synovial attacks and amyloidosis; (6) serosal attacks and amyloidosis; (7) full manifestation. The space between the outer circle and the inner ones indicates the homozygotes for the abnormal gene of people who show no symptoms, in most cases, that is, prior to their onset. As a schematic diagram this figure overlooks such points as differential frequencies and severities of the individual features or their combinations. (From Sohar et al., 1967; courtesy of J. Gafni and the *American Journal of Medicine*.)

Table 5-4 Frequency, in percent, of characteristic symptoms of the Marfan Syndrome (Based on 50 consecutive patients, unless indicated otherwise, observed by Pyeritz and McKusick, 1979)

Clinical Feature	Percent
Ocular	70
Ectopia lentis	60
Myopia	34
Cardiovascular	98
Midsystotic click only	30
Midsystotic click and late-systotic murmur	18
Aortic regurgitant murmur	10
Mitral regurgitant murmur only	6
Prosthetic aortic valve	10
Abnormal echocardiogram	96
Aortic englargement	84
Mitral-valve prolapse	58
Prosthetic aortic valve	10
Musculoskeletal	100
Arachnodactyly	88
Upper segment/lower segment at least 2 SD below mean for age	76.6[a]
Pectus deformity	68
High, narrow palate	60
Height >95 percentile for age	58
Hyperextensible joints	56
Vertebral-column deformity	44
Pes planus	44
Striae distensae	24
Inguinal hernia	22
Family history	
Additional documented cases of syndrome	80
Sporadic cases (new mutations)	14
Unclear or unknown pedigree	6

[a]Based on 47 cases.

Fig. 5-15A The Marfan syndrome in an 11-year-old boy. Note the pronounced arachnodactyly, long extremities, and thoracic cage deformity (due to excessive growth of the ribs). Both lenses are ectopic. Less constant features present are nystagmus, rocker-bottom feet (extreme flatness with protruding heels), and sparse subcutaneous fat. There are indications of kyphoscoliosis. Intelligence is normal. **B.** Eye with displacement of the lens (ectopia lentis), a quite characteristic feature of the Marfan syndrome, as well as homocystinuria and several other enzympopathies. In this case the lens is in the anterior chamber. (**A** from McKusick, 1972. Courtesy of V. A. McKusick and the C. V. Mosby Co., St. Louis; with the assistance of R. B. Bressler. **B** courtesy of I. H. Leopold, T. W. Lieberman, and D. Wong.)

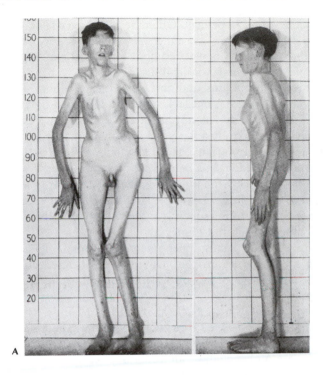

A

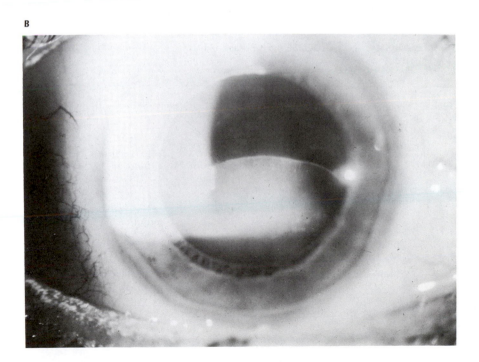

B

had a higher frequency than 88 percent. Often the expressed effects are so slight and occur in so many other disorders that either they could be easily overlooked or, in the absence of other evidence, they would not be diagnostic of Marfan. The story is told, for example, of a woman who had married twice. Of her 10 children, four were Marfans, three with one husband and one with the other. She was severely myopic and was fairly tall (5'8") but lacked cardiac abnormalities, ectopic lenses, or any other rank defects. Had she not had any children who were Marfans, she would have been considered only a fairly tall myopic woman. She would certainly not have been considered a Marfan. Many cases must indeed escape detection. A similar situation obtains in Fig. 1–7.

Other forms these phenomena may take are (1) variations in age of onset of a disorder in different individuals or families and (2) a tendency for an autosomal disorder to manifest itself more frequently in one sex than in the other. The latter point will be discussed further in Chapter 7.

As an aid in reconciling these phenomena with our understanding of gene action, a leading American pediatrician, David Y.-Y. Hsia, effectively publicized the point that the clinical symptoms of the final phenotype are often far removed from the basic biochemical defect. By constructing a "pedigree of causes," as he termed it, one could perhaps trace back, as in tracing a family tree, how the phenotypic manifestations are derived from the basic defect. Figure 5–16 illustrates this technique for type I (von Gierke) glycogen storage disease. The basic defect is a deficiency of glucose-6-phosphatase, an important enzyme in the mobilization of glucose from glycogen. One can readily see from such a chart how many physiological systems may be affected by a single defect.

Lionel S. Penrose, whom we encountered also in Chapter 3, pointed out that we are most apt to encounter difficulties in classification when we study aspects of

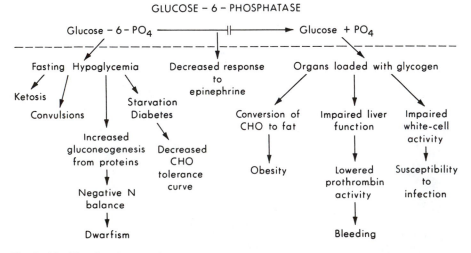

Fig. 5-16 The "pedigree of causes" in type I (von Gierke) glycogen storage disease, a usually fatal recessive disorder. (From Hsia, 1966; courtesy of Year Book Medical Publishers, Inc.)

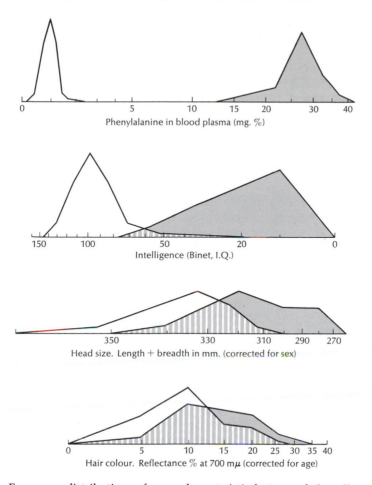

Fig. 5-17   Frequency distributions of some characteristic features of phenylketonuria in affected populations (right) and control (left) populations. The two populations overlap in the cross-hatched areas. (From Penrose, 1951; courtesy of L. S. Penrose, W. E. Knox, and *The Annals of Human Genetics,* successor to *Annals of Eugenics.*)

a phenotype that are farthest away from the basic effect of the gene. This is brought out beautifully in Fig. 5–17. As we get closer to fundamental gene products, the measurable aspects of phenotype become more and more clearly discontinuous, and genetic counts become easier.

Another important step forward has come from the realization that "heredity is not all" in the determination of the phenotype, that the chemical processes involving any one gene and its products do not occur in a vacuum but are influenced by the environment, especially by other reactions going on in the body. As a result of these factors, two individuals with the same basic reaction involving a given gene will not necessarily end up with the same final product, the same amount of it, or, in general, the same phenotype.

Three main elements of environmental variability are responsible for phenotypic differences among individuals having the same genotype:

1. Variations in the rest of the genome.
2. Variations in available substrate and ingested materials of the cells.
3. Variations in what might be summed up as the ecological conditions of life, both inside and outside the body.

PHENOCOPIES

Environment can also complicate genetic analysis by giving rise to a phenotype indistinguishable from that usually produced by a specific genotype had it been present. Such a phenotype is called a phenocopy, a term coined by the geneticist Richard Goldschmidt in his studies of butterflies and moths. Thus the environment can not only mask a gene's presence but, by means of phenocopies, it can also mislead the investigator into believing that a gene is present when it is not. A diet high in saturated fatty acids and cholesterol, for example, can cause a reduction in LDL receptors, and resultant hypercholesterolemia, very similar to that seen in genetic FH (p. 130).

Often the phenocopy is the "sporadic" case seen only once in a large family, but many genetic causes, notably rare recessives, can also give rise to sporadic cases. In addition, a persistent and pervasive environmental influence can cause relatives to be affected by the same trait and make it appear to be "familial," in the absence of any genetic predisposing factors.

Deafness, for example, may be caused by many different loci. It may have many other etiologies, however, among them being:

1. Birth injuries
2. Prematurity
3. Postnatal trauma
4. Factors producing hypoxia or hypoglycemia of the fetus, such as:
   (a) erythroblastosis fetalis (Chapter 16)
   (b) neonatal diabetes
   (c) maternal diabetes
5. Viral infections of the mother, especially measles and rubella
6. Infectious diseases of the infant, especially meningitis and respiratory ailments
7. Advancing age

Particularly likely to confuse the genetics investigator are the phenocopies in which the deafness is congenital, as it is in most inherited forms.

Sometimes a gene or a gene product normally can act only in the presence of a particular environmental factor (a substrate, for instance, or a certain temperature). Absence of the environmental factor or substitution of another one can then mimic the phenotype which usually results from a different gene, oftentimes that of an allele which is not present.

In this light, a prime object of medicine and allied professions can be to convert individuals afflicted with genetic disorders into phenocopies of those having the normal alleles of the locus.

Phenocopies point up the caution that must be exercised at all times against jumping to the conclusion that a disorder is inherited in a given family merely because a very similar disorder has been shown clearly to be inherited in other families. Above all, phenocopies accentuate the need to understand clearly that the terms "hereditary," "familial," and "congenital" are not synonymous, even though many conditions do fit all three.

SUGGESTED EXERCISES

5–1. The first six amino acids of the gamma chain in Hb F are: (1) glycine; (2) histidine; (3) phenylalanine; (4) threonine; (5) glutamic acid; (6) glutamic acid. The structural gene for gamma probably represents a duplicated beta gene that has undergone changes with time.

(a) If so, what is the minimum number of codon substitutions needed to effect the change from beta to gamma for the first six amino acids?

(b) Using the most similar codons available, what is the minimum number of nucleotide (base) substitutions needed to effect the necessary changes for these six amino acids?

5–2. Outline the steps involved in mutagenesis by 2-aminopurine.

5–3. What are the usual mechanisms of modification of the genetic material by (1) acridine, (b) ultraviolet light, (c) X-rays?

5–4. Outline the steps in repair of the usual changes caused by ultraviolet light to the genetic material.

5–5. Using the same codons as in Exercise 5–1(a), assume a deletion of the third nucleotide of the codon at position 2 of the locus (or cistron) for beta globin. What amino acids might then be incorporated at positions 2 through 8? Compare these to the usual ones.

5–6. Diagram the change responsible for Hb Tak and show the probable composition of amino acids 144–149 in its beta globin.

5–7. On the basis of what is known about Hb Wayne, show the probable mRNA and amino acid sequence at alpha positions 139–145 of Hb Koya Dora.

For the next five exercises refer to Fig. 1–9. Call this the *ec* locus. Assume every spouse not shown is homozygous normal unless there is some evidence to the contrary.

5–8. If you were asked to state the genotypes of the persons in generations I and II, how would you answer?

5–9. Suppose it were known that the ectrodactyly gene is 90 percent penetrant, would you modify your answer to Exercise 5–8, and, if so, how?

5–10. If it could be assumed that the gene were fully penetrant in this pedigree unless there was some evidence to the contrary, what percentage penetrance would you calculate?

5–11. Suppose II-3, an unaffected female, and one of her unaffected male cousins, II-10 or II-17, came to you for counseling, stating that they wished to marry and have children. What would you tell them?

5–12. Suppose the affected brother of II-3 wished to marry an unaffected unrelated female from a different town. What would you tell this couple if they came to you for counseling?

Note: Exercises 5–13 and 5–14 are to be considered as a unit.

5–13. If the genes of a locus are known to exist in six allelic forms, how many different genotypes are theoretically possible for this locus in the populations? How many of these are homozygotes?

5–14. Assuming that all the genotypes are viable,

   (a)   What is the minimum number of phenotypes possible for the trait determined by this locus?

   (b)   What is the maximum number?

   (c)   What besides the number of available genotypes determines the actual number of phenotypes?

6

The Molecular Biology
of Human Genes

In Chapter 5 we saw that the phenotype was the result of a complex series of events between the basic function of the gene to pattern an mRNA, its translation into a product, usually a polypeptide, and the eventual effects of that product in the cellular and body environment. This still left much to be desired for a good understanding of human genes. Most of the mutational changes in the gene discussed in Chapter 5, for instance, were inferred from the structure of the product, the globin molecules in the case of hemoglobin. In a very large number of genetic conditions, however, we do not know what the gene product is. Moreover, for many disorders in which we know (or surmise) the identity of the gene product, it appears to be unchanged in a large number of the affected; how then are we to determine the basic defect? Even when the product is known to be changed, as in sickle cell anemia, further complications arise when the cells that are readily available for, say, prenatal diagnosis, do not produce it, and the cells that do must be obtained at substantial risk to the patient.

Solutions to these and similar problems have been coming more and more from the application to human genes of new technologies that enable the geneticist to examine the gene itself, bypassing the phenotype as it were. These are commonly referred to as molecular methods.

The major steps in these methods involve preparing DNA from appropriate cells, cutting it into pieces in a meaningful way, identifying which of the pieces contains the genes under study, isolating this piece, finding out on which chromosome (and where on that chromosome) it is located, and determining its structure.

By being able to detect the presence or absence of the gene itself rather than its product, these techniques are enhancing our ability to locate and study loci involved in previously intractable genetic problems. They are also extending the domain of prenatal and presymptomatic diagnosis. In many cases we are learning not only a great deal more about how gene structure is correlated with observed abnormalities but also about the normal biological action of many loci. Some of these methods may even lend themselves to the cure of genetic disorders by the replacement of abnormal alleles in the tissues with their normal counterparts.

Some of the methods we will describe here were developed prior to the ones that examine the individual genes, and often for other purposes, but it is necessary to introduce them at this time because they have become essential parts of the molecular techniques. We will do this in three main sections concerning: (1) the tissue culture methods of determining on which chromosome a given gene lies; (2) the methods of hybridizing DNA and RNA fragments that enable us to identify the DNA fragment containing the gene; and (3) the methods of cutting up the DNA and multiplying, preserving, and analyzing the fragments.

SOMATIC CELL HYBRIDIZATION

Somatic cell hybridization involves getting cells from two tissue culture lines to unite *in vitro* and the hybrids to form a new viable tissue culture line that can be separated from the parental lines. Discovered originally when it was noted that cells from two mouse heteroploid lines grown together occasionally fused, hybrid lines can be produced also between lines of the same species where one or both parent lines have normal chromosome sets (but, if both lines are diploid, they differ in certain genes) and between lines of different species, such as man and mouse (Fig. 6–1).

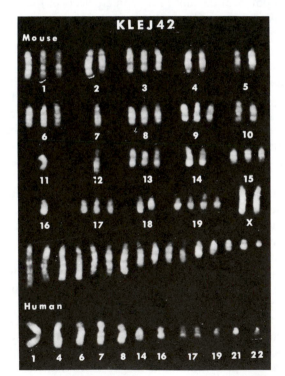

Fig. 6–1 Q-banded karyotype of a cell from a man–mouse hybrid line, Klej 42, several cell divisions after its establishment. Shown numbered are the apparently normal mouse and human chromosomes present. Note that most of the human chromosomes have already been lost. The unnumbered chromosomes are not readily identifiable, presumably abnormal ones of mouse origin produced by various interchanges and deletions. (From Miller et al., 1974, courtesy of D. A. Miller, O. J. Miller, and *Cell.*)

For somatic cell hybridization to become a useful technique two major obstacles had to be overcome: (1) the number of cells that actually fused when the dissimilar lines were grown together was very low: and (2) even if fusion occurred and the hybrids grew, it was often difficult to obtain (and make certain one had) a pure line of the hybrid cells for study and experimentation.

The first obstacle has been overcome by a number of techniques, usually involving the addition of inactivated Sendai virus or a chemical such as polyethylene glycol. These agents increase fusion of cells from the different cultures by modifying their cell membranes. Sendai virus, which belongs to the myxovirus group that cause parainfluenza, has to be inactivated, that is kept from multiplying, because otherwise the tissue culture cells, including the new hybrids, would become infected with it and this would cause complications in later generations of the study (fusions of hybrids, etc.). The inactivation can be accomplished by treating the virus with ultraviolet light or with a substance called β-propiolactone; these stop replication of the virus effectively, though they do not interfere with its fusion activity.

The second obstacle, that of selectively isolating pure lines of the hybrid cells, was first overcome by the development of an elegant technique by Littlefield (Fig. 6–2) and by variations on his basic method since then. The idea is to first develop a subdivision of each cell line which is resistant to a lethal drug because, by mutation, it lacks an enzyme; the absence of the enzyme makes it unable to use the drug (whereas the cells that have the enzyme incorporate the drug and die). In Littlefield's method, a strain of one parent line is selected by its ability to grow in the presence of azaguanine because the strain lacks the enzyme hypoxanthine-guanine phosphoribosyl transferase (so the strain is referred to as HGPRT−). From the other parent line a strain is selected that is resistant to the drug 5-bromo-deoxyuridine (BDUR or BdUR) because it is deficient in the enzyme thymidine kinase (hence TK−). Neither of these strains can grow in a medium that contains hypoxanthine, aminopterin, and thymidine (HAT medium). Aminopterin blocks *de novo* purine or pyrimidine synthesis by the cells. With aminopterin present the cells must use the hypoxanthine or thymidine supplied by the medium for DNA synthesis and growth. But the HGPRT− cells cannot use hypoxanthine, and the TK− cells cannot use thymidine. However, if there are any hybrid cells, these have received genes for making HGPRT from the TK− line and genes for making TK from the HGPRT− line, so they, and they alone, are able to grow in the HAT medium.

Some modifications of this technique (called "half-selection" methods) use one strain which is HGPRT− or TK− as in the Littlefield system and hybridize it in HAT medium with a parental line that grows very poorly or not at all in culture; hence this parental line is quickly overgrown by the hybrid cells.

The ability to determine chromosomal localizations from somatic cell hybridization derives from the observation that when a hybrid line is produced between human cells and cells from a rodent, the human chromosomes are progressively lost in successive cell divisions (Fig. 6–1). Apparently the human chromosomes do not attach well to the hybrid cell spindle and therefore lag behind the others during anaphase. When the new nucleus is formed in telophase around the chromosomes that have arrived at the poles of the spindle, the lagging human chromosomes

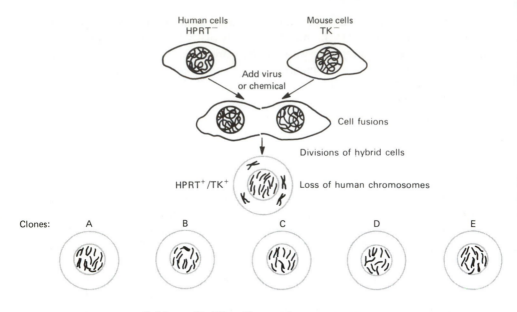

Cell lines with different human chromosomes present

Fig. 6-2 The Littlefield selection system for somatic cell hybridization. In this case the human cells are HPRT-, and the mouse cells are TK-; neither can grow in HAT medium. When plated together, fusions between them are enhanced by addition of Sendai virus or a chemical such as polyethylene glycol. The fused cells can grow in HAT medium because they receive a normal HGPRT gene from the mouse genome and a normal TK gene from the human genome. However, with each cell division some human chromosomes are lost, with the result that when stabilized cell lines develop they contain very few—sometimes only one—human chromosomes. (From Rothwell, 1982, courtesy of N. V. Rothwell and Oxford University Press.)

remain in the cytoplasm and disintegrate. After several cell divisions there may be only one or two human chromosomes left. Which chromosomes remain seems to be a matter of chance, so that different subclones of the same hybrid line will have different human chromosomes present. These chromosomes can be identified precisely by the methods described in Chapter 2.

If a hybrid line loses the ability to produce a certain human enzyme or some other protein *except* in those subclones which retain a certain chromosome, this is good evidence that the gene which normally is responsible for producing that enzyme or protein is located on the retained chromosome.

Figure 6–3, for example, shows a cell from a man–mouse hybrid line on HAT medium to which the human cells had contributed the TK gene (the mouse line having been TK−). The only subclones that retained the ability to produce thymidine kinase (and grow on HAT medium) were the ones in which at least one group E chromosome, either 17 or 18, was present. Conversely, whenever both of these chromosomes were absent the hybrids would grow in medium containing the drug BDUR. This indicates that thymidine kinase was absent; if it were present, the cells could incorporate BDUR and would die. Later, newer staining techniques

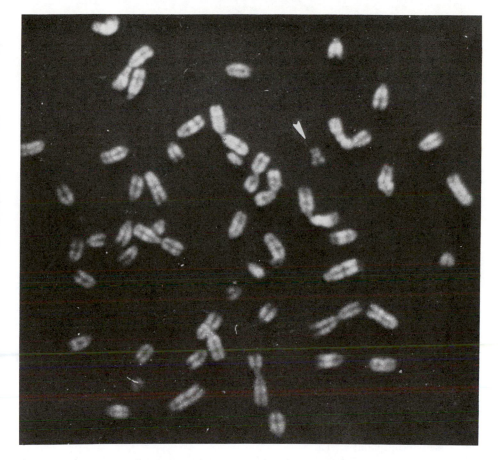

Fig. 6-3 Quinacrine fluorescent metaphase from man–mouse hybrid containing only a single human chromosome (arrow) but retaining the ability to produce human thymidine kinase. This indicates that the human TK locus is on this chromosome. (From Miller et al., 1971; courtesy of O. J. Miller and *Science*. Copyright 1971 by the Am. Assn. for the Advancement of Science.)

showed that chromosome 17 had to be present for TK to be produced (Figs. 6–3 and 6–4).

ABERRANCY MAPPING

This technique generally takes one of these forms:

1. Consistent segregation in families or somatic cells of a chromosomal variant (or a portion of one) and a gene locus.
2. Coincident absence of a gene and the absence (deficiency) of a portion of a chromosome: so-called "deletion mapping."

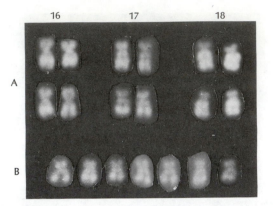

Fig. 6–4 Identification of the human chromosome in Fig. 6–3. Comparison of this chromosome from seven hybrid cells **(B)** with the group E chromosomes from two normal human cells **(A)** shows that it is a number 17. (From Miller et al., 1971. Courtesy of O. J. Miller and *Science*. Copyright 1971 by the Am. Assn. for the Advancement of Science.)

Though they were at first principally employed in family studies, these techniques are now extensively used in somatic cell hybridization experiments to pinpoint the localization of genes.

The first definite localization of a human gene to a specific autosome occurred by means of the first form. In 1968 two groups of investigators reported that Duffy (*Fy*) blood group genes (Chapter 16) segregated consistently in several families (Fig. 6–5) with the chromosome 1 variant 1qh+ (Fig. 6–6). The 1qh+ chromosome is enlarged near the beginning of the longer of its two arms, and the presence of the Duffy locus in this vicinity has since been corroborated by family studies of the type discussed in Chapter 13.

In another use of aberrancy mapping, a man-mouse hybrid clone was found with a translocation involving part of a mouse chromosome and the long arm of human chromosome 17. Only the subsequent clones that retained this aberrant chromosome maintained the ability to grow in HAT medium (for which human thymidine kinase had to be present). Thus aberrancy mapping in hybrid cells not only has corroborated the placement of TK on number 17, as described above, but it has placed the locus on 17q.

Comparing the amount of 17q persistent in experiments using a number of different translocations can lead to further refinement of the localization to a specific band on that arm.

Having observed its extensive use in *Drosophila* and other organisms, human geneticists saw the value of the second aberrancy technique, deletion mapping, almost as soon as the first chromosomal deficiencies were discovered. It is an unfortunate commentary on the technique, however, that its early applications have proved to be incorrect. Since its efficacy depends on two negative observations, namely, that both a certain piece of chromosome and a certain gene are absent, the method is subject to the previously mentioned pitfalls of such observations: the apparently absent chromosome piece may be intercalated elsewhere in the genome or its absence may be confined to one line of cells, and the apparently absent gene

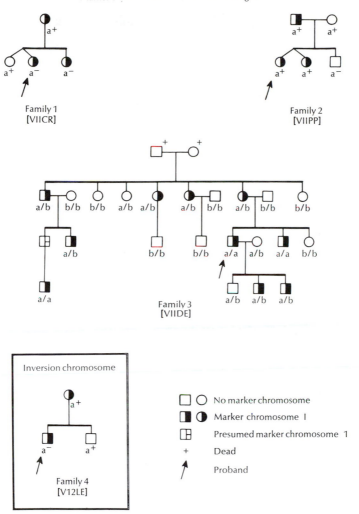

Fig. 6-5   Four families that demonstrate concordant segregation of 1qh+ and Duffy (Fy) blood group genes. In families 1 and 4, 1qh+ is associated with the Fl(a−) phenotype, presumably with gene Fy^b. In the other two, it segregates with Fy(a+), in family 3 clearly with Fy^a. The "genotypes" of pedigree 3 use a simplified notation. (From Donahue et al., 1968; courtesy of R. P. Donahue and the *Proceedings of the National Academy of Sciences*.)

may be present but not expressed. These are a greater problem in man than in most other organisms, because in the latter it is often possible to eliminate these pitfalls by planned experiments.

Despite these handicaps deletion mapping adds constantly to the assignment and localization of genes on the chromosomes. An individual with a deletion of approximately one-third of 12p, for example, was found to apparently also lack one

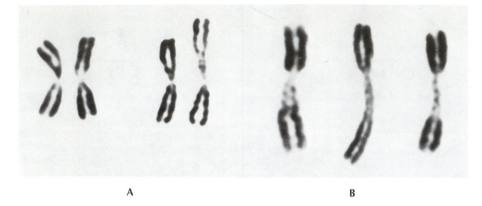

A   B

Fig. 6–6 Variant chromosome 1 due to elongation of the centromeric heterochromatin of the long arm (1qh+). **A** shows, on the left, the normal chromosome 1 pair of a sister of the proband in family 3 of Fig. 6–5, and, on the right, the pair of the proband's uncle, who has one normal chromosome and one with 1qh+. B shows the varied forms that 1qh+ can take in the same family. (From Donahue et al., 1968; courtesy of R. P. Donahue and the *Proceedings of the National Academy of Sciences.*)

allele at the B locus of lactate dehydrogenase (see p. 311). This corroborates data concerning LDH-B from somatic cell hybrids.

Deletion mapping can lead to a class of negative, but very significant, inferences. It was noted, for instance, that the person with the above-mentioned 12p deletion was heterozygous for codominant alleles at the loci for M-N blood groups, red cell acid phosphatase (ACP_1), and the Hp and Gc serum proteins. Therefore these four loci *cannot* be located in the deletion area. This kind of evidence was adduced also to prove that the alpha haptoglobin locus is not, as claimed in several earlier reports, on 13p. (The most recent evidence places *Hp* on chromosome 16.)

NUCLEIC ACID HYBRIDIZATION

Workers in microbial and viral genetics developed this elegant technique to combine nucleic acid strands from disparate sources. At first these were DNA-DNA duplexes in which the two strands were derived from different organisms. The basic process, referred to as "annealing," involves separation of strands by heat (denaturation) and then renaturation by slow cooling. Combination occurs only if the nucleic acids being annealed contain similar base sequences. Generally the complementary portion is detected by making one of the DNA strands radioactive.

A major advance occurred with the development of analogous procedures to anneal RNA and DNA. Here successful combination indicates the presence—and position—of DNA complementary to the RNA used. Further progress came when RNA and DNA could be hybridized in cytological preparations. This has led, for example, to the demonstration of the introns of most eukaryotic genes.

Figure 6–7 illustrates the use of nucleic acid hybridization to localize genes responsible for production of the 5S RNA that is so important in the ribosomal

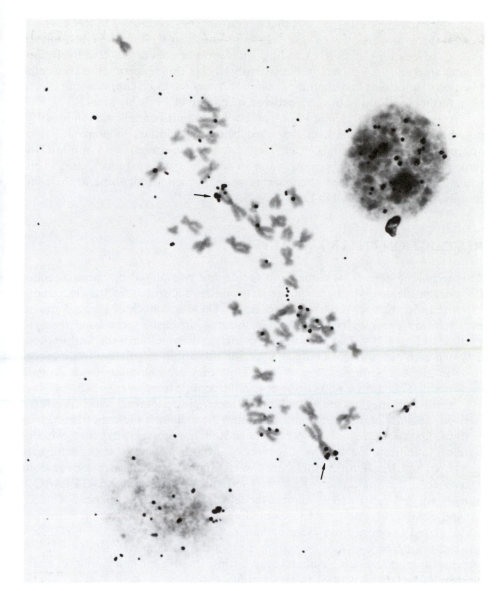

Fig. 6–7 Localization of genes governing production of 5S RNA by nucleic acid hybridization techniques. Note the clustering of black dots (silver grains) near the distal tips of lq (arrows). Other clustering occurs in the nucleoli, where ribosomal RNA is stored (Courtesy of D. M. Steffensen.)

assembly of proteins. 5S from human tissue culture cells was labeled with iodine-125 (a radioactive isotope) and incubated with live human leukocytes. Upon fixation of the cells and exposure to a photographic emulsion, the investigators found that the distal end of the long arm of chromosome 1 was consistently radioactive. (Note the intensive spotting with dark grains near the arrows in Fig. 6–7.) The evident complementarity indicates that a gene (or genes) coding for 5S RNA is (are) located there. Since, however, other chromosomes also took up the label, further analysis of locations of 5S RNA-coding genes must be conducted. Two likely candidates are 9 and 16, which quite consistently label in these experiments. By a combination of annealing and aberrancy mapping, genes for 5S on chromosome 1 have been further localized to the area between q32 and q44, probably at q43.

Annealing with DNA and RNA "probes" is an indispensable step in identifying chromosome fragments, as described below. In addition to preparations of appropriate cellular materials, chiefly denatured (single-strand) DNA and mRNA, molecular biologists have been ingenious in devising synthetic probes, such as oligonucleotides (small groups of connected bases), which mimic some of the common base sequences found in DNA.

RESTRICTION ENZYME ANALYSIS

This technique derives its name from the central role played by bacterial endo-deoxyribonucleases, which recognize specific nucleotide sequences and cleave both DNA strands wherever these sequences occur. These endonucleases are referred to as *restriction* enzymes because they enable the organisms possessing them to exclude foreign DNA. The most useful restriction enzymes have the further property that each cuts the DNA only at a specific site within or adjacent to the recognized nucleotide sequence (Fig. 6–8A). Thus they are analogous to proteolytic enzymes that cut amino acid chains at specific peptide bonds.

Restriction enzymes are named for the bacterial species from which they were derived. The first part of each name combines the first letter of the bacterial genus with the first two letters of the species. Then Roman numerals are added, without spacing, to indicate the order of discovery of several enzymes from the same species. *Hpa*I and *Hpa*II, for example, are two restriction endonucleases derived from *Haemophilus parainfluenza.* The former recognizes the sequence 5'-GTTAAC-3' and cleaves between T and A, whereas the latter recognizes the sequence 5'-CCGG' -3' and cleaves between C and G. Sometimes additional identification letters are added: *Hin*d enzymes from *Haemophilus influenzae* serotype d, are thus distinguished from *Hin*c enzymes from serotype c of the same species; similarly, *Eco*R enzymes from *Escherichia coli* are thus distinguished from nonrestriction endonucleases from the same species, for example, *Eco*B.

After addition of the restriction endonuclease to the DNA of a cell, the resulting DNA fragments, which are of varying sizes, can be separated by gel electrophoresis. With suitable DNA or RNA probes, one can then use various transfer and annealing techniques to identify the DNA fragments as containing specific human genes.

In a particularly efficient procedure for doing this devised by E. M. Southern (hence commonly called the "Southern blot"), the separated fragments are denatured and transferred to a sheet of nitrocellulose. This is then exposed to a radioactive probe related to the gene in question. The probe binds only to fragments on the nitrocellulose that contain the appropriate complementary DNA, and the rest of the radioactive material is washed away. Subsequent radiography reveals the

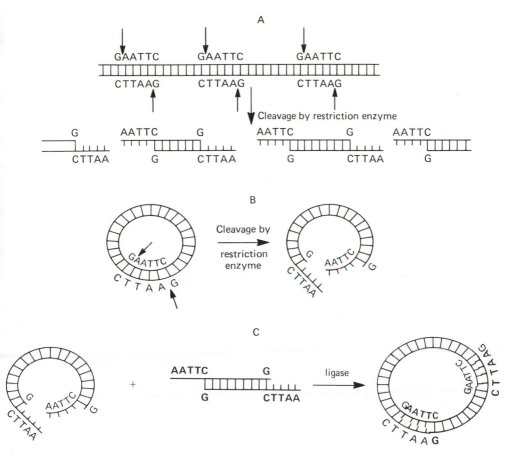

Fig. 6–8 Cloning of chromosomal fragments obtained by use of restriction enzymes. **A** diagrams a chromosome containing a number of the symmetrical sequences (called *palindromes*) that are recognized and cut by *Eco*Rl. Note that this leaves each complementary strand of the resulting fragments with characteristic single-stranded projection. In **B** a bacterial plasmid containing the same palindrome has been cut with *Eco*Rl. This opens the ring and exposes its strands to union with the complementary strands of a human chromosomal fragment from **A**. After incorporating the human material, ligases close the plasmid again **(C)**, thus forming a recombinant molecule. When the recombined plasmid enters a bacterial cell, the human chromosome fragment multiplies along with the bacterial DNA. The resultant multiple copies of human DNA fragments can be maintained for long periods of time. (Adapted from Rothwell, 1982, courtesy of N. V. Rothwell and Oxford University Press.)

electrophoretic positions (and therefore the sizes) of the gene fragments that bound to the probe.

The DNA identified in this way may be amplified and preserved for further study by cloning, that is, by incubating it with bacteria that can incorporate it into their genomes or plasmids (Fig. 6–8B), producing a recombinant DNA molecule. This part is related to "genetic engineering." As the bacteria divide, they reproduce the incorporated bits of human genetic material as well. The set of cloned fragments maintained in bacterial cultures is called a DNA "library."

To localize it, one can test concordance of the gene detected by this technique and the persistence of a given human chromosome in somatic cell hybrid cultures. Somatic cell studies involving chromosomal aberrations can then be used to refine the localization of the gene by observing concordance between its presence and the presence or absence of specific chromosomal bands.

Further enhancement of the value of this technique has come from the discovery of "restriction site polymorphism." It appears that in some individuals a given gene is *not* cut by a restriction enzyme that does cleave it in others. This is exactly what would be expected from what we know about the process of mutation. Where, for example, most individuals have the sequence GTTAAC, which is cleaved by *Hpa*I, some individuals may have the sequence *T*TTAAC, which is not.

Those who lack the site usually cleaved by the restriction enzyme will pass on intact (uncut) an area of DNA that *is* cut in the individuals who have that site. As illustrated in Fig. 6–9, chromosome C possesses two approximate cleavage sites. One of these is absent in this area of a homologous chromosome, D, the other in the same area of chromosome E; and both are absent in the corresponding portion of chromosome F (which may, however, be cleaved by this enzyme in areas flanking the discussed portion in the figure). The result is that the pieces of DNA which anneal to a probe that recognizes an area (which may be larger or smaller than a gene) between the restriction sites will be of different sizes. The piece lacking both recognition sites (usually referred to as − −) will be the largest fragment (most kb in length), those with only one (− + or + −) will be smaller, and the piece with both sites present (+ +) will be the smallest fragment.

When individuals are variable at two sites that are very close together, as in the illustrated example, the combination (+ +, + −, etc.) is often described as a restriction haplotype. In many other instances only one of restriction sites is variable, so the family members are designated as simply + or − with respect to it.

Because they result in fragments of different size, presence or absence of cleavage sites is commonly referred to as "Restriction Fragment Length Polymorphism" (RFLP or riflip). As with any polymorphism, the most useful markers are those which exist at frequencies that ensure that many individuals will be heterozygous for them (Chapter 8).

The method expands tremendously our ability to detect additional DNA variation, even in DNA in *terra incognita,* in genes whose functional or pathological relationships are unknown. Indeed, it can detect variation in introns, which are not translated.

A specific example of the analysis of restriction polymorphism is given by Fig. 6–10. DNA from a woman, her husband, and their daughter was subjected to digestion with the restriction enzyme *Pst*I, which cleaves DNA between A and G in the sequence 5′-CTGCAG-3′. Agarose gel electrophoresis, Southern blotting, and hybridization with an isotopically labeled probe for DNA of the gene producing antithrombin III, an inhibitor of serine proteases in plasma, resulted in the fragments of various sizes shown on the strip below each member of the family. All three have the 1.8 and 2.5 kilobase fragments. The father and daughter also have a 5.0 kb and a 5.5 kb fragment. The mother lacks both of these. She has, instead, a

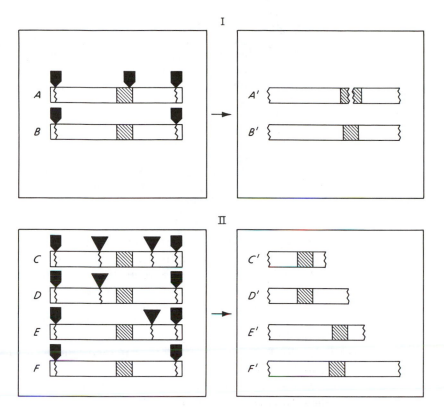

Fig. 6–9 Production of DNA fragments of different sizes as a result of restriction site polymorphism. Part I diagrams the two possibilities with respect to cleavage by a restriction enzyme at a site within a given gene: chromosomes containing the palindrome recognized by the enzyme at that site are cut by it there (A), whereas those lacking the palindrome there are left uncut at that point (B). A suitable probe that hybridizes to the gene, indicated by the cross-hatched material, will detect fragments of two different lengths in terms of kilobases. The largest will be the one lacking the restriction site in question (B'), whereas this piece of chromosome will be represented by two fragments from chromosomes that possess the palindrome at that site (A'), the total kb's of the two fragments in A' adding up to the kb's of the single fragment in B'. This is the situation in Fig. 6–10; similar situations in which the site in question is *close to* the gene under study will be described in Chapter 13. Part II diagrams the four possibilities with respect to cleavage by the same restriction enzyme at two nearby sites: some chromosomes are cut by it at both sites (C, containing haplotype + +), some at one (D: + −, or E: − +), and some at neither (F: − −). A suitable probe that hybridizes to the area between them, indicated by the cross-hatched material, will detect fragments of four different lengths in terms of kilobases. The largest will be the one lacking both restriction sites (F'), the smallest from the chromosome possessing both (C'). To be useful as a genetic marker, one haplotype has to be closely linked to the gene for a hereditary disorder in the family being studied, as, for example, in the pedigree in Fig. 13–6. (Adapted from Merz, 1985; courtesy of the *Journal of the American Medical Association*.)

Genotypes −/−   −/+   +/+

10.5▶
5.5▶
5.0▶
2.5▶
1.8▶

Fig. 6–10 Results of restriction site analysis of the antithrombin III gene in one family. Note that the husband has 5.0 and 5.5 kb fragments that his wife lacks. Instead she has a 10.5 kb fragment. Apparently his gene contains a site cleaved by the enzyme used (*Pst*I), whereas hers does not. The daughter has all three fragments, indicating that she has both genes (is heterozygous). These conclusions are verified by sequence analysis of the genes, as described in the text. (From Prochownik et al., 1983; courtesy of E. V. Prochownik and the *New England Journal of Medicine*.)

10.5 kb fragment that is also present in the daughter but absent in the husband. Analysis of the fragments shows that the 10.5 kb fragment, which constitutes the main body of the antithrombin III gene, lacks the above-mentioned *Pst*I restriction site. It has the sequence 5′-CTGCAA-3′ at the codons for amino acids 304 and 305 of the product; hence it is not cleaved. This part of the DNA of the husband is encoded, however, by 5′-CTGCAG-3′; hence, it *is* cleaved, so that the 10.5 kb fragment is replaced by 5.0 and 5.5 kb fragments. The husband's genotype is denoted as +/+, homozygous for the *Pst*I restriction site, and the wife's is −/−. The daughter, who has inherited a gene with the CAA codon from the mother and a gene with the CAG codon at this point from the father, exhibits all five fragments. She is, in other words, heterozygous (+/−) for this restriction site polymorphism.

Suppose, now, that the daughter's strip had been identical to the mother's (or to the father's). Our first guess would be that she, too, was homozygous −/− (or +/+). But that is impossible if one of the parents is −/− and the other is +/+. The inescapable conclusion would be that the antithrombin III gene on one of her chromosomes was deleted. If her strip was like that of the mother, this would indicate that she had inherited the deletion chromosome from the father. The genotypes would then be: mother, −/−; father, +/del; daughter, −/del, subject to confirmation by appropriate sequencing.

Such a study has indeed demonstrated that antithombin III deficiency, an autosomal dominant that results in recurrent, often fatal, thromboembolitic epi-

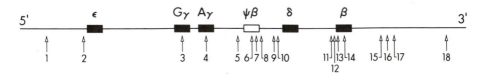

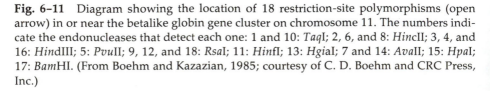

Fig. 6–11 Diagram showing the location of 18 restriction-site polymorphisms (open arrow) in or near the betalike globin gene cluster on chromosome 11. The numbers indicate the endonucleases that detect each one: 1 and 10: *Taq*I; 2, 6, and 8: *Hinc*II; 3, 4, and 16: *Hind*III; 5: *Pvu*II; 9, 12, and 18: *Rsa*I; 11: *Hinf*I; 13: *Hgia*I; 7 and 14: *Ava*II; 15: *Hpa*I; 17: *Bam*HI. (From Boehm and Kazazian, 1985; courtesy of C. D. Boehm and CRC Press, Inc.)

sodes, is heterogeneous. In some families it is due to a deleted gene, whereas in other families the gene is present but abnormal.

Similar findings with these techniques have demonstrated that certain defects are recessive but can nevertheless by expressed in the presence of only one mutant gene. As in several cytologically visible deletions discussed in Chapter 4, the affected are hemizygous for an abnormal gene because the homologous chromosome is deficient at that locus. The molecular methods show that in other cases the same defect appears because the person who was born with only one copy of the abnormal allele becomes secondarily homozygous for it in some tissues by means of somatic recombination, mutation, or other modification of the chromosomes.

Thus RFLPs have significantly strengthened the evidence mentioned in Chapter 4 for recessive forms of retinoblastoma and Wilms tumor. They indicate that it is also true for a urinary cancer, the locus being, like that of Wilms, on 11p. RFLPs have disclosed similar "genetic" bases for many seemingly sporadic cases of these disorders. Sporadic retinoblastoma usually involves only one eye, whereas familial forms are usually bilateral.

Among the earliest significant findings of the restriction enzyme technique were that the human alpha globin gene is on chromosome 16 and that the gamma-delta-beta complex, NAG (= nonalpha globin), is on chromosome 11. Further refinements have assigned the NAG complex to the region 11p1205–11p1208. Although this would appear to narrow down the localization tremendously, it must be noted that this small region contains about 4500 kilobases, about 75 times larger than the NAG complex. Similar studies show, incidentally, that the structural gene for human insulin is probably also on 11p. There is, furthermore, widespread restriction site polymorphism associated with both loci, which is proving very useful. One in the 5' flanking region of the insulin locus appears to be correlated with susceptibility to Noninsulin Dependent Diabetes Mellitus (NIDDM); and a number in the NAG region, some inside, some between, and some flanking the structural genes (Fig. 6–11), have been used accurately in prenatal diagnosis of sickle-cell anemia *without need to obtain fetal blood* for the procedure (Chapter 13).

Perhaps the most dramatic advances of molecular genetics have come in work on (a) thalassemia, (b) human oncogenes, and (c) linkage relationships, including data on two common disorders that have in the past been among the most resistant to localization and determination of the primary genetic defect: Huntington's chorea and cystic fibrosis. We shall discuss the linkage material in Chapter 13, thalassemia in Chapter 14, and oncogenes in Chapter 17.

$$7$$

Sex-Related Inheritance

Heretofore our discussion has been concerned with autosomal loci. These are the genes on the 22 pairs of chromosomes that are normally alike in the two sexes. One of the first findings of the geneticists who tested Mendel's laws early in this century was that in most animals and a few plants the genes on the X-chromosome did not yield quite the same results as those on the autosomes.

The major reason X-chromosome inheritance is different from autosomal is that one of the forms (sexes) in these organisms has only one X-chromosome. In humans, in most other mammals, and in many other animals this occurs in the male. Usually this sex has another chromosome, the Y-chromosome, not found in the female, that pairs to some extent with the X-chromosome, as, for example, in Fig. 7-1. Pairing between the X- and Y-chromosomes is so poor because they share few loci.

Many implications follow from these facts. For one, in meiosis the sex with the two X-chromosomes, the female, has received one from each parent and distributed them to the gametes in the same way as it does it autosomes. Since each gamete contains an X-chromosome, this is referred to as the *homogametic* sex.

The male, however, normally receives an X-chromosome only from his mother. From his father he receives the Y-chromosome. And when he in turn is producing gametes, half are expected to contain an X-chromosome and half a Y-chromosome. The human male is, therefore, the *heterogametic* sex.

Another important consideration enters here. In the female the action of a deleterious gene can be masked by an allele on the other X-chromosome. An X-chromosome gene that cannot make a specific enzyme or structural protein may have little or no effect because the allele on the other X-chromosome produces sufficient amounts of the material. In the male, however, there is usually no homologous allele on the Y-chromosome. Almost without exception, any X-chromosome gene present, whether beneficial or deleterious, is, therefore, fully expressed.

X-chromosome genes have often been referred to as *sex-linked.* This term implies, unfortunately, that these genes are necessarily involved in the reproductive system or other aspects of sexual differentiation. More and more, therefore, the loci of the X-chromosome are being referred to as *X-linked* rather than sex-linked.

Inheritance determined by Y-chromosome genes in humans is *holandric,* that is, these genes are ordinarily passed on only from male to male, from father to son.

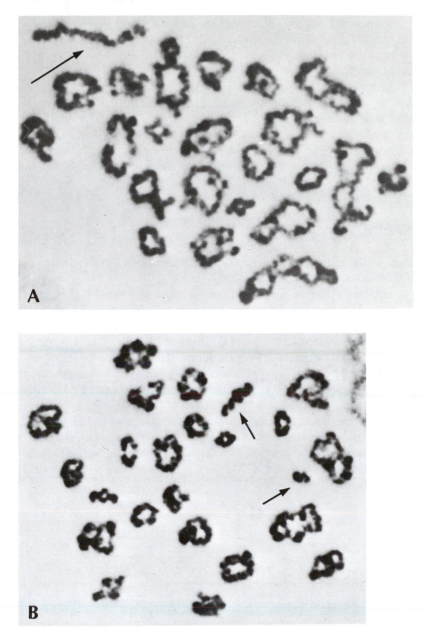

Fig. 7-1 Evidence of poor pairing between X- and Y-chromosomes (arrows) during human spermatogenesis. The figure is from diakinesis, the last part of Prophase I. In **A** the X- and Y- are seen associated in end-to-end fashion. (From Hulten et al., 1966. Courtesy of M. Hulten and the *Annals of Human Genetics*.)

Loci whose actions are influenced by the sexual environment are generally referred to as *sex-influenced* or *sex-limited.* They may be autosomal or X-linked. The majority are autosomal, of course, because there are about 19 times as many autosomal genes as X-linked ones.

The phenotypic counterpart of holandric is *maternal inheritance,* genes passed on solely from mother to daughter, to be discussed at the end of the chapter.

Molecular studies indicate that homology exists between a small amount of DNA on the X- and Y-chromosome. It may be termed *incompletely sex-linked.* To date only one such gene has been established in humans: MIC2, which encodes a cell surface antigen. On the Y-chromosome the locus is very close to the holandric TDF gene(s) (see p. 169)

X-LINKED LOCI

McKusick's 1983 catalog of inherited disorders mentions 243 as possibly X-linked, 115 of them considered well-established.

The primary criterion for establishing a locus as X-linked is the absence of male-to-male transmission. Barring a chromosomal aberration, a male receives X-chromosome genes only from his mother, never from his father.

One resulting inheritance pattern is illustrated by Fig. 7–2. Typically, a male manifesting the trait marries a woman whose family is free of it. None of their children show it. Their mates are also usually from families lacking the trait. In the next generation, none of the sons' children have the trait. Neither do the daughters' daughters, but the trait reappears in about half of the daughters' sons.

The proper notation for diagramming these results is indicated in Fig. 7–3. "cb" is taken as a general symbol for the gene for red-green colorblindness, "+" its normal allele. In the male a "Y" is written in place of the second allele.

Several additional features of X-linked inheritance are demonstrated in Fig.

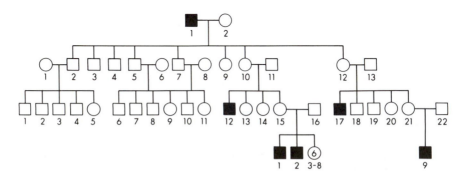

Fig. 7–2 The de Fontenay pedigree of red-green color blindness, illustrating the expected results when a man with an X-linked recessive trait marries a woman from an unaffected family. None of their children show the trait, nor do those of their sons. In their daughter's progeny half the sons are expected to be affected but none of the daughters; however, half of the daughters are expected to be carriers (e.g., III-15 and III-21). Redrawn from Bell (1926) after de Fontenay (1881).

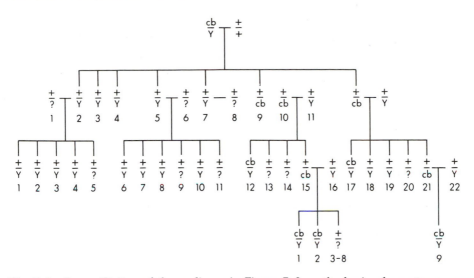

Fig. 7-3 Reconciliation of the pedigree in Figure 7–2 on the basis of genotypes predicted by the X-linkage hypothesis.

7–4. This shows that the results expected when an X-linked trait is introduced in the pedigree by a female (Fig. 7–4B) is different from the situation in Fig. 7–2 (and Fig. 7–4A), where it is introduced by a male. Thus, *reciprocal crosses* for X-linked traits produce different results, whereas it usually makes no difference for autosomal traits whether the condition is introduced by the male or by the female. When the female parent manifests a recessive X-linked trait, and the male parent lacks it, the offspring commonly demonstrate the "criss-cross" inheritance noted in Fig. 7–4: the sons phenotypically resemble the mother, showing the trait, the daughters resemble the father in not showing it.

Note, however, that all the daughters in Figure 7–4B are carriers. Were they to marry affected males the trait would have equal likelihood of appearing in their daughters as in their sons (Fig. 7–5).

This explains why females with relatively debilitating X-linked recessive traits are so rarely encountered in practice. Barring mutation, for such an X-linked homozygote to be produced, not only must the mother be a carrier but the father must be affected (Fig. 7–6).

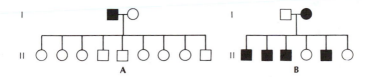

Fig. 7-4 Reciprocal crosses for red-green color blindness, illustrating the differential results in such crosses for X-linked traits (recessives in this case). B also illustrates "criss-cross" inheritance. (From Bell, 1926: **A** from pedigree 409 after Nettleship, 1914, **B** from pedigree 410 after Schiotz, 1922.)

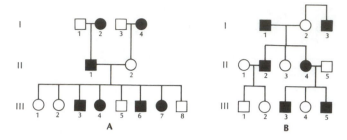

Fig. 7–5A Hypothetical pedigree in which a female heterozygous for an X-linked recessive, II-2, marries an affected male, II-1. Normal and affected progeny of both sexes are expected. The marriage of I-1 and I-2 in **B** is also of this type even though none of the parents in the previous generation are known to show the trait. The mating of II-4 × II-5 is akin to that in Fig. 7–4B. (**B**, redrawn from Stern, 1960, after Scott, 1778, is often referred to as the Lort or Lort and Whisson pedigree.)

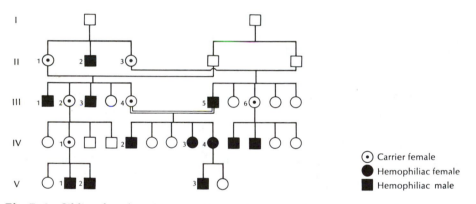

Carrier female
Hemophiliac female
Hemophiliac male

Fig. 7–6 Sibling females (IV-3 and IV-4) with hemophilia. Note that IV-3 and IV-4 are children of double first cousins. This would not influence the occurrence of the disorder in males but can be a factor increasing its likelihood in females, as will be discussed further in Chapter 10. (From Pola and Svojitka, 1958. Courtesy of V. Pola and *Folia Haematologica*, Leipzig.)

THE LYON HYPOTHESIS

From time to time reports do appear of "exceptional" females who manifest a rare, or at least uncommon, trait that has been generally accepted as being an X-linked recessive. They appear to be exceptional because at least one of the conditions just stated is not met—either the father is not affected or the mother's family contains no affected members (brothers or uncles). The possibility that a mutation has supplied a second gene that would make her a homozygote can often be ruled out by the birth to the "exceptional" woman of one or more unaffected sons (Fig. 7–7). In her classic study of red-green colorblindness for example, Julia Bell noted that about 75 percent of colorblind women are known to have colorblind fathers, and about 85 percent of the sons of colorblind women are known to be colorblind. From what was said above both figures should be 100 percent; this is especially true for the sons of colorblind females.

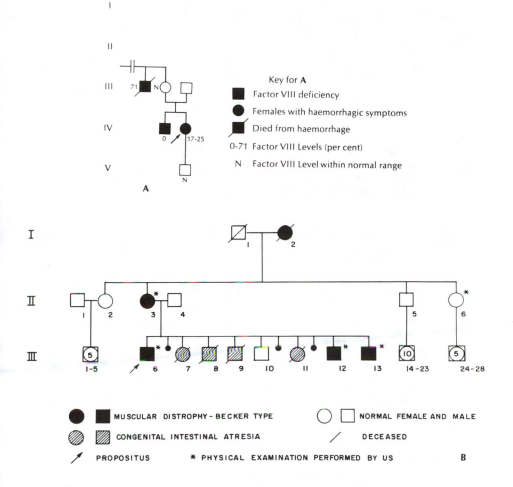

Fig. 7-7 Pedigrees containing females who manifested fully a trait ordinarily considered an X-linked recessive even though they are probably heterozygous, not homozygous, for it. Their heterozygosity is indicated by having a normal father, a normal son, or both. **A.** Hemophilia A. **B.** Becker type muscular dystrophy. The coincidental findings of congenital intestinal atresia should be ignored in studying the pedigree. **A** is from Kerr, 1965 after Taylor and Briggs, 1957; **B** from Aguilar et al., 1978. Courtesy of C. B. Kerr **(A)**, R. Lisker **(B)**, and the *Journal of Medical Genetics.*)

Such cases have frequently sown confusion in the literature. They have suggested that either the previous reports were interpeted incorrectly, that is, that the trait is in fact autosomal, or, at best, that two loci exist for the same trait, one X-linked and one autosomal. Although a number of well-authenticated instances do exist of similar traits that are autosomal in some families and X-linked in others, most apparent contradictions to X-linkage of the sort described in the previous paragraph have now been clarified by the Lyon hypothesis.

On the basis primarily of her work with mice, Mary Lyons postulated that at

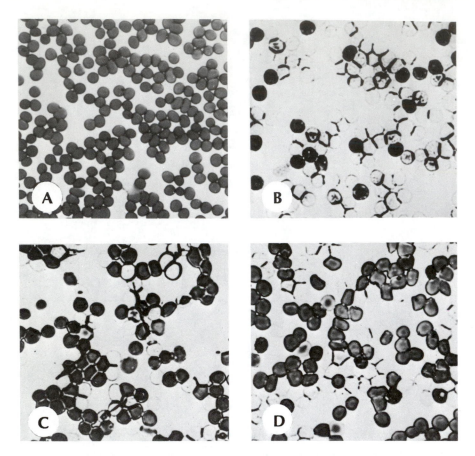

Fig. 7-8 Evidence for the Lyon hypothesis from the differential staining of normal and enzyme-deficient erythrocytes after 2 to 5 hours' incubation with Nile blue sulfate. **A.** Blood from a normal, nonenzyme-deficient individual showing all cells stained. **B.** Blood from G6PD-deficient (hemizygous) Negro male, showing approximately 17 percent of the cells stained. **C.** Artificial mixture of equal parts of **A** and **B** showing approximately 60 percent of cells stained. **D.** Blood from heterozygous Negro female with approximately half-normal enzyme activity showing approximately 60 percent of the cells stained. Note the close resemblance of **D** to mixture **C**. (From Gall et al., 1965. Courtesy of G. J. Brewer and the *American Journal of Human Genetics.*)

an early stage of development one X-chromosome of the female's cells becomes inactivated, so that thereafter only one X-chromosome allele in each cell is active. Which X-chromosome of each cell becomes inactivated is usually a matter of chance. The hypothesis implies, therefore, that the mammalian female becomes in effect a mosaic of cells in the expression of her X-linked genes.

Although subject to a number of modifications and exceptions—for example, it affects only somatic cells (does not affect oogonia or oocytes)—the Lyon hypothesis has become almost universally accepted since it was enunciated in 1961. Some of the best evidence for it has come from human X-linked genes whose manifes-

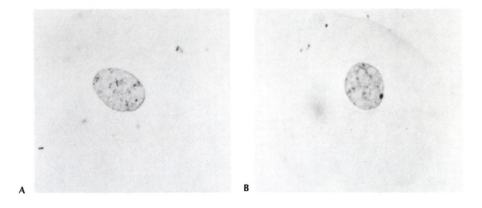

A   B

Fig. 7–9 Cells from a smear of human buccal epithelium. The cell on the right, from a female (XX), shows the typical single dark chromatin mass lying near the nuclear membrane; hence it is said to be "chromatin positive." The cell on the left, from a normal male, is "chromatin negative." (From Moore and Barr, 1955. Courtesy of M. L. Barr and *Lancet.*)

tations can be detected at the cellular level. As indicated by Fig. 7–8, females heterozygous for glucose-6-phosphate dehydrogenase (G6PD) tend to be mosaics of cell populations with respect to activity of this enzyme. Similar data have appeared for iduronate sulfatase, HGPRT, PKG, α-galactosidase, phosphorylase β kinase, and others.*

A particularly striking example, albeit one whose biochemistry is not yet understood, occurs in ocular albinism, an X-linked recessive. Males with the gene lack retinal pigment, but heterozygous females have irregular retinal pigmentation, with patches of pigment and patches lacking pigment, so that the fundus has a stippled appearance.

Further evidence for the hypothesis in humans has come from the chromatin (Barr) bodies (Fig. 7–9). As we noted in Chapter 3, in persons with abnormal numbers of X-chromosomes, the number of Barr bodies is always one less that the number of X-chromosomes present (Figs. 7–10, 3–13, and 3–15). Each Barr body represents an heterochromatic or inactivated X-chromosome; hence, in each case only one active X-chromosome remains. The X-chromatin bodies first appear just prior to or at the time of implantation of the embryo (the sixth or seventh day).

Since only chance determines which X-chromosome of the cell is inactivated, an occasional female heterozygous for an X-linked trait might have most (or, in a particular tissue, virtually all) cells in which the inactivated X-chromosome carries the normal allele. The phenotype of such a female would then resemble closely the phenotype of affected males or homozygous females. Hence, many investigators believe that the fully manifesting "exceptional" females referred to above are not

---

*Noninactivation has been reported, however, for steroid sulfatase, the enzyme deficient in X-linked ichthyosis, and for the Xg(a) blood group system; so part of the chromosome may not follow the Lyon hypothesis.

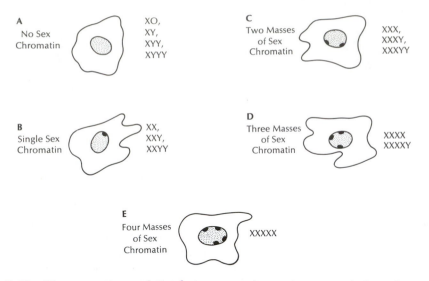

Fig. 7–10 Diagrammatic correlation between sex chromatin patterns in interphase cells and sex chromosome patterns in the karyotype. (From Barr, 1966. Courtesy of M. L. Barr and the *Canadian Medical Association Journal*.)

only explained by the Lyon hypothesis but their very existence is evidence for its correctness.

The heterozygous female who fully manifests an X-linked trait because the inactivated X-chromosome in nearly all her cells carries the normal allele or, on the contrary, resembles the *normal* male because in nearly all cells the inactivated X-chromosome carries the *abnormal* allele, is said to be "lyonized," and the phenomenon is called *lyonization*. (Some people use lyonization as a synonym for all X-inactivation.)

Recent studies indicate that about 5 percent of females heterozygous for a given X-linked locus are lyonized, or, as it is sometimes stated in the literature, show "an extremely unbalanced mosaic phenotype." Indeed, when the frequency of one of the two extreme phenotypes, the normal and the abnormal, in such heterozygotes is much greater than 5 percent, the investigator often feels impelled to seek a special explanation (usually somatic selection, either intrinsic to the locus in question or due to a nearby gene). The females heterozygous for "fragile X" chromosomes (p. 30, Fig. 2–6) who show some mental retardation may represent such lyonizations.

The Lyon hypothesis also explains neatly the phenomenon of "dosage compensation." This means that, unlike the situation for autosomal genes, females with two doses of an X-linked gene tend to have similar manifestation of the trait as the male with only one dose. Females homozygous for hemophilia A (classical hemophilia: AHG—factor VIII—deficiency), for example, have clotting times similar to those of affected hemizygous males. Similarly, Fig. 7–11 shows that the enzyme levels of females who do not have a deficiency of G6PD, most of them homozygotes, resemble closely those of normal hemizygous males.

An interesting extension of the Lyon hypothesis concerns the number of cells

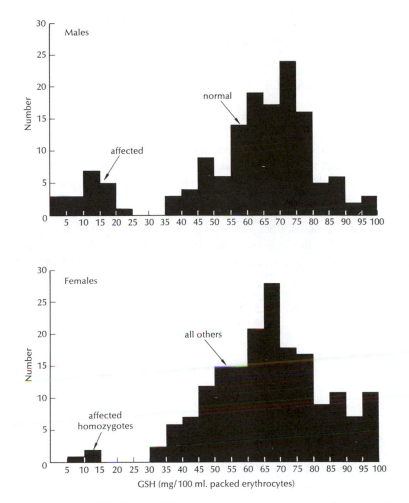

Fig. 7-11 Reduced glutathione (GSH) concentrations (after incubation with acetyl-phenylhydrazine) in the red blood cells of a random series of American Negroes. The GSH reflects the amount of glucose-6-phosphate dehydrogenase (G6PD) present. (From Childs et al., 1958. Courtesy of B. Childs and the *Bulletin of the Johns Hopkins Hospital*.)

from which tumors arise. If a female is heterozygous for an X-linked locus, such as G6PD, the presence of only one type in the tumor would indicate that it originated from a single cell, whereas the finding of both types would suggest an origin from more than one cell.

Perhaps the most interesting finding to date is that tumors such as common warts, which have a viral etiology, can be clonal (unicellular) in origin. Similar results have been reported for Burkitt lymphomas, which have been associated with Epstein–Barr viruses, leiomyomas, which are benign tumors of the uterus, and for the cells in chronic myelocytic leukemia, which carry the Philadelphia chromosome (Chapter 4). On the other hand, the tumor syndromes neurofibromatosis and multiple trichoepithelioma, which are inherited, and malignancies of the cervix or colon, which are probably not inherited, appear to be multiclonal in origin; however, the samples studied may have included cells besides those of the tumor.

X-LINKED DOMINANTS

Unlike X-linked recessives, X-linked dominants are expected to be more frequent in females than in males (Table 7–1, based on the random principles to be discussed in a later chapter). The proportion of females is never expected to be more than twice the number of males, but the discrepancy becomes larger as the frequency of the trait decreases. A preponderance of females is to be expected, inasmuch as one dose of the gene is sufficient for expression of a dominant trait. A female would have to have two doses of the normal allele *not* to show the trait. A preponderance of females does not establish a trait to be an X-linked dominant, however. Again, the only reliable criterion is the absence of male-to-male transmission. A typical pedigree of one such trait, vitamin-D resistant rickets, is shown in Fig. 7–12**A**.

Note also from Table 7–1 that most of the females manifesting an X-linked dominant trait are heterozygotes, and the discrepancy between heterozygotes and homozygotes also increases as the trait becomes rarer. When such a trait is seen in 25 percent of the males, for example, 37.5 percent of the females are expected to be heterozygotes and 6.25 percent homozygous dominant, for a total of 43.75; the ratio of heterozygotes:homozygotes is 6:1 (shown in the table as 85.7 percent heterozygous). When the frequency falls to 1 percent in males, 1.98 percent of the females are expected to be heterozygotes and 0.01 percent homozygous dominant, a ratio of 198:1. In that case almost all the females with the gene, being functional mosaics, are expected to exhibit an intermediate phenotype, whereas all the males are expected to show the complete defect. Since it would not be expected for an autosomal trait, such a consistent difference in expression between the two sexes

Table 7–1   Comparative proportions of females and males showing an X-linked trait when it is a recessive trait and when it is a dominant

| Percent Frequency in Males | Expected Frequency in Females | | | If Recessive | | If Dominant | |
	If Recessive	If Dominant	D/R	M/F	F/M	Percent Manifesting Females Heterozygous
75	56.25	93.75	1.67	1.33	1.25	40.0
50	25.00	75.00	3	2.00	1.50	66.7
25	6.25	43.75	7	4.00	1.75	85.7
10	1.00	19.00	19	10.00	1.90	94.7
5	0.25	9.75	39	20.00	1.95	97.4
1	0.01	1.99	199	100.00	1.99	99.5
0.5	0.0025	0.9975	399	200.00	1.995	99.7
0.1	0.0001	0.1999	1999	1000.00	1.999	99.9
Limit as → 0					2.000	100.0

can also be a good clue to probable X-linked dominance (Fig. 7–12**B**), provided, of course, that no instances of father-to-son transmission are encountered. The proviso is very important because a number of autosomal disorders, several of them mentioned below, also show a preponderance of females.

SEX-INFLUENCED TRAITS

The pitfalls of basing a diagnosis of X-linkage on the male:female ratio for a trait is well illustrated by early pattern baldness (Fig. 7–13). As occurs so frequently for X-linked recessives (e.g., Fig. 7–2), all the affected in Fig. 7–13**B** are males. The trait must be autosomal, however, because it is transmitted from father to son. Why, then, does it appear so much more frequently in males than in females? The answer lies in gene physiology rather than gene transmission: the gene for early pattern baldness acts as a recessive in the female body, but a dominant in the male. The action of this baldness gene has been shown to depend on the androgen level of the body. Male eunuchs, for example, do not become bald, but, if they have the requisite genotype at this locus, baldness can be induced by giving them testosterone. Females have normally only a minor concentration of androgens, of adrenocortical origin. They express the trait to any extent only when homozygous, and even then it is manifested only as excessively thin hair rather than the full expression seen in both heterozygous and homozygous males.

Traits determined by genes that act differently in the two sexes are said to be "sex-influenced." As explained earlier, they can be autosomal or X-linked. Primary hyperoxaluria with formation of oxalic kidney stones resembles baldness in having a preponderance of males affected (Fig. 7–14). Portuguese amyloidosis is another condition with a heavy preponderance of males affected, presumably because the gene penetrates only poorly in females. On the other hand, several genetic disorders such as Graves's disease, the Wildervanck syndrome, Alport's syndrome, Spiegler–Brooke tumors, focal dermal hypoplasia, and incontinentia pigmenti (Fig. 7–15) show a preponderance of females. Whether X-linked or autosomal, the responsible genes apparently cause a more severe disorder in the males, with resultant differential mortality. Incontinentia pigmenti, for example, is usually an embryonic lethal in the male.

Sex-influenced or sex-modified traits that can manifest themselves only in one sex are often called "sex-limited." Milk production in cattle, for example, manifests itself only in females, but every dairy farmer knows that the performance of his herd will depend every bit as much on the genes contributed by its sire as on its inheritance from the dam. Hydrometrocolpos (Fig. 7–16) is a trait of this type.

DOUBTFUL X-LINKAGE

When a trait is lethal in the male (e.g., Figs. 7–15 and 16–8), the best evidence for X-linkage, namely, the absence of male-to-male transmission, is unobtainable. The same is true when the male, though viable, cannot reproduce, as in the Reifenstein

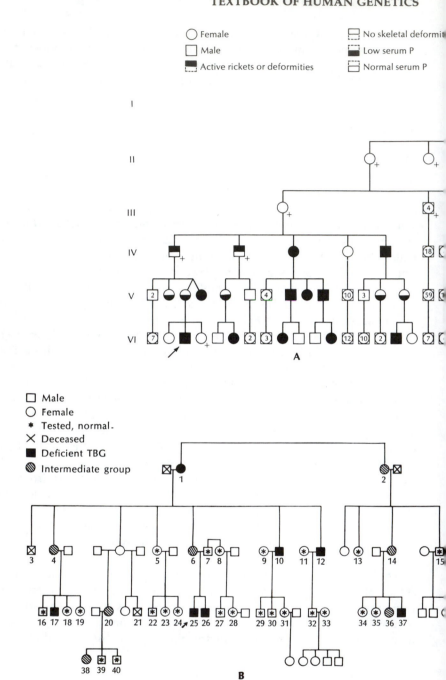

○ Female   ⬚ No skeletal deformit

□ Male   ▰ Low serum P

▪ Active rickets or deformities   ⬚ Normal serum P

A

□ Male
○ Female
* Tested, normal.
X Deceased
■ Deficient TBG
◍ Intermediate group

B

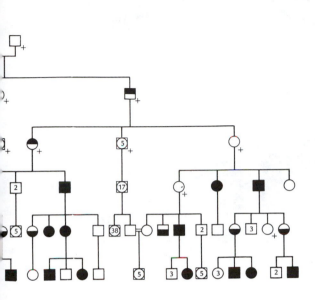

Fig. 7-12 Two kindreds exhibiting disorders probably due to X-linked dominant genes. **A.** Vitamin D-resistant rickets. **B.** Thyroxine-binding globulin deficiency. In **A** note that all examined daughters and none of the sons of affected males have low serum phosphorus, the basic defect, even though not all the daughters show the skeletal defects. Thus the main evidence of X-linkage comes from the inability of affected males to transmit it to their sons. This being the case, the frequency of the trait in females indicates the dominance of the abnormal allele. In **B** the main evidence stems from the fact that males show the complete defect, their mothers and daughters exhibiting the intermediate phenotype of heterozygotes. III-31 in **B** is contrary to rule, apparently an example of incomplete penetrance or possible lyonization of the normal allele. In **A** deceased members are indicated by + outside the square or circle, in **B** by an x inside. (**A** from Graham and Winters, 1961. Reprinted by permission of J. B. Graham and the New York Academy of Sciences. **B** from Marshall et al., 1966. Courtesy of J. S. Marshall and the *New England Journal of Medicine*.)

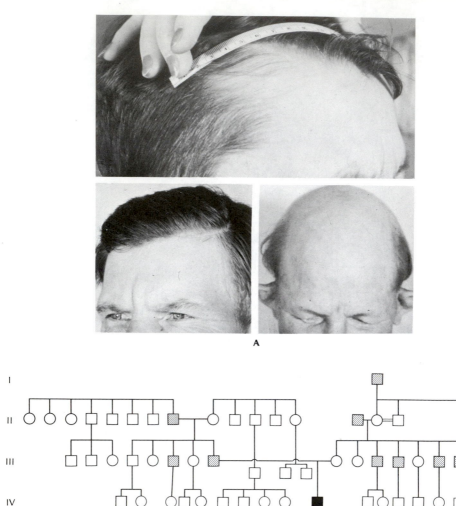

Known to be bald
Propositus (seen)

Fig. 7-13 Variable expressivity **(A)** and pedigree **(B)** of early pattern baldness. (From Hamilton, 1951. Reprinted by permission of J. B. Hamilton and the New York Academy of Sciences.) The relationship between II-15 and II-16 was not clarified by the original author.

syndrome (Fig. 7–17). Testicular feminization (Fig. 7–18) belongs in the same category. The affected are XY even though their outward appearance is decidedly feminine.

In these situations the final decision between X-linked and autosomal inheritance will be from linkage studies, aberrancy mapping, or from molecular genetics. In the case of testicular feminization strong support for X-linkage came, even

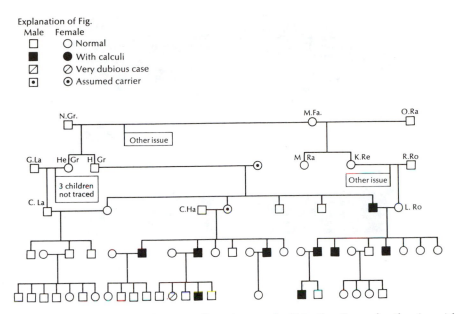

Fig. 7–14 Pedigree of hereditary oxalic urinary calculi in the Gram family. As with premature pattern baldness, there is a preponderance of affected males. Many receive the gene from the maternal side, as would be characteristic of X-linked inheritance, but the frequent male to male transmissions of this relatively rare trait attests to its autosomal sex-influenced basis. (From Gram, 1932. Courtesy of *Acta Medica Scandinavica*.)

before molecular studies, from the finding that a similar condition is X-linked in the mouse. Ohno and others have demonstrated that the X-chromosome of mammals tends to be very conservative: what is X-linked in one species is almost certain to be X-linked in all the species.

HOLANDRIC INHERITANCE

The Y-chromosome contains a number of "male-determining" factors. These include the TDF (testis differentiating factor) gene(s) that cause the gonad to become a testis. These are very near the genes that encode for the H-Y antigen, a cell surface protein present in males of all mammalian species tested. These loci are usually active even when the XY individual has a feminine appearance. In testicular feminization, for example, H-Y is present, and testosterone is produced by the gonad (a testis); the defect lies in the inability of testosterone receptors in the tissues to function properly. These male-specific genes are often found in XX males with no, or very little, Yp present.

A number of geneticists believe that hairy pinnae ("hypertrichosis of the ear": Fig. 7–19) is holandric, but this is not certain.

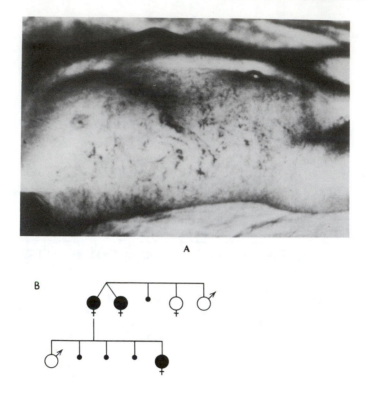

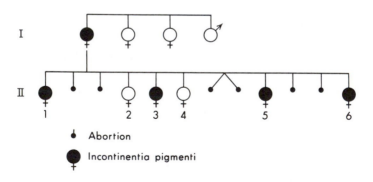

Fig. 7-15 Appearance of the skin **(A)** and typical pedigrees **(B)** in incontinentia pigmenti. The affected individual in **A** is II-6 of the lower pedigree. The large number of abortions coupled with the apparent tendency of the trait to be manifested only in females suggest that it is a dominant, possibly X-linked, and that males with the gene die before birth. (From Lenz, 1963).

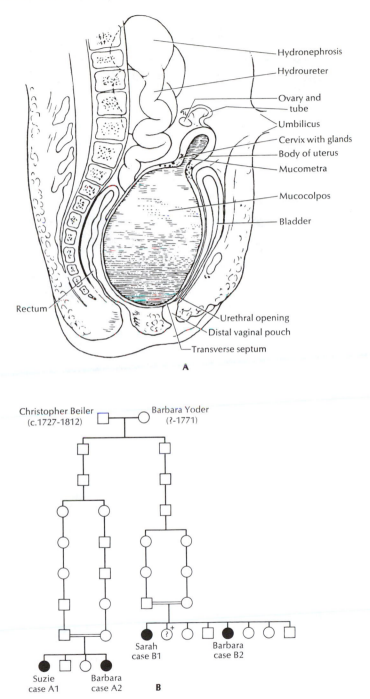

Fig. 7–16A Artist's sketch of hydrometrocolpos, prolapse of the uterus with accumulation of fluid. The disorder is due to homozygosity for an autosomal recessive gene but is sex limited. **B.** Occurrence of the trait in related inbred sibships. (From McKusick et al., 1964. Courtesy of V. A. McKusick and Cold Spring Harbor Laboratory, publishers of the *C.S.H. Symposia on Quantitative Biology.*)

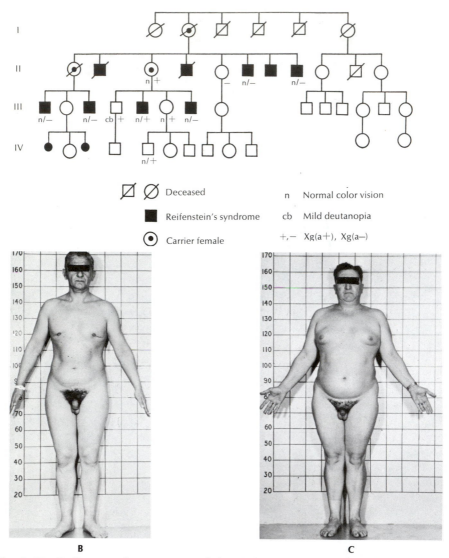

Fig. 7–17 Pedigree and appearance of the Reifenstein syndrome, male gender with hypogonadism (small testes), gynecomastia (breast development), and hypospadias (urethral opening on the ventral surface of the penis). The photos show the propositus **(B)**, III-3, at age 44 following mastectomy for cosmetic reasons and **(C)** his maternal uncle, II-8. Note the feminine type of distribution of fat and body hair. The penis is within normal size, and the hypospadias does not interfere with normal sexual relations. Although the pedigree does not show it, all the affected married; in the single instance in which the wife had a child, it was probably illegitimate. The brothers of I-2 died of infections before puberty, and, except for IV-5, the males of generation IV were too young to determine whether they were affected (and their mothers, carriers). None of the descendants of I-6 are affected. (From Bowen et al.,1965. Courtesy of E. C. Reifenstein, Jr., by permission of the authors and the *Annals of Internal Medicine*.)

MATERNAL INHERITANCE

In other organisms some traits are transmitted exclusively, or nearly exclusively, through females even though the trait may not be X-linked or sex-influenced, that is, both sons and daughters of carrier females may show the trait and to the same degree. Although other bases have been postulated, most cases are thought to result from the transmission of some cytoplasmic, rather than nuclear, element. Such transmission would not be expected to follow Mendelian principles, of course.

DNA in the mitochondria encodes for a number of proteins, chiefly parts of respiratory-enzyme complexes. Mutations in the mitochondrial DNA would be inherited in this non-Mendelian fashion. Indeed such a mitochondrial cytopathy has been reported in six families. Fifty one mothers but only 3 fathers passed it on to their children. Furthermore, of 130 siblings in 21 sibships, 89 were affected, a significant deviation from the expected number (65) for a Mendelian autosomal dominant. The clinical symptoms varied greatly in these cases—short stature, ptosis, muscle weakness, and deafness were particularly frequent—with attendant diagnostic difficulties, but they exhibited similar enzymatic deficiencies.

Maternal inheritance is also suspected in Leber's hereditary optic atrophy. This is usually listed as X-linked, because no male-to-male transmission is known. Recently, however, it has been determined that it involves deficiency of a mitochondrial enzyme, thiosulfate sulphurtransferase (Rhodanese). Chloramphenicol-induced blood disorders may also represent mitochondrial defects.

SUGGESTED EXERCISES

7–1. Call the structural locus of G6PD *Gd*. In most whites the normal enzyme is a form called G6PD B; in most blacks it is G6PD A. Males hemizygous or females homozygous for a number of variants, chiefly Gd^{A-} or $Gd^{Mediterranean}$, suffer from a hematologic disorder, G6PD deficiency, particularly if they ingest certain drugs.

An affected male marries an apparently normal female. Their first child, a girl, exhibits G6PD deficiency of the A− variety.

(a) Diagram the marriage using the stroke system.

(b) If their next child is a boy, what are the possibilities that he will also show the enzyme deficiency?

(c) If the first child, the girl, were to marry a normal man, show the expected genotypic and phenotypic ratios among their offspring.

7–2. Suppose the female parent of the previous exercise were to marry a man with normal enzyme production. Would the prognosis for her children from the second marriage differ from the prognosis from her first marriage? If not, why not? If so, how?

7–3. When G6PD deficiency involves the Mediterranean allele, affected subjects commonly develop hemolytic symptoms after ingesting the broad bean, *Vicia fava;* this form of the disorder is called favism.

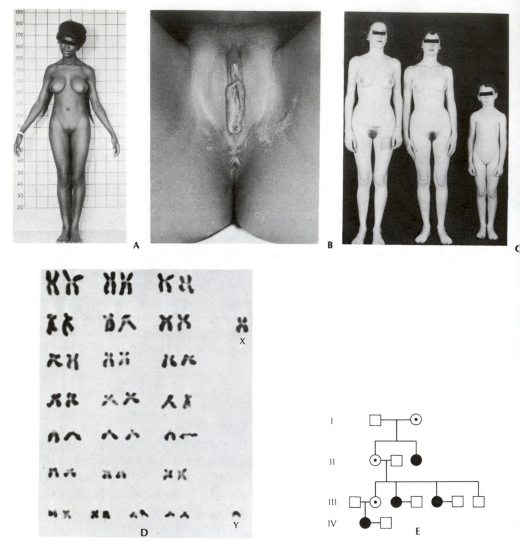

Fig. 7–18　Testicular feminization. **A** and **B** show the typical feminine appearance and genitalia of the syndrome. Note the absence of pubic and axillary hair. **C** shows three sisters with the syndrome; in this form pubic and axillary hair is present, though less than usual. All subjects had inguinal testes and blind shallow vaginas and were chromatin negative, the latter corresponding to the typical XY karyotype **(D)** present. **E.** A pedigree in which the responsible gene was transmitted through at least four generations. The sex ratio in the represented sibships appears to be 6 females: 1 male; in reality it is 2 XX: 5 XY. (**A** and **B** from Zourlas and Jones, 1965, courtesy of H. W. Jones, Jr., T. A. Baramki, and *Obstetrics and Gynecology,* journal of the American College of Obstetricians and Gynecologists. **C** from McKusick et al., 1964, courtesy of H. W. Jones, Jr., V. A. McKusick, T. A. Baramki, and C. B. Mosby Co., publishers of the *American Journal of Obstetrics and Gynecology.* D from Jacobs et al., 1959b, courtesy of P. A. Jacobs and *Lancet.* **E** from Taillard and Prader, 1957, based on data in Morris, 1953, courtesy of W. Taillard and the *Journal de Genetique Humaine.*)

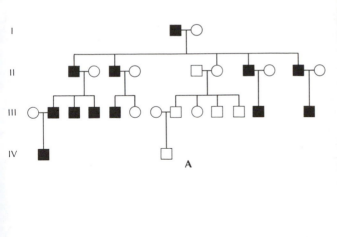
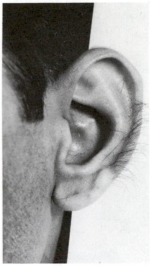

B

Fig. 7-19A Hypothetical pedigree of a completely Y-linked (holandric) trait. **B.** Left ear of a 28-year-old man from Andhra Pradesh, India, with hypertrichosis of the ears (hairy pinnae), which may be a holandric trait in humans. (From Dronamraju, 1965. Courtesy of K. R. Dronomraju and Academic Press, Inc., publishers of *Advances in Genetics*.)

A man with G6PD A marries a normal woman whose father and maternal grandfather both suffered from favism and whose brother has G6PD B.

(a) Diagram the marriage using the stroke system and a sensible nomenclature for the alleles involved.

(b) What are the expectations in their progeny?

(c) If one of their daughters who is known to carry at least the same G6PD allele as her mother's normal brother were to develop chronic myelogenous leukemia, what results are expected from G6PD analysis of the malignant marrow cells?

7-4. The last czarevitch (crown prince) of Russia suffered from hemophilia A (Factor 8 deficiency), an X-linked recessive disorder. By stroke diagrams show the probable genotypes (and names where you know them) of his great-grandparents, grandparents, and parents to indicate the transmission of the gene to him. Base your answer on Figure 10-7. The czars preceding Nicholas II were Alexander III and Alexander II.

7-5. The gene for hemophilia B, factor IX (PTC or Christmas factor) deficiency, is also an X-linked recessive, but it is at a different locus than hemophilia A. What result would be expected from the marriage of a man with hemophilia A and a woman who is homozygous normal at the A locus but who happens to be heterozygous for the B gene? Assume the two loci concern entirely unconnected metabolic processes that are related only in that they both affect clotting.

7-6. Consider Fig. 7–12. In both pedigrees the trait appears with nearly equal frequencies in both sexes.

(a)   Why, then, is X-linkage postulated for the responsible loci?

(b)   Look for critical matings and criticize the genetic basis for this hypothesis in Fig. 7–12**B.**

7-7. One of the implications of the Lyon hypothesis is that there should not really be any such thing as an X-linked recessive, for all X-chromosome genes should be manifesting themselves in some cells of the heterozygous females. If this were true, show how it would affect the peace of mind of married clinically normal sisters of a boy who manifests an X-linked disorder?

8

Chance and the Distribution of Families

In genetic experiments with plants and other animals, the most direct inferences as to method of inheritance come from a count of the progeny. For example, if one were to make a cross between two pure lines, intercross the F_1, and from the intercross obtain approximately three-fourths of one parental type and one-fourth of the other in the F_2, a simple Mendelian model, one locus with two alleles and dominance, would be inferred. This conclusion would be reinforced if the backcross of an F_1 hybrid (to the pure-line parental type that had not appeared in the F_1) produced progeny of which approximately one-half resembled the aforementioned parental types and one-half the F_1 hybrid.

In man, the number of progeny from any single family is usually so small that these conclusions would not be warranted. A mating of two heterozygotes for a recessive defect can produce 4:0, 2:2, 1:3, and 0:4 ratios, as well as the expected 3:1, in families of four children. Similarly, the mating $A/a \times a/a$ having two children, can produce 2:0 and 0:2 ratios as well as the expected 1:1.

A bit of reflection will convince the reader that this is not surprising. Consider, for example, the couple with genotypes A/a and a/a, respectively, having two children. Genetic theory expects them to have one A/a child and one a/a child because the A/a parent is expected to produce $1/2$ A gemetes and $1/2$ a gametes. If the A/a parent is the male, this ratio will usually be realized among the sperm. Is there, however, any guarantee that these sperm will take turns, so to speak, in fertilizing the egg? Obviously not. The sperm involved in producing the two children could well be A sperm in both cases or a sperm in both. If the A/a parent is the female, there is not even a guarantee that the gametic ratio will be $1/2$ A and $1/2$ a, since each meiosis ordinarily produces only one gamete and the various meioses are independent events: what happens in one meiosis does not influence what is to happen the next or any subsequent one. Hence, it could happen easily that the two children of this $A/a \times a/a$ mating are both A/a or both a/a.

Clearly the prediction of genetic results is fraught with uncertainties, events over which no one has control. Such uncertainty is generally referred to as "chance." One author has recognized the large element of chance involved by entitling his book on genetics *The Dice of Destiny*. The reader may well ask: how can genetics pretend to be a science if it cannot really predict the results of a given mating? Or, to put it more concretely, since chance plays such a large part in genetic transmission, of what value are the stated Mendelian ratios? The question becomes especially pertinent, we shall discover below, when the family size becomes greater than two; *most* families then will *not* yield the stated ratios of offspring.

Before answering this question it is necessary to understand that genetics in being beset with uncertainties is not singular among the sciences. Every scientist knows that in the real world absolute certainty does not exist; there are only relative degrees of uncertainty. To pick a rather absurd example, one could ask the following two questions of a meteorologist: (1) will the sun rise tomorrow? and (2) will tomorrow be a sunny day? He cannot answer either question with absolute certainty, but it is clear that he can answer the first with much more confidence than the second.

A great stride in the progress of a science is made when it can ascertain or measure these relative degrees of uncertainty. The meteorologist feels a sense of achievement when he can improve his forecast from "it may rain" or even "it will probably rain" to "there is a 90 percent chance of rain." The measurement or quantitation of uncertainty is called *probability.*

Usually the positive aspect of probability is emphasized. We are more interested in the degree we have moved toward certainty than in the amount of uncertainty left. Hence we think of probability as the likelihood of a desired event rather than as the degree to which we fall short of certainty in attaining it.

Let us examine some of the basic properties of probability. Perhaps we should begin with a well-known example. If a coin were to be tossed and we were asked the probability of its turning up "heads" the immediate answer would be some variant of "fifty-fifty," "one to one" or "one-half." If we asked why we gave this answer the reply would be roughly: why, it stands to reason; there are two ways the coin may fall and one of these is heads, so the chance is 1 out of 2, one-half or one to one. If we had an evenly weighted die and wished to know the probability of its upright face showing five dots when thrown, it does not seem difficult to extend the logic of this answer: since any of the six sides of the cube could turn up and the face with five dots is only one of these, there is one chance out of six of obtaining the "five." Clearly, the probability of success, that is, the likelihood that a desired event will happen, depends on the number of alternative events that could happen and on the number of these that spell "success."

Merely saying "the number of alternative events" can be misleading, however, because one could argue that in throwing the die on a given throw there are only two alternatives, success or failure, obtaining a five or not obtaining a five, and this might lead to the belief that the probability of success was one of two. Obviously this is not true: for every chance of obtaining a five there are five chances of obtaining something else. We must modify our statement, therefore, to state that the probability of success depends on the number of *equally probable* (or equally likely, as the mathematicians say) events possible and the number of these that spell success.

The probabilities discussed above may be stated "one chance out of two" and "one chance out of six." They could also be phrased as relative odds of success and failure. The chance of tossing a coin heads, for example, is 1:1, one chance of success to one chance of failure; similarly the odds of obtaining a five in the toss of a die are 1:5, one chance of success to five chances of failure. For arithmetic manipulation, however, the best way to state the probability is the way it is often instinctively given for the coin example: as a *fraction* whose denominator is the number of equally likely events possible in the situation under discussion and whose numerator is the number of these that constitute the event whose likelihood is in question.

Example: Suppose an urn contains five balls of identical size and shape. Two are black, marked B1 and B2, and three are white, marked W1, W2, and W3, respectively. We reach in to take out one ball. (1) What is the probability of obtaining the ball marked W2; and (2) what is the probability of obtaining a white ball?

$$(1) \text{ Probability of W2} = \frac{\text{number of W2 balls}}{\text{total number of balls present}} = \frac{1}{5}$$

$$(2) \text{ Probability of white} = \frac{\text{number of white balls}}{\text{total number of balls present}} = \frac{3}{5}$$

Mathematically, these statements would be written:

$$P(W2) = 1/5;$$
$$P(\text{white}) = 3/5.$$

P represents the phrase "probability of" the item in parentheses.

How large or how small may probabilities be? The maximum probability would be reached if we were satisfied with obtaining any ball present, whether it was white or black. Thus,

$$P(\text{white or black}) = 5/5 = 1.$$

Similarly, the minimum probability would come from wishing to obtain some other color than white or black from this urn:

$$P(\text{neither white nor black}) = 0/5 = 0.$$

This indicates that probability is a positive number between 0 and 1.

The sophisticated reader will suggest that probabilities of 1 and 0 represent "certainty," certainty of success and certainty of failure, respectively. This is correct. Certainty is possible in a mathematical sense, since a mathematical system assumes that only the conditions postulated will occur. In a few simple real situations this degree of simplicity may be approximated—but there is never a guarantee that the postulated condition will prevail. Thus we may feel secure that there are two black and three white balls in the urn, and this usually does approximate a mathematical system, but we really cannot guarantee absolutely, for example, that one or another of the balls did not disintegrate after we placed it in the urn. In practice, the likelihood of such an unexpected event is often so small that we ignore it, and we do speak of probabilities of 1 or 0 even for living things. Thus we have seen already that we ignore the probability of new mutations when we predict that the cross:

$$A/A \times A/A \to \text{all } A/A.$$

In probability terms we are saying

$$P(A/A \times A/A \to A/A) = 1,$$

and this cross is therefore usually written

$$A/A \times A/A \to 1 \ A/A.$$

Implicit in asking the probability of obtaining a *white* ball from the urn is the idea that it does not matter whether we obtain W1, W2, or W3. Any of these alternative events spells success. Thus,

$$P(\text{white}) = \frac{1 + 1 + 1}{5}$$
$$= 1/5 + 1/5 + 1/5.$$

But,

$$P(\text{W1}) = 1/5,$$
$$P(\text{W2}) = 1/5, \text{ and}$$
$$P(\text{W3}) = 1/5.$$

Hence,

$$P(\text{white}) = P(\text{W1}) + P(\text{W2}) + P(\text{W3}).$$

In other words, *if an event has several alternative forms* and attainment of any alternative is considered attainment of the desired event, the *probability of success is the sum of the probabilities of these alternative forms.* In commonsense terms, when we are not particular or choosy the chances for success are increased.

An equally interesting probability is that of a success which is composed of several events that must happen simultaneously or in succession. Clearly, this probability must be smaller than the likelihood of attaining any one of the events alone. How much smaller? To solve this problem let us return to the urn with the two black balls and the three white ones and set up a second urn with three black balls, B3, B4, B5, and three white ones, W4, W5, and W6. If a ball is to be removed from each urn, how likely is it, for example, that both will be black? To answer this we may return to our basic concept of probability and enumerate how many equally probable events, each consisting of one ball from urn A and one ball from urn B, can happen and note how many of these consist of a black ball from each urn. The equally probable events are shown in Fig. 8–1.

There are 30 equally probable events and 6 of these represent pulls of two black balls. Thus,

$$P(\text{black, black}) = 6/30 = 1/5.$$

Note that the 30 in the denominator is the product of the number of balls in urn A and the number of balls in urn B; likewise, the 6 in the numerator is the product of the number of black balls in urn A and the number of blacks in urn B.

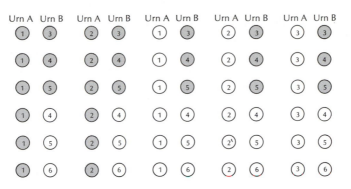

Fig. 8-1 The 30 combinations possible when a ball is drawn from each of two urns if the first urn contains 2 black balls and 3 white balls, the second contains 3 black ones and 3 white ones, and the balls are equal in size but distinguishable by number.

Thus,

$$P\text{ (black, black)} = \frac{2 \times 3}{5 \times 6}$$

$$= \frac{2}{5} \times \frac{3}{6} .$$

But,

$$\frac{2}{5} = P\text{ (black from urn A)}$$

and

$$\frac{3}{6} = P\text{ (black from urn B)}.$$

Thus, the probability of obtaining black balls from both urns is the product of the probabilities of obtaining a black ball from each urn.

We may generalize this into a rule: *The probability of obtaining certain simultaneous* (or successive) *events is the product of the probabilities of the events involved.* To check this generalization, we may note that

$$P\text{ (white, white)} = \frac{3}{5} \times \frac{3}{6}$$

$$= \frac{9}{30}$$

and this corresponds to the enumerated proportion.

This rule too, fits our commonsense expectations. The likelihood that both will happen must be smaller than the likelihood of either one alone, for each could often happen without the other. Since probabilities are fractions less than one, multiplying them has the effect of producing a still smaller fraction, that is, decreasing the probability.

This "multiplication rule" is valid whether the desired events occur simultaneously or in a particular order. Furthermore, it is applicable whether the probabilities of successive events are independent or dependent. Drawing balls from the two urns—described above—is an example of independent probabilities, where the probability of one event does not influence the probabilty of another in the series. Likewise, if only one urn is used and the ball replaced between pulls, the probabilities of successive choices are independent. To illustrate *dependent* probabilities we may consider only the first urn and calculate, for example, the probability of picking a black ball twice in succession if the first one removed is *not* seen and *not* replaced before pulling out the second.

For the first choice, as before,

$$P(B1 \text{ or } B2) = 2/5.$$

If the first choice is successful, only four balls remain in the urn and only one of these is black. Therefore, for the second choice

$$P(\text{black}) = 1/4$$

The probability that *both* events happen is, then

$$2/5 \times 1/4 = 2/20 = 1/10$$

The student is often disturbed by dependent probabilities because it seems more necessary than for independent probabilities to suppose that the first choice is successful before calculating the probability of the second. He should keep uppermost in mind that we are seeking the likelihood that both events *do* happen. We wish to calculate the probability of *success,* not the probability of failure. Failure, not obtaining the desired result, includes all the other results that could occur: the first choice is "right" but the second "wrong," the first wrong even if the second is right, or both choices are wrong. Calculating the probability of failure on the same basis used for the probability of success verifies our result:

$$P(\text{black, white}) = 2/5 \times 3/4 = 6/20$$
$$P(\text{white, black}) = 3/5 \times 2/4 = 6/20$$
$$P(\text{white, white}) = 3/5 \times 2/4 = 6/20$$

Since any of these alternative spells failure,

$$P(\text{Failure}) = 6/20 + 6/20 + 6/20 = 18/20.$$

Since

$$P(\text{Success}) + P(\text{Failure}) = 1*$$
$$P(\text{Success}) = 1 - P(\text{Failure})$$
$$= 1 - 18/20$$
$$= 2/20 = 1/10 = \text{the same result obtained directly.}$$

*This is a useful relation to keep in mind. Unlike the case above, it is often easier to calculate the probability of *not* obtaining the desired result, and then subtracting from unity, than to calculate directly the probability of the desired result.

WHAT THE GENETIC RATIOS MEAN

We may now consider the meaning of the Mendelian ratios.

Meaning 1: A genetic ratio states the probability for a single birth. When we state

$$A/a \times a/a \rightarrow 1/2\ A/a,\ 1/2\ a/a$$

we are saying that at any given birth from these parents the odds are 1:1 that the child will be a/a. On the other hand, for the mating

$$A/a \times A/a \rightarrow 1/4\ A/A,\ 1/2\ A/a,\ 1/4\ a/a,$$

the stated ratio means that at any given birth there is twice as much chance that the baby will be A/a than that it will be A/A. Likewise the odds are 2:1 for A/a versus a/a and 1:1 for A/A versus a/a. If A is dominant over a, the probability is 3/4 that a child from the last mating will show the A phenotype, 1/4 that it will show a phenotype, in other words, three times as much chance for gene A to be present at least once than for its complete absence, a/a.

Meaning 2: In any sibship, the result suggested by the genetic ratio has the modal probability. This probability is usually *not* the probability in the Mendelian ratio, but must be calculated for each case.

The genetic ratio leads us to expect that the distribution of children in a family will conform to this ratio, but we know it usually will not do so. For example, if the parents in the mating

$$A/a \times a/a \rightarrow 1/2\ A/a,\ 1/2\ a/a$$

decide to have two children the ratio "predicts" that they will have one A/a child and one a/a child. But our biological knowledge, and observation of actual families, tells us that such families will consists of two A/a children or two a/a children as well as one A/a and one a/a. Using our rules of probability and the first meaning for the genetic ratio, we can calculate the probability or expected relative frequency of these sibships.

$$P(2A/a) = P(A/a, A/a) = 1/2 \times 1/2 = 1/4.$$

Likewise,

$$P(2a/a) = P(a/a, a/a) = 1/2 \times 1/2 = 1/4.$$

For one A/a and one a/a, we should note that this may happen in two ways, the A/a birth first or the a/a first.

Therefore,

$$P(A/a, a/a) = 1/2 \times 1/2 = 1/4,$$
$$P(a/a, A/a) = 1/2 \times 1/2 = 1/4,\ \text{and}$$
$$P(1\ A/a\ \text{and}\ 1\ a/a) = 1/4 + 1/4 = 1/2.$$

The previous line is unique because the probability of obtaining the "expected" ratio is the same as a fraction in the ratio.

Consider the parents with *four* children. All four births may result in A/a progeny. The likelihood of this is

$$1/2 \times 1/2 \times 1/2 \times 1/2 = (1/2)^4 = 1/16.$$

Having three A/a and one a/a children in a family of four may occur in four different ways since the a/a child could be the first-born, the second-, the third-, or the fourth-born. These different families are:

	Probability
$a/a, A/a, A/a, A/a$	1/16
$A/a, a/a, A/a, A/a$	1/16
$A/a, A/a, a/a, A/a$	1/16
$A/a, A/a, A/a, a/a$	1/16
(3 A/a, 1 a/a)	4/16 = 1/4

Each birth order has a probability of 1/16. Since we are interested only in the probability of obtaining 3 A/a and 1 a/a, irrespective of the birth order, the probability is the sum of the probabilities of the alternative orders, or 4/16.

Families of 2 A/a and 2 a/a children may be achieved by any of 6 birth orders:

$A/a\ A/a\ a/a\ a/a$
$A/a\ a/a\ A/a\ a/a$
$A/a\ a/a\ a/a\ A/a$
$a/a\ A/a\ A/a\ a/a$
$a/a\ A/a\ a/a\ A/a$
$a/a\ a/a\ A/a\ A/a$

Again each birth order has a probability of 1/16, so the probability of $A/a \times a/a$ parents having two A/a and two a/a children is 6/16. By argument similar to the case of three A/a and one a/a, having one A/a and three a/a has a probability of 4/16, and the probability of four a/a is identical to the probability of four A/a: 1/16.

The most remarkable result of this analysis is that the family predicted by the genetic ratio, two A/a and two a/a, has less probability of being achieved (6/16) than of *not* being achieved (10/16). This will be true for any family size greater than two. Of the five kinds of families with four children possible, however, this family does have the *highest single probability*. Thus, the genetic ratio does not tell us the likelihood of attaining such a ratio in a sibship of given size. It does tell us, though, that the sibship indicated by the genetic ratio is the one we are *most likely* to encounter. Therefore, when we say that the cross $A/a \times a/a$ is "expected" to produce a family of half A/a and half a/a, we mean this family is the "*most often expected*" one.*

Meaning 3:   If progeny of a large number of couples with the same genotype are counted, the total are expected to equal the genetic ratio, provided that all the various sibships can be ascertained in their expected proportions. The proviso simply

---

*If the theory leads to an unreal expectation, say 3 1/2:3 1/2 in a family of 7, the most expected families are the real ones which are closest (3:4 and 4:3 in the example).

means the genetic ratio is expected only if the sampling procedures are unbiased. Examples of the most likely forms of biased sampling will be described later.

Consider again the parents A/a and a/a having four children each. The results expected in a random sample of the five kinds of families are given in Table 8–1. The progeny are calculated in two ways: (1) actual numbers expected in a typical sample of 1600 families and (2) fractional proportions of the total sample. Either way the calculations are made, the table shows the expected result is the same as the genetic ratio: half A/a and half a/a.

A similar conclusion is demonstrated by Table 8–2 concerning the four-children families expected from a cross of two normal heterozygotes for a recessive trait, for example, alkaptonuria. Again there are five kinds of families, but these have different probabilities than in the previous cross.

Here the classical expected ratio is 3/4 normal $(A/-)$:1/4 alkaptonurics (a/a). By our first meaning of the ratio, this means that at each birth there is a probability of three-fourths that the child will be normal, one-fourth that he will be an alkaptonuric. Hence the probability that all four children will turn out to be normal is $(3/4)^4$ or 81/256, a very substantial likelihood, that all four will be abnormal is $(1/4)^4$, or only 1/256.

Having three normal and one alkaptonuric can occur in four ways:

$$n\ n\ n\ a$$
$$n\ n\ a\ n$$
$$n\ a\ n\ n$$
$$a\ n\ n\ n$$

Each birth order has probability of $(3/4)^3 \cdot 1/4$, or 27/256, so the probability that any one of the four alternatives will be achieved is 4(27/256), or 108/256. Obtaining one normal and three alkaptonurics can also occur in four alternate birth orders, but each has a probability of $(3/4) \cdot (1/4)^3$, or 3/256, for a total of 12/256.

Table 8–1   Expected progeny in a random sample of four-children families where one parent is A/a and the other a/a, locus A being autosomal

Kind of Family	Probability[a]	Number of Families[b]	In Numbers[b]		As Proportions of Next Generation	
			A/a	a/a	A/a	a/a
4 A/a	1/16	100	400		1/16	
3 A/a, 1 a/a	4/16	400	1200	400	3/16	1/16
2 A/a, 2 a/a	6/16	600	1200	1200	3/16	3/16
1 A/a, 3 a/a	4/16	400	400	1200	1/16	3/16
4 a/ans	1/16	100		400		1/16
Total	16/16	1600	3200	3200	8/16	8/16
					1/2	1/2

[a]Calculated in the text.
[b]Calculated on the basis of 1600 families.

Table 8-2 Expected progeny in a random sample of four-children families where the parents are heterozygous for a recessive gene *a*

Kind of Family	Probability[a]	Number of Families[b]	In Numbers[b] A/—[c]	In Numbers[b] a/a	As Proportions of Next Generation A/—[c]	As Proportions of Next Generation a/a
4 A/—	81/256	2025	8100		81/256	
3 A/—, 1 a/a	108/256	2700	8100	2700	81/256	27/256
2 A/—, 2 a/a	54/256	1375	2700	2700	27/256	27/256
1 A/—, 3 a/a	12/256	300	300	900	3/256	9/256
4 a/a	1/256	25		100		1/256
Total	256/256	6400	19200	6400	192/256	64/256
					3/4	1/4

[a]Calculated in the text.
[b]Calculated on the basis of 6400 families.
[c]A/— means that the genotype is either A/A or A/a.

The remaining type of family, half normal and half alkaptonuric, may take any of six forms (as on page 184), each with probability of $(3/4)^2 \cdot (1/4)^2$, or 9/256, so the total is 54/256.

Note that our "expected" family, three normal:one alkaptonuria, is again the family with the highest single probability, in conformity with Meaning 2.

Again we calculate the progeny in Table 8-2 in two ways: by counting a specified number of families any by proportions. In either case the expected progeny from the random sample conform to the genetic ratio: 3/4 normal and 1/4 alkaptonuric.

In actual practice the expected results will rarely be attained exactly. The likelihood of finding precisely 25 families out of 6400 with all four members alkaptonurics, for example, is very small. Had there been 24 or 26 such families, the exact "expected" results would not have been attained. Similarly, if the number of families counted were not a multiple of 256, these exact results could not be expected. This type of deviation from the expected result is referred to as "sampling error." It is considered due to chance, since it results from the accidents of sampling and not from any change in our biological model or any purposeful deviation from random sampling procedures.

Several statistical methods are availabe to calculate how large a deviation must be before it may be considered significant, that is, before we suspect that perhaps our expectation is based on the wrong biological model or that random sampling procedures were *not* followed in obtaining the data.

It suffices at this point to note (1) that random sampling errors tend to cancel each other out; and (2) the relative magnitude tends to vary inversely with the sample size: as the sample size becomes larger the chance deviations from expected tend to become less important.

METHODS OF ASCERTAINMENT

The method of collecting data in Tables 8–1 and 8–2 is generally referred to as *complete ascertainment* (or complete selection). In complete ascertainment the sibships to be included (selected) are ascertained through the parents or, for X-linked traits, the grandparents. It is "complete" because an attempt is made to study all the members of the sample. When all the genotypes can be differentiated easily, almost all collections of families constitute completely ascertained samples. Thus the data in Table 1–3 for relatively rare dominants are pools of completely ascertained families, and, as we noted there, fit the Mendelian ratios very well.

A problem arises in attempting complete ascertainment for a recessive trait: We are unable to recognize $A/a \times A/a$ matings when they happen to have all normal offspring. The technical term for this error is *truncate selection,* since what we are really doing in such a case is cutting off a portion of the sample by selecting only those families with at least one affected child for our data. The older term "complete selection," that is, of affected individuals, was obviously unsatisfactory, but a combination of the two, complete truncate selection, may be best. Note, however, that the word, "selection" is used here in a very different sense from the Darwinian "selection" of Chapter 11.

One has to be very careful in reading the literature to note whether truncate selection was the method of collecting the data even though another criterion may be suggested by the title of the table or the article. For example, an opthalmologist was testing the hypothesis that in one series of families retinoblastoma was inherited as a dominant. Many affected persons now survive through early recognition of the disease and surgical removal of the affected eye. In the study in question, data were collected concerning the proportion of retinoblastoma among the children of such survivors. Ostensibly this should involve no problem of ascertainment since the retinoblastoma parent in each case was heterozygous and one parent was normal, leading to an expected ratio of 1 normal:1 retinoblastoma among the progeny just as for the similar dominants in Table 1–3. In the data presented, the ratio was 20 normal:63 retinoblastoma, an apparent 3:1 ratio in favor of the dominant

Table 8–3 Expected progeny in truncate sample of four-children families of which the parents are both heterozygous for a recessive gene *a*

Kind of Family	Proportions of all A/a × A/a Families[a]	Proportions of the Observed Families	Progeny in the Observed Sample	
			A/−	a/a
3 A/−, 1 a/a	108/256	108/175	81/175	27/175
2 A/−, 2 a/a	54/256	54/175	27/175	27/175
1 A/a, 3 a/a	12/256	12/175	3/175	9/175
4 a/a	1/256	1/175		1/175
Total	175/256	175/175	111/175	64/175
			63.4%	36.6%

[a]See Table 8-2.

trait. The difference from expected is highly significant. It turned out that the sib-ships were almost always identified through a patient with retinoblastoma and then finding that he had had a parent who had survived the condition. Thus the ascer-tainment was by way of the affected offspring rather than through the surviving parent. Sibships with no affected individuals were not being counted at all, a clear case of truncate selection for a *dominant* trait. To set the record straight, a few of the families of Table 1–3 were originally ascertained through an affected child. For this table, however, sibships from these families were collected on the basis of an affected parent, so that sibships having no affected children were as likely to be counted as sibships containing one or more affected.

For the effect of truncate selection on a recessive trait, let us reexamine the mating of two heterozygotes, A/a, studied in Table 8–2. Since both parents are nor-mal, how do we know they are heterozygotes so that their families should be counted in our sample? Usually our only clue has come from the presence of at least one affected child among their progeny. In other words, the families with all four children normal, being indistinguishable from the rest of the normal popula-tion, are not counted at all!

Table 8–3 shows the effect this has on the observed ratio even if the *ascertained* families are obtained without bias, that is, families with four affected children are no more likely to be counted than families with only one affected child. Clearly, the 3:1 ratio should *not* be expected when data are collected in this way.

Very soon after Mendel's laws were rediscovered in 1900 many geneticists real-ized that truncate selection posed a major obstacle to attempts to determine whether human traits followed the Mendelian ratios. If a trait was suspected to be dominant, sampling bias could be minimized by increasing the size of the sample and taking as great pains to find the families with only one or two affected members as the families with many affected. However, even the most assiduous and pains-taking effort could not avoid truncate selection for a suspected recessive trait. Often there was simply no way to identify the heterozygotes who had no affected children.

CORRECTIONS FOR TRUNCATE COMPLETE SELECTION

Fortunately for the history of human genetics, geneticists and mathematicians quickly developed methods to correct for this vexing problem. Three methods in particular are widely used. The first was suggested by a German physician, W. Weinberg, in 1912, only 12 years after the rediscovery of Mendel's work. He noted that the complete ascertainment sample was truncate because of a bias in favor of the affected progeny. These were the individuals that called attention to the sibship, that is, they were the *probands* or *propositi* (singular, *propositus*). Another synonym in "index case."

The normal progeny, on the other hand, could not identify the family as belonging in the data; hence, they were deficient in the final totals. To correct this imbalance he suggested the probands be removed, and the count among the siblings of the probands should show the correct ratio. This correction is referred to as *Weinberg's proband method;* unfortunately, the latter term has also been used for other methods, so that the consensus nowadays is to call it the "direct sib" method.

An illustration of how it works is given in Table 8–4 for families of Table 8–3.

It should be noted that the method involves eliminating the proband, but that each of the affected progeny must be considered a potential proband. Thus, each of the four affected (probands) in the last row of Table 8–4 has three affected siblings, or a total of 12, that must be counted. Similarly, each of the three probands in the families with three affected has one normal and two affected sibs, or a total of three normal and six affected per family; since there are 12 such families per 256 in the population, the progeny counted are 72 affected:36 normal, etc.

Calculation of the direct sib correction is simplified by handling the data as in Table 8–5. Usually the data contain a mixture of families of different sizes. For example, Lundin and Olow studied an early onset form of polycystic kidneys. The disease is present at birth and the infant rarely survives more than a few hours. They found nine cases in six families. Although the ratio of normal:affected children in these families was 12:9, Lundin and Olow concluded from the direct sib correction that the data suggest a 3:1 ratio (Table 8–6).

The weakness of the direct sib method lies in the difficulty of obtaining data with which to use it. Generally, the literature does not describe the numbers of affected:normal per sibship as was provided by Lundin and Olow; rather, the total data in a collection of sibships of given size is given. Breaking down the data into expected random numbers of different types is not only laborious but also susceptible to error. Furthermore, the method wastes considerable collected data if the bulk of it derives from sibships of three children or less. All one-sib families must be thrown out. Similarly, in a random sample of $A/a \times A/a$ marriages, only 8 items (2 affected:6 normal) can be salvaged from the 14 progeny of each 7 two-sibling families, and 96 from the 111 progeny of 37 three-sibling families. Note that the 6 children in the 3 two-child families in Table 8–6 contribute only 3 items of data. These considerations hamper calculations of statistical parameters to test the random sampling error of the data and the validity of pooling data from various sources.

The direct sib method does have the virtue of pointing out its own unbiased ratio of affected:normal in the progeny. This is not true in the second method of correcting complete ascertainment data: the so-called "direct *a priori*" method.

Table 8–4 Analysis of the data in Table 8–3 by the direct sib method (Weinberg's general proband method)

Affected	Expected Proportion[a]	"Observed" Proportion	Probands	Sibs/Proband Affected:Normal	Total Sibs of Probands Affected:Normal	Corrected Progeny Affected:Normal
0	81	0	0	0:0	0:0	0:0
1	108	108	1	0:3	0:3	0:324
2	54	54	2	1:2	2:4	108:216
3	12	12	3	2:1	6:3	72:36
4	1	1	4	3:0	12:0	12:0
					Total	192:576
					Ratio	1:3

[a]Per 256 four-children families of $A/a \times A/a$ marriages in the population.

Table 8-5 Suggested calculation of the direct sib method. Illustration is for a theoretical truncate distribution of four-child families from $A/a \times A/a$

Family Type	Number of Unaffected/Family (U)	Number of Affected/Family (A)	Number of Families (N)	Corrected Progeny	
				Normal UAN	Affected A(A − 1)N
3:1	3	1	108	324	0
2:2	2	2	54	216	108
1:3	1	3	12	36	72
0:4	0	4	1	0	12
				Total 576	192
				Ratio 3	1

The *a priori* method derives from the observation that a certain amount of data is missing (truncated) from the sample. How much is missing depends on the assumed ratio that the collected data were expected to fit. For example, in four-children sibships, the data missing consist of the families with all four normal. If the expected ratio is 3:1, this class has a probability of $(3/4)^4$, or 81/256 of the families; if, however, the expected ratio were 1:1, the missing group would be only $(1/2)^4$, or 1/16 of the families. If the actual total observed is increased by the missing fraction then the number of affected divided by the "true" total should equal the correct ratio.

In general,

$$\text{if } p = \text{probability of normal}$$
$$\text{and } q = \text{probability of affected}$$
$$\text{and } n = \text{the number in the sibship,}$$
$$\text{and the proportion of data missing} = p^n,$$
$$\text{the proportion of data present} = 1 - p^n.$$

This is the proportion of a true total, T.

If the actual total data = T_a, an estimate of T, T_c, may be obtained by equating

Table 8-6 Direct sib correction in six families of spongy type polycystic kidneys of early onset. (Data from Lundin and Olow, 1961)

Family Type	Unaffected Per Family (U)	Affected Per Family (A)	Number of Families (N)	UAN	A(A − 1)N
A	1	1	3	3	0
B	2	2	2	8	4
C	5	2	1	10	2
Totals	8	5	6	21	6
			Ratio	0.778	0.222
			Expected ratio	0.75	0.25
			Expected numbers	20.25	6.75
			$\chi^2 = 0.106$		
			$P > 0.70$		

$T_a = (1 - p^n)T_c$, or $T_c = T_a/(1 - p^n)$. If this were the correct total, the proportion of affected in the total data would be:

$$\hat{q} = \frac{\text{number affected}}{T_c}.$$

This may be compared with the theoretical probability of affected, q.

This method may be illustrated by an actual count of nine children with Friedreich's ataxia among eight sibships of two each from normal parents. If Friedreich's ataxia is inherited as a single locus recessive,

$$p = 3/4$$
$$q = 1/4$$
$$p^n = (3/4)^2 = 9/16$$
$$1 - p^n = 1 - 9/16 = 7/16$$
$$T_c = \frac{(8)(2)}{7/16} = \frac{256}{7} = 36.6$$
$$\hat{q} = \frac{9}{36.6} = 0.246.$$

Since $q = 0.250$, this is a very close fit.

To extend the method for a series of families of different size, it is necessary merely to calculate a T_c for each size. Adding these gives an overall T_c. The total affected divided by this T_c constitutes the calculated q to be compared with the *a priori* q from the hypothesis. The data of Table 8–6 may be used to illustrate the method (Table 8–7).

Again $\hat{q}$ is very close to the theroetical q and thus strengthens the hypothesis that this form of polycytic kidneys is determined by the recessive allele of a single locus.

Calculating the divisor, $1 - p^n$, each time is laborious. Table 10–6 gives these

Table 8–7 The direct *a priori* method used to correct the truncate data of Table 8–6

Size of Sibship (A)	Number of Sibships (B)	Divisor $(1 - p^A)$ (C)	T_c $(A \cdot B/C)$	Affected (D)	Expected $T_c/4$	χ^2
2	3	$\frac{7}{16}$	13.7	3	3.4	
						0.05
4	2	$\frac{175}{256}$	11.7	4	2.9	
						0.73
7	1	$\frac{14197}{16384}$	8.7	2	2.02	
						0.01
		Total	33.5	9	8.3[a]	0.78[b]
		$\hat{q} = \left(\dfrac{\Sigma D}{\Sigma T_c}\right)$		0.268		
		Expected q		0.25		

[a]χ^2 for difference between 8.3 and 9 = 0.05 with 1 d.f.; P > 0.80.
[b]χ^2, with 3 degrees of freedom; P > 0.80.

values to three decimal places when $p = 1/2$ or $p = 3/4$ and family size is 12 or less.

Before leaving the direct *a priori* method, it might be well to note a slightly different manner of checking whether a truncate set of data fits the hypothesis. Table 8–3 states that the proportion of affected (a/a) in a random but truncate sample of four-child sibships is

$$q_{tr} = \frac{64}{175} = 0.3657.$$

We can refer to this as the expected truncate q, q_{tr}. This means that if there has been complete ascertainment but we know the 4-child families in the sample do not include the ones with 0 affected, we *expect* 0.3657 affected and not one-fourth. On average the families that *are* in the sample should contain $4 (0.3657) = 1.463$ affected instead of 1, which is $4 (0.25)$. Instead of calculating the expected truncate q, as in Table 8–3, it can be calculated directly by noting that

$$q_{tr} = \frac{a \; priori \; q}{1 - p^n}$$

where n is the size of the sibship. Thus when the *a priori* $q = 1/4$, and sibship size is 3,

$$q_{tr} = \frac{1/4}{1 - (3/4)^3} = \frac{1/4}{37/64}$$
$$= 16/37$$
$$= 0.4324, \text{ so that:}$$

$$\text{average expected } (a/a) = 3(0.4324) = 1.297/\text{family}.$$

When n becomes larger than 4, the arithemetic becomes laborious, so the divisors in Table 8–8 can be used in the denominator. The expected truncate q and the average number of affected are shown in Table 8–9 for sibships with 1 to 16 members.

Note that q_{tr} approaches the *a priori* q as the family size increases. This is exactly what is expected from the previously noted fact that the divisor, $1 - p^n$, becomes almost indistinguishable from 1 as n grows larger. Hence, for families larger than 10, $q_{tr} \sim$ *a priori* q for the calculations. This would not be permissible if the *a priori* q were one-fourth and the data included a substantial number of large families. However, even if the data contained as many as five sibships of 10, the error would not be very great. Using $q = 1/4$ leads to 12.5 expected, whereas the correct expected number is $5 (2.649) = 13.2$, a difference of only 0.7.

This form of the *a priori* method may be illustrated by data for the Australia lipoprotein antigen (Table 8–10). Note the similarity of observed and expected positives (homozygous recessives), as well as the excellent fit of q to the theoretical 25 percent.

The example should caution us that such a good fit does not necessarily mean the hypothesis is correct. Subsequent research by Blumberg and others has demonstrated that the Australia antigen reflects infection by hepatitis virus. These data

Table 8-8 Divisors, $1 - p^n$, for the direct *a priori* correction when $q = 1/2$ or $q = 1/4$

Sibship Size (n)	$q = 1/2$ p^n	$1 - p^n$	$q = 1/4$ p^n	$1 - p^n$
1	0.500	0.500	0.750	0.250
2	0.250	0.750	0.5625	0.4375
3	0.125	0.875	0.422	0.578
4	0.0625	0.9375	0.316	0.684
5	0.031	0.969	0.237	0.763
6	0.016	0.984	0.178	0.822
7	0.008	0.992	0.133	0.867
8	0.004	0.996	0.100	0.900
9	0.002	0.998	0.075	0.925
10	0.001	0.999	0.056	0.944
11	< 0.001	~ 1.000	0.042	0.958
12			0.032	0.968
13			0.024	0.976
14			0.018	0.982
15			0.013	0.987
16			0.010	0.990

may therefore indicate an inherited differential susceptibility to such infection, but this has not been established with certainty.

It is a bit disturbing that the two methods of correcting truncate complete ascertained samples in Tables 8–6 and 8–7 do not arrive at the same estimate of q from the data. This shows that they may be consistent in pointing to the underlying

Table 8-9 Expected truncate $q(q_{tr})$ under complete ascertainment and average number of affected per sibship when a priori $q = 1/2$ or $1/4$

Sibship Size (n)	A priori $q = 1/2$ Expected q_{tr}	Expected Number of Affected/Sibship	A priori $q = 1/4$ Expected q_{tr}	Expected Number of Affected/Sibship
1	1.0000	1.000	1.0000	1.000
2	0.6667	1.333	0.5714	1.143
3	0.5714	1.714	0.4324	1.297
4	0.5333	2.133	0.3657	1.463
5	0.5161	2.581	0.3278	1.639
6	0.5071	3.043	0.3041	1.825
7	0.5039	3.527	0.2885	2.020
8	0.5020	4.016	0.2778	2.222
9	0.5010	4.509	0.2703	2.433
10	0.5005	5.005	0.2649	2.649
11	0.5002	5.502	0.2610	2.871
12	0.5001	6.001	0.2582	3.098
13	0.50006	6.5008	0.2561	3.329
14			0.2545	3.563
15			0.2539	3.808
16			0.2525	4.040

Table 8-10   Correction of truncate data by Bernstein's form of the *a priori* method: data from Blumberg et al. (1966) of 24 sibships in which both parents were negative for the Australia lipoprotein antigen but had at least one positive child

Size of Sibship	Number of Sibships	Observed Number of Positive Children	Expected Number[a]
1	8	8	8.000
2	3	4	3.429
3	3	3	3.891
4	3	5	4.389
5	2	3	3.278
6	3	5	5.475
7	1	1	2.020
8	1	4	2.222
		33	32.704[b]

$$\chi^2, 1 \text{ d.f.} \simeq 0.004$$
$$P > 0.90$$

[a]Number of sibships multiplied by appropriate number from column 5 of Table 10-7.
[b]It may be noted also that T_c as per column 6, Table 8-7 is 4(32.704), so that $\hat{q} = 33/130.816 = 0.252$.

ratio but are not very efficient from the statistical point of view. Several methods that have been developed to obtain more efficient estimates of q use maximum likelihood mathematics that are beyond the scope of this book. Li and Mantel, however, have described a relatively simple method that seems to be as efficient as the maximum likelihood methods. It harks back to Weinberg's direct sib (proband) method. Instead of removing all probands, however, it concentrates on the sibships reporting but a single affected child, and it removes the number of these affected children (referred to as "singletons") from both the total affected and the total progeny in the reported families. It is not suitablle for small amounts of data such as those of Table 8–6, but works well with large amounts. For example, one of the most extensive studies on albinism from normal parents found 864 albinos among 2435 children in 411 sibships of two or more children. 171 sibships contained only singleton albinos. Hence,

$$\text{Est. } q = \frac{864 - 171}{2435 - 171}$$
$$= \frac{693}{2264}$$
$$= 0.306.$$

This compares very well with the maximum likelihood estimate for the same data, 0.308. The standard error by both methods comes out to be 0.011. The deviations from 0.25 are highly significant, presumably because of the concentration on "interesting" families with many albinos in the older literature.

SINGLE SELECTION

Even when truncate selection is recognized, proper correction of the error by the methods described above assumes that the portion of the total sibships that have been ascertained have been identified in a random manner, so that their relative proportion will correspond well with the expected frequencies (108:54:12:2, for example, in the four-children families of Table 8–2). In actuality, families with many affected are more likely to come to the attention of the physician or geneticist than families with only one affected. This is apt to be especially true if the data are collected from the cases reported in the literature. Similarly, a family with many affected may be counted more than once, particularly if the data are accumulated by encountering an affected person and asking him how many normal and affected siblings he has. If there is only one affected in a family, this family would be counted only once; if there are three affected, however, each of the three may be encountered independently by the investigators, in which case the family might be counted three times.

To avoid some of these possible errors, but especially to avoid the onerous choice of examining a whole population and locating every sibship of the desired type, some geneticists have used an incomplete ascertainment method of sampling often called "single selection of affected individuals," or simply "single selection." The pertinent sibships are identified by studying all persons of a certain age, for example, or all children in a certain grade in school. No family could be counted more than once (The rare exception, the family with one or more affected twins, could be identified and the data corrected accordingly.) Many collections of data based on affected first seen in hospital clinics fall into this category.

While considerably more economical, single selection also requires to be corrected. In the single selection method, the relative number of families with different numbers of affected will depend not only on the relative proportions of these families in the population but also on the relative number of affected children in the sibship. To illustrate: if we try to ascertain by single selection the number of albinos in four-children sibships born to heterozygous parents, we might survey all the fifth-grade children in a given town to determine if any are albinos having three siblings and normal parents. According to Table 8–2, the expectation is that a sibship with three normal and one albino would have 108 times as much chance of being represented by a child in the fifth grade as a family with all four children albinos. However, the family with four albinos has four times as much chance that their representative in the fifth grade will be an albino child as any family with three normal and only one albino. Hence, only 27 families with 3 normal:1 albino will be counted for every family with 0 normal:4 albinos counted. The appropriate calculations are illustrated in Table 8–11.

Single selection is automatically truncate, since the family with all normal offspring has no chance of being counted. This would be true even for situations that would not be truncate under complete selection. (For some conditions, single selection might be truncate at both ends. Thus, for a condition in which the affected child is not available, ascertainment might be made by asking each normal person in the sample whether he had at least one affected sibling.) Notwithstanding these

Table 8-11 Relative proportion of sibships counted under single selection, illustrated by sibships of four for a recessive condition with both parents heterozygous

Number Affected	True Relative Proportion (A)	Relative Count Frequency (B)	A · B	Relative Proportion in Sample	Apparent Count Affected:Normal
0	81	0	0	0	0:0
1	108	1	108	27	27:81
2	54	2	108	27	54:54
3	12	3	36	9	27:9
4	1	4	4	1	4:0
					112:144
Totals	256			Ratio	0.4375:0.5625

apparent deficiencies, single selection has proved to be a very useful tool in genetic analyses. As with complete ascertainment, one need only be aware of the theoretical basis for expecting distortions of the true ratio in single selection studies to be able to understand the methods that have been developed to correct them.

CORRECTION FOR TRUNCATE COMPLETE SELECTION

Proband removal will also reveal the correct ratio in a sample collected by single selection. Since it is *single* selection, however, only one affected need be eliminated from each family.

What we are doing in effect is converting our sample of four-children families, which is truncate, to a "complete ascertained" sample of three-children families. Justification for this procedure may be readily understood by inspection of Table 8-4. Note that the distribution of counted sibships is 27:27:9:1. These are exactly the coefficients of the expansion $(3/4 \, A/- + 1/4 \, a/a)^3$, which is:

$$27/64(A/-)^3 + 27/64(A/-)^2(a/a) + 9/64(A/-)(a/a)^2 + 1/64(a/a)^3.$$

The conversion of the singly selected random sample of four-child families to a completely ascertained sample of three-child families by removing the single proband from each family looks like this:

Number of Affected (A)	Relative Frequency in Singly Selected Sample (B)	Before Correction Progeny Count per Sibship (C) Normal:Affected	After Correction Progeny Count (D) Normal:Affected	Total (B · D) Normal:Affected
0	0	4:0	4:0	–
1	27	3:1	3:0	81:00
2	27	2:2	2:1	54:27
3	9	1:3	1:2	9:18
4	1	0:4	0:3	0:3
			Total	144:48
			Ratio	3:1

Rather than removing the proband from each sibship separately, it may be done from the total data in one step, as illustrated below for a theoretical composite of three- and four-child families:

Sibship Size	Number of Affected	True Proportion in Its Sibship Size	Sibship of Each Size Relative Proportion in 256	Count Frequency under Single Selection	Relative Number of Sibships in Sample	Progeny Count	
						Normal	Affected
3	1	27/64	108	1	108	216	108
	2	9/64	36	2	72	72	144
	3	1/64	4	3	12	0	36
4	1	108/256	108	1	108	324	108
	2	54/256	54	2	108	216	216
	3	12/256	12	3	36	36	108
	4	1/256	1	4	4	0	16
				Total	448	864	736

$$q = \frac{\text{affected} - \text{probands}}{\text{total} - \text{probands}}.$$

For single selection, number of probands = number of sibships. Hence,

$$q = \frac{736 - 448}{1600 - 448} = \frac{288}{1152} = \frac{1}{4}.$$

EMPIRIC PROBABILITY

Our basic definition of probability assumed that once we have formulated a hypothesis about the system, mathematical or biological, under study, we knew the number of alternative events and the number that spell success or failure. Unfortunately, we are not always able to formulate so precise a hypothesis. To take a very important example from the field of insurance: we might ask what are the odds that a given person presently aged 20 will live till the age of 25? Clearly, we have no theoretical hypothesis to rely on in answering this question, which is so important in deciding how much premium he should pay for insurance. We feel certain the insured will die, but cannot be certain how long he will pay these premiums. Similarly, in genetics we are often faced with situations where inheritance seems definitely to play a part, but we cannot understand the exact mechanism responsible. In such cases we are unable to make probability statements based on the Mendelian ratios.

Ignorance of the underlying mechanism need not be a complete bar to making some estimate of probability, however. The viability and robustness of the insurance industry all over the world sufficiently testify to that point. We must recognize, though, that the kinds of probability statement possible in these situations are not the same as the kind we have thus far been making in this chapter. Instead of being based on a theoretical scientific formulation, our probability statements rely pragmatically on past experience as a guide. The assumption is that a given event will happen as often in the future as it did in the past. If, for example, in the past ten years 5 percent of men aged 20 died before the age of 25, we would say that the probability that any particular 20-year-old person will be alive on his twenty-fifth birthday is 95/100, etc.

Probability based on past experience rather than theory is referred to as *empiric* or *inductive* probability. Some workers refer to such statements as "empiric risk figures" (Chapter 18) rather than probability, but they manipulate them in the same way as probabilities based on knowledge of the underlying mechanism. To continue the previous example, if we wished to calculate the probability that two persons aged 20 would both be alive at age 25, the answer would be $(95/100)^2$, or 90.25 percent. This type of calculation would be important for group insurance.

Empiric probabilities have the disadvantage that they are only as good as the methods of collecting the data responsible for them. Obviously, they are subject to change whenever we collect more data. Despite this serious drawback we shall find them extremely useful in several areas of genetics. Even the application of statistical tests based on *theoretical* probability distributions we will find depends a great deal on *empiric* practical factors.

POSTERIOR PROBABILITY

Probability based on an analysis of equally likely events and what proportion of these would spell success has sometimes been called *a priori* or *prior* probability. On the other hand, probability whose approximate value is obtained from actual statistical data from repeated trials was called *a posteriori* or *posterior* probability. In recent years the term posterior probability has been expanded to include also situations where the prior probability should be modified by events subsequent to its formulation. This is the application of what statisticians refer to as Bayes' theorem.

Rather than burden the student with another formula let us illustrate the thinking and arithmetic involved with an example. A woman has a brother affected by a recessive disorder, say, galactosemia. *A priori* we say the probability is 2/3* that she is heterozygous for this trait.

If she were to marry a man with a similar history, the *a priori* probability that they would have an affected child is:

$$\frac{2}{3} \times \frac{2}{3} \times \frac{1}{4} = \frac{1}{9}.$$

If, however, they have three children, all free of galactosemia, what is the probability for their fourth child?

To calculate this we must take into consideration that the three normal children make it less likely that they are both heterozygous. The probability that the

---

*She cannot be homozygous recessive, so the odds are 2:1 that she is heterozygous.

two are heterozygotes and would produce three normal children and no affected child is:

$$\frac{2}{3} \times \frac{2}{3} \times \frac{3}{4} \times \frac{3}{4} \times \frac{3}{4} = \frac{3}{16}.$$

This is sometimes called a *joint* probability, because it is a combination of the prior probability that both parents are carriers and a conditional probability that if they are carriers they would have normal children. The corresponding joint probability based on the assumption that at least one of the parents is *not* a heterozygote is:

$$\left(1 - \frac{4}{9}\right) \times 1 = \frac{5}{9}.$$

Since these are now the only two possibilities, their sum becomes the denominator, that is, the posterior probability that both parents are heterozygous is:

$$\frac{3/16}{3/16 + 5/9} = 0.252.$$

Therefore, the posterior probability that the fourth child will be affected is only:

$$0.252 \times \frac{1}{4} = 0.063,$$

that is, about 1/16, as compared to 1/9 prior to the birth of the three normal children. The concept is clearly useful in genetic counseling.

The reader should consider this chapter, as in the case of many others, merely an introduction to a very complex subject. It does not consider, for example, how to correct for data that have been collected by a mixture of the two methods, referred to as "multiple" or "incomplete" selection. Here the method of choice is the maximum likelihood method of Bailey (1951) or the "segregation analysis" method of Morton (1958a, 1959, 1962). Those who are mathematically adept will find Morton's formulas to constitute a particularly comprehensive attack on the problems of ascertainment. They are, however, too complex for this book.

APPENDIX

TESTS FOR SIGNIFICANCE

Over the years scientists have found that events having less than 5 percent probability of occurring by chance ought to be looked at with some suspicion. We should wonder in such an event whether chance was really responsible for the observed deviation from expected frequency. Perhaps our assumption as to the basic mechanism is wrong. Or perhaps the hypothesis was correct, but some bias factors were at work between the fundamental biological activity and our observations. Whatever the real cause of our aberrant result, we should not accept it as merely the vagary of chance, though that is all that it might be.

The chance probability at which we lose confidence in our hypothesis, and suspect, instead, that perhaps some factor other than chance may be responsible for a difference between observation and expectation, is called a *level of significance.*

Scientists ordinarily advise accepting chance as responsbile at least until its probability falls below 5 percent. Where much is at stake on the conclusion drawn, they find that chance should be held responsible until its likelihood falls below 1 percent.

Although an investigator may define the terms in any way he chooses, a result that without further explanation is said to be of

"Borderline significance" has a chance probability at or slightly above 5 percent.

"Significant" has a chance probability which is below 5 percent.

"Highly significant" has a chance probability below 1 percent.

"Very highly significant" has a chance probability below 0.1 percent.

When n is small the probabilities above are not difficult to calculate, but even $(3/4)^8$ demands use of logarithms or a calculating machine. Moreover, no method we have studied thus far is suitable when we have more than two classes of data. Fortunately, statisticians have developed several relatively simple tests that enable the investigator to determine whether the chance probability is near the significance level.

The essence of each of these statistical tests is finding a generalized distribution of chance probabilities, one that does not have to be calculated for each different sample size. To apply the test we need to do a few relatively simple arithmetical operations that tell us approximately where in this distribution our observed data would lie if they *did* arise from chance.

Usually the generalized distribution is, or can serve as, a chart or graph of the relative likelihood that results differ, by chance, from some theoretical expectation. This is called testing the null hypothesis. To do so we calculate how far our results are from the "expected" results, and the chart or graph tells us whether this deviation from expected has high or low probability of happening by chance. If the probability is high, we assume chance is responsible for the deviation from expected, and that our data therefore fit the theoretical expectation. We say that the null hypothesis is accepted. If the probability is low, the null hypothesis is rejected. In that case, some other factor, we think, not chance, is responsible for the deviation from the "expected" result.

Note that the statistical test does not prove anything. Merely because the probability is high that a deviation resulted from chance constitutes no proof that it did—or that the theoretical "expected" result is really the one that should have been expected in the first place.

One of the most useful generalized chance distributions grows directly out of the binomial theorem. If there are but two classes of events (hence the term *binomial*) and they have equal probability of occurring by chance, as n becomes larger many of the chance probabilities change very little, that is, the values are approaching limits. The limits that are being approached are the ordinates of the curve of the binomial expansion when n is infinite, that is, of the situation

$$(a + b)^n$$

where

$$a = b = 1/2,$$

and

$$n \to \infty.$$

The bell-shaped graph of this chance distribution (Fig. 8–2) is well known to most of us as the "normal" curve. Its true mathematical formula, much more complicated that the form we have shown, was derived around 1730 by the French mathematician De Moivre, and, independently, about 50 years later, by Laplace and by Gauss. Many mathematicians call it the Gaussian distribution. It probably achieved its popular name because it describes the relative numbers of typical (i.e., "normal") deviations from expected, not only in many games of chance but also in comparing data when the same scientific measurements or experiments are repeated over and over. Deviation from the expected mean, or "true" result, in such cases is often referred to as the "error," so the distribution is also often called the curve of normal error.

After n is an appreciable number, say, 40, the expansion of $(a + b)^n$, where $a = b = 1/2$, and n is finite, are so close to the normal curve that very little error is introduced by assuming that our theoretical expectations do indeed follow that curve. When n is fairly large, even expansions of $(a + b)^n$ where $a \neq b$ come quite

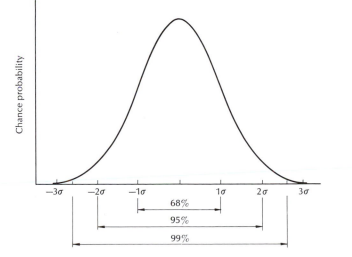

Fig. 8–2   A representation of the normal curve, showing approximately the relative areas (integrated sums of the probabilities) included between $\pm$ 1, 2, and 3 standard deviations or standard errors (σ) from the mean.

close to the normal curve, provided that the most expected result—indicated by the relation of *a* and *b*—is placed at the middle position (the 0 deviation point) of the normal curve. This means that for large samples the generalized probabilities based on the 1:1 ratio can be used for 2:1, 3:1, and even 15:1 ratios.

In conformity with the properties of the normal curve, mathematicians have devised a unit—called in some circumstances "standard deviation" and in others—"standard error," which allows us to determine exactly where a given result belongs on the curve. No matter what the sample size, a deviation of one standard error from the expected result always places the result at the *x*-axis point marked +1 or −1 on the curve, two standard errors at the points marked +2 or −2, etc. Reference to the height of the curve or, better yet, to a table summarizing these heights thereby immediately enables us to determine the probability of attaining that result by chance alone.

The general formula for the standard error of the binomial distribution is:

$$\text{S.E.} = \sqrt{\frac{pq}{n}}$$

where

p = the theoretical probability of one of the two possible events (corresponding to a in the formula $(a + b)^n$;

q = the theoretical probability of the other possible event; and

n = the sample size.

To avoid working with fractions, which most individuals find confusing, it is suggested that *p* and *q* be expressed as decimals. Another alternative is to use the *numbers* of expected, but it is important to be consistent throughout the whole operation.

The next step is to determine how many standard errors the result being tested is from the expected result. This statistic is often referred to as *t*, and this statistical test based on the normal curve is called a *t-test*.* Once we have found how far away the observed result is from the theoretical expectation or midpoint of the curve we can tell at a glance whether it would be likely for the observed result to be attributable to chance alone.

For a more exact determination a table of the distribution is more desirable than the curve itself. It turns out to be inconvenient, however, to show the probability of every single whole and fractional number of standard deviations on our table (though very extensive tables of this kind are available). A table of cumulative probabilities, such as Table A2 at the end of this chapter, is more practical.

The critical points in this table are related to the levels of significance: where

---

*The original *t*-test was devised by W. S. Gossett, an English research chemist in the Guinness brewery in Dublin, who wrote statistical papers under the pseudonym "Student" (hence, often referred to as "Student's *t* test"). It was designed for non-normal distributions, when the number of variates is less than infinite. As mentioned in the text, the probabilities he calculated for real samples of 31 or greater do not deviate critically from the infinite curve, and it is a test based on the infinite curve that is presented here. For a more exact result with smaller samples, the curves in the right half of Figure 8–3, which are based on his calculations, may be used.

Table A1 Squares, Factorials, and Square Roots of the Whole Numbers 1–50

n	n^2	n!	$\sqrt{n}$	n	n^2	n!	$\sqrt{n}$
1	1	1	1.000	26	676	4.03291×10^{26}	5.099
2	4	2	1.414	27	729	1.08889×10^{28}	5.196
3	9	6	1.732	28	784	3.04888×10^{29}	5.292
4	16	24	2.000	29	841	8.84176×10^{30}	5.385
5	25	120	2.236	30	900	2.65253×10^{32}	5.477
6	36	720	2.449	31	961	8.22284×10^{33}	5.568
7	49	5 040	2.646	32	1024	2.63131×10^{35}	5.657
8	64	40 320	2.828	33	1089	8.68332×10^{36}	5.745
9	81	362 880	3.000	34	1156	2.95233×10^{38}	5.831
10	100	3 628 800	3.162	35	1225	1.03331×10^{40}	5.916
11	121	39 916 800	3.316	36	1296	3.71993×10^{41}	6.000
12	144	479 001 600	3.464	37	1369	1.37638×10^{43}	6.083
13	169	6 227 020 800	3.606	38	1444	5.23023×10^{44}	6.164
14	196	87 178 291 200	3.742	39	1521	2.03970×10^{46}	6.245
15	225	1 307 674 368 000	3.873	40	1600	8.15915×10^{47}	6.325
16	256	20 922 789 888 000	4.000	41	1681	3.34525×10^{49}	6.403
17	289	3.55687×10^{14}	4.123	42	1764	1.40501×10^{51}	6.481
18	324	6.40237×10^{15}	4.243	43	1849	6.04153×10^{52}	6.557
19	361	1.21645×10^{17}	4.359	44	1936	2.65827×10^{54}	6.633
20	400	2.43290×10^{18}	4.472	45	2025	1.19622×10^{56}	6.708
21	441	5.10909×10^{19}	4.583	46	2116	5.50262×10^{57}	6.782
22	484	1.12400×10^{21}	4.690	47	2209	2.58623×10^{59}	6.856
23	529	2.58520×10^{22}	4.796	48	2304	1.24139×10^{61}	6.928
24	576	6.20448×10^{23}	4.899	49	2401	6.08282×10^{62}	7.000
25	625	1.55112×10^{25}	5.000	50	2500	3.04141×10^{64}	7.071

[a]This table may be used also to approximate squares and square roots of larger numbers. For example,

$$(a + 1)^2 = a^2 + 2a + 1 \qquad \text{alternatively, } (a + b)^2 = a^2 + 2ab + b^2$$
$$\therefore 73^2 = 72^2 + 2(72) + 1 \qquad \therefore 73^2 = (70 + 3)^2 = 70^2 + 2(70)(3) + 3^2$$
$$= (36 \cdot 2)^2 + 145 \qquad\qquad\qquad = 4900 + 420 + 9$$
$$= (1296 \cdot 4) + 145 \qquad\qquad\qquad = 5329.$$

Therefore, $\qquad\qquad\qquad 73^2 = 5184 + 145 = 5329.$

Similarly, $\qquad\qquad\qquad \sqrt{73} = > \sqrt{72}$ and $< \sqrt{74}$ $\sqrt{72} < \sqrt{73} < \sqrt{74}$
$$\sqrt{72} = \sqrt{36(2)} = 6\sqrt{2} = 8.484$$
$$\sqrt{74} = \sqrt{37} \sqrt{2} = 8.601$$

Therefore, $\qquad\qquad\qquad \sqrt{73} \simeq 8.542$, the mean of 8.484 and 8.601.

Actually, $\qquad\qquad\qquad \sqrt{73} = 8.544$, to which 8.542 is very close.

For less arithmetic, $\qquad\qquad \sqrt{72} = 6\sqrt{2} = 6(1.4) = 8.40$
$$\sqrt{74} = (6.1)(1.4) = 8.54$$

Therefore, $\qquad\qquad\qquad \sqrt{73} \simeq 8.47$

Answer $\qquad\qquad\qquad \sqrt{73} \simeq 8.5$, correct at the same level of exactness.

[b]Larger tables of these factors may be found in such handbooks as Fisher and Yates (1949) and Beyer (1966).

the chance probability that a given t is 5 percent and 1 percent. The 5 percent level is attained when $t = 1.96$, and the 1 percent is $t = 2.58$. For the sake of simplicity we ususally consider these critical levels as $t = 2$ and $t = 2.5$, respectively.

Let us illustrate this t-test by an example. 22 marriages between blood type M and MN persons (Table 1–4) produced 228 children of which 127 were type M and 101 MN. Our theorectical expectation is a ratio of 1 M:1 MN. Do the observed results differ significantly from theory? Here,

$$\text{Each expected result} = \frac{1}{2}(228) = 114$$

$$\text{Standard error} = \sqrt{\frac{(114)(114)}{228}}$$

$$= \sqrt{57}$$

$$1 \text{ S.E.} = 7.5\dagger$$

$$\text{Deviation from expected} = \text{Observed} - \text{Expected}$$

$$= 127 - 114 = 13$$

$$= 101 = 114 = -13$$

$$t = \frac{\text{deviation}}{1 \text{ S.E.}}$$

$$= \frac{\pm 13}{7.5}$$

$$t = \pm 1.73$$

From our table, we see that the probability of obtaining this much deviation by chance is greater than 5 percent. In fact a difference of this amount or more would be found by chance about 10 percent of the time. We may conclude therefore that we do not need any other explanation than chance sampling error to explain why we did not find exactly 114 M and 114 MN.

On the other hand, Sanders (1938) found that his 140 Dutch families of normal parents that had at least one albino child contained altogether 486 normal and 216 albino children. Let us test the hypothesis that this fits a 3:1 ratio. In this example let us use decimals, to illustrate a different computational method.

$$\text{Expected results: } p = 0.75$$

$$q = 0.25$$

$$\text{S.E.} = \sqrt{\frac{(0.75)(0.25)}{702}}$$

$$= \sqrt{\frac{0.1875}{702}}$$

$$1 \text{ S.E.} = \sqrt{0.00267}$$

$$= 0.0163$$

---

†To use *Appendix* Table A1, we would say $\sqrt{57} = \sim \sqrt{4 \times 14} = \sim 2\sqrt{14} = \sim 2(3.742) = \sim 7.484 = \sim 7.5$. Or, $\sqrt{57}$ is about halfway between $\sqrt{56}$ and $\sqrt{58}$; $\sqrt{56} = 2\sqrt{14} = 7.48$, and $\sqrt{58} = \sqrt{29}\sqrt{2} \cong 7.56$; so $\sqrt{57} \cong 7.52$.

Actual results: normals = 0.6923
albinos = 0.3077
deviation = 0.3077 − 0.2500 and 0.6932 − 0.7500

$$t = \frac{\text{Deviation}}{\text{S.E.}}$$

$$= -\frac{0.0577}{0.0163}$$

$$t = \pm 3.540$$

Checking Table A2 we find that the probability that a deviation this large would arise by chance alone is less than 0.001, hence, very highly significant.

Table A2 Cumulative probability and t in the normal distribution;[a] column A shows P for a given t and column B the magnitude t needs to be for a given P

A		B	
t	P[b]	P[b]	t
0.0	1.000	0.9	0.126
0.2	0.840	0.8	0.253
0.5	0.617	0.7	0.385
0.8	0.423	0.6	0.524
1.0	0.317	0.5	0.674
1.2	0.230	0.4	0.842
1.5	0.133	0.3	0.036
1.8	0.071	0.2	1.282
1.9	0.057	0.1	1.645
2.0	0.045	0.05	1.960
2.2	0.027	0.02	2.326
2.3	0.021	0.01	2.576
2.5	0.012	0.001	3.291
2.6	0.0093	0.0001	3.89
2.8	0.0053		
2.9	0.0037		
3.0	0.0027		
3.2	0.0014		
3.3	0.0010		
3.4	0.0007		
3.9	0.0001		

[a]More fully: the probability due to chance alone that the number of standard errors in an observed deviation from expected in a large normally distributed population will be a number at least as great as $\pm t$ (greater than $+t$ or less than $-t$).

[b]Strictly speaking these P values are derived from a normal distribution of an infinite number of variates and are exactly correct only for infinitely large samples. They are closely approximated, however, in most samples from such a distribution, especially if they contain 30 variates or more. For example, in the usual sample of 30 (29 degrees of freedom), P is 0.05 when $t = 2.045$, instead of 1.960 shown here; when t is 1.960 for such a sample, the true P is about 0.062. The approximation is nearly perfect when the sample size is 60 or more. Some of the more exact readings for small samples can be found in table III of Fisher and Yates (1949), and a close approximation gained from the curves in the right half of Figure 8–3.

Clearly, it is highly unlikely that the data as shown fit a 3:1 ratio. We have already discussed the probable reason for this discrepancy.

Despite its simplicity, the t-test has only limited usefulness in genetics, because it is not particularly suitable when there are more than two alternatives in the data. For multivariated data we usually use the chi-square (χ^2) test, based on chance distributions that are special derivations from the normal curve. Developed by Karl Pearson, about the same time Mendel's work was rediscovered, and publicized by R. A. Fisher (1925 and subsequent editions), this test is one of the most widely used by geneticists. It may be applied to binomial data as well as more complex series.

As a first step, a hypothesis is formulated to explain a set of measurements or counts. Each observed value is compared with the one expected under the hypothesis. The deviation between them is squared and then divided by the expected value. The sum of these quotients is called chi-square, that is,

$$\chi^2 = \sum \frac{(\text{observed-expected})^2}{\text{expected}}$$
$$= \sum \frac{d^2}{e}$$

Σ is the Greek letter used to indicate summation. Unlike the t-test, ratios cannot be used in the calculations. Only the actual counts or measurements are permissible.

Since it represents a sum of positive numbers, chi-square is bound to be larger as the number variates or items of data increases, even were every one very close to the figure expected in the tested hypothesis. Therefore, there are many chi-square distributions, depending on the number of items of data (Fig. 8–3). Technically, we say that the chance distribution of chi-squares is different for each number of "degrees of freedom," defined as the number of items of data that may be arbitrarily introduced and still have the same totals. To show how to find the number of degrees of freedom and determine which chi-square distribution applies, we will work out examples of the two types of tests for which χ^2 is mainly used: (1) heterogeneity and (2) goodness of fit.

As an example of the first, we might wish to compare the progeny from the aforementioned M × MN matings on the assumption that they are homogeneous, that it makes no difference whether M is the father or M is the mother. Putting the data into a tabular form with totals, we have:

| | Progeny | | |
Mating	M	MN	Total
M father × MN mother	67	46	113
M mother × MN father	60	55	115
Total	127	103	228

We see that 127/228 of all the children are M. If our hypothesis is correct, the children of M fathers have as much chance of being M, relative to their numbers, as the children of M mothers. If so, 127/228 of the 113 children of M fathers and

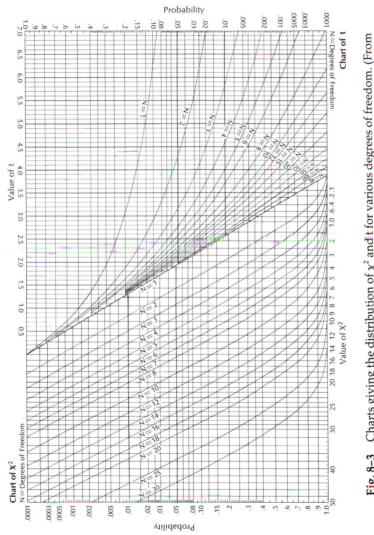

Fig. 8-3 Charts giving the distribution of χ^2 and t for various degrees of freedom. (From James F. Crow, *Genetic Notes*, 8th ed., 1983, Reprinted by permission of Burgess Publishing Company.)

127/228 of the 115 children of M mothers should be type M, etc. Our expected values on this hypothesis, therefore, are:

	M	MN	Total
M father	62.9*	50.1*	113.0
M mother	64.1	50.9	115.0
Total	127.0	101.0	228.0

This is known as a *contingency* table, and the items of data (not the totals) are referred to as *cells* of the contingency table.

How many degrees of freedom are there? The cell "M children of M fathers" certainly can vary arbitrarily. Suppose there were 20. Once this number was known all the other cells would be fixed by the totals. MN from M fathers would have to be 93; M children from M mothers would have to be 107; and MN children from MN mothers would have to be 8. Therefore, for this hypothesis (and contingency table) the four items of data have but *one* degree of freedom.

Note that the data in the above example contained two rows and two columns. For most situations of this type,

$$N = \text{degrees of freedom} = (r - 1)(c - 1).$$

For our 2 × 2 table, $\quad\quad r = 2 \text{ and } c = 2;$

so, $$N = (2 - 1)(2 - 1)$$
$$= 1.$$

Where there is only one column, generally, $N = r - 1$. However, one must be careful to examine each set of data and hypothesis being tested to determine the number of degrees of freedom.

In the example cited above, the calculations may be set up in the tabular form thus,

Variant	Observed o	Expected e	Deviation $o - e$	$\dfrac{d^2}{e}$
M from M father	67	62.9	+4.1	0.27
M from M mother	60	64.1	−4.1	0.26
MN from M father	46	50.1	−4.1	0.34
MN from M mother	55	50.9	+4.1	0.33
Totals	228	228.0	0.0	$1.20 = \chi^2$

Looking on the $N = 1$ of the χ^2 table (Table A3), we do not find 1.20. However, 1.20 is between 1.074 and 1.642, indicating that P is between 0.20 and 0.30. Similarly on the chart (Fig. 8–3) we find the approximate position of 1.20 on the horizontal line and direct a perpendicular to it at that point until we reach the curve of $N = 1$. At the intersection we read P on the left to be about 0.25. Since P is more than 0.05, we conclude that the observed deviations stem from chance alone, and we may accept the hypothesis that the progeny of these M and MN matings pro-

*Although it seems absurd to expect 9/10 to 1/10 of a person to be M, we must remember these are theoretical figures.

Table A3 Distributions of χ^2 (Based on Fisher and Yates, 1949, Table IV, courtesy of Oliver and Boyd, Ltd.)

N	Probability											
	.99	.90	.80	.70	.50	.30	.20	.10	.05	.02	.01	.001
1	0.03¹57	0.0158	0.0642	0.148	0.455	1.074	1.642	2.706	3.841	5.412	6.635	10.827
2	0.0201	0.211	0.446	0.713	1.386	2.408	3.219	4.605	5.991	7.824	9.210	13.815
3	0.115	0.584	1.005	1.424	2.366	3.665	4.642	6.251	7.815	9.837	11.345	16.268
4	0.297	1.064	1.649	2.195	3.357	4.878	5.989	7.779	9.488	11.668	13.277	18.465
5	0.554	1.610	2.343	3.000	4.351	6.064	7.289	9.236	11.070	13.388	15.086	20.517
6	0.872	2.204	3.070	3.828	5.348	7.231	8.558	10.645	12.592	15.033	16.812	22.457
7	1.239	2.833	3.822	4.671	6.346	8.383	9.803	12.017	14.067	16.622	18.475	24.322
8	1.646	3.490	4.594	5.527	7.344	9.524	11.030	13.362	15.507	18.168	20.090	26.125
9	2.088	4.168	5.380	6.393	8.343	10.656	12.242	14.684	16.919	19.679	21.666	27.877
10	2.558	4.865	6.179	7.267	9.342	11.781	13.442	15.987	18.307	21.161	23.209	29.588
11	3.053	5.578	6.989	8.148	10.341	12.899	14.631	17.275	19.675	22.618	24.725	31.264
12	3.571	6.304	7.807	9.034	11.340	14.011	15.812	18.549	21.026	24.054	26.217	32.909
13	4.107	7.042	8.634	9.926	12.340	15.119	16.985	19.812	22.362	25.472	27.688	34.528
14	4.660	7.790	9.467	10.821	13.339	16.222	18.151	21.064	23.685	26.873	29.141	36.123
15	5.229	8.547	10.307	11.721	14.339	17.322	19.311	22.307	24.996	28.259	30.578	37.697
16	5.812	9.312	11.152	12.624	15.338	18.418	20.465	23.542	26.296	29.633	32.000	39.252
17	6.408	10.085	12.002	13.531	16.338	19.511	21.615	24.769	27.587	30.995	33.409	40.790
18	7.015	10.865	12.857	14.440	17.338	20.601	22.760	25.989	28.869	32.346	34.805	42.312
19	7.633	11.651	13.716	15.352	18.338	21.689	23.900	27.204	30.144	33.687	36.191	43.820
20	8.260	12.443	14.578	16.266	19.337	22.775	25.038	28.412	31.410	35.020	37.566	45.315
21	8.897	13.240	15.445	17.182	20.337	23.858	26.171	29.615	32.671	36.343	38.932	46.797
22	9.542	14.041	16.314	18.101	21.337	24.939	27.301	30.813	33.924	37.659	40.289	48.268
23	10.196	14.848	17.187	19.021	22.337	26.018	28.429	32.007	35.172	38.968	41.638	49.728
24	10.856	15.659	18.062	19.943	23.337	27.096	29.553	33.196	36.415	40.270	42.980	51.179
25	11.524	16.473	18.940	20.867	24.337	28.172	30.675	34.382	37.652	41.566	44.314	52.620
26	12.198	17.292	19.820	21.792	25.336	29.246	31.795	35.563	38.885	42.856	45.642	54.052
27	12.879	18.114	20.703	22.719	26.336	30.319	32.912	36.741	40.113	44.140	46.963	55.476
28	13.565	18.939	21.588	23.647	27.336	31.391	34.027	37.916	41.337	45.419	48.278	56.893
29	14.256	19.768	22.475	24.577	28.336	32.461	35.139	39.087	42.557	46.693	49.488	58.302
30	14.953	20.509	23.364	25.508	29.336	33.530	36.250	40.256	43.773	47.962	50.892	59.703

For larger values of N, the expression $\sqrt{2\chi^2} - \sqrt{2N - 1}$ may be used as though it were t in a standard t-test, remembering that the probability of χ^2 corresponds with that of a single tail of the normal curve. This means that P is half of that shown in Table A2, part A.

duce essentially the same results. In technical parlance we would say, "the chi-square test indicates no significant *heterogeneity* between the progeny of M × MN and MN × M matings."

Absence of heterogeneity is a prerequisite before we can pool these two items of data to determine how well the backcross *fits* the 1:1 ratio expected under Mendel's first law. Our "goodness of fit" test would look thus:

Progeny	o	e	d	$\dfrac{d^2}{e}$
M	127	114.0	$+13.0$	1.474
MN	101	114.0	-13.0	1.474
Total	228	228.0	0.0	$2.948 = \chi^2$

Again we have one degree of freedom. From our table we see that P is slightly less than 0.10, but greater than 0.05, thus confirming the t-test.

Another way of looking at these data illustrates how the same set of data can have different degrees of freedom depending on how the contingency table, that is, the underlying hypothesis, is propounded. Consider the chi-squares testing, individually, the goodness of fit of the M × MN and MN × M matings:

	chi-square testing fit to 1:1 ratio	N
M × MN	3.902	1
MN × M	0.218	1
Total	4.120	2

Fisher showed that the sum of chi-squares also have a chi-square distribution. Its number of degrees of freedom is equal to the sum of degrees of freedom of the added chi-squares. The chi-square above of 4.120 with two degrees of freedom has a probability between 0.10 and 0.20 of arising by chance alone, another indication that we may accept the hypothesis that these data fit a 1:1 ratio.

Textbooks usually warn the student not to use the chi-square test unless every cell of the contingency table of expected values is 5 or more. When one of the cells has a value of less than 5, the true probability is usually larger than the P given in the χ^2 table. Even when there are only two degrees of freedom and the smallest expectation is 0.5, however, the true probability rarely exceeds the tabular P by more than 0.01, so that it is still about the same order of magnitude. For example, if there are three degrees of freedom and there are two expectations as small as 1.0, the χ^2 that has P of 0.0500 in the table really has a P of 0.0592, and the χ^2 that has P of 0.01 in the table really has a P of 0.0177. Therefore, if we did a test that contained two expectations that small and obtained a χ^2 whose P seemed to be slightly less than 0.01, the χ^2 would not really be highly significant, *but it would be very close to it.* If the calculated χ^2 seemed to be just below 0.05, it might really be just above 0.05.

The upshot is that we need not desist from doing χ^2 tests when a few of the cells have expected values less than 5; we should just be a bit more cautious about our conclusions. A safe rule of thumb would be to tack on an extra 0.01 (1 percent if expressed as a percent) to the tabular P when there are small cells. In general, the conclusion will be about the same. If P seems to be about 0.04, assuming that it is really 0.045 or 0.05 doesn't change the conclusion that the deviations are of borderline significance.

Expectations below 0.5 seem to cause more error in reading the tables, so they should probably be avoided. They should be coalesced with adjacent cells, if this can be done meaningfully.

If there is only one degree of freedom, a correction "for continuity" devised by Fisher's colleague Yates should be employed if there are cells with values less than 5. One-half (0.5) is subtracted from each deviation and the rest of the test performed as before.

CONFIDENCE INTERVALS

Very frequently the results of an experiment or a survey are shown as a number followed by another number preceded by $\pm$, for example, 8.75 ± 0.83, where $\pm$ 0.83 represents *confidence limits* for the main result (8.75). Confidence limits usually indicate the values or results of the experiment for which we will accept the null hypothesis. To put it another way, when we accept the null hypothesis we are in effect saying that we are confident that the observed deviations from our hypothesis are ascribable to chance (and therefore need not be attributed to any mistake in our hypothesis or the way the experiment was done). The confidence limits tells us in what range we can feel this confidence.

For example, in a mating of MN $\times$ N genetic theory tells us to expect 50 percent N children and 50 percent MN. If we count 100 progeny from such matings, we can calculate

in decimals

$$\text{S.E.} = \sqrt{\frac{0.50 \times 0.50}{100}}$$
$$= \pm 0.05$$

in whole numbers

$$\text{S.E.} = \sqrt{\frac{50 \times 50}{100}}$$
$$= \pm 5.$$

According to the normal curve, we expect that by chance roughly 95 percent of all the times we count 100 progeny we would differ from the expected result by less than two standard errors. In other words we feel 95 percent confident that chance will cause our fraction of either type to fall in the range 0.40 to 0.60 or, in whole numbers, between 40 of one type and 60 of the other. We say, "the 95 percent confidence limits of this study are 40 and 60."

However, one would often not wish to prejudice the reader as to what level of significance he should choose. He may not be the same kind of gambler, as it were.

Therefore the convention in this type of case is simply to state the result and the standard error (or, less often, the standard deviation).

In a way, the progeny count from an MN × N mating is an unfortunate example with which to introduce the idea of confidence limits because the standard error is based on an *expected* rather than an actual result. Hence, the usual method of reporting the result could be misleading. If we actually obtained 57 MN and 43 N, and we reported this as: 57 ± 5 percent MN, we would be implying, incorrectly, that the null hypothesis is acceptable at the 95 percent level between 47 and 67. Where we base our expected value on an *a priori* probability, therefore, the best way to report these data is: "57 percent MN when we expect 50 ± 5 percent," or, "57 percent MN with 95 percent confidence limits between 40 and 60 percent."

Since it is so easy for the knowledgeable reader to calculate his own standard error when the hypothesis establishes a clear *a priori* probability, it is even possible to dispense with confidence limits in such a case. Confidence limits are more important when the researcher ventures into uncharted seas, with no preformed numerical hypothesis to test. Here two related measures of spread (variance) in the data are commonly encountered: the standard deviation and the standard error of the mean. When they are not expressly defined, stated confidence limits almost always refer nowadays to the latter, the standard error.

The standard deviation measures how likely it is that possible variates (measurements or items of data) could have appeared in the same sample. The standard error measures how likely it is that other samples derived from the same population would have means that are much different from the mean of this sample.

The standard deviation of a sample is the square root of its variance. How is the standard deviation or its square, the variance, calculated when there is no *a priori* probability? In effect the variance is an average of the second moment of the deviations, that is, an average of the squares of differences between each measurement and the sample mean. If we have N measurements, any given one of which is X_i, whose mean is $\overline{X}$

$$s = \text{S.D.} = \sqrt{\frac{\sum_{i=1}^{N} (X_i - \overline{X})^2}{N - 1}}$$

If, for example, we had the following eleven measurements: 8, 9, 5, 4, 6, 17, 9, 3, 12, 8, 7,

$$\overline{X} = \frac{88}{11} = 8.0$$

$$\sum (X - \overline{X})^2 = 154$$

$$N - 1 = 10$$

$$s^2 = \frac{154}{10} = 15.4$$

$$s = \pm 3.9$$

Using the sample standard deviation allows the *t*-test to be used even when the *a priori* probability or the whole populational distribution is unknown, provided that it is reasonably likely that the sample is a random one. We might ask, for example, what is the probability that a measurement of one belongs to the same distribution set.

$$d = X - \bar{X} = 1 - 8 = -7$$

$$t = \left| \frac{d}{s} \right|$$

$$t = \left| \frac{-7}{3.9} \right| = 1.89$$

This deviation would not be significant even for a very large sample (Table A2), and certainly not so when S.D. has been calculated from a sample of 11. For such a sample t would need to be 2.228 or more for significance (table III of Fisher and Yates, 1949, or right side Fig. 8–3 for $N = 10$).

Thus the standard deviation, by taking into account the way the data "clusters," is a more meaningful measurement of spread than the range. The variate one, for example, is outside the range of this sample (from 3 to 17), but well within the spread of two standard deviations. Hence the standard deviation can be useful to indicate whether related samples overlap. Consider Table 5–3, for instance. The data on diaphorase activity may be taken as representative. In the original report (Scott, 1960) these results are presented as follows:

Sample	Number Studied	Mean Activity	Standard Deviation	Range
Abnormal homozygotes	14	0.9	2.1	−3 to 5
Heterozygotes	13	21.8	4.4	15 to 28
Normal homozygotes	88	45.5	8.5	28 to 81

The report tells us that the standard deviation of the heterozygote measurements is 4.4. If we can assume that observed variations from the mean are due to chance and are, therefore, normally distributed, then approximately 95 percent of variates would be expected to fall by chance in the group

$$21.8 \pm 2(4.4)$$
$$= 21.8 \pm 8.8,$$

or to range *between 13.0 and 30.6.*

The same study shows that the 95 percent probability range of the normal homozygotes is $45.5 \pm 2 (8.5)$, or between 28.5 and 62.5. Since the lower 95 percent limit, 28.5, overlaps the upper 95 percent limit for the heterozygotes, we cannot really feel secure that all the variates in the two samples are classified correctly. A person with a measurement of 29, for example, could easily belong to either group if no other information is available. On the other hand, the 95 percent probability range of the abnormal homozygotes is $0.9 \pm 2 (2.1)$. These 95 percent limits are between -3.3 and 5.1. This upper limit is considerably less than the corresponding lower limit for the heterozygotes (13.0), indicating that any person with a measurement in the abnormal homozygote range is not very likely to be mistaken for a member of the heterozygote sample.

When measurements of this type are made, it is hoped that the observed mean will give a clue to the true mean of all the members of the class, not just the persons that were tested. In short, it is hoped that the population mean (say, of the whole population of heterozygotes) is indicated by the mean of the sample (of heterozygotes). However, we do not know what the true population mean is, nor do we have any *a priori* expected value for it. The *standard error of the mean* gives us some idea of how close the observed mean brings us to a characterization of the real mean of the category. Its statistical usefulness stems from the fact that the sample means from a randomly distributed population are themselves randomly distributed. The variance of *this* population (the population of means), σ^2, is the square of the aforementioned standard error of the mean. It can often be calculated from the standard deviation of the sample by the relation,

$$\sigma^2 = \frac{s^2}{N}$$

or

$$\text{S.E.}_m = \sigma_m = \frac{s}{\sqrt{N}}$$

Strictly speaking, σ should refer to the true standard deviation of the whole population (which is, of course, unknown), and a σ calculated from the sample s is not really that of a normal distribution. It closely approximates that of a normal distribution, however, especially if N is 30 or greater (see footnotes to Table A2), so that this calculation of the standard error of the mean is valid for all practical purposes. In fact, the distribution of sample means generally approaches a normal distribution even in situations where the sample is drawn from a population that is not normally distributed.

One could calculate standard errors of the means in the data on p. 000 and obtain some idea whether the method used leads to significantly different samples. The tabulation would then be as follows:

Sample	Number	Mean	s	σ
Abnormal homozygotes	14	0.9	2.1	0.56
Heterozygotes	13	21.8	4.4	1.22
Normal homozygotes	88	45.5	8.5	0.91

These figures mean that 95 percent of time that we sample normal homozygotes for this locus by this method we would probably obtain a mean which is

$$45.5 \pm 2(0.91),$$

that is,

$$45.5 \pm 1.82,$$

or, *between 43.7 and 47.3.*

Similarly, 95 percent of the time the means of samples of heterozygotes would be expected to range between 19.4 and 24.2. Clearly, the means of the heterozygote and normal homozygote samples are significantly different at the 5 percent level since there is no overlap at that level. Theoretically, chance could produce a sample of one group with a mean that overlapped the sample mean of the other, but the calculated parameters state that this would be expected to happen by chance less than 5 percent of the time.

SUGGESTED EXERCISES

Several forms of intestinal polyposis are inherited in a manner similar to the traits in Table 1–3. One of these, multiple polyposis of the colon tends to be premalignant. Although the cancer development varies in age of onset, polyps are almost always present in an affected person (and the trait may be diagnosed confidently) by the third decade. In working the exercises it should be assumed that these points are always true: that the trait is 100 percent penetrant by a certain age.

8–1. The mother and the wife of a man with multiple polyposis of the colon are free of the trait. His eldest child exhibits the trait.

   (a)   What is the probability that his next child will prove to exhibit the trait?

   (b)   If the aforementioned second child (a boy) proves to be free of the disease, what is the probability that of the next two children after him one will have the disease and one be free of it?

   (c)   What would have been your estimate of the probability of this four-child sibship, two affected and two not, had you been asked before any children had been born to this couple?

   (d)   If your answer to (c) differs from the answers to (a) or (b), explain in a few phrases why this is so.

8–2. From the chromosomal considerations outlined in Chapter 1 it is expected that the primary sex ratio, the ratio of males to females conceived ought to be 1:1. If this is in fact true, what is the probability

   (a)   that two conceptions in a row will be male?

   (b)   that the first will be male and the second female?

   (c)   that one of the two will be male and one female?

   (d)   that two out of four consecutive conceptions will be male and two female?

8–3. The actual primary sex ratio is not known, but the human secondary sex ratio, the ratio of males to females at birth, is known to vary in different populations. In almost all of them it is greater than unity (one). In one population the secondary sex ratio has been consistently very close to 1.05 for the past two decades.

   (a)   What is the probability that the next child born in this group will be a boy? a girl?

   (b)   How would you characterize this type of probability?

   (c)   Answer the questions in exercise 8–2 (b), (c), and (d) on the assumption that they were referring to births in the population of exercise 8–3 instead of conceptions.

   (d)   What percentage of error would be introduced by assuming the secondary sex ratio was 1:1?

8–4. (a) If one had been asked to calculate the probability of the entire sequence of births in generation IV of Fig. 8–4 prior to their occurrence what would have

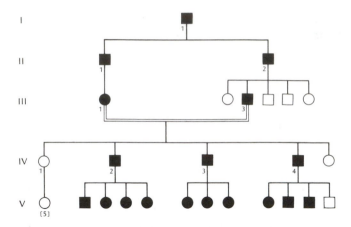

Fig. 8-4 A pedigree of congenital cataract. After Komai (1934). (From Roberts, 1967.)

been the answer? The desired answer is in terms of the trait only and is not concerned with the sex of the offspring.

(b) Answer the same type of question for the sequence of births in generation V of the same pedigree. You may assume that the affected members of generation IV married persons who lacked the trait.

8-5. A couple's first child shows the Aldrich (Wiskott–Aldrich) syndrome, an X-linked recessive lethal.

(a) What is the probable sex of this child?

(b) If the couple's next four children were 2 boys and 2 girls, what is the probability that two of the children would show the same disorder as the first child and two would not?

8-6. In two different families a trait has appeared in male siblings who die before reaching reproductive age. How many births of this type should be recorded before one feels secure at the 1 percent level that if a lethal gene is responsible it is probably X-linked?

8-7. A woman had two brothers with Duchenne type muscular dystropy, another X-linked recessive. Her husband is normal, and they have five children. If her five children—3 girls and 2 boys, turn out to be normal, what is the posterior probability.

(a) That all 3 girls are heterozygous for the dystrophy gene?

(b) That two of the three are heterozygous for it?

8-8. A hemophiliac (AHG deficiency) boy is born. Neither of his parents nor his grandparents exhibit the disorder, but his maternal great-uncle (grandmother's brother) did. The boy's older sister has had two daughters, neither of whom suffer from hemophilia. She is worried, however, about having another child. She asks you about it.

(a) How could you answer her?

(b) Suppose she does not have any further children (because of or in spite of your counseling). What is the probability that if the hemophiliac boy's nieces marry

history will repeat itself in this case, namely, that the boy will have a grand-nephew with hemophilia?

8-9. Determine whether the four sets of data in Table 1-3 are homogeneous.

8-10. Determine in two ways whether the four sets of data in Table 1-3 fit the expected ratio: (a) by a chi-square test of the total; (b) by adding the chi-squares for the individual reports.

8-11. Assuming a secondary sex ratio of 1:1, what sex ratio would you expect to find in a compilation of all the families of two children having at least one boy?

8-12. Cystic fibrosis of the pancreas (Chapter 13) appears to be due to homozygosity for an autosomal gene that is recessive to its normal allele.

What ratio of normal to affected offspring would be expected in a random sample of five-child sibships in which at least one child was born with the disorder?

8-13. The data of Blumberg et al. (1966) quoted in Table 8-10 contain the following distribution of sibships:

A Negative	B Positive	C Number of Sibships
0	1	8
1	1	2
0	2	1
2	1	3
2	2	2
3	1	1
4	1	1
3	2	1
5	1	1
4	2	2
6	1	1
4	4	1

Analyze these data by (1) the direct sib method and compare with the analysis in Table 8-10; (b) on the assumption that the data were obtained by single selection. If the responsible gene really is a recessive, do the data contradict the hypothesis of single selection?

8-14. Familial dysautonomia (Riley–Day syndrome) is a severe neuromuscular disorder whose major symptoms include a characteristic facies with wide mouth, difficulty in feeding and swallowing, relative insensitivity to pain, absence of tears, skin blotching, excessive sweating, breath-holding attacks, episodic vomiting, motor uncoordination, and often include posterior or paroxysmal hypertension and scoliosis. About 50 percent have died by the age of 20, most of these from pulmonary infections. It is one of the genetic diseases* found much more often

---

*Including also polycythemia vera, at least one form each of Tay-Sachs disease and Gaucher's disease, Niemann–Pick's disease, diabetes, and pentosuria, among others.

among persons of Ashkenazi Jewish descent than among their non-Jewish neighbors.

McKusick et al (1967) sought all of the families in the United States and Canada with at least one child with the disease born to normal parents. Their 164 reported sibships were distributed as follows:

Affected Children	Normal Children	Number of Sibships
1	0	28
1	1	58
2	0	13
1	2	30
2	1	8
3	0	1
2	2	5
1	3	8
3	2	2
1	4	3
3	3	1
2	4	1

Compare the Bernstein *a priori* (using Table 8–9) and Li–Mantel methods to test the hypothesis that the trait is due to homozygosity for a recessive gene in these families.

8–15. Test the hypothesis that the sibships with two, three, and four children in the familial dysautonomia data represent a random sample of sibships of that size under the circumstances in which the data were collected.

8–16. You have a completely ascertained sample in which each sibship contains at least one boy. If the sex ratio to be expected were 1.05:1, what would be the expected frequency and number of boys per sibship of three? The sex ratio is usually stated as boys:girls.

9

The Random Mating Law

A great deal of information about genetics can be obtained by studying the distribution of traits in a population without looking into the situation in specific families. One of the commonest findings is that human populations usually fit the results that would be expected if their progenitors had mated at random.

A population is characterized by random mating if the probability that two given genotypes will mate can be calculated in the same way as the probability that any two independent events will happen simultaneously by chance; namely, if it is the product of the proportions of the population that the genotypes in question constitute. If 50 percent of a group are A/a and 20 percent are a/a, for example, it would constitute a random mating population if the proportion of marriages in which both husband and wife are A/a is $(0.50)^2$ or 0.25, the proportion in which the husband is A/a and the wife a/a, 0.10 ($= 0.50 \times 0.20$), and so forth.

The student may well be disturbed by this statement. How can one assume human marriages are similar to chance events? Is it not well known that human beings choose their mates with great care, often only after prolonged courtships? This is, of course, in general true, but the evidence indicates that these meticulous choices are rarely based on genetic criteria. The parties to a marriage do not usually evaluate each other's genes. Generally, their concern is with social position, worldly goods, and such intangible qualities as "character," ability to be a good provider (or a good cook), "social compatibility," and the like, in which genetic factors, to the extent that they are involved at all, probably play only a small role. Considerations of physique, height, weight, beauty, hair color, and eye color, probably include a greater degree of genetic involvement, but subjective factors play such a large part that the bias reaches in all directions. Whatever genetic factors may in fact be discriminated against in marriage practices, they must be independent of the bulk of gene loci that have been studied, for by and large the assumption of random mating has been found to fit human population data amazingly well. The only significant exceptions have come, as expected, in the occasional pockets of population ("isolates") where the choice of mates is limited to a small number of families. These will be discussed later, in the chapter concerned with *assortative* mating, in which certain genotypes mate much more frequently than expected by chance.

A population undergoing random mating is often referred to as a *panmictic* population, or it is said to be in a state of *panmixia.*

Several additional assumptions are necessary for a theoretical demonstration of the effect of random mating. These are:

1. *No natural selection.* This means that no type of marriage produces a greater proportion of the progeny of the following generation than would be expected by the probability of the marriage. If the marriages between heterozygotes are 25 percent of the total marriages, they produce 25 percent of the progeny. Were they to produce 30 percent of the progeny, some other genotypes (marriages) would be producing less than their share and therefore selected against. Similarly, 12.5 percent of the progeny (half of 25) must be assumed to be heterozygotes stemming from these marriages between heterozygotes. Were 15 percent of the progeny heterozygotes from these marriages, that would again constitute natural selection because the A/A or a/a progeny (or both) would account for less than their expected share, one-fourth of 25 or 6.25 percent each.

2. *No changes in the proportion of alleles* due to differential mutation, migration, or chance factors.

3. *No differences between the two sexes in proportions of alleles.* That this would be true for most autosomal loci is obvious enough, but we shall see later that the populations of males and females generally have or would quickly obtain similar amounts of X-linked and sex-influenced genes as well, and this is true even though the two sexes differ greatly in the numbers exhibiting the traits determined by these genes.

4. *Large populations.* The theoretical need for this assumption seems apparent when we consider that a trait such as albinism has a frequency of about 0.00005, one per 20,000 individuals, and albinism is by no means the rarest trait for which the random mating law seems to fit rather well in human populations. Random mating between two albinos, for example, would be expected only once in four billion (1 per 4×10^9, or 2.5×10^{-10}) marriages. In reality, the population need not be so forbiddingly large. As a matter of fact, we shall note in our examples that data from populations with amazingly small numbers often fit the random mating law very closely.

Let us now examine what would be expected under random mating in several hypothetical populations. For simplicity, we shall consider first an autosomal locus with two alleles, A and a. Suppose a population contains 85 percent A/A, 10 percent A/a, and 5 percent a/a and now undergoes random mating. The various matings and expected progeny are given in Table 9–1. The expected result is a new set of genotype frequencies: 81 percent A/A, 18 percent A/a, and 1 percent a/a. Each homozygous type decreased, and the heterozygotes increased.

The student may verify (exercise 9–14) that the same result, 81:18:1, would be expected if we had begun with, say, 88 percent A/A, 4 percent A/a, and 8 percent a/a. On the other hand it is possible for the homozygous types to increase and the heterozygotes to decrease, as would be expected, for example, to occur if our initial values were 80 percent A/A, 20 percent A/a, and 0 a/a.

The next question might be: What would happen if you had random mating

Table 9-1 Progeny expected from random mating in a population initially consisting of 85 percent A/A, 10 percent A/a, and 5 percent a/a

Mating	Frequency	Expected Progeny		
		A/A	A/a	a/a
$A/A \times A/A$	0.7225	0.7225		
$A/A \times A/a$	0.0850	0.0425	0.0425	
$A/A \times a/a$	0.0425		0.0425	
$A/a \times A/A$	0.0850	0.0425	0.0425	
$A/a \times A/a$	0.0100	0.0025	0.0050	0.0025
$A/a \times a/a$	0.0050		0.0025	0.0025
$a/a \times A/A$	0.0425		0.0425	
$a/a \times A/a$	0.0050		0.0025	0.0025
$a/a \times a/a$	0.0025			0.0025
Total	1.0000	0.8100	0.1800	0.0100

in the 81:18:1 population attained in each of these cases? A similar bit of arithmetic would show that the result would again be 81 percent A/A, 18 percent A/a, and 1 percent a/a. Clearly, once this populational distribution has been reached random mating would produce no further change. Such a phenomenon, where there is considerable activity but no overall change, is a state of equilibrium. Random mating, then, leads to an equilibrium in genotype frequencies.

Does random mating always lead to the same equilibrium? The student can readily verify that it does not. A population consisting initially of 20 percent A/A, 20 percent A/a, and 60 percent a/a, for example, will reach equilibrium at 9 percent A/A, 42 percent A/a, and 49 percent a/a after a single generation.

So would an initial 5 A/A:50 A/a:45 a/a. Likewise, 1:58:41. And many others.

The student might ask, wherein did these populations differ, that one group leads to an equilibrium at 81:18:1, whereas the others reach 9:42:49? It turns out that the question would be most fruitfully rephrased thus: What do the populations of the first group have in common that they reach equilibrium at 81:18:1, and what do the second group have in common that they change to 9:42:49?

The answer—and key factor in understanding random mating—comes from the ratio of A to a genes in each population. The proportion of each allele in the population is known as its *gene frequency*.

The simplest way to calculate gene frequencies is to ask "What proportion of the gametes produced by the population will contain the allele in question?" Consider the population with 85 percent A/A, 10 percent A/a, and 5 percent a/a. If there is no selection or mutation, the A/A individuals are expected to produce 85 percent of all the gametes produced in the population, and these would all contain the A gene. The A/a people would produce 10 percent of all the gametes, but half of them are expected to contain A and half a. Hence, the total production of A gametes is expected to be 85 percent plus 5 percent, or 90 percent. Likewise, the expectation of a gametes is 5 percent plus 5 percent, a total of 10 percent. A similar calculation for the 81:18:1 population is shown in Table 9–2.

The student may verify that the population with 80 percent A/A and 20 percent

Table 9–2 Proportion of A and a gametes expected in a
population consisting of 81 percent A/A, 18 percent A/a,
and 1 percent a/a

Genotype	Proportion of Gametes	Gametes Produced	
		A	a
A/a	0.81	0.81	
A/a	0.18	0.09	0.09
a/a	0.01		0.01
Total	1.00	0.90	0.10

A/a also has a 9:1 ratio of A and a gametes. On the other hand, all of the populations in the group leading to the 9:42:49 equilibrium contain gene frequencies of
30 percent A and 70 percent a.

If the student will now realize that random mating implies nothing more than
a random combination of the gametes produced by a population, he can see at a
glance why any population with a gene frequency of 90 percent A:10 percent a produces a population of 81 percent A/A, 18 percent A/a, and 1 percent a/a. A Punnett
square diagram, Figure 9–1, illustrates the point.

Similar calculations with the 3 A:7 a of the second set lead to 9 percent A/A,
42 percent A/a (21 percent from the union of A eggs and a sperm, plus 21 percent
from a eggs and A sperm), and 49 percent a/a.

Note that the probability of A/A progeny is, in each instance, the square of the
probability of the A gamete; the probability of the other homozygote, a/a, is the
square of the a proportion; and the probability of the heterozygotes is twice the
probability of A multiplied by the probability of a. This lends itself to a very neat
generalization: random mating under the conditions outlined will always result in
a population in which the proportion of each homozygote is the square of the probability of the allele involved, and the proportion of heterozygotes is twice the product of the probabilities of the alleles present.

This conclusion may be put in algebraic terms. Call the proportion of A genes
in a population p, and the proportion of a genes q. If these proportions are the same
in both sexes, then, with random mating:

$$(A/A) = p \cdot p = p^2$$
$$(a/a) = q \cdot q = q^2$$
$$(A/a) = p \cdot q + q \cdot p = 2pq.$$

MALE

Gametes	.90 A	.10 a
.90 A	.81 A/A	.09 A/a
.10 a	.09 a/A	.01 a/a

FEMALE

Final result: .81 A/A: .18 A/a: .01 a/a

Fig. 9–1 Random combinations of
gametes expected in a population containing 90 percent A and 10 percent a
genes.

If $p + q = 1$, which is merely a fancy way of saying that they are the only alleles present at this locus in the population, the general result may be written:

$$p^2 \; A/A{:}2pq \; A/a{:}q^2 \; a/a$$

or,

$$p^2 \; A/A{:}2p(1 - p) \; A/a{:}(1 - p)^2 \; a/a$$

or,

$$(1 - q)^2 \; A/A{:}2q(1 - q) \; A/a{:}q^2 \; a/a.$$

Of course, this is true no matter what the relative actions of A and a are, but we shall see later that the last form is particularly useful when A is dominant to a.

Note that $p^2 + 2pq + q^2$ is $(p + q)^2$. For this reason some refer to the random mating equilibrium as the binomial square law. More commonly it is spoken of as the Hardy–Weinberg equilibrium to honor the two men who formulated it almost simultaneously in 1908: G. H. Hardy, a British mathematician, and Wilhelm Weinberg, whom we met in Chapter 8. Others use the term "Castle–Hardy–Weinberg," in recognition of an even earlier, though less explicit, statement of the effects of random mating by William Castle, a pioneer American mammalian geneticist.

Table 9–3 presents a formal demonstration that $p^2{:}2pq{:}q^2$ is an equilibrium.

Our random mating generalization applies just as well when there are more than two alleles at a locus, as illustrated by the Punnett square, Figure 9–2, for three alleles, A^1, A^2, and A^3, with probabilities p, q, and r, respectively.

The Hardy–Weinberg law may also be applied to X-linked loci. Suppose 90 percent of all the X-chromosomes of a population contain a gene B and 10 percent its allele, b. This means that 90 percent of the gametes of each sex that contain an

Table 9–3 Proof that $p^2 \; A/A + 2pq \; A/a + q^2 \; a/a$ represents an equilibrium state

Mating	Frequency	Expected Progeny		
		A/A	A/a	a/a
$A/A \times A/A$	p^4	p^4		
$A/A \times A/a$	$2p^3q$	p^3q	p^3q	
$A/A \times a/a$	p^2q^2		p^2q^2	
$A/a \times A/A$	$2p^3q$	p^3q	p^3q	
$A/a \times A/a$	$4p^2q^2$	p^2q^2	$2p^2q^2$	p^2q^2
$A/a \times a/a$	$2pq^3$		pq^3	pq^3
$a/a \times A/A$	p^2q^2		p^2q^2	
$a/a \times A/a$	$2pq^3$		pq^3	pq^3
$a/a \times a/a$	q^4			q^4
Total		p^2	$2pq$	q^2

Calculation of totals, noting that $p^2 + 2pq + q^2 = 1$:
$$p^4 + 2p^3q + p^2q^2 = p^2(p^2 + 2pq + q^2) = p^2$$
$$2p^3q + 4p^2q^2 + 2pq^3 = 2pq(p^2 + 2pq + q^2) = 2pq$$
$$p^2q^2 + 2pq^3 + q^4 = q^2(p^2 + 2pq + q^2) = q^2$$

MALE

Gametes	$p\,A^1$	$q\,A^2$	$r\,A^3$
$p\,A^1$	$p^2\,A^1/A^1$	$pq\,A^1/A^2$	$pr\,A^1/A^3$
$q\,A^2$	$pq\,A^1/A^2$	$q^2\,A^2/A^2$	$qr\,A^2/A^3$
$r\,A^3$	$pr\,A^1/A^3$	$qr\,A^2/A^3$	$r^2\,A^3/A^3$

Total result: $p^2\,A^1/A^1 + q^2\,A^2/A^2 + r^2\,A^3/A^3$
$+ 2pq\,A^1/A^2 + 2pr\,A^1/A^3 + 2qr\,A^2/A^3$

Fig. 9-2 Random combinations of gametes expected in a population containing $p\,A^1$, $q\,A^2$, and $r\,A^3$ alleles.

X-chromosome will have the B gene and 10 percent of X-bearing gametes of each sex will contain the b gene. Our Punnett square would then appear as in Figure 9–3.

Note that the male types are the same as the gene frequencies whereas the female genotypes have the same frequencies that they would have for an autosomal locus.

In general terms, if an X-linked locus has alleles B^1 and B^2 with frequencies p and q, respectively, a random mating population will consist of:

$$p\,B^1/Y + q\,B^2/Y \text{ males, and}$$
$$p^2\,B^1/B^1 + 2pq\,B^1/B^2 + q^2\,B^2/B^2 \text{ females.}$$

In practice, this means that we need not calculate the gene frequency for an X-linked locus in the usual way: we can simply read it from the distribution of the trait among the males. If the random mating conditions hold, the frequency of each homozygote in the females is then the square of the frequency of the corresponding trait among the males, and the frequency of heterozygous females is twice the product of the male frequencies for the pertinent alleles.

Since the square of a fraction is always a still smaller fraction, this explains very readily why females exhibiting a trait determined by an X-linked recessive gene are less likely to be found than males with the trait. A number of ramifications of this point have been discussed in Chapter 7. Note especially in Table 7–1 that

MALE

X-bearing

	Gametes	$.90\,B$	$.10\,b$	Y
FEMALE	$.90\,B$	$.81\,B/B$	$.09\,B/b$	$.90\,B/Y$
	$.10\,b$	$.09\,B/b$	$.01\,b/b$	$.10\,b/Y$

Totals: Females $.81\,B/B$: $.18\,B/b$: $.01\,b/b$
Males $.90\,B/Y$: $.10\,b/Y$

Fig. 9-3 Random combinations of gametes expected in a population in which 90 percent of the X-chromosomes contain B and 10 percent b.

the disproportion between the two sexes increases rapidly as the trait becomes rarer. Whereas only twice as many males as females are expected to have a recessive X-linked trait present in half of the males, 100 times more males than females would show a trait present in 1 percent of males. The difference reaches extreme proportions for very rare traits. An X-linked character found in one out of 10,000 males, for example, would be encountered only once in 100 million females. Thus, a physician practicing in a city with a million inhabitants would expect to be able to find 50 males with such a condition at any time, but over an entire lifetime he might not expect to see even one female with it.

Attainment of equilibrium after one generation of random mating presupposes that the initial gene frequencies in the two sexes are equal. If they are not, they become equal once equilibrium is reached, but more than one generation of random mating is necessary before this is attained. For autosomal genes, two consecutive generations of random mating are necessary to accomplish this, and the gene frequencies at equilibrium are the arithmetic averages of the initial ones. Thus, if the initial frequency of A in the males is 0.52 and that of the females is 0.54, at equilibrium (in the F_2) the frequency in each sex is 0.53 and the genotype proportions are $(0.53)^2$ A/A, $2(0.53)(0.47)$ A/a, and $(0.47)^2$ a/a. For X-linked genes attainment of equilibrium (and with it equal gene frequencies) takes longer. The eventual gene frequency in both sexes is a weighted average based on the number of X-chromosomes. If the initial frequencies of A and a in females are m and n, respectively, and in males they are p and q, equilibrium is reached when the gene frequency of A in both sexes is $(2m + p)/3$, that of a, $(2n + q)/3$.

USING THE RANDOM MATING LAW

Subsequent chapters will discuss other departures from the assumptions stated on page 220, such as natural selection, changes in gene frequency due to mutation pressure, and matings between relatives more frequent than expected under random mating. It will be seen that the Hardy–Weinberg formulation is used as a basis for analyzing their effects on the population.

Another important use is to answer questions similar to the following: The frequency of children with a given recessive trait is 1 in 14,400 births; what proportion of the normal population are probably carriers? If we can assume random mating, the gene frequency can be derived by setting the birth frequency, 1/14,400, equal to q^2 in the Hardy–Weinberg equation. Thus,

$$q = \sqrt{1/14,400} = 1/120 = 0.0083.$$
$$p = 1 - q = 0.9917.$$

Now,

$$\frac{(A/a)}{\text{normal pop.}} = \frac{2pq}{p^2 + 2pq} = \frac{2q}{p + 2q} = \frac{2q}{1 - q + 2q} = \frac{2q}{1 + q}$$

So, the answer is 0.0166/1.0083, or about 0.015. This states that about 1.5 percent, about 1 in 67 normal persons, is a carrier. Note that there are about 215 times as many carriers as "show"-ers. This is bound to have important implications for any attempt to reduce the number of affected by a negative eugenics program of eliminating the affected or preventing them from mating.

Another type of analysis is exemplified by finding that a particular population sample consists of 90 persons with blood type M, 162 MN, and 48 N. What can be said about the mating structure of this population? Converting to percentages, 30 M:54 MN:16 N, we note immediately that something is amiss: under random mating, no equilibrium population should have more than 50 percent heterozygotes (the figure expected when $p = q = 0.5$).

In any case we cannot assume that the data result from random mating, since that is the question being posed; therefore we cannot determine p or q from taking the square root of the respective homozygote frequencies. By direct count in the sample, as in Table 9–2, however, we find that

$$p = 0.57 \text{ and } q = 0.43$$

For these gene frequencies the expected equilibrium is:

$$32.49\% \text{ M}:49.02\% \text{ MN}:18.49\% \text{ N.}$$

In a sample of 300 from such a population we would expect:

$$97.5 \text{ M}, 147.1 \text{ MN}, \text{ and } 55.5 \text{ N.}$$

Comparing this to the actual sample, we find that chi-square for 1 degree of freedom* is 3.1, with P greater than 5 percent. Hence, despite the suspicious excess of heterozygotes, the data fit the hypothesis of random mating.

Conformity to Hardy–Weinberg expectations can be considered additional evidence that the genes in question are alleles fulfilling Mendel's first law, for that is an underlying assumption in deriving the formulations in Tables 9–1 to 9–3. Quite often populational data can be the first extensive material for testing such an hypothesis when new variation is discovered, and it is especially useful when one of the alleles appears to be dominant, as in the following example (Table 9–4).

Two groups working independently, Knight, Selin, and Harris at the Veterans Administration Hospital in Salt Lake City, Utah, and Price Evans, Manley,

---

*Although there are three items of data, there is only 1 d.f. because one is taken away by the need to conform to the total and one by the need to conform to the gene frequencies.

Table 9–4   Speed of inactivation of the drug isoniazid by seventy-three U.S. Causasoid families (composite[a] of independent investigations by Knight et al. 1959, and Evans et al., 1959, 1960)

Matings			Progeny				
			Rapid		Slow		Chi
	Number	Expected	Obs.	Exp.	Obs.	Exp.	Square
Rapid × Rapid	18	15.9	42	47.0	15	10.0	2.20
Rapid × Slow	34	36.3	60	61.6	46	44.4	0.10
Slow × Slow	21	20.7	0		70	70	0
Total	73						

[a]Tests of the two sets of data for heterogeneity were not significant.

McKusick, Merryman, and M. A. Ferguson-Smith at Johns Hopkins University, Baltimore, Maryland, were checking reports that the speed at which a powerful new antituberculosis drug, isoniazid, was broken down by the body was inherited. The authors noted that the expected progeny corresponded very well with the observed data and concluded that these results confirmed the hypothesis that the speed of inactivation of isoniazid is inherited via a single locus, the gene for rapid inactivation being dominant to its allele for slow inactivation. Later work demonstrated that the alleles were really codominant. With the techniques available to them, however, these investigators could not distinguish the homozygous rapid inactivators from the heterozygotes.

Here we cannot calculate the gene frequency by "counting" the genes in the raw data, for, if the hypothesis is correct, we do not know how many of the rapid inactivators are homozygotes and how many are heterozygotes. We may argue, however, that if the data fit the hypothesis, the slow inactivators, tentatively assigned the genotype ri/ri, should correspond to a/a in our formula. An estimate of their proportion of the population can be made from the parents shown on the left in Table 9–4. Of the 146 parents in the 73 matings, 76 (the sum of 34 plus two times 21) are slow inactivators, 52.1 percent. Hence, if the data fit the random mating law,

$$q^2 = 0.521,$$
$$q = 0.722.$$

If so,

$$p = 1 - q = 0.278.$$

We may now analyze the progeny side of the table. The 70 slow from slow × slow fit expectation. To find the number of slow inactivators expected from the other two matings, we can use the ratios first derived by L. H. Snyder, a pioneer American human geneticist. For the proportion of recessives (R) expected from the mating of two dominants, note the appropriate entries in Table 9–3:

$$R = \frac{p^2 q^2}{p^4 + 4p^3 q + 4p^2 q^2},$$

which can be reduced to:

$$R = \frac{q^2}{(1 + q)^2}.$$

Similarly, for the recessives from $D \times R$ matings:

$$R = \frac{2pq^3}{2p^2 q^2 + 4pq^3} = \frac{q}{1 + q}.$$

Here, from $D \times D$, the expected R fraction is $0.521/(1.722)^2 = 0.176$. Out of 57 offspring from rapid × rapid we therefore expect 10.0 to be slow inactivators, 47.0 rapid. Similarly, from $D \times R$ the expected R fraction is $0.722/1.722 = 0.419$; so, of the 106 offspring from rapid × slow, we expect 44.4 slow, 61.6 rapid.

As may be seen from the rightmost column of Table 9–4, neither set of progeny deviates significantly (each with 1 degree of freedom) from expectation, and this is borne out by the combined χ^2 of 2.30 for 3 or for 2 degrees of freedom, the number of d.f. depending on whether the slow $\times$ slow data are included in the analysis. Thus the data fit the Hardy–Weinberg expectations for a single locus very well, and the hypothesis is confirmed.

The calculation of the expected numbers of marriages in the left-hand side of Table 9–4 is not crucial to the test of the hypothesis, but is a useful check as to whether the families studied are a random sample of the mating population. In an independent sample from these populations, 53.3 percent were slow inactivators. Hence we expect:

$$\text{marriages of slow and slow} = (0.533)^2(73) = 20.7$$
$$\begin{aligned}\text{marriages of rapid and slow} \\ \text{and slow and rapid} &= 2(0.533)(0.467)(73) = 36.3 \\ \text{rapid and rapid} &= (0.467)^2(73) = 15.9.\end{aligned}$$

These are very close to the actual numbers reported.

The expected progeny in Table 9–4 could also have been calculated on the basis of the independent sample, with the same conclusions.

One of the most famous applications of the Hardy–Weinberg formula was its use by Felix Bernstein, a German mathematician and writer, to demonstrate conclusively how the ABO blood types are inherited.

Much of the knowledge of blood types can be traced to the pioneering work of Karl Landsteiner. Over a span of more than 40 years he was involved in the discovery of four blood group systems in man, ABO, M-N, P, and Rh. It was primarily for his discovery of the ABO system in 1900 that Landsteiner was awarded the Nobel Prize in Medicine in 1930. Not only did this discovery make blood transfusions a great deal safer and, in recent years, lead us to understand some anomalous cases of hemolytic disease in the newborn, but it created the fundamental knowledge on which all subsequent blood type work has been based.

When the inheritance of the A and B antigens was demonstrated, the first hypothesis was that each was determined by an independent locus. The genotype of type O was supposedly $a/a\ b/b$, and type AB could have various possibilities, summarized by $A/-\ B/-$. It was disturbing that AB $\times$ O matings seemed to produce only type A and type B offspring, never O or AB, but, in view of the rarity of AB, the family evidence was considered inconclusive. The hypothesis was fully rejected only when Bernstein showed in 1924 and 1925 that *population* data do not fit the expectations of a two-locus hypothesis but do fit well the expectations for one locus with multiple alleles. The data in Table 9–5 are typical.

Under the single-locus hypothesis, we assume three alleles: (1) I^A for production of the A antigen; (2) I^B for production of the B antigen; and (3) I^O which results in neither A nor B.* I^O appears to be recessive to I^A and I^B, but I^A and I^B are codom-

*This is called the *I* locus because persons lacking one or another of the antigens almost invariably produce natural antibodies against it. Since these are against antigens of another member of the same species, they are called *iso*antibodies. In this case, as for the Rh group, they are *isoagglutinins,* and the A and B substances are *isoagglutinogens.* The locus name derives from the first letter of

Table 9-5 Frequencies of ABO blood types in Great Britain, compared with the expected values under two genetic hypotheses. (Data from Dobson and Ikin, 1946, quoted by Race and Sanger 1950)

Blood Type	Number	Actual Frequency (in %)	Expected Frequency Under Two Locus Hypothesis[a]	Expected Frequency Under Multiple Alleles
O	88,782	46.684	48.84	46.65
A	79,334	41.716	39.56	41.71
B	16,280	8.560	6.41	8.56
AB	5,781	3.040	5.19	3.08
Total	190,177	100.000	100.00	100.00
x^2 (testing goodness of it)			3570.7	1.05
P			infinitesimal	>0.70

[a]Basis described in Levitan and Montagu (1977), pp. 451-453.

inant. Table 9-6 shows the expected frequencies of the four types under random mating.

To calculate the gene frequencies in an actual population, note that

$$\text{Frequencies of A and O} = (A) + (O) = p^2 + 2pr + r^2$$
$$= (p + r)^2.$$

Hence,

$$p + r = \sqrt{(O) + (A)}.$$

so,

$$p = \sqrt{(O) + (A)} - r.$$

Since $(O) = r^2$,

$$p = \sqrt{(O) + (A)} - \sqrt{(O)}$$

Likewise,

$$(B) + (O) = q^2 + 2qr + r^2$$
$$= (q + r)^2.$$

So that

$$q + r = \sqrt{(B) + (O)}$$

and

$$q = \sqrt{(B) + (O)} - r$$
$$= \sqrt{(B) + (O)} - \sqrt{(O)}.$$

these words. It can stand also for the "International" accepted ABO nomenclature as opposed to the obsolete I–IV nomenclature of Moss and Jansky. It should not be confused with the locus for the nearly universal ("public") blood group I, whose determining alleles are, unfortunately, written I, I^2, and I^3, ..., and i.

Table 9-6 Genotypes and proportions of each expected under random mating of ABO blood types are inherited by means of the multiple alleles described in the text. $(I^A) = p$, $(I^B) = q$, and $(I^O) = r$

Blood Type	Genotype(s)	Expected Frequencies
O	I^O/I^O	r^2
A	I^A/I^A and I^A/I^O	$p^2 + 2pr$
B	I^B/I^B and I^B/I^O	$q^2 + 2qr$
AB	I^A/I^B	$2pq$

Having found p and q, we can then check the observed frequency of type AB against its expected frequency. If our hypothesis is correct, $(AB) = 2pq$; also, $p + q + r$ should $= 1$.

Applying these derivations to the population shown in Table 9–5, we get

$$(I^O) = r = \sqrt{(O)}$$
$$= \sqrt{0.46684}$$
$$= 0.683,$$
$$(I^A = p = \sqrt{(O) + (A)} - \sqrt{(O)}$$
$$= \sqrt{0.88400} - \sqrt{0.46684}$$
$$= 0.940 - 0.683,$$
$$(I)^A) = p = 0.257,$$

and

$$(I^B) = q = \sqrt{(O) + (B)} - \sqrt{(O)}$$
$$= \sqrt{0.55244} - \sqrt{0.46684}$$
$$= 0.743 - 0.683,$$
$$(I^B) = q = 0.060.$$

Note that $p + q + r = 0.257 + 0.060 + 0.683 = 1.000$.

As a further test we may ask if

$$(AB) = 2pq.$$

From Table 9–5,

$$(AB) = 0.0304.$$
$$2pq = 2(0.257)(0.060)$$
$$= 0.0308,$$

a very close fit.

In many studies, the sum $p + q + r$ does not equal 1.00 exactly, probably because (1) not all the data are used in calculating the gene frequencies; and (2) gene frequencies should not really be estimated from the same sample in asking whether a sample fits the random-mating law. To apply a commonly used correction, first suggested by Bernstein, p and q are found by alternative formulas:

As noted above,

$$p + r = \sqrt{(O) + (A)}.$$

Now,

$$r = 1 - p - q.$$

Therefore,

$$p + 1 - p - q = \sqrt{(O) + (A)},$$
$$-q = \sqrt{(O) + (A)} - 1,$$
$$(I^B) = q = 1 - \sqrt{(O) + (A)}.$$

Similarly,

$$(I^A) = p = 1 - \sqrt{(O) + (B)}.$$

The raw p and q are then multiplied by a correction factor,

$$1 + \frac{D}{2},$$

where $D = \sqrt{(O) + (A)} + \sqrt{(O) + (B)} - \sqrt{(O)} - 1$.

In this method, r is found by the identity $1 - p - q$, using the corrected p and q. (In our example $D = O$.)

Workers have developed more refined methods of estimating the gene frequencies. One such method is alluded to below. Recent further improvements use high-speed computers.

Further evidence for the multiple allele theory is found when we include the subtypes of group A. Some anti-A sera (from a type B) that have been absorbed by certain group A red blood cells retain ability to agglutinate other group A bloods, but do not agglutinate more red blood cells from the original source. The type that agglutinates the anti-A both before and after such absorption is labeled type A_1 (read "A-one"), and the ones that do not are called type A_2. Type A_2 cells will not react at all to certain anti-A sera. Apparently some anti-A sera contain two different antibodies, conventionally referred to as α and α_1, whereas others contain only α_1. A_1 blood reacts with both, whereas A_2 reacts only with α. Virtually all type B have both α and α_1 in their serum. When A_2 cells have absorbed all the α from such an anti-A serum, A_1 can still react with the antiserum (because it can react with the α_1), but additional A_2 cells cannot. About 26 percent of type A_2B persons and a smaller proportion, about 1 to 2 percent, of type A_2 produce α_1 (but no α, of course) in their sera. Such an anti-A_1 serum will react only with A_1 or A_1B cells. We can diagram the reaction as follows:

	Serum	
	anti-A	anti-A_1
Antibodies present	$\alpha + \alpha_1$	α_1
Reaction of type A_1 and A_1B cells	+	+
Reaction of type A_2 and A_2B cells	+	−
Reaction of type O and type B cells	−	−

The simplest hypothesis to explain these data is that there are two different kinds of I^A alleles, I^{A_1} and I^{A_2}. Both substitute for I^A in being codominant with I^B and dominant to I^O. Since some $A_1 \times O$ marriages produce both A_1 and A_2 children, it appears that these A_1 are heterozygotes, I^{A_1}/I^{A_2}, and the I^{A_1} gene is dominant to

I^{A_2}. Let $p_1 = (I^{A_1})$ and $p_2 = (I^{A_2})$, with q and r equal to (I^B) and (I^O) as before. Since, under the random mating law,

$$p_1^2 + 2p_1p_2 + 2p_1r = A_1,$$
$$p_2^2 + 2p_2r = A_2,$$

and

$$r^2 = O,$$

it follows that

$$(p_1 + p_2 + r)^2 = A_1 + A_2 + O$$

and

$$(p_2 + r)^2 = A_2 + O,$$

then

$$(p_1 + p_2 + r) - (p_2 + r) = \sqrt{A_1 + A_2 + O} - \sqrt{A_2 + O}.$$

Hence

$$(I^{A_1}) = p_1 = \sqrt{A_1 + A_2 + O} - \sqrt{A_2 + O}$$

and

$$(I^{A_2}) = p_2 = \sqrt{A_2 + O} - \sqrt{O}.$$

Analogous methods can be employed whenever we add a new allele of this type to a locus. In a sample of 3459 from South England, Ikin et al. (1939) found the following distribution:

Type	Frequency (percent)
O	43.45
A_1	34.81
A_2	9.89
B	8.59
A_1B	2.62
A_2B	0.64

From this we can calculate:

By methods described here	By maximum likelihood method (Stevens, 1938)
$(I^O$ = 0.659	0.66023
$(I^{A_1}) = 0.209$	0.20896
$(A^{A_2}) = 0.071$	0.06965
(I^B) = 0.062	0.06117
If so $p_1 + p_2 + q + r = 1.001$,	1.00001
and expected $(A_1 B) = 2.59$ percent	2.556 percent
and expected $(A_2 B) = 0.88$ percent	0.852 percent

Neither AB type deviates significantly from the actual numbers observed. The fancier methods which gave the results in last column seem in this instance hardly worth the additional effort.

SUGGESTED EXERCISES

In all the following problems assume that the population is panmictic unless some question about this is indicated. (Some parts can await study of Chap. 12.)

In a sample of 220 parents of children with congenital heart disease, Gershowitz and Neel (1965) found that the frequency of gene L^M was 0.58 and that of L^N was 0.42. M-N and ABO are on different chromosomes (Chap. 16).

9-1. If these frequencies were typical of the large panmictic population from which these parents were derived and they were alike in the two sexes, what proportion of the progeny would be expected to be (a) type M; (b) type MN; (c) type N?

9-2. Suppose a sample of 200 progeny from this population contained 29.5 percent M, 56.5 percent MN, 14.0 percent N.
   (a)   What result in the sample should make you suspicious immediately that this may not come from a random mating population (or be a random sample from one)?
   (b)   Is this sample consistent with our previous statement that the population was reproducing by random mating?

   In the same population (which applies to exercises 9-3 through 9-8) Gershowitz and Neel found the following frequencies of the genes at the ABO locus:

Gene	Frequency
I^{A_1}	0.19
I^{A_2}	0.06
I^B	0.08
I^O	0.67

9-3. What proportion of the gametes produced in this population are expected to contain the following:
   (a) I^{A_1}?
   (b) I^{A_1} and I^{A_2}?
   (c) I^{A_1} or I^{A_2}?
   (d)   both I^O and L^M?
   (e)   both I^{A_2} and L^N?

9-4. What proportion of the progeny are expected to be of the following genotypes:
   (a) I^{A_1}/I^{A_1}?
   (b) I^{A_1}/I^{A_2}?
   (c) I^{A_1}/I^O?
   (d) I^A/I^B, L^M/L^N?

9–5. What proportion of the progeny are expected to be of the following blood types:
  (a)   O?
  (b)   B?
  (c)   A (any form)?
  (d) A_1?
  (e) A_2B?

9–6. What proportion of the progeny are expected to have the following blood type combinations?
  (a)   O, MN,
  (b)   B, M,
  (c) A_2, N,
  (d)   AB, N.

9–7. (a) What proportion of type B persons in this population is expected to be heterozygous?
  (b)   What proportion of type A persons is expected to be heterozygous?
  (c)   What generalization can be made from the comparison of the answers to (a) and (b)?

9–8. A woman who is O, M has an A, M child. She accuses a certain man of being the father of the child. If he is a member of the population mentioned in the foregoing problems, what is the probability that these two blood type systems will exonerate him if he is being accused unjustly? Hint: what we desire is the probability that he has the combinations of these types that cannot be paternal to this child (because of one, the other, or both).

About 56 per million births in a random mating population have galactosemia.

9–9. A man who had an older brother with galactosemia marries a first cousin, his mother's sister's daughter. What is the probability that their first child will have galactosemia? (Assume that all the grandparents except the barest minimum necessary to explain the galactosemic brother are homozygous for the normal allele.)

9–10. Suppose that instead of his first cousin the man had married a woman from the general population. What is the probability that their first child would have galactosemia?

9–11. If exercises 9–9 and 9–10 had concerned a more common condition, one appearing in every 100 births, what would be the relative probabilities of an affected child in the two marriages?

9–12. How much error is introduced in exercise 9–9 by assuming that the cousin's paternal grandparents were homozygous normal. Hint: The total probability is the sum of the probabilities from all three possibilities—that both are homozygous, that one is heterozygous, or both are heterozygous.

9–13. A representative U.S. Caucasoid population consisted of 44.9 percent type O, 41.6 percent type A, 9.9 percent type B, and 3.6 percent type AB.
  (a)   Calculate the frequencies of I^O, I^A, and I^B on the assumption of panmixia.
  (b)   Does the observed frequency of AB correspond to the frequency expected on this assumption?

9-14. Verify the statement on p. 220 concerning random mating in populations with (1) 88 percent A/A, 4 percent A/a, and 8 percent a/a, (2) 80 percent A/A and 20 percent A/a, (3) 81 percent A/A, 18 percent A/a, and 1 percent a/a.

9-15. About the same time that they discovered the M-N blood groups, Landsteiner and Levine found another blood group system, P. Like M-N, it presents limited clinical problems, but is useful for medico-legal studies. The system has since proven more complex, but the basic findings hold. In a study of 563 German families in Cologne, Dahr (1942) found the following distribution:

| | Number of | | Progeny | |
Parents	Couples	$P+6\times$	$P-$	Total
$P+ \times P+$	319	980	131	1111
$P+ \times P-$	194	505	277	782
$P- \times P-$	50	4	173	177
Totals	563	1489	581	2070

Three of the 4 P+ progeny from $P- \times P-$ matings were admittedly illegitimate.

For ease of calculation assume these data were derived from a population which is 72.96 percent $P+$ and 27.04 percent $P-$ (an actual sample of 6478 in Cologne was 73.62 $P+$).

(a)   Test the conclusion that the distribution of the types among the parents fits the postulated frequencies in this population.

(b)   Test the conclusion that the distribution of marriages in the sample fits a hypothesis of random mating in the population.

(c)   Test the conclusion that the distribution of progeny fits a hypothesis of a single locus with the gene for the P antigen dominant to its allele for no P antigen.

10

Relationship and Consanguinity

The opposite of random mating is *assortative,* that is, preferential, mating. We are interested in this, of course, when the preference is based on inherited characteristics. Genetically significant *positive* assortative mating occurs, therefore, when like genotypes mate more frequently than they would be expected to under random mating, *negative* assortative mating when unlike genotypes prefer one another more often than expected by chance.

Consanguinity, the marriage of close relatives, is almost always a form of positive assortative mating because their relationship increases the likelihood that the mates have the same genotype. We noted in Chapter 1 that such marriages can confound the analysis of recessive pedigrees. In fact consanguinity of the parents is sometimes the prime criterion for deciding that the trait of an affected person is inherited as a recessive. In this chapter we will consider the theoretical basis for these statements, measurements of relationship, and the effects of consanguinity.

RELATIONSHIP

The likelihood that two persons have the same genes derived from a common ancestor is called the coefficient of relationship. A more technical definition is that it measures the degree of correlation between their genotypes.

For a simple way to calculate it one asks: If a person has any given gene, how likely is it that a specific relative also carries it? Consider, for example, a brother and sister. If one has autosomal gene A^1, one of the parents must have the same gene; so the chance that the sibling also inherited it is 1/2. Generalizing, one can say full siblings who are not identical twins have half their genes in common by descent: The correlation of their genotypes is 0.5. Similarly the correlation of parent and child is 1/2.

Consider now the correlation of III-1 and his uncle, II-3, in Fig. 10–1. If III-1 has A^2, there is equal likelihood that he got it from II-1 or from II-2; hence, the probability that II-1—and one of *his* parents—has A^2 is 1/2. It follows that the probability that II-3 also has A^2 is 1/4. Thus the coefficient of relationship between a person and an uncle or aunt for autosomal genes is 1/4. Figure 10–1 shows that the same correlation holds for a person and a grandparent; it holds true as well for

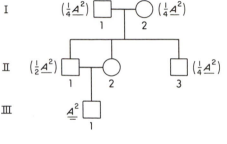

Fig. 10–1 Hypothetical pedigree for calculating the coefficients of relationship of some second degree relatives. Note that the probability that I-1 *or* I-2 has A^2 is 1/2; for each one it is 1/4.

half-sibs (persons with only one parent in common), and for double first cousins (e.g., their mothers are sisters and fathers are brothers). The coefficient for ordinary first cousins is 1/8.

One can see from the cited example in Fig. 10–1 that the coefficient of relationship need have nothing to do with breeding. (The correlation of identical twins is 1.) It turns out to be particularly useful in traits involving many loci and considerable environmental effects that obscure the Mendelian ratios (Chapter 15). In such discussions those with coefficients of 1/2 are often referred to as relatives of the first degree, those with 1/4, that is, $(1/2)^2$, as second-degree relatives, those with 1/8 as third-degree, and so forth.

THE COEFFICIENT OF INBREEDING

To measure the effect of relationship on breeding we use a different figure, the coefficient of inbreeding. This measures the likelihood that any two persons with common ancestors have received the same genes from them and, if mated, pass these to their offspring. When we know how often matings with various coefficients of inbreeding take place in a population, we can also calculate the average coefficient of inbreeding of the whole population. Generally the coefficient of inbreeding is denoted by F, the average coefficient of a population by α.

Essentially, calculation of F involves finding the probability that a child born to related parents will be homozygous for a gene of their common ancestor, that this gene will "meet itself," so to speak, in the child.

Consider first the simplest situation: an incestuous brother–sister union, such as produced the affected child in the pedigree in Figure 10–2A.

In this case both parents apparently inherited a gene for osteogenesis imperfecta from one of their parents and this gene then "met itself" in their child. Suppose we are estimating, before they had the child, the likelihood that they would produce a homozygote for any given locus without knowing what genes the grandparents carried. What, in other words, is F for a brother–sister union?

Assume one grandparent has genotype A_1/A_2 and the other A_3/A_4. In reality these could be identical alleles, but it is easier for working out the theory to identify them separately. The pedigree would be as in Figure 10–3. We want to know the likelihood that III-1 is A_1/A_2, A_2/A_2, A_3/A_3, or A_4/A_4.

The probability that II-1 has gene A_1 is one-half. If II-1 has A_1, the probability that he will pass it on to III-1 is one-half. Similarly, the probability that II-2

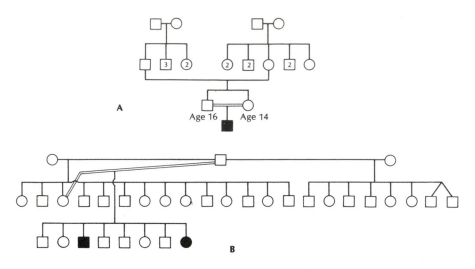

Fig. 10–2A A pedigree of osteogenesis imperfecta congenita (Vrolik type), product of a brother-sister mating. **B.** Two cases of hereditary ataxia born to a father-daughter union. Both disorders are due to homozygosity for rare recessives (**A** from Rohwedder 1953: courtesy of *Archiv für Kinderheilunde*. **B** courtesy of F. E. Stephens.)

received A_1 from her father is one-half; if so, the chance that she will pass it on to III-1 is one-half. All of these eventualities must come to pass for III-1 to be A_1/A_1. Therefore, the probability that this will happen is:

$$1/2 \cdot 1/2 \cdot 1/2 \cdot 1/2 = 1/16.$$

In other words,

$$P(\text{III-1 is } A_1/A_1) = 1/16.$$

By analogous reasoning,

$$P(\text{III-1 is } A_2/A_2) = 1/16$$
$$P(\text{III-1 is } A_3/A_3) = 1/16$$
$$P(\text{III-1 is } A_4/A_4) = 1/16.$$

Since for the theory we do not care which homozygosity results,

$$P(\text{III-1 is } A_1/A_1, A_2/A_2, A_3/A_3, \text{ or } A_4/A_4) = 1/16 + 1/16 + 1/16 + 1/16$$
$$= 1/4.$$

Therefore, the coefficient of inbreeding of a brother–sister mating is 25 percent.

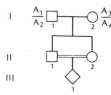

Fig. 10–3 Hypothetical pedigree of brother-sister mating to calculate coefficient of inbreeding.

Next, let us diagram the most frequent consanguineous union frowned on by law in many parts of the United States, marriages of first cousins. As the diagram (Fig. 10–4) shows, they are members of the same generation who have one pair of grandparents in common.

$$P(\text{II-2 has } A_1) = 1/2,$$
$$P(\text{II-3 has } A_1) = 1/2.$$

If so,

$$P(\text{III-1 has } A_1) = 1/4,$$

and

$$P(\text{III-2 has } A_1) = 1/4.$$

If so,

$$P(\text{IV-1 receives } A_1 \text{ from III-1}) = 1/8,$$
$$P(\text{IV-1 receives } A_1 \text{ from III-2}) = 1/8.$$

Therefore,

$$P(\text{IV-1 received } A_1 \text{ from both}) = 1/64.$$

Hence,

$$P(\text{IV-1 is } A_1/A_1, A_2/A_2, A_3/A_3, \text{ or } A_4/A_4) = 1/16,$$
$$F = 1/16.$$

A representative pedigree of first-cousin marriage is shown in Figure 10–5.

If a first cousin marries the child of his first cousin, the couple are first-cousins-once-removed (also referred to as 1-1/2 cousins). Second cousins have one parent each of whom are first cousins to one another; if both of their parents are first cousins the couple are double second cousins. Third cousins are the children of one pair of second cousins, etc.

Table 10–1 summarizes the coefficients inbreeding and relationship of relatives through third cousins. Beyond third cousin both the likelihood of tracing correct relationship and the inbreeding coefficient are so small that most analyses of consanguinity do not delve farther.

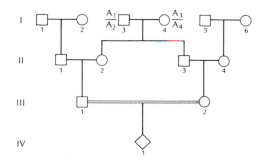

Fig. 10–4   Theoretical pedigree of a mating between first cousins.

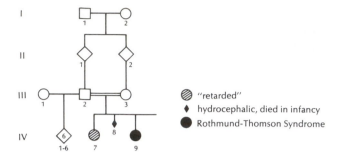

Fig. 10-5 After having six normal children with his first wife, III-2 married his first cousin, with the results shown. For some unknown reason the rare Rothmund–Thomson syndrome (poikiloderma atrophicans and cataract) appears predominantly in females, as in this family. (Data from Castel et al., 1967.)

Note the constant relationship between the coefficients for autosomal genes: The coefficient of inbreeding is always half the corresponding coefficient of relationship.

For a population, the mean (or average) inbreeding coefficient, α, is calculated by:

1. Multiplying the proportion of marriages of each class times the appropriate inbreeding coefficient F, and
2. adding together the results of step 1.

In general, if there are M marriages of a type i that has inbreeding coefficient F, out of a total of N marriages, so that the proportion of marriages of this type is c_i,

$$\text{Step 1: } c_i = \frac{M_1}{N},$$

$$\alpha_i = c_i F_i.$$

$$\text{Step 2: } \alpha = \sum \alpha_i.$$

Table 10-1 Coefficients of inbreeding and relationship for autosomal genes

Relationship	Coefficient of Relationship	Coefficient of Inbreeding
Monozygotic twins	1	—
Self-fertilization	1	1/2
Dizygotic twins; other full sibling; parent–child	1/2	1/4
Half sibling; uncle–niece; aunt–nephew; grandparent–grandchild; double first cousins	1/4	1/8
First cousins	1/8	1/16
First cousin once removed; double second cousins	1/16	1/32
Second cousins	1/32	1/64
Second cousins once removed; double third cousins	1/64	1/128
Third cousins	1/128	1/256

For example, 6755 marriages in 1948–1949 in Hiroshima, Kure, and Kumamoto City, Japan, included 290 between first cousins, 100 of 1-1/2 cousins, 132 of second cousins, 29 of 2-1/2 cousins, and 8 of third cousins; therefore,

$$\alpha = \frac{290}{6755}\left(\frac{1}{16}\right) + \frac{100}{6755}\left(\frac{1}{32}\right) + \frac{132}{6755}\left(\frac{1}{64}\right) + \frac{29}{6755}\left(\frac{1}{128}\right) + \frac{8}{6755}\left(\frac{1}{256}\right)$$
$$= 0.002683 + 0.000463 + 0.000305 + 0.000034 + 0.000005$$
$$= 0.003490$$

Table 10–2 summarizes some representative α's. Though they have some validity for comparative purposes, all the listed results are underestimates, because degrees of relationship are often not known or forgotten and incestuous matings are neither registered nor generally disclosed in surveys. In the United States data this is somewhat counterbalanced by the emphasis on rural areas, which have relatively large amounts of inbreeding, in the lists.

The Wautauga County, North Carolina, data show some of the highest degrees of inbreeding that have been recorded in the United States, and the Japanese data are among some of the highest found in the world. Perhaps the highest reported rate has come from the state of Andhra Pradesh, India, where not only cousin marriage but also uncle–niece union is frequent.

Table 10–2 illustrates some general tendencies about biological inbreeding:

1. Urban areas tend to have lower consanguinity rates than rural areas.
2. The comparison of the accessible vs. isolated villages shows that the size of the town is not as significant as the size of the overall population from which mates are drawn. Thus, a small town near a big one will have almost as little inbreeding as the city and much less inbreeding than an isolated town of the same size.
3. The rate of inbreeding in the United States has been decreasing in recent

Table 10–2 Some comparative average coefficients of inbreeding (α) (Based on data in Woolf et al., 1956; Dewey et al., 1965; Neel et al., 1949; and Dronamraju and Khan, 1963)

Locality	Period	$\alpha \times 10^4$
Utah (whole state)	1847–1869	5.75
	1870–1889	8.00
	1890–1909	2.80
	1910–1929	1.15
Utah-Nevada (rural)	1930–1950	16.31
North Carolina (Wautauga County)	1910–1929	17.61
	1930–1950	5.86
Wisconsin	1941–1955	0.50
Japan		
3 cities	1948–1949	34.90
2 accessible villages	1948–1949	50.45
3 isolated villages	1948–1949	62.48
3 other isolated villages	1948–1949	93.73
India (Andhra Pradesh)	1959	209.3

years. This is especially evident in the comparison of the two sets of North Carolina data and, in the Utah data, 1910–1929 as compared with 1870–1889 (the peak period here).

In recent years the rate of consanguinity in the United States has been among the lowest in the world. By contrast, consanguinity rates did not change materially in Japan in the 60 years prior to the collection of the data in Table 10–2. Apparently different factors govern the frequency of consanguineous unions in different localities. In the United States the distribution of population has been a major factor, whereas social custom has played a greater role in Japan. However, social custom can create effective inbreeding isolates even in the United States.

THE EFFECT OF INBREEDING

To understand better the effect of consanguinity (and to gain incidentally a deeper meaning of the coefficients of inbreeding), let us consider what to expect under the most extreme positive assortative mating imaginable, when a genotype can mate *only* with the like genotype. This could actually happen naturally in some plants which are facultatively self-pollinating and is, in fact, closely approached by peas and other legumes. (To prevent this in his P_1 crosses, Mendel had to enter the closed buds, destamenate them, and artificially dust pollen from the "male" plant onto the pistils; later, self-fertilization was exactly what he wanted to obtain his F_2, the ones with the famous 3:1 ratio.)

Suppose we have a population in random-mating equilibrium of:

36 percent A/A, 48 percent A/a, 16 percent a/a,

so that

$$p = 0.60 \; q = 0.40,$$

and suddenly instituted complete positive assortative mating. The results would be as follows:

Mating	Proportion of Matings	Expected Progeny		
		A/A	A/a	a/a
$A/A \times A/A$	0.36	0.36		
$A/a \times A/a$	0.48	0.12	0.24	0.12
$a/a \times a/a$	0.16			0.16
Totals	1.00	0.48	0.24	0.28

If the extreme mating procedure is maintained, the expected constitution of the successive generations will be as shown in Table 10–3.

Thus complete assortative mating results in an increase of homozygotes with a concomitant decrease in heterozygotes. If the system is carried on long enough, the latter would be reduced to the point where it would take but a minor accident

Table 10-3 Complete positive assortative mating. Top: beginning with a population of 36 percent A/A, 48 percent A/a, and 16 percent a/a. Below: the general case

Generation	A/A	A/a	a/a
0	0.36	0.48	0.16
1	0.48	0.24	0.28
2	0.54	0.12	0.34
3	0.57	0.06	0.37
4	0.585	0.03	0.385
5	0.5925	0.015	0.3925
6	0.59625	0.0075	0.39625
7	0.598125	0.00375	0.398125
8	0.5990625	0.001875	0.3990625
n	$0.60 - \dfrac{(A/a)}{2}$	$(0.48)\left(\dfrac{1}{2}\right)^n$	$0.40 - \dfrac{(A/a)}{2}$
As $n \to \infty$	$\to 0.60$	$\to 0$	$\to 0.40$
For the general case,	$p - \dfrac{(A/a)}{2}$	$(2pq)\left(\dfrac{1}{2}\right)^n$	$q - \dfrac{(A/a)}{2}$
As $n \to \infty$	$\to p$	$\to 0$	$\to q$

of progagation or chance to eliminate them completely. The population that began originally as

$$p^2 \, A/A, \; 2pq \, A/a \text{ and } q^2 \, a/a$$

would then become

$$p \, A/A \text{ and } q \, a/a.$$

As indicated in Table 10-1, self-fertilization has $F = 1/2$, the sum of the probabilities that each of the genes of the parent genotype will "meet itself" in the offspring (each homozygote has probability of 1/4). Note that the effect of this system of mating is to decrease the frequency of heterozygotes by 1/2 of each generation (Table 10-3). This leads us to the true meaning of F and α: they indicate the extent that heterozygosity is decreased, and homozygosity increased, by consanguinity for each generation. The other rates shown in Table 10-3 would do this at a slower pace, of course, but we could expect that inbreeding in human beings, too, would lead to more homozygotes and fewer heterozygotes than would be expected under random mating.

It should be emphasized that this theory does not predict whether inbreeding is "good" or "bad." That depends on the nature of the homozygotes. Many instances can be cited of talented persons whose parents were first cousins or otherwise closely related. Presumably consanguinity made it easier for "good" genes to come together in these cases. On the other hand, there is considerable evidence that rare recessives are encountered with greater frequency in consanguineous marriages than in marriages of unrelated persons. For example, a study found 14 cases of autosomal-recessive progressive muscular dystrophy in a small midwestern religious group. In the century from 1850 to 1949, more than one out of every five (21.5 percent) of the marriages in this group were between second cousins or closer, almost 25 percent between third cousins or closer. By contrast, the incidence of this type of muscular dystrophy is only 38 per million births in the general population. The 14 affected in the religious group were born to 7 couples, six of whom (83 percent) were known to be consanguineous. Similarly, about 20 percent of the parents of European albinos and 40 percent of the parents of Caucasian Gentiles with Tay–Sachs disease in one study were first cousins. Among Japanese the incidence of first-cousin marriages among parents of similarly affected children is even higher: 37 to 59 percent for albinism and 55 to 85 percent for Tay–Sachs disease.

DAHLBERG'S FORMULA

When we know, as in the above-mentioned cases, the proportion of homozygotes born to consanguineous couples, the inbreeding coefficient enables us to calculate the frequency of a recessive gene, q. Conversely, if we know q we can predict how often the homozygotes will have consanguineous parents. Both predictions stem from a mathematical expression first derived by Weinberg, whom we first encountered in Chapter 8, in 1920 but usually named for the Swedish geneticist, Gunnar Dahlberg, who derived it independently in 1929. Its most frequently quoted form is for first-cousin marriages. If c is the proportion of first-cousin marriages in a population, and k is the proportion of the births of affected that come from marriages of first cousins,

$$k = \frac{c(15q + 1)}{c + q(16 - c)}.$$

For example, if a gene had a frequency of 0.001 in Wautauga County, North Carolina, from 1910 to 1929, where $c = 0.0091$ (4 first-cousin marriages out of 439),

$$k = \frac{(0.0091)[15(0.001) + 1]}{0.0091 + (0.001)(16 - 0.0091)}$$
$$= \frac{(0.009)(1.015)}{0.0091 + 0.0159909}$$
$$= \frac{0.0092365}{0.0250909}$$
$$k \simeq 0.36.$$

The formula predicts that about 36 percent of all cases of the disease would be born to first cousins.

Figure 10–6 relates k, c, and q when q is between 1 and 0.0001 and c between 0 and 0.12. According to this graph, in a population where c was 0.01 and q_a was 0.0001, almost 90 percent of the a/a would result from first-cousin marriages; k is even higher as c increases, being over 95 percent when c is 0.03 for genes with $q = 0.0001$.

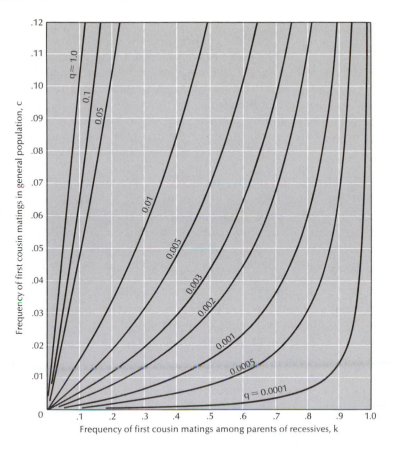

Fig. 10-6 Recessive gene frequency *(q)* as a function of the frequency of first cousin mating among the general population *(c)* and among the parents of recessives *(k)*, based on Dahlberg's formula (From Neel et al., 1949. Courtesy of J. V. Neel and the *American Journal of Human Genetics.*)

These and other high values of k have an important bearing on genetic inference:

> If a trait is rare, a high incidence of consanguineous marriages among the parents can be considered quite conclusive evidence (1) that it is inherited and (2) that the responsible gene is an autosomal recessive, even if only sporadic cases are known and counts to fit genetic ratios are not attainable.

Many of the classifications of the rare disorders as autosomal recessives have been based on this rule. Thus, the fact that his parents were first cousins is one of the leading arguments for the belief that the French painter Toulouse–Lautrec suffered from pycnodysostosis, conditioned by a rare autosomal recessive, rather than, as had been widely believed, achondroplasia, which is due to a dominant.

The above rule is strong even if the few known cases affect only males. If the gene is X-linked, inbreeding has no effect on its incidence in males. They get the gene only from the mother, so it does not matter how many common ancestors the mother and father have. (The presence of consanguinity in parents of a child with a rare malady therefore suggests *autosomal* recessive inheritance.) The idea that hemophilia was prevalent in the royal houses of Europe as a result of so-called "inbreeding" is, therefore, quite erroneous. Although there were several cousin marriages, its incidence in these families is clearly ascribable to the normal transmission of an X-linked gene by some of the daughters and granddaughters (and one son) of Queen Victoria of England (Fig. 10–7), and they would have transmitted it in this manner no matter whom they had married.

Consanguinity can increase the incidence of an X-linked trait in females. The pedigree in Figure 10–8 shows two females with rare X-linked icthyosis, presumably because an affected male, III-5, married his first cousin once removed, IV-1. Similarly, the female with hemophilia in Figure 7–6 is the child of double first cousins. However, it would be less likely to be a factor in X-linked inheritance because even for females many consanguineous unions do not increase the likelihood that they will receive the gene from the common ancestor. For example, a first-cousin relationship is significant for an X-linked gene only if the common ancestry came through (a) both parents' mothers (**A** in Fig. 10–9); or (b) the mother's father and the father's mother (**B** in Fig. 10–9). **C** and **D** in Figure 10–9 would not increase the likelihood that a girl would receive an X-linked trait, since her father could not obtain his gene from the common ancestor. The relationship in Figure 10–8 is of the **A** type. Clearly the calculation of the inbreeding coefficient will be different in the four situations. Thus F for female progeny in **C** and **D** is 0, in **A** it is 3/16, and in **B** 1/8. F will also be modified if the trait is of late onset in the male. In any case, the pattern of X-linked pedigrees is usually so straightforward that even a few cases will usually allow clear inference without resort to other considerations.

In most populations the big problem is not finding k (which can be obtained from a survey), but finding q. If there is an appreciable amount of inbreeding, we cannot estimate q by taking the square root of the incidence of the trait, because the incidence is equal to q^2 only in a true random mating population. However, Dahlberg's formula can be solved for q in terms of c and k:

$$q = \frac{c(1 - k)}{16k - 15c - ck}$$

This leads to interesting conparisons of gene frequency and the relation between gene frequency and degrees of inbreeding. For example, 7.7 percent of U.S. Gentile couples who gave birth to children with Tay–Sachs disease between 1954 and 1957 were first cousins. Let us assume the general rate of first-cousin marriage in this population is about 0.2 percent. Hence, $c = 0.002$, $k = 0.077$, and

$$q_G = \frac{(0.002)(1.077)}{16(0.077) - 15(0.002) - (0.002)(0.077)}$$
$$= \frac{(0.002)(0.923)}{1.232 - 0.030 - 0.00154}$$

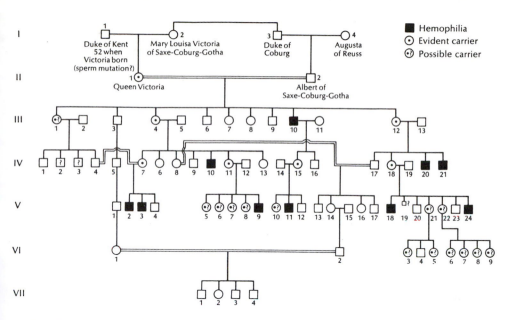

Fig. 10-7 Partial pedigree of descendants of Queen Victoria and resultant appearance of hemophilia A in one of her sons and his descendants, and, via her daughters and granddaughters, in the royal families of Prussia, Hesse, Battenberg (Mountbatten), Russia, and Spain. Note that present royal family of England is free of the gene despite inbreeding.

III-1. Princess Victoria, wife of Emperor Frederick III of Germany (III-2).

III-3. King Edward VII of England.

III-4. Princess Alice, wife of Grand Duke Ludwig IV of Hesse–Darmstadt (III-5).

III-10. Prince Leopold, Duke of Albany, died, age 31, of hemorrhage after a fall.

III-12. Princess Beatrice, wife of Prince Henry Maurice of Battenberg (III-13).

IV-1. Kaiser Wilhelm II of Germany.

IV-2. and IV-3, Prince Sigismund (d. age 2) and Prince Waldemar (d. age 11) of Prussia.

IV-7. Princess Irene of Hesse, wife of Prince Henry of Prussia (IV-4).

IV-8. Princess Victoria of Hesse, wife of Prince Louis Alexander of Battenberg (IV-17), founder of English Mountbatten family.

IV-10. Prince Friedrich of Hesse, died as a child of hemorrhage after a fall.

IV-11. Princess Alix, later Queen Alexandra, wife of Tsar Nicholas II of Russia (IV-12).

IV-15. Princess Alice, wife of Alexander, Prince of Teck (IV-14).

IV-18. Princess Victoria Eugenie of Battenberg, wife of King Alfonso XIII of Spain (IV-19).

IV-20. Prince Leopold of Battenberg, died, age 33, presumably of hemorrhage, after surgery.

IV-21. Prince Maurice of Battenberg, died, age 23, in Battle of Ypres.

V-2. Prince Waldemar of Prussia, lived to be 56 but had no children.

V-3. Prince Henry of Prussia, died age 4.

V-1. King George V of England.

V-9. Tsarevitch Alexis of Russia.

V-11. Rupert, Lord Trematon, died of hemorrhage following auto accident.

V-14. Alice Mountbatten, married to Prince Andrew of Greece (V-15).

V-18. Alfonso Pio, Prince of Asturias, died age 31, of hemorrhage after auto accident.

V-24. Prince Gonzalo of Spain, died age 20, of hemorrhage after auto accident.

VI-1. Queen Elizabeth II of Gt. Britain, married to Prince Philip Mountbatten, Duke of Edinburgh (VI-2), slightly more closely related than third cousins.

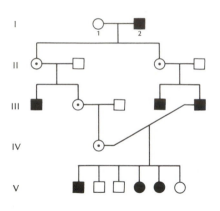

Fig. 10-8 Pedigree of X-linked ichthyosis vulgaris in which the appearance of the trait in females is probably enhanced by consanguinity. (From Stern, 1973 after Gates, 1946.)

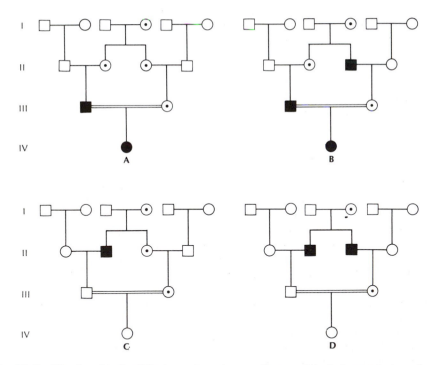

Fig. 10-9 The four kinds of first-cousin unions as they pertain to transmission of an X-linked trait. **A** and **B** increase the likelihood that a female will be homozygous for an X-linked gene present in one of the common grandparents, **C** and **D** do not. This is most clearly evident by considering one of the genes of the common grandmother as determining a clinically significant trait in the hemizygous male and homozygous female.

$$= \frac{0.001846}{1.20038}$$
$$q_G = 0.0015.$$

At the same time, for Americans of Jewish descent the rate of the first-cousin marriages among parents of children with this disease was quite a bit lower, 1.8 percent, even though the over-all rate of first-cousin marriages among American Jews has in the recent past been considerably higher than among the Gentiles, perhaps as high as 1 percent. Under these circumstances,

$$q_J = \frac{(0.01)(1 - 0.018)}{16(0.018) - 15(0.01) - (0.01)(0.018)}$$
$$= \frac{(0.01)(0.982)}{0.288 - 0.15 - 0.00018}$$
$$= \frac{0.00982}{0.13782}$$
$$q_J = 0.071$$

These estimates indicate that the T–S gene is about 50 times more frequent among Jewish people in the United States than it is among gentiles. They also confirm the general rule that the effect of inbreeding is inversely proportional to the frequency of the gene. If a gene is common, there is no pronounced tendency for it to appear from consanguineous unions.

Several studies have attempted to assess the effects of inbreeding on a broad spectrum of important traits, such as perinatal and juvenile deaths (Table 10–4), measurements of children at birth, length of gestation, and four growth characteristics of infants (Table 10–5): height, weight, and several body measurements at 8 to 10 months. Although there are exceptions, ascribed mainly to such technical problems as obtaining adequate controls, mortality of fetuses and infants is clearly related to the amount of inbreeding. It appears to be approximately doubled by first-cousin parentage (Table 10–4).

It has been estimated from such data that most individuals carry at least one recessive gene which would cause severe impairment or death if it were to meet

Table 10–4 Effect of consanguinity on fetal, infant, and juvenile mortality rates (Based on Morton, 1961)

Trait	Authority[a]	Relationship of Parents	
		Unrelated	First Cousins
Stillbirths and neonatal deaths	Sutter and Tabah (1958)	0.044	0.111
Infant and juvenile deaths	Sutter and Tabah (1958)	0.089	0.156
Early deaths (Hiroshima)	Schull and Neel (1958)	0.031	0.050
Early deaths (Kure)	Schull and Neel (1958)	0.035	0.041
Juvenile deaths	Bemiss (1958)	0.160	0.229
Postnatal deaths	Slatis et al. (1958)	0.024	0.081
Miscarriages	Slatis et al. (1958)	0.129	0.145

[a]As cited by Morton.

Table 10-5   Effect of consanguinity on averages for certain metrical traits in Japan (From Morton, 1958b)

Trait	Unrelated	Second Cousins	1-1/2 Cousins	First Cousins
Weight of live births (grams)	3074	3071	3071	3046
Length of gestation (weeks)	40.13	40.22	40.11	40.13
Weight at 8–10 months (grams)	7818	7785	7765	7722
Height at 8–10 months (mm)	689.6	689.3	689.8	687.3
Head girth at 8–10 months (mm)	442.8	444.0	442.5	442.8
Chest girth at 8–10 months (mm)	427.8	427.6	428.3	426.8

another like itself and become homozygous. The exact number of such genes, termed "lethal equivalents," is not known, especially since some of them are sem-ilethals and subvitals rather than outright lethals and are therefore difficult to assess. In many discussions these genes are referred to as our "genetic load."

Although effects of inbreeding on some of the metrical traits studied are significant, they are, clearly, very small. Accordingly, considerable doubt is cast on studies that have appeared from time to time which attribute improvements in such traits as height and weight to the general reduction in the inbreeding coefficient that we noted earlier in United States and European populations. Such factors as improved nutrition and medical practices probably better account for the improvements than the decrease in homozygosity resulting from the decrease in consanguinity.

SUGGESTED EXERCISES

Assume all questions relate to autosomal inheritance unless stated otherwise.

10-1. Demonstrate with appropriate diagrams and arguments
  (a)   that the coefficient of inbreeding for a parent–child mating is the same as that for a mating between full sibs;
  (b)   the coefficient of inbreeding for a mating of double first cousins;
  (c)   the coefficient of inbreeding for a mating of first cousins once removed;
  (d)   the coefficient of inbreeding for a mating of third cousins.

10-2. In a similar manner demonstrate the correctness of the stated coefficients of relationship for the pairs in exercise 10–1.

10-3. Two cousins wish to marry. Their fathers are brothers and their maternal grandmothers are sisters. What is the coefficient of inbreeding?

10-4. Demonstrate the correctness of the X-linkage coefficients of inbreeding stated in the text for the pedigrees in Fig. 10–9.

10-5. Describe the relationship and state (or calculate) F for the mating of II-3 and III-1 of Fig. 10–10.

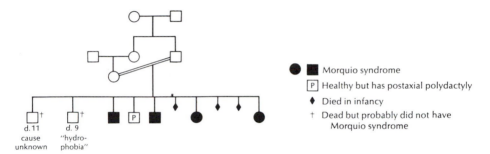

Fig. 10-10   Pedigree of Morquio syndrome, a mucopolysaccharidosis, often referred to as a type of "gargoylism." There is no history of the disorder in the family on either side, but at least four siblings with the disorder were born to this uncle-niece marriage. (Based on Gupta, 1967.)

10-6. In recent years, Spain appears to have the highest frequency of consanguinity in Europe. Obtaining accurate records is aided by the detailed records kept by the Roman Catholic diocesan offices, since all marriages of second cousins or closer require special dispensation of the bishop. In one study in a northwestern part of that country Valls (1967) found that 3988 of 65,555 marriages contracted between 1922 and 1964 were consanguineous, distributed as follows:

		Percent of All Marriages
First cousins	1681	2.56
First cousins once removed	412	0.62
Second cousins	1693	2.58
Other (not detailed)	202	0.31

Calculate:

(a)   The frequency of consanguineous marriages.

(b)   The average inbreeding coefficient for this area during this period. For (b) ignore the 202 not described as to degree.

If there is a mixture of random and consanguineous mating in a population, the distribution of genotypes can be shown to be:

$$[(1 - \alpha)p^2 + \alpha p] \; A/A : (1 - \alpha)(2pq) \; A/a : [(1 - \alpha)q^2 + \alpha q] \; a/a$$

Note that under complete random mating $\alpha = 0$, so this becomes the standard Hardy–Weinberg formula.

10-7. If the average coefficient of inbreeding in an otherwise random mating population is 0.05 (5 percent), what distribution of genotypes is expected if the frequency of gene A is 80 percent, that of its allele, a, 20 percent?

10-8. Freire-Maia (1957a, 1957b) found large contrasts in the degree of inbreeding in Brazil. The following, for example, are his findings in two localities, Porto

Alegre, Rio Grande de Sul, representative of the southern part of the country, and Oeiras, in the state of Piaui, representative of the northeastern part:

	Porto Alegre		Oeiras	
	Number	Percent	Number	Percent
Total marriages	4032		1931	
Uncle-niece and aunt-nephew	2	0.05	11	0.57
First cousin	47	1.17	206	10.67
1-1/2 cousins	12	0.30	72	3.73
Second cousins	11	0.27	116	6.00
All consanguineous listed	72	1.79	405	20.97

If a gene, a (recessive to its only allele, A), was present in both localities with the same frequency, 10 percent, contrast the expected frequency of a/a births in the two localities. Assume random mating in all marriages except the inbred ones shown.

10–9. Using Dahlberg's formula,

(a) Calculate the proportion of the a/a individuals in Porto Alegre (see exercise 10–8) whose parents were first cousins.

(b) Make the same calculation for Oeiras.

(c) Compare these results with those for another recessive whose gene frequency is only 0.1 percent.

11

Factors Causing Changes in Gene Frequencies

Random mating and consanguinity share the property that they can modify the genotype frequencies of a population without any concomitant change in gene frequencies. In this chapter we shall examine the forces capable of changing gene frequencies as well. These are mutation, natural selection, migration, and genetic drift. The first three are considered directional forces, that is, they often maintain regular rates which move the gene frequency in a predictable direction; the last follows the vagaries of chance, so that any directional effect from it would be not only unpredictable but also accidental.

MUTATION

We discussed the basic nature of mutation in Chapter 5. Here we are interested in its quantitative aspects: how frequently it occurs and how it affects gene frequencies.

Although mutations are rare events, they apparently happen in the same way again and again during the lifetime of a species. But they do not happen equally often. Not only do different loci mutate at different frequencies, but even alleles of the same locus do not mutate at the same rate.

Mutation rates are usually stated in terms of the number of changed genes per locus per generation. This is a rather technical way of stating the relative numbers of changed and unchanged genes present in the *gametes* that produced a given generation; as a matter of fact, some geneticists prefer the expression "mutant genes per given number of gametes."

Most mutation rate measurements in man are based on one or both the following points:

1. A gene present in a child that was not present in his parents must have arisen by mutation.
2. If a gene persists in the population at a steady rate even though some, or, in certain cases, all, of its carriers leave no offspring (usually because the

gene is lethal), the recurring cases of the condition must be due to new mutations to that gene.

The first point is the rationale behind the so-called *direct method* of measuring mutation rates, the second, the *indirect method.*

Human mutation rates can be measured most accurately for abnormalities caused by dominant genes, especially if the gene in question is fully penetrant. If we can feel secure that everyone who has the gene would manifest the condition, every sibship in which normal parents have a child with the abnormality represents a new mutation. This is the usual application of the *direct method* of estimating mutation rates.

One of the most thorough studies of this type found that 10 chondrodystrophic dwarfs were born over a period of 30 years, out of a total of 94,073 births, in the Rigshospital in Copenhagen. Chondrodystrophy, also known as achondroplasia, is a disorder of the bone which develops from cartilage. It particularly affects the cartilage at the junction of metaphyses (shafts) and epiphyses (ends) of the long bones, where these bones normally grow in length, with the result that the legs and arms remain abnormally short. In contrast with metabolic dwarfs (cretins), other bones (the so-called "membrane bones") develop normally, so the dwarf's trunk and head are essentially normal in size. It is inherited as a simple dominant with close to 100 percent penetrance, though many cases are stillborn or die in early infancy because of associated defects. In the Danish data, two of the chondrodystrophic births had a parent with the same condition. The other 8, born to normal parents, probably betoken the new mutations. The 94,073 births to normal parents represent 188,146 gamete alleles of this locus, so:

$$\text{Mutation rate} = \frac{8}{188,146}$$
$$= \frac{4.252}{100,000}$$
$$= 4.252 \times 10^{-5},$$

or one mutant allele in each 23,518 gametes.

The indirect method involves both mutation and selection, so we shall discuss it later. We shall note that it is the method used for recessive and X-linked genes. In addition to the problems of heterogeneity and penetrance mentioned above both methods share the pitfall of distinguishing true mutants from phenocopies. They are given some credence, however, by the essential similarity of the rates obtained. A sample of these are shown in Table 11–1.

However credible the rates may be for these loci, they are considered too high to be representative. The rates obtained for bacteria and other laboratory organisms, with more objective and more accurate methods available, are usually several magnitudes lower (Table 11–2). It is felt that only the higher mutation rates of human loci are known because those are the easiest to measure. Hence many geneticists take 1×10^{-6} (one per million) as a more likely average mutation rate.

Table 11–2 illustrates another point. Mutations from a very rare allele to a more common one happen so seldom that we tend to think solely in terms of mutations to produce so-called abnormal alleles. At most loci, mutations are occurring

Table 11-1 Some estimated spontaneous mutation rates in man (For references see Levitan and Montagu, 1977)

Gene	Estimated Mutation Rate (per Million Gametes per Generation)
Autosomal dominant	
Muscular dystrophy, facioscapulohumeral type	0.5
Nail-patella syndrome	2
Multiple telangiectasia (Osler disease)	2–3
Acrocephalosyndactyly	3
Waardenburg's syndrome	4
Aniridia	4–5
Marfan's syndrome	5
Tuberous sclerosis	8
Pelger anomaly	10
Multiple polyposis of the colon	13
Amyotrophic lateral sclerosis	30
Achondroplastic dwarfism	43–70
Autosomal recessive	
Tay Sachs disease	11
Ichthyosis congenita	11
Congenital total color blindness	28
Albinism	28–70
Epidermolysis bullosa letalis	50
X-linked recessive	
Hemophilia B	0.5–2
Hemophilia A	13–32
Muscular dystrophy, Duchenne type	43–49
Muscular dystrophy, Becker tardive type	47

Table 11-2 Some rates of mutation and back mutation in bacteria (*E. coli*) (For references see Levitan and Montagu, 1977)

Mutation Studied[a]	Rate	$\mu:\nu$
$his^+ \rightarrow his^{-a}$	1.2×10^{-6}	
$his^- \rightarrow his^+$	2.4×10^{-8}	50:1
$+ \rightarrow$ strepto-	1.1×10^{-9b}	
mycin resistance[c]		1:13
streptomycin resistance $\rightarrow +$	1.4×10^{-8}	

[a] + refers to the normal allele, his+ means the organism is an autotroph, can produce the substance (in this case, histidine) from minimal medium; − means it is an auxotroph: the substance must be added if the organism is to live and reproduce.

[b] Average of several experiments.

[c] In these cases, the resistant strains were actually *dependent* on streptomycin for growth.

in the reverse direction as well. The production of "normal" alleles from the genes for abnormal conditions is called *reverse mutation* or *back mutation.* When neither of the alleles may properly be referred to as "abnormal," the choice of terms becomes a matter of semantics, but the change from the rarer allele to the more common one is usually considered the reverse mutation.

Most authors diagram the process in this way:

$$A \overset{\mu}{\underset{\nu}{\rightleftarrows}} a$$

This is read "*A* mutates to *a* at a rate μ, and the reverse mutation occurs at rate ν." As Table 11–2 shows, μ and ν may be different. Sometimes one is 100 times as frequent as the other.

Reverse mutation is very important for genetic theory, particularly in applying the results from studies of induced mutagenesis. Without it, all such mutations would be open to the criticism that they are not comparable to spontaneous mutations, but instead represent deletions or otherwise irreversible damage to the chromosome. Biochemical geneticists have been especially effective in proving not only that reverse mutations occur but that the new normal alleles resemble the original ones in every way (dominance, chemical activity, etc.).

Let us examine what effect the interplay of mutation and back-mutation exerts on the frequency of each allele in the population. We will assume that all other factors are equal and that the mutation *rates* remain constant whether the alleles are common or rare.

If *a* has frequency *q* and *A* and *a* are the only two alleles at that locus, then the *A* fraction is $1 - q$. Considering only mutation, if there are *N* people with $2N$ of these loci, each generation,

$$\text{New } a = 2N \times (1 - q) \times \mu,$$

and

$$\text{New } A = 2N \times q \times \nu$$

In other words, mutation adds $2N(1 - q)\nu$ *a* genes and causes the loss of $2Nq\nu$ *a* genes each generation. If we denote the new frequency of q by q_1 and the previous one as q_0,

$$2N_{q1} = 2N_{q0} + 2N(1 - q)\mu - 2N_q\nu$$

Dividing through by $2N$,

$$q_1 = q_0 + (1 - q_0)\mu - q_0\nu.$$

The change in proportion of *a* each generation, Δq, is,

$$q_1 - q_0 = (1 - q_0)\mu - q_0\nu.$$

At any point in time

$$\Delta_q = \mu - q\mu - q\nu$$
$$= \mu - q(\mu + \nu).$$

The change in q will stop when $\Delta q = 0$:

$$0 = \mu - q(\mu + v)$$
$$q(\mu + v) = \mu$$
$$q = \frac{\mu}{\mu + v}.$$

This says that once q reaches a value which is the ratio of the mutation rate divided by the sum of this rate and the reverse mutation rate, there will be no further change in the ratio of $a:A$ in the population.

To illustrate this, suppose autosomal gene A mutates to a at a rate of 1.5×10^{-6}, but mutations from a to A take place at the lesser rate of 1×10^{-6}. When 80 percent of the genes are A and 20 percent are a, in a population of five million persons, there are 8,000,000 A and 2,000,000 a genes. The new gene production is:

$$A \rightarrow a = (1.5 \times 10^{-6})(8 \times 10^{6}) = 12$$
$$a \rightarrow A = (1.0 \times 10^{-6})(2 \times 10^{6}) = 2$$
$$\text{Net decrease in } A = 10$$
$$\text{Net increase in } a = 10.$$

When will the increase in a and decrease in A stop? According to our formula, this will happen when q, the frequency of a, is given by

$$q = \frac{1.5 \times 10^{-6}}{1 \times 10^{-6} + 1.5 \times 10^{-6}} = \frac{1.5 \times 10^{-6}}{2.5 \times 10^{-6}} = \frac{3}{5} = 0.6$$

When the proportion of the genes that are A has fallen to 40 percent and the proportion of a has risen to 60 percent, the new gene production in a given generation in the population is:

$$A \rightarrow a = 1.5 \times 10^{-6} \times 4 \times 10^{6} = 6$$
$$a \rightarrow A = 1.0 \times 10^{-6} \times 6 \times 10^{6} = 6$$
$$\text{Net change} = 0.$$

The mutation rates produce exactly equal numbers of the two alleles, and there is no further change in their relative proportions. In other words, mutation and back mutation alone lead to an equilibrium of the alleles, the exact figure being governed by the relation between the rate of mutation and back mutation. The gene frequency of a at equilibrium is generally written $\hat{q}$, read q-hat.

The very fact that reverse mutations take place ensures polymorphism.* Neither allele can completely replace the other as long as mutations are produced in both directions. If these are the only factors operating, the polymorphism is said to be maintained by the recurrent mutations, or *mutation pressures,* in both directions. In theory this could explain most of the gene frequencies in "normal" variations (blood groups, PTC-taste sensitivity, serum types, etc.) without resort to other factors, provided of course that we had confidence (as we do not) that muta-

---

*Defined usually as the existence of at least one allele at a given locus with a frequency of 1 percent or more.

tion pressures of this type were actually available and the other factors were not. Intergroup variations would presumably result from variations in the $\mu{:}\nu$ ratios.

However, the interplay of mutation and back mutation alone cannot explain the situations in which one trait, usually the abnormal one, is rare. For some loci, we know ν must be 0, since the persons manifesting the trait do not reproduce at all. Here we need the combination of mutation with other evolutionary factors, notably, selection. In many cases selection is so severe that the abnormal allele would disappear completely were it not for the ability of mutations to replenish the losses.

NATURAL SELECTION

Natural selection is the increase or decrease of gene or genotype frequency as a result of differential fertility or differential survival of its bearers. The extent of natural selection is judged by a comparison between the frequency of the allele or genotype in a mating population and the frequency of that allele in the mating population of a subsequent generation. An allele or genotype whose frequency has diminished between the generations is said to be selected against, and the disparity is referred to as its *selective disadvantage.* This is usually indicated by the letter *s*.

Instead of speaking of the selective *dis*advantage of a gene or genotype, it is often convenient to look at it from the positive side and speak of its *adaptive* value or fitness, *W*. If there were no selective disadvantage, the adaptive value of a genotype would be the same in both generations, or one. A genotype with selective disadvantage *s* has an adaptive value $1 - s$, etc. By convention the other genotypes manifest their relatively increased adaptive values through increased contributions to the total rather than through numerical changes in their *W*'s.

To illustrate, consider selection against one homozygote. Suppose a population consists of

64 percent A/A, 32 percent A/a, and 4 percent a/a

and three-fourths of the *a/a* do not survive to reproduce, or for some other reason the *a/a* produce only one-fourth of the 4 percent gametes to create the next generation to which by their original numbers they appear entitled. The genotype *a/a* is said to have a selective disadvantage of 75 percent, that is, $s = 0.75$, and $W = 0.25$. The *W*'s of the other genotypes are still considered 1.00, but their relatively increased contribution is shown by having the proportions contributed add up to 0.97, that is $0.64 + 0.32 + 0.01$, instead of 1. Thus the *A/A* contribute 64/97, the *A/a* 32/97, and the *a/a* 1/97 of the next generation's gametes. Therefore, in the gamete pool,

$$q = \frac{0.16}{0.97} + \frac{0.01}{0.97} = 0.1649 + 0.0103$$
$$= 0.175,$$

instead of 0.20, etc.

Generalizing, we could schematize this kind of selection as follows:

	A/A	A/a	a/a	Total
Old population	p^2	$2pq$	q^2	1
W	1	1	$1 - s$	
Relative contribution to new population	p^2	$2pq$	$(1 - s)q^2$	$1 - sq^2$

Considering selection only, the new frequency of a,

$$q_1 = \frac{pq_0 + (1 - s)q_0 2}{1 - sq_0 2}.$$

Skipping the algebraic details,* we find that

$$\Delta q = -\frac{spq^2}{1 - sq^2}$$

Since Δq is negative (and q^2 cannot be greater than 1), a would tend to be eliminated. Mathematically, if selection alone is operating, the change in the frequency of a would stop when $\Delta q = 0 = spq^2$, that is, when either A or a is fixed ($q = 0$ or $p = 0$, respectively). Realistically this would be when $q = 0$; under the terms of selection p could be zero only by accident.

If we add mutation, a positive factor is brought in, namely,

$$\Delta q = -\frac{spq^2}{1 - sq^2} + \mu(1 - q) - \nu q.$$

After some appropriate simplifications,

$$\Delta q \simeq \mu(1 - q) - spq^2.$$

For equilibrium,

$$\Delta q = 0 \simeq \mu(1 - q) - s(1 - q)q^2.$$

At that time,

$$\mu(1 - q) \simeq s(1 - q)q^2.$$

This would be true when q is 1, but that would be begging the question. For all other situations $\Delta q = 0$ when mutation and selection are balanced, that is, when

$$\mu \simeq sq^2,$$

or

$$\hat{q} \simeq \sqrt{\frac{\mu}{s}}.$$

This equilibrium value is especially interesting when a/a is 100 percent lethal.

*The interested student may find them in Levitan and Montagu (1977).

Then, $s = 1$, so

$$\hat{q} \simeq \sqrt{\mu},$$

that is, the persisting frequency of a depends entirely on, and is indicative of, the mutation rate.

Some typical relations of s, Δq, q and q^2 are illustrated in Fig. 11–1. Note that Δq usually becomes progressively smaller as q decreases. This means that elimination of a is very difficult even if its losses were not kept in balance by recurrent mutations. This is merely another way of stating what was established in Chapter 9: When an allele becomes rare in a random mating population, almost all of these genes are in heterozygotes. If selection is directed only against the homozygotes, these genes become exposed to selection at an ever decreasing rate. If any mutations to a are occurring, its elimination becomes virtually impossible. This bit of theory is the stumbling block of many a poorly thought-out program of negative eugenics.

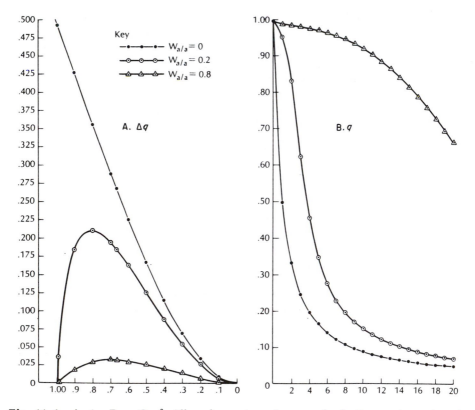

Fig. 11-1   A. Δq. B. q. C. q^2. All under various degrees of selection against a/a only. Graph **A** shows that the size of the decrease in gene frequency depends on the gene frequency at the time as well as on the adaptive value ($W = 1 - s$) of the homozygote under selection, but the effect of gene frequency is diminished (Δq becoming fairly uniform) as the selective disadvantage of a/a (s) becomes smaller. **B** and **C** trace the effect

The same point may be deduced by noticing the number of generations required to make changes in gene frequency when q is common and when q is rare. Consider, for example, the simplest situation, when a/a is lethal or otherwise completely restrained from mating ($s = 1$). With a bit of algebra it can be shown that, after n generations

$$q_n = \frac{q_0}{1 + nq_0},$$

To solve for n, the number of generations needed to effect a given change in q,

$$q_n + nq_0q_n = q_0$$

so that

$$n = \frac{q_0 - q_n}{q_0q_n}.$$

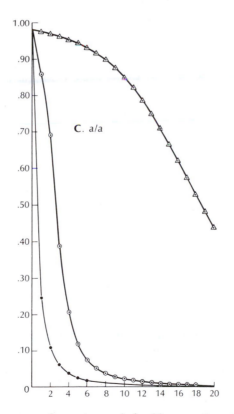

on the frequency of gene a and genotype a/a for 20 generations. Note in **C** that the a/a have virtually disappeared from the population after a few generations of strong selection, but the further diminution of a/a per generation becomes more difficult thereafter even though all or virtually all a/a are eliminated each generation. The graph for $W = 0.8$ will take longer to, but will eventually also, reach this stage.

If $q_0 = 0.01$ and we wish to know how many generations of complete selection against a/a it would take to make $q_n = 0.005$,

$$n = \frac{0.005}{(0.01)(0.005)} = 100.$$

In 100 more generations, q would move only to 0.0033, since

$$q_n = \frac{0.005}{1 + 100(0.005)} = 0.0033,$$

and it would take 100 generations more to decrease q half of 0.005, from 0.0033 to 0.0025.

The converse is also true. If the direction of selection against a formerly deleterious recessive gene is changed, the rate of increase of the gene will be very slow until it reaches a much higher frequency. Some persons inadequately grounded in this theory have expressed the fear that the development of treatments that would enable individuals with such conditions as phenylketonuria and galactosemia to lead normal lives would result in large increases in the number of children born to them. Such fears are clearly groundless. Even if every afflicted person were salvageable, the increase in q from 0.001 to 0.01 would take just as long as the decrease from 0.01 to 0.001 would take when none could be saved. Crow has estimated that it would take about 40 generations, or 12 centuries, to double the incidence of phenylketonuria, even if one were to assume (as is unlikely) that all persons presently born with the defect were to enjoy normal fertility as well as normal survival. As he so aptly remarks, "In comparison with the rate at which knowledge is changing, that is a long time." The rate of increase, however, would be much faster for currently deleterious *dominant* genes.

These points about recessives affect also the ability to derive meaningful mutation rates by the indirect method from the indicated equilibrium. We are in effect estimating the mutation rate by calculating how many genes have to be replaced each generation because of the selective disadvantage of the homozygote. Indeed, several rates for recessives in Table 11–1 were derived from slightly refined forms of the equation for q on page 259, assuming $s = 1$ for congenital ichthyosis and Tay–Sachs disease and 0.5 for albinism and congenital total color-blindness.

Such calculations, however, must be taken with a great deal of caution. When the reproductive performance of the heterozygotes is also lower than the normal homozygotes, additional genes besides the ones accounted for in the equation are being lost, and these, too, have to be replaced by mutations for the trait to remain stable. If so, the calculated mutation rate underestimates the true rate. On the other hand, good evidence exists that the heterozygotes for some recessive genes leave more offspring relative to their numbers than do the normal homozygotes. As a result, fewer new mutations are required to counterbalance the losses by the homozygous recessives. The true mutation rate to the autosomal recessive gene will therefore be much smaller than a rate the calculation of which ignores this possibility. Because of these serious sources of error, many authors believe that the few autosomal recessive mutation rates obtained by the above methods that have been published have no value even though their orders of magnitude correspond well to those of the dominants.

Although partially subject to the same criticism, rates for X-linked recessives find better acceptance, primarily because, like the autosomal dominants, they can be manifested in single dose (in the male) and thereby frequently exposed to natural selection. Consequently, selective advantages or disadvantages of the heterozygotes constitute a smaller source of error. In this calculation, it need be kept in mind that if the number of this gene that was being lost in the males were mutating in the female X-bearing gametes that produced males, in the female X-bearing gametes that produced females, and in the male X-bearing gametes, three times as many mutations would be produced as were needed. Exactly the number needed will be obtained, however, if the number produced at all of these three locations of the gene, the mutation rate of the locus, is equal to *one-third* the number lost through reproductive disadvantage of the male. The very first mutation rate calculation for human beings, that for hemophilia, was made by Haldane with this formula. The subsequent discovery that there were two different X-linked loci for hemophilia has forced recalculation of this historic rate.

Let us now consider the expectations if both A/A and a/a are selected against so that the heterozygote, A/a, has the superior fitness. To avoid confusion, we shall continue to refer to the selective disadvantage of the a/a as s and refer to the selective disadvantage of the A/A as t: in the literature these are often called s_1 and s_2. The scheme looks like this:

	A/A	A/a	a/a	Total (T)
Previous generation	p^2	$2pq$	q^2	1
Selective disadvantage	t	0	s	
Relative fitness	$1 - t$	1	$1 - s$	
Relative contribution to new generation	$(1 - t)p^2$	$2pq$	$(1 - s)q^2$	$1 - tp^2 - sq^2$

Here

$$\Delta q = \frac{pq(tp - sq)}{T},$$

and it turns out an equilibrium is reached without calling on mutation, for $\Delta q = 0$ when

$$\hat{q} = \frac{t}{s + t}.$$

This is a stable equilibrium, because whenever q is different from $\hat{q}$ the change in q has a sign that will move q toward the equilibrium point, as is illustrated well by a graph of the values of Δq for $t = 0.1$ and $s = 0.4$ (Fig. 11–2). The resultant persistence of both genes in the population is referred to as *balanced polymorphism*.

Generally the effect of mutations here is minimal as compared with the effect of selection. This is particularly true during the large portion of the curve (Fig. 11–2) in which Δq is almost linear in relation to q. Hence, they will have little chance

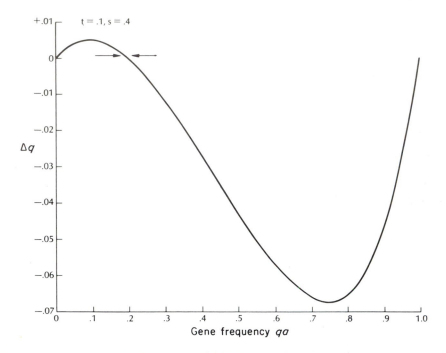

Fig. 11-2 Changes in the frequency of a (Δq) when the selective disadvantage of the A/A is 0.1 and that of the a/a is 0.4. Note that the changes stop when q is 0.2. At other values of q the changes push it toward 0.2 (arrows), so this is a stable equilibrium point.

of upsetting the drive toward the selectional equilibrium point even if their own projected equilibrium point is far away.

The best established balanced polymorphism in humans is the persistence of the gene for S hemoglobin even though the S homozygote, afflicted with sickle cell anemia, has until recently rarely survived till maturity. Evidence is strong that in areas of Africa with large amounts of the kind of malaria caused by *Plasmodium falciparum* the heterozygotes (AS), with sickle cell trait, are adaptively superior not only to the SS but also to the normal homozygotes (AA). AS are far less likely than AA to develop severe *falciparum* infections (Table 11–3). Apparently the sickling that occurs under the relatively anoxic conditions in some of the AS's smaller blood vessels hinders the multiplication of the parasite. The situation—and the algebra— is complicated by the persistence of another abnormal allele, for Hb C, in many of these areas. Evidently the adaptive superiority of both AS and AC counterbalances not only the various homozygotes but also the heterozygotes with SC disease, who are almost as seriously affected as the SS.

American blacks are largely derived from areas of high S frequencies. The pro- portion of AS has stabilized here at about 9 percent as a result of white admixture (p. 267) and the better medical care that has enabled more SS to reproduce.

In other malarial areas heterozygote superiority is thought to similarly main- tain β-thalassemia (Chapter 14), G6PD deficiency, and hemoglobin E.

Table 11-3 Comparison of hemoglobin types in samples of 100 children with severe *falciparum* malaria and 200 matched controls in southwestern Nigeria (From Gilles et al., 1967)

	Number	Hemoglobin Types (in percent)	
		AA	AS
Children with severe *falciparum* malaria	100	96	4
Control children	200	82	18

Now let us consider what happens when both homozygotes are adaptively *superior* to the heterozygotes. The scheme is:

	A/A	A/a	a/a	Total
Initial population	p^2	$2pq$	q^2	1
Selection coefficient	0	h	0	
Fitness	1	$1 - h$	1	
Relative contribution to next generation	p^2	$(1 - h)(2pq)$	q^2	$1 - 2hpq$

The notation h is used here for the selection coefficient to avoid confusion with s, which is generally used for a/a.

$$\Delta q = \frac{hpq(2q - 1)}{1 - 2hpq}$$

$\Delta q = 0$ when p or $q = 0$, but also when $\hat{q} = 1/2$.

This "equilibrium" is unstable, however, because when q does *not* equal 1/2, the sign of Δq is such as to pull q *away* from the equilibrium point. Since hpq and $1 - 2hpq$ are always positive, the sign of Δq depends entirely on the factor $2q - 1$. Thus, if

$$q > 1/2,$$
$$2q - 1 > 1,$$

and

$$\Delta q > 0,$$

that is, it has a plus sign, so that the new q is even larger. If the same selection continues, q would reach 1 and a, the commoner allele, would be fixed. On the other hand, if a is the rarer allele, that is, if

$$q < 1/2,$$
$$2q - 1 < 1,$$

and

$$\Delta q < 0,$$

that is, it has a minus sign, so that the new q is even less than 0.5 than the previous one. If continued, q would reach 0 and a, the rarer allele, would be lost. Again the more common allele, A this time, would be fixed.

Clearly, since selection always takes q away from 0.5, it would take a fortuitous combination of events for q to ever hit the equilibrium point. Once it did, theoretically it would stay there, but Fig. 11–3 shows that the slightest nudge away by mutation or chance would bring selection into play immediately and move q toward 0 or 1. Therefore, when selection is against heterozygotes only, it may be taken for granted that no equilibrium would be reached unless the selection against the rarer allele was counterbalanced by mutation or some other factor. This is exactly the difficulty of accounting for the Rh polymorphism; we shall return to this problem later.

Two other selectional systems could sometimes result in a stable polymorphism:

1. If the species can occupy several ecological niches, the heterozygotes need not be adaptively superior in any of them if the different homozygotes can find niches in which each is superior.
2. Frequency-dependent selection, whereby a gene or genotype has a higher adaptive value when it is rare than when it becomes frequent again.

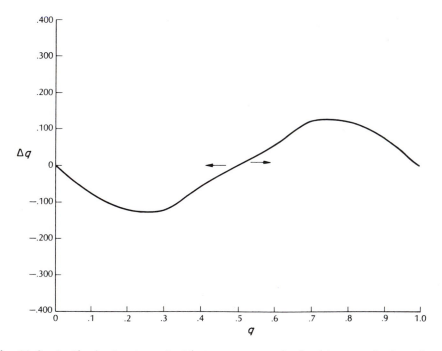

Fig. 11–3 Δq if selection is against heterozygotes only. In this example the selective disadvantage of A/a is 0.9. Note that Δq is always positive when $q > 0.5$, always negative when $q < 0.5$, thus making the apparent equilibrium point ($q = 0.5$) unstable and never reachable by selection alone. The arrows point to the direction in which q is being pushed as a result of selection.

MIGRATION

Migration to and from populations, whether of whole groups or of individuals (in which case the term "gene flow" is more appropriate) has been an important phenomenon in humans. When it goes in both directions, the effect is very similar to that of mutation and back-mutation. More often, however, it is in only one direction. If q_{0A} and q_{0B} are the frequencies of a gene in groups A and B, respectively, prior to the migration, m the proportion of group A that come from group B, and $1 - m$ the proportion from the original group A, the new frequency, q_{1A}, is:

$$q_{1A} = mq_{0B} + (1 - m)q_{0A}$$
$$\Delta q = q_{1A} - q_{0A} = -m(q_{0A} - q_{0B}).$$

The process can easily cause some large changes in gene frequency. If continued long enough, it would tend to equalize the gene frequencies in the two populations, as $\Delta q = 0$ when $q_A = q_B$.

Migration analysis has been used mostly to estimate the degree of racial admixture that has occurred, usually thought of in terms of "white" genes changing aboriginal black frequencies. Thus calculation of the effect of relaxation of selection on the frequency of the S globin gene in America must take into account the decrease due to intermarriage. Some believe that gene flow can also explain many observed variations in gene frequencies. For example, one hypothesis for the larger amount of the B gene in the ABO blood group system in eastern Europe than in the western countries is that it is related to the invasions of Mongols and other Asiatic groups carrying high amounts of B.

GENETIC DRIFT

In Chapter 8 it was demonstrated that chance could play a large part in determining genetic results. Thus in the matings

$$A/a \times A/a$$

or

$$A/a \times a/a$$

with A dominant to a, the offspring could by chance vary between all $A/-$ and all a/a. The probabilities of the different kinds of families that could result is given by the binomial expression

$$[p(A/-) + q(a/a)]^n,$$

where p is the probability of an $A/-$ child and q the probability of an a/a child.

In a fundamental paper published in 1931, Sewall Wright pointed out that a similar factor could be responsible for gene frequency changes in populations as well. Where there are pA and qa genes at a locus distributed among N individuals (who produce $2N$ gametes) it is possible for chance to distribute any proportion of these genes into the gametes (and therefore to the next generation) between all A

and all a. The probability of any combination of A and a genes in the next generation is again given by the binomial, in this case

$$[p(A) + q(a)]^{2N}.$$

As before, most of the time the result will be at or very near the previous one, but sometimes it will not. When a significantly different p or q results, it is said to have been produced by "genetic drift."

The extent that this will actually happen by chance is predicted by the graph of this binomial, as determined especially by the standard error:

$$\sigma = \sqrt{\frac{pq}{2N}}$$

Clearly, the likelihood of any significant deviation by chance from the frequencies of the previous generation depends somewhat on the relative magnitudes of p and q. If p and q are nearly equal, the variance for the same population size will be greater than when they are very different. Thus

$$\frac{1}{2} \times \frac{1}{2} = \frac{1}{4} = 0.2500$$

to enter into the numerator, but

$$\frac{1}{100} \times \frac{99}{100} = \frac{99}{10,000} = 0.0099.$$

For the same N, σ is about eight times as large when $p = q = 0.5$ than when $p = 0.99$. Hence, chance fluctuations will tend to be smaller when one of the alleles is much rarer than the other. At the same time it must be recognized that even though the theoretical magnitude of change is smaller the danger that mere chance fluctuations will erase the polymorphism (that p or $q = 0$) is greatly enhanced when p or q is already near to zero, either as a result of selective forces or of chance fluctuations in previous generations.

An even more important factor in the possibility of chance fluctuations in p and q is the population size, N. For example, if $p = 0.4$ and $q = 0.6$ and $N = 1200$.

$$\sigma = \sqrt{\frac{(0.4)(0.6)}{2400}}$$
$$= 0.01.$$

This means that 68 percent of the time the next generation p is expected to be between 0.39 and 0.41 *by chance alone.* About 95 percent of the time, chance would produce $0.38 < p < 0.42$. Less than 1 percent of the time is it expected that p would be less than 0.37 or more than 0.43. On the other hand, for the same p and q, if $N = 60$

$$\sigma = \sqrt{\frac{(0.4)(0.6)}{120}}$$

$$= \sqrt{0.002}$$
$$\sigma = 0.045.$$

Now about 5 percent of the time the next generation p might by chance be less than 0.31, or more than 0.49. The new possibilities have quite a spread, and at 99 percent or even the 95 percent limits represent an appreciable change in frequency without any selective, migrational, or mutational factors being involved.

The possibility that chance could produce even more extreme changes, that it could lead to "random walks" in one direction, and especially that it might cause extinction ($q = 0$) or fixation ($q = 1$) of a gene, has naturally attracted the widest attention. The implication is that chance factors alone could therefore be responsible for evolutionary changes. Wright has suggested that this is most likely to happen if the population is subdivided into a large number of small breeding groups (often referred to as "demes" or "isolates"). Such changes are also increased by inbreeding.

Wright has shown that the rate at which genes are fixed or extinguished by chance alone is: $\frac{1}{2N}$. Ordinarily, the probability of fixation is the same as the probability of extinction, so the rate of either one, fixation for instance, is: $\frac{1}{4N}$.

Wright cautions, however, that N in most aspects of population genetics is not the census of population, but the number of persons who contribute to the gene pool of the next generation, the reproductive individuals. He refers to these as the *effective size* of the population. As a result, populations that seem to be too large to produce substantial gene frequency changes by genetic drift may actually have much smaller effective sizes.

If the numbers of males and females contributing to the gene pool are not equal, this further depresses the effective size of the population. If N_F = number of female parents and N_M = number of male parents, then, the effective population size, $\hat{N}$, is approximated by

$$\hat{N} = \frac{4N_F N_M}{N_F + N_M}$$

Thus, if 200 females but only 40 males contributed to the next generation,

$$\hat{N} = \frac{4(200)(40)}{200 + 40}$$
$$= \frac{32000}{240}$$
$$= 133$$

instead of 240. This could have been a significant factor in some of the early subdivisions of the human species and in primitive societies in which polygyny and polyandry were more common than they are today.

In the literature, the tendency has been to ascribe to genetic drift all unusual increases in gene frequency in groups with small breeding populations, especially if the same gene has tended to be carried at a lower rate in another group living in substantially similar environments. The rationale is that if selective factors were responsible, the changes ought to have been the same in both groups.

One study, for example, found that the effective population size among the Dunkard (Dunker) sect in Pennsylvania was only about 90. The oldest members of the group have frequencies of the M-N blood type genes substantially similar to those of the German Rhineland population from which their ancestors were derived. However, the youngest members have significantly more M genes, and fewer N genes, the generation in between having intermediate frequencies. Very likely the changed frequencies are attributable to genetic drift, especially since the members of this isolate of whatever age live in a rather uniform environment.

Interestingly enough, the ABO blood type gene frequencies of the three generations of Dunkers were very similar, though all were slightly different (more I^A but less I^0 and I^B) from the frequencies in Germany. The ABO differences could be ascribable to natural selection or to chance factors in migration.

In later papers, Wright extended the concept of genetic drift to all chance fluctuations that could influence gene frequencies. Thus chance variations in the selective disadvantage, s, of a gene or genotype would be included, as would chance factors in mutation and migration.

Perhaps the most significant aspect of this extension is the inclusion of chance variations as a result of migrations of individuals or groups, or, as it is often referred to, "gene flow." Thus genetic drift would apply in cases in which the founders of a separate deme or isolate constitute a very small portion of a population and by chance contain very different frequencies of one or more genes than the population from which they originated. An unusually high number of persons among the Old Order Amish have four autosomal recessive conditions, the Ellis-van Creveld syndrome, pyruvate kinase deficiency (Table 5–3), cartilage-hair hypoplasia, and a form of limb-girdle muscular dystrophy (Troyer syndrome), and one X-linked gene, the one causing hemophilia B (Christmas disease). The investigators attribute this to the fact that genes for each of these traits were brought to the United States by small bands of the sect, often as few as 200 at a time, who established relatively isolated colonies in Pennsylvania, Ohio, Indiana, and Ontario. Similar factors may be responsible for the relatively high frequencies of porphyria variegata among the Dutch settlers in the Union of South Africa and albinism among the San Blas Indians of Panama. The factor of isolation/genetic drift may also explain some of the blood group differences between homeland and migrant population, such as the ABO types of the Dunkers referred to above.

Although he did not think of it as drift, R. A. Fisher showed that a mutant had a chance to survive in the population even if there were no further mutations to the same allele and it was adaptively neutral. It may then spread in the population because there is a chance that some of its carriers will pass it on to most or all of their children. According to Fisher's calculations there is a 10 percent chance that the single mutant could increase to 116 in 100 generations, and there is a 1 percent chance that this figure may even be twice as large (232) in that time, 0.1 percent chance of its being three times as much (348). By the time 40,000 generations have gone by there are only 25 chances in a million (probability of 0.000025) that the gene will have persisted, but *if it has,* there is a 10 percent chance that there are

46,400 copies of it in the population, and a 0.1 percent chance that there may be as many as 139,200 present.

In actuality it is unlikely that a mutant will occur only once; generally it has a consistent, albeit small, rate of appearance each generation. Thus it is theoretically possible for the combination of mutation and chance survival and spread to cause the production and persistence of polymorphism. This could take place even in a large population. Although the mutation rate might be the same in all populations, the chance survival factor could easily differ in different populations, so that this form of drift could also account for interpopulational variation which might be enhanced by occasional episodes of the more typical (small population) Sewall Wright effect and inbreeding.

Many geneticists are skeptical of genetic drift for the maintenance of polymorphism. The major flaw, as they see it, is that it implies that the genotypes are adaptively neutral. For a considerable number of loci, this is patently untrue, as has been shown already and will be documented further below. For others the hypothesis leads to considerable difficulties in view of known rates of mutation. From these and other considerations, these geneticists are inclined to believe that the number of loci for which the genotypes are indeed adaptively neutral must be very small. Once selection comes into the picture its effect per generation is usually so much larger than mutation or the chance survival and spread probabilities that it becomes the dominant evolutionary force.

The controversy concerning the relative significance of selection and genetic drift in human polymorphism took a dramatic turn as a result of the burgeoning of information concerning biochemical variation, primarily as a result of improvements in electrophoretic techniques. A 1972 review of the data on isozymes, for instance, found that 20 out of 71 loci investigated (28 percent) were polymorphic (Table 11–4). (Their criterion for polymorphism was that there exists at least one form of the enzyme with a frequency of 2 percent, equivalent to a gene frequency of 1 percent.) Furthermore, by use of the random mating law, they calculated that average heterozygosity for these loci was 6.7 percent. Since the sampling of loci is

Table 11-4 Data on the incidence of polymorphic loci and average heterozygosity per locus derived from electrophoretic surveys in various animal populations (From Harris and Hopkinson, 1972, which should be consulted for references)

Species	No. of Populations Studied	No. of Loci	Proportion of Loci Polymorphic per Population	Average Heterozygosity per Locus
Mus musculus				
Denmark	6	41	0.22–0.30	0.078
California	1	40	0.30	0.100
Peromyscus polionotus	18	32	0.23	0.058
Limulus polyphemus	4	25	0.25	0.057
Drosophilia persimilis	1	24	0.25	0.105
D. pseudoobscura	3	24	0.42	0.123
Man	1	71	0.28	0.067

considered essentially random, that is, not determined by a preconception of whether polymorphism is present or not, this figure indicates also that the average individual is heterozygous at 6.7 percent of his loci. Very similar data have come from other well-studied species (Table 11–4). If anything, these are probably underestimates because electrophoresis can reveal variation only when there is an underlying change in charge, and we have seen that many mutational amino acid differences do not result in charge differences.

Many have felt that these findings argue in favor of genetic drift as the major factor in maintenance of many, if not all, of these polymorphisms. If such a large number of polymorphisms, it is said, depend on adaptive superiority of heterozygotes—which implies the loss of many homozygotes each generation due to selection against homozygotes—the resultant genetic load would seem too burdensome for the species to bear.

Although much has been written on the question, it remains very much an open one, with no amount of theoretical and experimental evidence satisfying the proponents of either view.

SUGGESTED EXERCISES

11–1. According to Table 11–1 the mutation rate producing the gene for the Waardenburg syndrome is 4 per million.

(a) What is the probability that any gamete one of us produces contains such a mutation?

(b) How many such mutations would be expected to be produced by a population containing 504,000 females and 496,000 males?

11–2. Answer the questions of exercise 11–1 concerning the gene for hemophilia A.

11–3. The abnormal allele at a certain locus is lethal when homozygous. It was assumed, therefore, that the mutation rate was equal to the number of these homozygotes born (and whose genes, therefore, had to be replaced) each generation. Some evidence then develops that the heterozygotes for this locus are reproductively superior to the normal homozygotes. Would the new data change your opinion of the assumed mutation rate and, if so, in which direction? Explain your answer.

11–4. A certain trait was assumed to be due to an autosomal gene dominant to its normal allele. An estimate of its mutation rate was made by the direct method. Some years later evidence developed that the same trait can be produced by dominants at no fewer than three different loci. Would the new data change your opinion of the assumed mutation rate, and if so, in which direction? Explain your answer.

11–5. Phenylketonuria has never been known to have occurred on either side in a certain family. Assume the records of the family are good, that a correct diagnosis has always been possible, and so forth. A phenylketonuric child is now born to one couple in the family. A farmer friend of the family says he reckons that a "sport" (mutation) is responsible. Having had more genetic training, you are asked to comment on this remark. What would you say?

11–6. Define the following phrases: natural selection; genetic drift; directional factors; balanced polymorphism; stable equilibrium; unstable equilibrium; adaptive value; effective population size.

In the following exercises assume panmixia with but two alleles, A and a, and disregard other possible evolutionary forces unless they are specifically mentioned.

11–7. Suppose selection is acting only against the genotype a/a, with A/A and A/a reproducing according to previous expectation.

If $s = 1.0$, and $q = 0.1$, what are the expected proportions of homozygous recessives in the initial population and in the next three generations?

11–8. (a) Do exercise 11–7 taking into account the knowledge that the forward mutation rate, μ, $= 1 \times 10^{-5}$.

(b) Compare the results of exercises 11–7 and 11–8 in a table.

11–9. If q initially $= 0.4$ and s and t are the same as in Figure 11–2, calculate the expected proportions of the genotypes in the initial population and the next three generations.

11–10. Calculate the expected proportions of the genotypes in the next generation if selection is against A/a only, its selective disadvantage being 0.5, (a) if initially $q = 0.2$; (b) if initially $q = 0.8$.

11–11. Suppose q is 0.1 in both of two populations with an effective population size of 10,000. In one, chance factors move q in the same direction downward, for two generations in a row, each time the movement being the maximum amount expected at the 95 percent confidence level. In the other, the movement is again the maximum expected at 95 percent level, but the movement in the second generation is the opposite to that in the first. What proportions of recessives are expected in the two populations at the end of the second generation?

11–12. How much different would have been the expected change in the proportion of recessives in the first-named population in exercise 11–11 (a) if the initial q were 0.8; (b) if q were 0.1, but the effective population size were 100?

11–13. In a population with an initial $q = 0.5$, q rose to 0.6 after 10 generations. Diagram a likely pattern of genetic drift that could lead to this result even if no single change were larger than 0.04 and there were not a significantly larger number of "plus" than "minus" years.

11–14. According to Hansen et al. (1964) the frequency of galactosemia at birth in the United States is 5.6×10^{-5}. If this represents an equilibrium figure and galactosemia may be considered 100 percent lethal, (a) how long did it take the frequency of the disorder to fall from a frequency of 1×10^{-4} to its present level? (b) Before that how long did it take to drop approximately 100 times the same amount, from 4.9×10^{-3} to 1×10^{-4}? Hint: Note that $(7.5)^2 = 56.25$; 5.625×10^{-5} is a sufficient approximation to 5.6×10^{-5} for these purposes.

11-15. Assuming the present frequency of galactosemia represents an equilibrium between mutation and selection at a single locus, what is the approximate mutation rate to the galactosemia gene from its normal allele in the United States?

11-16. What selective disadvantage of the normal homozygote would need to be postulated in the United States if one were to assume that the galactosemia locus was being maintained by heterozygous advantage?

11-17. Schwartz et al. (1961) found the frequency of galactosemia in England was about one-fourth that in the United States, namely, 1.4×10^{-5}. Would the selective disadvantage of the normal homozygotes in England need to be less or greater than the corresponding value in the United States to maintain the polymorphism? By how much?

11-18. In a pioneer study, McIntosh et al. (1954) found that of 5739 babies born apparently free of congenital malformations, 5530 (96.4 percent) survived the neonatal period (defined as the first 30 days of life) whereas 386 (89.1 percent) of 433 babies born with known congenital malformations survived this period. Assuming these figures can be used without resort to coefficient of variation, what is the apparent selective disadvantage, based on survival in the neonatal period, of the babies born with congenital malformations?

12

Independent Genes

When one marriage partner has both Hb S and Hb C and the other partner has only Hb A, the offspring either have S and A, or they have C and A. None have both S and C; nor do any have only A, that is, neither S nor C. This is what we referred to as segregation (Mendel's First Law), and it shows that S and C are probably determined by variants of a single locus. Their allelic nature is reinforced by evidence that these hemoglobins involve variation in the same molecule: beta globin.

Conversely, whenever the hemoglobins represent changes in two different peptide chains, the evidence shows that two different loci are involved. For example, Hopkins-2 is an alpha globin variant. Figure 12–1 shows several matings of persons who have both Hb Hopkins-2 and Hb S and persons who have only normal hemoglobin. Note especially II-9 and III-1. Their offspring include children with neither abnormal hemoglobin and children with both of them.

These contrasting patterns of inheritance are diagrammed in Fig. 12–2. As indicated by parts II and III of this figure, there are two alternative possibilities to explain the results in the previous paragraph: independence (part II) or linkage (part III). This chapter is concerned primarily with the first of these two.

MENDEL'S SECOND LAW

The basic principles of independence were discovered by Mendel and are incorporated in his Second Law. Like the First Law, it can be inferred from the chromosomal theory and the behavior of the chromosomes in meiosis. Generally referred to as the "law of independent assortment," it may be stated thus: *When gametes are being formed, the genetic material contributed by one parent for several traits need not remain together; rather, these materials have as much likelihood of passing into different gametes as of passing into the same one.* This is exactly what would be expected whenever the genetic material for several traits is on *different* pairs of homologous chromosomes.

Consider, for example, the A, B parent in part II of Fig. 12–2. Suppose he had received the A and B genes from one parent and the corresponding A^+ and B^+ genes from the other. (This is analogous exactly to the formation of III-15, III-17,

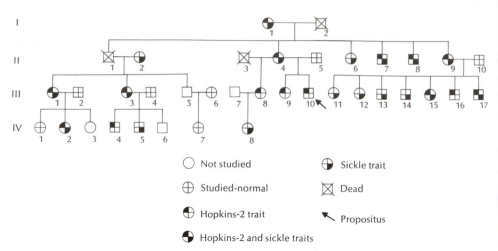

Fig. 12–1 Pedigree demonstrating independent assortment of the genes for two abnormal hemoglobins, S and Hopkins-2. Particularly noteworthy are the two progeny of II-9 × II-10 with both abnormal hemoglobins and the daughter of III-2 who lacks both. (From the revision by Bradley et al., 1961, of a family originally presented by Smith and Torbert, 1958. Courtesy of T. B. Bradley, Jr. and the *Bulletin of Johns Hopkins Hospital*.)

IV-2, and probably also II-4, -7, -8, and -9, of Fig. 12–1.) During Metaphase I of meiosis, if both of the marked chromosomes, containing genes A and B, respectively, are turned toward the same pole, the gametes this individual produces will transmit these genetic materials exactly as he received them, with either A and B together or A$^+$ and B$^+$ together. If one marked chromosome faces a different pole from the other, however, the A, B parent transmits either A and B$^+$ or A$^+$ and B in the resulting gametes. Since these combinations are new, that is, different from the combinations the A, B parent had received from his parents, production of these gametes constitutes *recombination* of the genes.

Since the direction in which the members of each pair face at Metaphase I

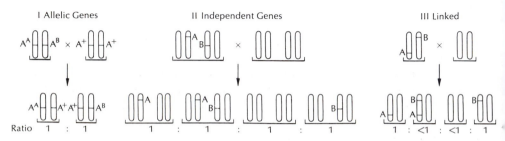

Fig. 12–2 Contrast in the pattern of inheritance expected from marriages of persons with two codominant genes to individuals containing neither one if the two are (I) determined by allelic genes or (II and III) by different loci. The normal alleles A$^+$ and B$^+$ are omitted from II and III. (Modified from a figure in W. W. Zuelzer et al., 1956. Reprinted by permission of Grune and Stratton, Inc., publishers of *Progress in Hematology*.)

appears to be completely a matter of chance, the marked chromosomes may be turned toward different poles in as many meioses as toward the same one. As a result, the gametes of an A/A^+, B/B^+ may contain four possible combinations of these genes, and any one of the four is as likely as the other. This is the essence of the law of independent assortment. To put it another way, under independent assortment, new and old combinations of the genes are equally likely.

As in the case of the first law, the best test comes from the backcross (testcross) indicated in Fig. 12–2. Four certain matings of this type in Fig. 12–1 produced 5 S, 4 Hopkins-2, 1 A, and 3 with both S and Hopkins-2. Thus all four combinations predicted by the law of independent assortment were produced. Their proportions are not exactly 1:1:1:1, but even for such a small sample they do not deviate significantly from the 3.25 expected in each of the four classes. In a much larger series, Levitan and Montagu (1971, 1977) were able to determine the composition of the gametes produced by persons who were (1) blood type MN and (2) heterozygous for the Rh blood groups by having a gene that enabled them to produce a factor called rh' and an allelic gene that produced the factor hr' (Chapter 16). These double heterozygotes transmitted the following combinations in their gametes:

514 with genes for M and rh'
516 with genes for M and hr'
498 with genes for N and rh'
526 with genes for N and hr'

The fit to the 513.5 expected in each class is very close.

Figure 12–3 diagrams the combinations of gametes expected in a mating of two heterozygotes for these loci. The 16 different combinations of gametes represent nine different kinds of offspring. Collecting together those that are alike, the relative likelihoods of the offspring are:

1 M, rh'+: 2 MN, rh'+: 1 N, rh'+:
2 M, rh'+, hr'+: 4 MN, rh'+, hr'+: 2 N, rh'+, hr'+:
1 M, hr'+: 2 MN, hr'+: 1 N, hr'+

Note that if we add up the expected progeny for each trait separately, we obtain the results predicted for each one by the law of segregation: 4 M: 8 MN: 4 N = 1/4 M: 1/2 MN: 1/4 N, and 4 rh'+: 8 rh'+, hr'+: 4 hr'+ are also in a 1/4:1/2:1/4 ratio. Furthermore, the combined results, 1/16 M, rh'+: 1/8 MN, rh'+, and so forth can be thought of as the product of these two segregation ratios.

SIMPLIFYING THE CALCULATIONS FOR MULTIPLE LOCI

The observations in the previous paragraph suggest a method for simplifying the calculation of expected results when more than one locus is involved. The traditional method of first figuring out the gametes and then the kinds of fertilizations, illustrated in Fig. 12–3, is fundamentally sound and should be understood as a first step by every student. The labor involved becomes even more onerous, however, as the number of loci being considered increases, and the method is prone to com-

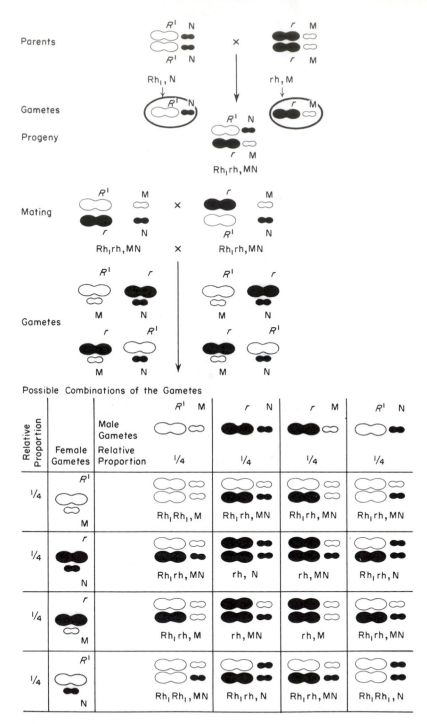

Fig. 12-3 Gametes and Punnett squre diagram of fertilizations in certain marriages between MN individuals who are both rh′+ and hr′+ (positive for C and c in the Fisher–Race terminology). The assumed Rh genotype, R^1/r (or CDe/cde), is the commonest with this phenotype among Caucasoids.

putational error even for a small number of loci. Suppose, for example, we had a mating of individuals heterozygous for three loci:

$$\frac{A}{a}\frac{B}{b}\frac{C}{c} \times \frac{A}{a}\frac{B}{b}\frac{C}{c}$$

Each can produce eight different kinds of gametes of equal probability. If we were interested in the proportion of their children that were expected to be A/A, b/b, C/C, for instance, the Punnett square method would force us to diagram the 64 (8 $\times$ 8) different possible fertilizations and pick out how many had this genotype. It happens that this would almost be a needle-in-the-haystack proposition, because only one out of the 64 is the desired type. If, on the other hand, we wished to know how many to expect (assuming dominance of all three loci) with the A, b, and C phenotypes, we would have to ferret out how many of the 64 were A/A b/b C/C, how many A/a b/b C/C, how many were A/A b/b C/c, and how many were A/a b/b C/c, and then add these together (there would be nine altogether out of 64) to obtain the desired result.

Understanding the rules of probability leads to considerable simplification of these chores. As soon as we know that the three loci in question are on different chromosomes and, therefore, each performs according to Mendel's first law independently of the other, we can apply the probability multiplication rules. In other words, what happens at the three loci are really simultaneous combinations of independent events. To answer the first question we posed above, then, we need merely ask:

1. What proportion of an $A/a \times A/a$ mating is expected to be A/A? Answer: 1/4.
2. What proportion of a $B/b \times B/b$ mating would be b/b? Answer: 1/4.
3. What proportion of C/C children from a $C/c \times C/c$ mating? Answer: 1/4.
4. Therefore, the expected proportion of A/A b/b C/C children is:

$$\frac{1}{4} \times \frac{1}{4} \times \frac{1}{4} = \frac{1}{64}$$

Asking the corresponding questions for the phenotype problem, we realize that the expected proportion of A b C children (assuming dominance at all three loci) is:

(A from $A/a \times A/a$ $\times$ (b from $B/b \times B/b$) $\times$ (C from $C/c \times C/c$)
=   3/4 $\times$ 1/4 $\times$ 3/4
=   9/64.

For a slightly more complex problem we could ask: What proportion of those with the A b C phenotype from this mating would be expected to be homozygous at all three loci? By the multiplication rule independent events for the answer is quickly available:

(Prob. that A phenotype from $A/a \times A/a$ is A/A)
$\times$ (Prob. that b phenotype from $B/b \times B/b$ is b/b)

$\times$ (Prob. that C phenotype from $C/c \times C/c$ is C/C)

$$= \frac{1^*}{3} \cdot 1 \cdot \frac{1}{3} = \frac{1}{9}$$

This is much quicker and less prone to error than the indirect way we would have to work the problem if we used a Punnett square. Then we would first have to realize that what we wished to know was: What proportion of the 9/64 expected to be A b C are the 1/64 expected to be A/A b/b C/C? 1/64 out of 9/64 is 1/9, of course, the same as the answer we obtained much more directly above.

SYNTENIC INDEPENDENCE

When loci are on the same chromosome they are said to be *syntenic,* from Greek words which mean "same ribbon." *A priori* one expects syntenic loci to be pulled toward the same pole during meiosis. As we have noted, earlier, however, homologous chromosomes regularly interchange pieces during prophase of the first meiotic division. These interchanges are manifestations, as it were, of the chiasmata, the cross-shaped figures between the homologues, which are often seen as early as late zygotene but are most clearly visible in diplotene (Figs. 1–1 and 1–2). When the interchanges result in new combinations of the genes, these are referred to as *crossovers.* If the parent undergoing meiosis has the genotype ab/AB, for example, aB or Ab gametes that he or she produces represent new combinations or crossovers. The process that produced them is called *crossing over.*

Crossing over is a form of recombination. For many pairs of loci it differs from the recombination of independent assortment because the new and old combination gametes are not equally likely. For some syntenic loci, however, the results are not distinguishable from those of independent assortment, as equal (or nearly equal) numbers of new and old combinations are produced.

To understand this, it should be noted that crossing over is essentially random along the chromosome. As indicated diagrammatically in Fig. 12–4, it may take place at different points in successive meioses. For most of the loci in the diagram, less than half of the resulting gametes would contain new combinations. Between C and F, for instance, crossing over occurs in only three of the 10 meioses. In the male these three would produce 12 gametes, six of which contain new combination (Cf or cF). None of the 28 gametes from the other seven meioses would contain these combinations. Hence, only six of the 40 gametes, 15 percent, would contain new combinations between C and F. Similar considerations would apply to oogenesis. The recombination frequency, 15 percent, is clearly different from the 50 percent frequency in independent assortment. It stems from the fact that C and F are quite close to one another on the chromosome.

When loci are farther apart it is conceivable that crossing over between them would occur in *every* meiosis. In that case equal numbers of new and old combinations would be produced in the gametes. To put it another way, syntenic genes that are far apart may also manifest independent assortment.

---

*In the A phenotype the ratio of A/A:A/a is 1:2.

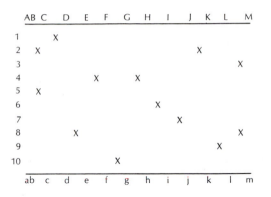

Fig. 12-4   Diagrammatic representation of chiasmata locations on one pair of homologous chromosomes in 10 successive meioses. The letters above and below represent alleles. For simplicity the entire chromosome is shown in coupling, but the chiasmata could occur in the same way even if all the alleles were alike.

Even when they are so far apart that chiasmata between them occur in every meiosis, syntenic genes frequently do not produce 50 percent new combination gametes because some meioses would contain an even number of chiasmata between them (e.g., meiosis 4 in Fig. 12-4, with two chiasmata: in intervals E–F and G–H). Such crossovers would restore some old combinations. This is one reason, incidentally, why the term "recombination frequency" is preferable to "crossover frequency." The number of double crossovers is relatively small, however, being almost universally less than the number expected on probability considerations. (The discrepancy from the expected number of multiple crossovers is called *interference*.) Hence, many genes which are on the same chromosome mimic independence when pedigree data are gathered to determine whether they are syntenic.

In some instances such loci can nevertheless be proven syntenic. One method is to find a third gene which lies between them but sufficiently close to each one to produce significantly less than 50 percent recombinants in pedigree data. Another method is to find a chromosomal variant that segregates concordantly with these loci. In addition, as we have seen in Chapter 6, a number of *in vitro* methods have been developed. All of these techniques will be expanded upon in the next chapter.

POPULATIONAL INDEPENDENCE

It can be shown (see, for example, pp. 464–465 of Levitan and Montagu, 1977) that all separated loci should exist in *populational independence*. This means that the frequency of any combination of the genes at the two loci in the population should equal the product of the frequencies of the genes involved. If, for instance, 85 percent of a population are Rh-positive and 10 percent are type B of the ABO system, then 8.5 percent of the population ($0.85 \times 0.10 \times 100$) should be B, Rh-positive. Similarly, if 40 percent of the gametes in a population are expected to contain an r gene, for the Rh-negative condition, and 30 percent the Fy^b gene, for Duffy-b blood type, then 12 percent of the gametes are expected to contain both the r and Fy^b genes.

The expectation of populational independence holds true whether the loci are on different chromosomes, as in the case for Rh and ABO, or on the same chromosome, as in the case for Rh and Duffy, so long as any recombination occurs between them. Unlike the random mating equilibrium for single loci (Chapter 9), it takes more than one generation to attain the state of populational independence. Also, the smaller the recombination rate the longer it takes to attain it. Most polymorphic loci of humans, however, have probably coexisted sufficiently long— indeed, some alleles were probably together in our primate ancestors, if not further back—that populational independence should be the rule even when the recombination frequency is very low, and any discrepancy from this rule demands special explanation.

Populational independence of syntenic genes is often referred to as *linkage equilibrium*. If the data contradict such independence, the population is said to exhibit *linkage disequilibrium* for the genes in question. We shall note some important instances of this in Chapter 16.

SUGGESTED EXERCISES

12–1. Considering the results of a number of meioses under the same conditions as in exercise 1–5,

(a) What proportion of the gametes are expected to contain the paternal large metacentric and the paternal large acrocentric?

(b) In what proportion of the gametes would you expect both of these chromosomes to be the maternal ones?

(c) In what proportion would one of them be expected to be paternal and one maternal?

12–2. The disposition of the chromosomes at which critical stages of meiosis determines the answers to exercise 12–1?

12–3. The genes for ovalocytosis, a certain form of epidermolysis bullosa, and the nail-patella syndrome are known to be dominant to their normal alleles (Table 1–3). A man with this type of epidermolysis marries a woman with ovalocytosis. Their first child is normal in every way, but their second child has the nail-patella syndrome.

(a) How do you explain the absence of the parental traits in the children and the presence of traits in the children not represented in the parents?

(b) Can you predict what proportion of further children in this sibship would be expected to resemble the first child for these traits and what proportion the second child? Explain. Assume the loci are on different chromosomes.

12–4. Figure 12–5 is a rare pedigree in which two different abnormal genes are segregating. What are the probable genotypes of all the members of the pedigree?

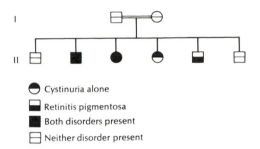

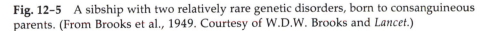

○ Cystinuria alone
▬ Retinitis pigmentosa
■ Both disorders present
▤ Neither disorder present

Fig. 12-5 A sibship with two relatively rare genetic disorders, born to consanguineous parents. (From Brooks et al., 1949. Courtesy of W.D.W. Brooks and *Lancet*.)

Note that the pedigree suggests independent assortment. Call the cystinuria locus cy, retinitis pigmentosa, rp.

12-5. The indicated genes at the Lutheran (Lu^a and Lu^b), Duffy (Fy^a and Fy^b), and Kidd (Jk^a and Jk^b) blood group loci are codominants, just as M and N, but the resultant types are indicated by showing whether antigens a and b in each case are present. Thus the person who is Fy^a/Fy^a is said to be $Fy(a+b-)$ and the heterozygote Jk^a/Jk^b is Jk(a+b+). The possibility that a person is Jk(a−b−) or $Fy(a−b−)$ may be ignored for these problems. These loci and the one responsible for M-N appear to be on four different chromosomes.
What progeny are expected from the following marriages?
    (a) Lu(a+b+), Fy(a+b+) × Lu(a−b+), Fy(a+b−)
    (b) M, Lu(a+b−), Jk(a+b+) × N, Lu(a+b+), Jk(a−b+)
    (c) N, Lu(a−b+), Fy(a−b+), Jk(a+b−) × MN, Lu(a+b−), Fy(a+b+), Jk(a+b+).

Whether a person is Rh-positive or negative depends on the reaction to an antiserum, anti-Rh$_0$ (called by some anti-D). The responsible gene is dominant to an allele, r, which no known antiserum can identify, but codominant to other genes of the series (Chapter 16).

12-6. A man with multiple polyposis of the colon is Rh-positive. His wife is also Rh-positive, but she is free of the intestinal disease (as are his mother and mother-in-law, who are Rh-negative). Using the methods outlined in this chapter, what is the probability (assuming the loci are on different chromosomes)
    (a) That their first child will be Rh-positive and be affected by multiple polyposis of the colon?
    (b) That two of their first four children will resemble him for both traits and two will resemble his mother for both?
    (c) That their first child will resemble his wife in being a female who is Rh-positive and free of multiple polyposis of the colon? (Assume an expected secondary sex ratio of 1:1.)
    (d) If the wife in this question also had multiple polyposis of the colon, what is the probability that a child of theirs who was Rh-positive and had multiple poly-

posis of the colon was homozygous for both loci? (To make the question credible, either assume what is not known, namely, that homozygosity for multiple polyposis is viable, or else suppose that the exercise refers to conceptions and makes no assumptions as to eventual viability of the conceptus.)

12–7. A man who belongs to group MN and is Xg(a+) marries a woman who is type M and Xg(a+). Her father, however, was type MN and Xg(a−). What are the expected blood group combinations, including, of course, the relative proportions, among their progeny?

13

Linked Genes

Syntenic loci, genes that are on the same chromosome, were introduced in the previous chapter. We noted there that very often syntenic genes, particularly those that are far apart on the chromosome, mimic independence in family data because the percentage of new combinations in their gametes do not differ significantly from the 50 percent expected when loci are on separate chromosomes.

A great deal of effort is expended by geneticists to find which loci are syntenic. They are especially bent on discovering which genes are so close to one another that they always, or nearly always, go into a person's gametes in the same combination as the person inherited them. In technical language: they wish to know which pairs of loci have low recombination frequencies.

Loci with significantly fewer than 50 percent recombination between them are said to exhibit "measurable linkage," or, more simply stated, are "linked." When the recombination frequency is very low—about 5 percent or less—the loci are said to be "closely linked."

Linkage can have important implications for medicine. If a locus responsible for a genetic disease could be shown to be closely linked to a normal chromosomal or genetic variation, the latter could serve as a "marker" of the disorder. This would be especially helpful for anticipation of traits with late onset, such as Huntington's chorea. It can also aid the analysis of an amniocentesis when the aspirated material can be tested for the normal marker but not for the suspected disorder.

It must be emphasized that the usefulness of close linkage for these purposes generally applies only to families, not to populations. Thus, in the family shown in Fig. 13–1 whenever a person with elliptocytosis (Fig. 13–2 and Table 1–3) transmits to a child an R^2 gene of the Rh blood group locus, that child is likewise affected with elliptocytosis. Linkage is evidently very close. Nevertheless, in other families of the same population this elliptocytosis gene may be bound to other Rh alleles, to R^1, r, or R^0. Thus there is no populational marker, and the Rh gene that can serve as a familial marker must be ascertained anew in each kindred. This fits the rule of "populational independence" mentioned at the end of Chapter 12. The rare exceptions to it will be discussed later.

Usually intertwined with the question of which genes are linked is another question: Where on the chromosome are the genes located? This, too, could be

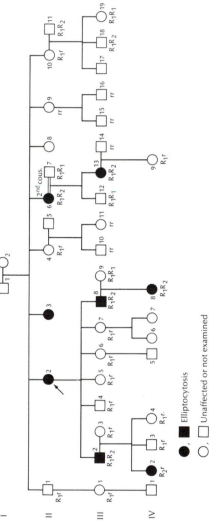

Fig. 13-1 An illustration of the Rh–elliptocytosis linkage. In this family every transmission of an R^2 gene (explained in Chapter 16) also transmits the gene for elliptocytosis. Linkage is, therefore, very close. In other families the elliptocytosis has been found traveling with genes R^0, R^1, or r with very little crossing over. In still other families a different gene for elliptocytosis exists which is not linked to the R locus. (From Roberts, 1967 after Goodall et al., 1953. Courtesy of J. A. Fraser Roberts, H. B. Goodall, and the *Annals of Human Genetics*, successor to the *Annals of Eugenics*.)

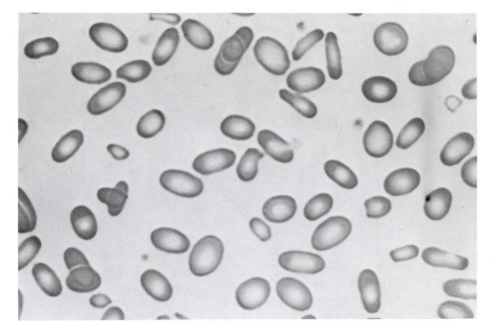

Fig. 13-2   The typical blood picture in elliptocytosis. (From Bannerman and Renwick, 1962. Courtesy of R. M. Bannerman and the *Annals of Human Genetics.*)

medically important. Knowing the exact location of a gene responsible for a serious disorder may make it possible in the not too distant future to engineer the substitution of a normal piece of chromosome for the aberrant one and thus prevent the genetic disease from being expressed.

PEDIGREE ANALYSIS

The time-honored method for detecting linkage is to search for pedigrees, such as those in Figs. 13-1 and 13-3, which contain possible recombinants, to count these, and thereby estimate the recombination rate.

   For many years two major drawbacks have impeded the success of this method in humans (1) the rarity of appropriate pedigrees; and (2) largely because of our small family sizes, the absence of robust statistical techniques that would differentiate between linkage and independence or, when linkage seemed likely, determine the probable recombination rate.

   The introduction of Morton's loci score method, to be described below, and its improvements have solved the second problem, but the first remains a severe obstacle to the development of this method of detecting linkage. The difficulty stems from the fact that even though crossing over generally occurs regardless of the genotype form, in *GT/GT* and *gT/gt* individuals, for example, *detectable* cross-

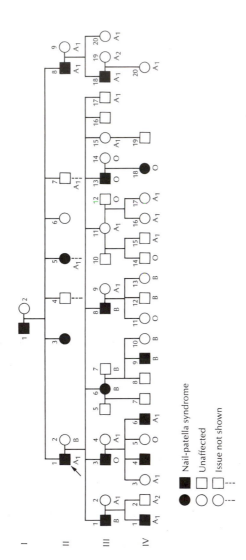

Fig. 13–3 An illustration of the ABO-nail patella linkage. In this family the abnormal nail patella gene is riding with gene O of the ABO locus. Two members of generation IV represent crossover gametes. Because of crowding, seven informative descendants of II-5 are omitted; none appear to be recombinants. (The full pedigree, family G, may be found in Jameson et al., 1956. See also Fig. 8–2**B**. Courtesy of J. H. Renwick and the *Annals of Human Genetics*.)

ing over occurs only in double heterozygotes. These occur in two forms, or phases:

"Coupling," exemplified by GT/gt

"Repulsion," Gt/gT

Coupling is also sometimes referred to as "cis" form, repulsion as "trans."

In Chapter 9 we learned that the maximum frequency of heterozygotes for a single autosomal locus with two alleles is 50 percent, attained when the alleles are equally frequent in the population. It follows that under these conditions the maximum frequency of double heterozygotes is 25 percent. This figure falls off rapidly if one of the alleles is rare. Consider the following example:

		Frequency
Locus G: allele G		0.99
allele g		0.01
Heterozygote: G/g		0.0198
Locus T: allele T		0.50
allele t		0.50
T/t		0.50
Double heterozygotes: GT/gt		0.00495
Gt/gT		0.00495
Total		0.0099

Note that when one gene is rare the total frequency of double heterozygotes is almost identical to the frequency of the rarest allele, g. Most genetic disorders, particularly the severe ones, are even rarer than 1 per 100 gametes.

The frequency of double heterozygotes is increased somewhat if the loci are represented by more than two alleles.

Even if a double heterozygote is found, not all of his or her progeny may be informative. Much depends on the genotype of the mate and whether there is dominance, as illustrated in Table 13–1. The greatest efficiency for linkage is found in the backcross, when the double heterozygote is mated to a homozygote for the recessive genes of both loci. Such homozygotes are generally rarer than the double heterozygotes.

The net effect of these considerations is that it has been possible to find a substantial number of pedigrees to seek possible linkages between codominant variants, such as blood groups or serum protein polymorphisms, but it has been difficult to ascertain informative families for possible linkage of these variants and genetic disorders, especially the rare recessives.

Recombination Frequencies and Map Distance

As noted in Chapter 12, the frequency of recombination between two loci reflects the distance between them on the chromosome. Indeed, recombination rates are

Table 13–1 Informative[a] progeny of a double heterozygote, when dominance obtains at both loci and when it obtains at only one

		Informative Progeny	
Type of Mating	Mate of Double Heterozygote	Dominance at One Locus	Dominance at Both Loci
Double intercross	GT/gt or Gt/gT	4	1
		of the 16 possible fertilizations	
Single intercross	GT/Gt, gT/gt, GT/gT, or Gt/gt	4	2
		of the 8 possible fertilizations	
(Double) backcross	gt/gt	4	4
		of the 4 possible fertilizations	

[a]Offspring are informative if all the progeny with the same phenotype can be classified unambiguously as to the combination of recombinant or nonrecombinant gametes that produced them. Thus, if dominance obtains at the G locus but not at the T locus, the G, T progeny from the mating $GT/gt \times GT/gt$ are not informative because the GT/GT, produced by nonrecombinant gametes, cannot be distinguished phenotypically from the GT/gT, produced by combination of recombinant and nonrecombinant gametes. The g, T/t progeny of the same mating, on the other hand, are informative: each is derived from the union of a recombinant and a nonrecombinant gamete.

often additive, following the geometrical principle that if A, B, and C are linear, $\overline{AC} = \overline{AB} + \overline{BC}$.

The matter is confused, however, by multiple crossovers, especially doubles, that restore the old combination and, by interference, the tendency of a crossover to diminish the likelihood of another nearby. (The fraction of expected multiple crossover gametes that are actually found is called the *coincidence.*) Double crossing over on chromosome 1 is not uncommon in the female, and this undoubtedly holds true for the other large autosomes; one certain double crossover has also been documented on the X-chromosome.

Because of interference and the fact that even loci that are very far apart cannot show more than 50 percent recombination, the distance between loci, the so-called "map distance," does not always coincide with the recombination percentage or sum of such percentages measured by testcross experiments. In the language of the mathematician, the curve showing the relation of map distance and recombination frequency is not always linear. It comes close to being a straight line when the loci are close together, but then departs drastically from linearity when they are far apart.

The famous British geneticist J.B.S. Haldane suggested that because of this the unit of map distance should be given a name other than the unit of recombination frequency. He suggested the name "morgan," honoring T. H. Morgan, in whose *Drosophila* laboratory many of the pioneering studies on linkage were done. Following the metric system, each morgan is subdivisible into 100 centimorgans, each centimorgan (cM) corresponding to the map distance between two loci showing 1 percent crossing over between them. For the close loci the recombination percentage can be translated directly into centimorgans, but this is not possible for more distant loci, especially those more than 30 centimorgans apart.

Chiasma Frequencies

An additional reason for the dearth of well-established autosomal linkages may be the relatively high frequency of chiasmata in human chromosomes. An authoritative study observed an average of 56 chiasmata per cell during meiosis. With 23 pairs of chromosomes this works out to be, on average:

$$\frac{56}{23} = 2.44 \text{ per chromosome.}$$

In view of the interference phenomenon, it may be assumed that each chiasma defines a space equivalent to 50 map units. Hence, it comes out that the average chromosome contains

$$(2.44)(50) = 120 \text{ centimorgans.}$$

It is no wonder, then, that even genes which may be on the same chromosome generally act as though they were not. To be recognized as being linked they must lie within at least 50 units; and with the statistical difficulties described above for human linkage analysis, they ought to be even closer, perhaps 30 units or less away.

The difficulties are obvious. First the chances are about 21.1 that another autosomal gene will be on a different chromosome. Even if it were on the same chromosome, there is about three times as much chance as not that it will be too remote for the relationship to be detected.

To compound the problem, evidence has appeared that the recombination frequencies may not be equal in the two sexes. On average, crossing over in females seems to be about 1.5 times as frequent as in males.

Results of this type have also been encountered in studies with other mammals. It has been pointed out that this phenomenon would work a particular handicap on X-chromosome mapping. Since our estimates are based entirely on recombination in females, the data would tend to make the X-linked genes seem far apart and therefore difficult to localize. According to one reliable estimate the X-chromosome may have a length of 250 to 300 map units.

The Lod Score Method

Since 1955 analysis of possible linkages has been aided greatly by a technique introduced by the American geneticist Newton E. Morton. His method takes advantage of available data from single and double intercrosses (e.g., $GT/gt \times GT/Gt$ and $GT/gt \times GT/gt$, respectively) as well as double backcrosses (such as $GT/gt \times gt/gt$). It asks, essentially, the following question of data collected from possibly informative matings: What are the relative odds that this sequence of births came from linked loci with a certain percentage of crossing over as compared with the probability that they would have been produced by independent loci?

In other words, we desire a relative probability or ratio between the probabilities of the two alternatives:

$$\text{Relative } P \text{ (linkage)} = \frac{\text{Probability of a sequence of births with recombination frequency } \theta}{\text{Probability of the sequence of births if unlinked}}$$

If the genes are not linked, the best fit of the data would be to a recombination frequency of 1/2. In that case numerator and denominator would be the same, so that the relative P would be 1. A relative probability of substantially more than 1 suggests that linkage is a better hypothesis for the data than nonlinkage, and the recombination frequency that produces the highest relative probability indicates the probable degree of crossing over between the loci.

Since the data consist of a *sequence* of births, the numerator and denominator are each products of the probabilities of the various births. To put this in symbols, if we let $p_1(\theta_1)$ represent the probability of the first birth on the assumption of a recombination frequency θ_1, and $p_2(\theta_1)$ = probability of the second birth on the assumption of θ_1, the probability that both births would occur is $p_1(\theta_1) \cdot p_2(\theta_1)$. For the sequence of births, then

$$\text{Relative } P \text{ (linkage)} = \frac{p_1(\theta_1) \cdot p_2(\theta_1) \cdot p_3(\theta_1) \cdot p_4(\theta_1) \cdots \text{etc.}}{p_1(1/2) \cdot p_2(1/2) \cdot p_3(1/2) \cdot p_4(1/2) \cdots \text{etc.}}$$

To shorten the phrase, we will call the relative probability of linkage, the relative *odds* for linkage. Now, the easiest way to multiply numbers is to add their logarithms, so:

$$\text{Log (odds for linkage)} = \frac{\log p_1(\theta_1) + \log p_2(\theta_1) + \log p_3(\theta_1) + \text{etc.}}{\log p_1(1/2) + \log p_2(1/2) + \log p_3(1/2) + \text{etc.}}$$

Morton calls the total relative probability his *lod* score, the word "lod" being the first letter of "logarithm" combined with the first two letters of "odds." He refers to the lod score as z, so that

z_{θ_1} = lod score based on θ_1.

z_{θ_2} = lod score based on another recombination frequency, θ_2.

z_{θ_3} = lod score based on θ_3, etc.

If more than one kind of mating is available, lod scores for a given recombination frequency may be calculated for each one ($z_1(\theta_1)$, $z_2(\theta_1)$, $z_3(\theta_1)$, $z_1(\theta_2)$, $z_2(\theta_2)$, ..., $z_i(\theta_j)$). The z's for each θ may then be added together to obtain a composite lod score for this recombination frequency, $Z(\theta_j)$.

If the genes are linked, it is expected that the lod score for at least one of the recombination frequencies will be considerably in excess of 0, the lod score if $\theta = 1/2$ (since the log of 1 is 0). Linkage is considered likely if a lod score is over 3, which is to say, that the odds are more than 1000 times greater that the loci are linked than that they are not. If one or more lod scores are quite large, the largest would give a clue as to the correct recombination frequency.

To illustrate the basic workings of this method, consider the mating II-1 × II-

2 in Fig. 13–3. At first glance the genotype of II-1 could be either (assuming linkage):

$$\frac{A_1 np}{O\ Np} \quad \text{or} \quad \frac{A_1\ Np}{O\ np}.$$

However, the two type O children are affected, but the three A_1 are not; this suggests strongly that the first is the most probable. Further evidence comes from the three type B children, all affected; they, too, must have received an O gene from their father (otherwise they would be A, B). The mother's genotype is $B\ np/O\ np$. This is a single intercross, so there are eight possible combinations in the offspring. If the probability of recombination is denoted by θ, these possibilities and their probabilities are:

$$\frac{1}{4}(1-\theta) \quad A_1 B, \text{ not affected} \qquad \frac{1}{4}\theta \quad A_1 B, \text{ affected}$$

$$\frac{1}{4}(1-\theta) \quad A_1, \text{ not affected} \qquad \frac{1}{4}\theta \quad A_1, \text{ affected}$$

$$\frac{1}{4}(1-\theta) \quad B, \text{ affected} \qquad \frac{1}{4}\theta \quad B, \text{ not affected}$$

$$\frac{1}{4}(1-\theta) \quad 0, \text{ affected} \qquad \frac{1}{4}\theta \quad O, \text{ not affected.}$$

Each crossover type has a probability $1/4\,\theta$, and each noncrossover type $1/4(1-\theta)$. The probability of obtaining the sequence of eight children of II-1 and II-2 mentioned above is, therefore,

$$1/4(1-\theta)^8.$$

On the assumption of nonlinkage each of the eight possible combinations has equal probability, or $1/8$. [Note that this is the same as $1/4(1-\theta)$ or $1/4\,\theta$ when $\theta = 1/2$.] Hence, the probability of the above-mentioned sequence is $(1/8)^8$, and the relative probability of linkage is

$$= \frac{1/4^8(1-\theta)^8}{1/4^8 \cdot 1/2^8} = 2^8(1-\theta)^8.$$

In terms of logs, for this sibship

$$z = 8 \log 2 + 8 \log (1-\theta).$$

When this is worked out for θ's between 0 and 0.50 (column 2 of Table 13–2), it is seen that the data are suggestive of linkage, but the largest lod score, for $\theta = 0$, is less than 3. A more realistic picture of the recombination frequency is obtained by taking into account the offspring of other double heterozygotes in Fig. 13–3. The informative progeny of II-5, 11-1, III-8, and III-18 appear to contain 11 noncrossovers and two crossovers. (The crossover status of the children of II-8 and III-6 is ambiguous.) For all the data the lod score formula is:

$$Z = 21 \log 2 + 19 \log (1-\theta) + 2 \log \theta.$$

Table 13-2   Lod scores for the data in Fig. 13–3. z_1 is based on the progeny of II-1, Z on all the informative progeny

θ	$z_1(\theta)$	$Z(\theta)$	$\lambda(\theta)$
0	2.408	$-\infty$	$-\infty$
0.05	2.230	3.296	1976.970
0.10	2.042	3.452	2831.392
0.15	1.844	3.333	2152.782
0.20	1.633	3.082	1207.814
0.25	1.409	2.744	554.626
0.30	1.169	2.333	515.278
0.35	0.912	1.855	71.614
0.40	0.633	1.311	20.464
0.45	0.331	0.695	4.955
0.50	0	0	1.000

Now several lod scores are more than 3 (Table 13–2, column 3), the largest for θ = 0.1. Calculation of lod scores for 0.09 and 0.11 (not shown) suggests that θ is between 0.09 and 0.1, as is indicated indeed by the raw data: two recombinants in 21 informative progeny, a rate of 9.5 percent. (The rate from a larger series turns out to be somewhat higher, 13 percent.)

C.A.B. Smith has introduced a method to determine precisely what the lod scores mean. How probable is linkage, for example, when the data give the results of Table 13–2? He noted that according to Bayes theorem, the probability that two genes are independent is

$$P\left(\theta = \frac{1}{2}\right) = \frac{21}{\lambda + 21},$$

where lambda (λ) is the average value of the quantity "$\lambda(\theta)$," the antilog of the total of the z's from all the available kindreds for a given recombination frequency θ, that is,

$$\lambda(\theta) = \text{antilog } Z(\theta)$$

The 21 in the formula derives from the fact that, for an autosomal gene, the initial average odds that a second gene is independent (as opposed to linked) is 21:1.

To find the *average* value of $\lambda(\theta)$, the antilogs of the z values of all θ's, in steps of 0.05, are substituted into Simpson's rule for averaging, that is,

$$\lambda = 1/30[\lambda(0) + 4\lambda(0.05) + 2\lambda(0.1)4\lambda(0.15) + 2\lambda(0.2) + 4\lambda(0.25) \\ + 2\lambda(0.3) + 4\lambda(0.35) + 2\lambda(0.4) + 4\lambda(0.45) + 1].$$

Applying this formula to the data of Table 13–2, we get

$$\lambda = 919.823$$

so that,

$$P\left(\theta = \frac{1}{2}\right) = \frac{21}{919.8 + 21} \\ = 0.022.$$

Hence,

$$P(\text{linkage}) = 0.978.$$

A P of at least 0.90 is desirable, so this is a substantial indication of linkage. It is increased, of course, by the larger series mentioned above.

Smith also pointed out how to calculate the probability that the recombination percentage is any particular value, c:

$$P(\theta/c) = \frac{\lambda(\theta)}{50(\lambda + 21)}.$$

If we substitute, say, the values for $\theta = 0.1$ into this formula, we are calculating the probability that θ is between 0.10 and 0.11. For practical purposes we can assume this means $P(\theta)$ is *about* 0.10.

From our data, noting column 4 at Table 13–2,

$$P(\theta/0.1) = \frac{2831.4}{50(940.8)}$$
$$= 0.060.$$

This does not seem to be a large number, but it is actually quite a high probability when one considers that (a) not just the 10 or 11 considered in the table but that every one of the 51 units between 0 and 50 have a finite probability of being the true θ, and (b) that 6 of the 10 values that can be calculated from Table 13–2 have probabilities of 0.012 or less of being the true θ.

In practice, tables of lod scores (z) for various kinds of testcross situations and progenies with instructions on how to use them have been published. Therefore, for most situations one need not calculate the lod scores as we did above to illustrate the basic method, but may merely gather them from the published tables.

Commonly, the data are presented in the form of a graph comparing the lod socres or the relative odds (the antilogs of the lods) of the different crossover percentages. A graph with significant evidence of linkage will usually show a major hump in the vicinity of the probable recombination frequency, as in Fig. 13–4.

Figure 13–4B shows the effect of using computerized methods, which are especially useful when there are large, complex pedigrees. In this instance these methods led to the same conclusion concerning probable recombination frequency as with the usual lod score method, but the result has a higher relative probability and is, therefore, much more reliable.

CELLULAR AND MOLECULAR METHODS

Despite the elegance of the methods for gaining linkage data from pedigree analysis, they led to very little progress in mapping the human genome, especially the autosomal portion. Fortunately, linkage studies have benefited greatly from the development of the *in vitro* techniques described in Chapter 6. Because they are "parasexual," that is, they bypass the meiotic process and other aspects of normal reproduction that are responsible for the many difficulties we encounter in obtain-

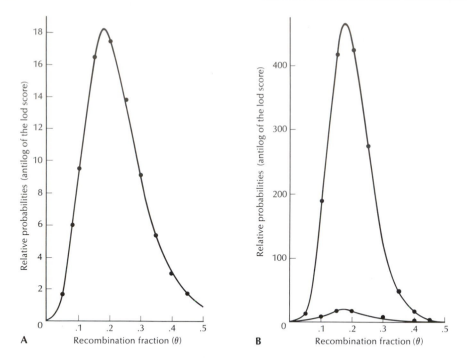

Fig. 13-4 Comparison of curves showing the relative probability of linkage calculated in two different ways. In **A** data concerning linkage of two X-linked traits, ocular albinism and Xg blood group, are scored by the conventional lod score method. In **B** the data of **A** are shown on a different scale (lower curve of **B**) along with data (upper curve of **B**) from the same families obtained by use of a computer. Note that the computer has extracted considerably more information from the data. As a result the relative probability at the highest point is 470 times that of no linkage in **B** as compared with 18 times that of no linkage in **A**. In both cases, however, the most likely recombination fraction (θ) is about 17.5 percent. (From Fialkow et al.,1967. Courtesy of P. J. Fialkow and the *American Journal of Human Genetics.*)

ing linkage information from family studies, these techniques have, in a very short time, led to hitherto undreamed of advances in three major aspects of the problem: (a) On which chromosome, and where on that chromosome, specific loci are situated; (b) what other loci are on the same chromosome; and (3) whether the relative positions of the loci make them likely to be closely linked.

We illustrated the basic methods of chromosomal localization by means of somatic cell hybrids in Chapter 6. Sometimes it can be inferred that two loci are on the same chromosome by the fact that their products (enzyme or other protein) either disappear together consistently or continue to be produced together in man–rodent hybrid clones.

This can occur even if the exact chromosome involved has not yet been determined. Figure 13–5 shows that the loci of the two enzymes are syntenic because they behave this way in hybrids between human and Chinese hamster cells.

Fig. 13–5 2 × 2 chart showing completely concordant segregation between the loci responsible for human phosphoglucomutase-1 (PGM₁) and 6-phosphogluconate dehydrogenase (PGD) in 83 man-Chinese hamster hybrid clones. Based on Westervald and Meera Khan (1972).

	PGM₁		
	+	−	Total
PGD → +	31	0	31
−	0	52	52
Total	31	52	83

Similarly, in man–mouse studies, human erythrocyte acid phosphatase (ACP₁, Fig. 5–9), the soluble or cytoplasmic form of NAD-dependent malate dehydrogenase (MOR-S), and the soluble form of NADP-dependent isocitrate dehydrogenase (ICD-S) were either all three present in a given subclone or all three absent. Hence, the structural loci for the three enzymes are presumably syntenic. In this instance a detailed examination was made of the human chromosomes remaining in the subclones. Typical findings are illustrated in Table 13–3. The only consistency among the clones lacking the three enzymes is that human chromosome 2 is missing. On the other hand, the clones retaining the three enzymes also retained chromosome 2. The data suggest, therefore, that the synteny of the three loci is on chromosome 2.

It should be noted that even if the loci concerned with these traits were invariant or variants were very rare (in which case heterozygotes informative for family studies are absent or rare) the cells can shed light on syntenic relationships as long as a gene product can be identified.

Aberrancy mapping greatly enhances the linkage information from somatic cell hybrids. Often it allows the investigator to pinpoint localization of several loci to the very same chromosome band by noting the concordant presence or absence with a translocation or deletion involving that band.

As we pointed out in Chapter 6, however, the early studies using tissue culture cells, whether obtained from amniocentesis (Chapter 18) or resulting from somatic

Table 13–3 Human enzyme and chromosome analysis of six subclones of a man-mouse hybrid studied by Povey et al. (1974). ACP₁ = red cell acid phosphatase; MOR-S and ICD-S are, respectively, cytoplasmic (soluble) malic and isocitric dehydrogenases

Clone	ACP₁ MOR-S ICD-S	Percentage of Cells with Chromosome Number[a]									
		2	4	7	10	12	15	19	21	22	X
9	0	0	33	0	87	87	0	40	0	40	87
14	+	69	0	88	44	0	0	0	100	25	94
15	0	0	22	48	65	74	0	0	57	26	78
24	0	0	27	73	0	73	46	0	96	69	81
27R	0	0	21	67	0	79	50	0	79	12	0
25	+	93	93	79	0	0	50	0	71	0	79

[a]Data on chromosomes positive or negative in all clones are omitted.

cell hybridization, had a serious drawback in that they could not yield any information concerning loci which are not expressed (do not produce a product) in these cells, not to speak of loci for the many traits and syndromes where the gene product is unknown.

In some instances this drawback has been overcome by finding that the locus under study is closely linked to a gene that *is* expressed in these cells. Thus some of the first intimations concerning deletions associated with recessive retinoblastoma at 13q11 were based on its close linkage to esterase D. If a culture containing chromosome 13 does not produce esterase D, the genes presumably missing, it is assumed that the retinoblastoma locus is also absent even though the deletion is not cytologically detectable.

Such close linkages became much more readily available with the advent of the molecular methods, specifically the restriction site variations described in Chapter 6. A remarkably large number of these variations have proven to be polymorphic, that is, present in the population in substantial frequencies. Moreover, many have proven to be associated with genes of considerable clinical interest.

Until 1978, for example, prenatal diagnosis of sickle cell anemia was possible only by analysis of hemoglobin in fetal blood. Fetal blood sampling not only demands great skill but even in the best of hands carries a 5 to 10 percent risk to the fetus. Furthermore the analysis of the globin is complex and subject to frequent diagnostic error. Y. W. Kan and A. M. Dozy reported in 1978 that the DNA from persons with Hb A digested with restriction enzyme *Hpa*I produced fragments 7.6 kb in length that hybridized with β-globin probes, whereas the DNA from individuals with Hb S generally yielded 13.0 kb fragments. The difference is due to an *Hpa*I cleavage site, flanking the 3′ side of the beta globin gene, that is present on Hb A chromosomes but absent on most Hb S chromosomes. The cleavage site (shown as number seventeen on Fig. 6–11) is about 5000 nucleotides beyond the globin genes. The close linkage to beta globin enabled the authors to determine that the fetus being diagnosed antenatally, like its parents, had sickle cell trait (genotype A/S), since the DNA contained both the 7.6 and the 13.0 fragments. Offspring with sickle-cell anemia, on the other hand, had only the 13.0 kb fragments (diagnosing S/S).

Use of the enzyme for prenatal diagnosis is hampered, however, by the fact that about 30 percent of S chromosomes in American blacks and in the inhabitants of most other places where Hb S exists are +, rather than −, for the *Hpa*I site. Indeed, in several countries *most* S chromosomes are + for it. Fortunately, Kan and others have found RFLPs, based on the enzymes *Dde*I and *Mst*II, which can distinguish directly between the base sequences (p. 113) in HbA and HbS genes. These enzymes cannot distinguish between HbA and HbC, however, so, if SC disease is a possibility, one must also use *Hpa*I, which is linked to the C gene over 95 percent of the time.

Such techniques have also solved a number of longstanding mysteries of X-chromosome localization: the positions on it of the genes for Duchenne muscular dystrophy (DMD), Becker muscular dystrophy (BMD), and Factor IX deficiency (F9, Hemophilia B, Christmas disease). In the case of DMD, the probable location had been surmised from an affected female who was heterozygous for a three-break aberration, an X:1 translocation plus an X inversion, which apparently resulted in effective deletion of Xp21 on her functional X-chromosome (the normal X being the late replicating one in all cells tested). RFLPs on both sides have narrowed the probable location to Xp21.2. One of these also has demonstrated that BMD is very close, probably allelic, to DMD. Similar methods have shown that the hemophilia B locus is located just proximal to Xq27. This is not far from hemophilia A (F8), but linkage between them is quite loose, suggesting unusually high recombination frequency in the portion of chromosome near the telomere; similar results occur near the tip of the short arm. As in Hb S, restriction polymorphisms have been detected within the F8 gene itself, making prenatal screening more reliable than dependence on linked DNA markers.

We noted in Chapter 6 that one of the most dramatic accomplishments of the molecular techniques has come in advances concerning two clinical conditions that have in the past been among the most resistant to localization and determination of the primary genetic defect: Huntington's chorea and cystic fibrosis.

As the name indicates, Huntington's chorea is a progressive motor abnormality, especially involuntary movements of the head, accompanied by intellectual deterioration and often also psychiatric symptoms. It has long been known to be inherited as an autosomal dominant, but its tendency to late onset creates considerable problems for the children of affected individuals in not knowing, at least during the early reproductive years, whether they will be affected and, if so, whether they would pass on the gene to half of their offspring.

Persistent family studies searching for a blood group or protein marker that would enable one to predict earlier who is likely to be affected were in vain. A 1983 study discovered, however, that the gene for this disorder is closely linked to an anonymous locus (that is, of unknown function) that hybridizes to a probe, called G8, that had been cloned some years before because it was one of several human chromosome fragments containing no repetitive sequences. The G8 locus was found to be associated with two *Hin*dIII RFLP sites that are inherited together as a unit (or haplotype), there being only 18.7 kb between them. Despite this short distance, the four possible haplotype combinations (Table 13–4) appear to exist in linkage equilibrium in the population. Using somatic cell hybrids, it was determined that G8, and therefore also the locus of Huntington's disease, is on chromosome 4.

The highest lod score for the relation between G8 and Huntington's disease in both the Venezuelan family (Fig. 13–6) and in a smaller American pedigree studied by the same group was 8.5 at a θ of 0.0, with no known recombinants. Subsequent studies have found some recombinants, and Huntington's disease has been found to "ride" with all of the possible *Hin*dIII haplotypes. Nevertheless, the best estimate of θ remains under 5 percent.

With such close linkage one could be close to 95 to 100 percent certainty in predicting whether a person at risk who is heterozygous for the G8 polymorphism carried the gene and would therefore probably develop the disorder, the gene being strongly penetrant. (Fortunately the frequency of G8 heterozygotes is quite high in the populations that have been studied thus far; indeed, with the finding of additional restriction sites at the G8 locus, the frequency of restriction site heterozy-

Table 13–4 *Hind*III haplotypes at the G8 locus, as designated by Gusella et al. (1983), and their frequencies in a sample of normal individuals. + and − denote presence or absence of the respective *Hind*III restriction sites. − at site 1 results in a 17.5kb fragment, + a 15.0kb one; + at site 2 yields fragments of 3.7 and 1.2kb, − one of 4.9kb (i.e., area uncleaved). Between sites 1 and 2 is an *Hind*III restriction site common to all halotypes (Modified from Harper et al., 1985, including also data of Gusella et al., 1983)

Haplotype	Hind III Polymorphism		Haplotype Frequency[a]	Expected Frequency[b]
	Site 1	Site 2		
A	−	+	.649	.647
B	−	−	.099	.101
C	+	+	.216	.218
D	+	−	.036	.034

[a] n = 111.
[b] On the assumption of linkage equilibrium.

gotes is over 80 percent in the populations studied thus far.) This would be very helpful for prenatal and presymptomatic detection. Perhaps even more important, this work can lead to further localization and cloning of the Huntington gene, determining the normal and abnormal biochemical actions of the locus, and eventually finding a way to reverse the action of the abnormal allele(s).

Cystic fibrosis (or fibrocystic disease) of the pancreas, a recessive trait, is a generalized disturbance of the exocrine glands. It derived its name from the fact that one of its earliest recognized symptoms, meconium ileus, results from deficiency of pancreatic enzymes. Meconium ileus appears in only about 15 percent of cases, but the name has persisted even though the symptoms in other systems, especially the respiratory tract, may be more constant and more life-threatening.

The respiratory symptoms usually also occur early in the disease. They start off as a severe nonproductive cough, which later becomes spasmodic and productive, often followed by vomiting. Because of these symptoms, the affected infant may be diagnosed as suffering from pertussis. Absence of the thin, watery secretions of mucus that normally lubricate the cilia of the bronchial epithelium causes the ciliary movement to be abolished. This results in the formation of thick, tenacious mucus within the trachea and bronchi, and the child coughs to expel the material. The lack of ciliary action also permits secondary bacterial invasion of the lungs by *Staph. aureus.* The pulmonary infiltration gives a characteristic X-ray picture, which is diagnostic. Frequently bronchiectasis and cor pulmonale follow.

Formerly the disease was usually lethal in the first year or two of life, with the respiratory symptoms major causes of death. The development of broad-spectrum antibiotics and other measures has, however, increased life expectancy in recent years, so that some victims are surviving into reproductive age. Affected males are sterile, however.

Carriers of cystic fibrosis have been estimated to be as frequent as 1 in 25 in populations of predominantly North European descent, with a frequency of the disorder in the vicinity of 1 in 2000 births. Geneticists have long puzzled over the

Venezuela HD Family

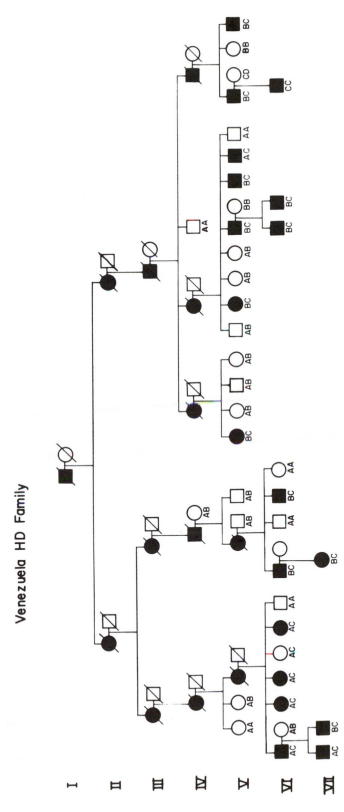

Fig. 13-6 Partial pedigree of a Venezuelan family with many members affected with Huntington's chorea. A,B,C, and D refer to restriction fragment length haplotypes (see text and Table 13–4). They indicate close linkage of the gene for this disorder with haplotype C in this family. (From Gusella et al., 1983, courtesy of J. F. Gusella; reprinted by permission from *Nature*, © 1983, Macmillan Journals, Ltd.)

ability of these populations to maintain such frequencies of a disease that has been essentially 100 percent lethal, genetically speaking, until recent years. Some evidence suggests heterogeneity, that is, that we may be dealing with a number of loci capable of producing clinically similar disorders when homozygous, but it is questionable whether this would be of sufficient magnitude, even if true, to solve the problem.

The high frequency of the disease has made all the more frustrating the hitherto fruitless search for the location and action of the responsible gene. A major breakthrough occurred in late 1985, however, when three reports in the same issue of *Nature* described close linkage between cystic fibrosis and loci identified by the restriction polymorphism technique. One group had previously found that cystic fibrosis was closely linked to a 17kb fragment, referred to as the DOCRI-917 locus, identified by a random probe; it now reported somatic cell hybridization data indicating that this locus, and therefore also cystic fibrosis, is on chromosome 7. A second group found linkage to another anonymous fragment, called *pj*3.11, and to the gene for the T-cell receptor beta chain, both located on 7q. (In another journal the same group also reported linkage with a probe to a collagen gene, COLIA2, on chromosome 7.) The third group showed that cystic fibrosis is closely linked to the locus of *met,* a human oncogene (Chapter 17), on 7q. The overlap between the various restriction sites identified in these studies indicates that the cystic fibrosis locus is probably in the middle third of 7q. These results should enable considerable progress in prenatal screening and biochemical analysis of the disease.

Noteworthy advances by similar methods have recently been made for some forms of polycystic kidney disease, retinitis pigmentosa, familial Alzheimer's disease, and manic-depressive psychosis.

THE CURRENT CHROMOSOME MAP

The ultimate achievement in the development of linkage information comes when all the techniques—pedigree studies, somatic cell hybridization, aberrancy mapping, nucleic acid hybridization, and restriction enzyme analysis—can be combined to extend and reinforce the conclusions made from each separately. Such a synthesis has produced a chromosome-1 linkage group, for instance, comprising over 80 loci, a feat that was undreamed of only a few years ago.

We shall indicate the recent status of the human linkage groups by means of Fig. 13–7. Many of the genes or traits identified by the symbols shown alongside the chromosomes are mentioned here and elsewhere in this book; the others may be found in the issue of *Cytogenetics and Cell Genetics* or the *Birth Defects: Original Article Series* that regularly publishes the proceedings of the International Workshops on Human Gene Mapping.

Figure 13–7 is most useful in showing on which chromosome a trait or gene appears to be located. In many cases it indicates also the arm, and in a few instances also the band, with which it is probably associated. The figure provides very little information, however, on the very critical factor of genetic distance. As more data accumulate the correspondence between structural and genetic maps should become clearer.

SUGGESTED EXERCISES

In the following exercises assume recombination frequencies wherever possible are alike in the two sexes.

13-1. Most of the well-established autosomal linkages involve a relatively rare trait such as the nail-patella syndrome or ovalocytosis and a blood-group or serum protein variation.

(a) Explain why this is so.

(b) What combination of traits might be expected to be even likelier than these to establish linkages? Give a possible explanation why they have not yet been found.

13-2. If G and T are dominant to their alleles, g and t, respectively, show by stroke diagrams

(a) The genotypes of the crosses that could be possibly informative for linkage.

(b) The technical term for each cross.

13-3 Again using G and T loci mentioned above, show the expected proportions of (a) gametes and (b) progeny from the most informative mating(s) if the recombination frequency between the loci is designated by the general term θ.

13-4. What would be the expected results of exercise 13-3 if $\theta = 0.5$? What is the technical name for that situation?

13-5. What would be the expected results of exercise 13-3 if θ were 20 percent?

13-6. (Extra credit) Do exercises 13-3, 13-4, and 13-5 for the other crosses that could be informative for linkage.

13-7. In Fig. 13-3 IV-2 and IV-11 represent crossovers; likewise IV-42 in Fig. 1–5B.

(a) Diagram the probable genotypes of the parents and all the offspring in their sibships, showing the gametes contributed to the children by each parent. Encircle the crossover gametes.

(b) What is the probability that three such crossovers in a row should show the normal trait (and none the nail-patella syndrome)?

13-8. The genes governing normal vision and normal production of the enzyme glucose-6-phosphate dehydrogenase (G6PD) are dominant to their alleles, dt, for deuteranopia (red-green color blindness), and gd for G6PD deficiency, respectively. The loci are X-linked with a maximum of 6 percent recombination, but, of course, there is no crossing over in the male for these loci. A man and woman, both normal in both respects, marry. Their two daughters are normal in both respects, one of their two sons has normal vision but is deficient in G6PD, and the other son has deuteranopia but has normal G6PD. Assuming 6 percent recombination were correct,

(a) What are the probable genotypes of the parents?

(b) If they have another son, how likely is it that he will show deuteranopia?

(c) If they have another son, how likely is it that he will show G6PD deficiency?

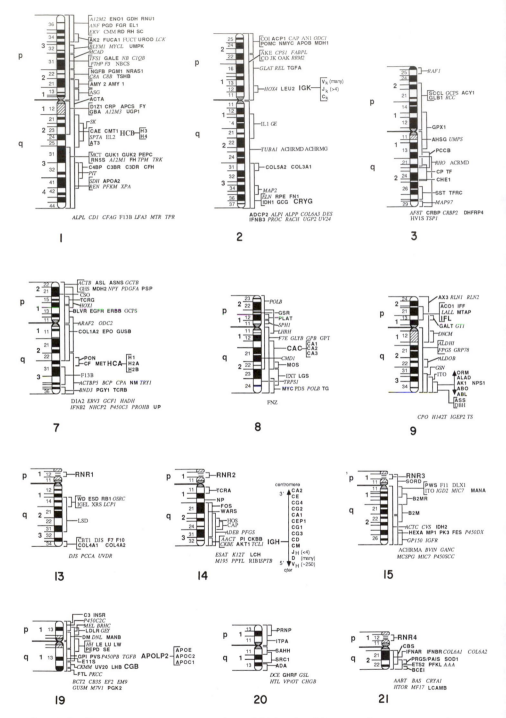

Fig. 13-7 Diagrammatic representation of 24 kinds of human chromosomes, showing on the left side of each one the enumeration of the bands observed with Q-, G-, and R-staining methods according to the Paris Conference (1971) and on the right side of each

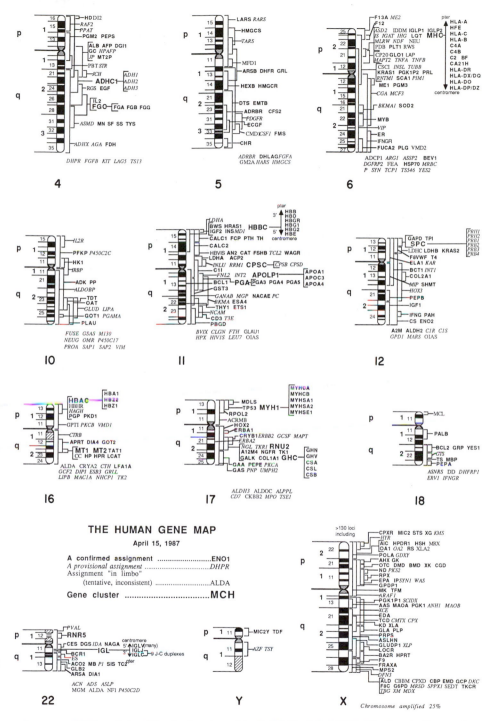

a January, 1987 update of the loci assigned to it (McKusick, 1986). The key indicates the relative degrees of certainty of these assignments. (Courtesy of V. A. McKusick.)

(d)   If they have another son, how likely is it that he will show both abnormal traits (have deuteranopia and G6PD deficiency)?

For (b), (c), and (d) assume the genotypes you answered in (a) are the correct ones.

13-9. What would be the probability of obtaining the sibship listed in the heading of the previous exercise if the woman in question had the alternative (the less probable) genotype?

13-10. Demonstrate, by use of a general term for recombination frequency (e.g., θ), that the proportion of the rarest class of offspring from a single backcross is expected to be one-fourth of this frequency.

13-11. Demonstrate that the formula for the relative probabilities, Z, of the 21 progeny on p. 293 is correct.

13-12. A boy has an X-linked variety of agammaglobulinemia, a very serious disorder because it diminishes his ability to fight infection. (In fact, most affected infants die from respiratory infections, usually soon after their maternal antibodies become exhausted.) He is Xg(a−). His healthy older sister is Xg(a+). If it were true (there is unfortunately no evidence that it is) that the loci governing Xg and this agammaglobulinemia were very close together, what is the prognosis for her sons who turn out to be Xg(a+)?

13-13. Expand Table 13-2 by adding to it lod scores based on the informative matings in Fig. 1–5**B**. Does this change our estimate of the probable recombination rate between ABO and Np?

14

Epistatic and Regulatory Interactions

In several previous chapters we have noted that the milieu in which a gene functions may be as important as the nature of the gene itself in influencing the development of the trait or phenotype. The ambient genes form a very important part of that milieu. Foremost, of course, is the nature of the gene's allele, particularly the degree of dominance. In addition, two or more loci may exert effects on the same trait: *gene interaction.**

We can subdivide interactions into three groups:

1. A number of loci work together to produce a trait in a complementary, yet independent, manner. If the nature of a variant or disorder turns only one of these loci, this locus is said to be *epistatic* to the others.
2. The epistatic locus has one of the special relationships to a structural locus called for by the operon theory of Jacob and Monod: operator, inducer, enhancer, repressor, derepressor, or regulator in some other way. Many of these genes are very close to the structural gene.
3. Many loci work together in a cumulative manner, though their contributions are not necessarily equal. This is often called quantitative, multifactorial, or polygenic inheritance.

This chapter will focus on the first two categories; the third is the subject of the next chapter.

EPISTATIC INTERACTIONS

The epistatic interactions that are easiest to describe are seen whenever we find that the final phenotypic product is the result of a *series* of reactions that must take place in the cell or the body, as, for example, the series in Fig. 14–1. Each of these reactions typically depends on a different enzyme, and each enzyme, in turn, depends on a different locus to produce it. Thus the final reaction depends on the *complementary* actions of all the enzyme-producing loci of the series; every locus in the

---

*We use the term "interaction" in the broad sense, as referring to all situations in which genes interact. The student should be aware, however, that geneticists studying polygenic inheritance (Chapter 15) often use the term in a narrower sense to refer to epistatic or nonadditive effects on the phenotype.

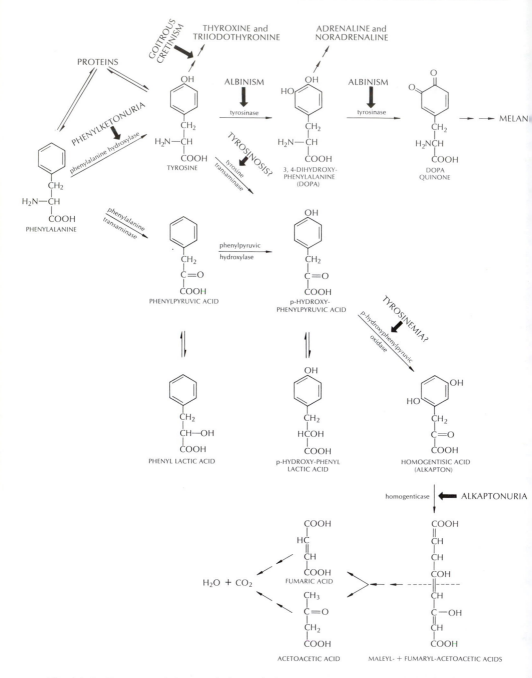

Fig. 14–1 Diagram of the metabolism of phenylalanine and tyrosine in man. The thickened arrows indicate the probable blocks, because of deficiency of the indicated enzyme, in several inborn errors of metabolism. In each case the normal allele is responsible for production of the enzyme, and affected individuals are homozygous for an abnormal gene, which appears to be recessive to its normal allele.

metabolic step series can be thought of as epistatic to all the others. The phenyl-ketonuria gene, for example, when it is homozygous prevents the normal alleles of most of the other steps in Fig. 14–1 from functioning. It is also epistatic to any genes for mental ability or intelligence that the person may have inherited. Similarly, a person may have genes for red, brown, or black pigment in eyes and hair, but homozygosity for the albinism locus is epistatic to all of them. In the same sense, a lethal gene can be thought of as epistatic to the rest of the genome, which may be otherwise normal in every way.

If we visualize a normal step series of reactions thus:

$$\text{Substance 1} \rightarrow \text{Substance 2} \rightarrow \text{Phenotype N}$$

	α	β
Depending on enzyme	α	β
Due to normal allele at	A	B

then if either α or β are not produced, due to absence of the normal allele at locus A or locus B, phenotype N would not be produced. Which gene is responsible can often be determined by which precursor substance accumulates in the body: substance 1 if locus A is abnormal, 2 if locus B is abnormal.

We become aware most dramatically of complementary loci when two abnormal individuals have a normal child. In the above example, two individuals could have an abnormal phenotype, not N, because both lack the enzyme α or both lack the enzyme β. Their marriage would generally result in children who lacked the same enzyme as their parents. In that event we would really have no cause to suspect that two different loci must interact to produce the normal phenotype. We would suspect complementary action only if two N-less individuals married and had an N child. A likely basis for such a result would be that one parent was N-less because he lacked the normal allele at locus A but had the normal allele at B, whereas the second parent normal at A lacked the normal allele at B. Thus their genotypes could be visualized as:

$$\frac{a\ B}{a\ B} \times \frac{A\ b}{A\ b}.$$

The child, being

$$\frac{A\ B}{a\ b},$$

produces both α and β and, therefore, phenotype N. Then we realize that to produce phenotype N, loci A and B must *complement* one another.

This is precisely the favored explanation for the albino parents who had four normal children. The data seem to contradict the hypothesis that albinism is determined by a recessive gene. Rather than postulate mutation or extensive incomplete penetrance, it is easier to assume that two different loci can produce albinism, and complementary action of their normal alleles produces the normal phenotype.

What we know about melanin production (Fig. 14–1) makes such a hypothesis good sense. Most albinos cannot produce the enzyme tyrosinase, but many albinos do produce both DOPA and tyrosinase. These are somehow unable to utilize the enzyme properly in oxidizing the DOPA to DOPA-quinone. Indeed, reinvestigation of the above-mentioned case disclosed that one of the parents was a typical

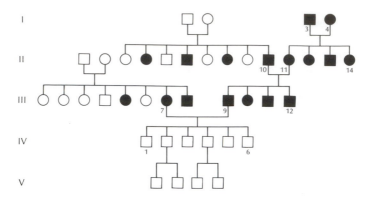

Fig. 14-2 One of several pedigrees published by Stevenson and Cheeseman (1956) in which a marriage of two persons with recessive deafness results in some or all children with normal hearing. (Courtesy of A. C. Stevenson and the *Annals of Human Genetics*.)

"can't make tyrosinase" albino and the other was the rarer "utilization" gene homozygote.

The existence of at least two different loci whose recessive mutant forms can produce Leber's congenital amaurosis, a form of blindness, has been inferred from pedigrees of normal children born to affected parents. A similar idea explains the fact that the children of a husband and wife with recessive deafness often have normal hearing (Fig. 14–2).

The complementation diagram on the previous page can also take the form:

$$\begin{array}{c} \text{Precursor} \xrightarrow[\alpha]{} \text{substance A} \\ \\ \text{Precursor} \xrightarrow[\beta]{} \text{substance B} \end{array} \Bigg\rangle \rightarrow \text{Phenotype N}$$

This is essentially the way the body produces those enzymes that are not monomers, which is to say, multimeric enzymes. These are not immediate gene products but are instead combination of several polypeptides, each of which is the product of a different locus. When an enzyme is able to assume different forms, depending on the number of molecules of each of the component polypeptides present, these forms are referred to as *isozymes* just as are the allelic (mutational) variants of the enzymes (pp. 123–125).* Often the different forms are unique to different tissues or different stages of development.

Two lines of evidence, biochemical and genetic, have established the foregoing statements, that these isozymes consist of several polypeptide components and that these are under independent genetic control. In the pioneer work on one of the best-studied systems, the lactate dehydrogenases (LDH), the two forms of beef LDH which have the most extremely different electrophoretic properties, LDH-1 and LDH-5, can be dissociated *in vitro* into their component polypeptides and then allowed to recombine (reassociate). This results in five different lactate dehydro-

*Not all enzymes that yield separable components on electrophoresis (and are therefore suspected of being isozymes, for example, Fig. 5–9) have proven to be composed of variable numbers of polypeptide subunits *in vivo*. Some separations are apparently based on artifactural, polymeric, or tertiary structural differences *in a single molecule*.

genases in 1:4:6:4:1 proportions, exactly the result expected if the enzyme were a tetramer consisting of two similar polypeptide chains which combine at random. If one of these is termed the A chain and the other the B chain, one extreme form apparently has 4A and 0B and the other extreme form 0A and 4B components. When the 4A and 4B are combined in the test tube, dissociated, and allowed to recombine (Fig. 14–3) the five types produced are

Isozyme	Composition	Symbol	Relative Frequency in Reassociation
LDH-5	4A 0B	AAAA or A_4B_0	1
LDH-4	3A 1B	AAAB or A_3B_1	4
LDH-3	2A 2B	AABB or A_2B_2	6
LDH-2	1A 3B	ABBB or A_1B_3	4
LDH-1	0A 4B	BBBB or A_0B_4	1

If there were four "slots" to be filled and each slot had equal chances of being filled with an A or a B, the probability of obtaining 3A and 1B is four times as likely as the probability of obtaining 4A and 0B, just as the probability of 3 heads and 1 tail is four times as likely as four heads in a row when tossing an equally weighted coin four times. Likewise, there is six times as much chance of obtaining 2A and 2B as of obtaining 4A and 0B. This type of *in vitro* analysis demonstrates that the isozyme contains at least two separate components. A similar distribution of LDH forms *in vivo* in man was observed in a family containing two allelic variants of the B polypeptide.

Genetically, the A and B components of LDH assort independently, the loci being on chromosomes 11 and 12, respectively.

As data concerning the prevalence of the complementary interactions producing isozymes have accumulated, it has become increasingly clear that these interactions have considerable developmental, functional, evolutionary, and even clinical significance. Somehow organisms are able to regulate the production of these enzymes so that different forms predominate in tissues at different stages of ontogeny and under different physiological stresses (Fig. 14–4).

Complementary action of genes may also be diagnosed by the relation of the gene products, often *in vitro,* even when we do not know the exact gene-enzyme relationship. Classical hemophilia and Christmas disease present a prime example. Classical hemophilia, or hemophilia A, was one of the first human diseases recognized to be X-linked; indeed, its general mode of inheritance was understood even in antiquity. In recent years, it has been famous because of the number of royal houses of Europe tainted by the disease (Fig. 10–7), but even in commoners it is one of the most frequent and most serious genetic disorders. Affected persons, usually males, have a much prolonged clotting time because their blood is deficient in a substance called antihemophilic factor, often also referred to as AHG (antihemophilic globulin) and as Factor VIII, needed for one of the steps in the normal conversion of prothrombin to thrombin. Thrombin is the enzyme that, in the presence of calcium ions, converts the soluble plasma protein fibrinogen into insoluble fibrin, the main structural component of the blood clot.

In 1952, British and American hematologists found that about 10 to 20 percent of presumed sufferers from classical hemophilia had normal amounts of AHG.

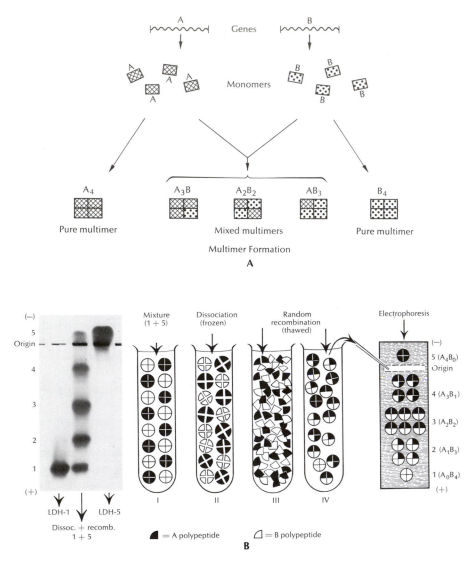

Fig. 14-3A Formation of mixed multimers. Two polypeptide chains, if allowed to aggregate randomly, will give rise to five types of tetramers; two "pure" and three "mixed." **B.** The lactate dehydrogenase isoenzymes are formed in this manner. The middle column in the electrophoresis picture at the left contains the five types expected from the diagram on the right. (**A.** from Epstein and Motulsky, 1965; courtesy of C. J. Epstein and Grune and Stratton, Inc., publishers of *Progress in Medical Genetics*. **B.** from Zinkham et al., 1966; courtesy of W. H. Zinkham and *Pediatrics*, the electrophoresis photograph being contributed originally by C. L. Markert.)

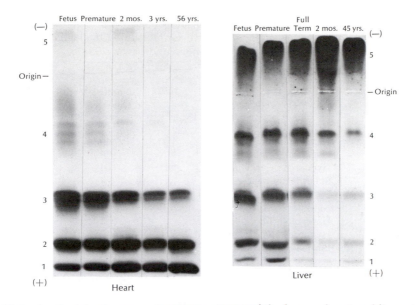

Fig. 14-4 Lactic dehydrogenase isozyme patterns of the human heart and liver at different ages. Note that the more rapidly migrating forms, LDH-1, LDH-2, and LDH-3, predominate in the adult heart, whereas LDH-5 is predominant in the adult liver. The fetal tissue appear to be less selective. Some of the banding areas contain subbands, apparently because the production of these isozymes is really determined by a more complex mechanism than suggested by Fig. 14–3, involving interaction of more than two loci. (From Zinkham et al.,1966. Courtesy of W. H. Zinkham and *Pediatrics.*)

Instead, they were deficient in a different substance needed to form thrombin properly. Both this substance and the new disease have been named for the British family in which the condition was recognized, whose surname happened to be Christmas. (By coincidence the report in the *British Medical Journal* appeared during Christmas week of that year!) The Christmas factor is also sometimes referred to as PTC (for plasma thromboplastin component), antihemophilic factor B, or simply Factor IX. Christmas disease, also known as hemophilia B, often resembles classical hemophilia in relative severity, and is also an X-linked recessive.

The interesting point for us is that when blood from a person with hemophilia A is mixed with blood from a person with hemophilia B, in the test tube or by transfusion, the combination clots normally. This proves that each blood lacks a factor present in the other. In the normal person two different normal alleles would presumably be necessary to produce these complementary factors.

Tests of this type have also been very useful to distinguish from one another many of the other inherited clotting disorders that are known (Table 14–1). Most of them are autosomal, incidentally, and so are easily proven genetically as well as physiologically distinct from hemophilias A and B. Contrariwise, if the mixture of bloods from two persons with clotting defect does not clot normally, this means usually that they suffer from the same disorder (or at least disorders determined by alleles of the same locus).

TABLE 14-1 Relative frequencies of various clotting disorders as judged from (1) studies in Pittsburgh, Pennsylvania, and North Carolina and (2) a larger compilation for the two most frequent forms (From Didisheim and Lewis, 1958)

1. Pittsburgh and North Carolina Data

Factor Deficiency	Common Term	Number Observed	Proportion (in Percent)
VIII	Hemophilia A	143	73
IX	Hemophilia B	40	21
II	Hypoprothrombinemia	4	2
V	Hypoproaccelerinemia	4	2
X	Stuart factor deficiency	4	2
XI	PTA deficiency, hemophilia C	2	1
I	Afibrinogenemia	1	0.5
XII	Hageman trait	1	0.5
VII	Hypoproconvertinemia	0	—
XIII	Fibrinase deficiency	0	—
	Total	199	

2. Hemophilia A vs. Hemophilia B

Type	Number of Families	Number of Individuals
Hemophilia A	505	705
Hemophilia B	97	136
Percent B	16.1	16.2

Even if the normal result is obtained in only one direction, the data can suggest complementary loci. For example, both persons with classical hemophilia (A) and those with von Willebrand disease may be deficient in clotting factor VIII. Transfusion of von Willebrand blood into hemophilia A is no help. However, transfusion of blood from a hemophilia A person will correct the clotting defect of a von Willebrand patient, even though the transfused blood also lacks factor VIII. Hence, the true hemophiliac must be able to make a factor which the von Willebrand cannot; that is, he is normal for the allele for which the von Willebrand is abnormal. The critical point seems to be that the von Willebrand cannot produce AHG because he lacks a factor for platelet adhesiveness. The classic hemophiliac has the platelet adhesiveness factor but nevertheless cannot produce AHG. Transfusing him with von Willebrand blood will therefore contribute nothing he lacks. On the other hand, when his blood brings the platelet adhesiveness factor to the von Willebrand patient, the latter can manufacture his own AHG, and the blood clots. von Willebrand disease is autosomal.

By similar applications complementation has proved to be a powerful tool to establish the important principle of biochemical genetics indicated in Chapter 5; namely, that allelic variation involves differences in the same structural protein whereas variation at different, though related, loci involves differences in different structural proteins.

As noted in Chapter 12, for example, none of the offspring of persons with hemoglobin S mated to persons with hemoglobin C have hemoglobin A. This may be considered evidence that the S and C genes are allelic. In marriages between carriers of Hb S and Hb Hopkins-2, on the other hand, the progeny who produce both abnormal hemoglobins *also* produce Hb A. This is understandable as complementation of two loci: the gamete with the S gene brings in an allele for normal α-chains, and the gamete with the Hopkins-2 gene brings in an allele for normal β-chains.

Evidence as to whether two hemoglobin variants involve the same chain (and therefore indicate whether their determining genes are allelic) can be obtained from complementation of gene products even though intercrosses of the carriers cannot be found. When two hemoglobins that involve the same chain are dissociated and recombined ("hybridized") in the test tube, only the two original types are recovered (line 3 of Fig. 14–5). If the two hemoglobins involve different chains, however, four types are recovered, including normal hemoglobin, Hb A (line 4 of Fig. 14–5). The *in vitro* results thus mimic exactly the corresponding results when such combinations are produced genetically.

It will be recalled that complementational methods in tissue culture are at the heart of the somatic cell hybridization discussed in Chapter 6. They are also the basis of the techniques whereby Neufeld and her associates have so brilliantly elucidated the genetics and biochemistry of the mucopolysaccharidoses in recent

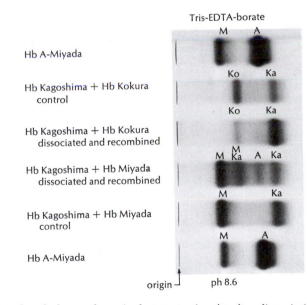

Fig. 14–5 Starch gel electrophoresis demonstrating *in vitro* dissociation and recombination of allelic and nonallelic hemoglobins. When Hb Kagoshima and Hb Kokura, both of which involve beta chain variants, are hybridized (line 3), the same hemoglobins are recovered as in the control (line 2). With Hb Kagoshima and an alpha chain variant, Hb Miyada, however, four hemoglobins appear (line 4), the two originals plus normal hemoglobin (Hb A), and a doubly abnormal hemoglobin whose electrophoretic position is intermediate between those of the Hb Miyada and Hb A. The appearance of Hb A is a form of complementation. (From Imamura, 1966. Courtesy of T. Imamura and *American Journal of Human Genetics*.)

years. They have shown by these means, for example, that the clinically severe Hurler's syndrome and the relatively mild Scheie's syndrome are allelic, being due to homozygosity for variants of the same enzyme, α-L-iduronidase. The same methods demonstrated, on the other hand, that Sanfilippo's syndrome really consists of two genetically and biochemically distinct disorders. These methods are also aiding greatly the analysis of heterogeneity in xeroderma pigmentosum and other diseases.

EPISTASIS IN BLOOD GROUPS

A number of more subtle epistatic interactions have also been found in man. Soon after the first major blood system, ABO, was discovered, it became evident that most persons have these antigens in their mucopolysaccharide-containing tissue fluids and secretions as well as in their red blood cells. Those who do are called secretors, those who do not, nonsecretors. The secretor property comes from an ability to produce mucoids that carry ABO antigens as well as the usual glycolipid forms of the antigens in the red cell membrane. Every type O persons can be secretors. Instead of A or B antigens they secrete one called H, often referred to as "H substance," which we shall see is a rudimentary building block of the other two antigens. (Unfortunately, heterozygous A and B individuals react poorly to anti-H, so H production cannot be used to diagnose the presence of the O(I^0) genes.) The capacity to secrete, that is, produce the water-soluble forms of A, B, or H antigens, is determined by a locus on a different pair of chromosomes than the one controlling production of the intracellular forms of these antigens. The secretor gene, Se, appears to be dominant to its allele for nonsecretion, se. Usually, secretor property is diagnosed in the saliva.

Thus as a first step, the major ABO and secretor genes maintain an epistatic relationship to one another. If the individual lacks an allele for production of A antigen, he cannot secrete A antigen in tissue fluids even if he has a secretor genotype (Se/Se or Se/se). On the other hand, if he has an A allele (I^A), he cannot produce the antigen in his tissue fluids if he is of the genotype se/se.

Even more interesting interactions occur between ABO, secretor, and another blood group system, Lewis. The latter is represented by three main types in the population: Lewis-a, generally written Le(a+b−), Lewis-b (Le(a−b+), and those negative for both, Le(a−b−). Lewis can be detected in tissue fluids, such as saliva or plasma, as well as on red blood cells. Unlike ABO, however, it is primarily a tissue fluid, and only secondarily a red cell antigen. It is not surprising, therefore, that one need not be a secretor to be Le(a+b−); one need only have an Le gene. Table 14–2 shows, however, that only persons with both Le and Se can be Lewis-b.

The biochemical basis of the interactions between ABH, secretor, and Lewis loci is now well understood. It appears that ABH and Lewis-a substances are merely different portions of the same oligosaccharide structure, and the antigenic specificity depends entirely on the kinds of terminal sugars present on the hapten (antigen-active) portion of this structure. The backbone structure of this oligosaccharide consists of N-acetylglucosamine (GluNac) and galactose, thus:

$$Gal-GluNAc-R \text{ (rest of oligosaccharide)}$$

TABLE 14–2 Correspondence between the genotypes for Lewis and Secretor traits and some antigenic specificities of red blood cells and tissue fluids

Genotype	Tissue Fluids			Red Blood Cells
	ABH[a]	Le-a	Le-b	
Le/– Se/–	+	+	+	Le(a–b+)
Le/– se/se	–	+	–	Le(a+b–)
le/le Se/–	+	–	–	
				Le(a–b–)
le/le se/se	–	–	–	

[a]Not shown for red blood cells because there the ABO system is independent of the Se trait.

The H locus controls an enzyme, possessed by almost everyone, which adds a molecule of fucose linked to this galactose, thus:

$$\begin{array}{c} \text{Fucose} \\ | \\ \text{Gal}-\text{GluNAc}-\text{R.} \end{array}$$

The oligosaccharide molecule at this stage is said to have H specificity.

The ABO locus controls enzymes which add sugars to the H structure. The oligosaccharide then has A or B specificity (which supersedes H specificity, though H substances may still be present elsewhere). The A enzyme adds a terminal N-acetylgalactosamine, thus:

$$\begin{array}{c} \text{Fucose} \\ | \\ \text{GalNAc}-\text{Gal}-\text{GluNAc}-\text{R.} \end{array}$$

The B enzyme adds a terminal galactose instead, that is,

$$\begin{array}{c} \text{Fucose} \\ | \\ \text{Gal}-\text{Gal}-\text{GluNAc}-\text{R.} \end{array}$$

O denotes the absence of either enzyme.

Persons with the *Le* gene produce an enzyme which enables them to attach fucose to the *N-acetylglucosamine*, thus:

$$\begin{array}{c} \text{Fucose} \\ | \\ \text{Gal}-\text{GluNAc}-\text{R.} \end{array}$$

The oligosaccharide then has Lewis-a specificity.

When the *Le* and the *H* genes are both present and active, both the GluNAc and the galactose of the backbone have fucose on them, thus:

$$\begin{array}{c} \text{Fucose} \quad \text{Fucose} \\ | \qquad | \\ \text{Gal}- \ \text{GluNAc}-\text{R.} \end{array}$$

The oligosaccharide with this combination loses all (for practical purposes) its H and Le-a specificities but now has instead *Lewis b* specificity. Therefore, Lewis-b does not call for the action of any additional gene or locus but is the result of complementary interaction of the *H* and *Le* genes. In this respect A and B supersede H and Lewis-b supersedes Lewis-a in the blood cells.

The foregoing applies to oligosaccharides in which Gal is bound to GluNac in $\beta1$–3 glycoside bond. Another bond, present as well in mucoids and present exclusively in red cell membranes, is $\beta1$–4 glycoside bonding. This, too, can have A, B, or H activity, but never Lewis. Thus red cell membranes cannot generate either Le-a or Le-b; they can only absorb glycolipoproteins from plasma that carry such activity.

This explains why *Le* acts only in the plasma and other body fluids. In the plasma, it can produce Lewis (and have some of it appear, secondarily, on the red blood cells) irrespective of whether molecules having the other fucose (fucose–galactose) linkage are present or not, that is, whether the individual is a secretor of ABH substances or not. To produce Lewis-b substance, however, he must have the other fucose linkage on hand as well, and this can happen only if he is a secretor.

Several epistatic genes suppress the activity of blood group genes. One of the best known has been found in persons who appear to be type O and transmit A or B genes (Fig. 14–6). Like other O's they produce anti-A and anti-B, but they also produce natural anti-H since they do not produce any H substance. They are said to have the "Bombay" phenotype, in honor of the locale of its first discovery. Bombay individuals are genetically *h/h*, that is, they lack the enzyme that attaches fucose to the galactose of the precursor disaccharide described above. *h/h* is, therefore, epistatic to A and B since these genes can only build on the H backbone. In the absence of precursors with the H (galactose-fucose) linkage, the body also cannot make Lewis-b substance. "Bombays" who have the *Le* gene, therefore, remain Le(a+) even if they inherit a dominant gene at the secretor locus, for example, II-6 in Figure 14–6.

The fact that a homozygote for Bombay will mimic type O with standard antisera even if he has inherited A and B can be dangerous for him because few labo-

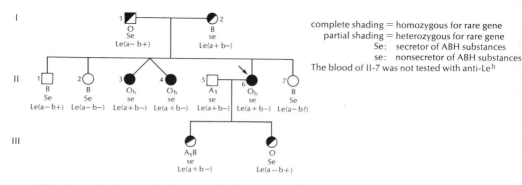

Fig. 14–6 Pedigree of a family with the rare Bombay gene epistatic to the A-B-O locus. Note that II-6 must carry an *Se* gene since her daughter III-2 is a secretor; she must also be the source of III-1's *I^B*. (From Levine et al., 1955. By permission of P. Levine and Grune and Stratton, Inc.)

ratories test routinely for anti-H. Thinking he is type O, an attempt may be made to give him type O blood. This could be fatal, which is one of the reasons for routine cross-matching bloods, even of apparently identical types.

REGULATORY INTERACTION

In prokaryotes a number of nucleotide sequences are known to control transcription of structural genes. They are called "promoters" if they contain the starting signals for transcription, "operators" if they interact with the product of a separate regulatory gene. These elements usually lie close to the structural gene, and the combination of this gene and its control elements is called an *operon.* If the product of a separate regulatory gene blocks transcription when it combines with the operator, it is called a "repressor" substance; removal of the block, thereby allowing transcription to proceed again, is often referred to as "derepression."

Control of transcription is very important. It is probably the major factor in differentiation of cells and in the rate at which the differentiated cell makes its unique product. What, for example, determines that the major oxygen transporting component of red blood cells shall stop being Hb F and start being Hb A? And what determines how much F shall be produced? And how could the F production be derepressed if that is desirable (e.g., when Hb A is not produced in normal quantities)?

The answers to these and many similar questions have thus far proved elusive because we lack good understanding of regulatory elements in eukaryotes.

Many believe that the best place to search for the answers to general as well as specific questions regarding the control elements in humans is indeed in the regulation of globin production. These studies have not yet solved the problem, but they have already yielded a rich by-product: better understanding of an important disorder, thalassemia, leading to considerable improvement in its diagnosis and treatment.

Essentially the story begins in 1925, when Cooley and Lee described a hereditary blood disorder that is particularly frequent among individuals who are, or are descended from, inhabitants of the countries bordering the Mediterranean Sea, especially Greece and Italy; hence its two common names: Cooley's anemia and thalassemia (from the Greek word for sea, *thalassa,* and anemia). The blood cells tend to be small (microcytic), elongated (leptocytic), and compensatorily increased in number (polycythemic), as in Fig. 14–7. Severe forms usually also display splenomegaly, characteristic changes in the bones (Figs. 14–7C,D), and skin pigmentation with a characteristic facies (Fig. 14–7B); they rarely survive past the second or third decade of life.

Our understanding of thalassemia has undergone a complex evolution that parallels in many respects the development of human genetics. At first the genetics seemed simple enough and somewhat similar to the sickle cell story: one locus with two alleles, with homozygotes for the abnormal allele having Cooley's anemia, generally referred to as "thalassemia major," and heterozygotes having a much milder disorder, "thalassemia minor."

This model was not completely satisfactory, however. Population geneticists

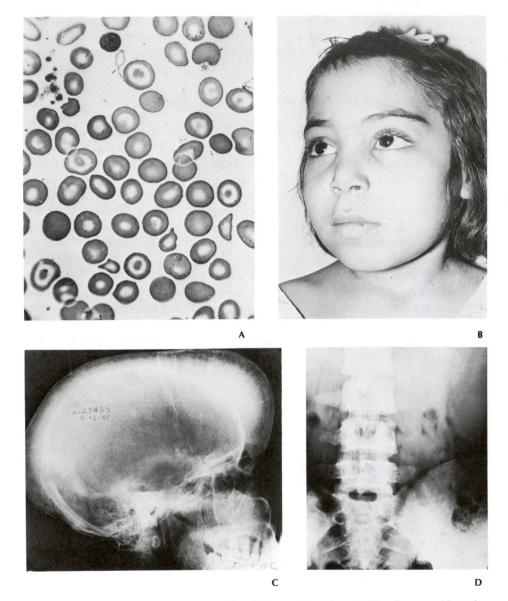

Fig. 14–7 Some diagnostic features of B-thalassemia major. **A.** Blood smear. Note the large number of target cells and small irregularly shaped cells. **B.** The characteristic facies, seen here in an Arabian girl. **C** and **D.** Bone changes: **C** shows the "hair-on-end" or "crew haircut" pattern in a lateral skull film; **D,** the analogous changes in the sacrum, lumbar vertebrae, and pelvis. (**A** and **B** from McNiel, 1967; courtesy of J. R. McNiel and the *American Journal of Human Genetics.* **C** courtesy of S. J. Baker and **D** courtesy of B. M. Jacobson and the *New England Journal of Medicine.* **C** appears also in *Clinical Hematology* by M. M. Wintrobe, published by Lea and Febiger.)

pointed out that the frequency of the postulated abnormal allele was so high in many groups that the rate at which it needed to be replaced (because it was semi-lethal) was much greater than known mutation rates. In addition, when the mutational basis of sickle cell anemia and other hemoglobinopathies (Chapter 5) was uncovered, there seemed to be no similar basis for thalassemia. The general consensus was then that inasmuch as thalassemia appeared to affect the *amount* of hemoglobin produced, rather than the production of abnormal hemoglobins, it must involve a defect in a hemoglobin controlling element rather than in a structural gene.

Subsequent findings, particularly of the wholesale heterogeneity of the disease, have shown that this, too, was an oversimplification. Instead of one disease, at least seven types of thalassemia are now recognized. Furthermore, most of these can have a number of subtypes or forms, and some of the subtypes can have multiple molecular bases.

What all the forms have in common is a genetically determined block in the synthesis of one or more of the globin chains. In some the block stems from complete or partial deletion of globin structural genes. Others involve less drastic changes in these genes that affect transcription or translation. In a large number, however, the absence of demonstrable change in the structural genes suggests that changes in regulatory or rate-determining genes are responsible. We will describe here the major findings for four of the more common thalassemias, as they illustrate the kinds of molecular evidence involved.

BETA-THALASSEMIA

Cooley's classic condition is now referred to as β-thalassemia, since the basic defect is in beta globin synthesis. It exists in two main forms. The most common, accounting for about 90 percent of cases, is called β^+-thalassemia. Most of the other cases are β^0-thalassemia. β^+- and β^0-thalassemia major are clinically very similar. The main difference between them is that in the β^0 form (often spoken of as β^{thal0} homozygotes) β-globin chains are completely absent, whereas in severe β^+-thalassemia ("β^{thal+} homozygotes") β-globin chains are present, at 5 to 30 percent of normal levels. The result is that those with β^+-major contain some Hb A, with, usually, large amounts of Hb F, whereas in those with β^0-major the hemoglobin is entirely fetal except for a small amount of A_2.

In either case there is a severe imbalance of α- to β-globin chain synthesis. The excess α-globin chains tend to precipitate, damaging the red cell membrane, with resultant ineffective erythropoiesis, destruction and phagocytosis of nucleated erythrocyte precursors in the bone marrow, and premature removal of surviving red cells by the spleen. This accounts for the above-mentioned microcytic hemolytic anemia and splenomegaly. Excessive destruction of red blood cells also leads to jaundice (hence the skin pigmentation) and icterus. The bone changes and characteristic facies are thought to be due to compensatory expansion of the marrow. Some of these symptoms can be relieved for a time by means of blood transfusions, but eventually there is a systemic iron overload and death, usually from arrhythmia or chronic congestive heart failure due to iron deposition in the cardiac conduction system and myocardium.

Those affected with β^0-thalassemia major are not all alike. Some produce small amounts of β mRNA, whereas others produce none at all. In β^+-thalassemia major, β mRNA production generally parallels the amount of β-globin produced.

It would appear, therefore, that there are three main forms of Cooley's anemia: (1) $\beta^{\text{thal}0}$ that produce neither normal β-globin nor normal β mRNA; (2) $\beta^{\text{thal}0}$ that produce small amounts of β mRNA but no β-globin; and (3) the $\beta^{\text{thal}+}$, that produce both β mRNA and β-globin, but in deficient amounts. A fourth class consists of individuals who have a clinically indistinguishable disorder but are genetically heterozygous, with one β^0 or one β^+ chromosome and a chromosome with a structural abnormality involving partial or complete deletion of the beta gene.

Recent evidence suggests that many, possibly all, the group 2 forms result from nonsense mutations in the β-globin exons that render them untranslatable. Single nucleotide mutations in the β exons could result in termination codons in 29 positions. Several such mutations have been identified. One at amino acid 39 (CAG, for glutamine, converted to UAG, amber) accounts for over 95 percent of β-thalassemias in Sardinia and probably most of the β^0-thalassemia major cases with mRNA in Mediterranean peoples. It can be readily diagnosed prenatally by several methods. Another nonsense mutation, at beta 17, has been identified in a Chinese case. The low level of mRNA produced suggests that the mRNA produced from these abnormal templates is unstable or is preferentially degraded. Similar mechanisms may be at work in Kurdish Jewish and Turkish β^0 patients who have nucleotide deletions that result in frameshifts of the β-globin gene with premature termination of translation.

The group 1 forms appear to be even more heterogeneous. In about 30 percent of Asian Indians the defect has been traced to a 619 nucleotide deletion/duplication rearrangement at the 3' end of the β globin gene which apparently renders it untranscribable. Two small deletions involving the β gene have been described in blacks, and a 10kb one including the entire β gene has been found in a Dutch family (the top 3 deletions in Fig. 14–9); all 3 appear to be rare. Other group 1 patients appear to have *intron* mutations that interfere with normal splicing of the several pieces of exon mRNA needed to produce mature globin mRNA. (Presumably transcription of precursor mRNA is not affected.) A number of other cases are attributable to several different mutations in normally highly conserved regions of the gene that apparently control transcription.

The molecular basis of beta$^+$-thalassemia, the most common form, is less well understood. The structure of the beta gene and of the beta globins and beta mRNA that are produced appear to be completely normal in most cases. In some people abnormalities similar to those observed in β^0-thalassemia have been found, though it is not clear why the β^+ produce β-globin but the β^0 with similar defects do not. Mediterranean peoples with homozygous β^+-thalassemia, for example, often have a single nucleotide substitution in the smaller intron of the beta gene. This base change results in anomalous splicing of the nuclear β-globin mRNA precursor and deficient production of mature cytoplasmic β-globin mRNA. Abnormal processing of precursor mRNA is also implicated in β^+-thalassemia among American blacks who have a base substitution at position 24 of the beta gene, even though the mutation causes no change in the amino acid introduced by this codon. Whether this mechanism is correlated with the relative mildness of β^+-thalassemia in American blacks is not known.

In general the β^+ story to date provides the strongest basis for postulation of a special β-thalassemia gene, though, as we shall note below, its structure and exact location are thus far unknown.

Further evidence for such a gene comes from heterozygotes with an abnormal β-globin gene and a β-thalassemia chromosome. Consider individuals with sickle cell trait (SA), for example. Since about 60 to 85 percent of their β-chains are normal (for Hb A), they are mildly affected, if at all, by the abnormal hemoglobins. If they are also heterozygous for β-thalassemia, however, they can make very little, if any, normal β-chains that are needed to produce hemoglobin A. Relatively speaking, therefore, the small amount of S hemoglobin they produce becomes 60 percent or more of the total hemoglobin. This is accompanied by an abnormal elevation of hemoglobins F and A_2 (Fig. 14–8). Hence such an S-heterozygote would often have a severe anemia that might even mimic sickle anemia, or, looked at the other way, such a thalassemia minor might be as ill as one with thalassemia major (one of those in class 4 of this condition as defined earlier). We say he or she is affected by sickle cell–thalassemia disease.

It should be realized that in all the double heterozygotes the S and β^{thal} have come from different parents (as in Fig. 14–8). In other words, the S and thal factors are on different chromosomes, that is, in "repulsion phase." Therefore, the thalassemia factor must be acting only in *cis*, that is, only on the β-gene on the same

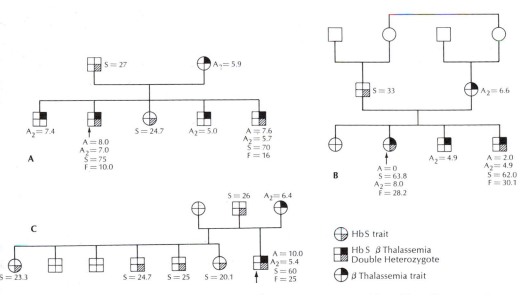

Fig. 14-8 Pedigrees containing marriages between a person with sickle-cell trait and one with β-thalassemia minor. Note the unusually high percentages of S, A_2, and F hemoglobins in the progeny affected by S-thalassemia disease (the double heterozygotes). (From McNiel, 1967. Courtesy of J. R. McNiel and *American Journal of Human Genetics*.)

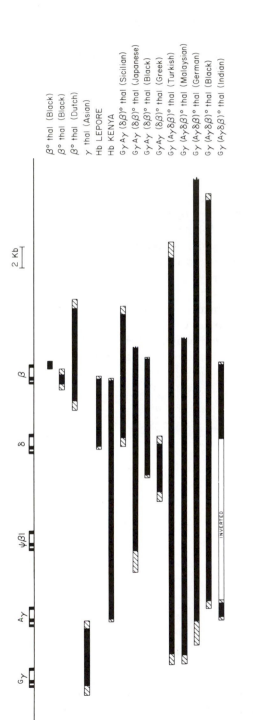

2 Kb

Gγ   Aγ   ψβ1   δ   β

β° thal (Black)
β° thal (Black)
β° thal (Dutch)
γ thal (Asian)
Hb LEPORE
Hb KENYA
Gγ Aγ (δβ)° thal (Sicilian)
Gγ Aγ (δβ)° thal (Japanese)
Gγ Aγ (δβ)° thal (Black)
Gγ Aγ (δβ)° thal (Greek)
Gγ (Aγδβ)° thal (Turkish)
Gγ (Aγδβ)° thal (Malaysian)
Gγ (Aγδβ)° thal (German)
Gγ (Aγδβ)° thal (Black)
Gγ (Aγδβ)° thal (Indian)

INVERTED

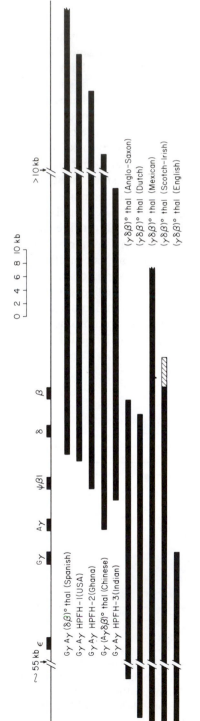

0 2 4 6 8 10 kb

~55 kb   ε   Gγ   Aγ   ψβ1   δ   β

>10 kb

Gγ Aγ (δβ)° thal (Spanish)
Gγ Aγ HPFH-1(USA)
Gγ Aγ HPFH-2(Ghana)
Gγ (Aγδβ)° thal (Chinese)
Gγ Aγ HPFH-3(Indian)

(γδβ)° thal (Anglo-Saxon)
(γδβ)° thal (Dutch)
(γδβ)° thal (Mexican)
(γδβ)° thal (Scotch-Irish)
(γδβ)° thal (English)

From: Bunn and Forget, Hemoglobin: Molecular, Genetic and
       Clinical Aspects, 1986, p250

chromosome, the one for normal chains. Otherwise the S gene would be repressed, too. Action only in *cis* bespeaks a very intimate relationship of the factors such as one would find in an operon.

The hypothesis is given further credence by evidence that the β^{thal} factors and the β and β-like structural genes are very close together on the chromosome. In matings of S-thalassemia double heterozygotes to normals, for example, the progeny either are SA or have thalassemia minor. None give certain evidence of crossing over by being normal in both respects or by having S-thalassemia disease. Indeed, no verified crossover has been found in several hundred matings of double heterozygotes for β-thalassemia and a β variant, all of whom were in *trans* phase. The β-thal factors are evidently part of the NAG complex, about 60,000 nucleotides (60 kb) long, shown in Fig. 14–9.

It may be noted that none of this DNA can at this time be positively designated as a thalassemia gene or controller element, but geneticists are generally convinced that it (or one for each of the structural genes) exists somewhere in the complex, and they constantly use the term "thalassemia gene" in the literature. It is interesting in this respect that a few recombinants have been found between β-thalassemia and the δ structural locus, also some between the β structural locus and a postulated controlling element of the gamma genes (see discussion of HPFH, below) which may be farther away from the gene(s) it controls than the others are.

ALPHA-THALASSEMIA

The α-globin locus is duplicated in most individuals. The two loci, which produce identical products, are designated $\alpha1$ and $\alpha2$. Like β, each gene has three exons and two introns (Fig. 5–1) and is part of a closely linked cluster with its ontogenetic predecessors. The α-like globin gene complex, on chromosome 16, also includes the structural gene for alphalike embryonic globin (ζ), several pseudogenes, and considerable intervening DNA. The 5′–3′ linear sequence is ζ, $\psi\zeta$, $\psi\alpha1$, $\alpha2$, and $\alpha1$ (Fig. 14–10).

Alpha-thalassemias are most frequently found in Southeast Asia, though some forms are also quite common in parts of the Middle East and the Mediterranean region. The severer forms are characterized by production of hemoglobin H, hemoglobin Bart's, or both. Hb H, which is manifested by characteristic inclusions of some red blood cells (Fig. 14–11A), has the formula β_4, and Bart's, so named because the first-described affected infant, of Oriental descent, was at St. Bartho-

Fig. 14–9 Chromosomal organization of the β-like (non-α) globin gene family and some of the deletions in it that cause various thalassemia syndromes. The intergene DNA is represented by the straight line between genes on the upper diagram of the cluster. In the gene diagrams, closed blocks represent exons, and open blocks, introns. Extents of various deletions are indicated by bars under the gene diagram; hatched regions of bars indicate regions where the precise endpoint of the deletions is indeterminate, and arrows indicate unmapped endpoints. kb = kilobases. (From Bunn and Forget, 1986. Courtesy of R. A. Spritz and the publishers, W. B. Saunders.)

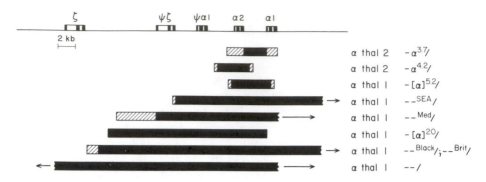

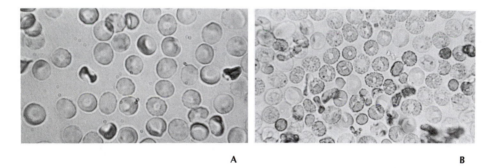

Fig. 14–10 The organization of the α-like globin gene family and deletions in it that cause α-thalassemia. See Fig. 14-9 legend for details. Med = Mediterranean. SEA = Southeast Asia. (From Bunn and Forget, 1986. Courtesy of R. A. Spritz and the publishers, W. B. Saunders.)

Fig. 14–11A Hb H blood picture in a Saudi patient. **B.** The nearly normal blood picture in the patient's mother. The blood of the father contained approximately one red cell in 1000 with Hb H. The mother and father are first cousins. (From McNiel, 1967. Courtesy of J. R. McNiel and *American Journal of Human Genetics*.)

lomew's (Bart's) Hospital in London, has the formula γ_4. Both can be understood from a reduction in α-chain synthesis: finding few α-chains with which to couple, the dimers of β-chains (in the case of Hb H) or those of γ-chains (in the case of Bart's) combine with dimers of the same types.

Like the β-thalassemias, α-thalassemia can be subdivided into α^+ types, in which there is reduced output of α chains, and α^0 types, with no α-chain synthesis.

These forms, too, display considerable heterogeneity, with a somewhat similar pattern: some cases attributable to deletions or other drastic changes in the DNA and other cases with no obvious molecular basis.

The molecular studies of Y. W. Kan and others point to a very interesting regularity: The variation in severity of α-thalassemia depends directly on the number of α-globin genes that are deleted or nonfunctional. Thus in the most severe α-thalassemia none of the four globin genes is present or functioning (often formulated --/--). No α-globin is produced, and the result is a syndrome, hydrops fetalis, which is lethal, often *in utero*. The blood picture is characterized by 80 to 100 percent Hb Bart's, the rest being Hb H and, if the ζ gene has not been deleted, Hb Portland ($\zeta_2\gamma_2$). Hb Bart's has a very high oxygen affinity, and therefore releases relatively little oxygen to the tissues (tissue hypoxia).

In a less severe condition known as hemoglobin H disease (Fig. 14–11A), three of the four α-genes appear to be missing or dysfunctional (--/-α). Patients with Hb H disease have a mild to moderate hemolytic anemia and occasionally exhibit a phenotype similar to that of severe homozygous β-thalassemia. Two α-genes are missing in α-thalassemia trait, also called α-thalassemia 1, usually characterized by a mild microcytic anemia, and one is missing in a generally asymptomatic ("silent carrier") condition referred to as α-thalassemia 2.

The deletions in these conditions are not all the same. The major ones are diagrammed in Fig. 14–10. They vary not only in the number of α-genes missing or rendered dysfunctional (where part of an α gene is still present) but also in how much additional DNA from the complex, or beyond it, has been removed.

In analyzing them a critical factor is whether the haplotype allows the production of one alpha globin or none. The ones that allow one to be produced are referred to as "α^+-thal" or as "α-thal 2" deletions (symbolized -α/) because they are the ones carried by persons with the deletion forms of α-thalassemia 2. The haplotypes producing no α-globins in *cis* are called "α^0" or "α-thal 1" deletions (symbolized --/). They are exemplified by the ones so marked in Fig. 14–10. A person affected with a deletion form of α-thalassemia 1 could be heterozygous for one of these, that is, --/$\alpha\alpha$. However, a deletion α-thalassemia 1 could be "homozygous α -thal 2," that is, -α/-α. (It is perhaps to minimize the possible confusion here that many authors prefer the name α-thalassemia trait over α-thalassemia 1.)

Some of the deletions occur in a number of geographic areas, whereas others appear to be confined to a single area or ethnic group. For example, the uppermost, 3.7 kb, deletion in Fig. 14–10, known as the "rightward α-thalassemia 2 deletion haplotype," is the most frequent case of α^+-thalassemia in blacks and Asians; it also occurs in Mediterranean peoples. By contrast, the 4.2 kb, "leftward," α-thal 2 deletion, just below it in the figure, appears confined to Asians. Both were probably formed by unequal crossing over. Indeed, chromosomes containing three α-genes, representing the reciprocal products of such crossing over, are known, though not with equal frequency. In Jamaica, where about 35 percent of the population have the rightward deletion, about 2.7 percent have the reciprocal, $\alpha\alpha\alpha^{3.7}$, haplotype.

Because the rightward α-thal deletion is the only one with any appreciable frequency in blacks, members of this ethnic group would rarely have any α-thalassemia disorder more severe than α-thalassemia 1. Hence Hb H disease (--/-α) is rare and hydrops fetalis (--/--) is completely unknown in blacks. The -α/ deletion is also known to ameliorate some cases of β-thalassemia in blacks: By decreasing the amount of α produced, the imbalance of α- to β-chains is reduced. As stated, the rightward deletion is also common in Asians, but this group contains so many other deletion chromosomes that loss of three or all four α-genes is quite frequent.

The characteristic --/ haplotype in Asians appears to be the second α-thal 1 chromosome in Fig. 14–10. Several of the others are known only from Mediterranean people. The two smallest of these appear to be rare, but the largest, the lowest one on the figure, is quite common. By contrast with the other --/ haplotypes, however, it does not result in hydrops fetalis, apparently because in it the zeta gene has also been deleted. Not being able to make the earliest embryonic hemoglobins, the homozygote for this haplotype does not survive long enough to present as hydrops.

So much emphasis is placed in the literature on the deletion forms of α-thalassemia that it is sometimes overlooked that in many cases all four genes are present. These "nondeletion α-thalassemias" are then attributed to "α-thalassemia alleles." (Unfortunately, the deletion haplotypes are also sometimes referred to as α-thalassemia alleles.) Some of these may actually be smaller modifications of the α structural genes than the ones detectable by restriction enzyme analyses. In one Italian family, for example, there was a five nucleotide deletion at the 5' splice junction of the first intron, with the result that no mature α-globin mRNA could be produced from this gene.

α-thalassemia often results from, or is mimicked by, abnormal hemoglobins produced by mutations in a single nucleotide. In a Chinese family, for instance, Hb H disease occurred even though the affected are --/$\alpha\alpha$ on the basis of the major deletions. It turns out that one of the "α's" has undergone a mutational change (proline in place of leucine at position 125) producing Hb Quong Sze, which is in effect nonfunctional. To all intents and purposes, therefore, a patient with genotype --/$\alpha\alpha^{QZ}$ has three missing α-genes, not two. Similar effects are seen in the case of Hb Suan–Dok (arginine in place of leucine at number 109) and Hb Petah Tikvah (aspartic acid in place of alanine at number 110). Also, Hb Constant Spring and other elongation variants resulting from mutations or frameshifts at the normal terminal α-gene codon (described in Chapter 5) result in α-thalassemia-like expression. Finally, there is an α-thalassemia that is actually due to an abnormality in a *beta* gene: The abnormal β-globins of Hb New York (glutamic acid in place of valine at β position 113) are produced at a faster rate, and unite with α-dimers more often than normal β-globins; however, the resultant hemoglobin is unstable and quickly degraded, so that there seems to be an α-chain deficiency.

Some Saudi Arabians carry a nondeletion haplotype that has such a detrimental effect on α-globin production that homozygotes for it exhibit Hb H disease, and persons who have one of these chromosomes and one -α/ (which is also common in that country) exhibit an α-thalassemia that is more severe than that of α-thalassemia 1 homozygotes (-α/-α). It is currently not clear whether this or any of the other "α-thalassemia alleles" that remain to be elucidated are true operonlike mutations, nor is it known exactly where they are located.

HPFH

Hereditary persistence of fetal hemoglobin (HPFH) is a generally asymptomatic thalassemic disorder characterized by very high levels of Hb F in heterozygotes as well as homozygotes.

It is often referred to as "pancellular HPFH" because synthesis of Hb F is uniform, in all red cells; in other conditions with increased F its synthesis is restricted to a selected population of red cells. In fact γ-globin synthesis is usually so efficient in HPFH that there is little or no imbalance of globin-chain production, whereas in $\delta\beta$-thalassemia (discussed below) the increased γ is usually insufficient to compensate for the diminution in β and δ.

Though relatively uninteresting as a clinical entity, HPFH has aroused a great deal of interest in medical geneticists interested in one of the fundamental mysteries of life: The nature and location of the controller elements that "turn on" and "turn off" genes in different cells and at different stages of ontogeny. The elevated Hb F of HPFH apparently results from a defect in such a switching mechanism, the one that normally turns off γ-chain production after fetal life. Recent work suggests that β-thalassemia can be alleviated by inducing this controlling element to be derepressed.

HPFH, too, is very heterogeneous. Some forms have very large (19 kb or more) deletions such as the three HPFH ones diagramed in the lower part of Fig. 14–9. Carriers of such deletions would, of course, produce no β- or δ-globins in *cis,* so that they are designated $^G\gamma^A\gamma(\delta\beta)^0$ HPFH.

In the homozygotes all the hemoglobin is F, in heterozygotes 25 to 30 percent. Some Black HPFH families, however, lack deletions or other rearrangements, at least those large enough to be detectable by such methods as restriction enzyme analysis.

In the so-called Greek and British forms there is no detectable deletion, so that β- and δ- as well as high amounts of γ-globins are produced. The two types differ in the levels of Hb F: about 15 percent in Greek form heterozygotes as opposed to 20 percent in homozygotes and 8 percent in heterozygotes of the British form.

HPFH γ-derepression may be highly selective. In the British and Greek forms most, or all, the F hemoglobin consists of $^A\gamma$-chains. $^A\gamma$ HPFH occurs also in a Chinese nondeletion form. In another nondeletion type, $^G\gamma$- and β-chains persist, but $^A\gamma$-globins are absent and δ-chains are deficient: $^G\gamma(\beta^+)$ HPFH. $^G\gamma$ predominance has also been observed in some Black HPFH families ($^G\gamma(\delta\beta)^0$ HPFH).

Linkage studies using restriction site polymorphisms have attempted to localize the γ-controlling element. One such study showed in both a family with the British form and in one with the Swiss type (another nondeletion form associated with small increases in Hb F), the HPFH determinant is closely linked to the NAG gene cluster. In one of these cases (the Swiss type) it is apparently *outside* the complex.

Heterozygosity for Hb Kenya is also considered to be a form of HPFH. Hb Kenya is produced by a Lepore-like fusion of the β- and $^A\gamma$-genes, with deletion of the intervening delta and pseudo-β loci as well as parts of the β- and $^A\gamma$-genes (Figs. 14–9 and 14–12). It follows that here, too, there is an elevation of $^G\gamma$ synthesis. Such a condition is often written in the literature as $^G\gamma^+(^A\gamma\delta\beta)^0$-thalassemia instead of being denoted as a form of HPFH, presumably because a single remaining $^G\gamma$ gene, even if fully active, may not be able to compensate for the lack of β-chain production. A similar situation occurs when part of the region has not been deleted but exists in inverted configuration (lowest diagram in the upper portion of Fig. 14–9).

4. $\delta\beta$-thalassemia

We noted above that one form of β^0-thalassemia involved a deletion of 619 nucleotides of the β-structural gene. In larger deletions in the nonalpha gene complex the whole β-globin gene and also the nearby δ-gene may be lost (Fig. 14–9). This is one of the bases for the condition known as $\delta\beta$-thalassemia.

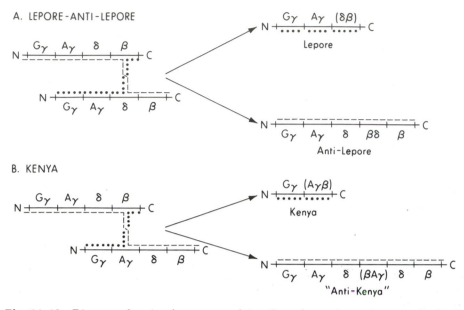

Fig. 14–12   Diagram showing how unequal (nonhomologous) crossing over in the β-like gene cluster could produce the Lepore, anti-Lepore, and Kenya polypeptides. Anti-Kenya has not yet been reported. N = aminoterminal (5') end, C = carboxyterminal (3') end. (From Nienhuis and Benz, 1977; courtesy of A. W. Nienhuis and *New England Journal of Medicine*.)

Surprisingly, the clinical picture in homozygous δβ-thalassemia resulting from such deletions is usually less severe than that of β-thalassemia major, the absence of hemoglobins A and A₂ being partially compensated for by the persistence of fetal hemoglobin into adult life. In fact, one of the early synonyms of this condition was F-thalassemia. Heterozygotes with one of these deletions and one normal chromosome produce some A, normal A₂, and a moderately increased amount of F (5 to 15 percent).

Homozygotes for the various forms of hemoglobin Lepore are also often referred to as having δβ-thalassemia. The Lepore chromosome cannot make normal δ- or β-globins because a portion of the δ-gene responsible for the carboxy (3') end of δ-globin and a portion of the β-gene responsible for the amino-terminal (5') end of β-globin are deleted (Fig. 14–9), probably as a result of unequal crossing over (Fig. 14–12). The fused remainders of these genes are expressed at a low level as Lepore globins, which therefore have only a variable amount of the N-terminal portion of δ-globin and of the C-terminal portion of β-globin (Fig. 14–13). Since the first one was found in a family named Lepore, at least six different forms have been reported. All are referred to as Hb Lepore, with the place of discovery as a subscript. The original one, for example, is now Lepore_Boston.

The δβ-thalassemia of Lepore homozygotes is more severe than in those with the complete deletion of the δ- and β-genes, inasmuch as the level of Hb F is normal. This suggests that the more complete deletions also remove portions of the

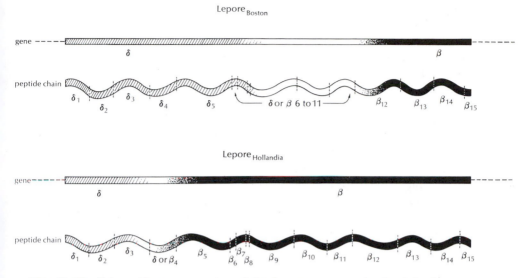

Fig. 14–13   Schematic representation of the Lepore$_{Boston}$ gene (top), of the Lepore$_{Helland}$ gene (bottom), and of the corresponding peptide chains. The shaded areas indicate that part of the Lepore genes appears to be derived from the δ gene and that part of the corresponding peptide chains is δ-like. The area in solid color indicates that part of the Leopore genes that appears to be derived from the B gene and that part of the corresponding peptide chains that is β-like. The empty areas between shaded and solid color areas indicate those portions of the genes and of the peptide chains that may be derived either from β or from δ. The postulated joining of part of the β gene to part of the δ gene has occurred presumably in this area. The dotted lines along the peptide chains indicate schematically the peptide bonds that may be split by trypsin. The resulting peptides are indicated below and are numbered consecutively starting from the N-terminus. The symbols β or δ, which precede the peptide numbers, indicate whether the corresponding peptides are β-like or δ-like. (From Baglioni, 1962; courtesy of C. Baglioni and the *Proceedings of the National Academy of Science,* U.S.)

nonalpha-gene complex that normally are responsible for repressing F synthesis in the adult.

Several other abnormal hemoglobins, such as Miyada, P-Congo, P-Nilotic, and Lincoln Park, are δ-β recombinants which represent the reciprocal products of the process that produced the Lepore hemoglobins, that is, in these the amino terminal end is from β and the carboxy terminal part from δ. Hence they are referred to as anti-Lepore (Fig. 14–12). They are not simply reverse-Lepores, however, because these chromosomes also contain normal β and δ-genes. Hb Lincoln Park has an additional deletion of one δ amino acid.

Recently an even more complicated ($\delta\beta\delta$) fusion chain, Hb Parchman, has been reported. It probably arose from a double nonhomologous interchange between δ and β structural genes.

The condition of heterozygotes for the various $\delta\beta$ chromosomes mentioned usually resembles thalassemia minor, since they produce normal β- and δ-globins as well. Those who also have a β-thalassemia chromosome, however, tend to have a clinical picture very similar to that of homozygous β-thalassemia. These account for some of the cases referred to earlier as class 4 of that disorder. Even the normal β-genes of the anti-Lepore chromosomes seem to be inhibited by the β-thalassemia factor in *trans*.

Recent molecular genetics studies indicate that a number of nucleotide groupings, totaling about 100 base pairs, located on the 5' side ("upstream") of mammalian globin genes are significant for regulation of transcription. Such groupings are called "promoters." Two types are recognized: (1) AT-rich regions, commonly referred to as "TATA boxes," important in initiating transcription; and (2) 8–12 base pair groups called "UPE's" (upstream promoter elements) that are important in determining its rate. Presumably mutations in such promoter elements could be instrumental in the interference with normal globin production in many thalassemias not ascribable to deletions or other defects in the structural genes. Promoters appear to operate only in cis.

15

Polygenic Inheritance

The hallmark of Mendelian traits discussed thus far is that the variants can be distinguished and classified in a clear-cut manner. The traits Mendel chose to study, such as round and wrinkled peas, serve as the classical paradigm of such discontinuous distributions. Similarly, the normal and affected for the human conditions listed in Table 1–3 fall into sharply differentiated classes that exhibit Mendelian ratios. Even when environmental factors caused some overlapping between phenotypes (review particularly Fig. 5–14), further analysis was able to show that a discontinuous distribution does exist and that, if we make small allowances for variable expressivity and incomplete penetrance, the Mendelian ratios do fit after all.

Some traits, however, are impossible to characterize in a discontinuous manner. For example, when in any group we measure the heights of normal individuals after they have stopped growing, we find that between the shortest and tallest of them stand individuals in every category we can devise with our measuring instruments. Table 15–1 is an excerpt from one such study: the heights of males whose fathers were between 67.5 and 68.5 inches in height. Most of the sons are close to the heights of their fathers, but they vary from 61.5 to 77.5 inches with every possible measurement in between. (One should not be misled by the fact that the data are presented in one-inch intervals.) Although we could agree that the individuals at the extremes be characterized as "short" or "tall," we would have great difficulty agreeing on how to label many of the persons in between and where to draw the line between categories.

A number of other traits show similar distributions. We call them quantitative or metrical traits or traits that show continuous variation. In the case of stature and many other such traits, even when we study the extremes, when, say, the fathers are 61 inches tall or 75 inches tall, the distribution of offspring in each case is continuous and there is much overlapping. The trait is clearly familial, for the sons of 61 inch men tend to fall in the lower end of the range, and those of 75 inch men in the high end. Nevertheless, the absence of Mendelian groupings seems to make the conclusion of inheritance uncertain and its nature unclear.

In addition, we encounter many situations that do exhibit discontinuous distributions but are nevertheless troublesome because even after our very best analysis the trait does not fall into Mendelian ratios. In some instances we are able to

Table 15–1 Distribution of heights among 154 males whose fathers were between 67.5 and 68.5 inches tall (From Neel and Schull, 1954, after Kendall, 1947 and Pearson and Lee, 1903)

Height in Inches	Percent of Total
61.5–62.5	0.3
62.5–63.5	0.8
63.5–64.5	0.8
64.5–65.5	3.6
65.5–66.5	10.4
66.5–67.5	12.7
67.5–68.5	15.3
68.5–69.5	15.6
69.5–70.5	12.7
70.5–71.5	12.4
71.5–72.5	5.0
72.5–73.5	4.9
73.5–74.5	3.4
74.5–75.5	0.6
75.5–76.5	0.8
76.5–77.5	0.8
Total	100.1

marshall ancillary evidence, such as a high rate of consanguinity among the parents of the affected, to support a Mendelian basis. Where strong data of this type are not available, we are tempted to conclude that the trait is apparently not inherited, but if we do so we seem to neglect considerable evidence that heredity *does* play a role. Data may show, for example, that close relatives of the affected, even those not sharing a common environment with them, are more likely to exhibit the same trait than unrelated persons. This is particularly noteworthy for a number of common clinical conditions, such as peptic ulcer and congenital heart defects.

Geneticists have found that many of these cases do follow Mendelian principles, except that in these cases the ratios are obscured by (a) environmental interactions and (b) the fact that the trait is determined by a large number of loci acting together. This is often referred to as the multiple factor hypothesis, and this type of inheritance is called *polygenic, quantitative,* or *multifactorial.* We shall first discuss cases that are clearly metrical, then cases that appear discontinuous but probably have a polygenic basis. We shall also include here a discussion of a method that many human geneticists have found useful in attacking problems of ambiguous inheritance: the study of twins.

CONTINUOUS VARIATION

When we study metrical traits in other organisms, the following results are typical: A cross between representatives of two extremes produces progeny that generally show some continuous variation about an intermediate point, which many not be an exact average of the original extremes. However, the variance is not particularly extensive: rarely are any of the progeny as different from this intermediate as either parent was. When the F_1 intermediates are intercrossed, the F_2 shows a similar average. The range of variation in the F_2 is much greater, however. In fact, some F_2 may differ from the F_1 and F_2 average as much as the original parents did.

The simplest explanation is that the parental extremes differ by many loci which in the main contribute additively to the phenotype. For example, suppose a dwarf line of plants is 12 cm tall on the average and the mean height of a tall line is 60 cm. If six loci were responsible for the height, each of the 12 genes at these loci in the dwarf line might contribute 1 cm of height and each gene of the tall line 5 cm. The F_1 would contain six "tall" genes, good for 30 cm, and six "dwarf" genes, good for 6 cm, for an average height of 36 cm. Not all the F_1 would be 36 cm tall—just as not all the P_1 were exactly 12 cm or 60 cm—because of environmental variables: chance variation of nutriments in the soil, moisture, predators, and the like. (Similar variations in diet, living conditions, etc. play a large part in determining the distribution of human metrical traits.)

In the F_2, the heights expected from these genetic factors follows the binomial distribution $(1/2 + 1/2)^{12}$ (Table 15-2). Note that the exponent of the binomial is the same as the number of alleles that contribute to the phenotype.

Though based on a relatively small sample, the distribution of heights in Table 15-1 resembles broadly the infinite (theoretical) one in Table 15-2. It shows that

Table 15-2 Expected results and their relative frequency in the F_2 of the hypothetical cross discussed in the text in which the F_1 are heterozygous for six additive loci

Number of "Tall" Genes	Number of "Dwarf" Genes	Height (Y)	Relative to the mean (Y')[a]	Probability (f) Exact	Percent
12	0	60	24	$1(1/2)^{12}$	0.02
11	1	56	20	$12(1/2)^{12}$	0.29
10	2	52	16	$66(1/2)^{12}$	1.61
9	3	48	12	$220(1/2)^{12}$	5.37
8	4	44	8	$495(1/2)^{12}$	12.08
7	5	40	4	$792(1/2)^{12}$	19.34
6	6	36	0	$924(1/2)^{12}$	22.56
5	7	32	−4	$792(1/2)^{12}$	19.34
4	8	28	−8	$495(1/2)^{12}$	12.08
3	9	24	−12	$220(1/2)^{12}$	5.37
2	10	20	−16	$66(1/2)^{12}$	1.61
1	11	16	−20	$12(1/2)^{12}$	0.29
0	12	12	−24	$1(1/2)^{12}$	0.02
		Total	0	1	99.98

$$V_P = \frac{\Sigma fY'^2 - \Sigma (fY')^2}{\Sigma f}$$

$$= \frac{196\ 608/4096 - 0}{1}$$

$$= 48.$$

[a]Using Y' instead of Y greatly simplifies the calculations.

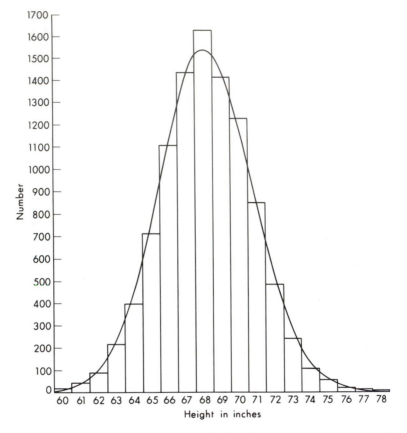

Fig. 15-1 Histogram showing the observed distribution of statures of 10,004 adult American Indian males, with a normal distribution having the same mean and standard deviation superimposed. (From Neel and Schull, 1954, after Davenport and Love, 1921. Courtesy of J. V. Neel and the University of Chicago Press.)

one does not really need an F_2 to approximate the distribution of phenotypes of a continuously varying trait. This is further borne out by Fig. 15-1, based on a larger sample.

If, in our plant example, there had been only three loci whose genes made the same contributions to the height, 5 cm by a "tall" allele and 1 cm by a "dwarf" allele, the F_1 and F_2 would have been expected to be 18 cm on average, and the distribution of F_2 would have been expected to be as it is in Table 15-3.

Note the differences between Tables 15-2 and 15-3. The probabilities of achieving the mean height and the extremes are smaller in Table 15-2, but more of the results are grouped around the mean and, above all, there are many more classes of phenotypes. As the exponent increases and the binomial distribution approaches the normal distribution, the curve tends to flatten downward and to spread outward. In other words, as the number of loci increases, the variability increases, so that, other things being equal, the measure of variability, the standard error (or, more conveniently, its square, the *variance*) can be an indication of the number of loci involved.

For the data of Table 15–3 the variance is 24, and for the data of Table 15–2 it is 48. The doubling mirrors the doubling of the number of loci having the same effects.

True, the mean was also doubled when the number of loci was doubled. The mean does not measure the variability well, however. Consider a case with three loci in which each "tall" gene contributed 4 cm and each "dwarf" gene 2 cm (Table 15–4). Comparing this to Table 15–3, there are again six classes, with the same frequency distribution. The interval between classes would be 2 cm, however, instead of the 4 in Table 15–3, and the extremes would be much closer to the mean (12 and 24 cm, as opposed to 6 and 30). Thus the variance is much less, even though the mean is the same.

A general formula denotes the genetic variance contributed by each locus: $2pqa^2$, where p and q are the frequencies of the two alleles (as in Chapter 8) and a is the incremental difference between the two alleles. (Strictly speaking, $a =$ the increase above midparent for each additional "tall" gene.) For F_2's, such as those in Tables 15–2 to 15–4, $p = q = 1/2$; and in the case where each "dwarf" gene contributes 1 cm and each "tall" gene 5 cm, a is 4. Hence, each locus variance in Tables 15–2 and 15–3 is $2(1/2)(1/2)16$, a total of 8.

In Table 15–3, with three such loci, the variance is $8 + 8 + 8 = 24$, and in Table 15–2, it is 8 added six times, or 48. In Table 15–4, however, each locus contributes a variance of $3[2(1/2)(1/2)4]$, for a total of 6.

The effect of environment can be seen by a simple example (Table 15–5) calculated by assuming three different environments: one-quarter of each genetic class of Table 15–2 fell into an environment that added 4 cm to whatever the genes contributed, one-half into an environment that made no change, and one-quarter into one that *reduced* 4 cm from whatever the genes produced. Note that the effect is to leave the mean unchanged but to further increase the spread of results. Fur-

Table 15-3 Expected F_2 heights if there are only three additive loci, each of whose alleles contribute the same amounts as those in Table 15–2

Number of "Tall" Genes	Number of "Dwarf" Genes	Height (Y)	Relative to the Mean (Y')	Probability (f) Exact	Percent
6	0	30	12	$1(1/2)^6$	1.56
5	1	26	8	$6(1/2)^6$	9.38
4	2	22	4	$15(1/2)^6$	23.44
3	3	18	0	$20(1/2)^6$	31.25
2	4	14	−4	$15(1/2)^6$	23.44
1	5	10	−8	$6(1/2)^6$	9.38
0	6	6	−12	$1(1/2)^6$	1.56
		Total	0	1	100.01

$$V_P = \frac{1\ 536/64 - 0}{1}$$

$$= 24$$

Table 15-4 Expected F$_2$ heights if the 3 additive loci of Table 15–3 produced an incremental interval of 2 instead of 4

Number of "Tall" Genes	Number of "Dwarf" Genes	Height (Y)	Relative to the Mean (Y')	Probability (f)
6	0	24	6	$1(1/2)^6$
5	1	22	4	$6(1/2)^6$
4	2	20	2	$15(1/2)^6$
3	3	18	0	$20(1/2)^6$
2	4	16	−2	$15(1/2)^6$
1	5	14	−4	$6(1/2)^6$
0	6	12	$\underline{-6}$	$\underline{1(1/2)^6}$
		Total	0	1

$$V_P = \frac{384/64 - 0}{1}$$

$$= 6$$

Table 15-5 Expected results in the F$_2$ if the Table 15–2 plants grew in the three environments described in the text

Height (Y)	Relative to the Mean (Y')	Probability (f)	
		Exact	Percent
64	28	$1(1/2)^{14}$	0.01
60	24	$14(1/2)^{14}$	0.09
56	20	$91(1/2)^{14}$	0.56
52	16	$364(1/2)^{14}$	2.22
48	12	$1001(1/2)^{14}$	6.11
44	8	$2002(1/2)^{14}$	12.22
40	40	$3003(1/2)^{14}$	18.33
36	0	$3432(1/2)^{14}$	20.95
32	−4	$3003(1/2)^{14}$	18.33
28	−8	$2002(1/2)^{14}$	12.22
24	−12	$1001(1/2)^{14}$	6.11
20	−16	$364(1/2)^{14}$	2.22
16	−20	$91(1/2)^{14}$	0.56
12	−24	$14(1/2)^{14}$	0.09
8	−28	$\underline{1(1/2)^{14}}$	$\underline{0.01}$
Total	0	1	100.03

$$V_P = \frac{917\,506/16\,384 - 0}{1}$$

$$= 56$$

thermore, when the example is worked out in detail, it will be noted that a number of different genotypes come out to have the same phenotype. A plant with 12 "tall" genes raised in the poorest environment, for example, will grow to the same height, 56 cm, as a plant with 11 "tall" and 1 "dwarf" genes in the neutral environment and a plant with 10 "tall" and 2 "dwarf" genes in the optimal environment. The overlapping of genotypes within the classes of phenotypes means, in other words, that these classes no longer have clear genotypic meaning.

It is little wonder, then, that the results range over the whole spectrum of possible measurements. It becomes difficult, in fact, to distinguish classes among the data, especially in the middle range of measurements.

The total variance of the data in Table 15–5 is 56. Since the environmental variance in this case is 8 and the variance contributed by the genes is again 48, it comes out that the total phenotypic variance is the sum of the variance contributed by the genes and the variance contributed by the environment. In symbolic terms,

$$V_P = V_G + V_E.$$

This is known as *partitioning the variance.*

The proportion of the total variance contributed by the genes is often referred to as the *heritability* of the trait, symbolized as h^2. So,

$$h^2 = \frac{V_G}{V_P}.$$

If the environment contributed nothing, heritability would be 100 percent; if the genes contributed nothing, it would be 0.

For the Table 15–5 case:

$$h^2 = 48/56 = 85.7 \text{ percent.}$$

In these examples the genetic variance has been simply additive, that is, the total has been the sum of the contributions of the individual loci. Furthermore, we have assumed no dominance at any loci: When any locus is heterozygous, the genetic contribution has been the sum of the contributions of the two alleles.

The actual situation may be more complicated. At some loci one allele may exert some degree of dominance, so that the heterozygotes for these loci falls closer to one homozygote than to the midpoint between the two homozygotes; in complete dominance, the heterozygote and one homozygote would be equal in height. Similarly, there may be epistatic interactions between loci that would cause their effects not to be the same. The phenotypic variance would then be the sum of the variances contributed by all these factors, or

$$V_P = V_A + V_D + V_{EP} + V_E,$$

where A = additive, D = dominance, EP = epistatic interaction, and E = environment. More complicated analyses would include also such factors as inbreeding and maternal effects.

To differentiate between heritability based only on the additive variance and one considering also other genetic influences, the former is often referred to as "heritability in the narrow sense" (h^2), whereas the latter is called "heritability in the broad sense" or "the degree of genetic determination" (symbolized as H). Usually in genetics estimates that use the word "heritability" without modifiers are referring to the one "in the narrow sense."

In addition to stature, a number of human traits exhibit continuous variation, either as binomial distributions, signifying that a relatively small number of loci are involved, or as normal distributions based on a large number of loci.

One that involves a relatively small number of loci is skin pigmentation. A pioneer human geneticist, C. B. Davenport, was particularly interested in this trait among the data he collected (in collaboration with his wife, Gertrude, and others) at the Eugenics Record Office at Cold Spring Harbor, New York. Although the scientific reputation of the group was sullied by work with racist overtones, it was the first to clarify the genetics of many human conditions, especially Huntington's chorea. Indeed, Davenport's study of skin color differences between Negroes and Caucasians is still considered classical by many writers. Basing his ascertainment on matches to various blends of pigments, he noted that almost all of the first generation ("mullatoes") from matings of light whites and dark blacks were more or less intermediate in skin color. The offspring of two mullatoes manifested a wide range of pigmentation, which he thought fell into five classes. A small number (4 out of 33) were as light as the white grandparent or as dark as the black grandparent. Since this was about one-eighth of the sample, Davenport thought that the probability of each F_2 extreme class was one-sixteenth. He concluded that skin pigmentation was determined by additive loci and, since $(1/2)^4 = 16$, that two loci (four alleles) were involved. This also fitted well with his finding of five classes in the F_2.

Basing the estimate of the number of genes on the size of the extreme classes in the F_2 is generally not reliable, for several reasons:

1. A small chance error in the fertilizations would cause a major error. Obtaining 3 out of 256, for example, one might assume the nearest meaningful fraction, 4/256 ($= 1/64$, the proportion expected for 3 loci) when the true result perhaps should have been 1/256 (the expected for 8 genes, 4 loci).
2. A small environmentally induced modification could cause an error akin to the one just mentioned.
3. Often we cannot see the entire F_2, but only a sampling of it in which the grandparental extremes do not even appear. Basing our results on the extremes that *are* observed only compounds the error.

More recent data, based on improved pigment measuring techniques, suggests that a minimum of three, possibly as many as six, loci are involved (Fig. 15–2). All agree, however, that skin color differences in human beings depend on additive interactions with little or no dominance.

This carries implications that are contrary to some widely held misconceptions among the lay public. It explains, for example, why marriages between two persons, each of whom has mixed black and white ancestry, can result in children who are darker than the darkest parent while others could be lighter than the lightest parent. If, for example, skin color differences depend on four loci on different chromosomes, A, B, C, and D, and we assume the higher case allele of each locus adds more pigment than the lower case one, a relatively dark person could have the genotype A/a B/B C/c D/d, and a relatively light one might be A/a b/b c/c D/d. A child of theirs with a genotype A/A B/b C/c D/D would probably be darker than the relatively dark parent, whereas one with genotype a/a B/b c/c d/d would be expected to be lighter than the relatively light parent.

However, marriage to a person with minimum pigment genes, a/a b/b c/c d/d (as we would characterize most whites) would never be expected to produce any child who was darker than the darkest parent. The mating A/a B/B C/c D/d

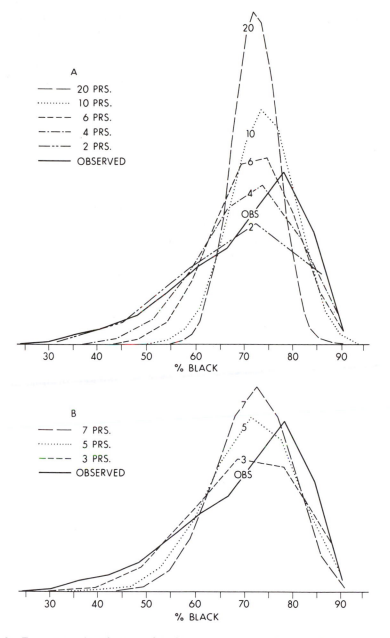

Fig. 15-2 Frequency distributions for skin pigmentation. In part **A** the observed distribution is compared to theoretical distributions based upon 2, 4, 6, 10, and 20 gene pairs, in part B upon 3, 5, and 7 gene pairs, on the assumption that the observed black population is an admixture of 30 percent white and 70 percent black ancestry. (From Stern, 1953; courtesy of S. Karger AG, Basel, publishers of *Human Heredity*, successor to *Acta Genetica*.)

$\times$ a/a b/b c/c d/d, for instance, could produce no child with more than 4 high pigment genes, A/a B/b C/c D/d. This is the hue expected in the first-generation mulatto between the darkest black and the whitest white. Although the variation observed among such mulattoes indicates that environmental variations play a role in determining human skin color, it is almost certain that the A/a B/b C/c D/d child would be lighter than his A/a B/B C/c D/d parent. The stories of marriages of two white persons that produced "black babies" have proved time and again to be false.

Variation in the amount of pigment in the iris, which determines "eye color," is independent of skin color. Here the absence of pigment in the outer part of the iris causes the eye to appear blue for the same reason that an uncloudy sky appears blue: as light is scattered (by the pure atmosphere in the clear sky or by the unpigmented iris diaphragm in the eye), the portion with shortest wave length, the blue, is scattered the most and reflected back to the eyes of the beholder. A pigmented iris absorbs light and reflects back a color, green, hazel, or brown, depending on the nature and intensity of the pigment present.

Several studies have shown that the amount of pigment deposition between blue and dark brown probably is in the nature of a continuous variation. Attempts to erect meaningful genetic classes such as blue, yellow, green, hazel, light brown, and dark brown within this continuous spectrum generally have been unsuccessful. This is especially true in the lower part of the range, where persons with small amounts of pigment and completely pigmentless eyes are very difficult to distinguish, all referred to as "blue" by the layman. Thus, if there are three loci that we could call P_1, P_2, and P_3 the marriage of two "blue-eyed" persons might involve a husband and wife with no uppercase (pigment) genes at all

$$\frac{p_1\ p_2\ p_3}{p_1\ p_2\ p_3} \times \frac{p_1\ p_2\ p_3}{p_1\ p_2\ p_3}$$

and produce all blue-eyed children. On the other hand, both of the "blue-eyed" parents may have a small amount of pigment (and a small number of uppercase pigment genes) thus:

$$\frac{p_1\ p_2\ P_3}{p_1\ p_2\ p_3} \times \frac{p_1\ P_2\ P_3}{p_1\ p_2\ p_3}$$

and they could have children with quite a few pigment genes, for example,

$$\frac{p_1\ P_2\ P_3}{p_1\ p_2\ P_3}$$

and might appear definitely light brown, hazel, or even distinctly brown-eyed.

The number of dermal ridges (in fingerprints) appears to be similarly determined by a relatively small number of additive loci. As we shall see below, the heritability is very high.

Blood pressure, glucose tolerance, and other medically significant traits exhibit continuous distributions that suggest the involvement of a large number of additive loci. Here, however, environment, too, plays a wide role, and geneticists have striven mightily to derive reliable methods of estimating the extent of their heritability. These may be subsumed under two headings: (1) regression systems based on degrees of relationship and (2) twin studies.

REGRESSION SYSTEMS

The conceptual basis of regressions systems is that if heredity is the sole determiner the degree of resemblance between relatives for a trait determined by a large number of additive loci without dominance should follow the coefficients of relationship (Chapter 10). It will be recalled that the coefficient of relationship measures the degree that relatives have genes in common. The more genes for a continuously varying trait that they have in common the more they should resemble one another for that trait. Conversely, the degree that relatives correlate for the trait should be an exact reflection of their degree of relationship. If the correlation is the same or nearly the same as the coefficient of relationship, this is a sign that the heritability of the trait is high. If, on the other hand, the correlation is much lower than the coefficient of relationship, environment must be playing a major role.

With 100 percent heritability due to additive genes and no dominance, the correlation between first degree relatives (parent–child or sib–sib comparisons) should be 0.5; second-degree relatives (comparisons of uncles and aunts to nephews and nieces or grandparents to grandchildren) should show 0.25 correlation; third-degree relatives (first cousins, for instance) 0.125 correlation; and so forth. The correlation between unrelated persons, such as between mates under random mating, should be zero.

This is essentially what Sarah Holt found to be the case for dermal ridge counts (Table 15–6). None of the parent–child or ordinary sib–sib correlations differ significantly from 0.5; and the parent–parent correlation is not only very close to zero, but it differs from zero by less than its standard error. The similarity of the sib-pair and parent–child correlations is evidence for the absence of dominance; dom-

Table 15–6 Correlations between relative for total finger dermal ridge count (Data from Holt, 1968, unless denoted otherwise)

Nature of Relationship	Number of Pairs	Observed Correlation	Theoretical Correlation[a]
Parent–child			
Mother-child	405	0.48 ± 0.04	0.5
Father-child	405	0.49 ± 0.04	0.5
Sib–sib	642	0.50 ± 0.04	0.5
Parent–parent	200	0.05 ± 0.07	0.0[b]
Twin–twin			
Monozygotic	80	0.95 ± 0.01	1.0
Male-Male[c]	129	0.953 ± 0.008	1.0
Female-Female[c]	143	0.966 ± 0.006	1.0
Dizygotic	92	0.49 ± 0.08	0.5
Male-Male[c]	95	0.463 ± 0.081	0.5
Female-Female[c]	90	0.464 ± 0.083	0.5
Male-Female[c]	127	0.423 ± 0.052	0.5

[a]On the assumption that the trait is determined by multiple additive loci without dominance.
[b]On the assumption of random mating.
[c]Data of Lamy et al. (1957) cited by Holt (1968).

inance would increase the sib–pair correlation but not affect the one between parent and child.

By contrast, the research team responsible for Fig. 15–3 found that the blood pressure correlations between first-degree relatives was 0.174 for diastolic pressures and 0.198 for systolic pressures. The figures are even smaller, 0.083 for diastolic and 0.125 for systolic, if the known hypertensives and their relatives are removed from the sample. These data indicate a very high influence of environment.

For simple models, heritability is related to the coefficients of regression and relationship by the formula

$$h^2 = \frac{b}{r}$$

where b = coefficient of regression (correlation) and r = coefficient of relationship. Therefore, for dermal ridge counts, using the weighted mean of all the data in Table 12–6 for first degree relatives,

$$h^2 = \frac{0.484}{1/2}$$
$$= 2(0.484)$$
$$= 0.968, \text{ or about 97 percent.}$$

For blood pressure, using the mean between the diastolic and systolic correlations for the "control" sample,

$$h^2 = 2(0.104)$$
$$= 0.208, \text{ or about 21 percent.}$$

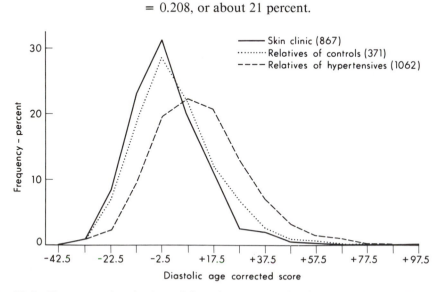

Fig. 15–3 Frequency distribution of diastolic pressures for three populations. The data have been adjusted for age and sex differences. The skin clinic patients are considered a control population. Note the distribution of the relatives of hypertensives resembles a normal distribution (an even better one than the control group) that has been shifted to the right as compared to the controls. (From Hamilton et al.,1954; reprinted by permission from *Clinical Science* © 1954, The Biochemical Society, London.)

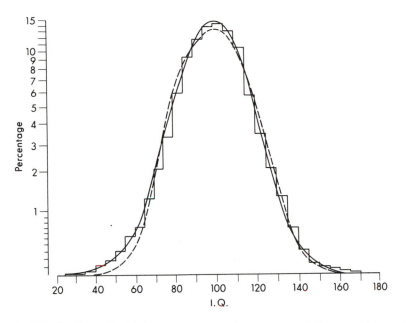

Fig. 15-4 Distribution of intelligence quotients in a representative population ($N =$ 4523). Superimposed on the observed data (the stepped figure) is a continuous line representation of these data and a normal curve (dotted line) based on the same mean and standard deviation. Note that the actual percentages exceed those expected by the normal curve at both tails, but the excess for IQ's below 70 is much greater than for those above 130, even though known cases of mental deficiency attributable to known nongenetic organic defects had been removed from the data. (From Burt, 1963; courtesy of the *British Journal of Statistical Psychology*.)

Heritability in the broad sense is probably much greater here, 70 percent or more, because of a considerable dominance factor. Hence, many cases of hypertension may be due to the chance accumulation of blood pressure genes that puts these persons beyond the demarcation line between "normal" and "hypertensive." If the population mean diastolic pressure were 70 mm of mercury, for instance, a diastolic pressure of 90 might be considered such a demarcation line by many clinicians. In effect we are saying that even though blood pressure basically exhibits continuous variation, we can divide the curve into two discontinuous groups.

A similar situation is encountered when we examine the distribution of intelligence at the lower levels. Using the rough and admittedly inaccurate estimate provided by the standard intelligence tests, the observed proportions of persons with IQ's between 70 and 130 and those with IQ above 130 correspond well to the normal curve (Fig. 15-4), but those with IQ below 70, the mentally retarded, are considerably in excess of "normal" expectation. Current thinking is that this group has not one but two hereditary components superposed on the usual environmental variables:

1. The additive component: persons who have by chance received too few of the "upper case" intelligence genes.

2. An epistatic component: persons whose additive components follow the normal range but who cannot express them because of a major defect locus (such as those for phenylketonuria, galactosemia, and other enzyme deficiencies) or a chromosomal derangement (Chapters 3 and 4).

Even though the additive one is probably the lesser of these two components, it is important not to lose sight of the multifactorial aspects of intelligence when discussing the group falling below the IQ of 70, but to realize instead that many members of the category "mental retardate" are there because they are below an arbitrary threshold level on a continuously variable curve.

A somewhat similar phenomenon is encountered with respect to diabetes mellitus. Although the matter is complicated by evidence for differing genetic components in the two major forms of the disease, as discussed further in Chapter 16, many medical geneticists lean toward the hypothesis of J. V. Neel and his co-workers that multiple genes are involved. Noting that the populational distribution of glucose tolerance test results resembles a normal curve, these authors have proposed that the glucose tolerance response is the result of additive interaction of multiple loci. Diabetics would then represent one extreme section of the curve, those below a minimal normal glucose tolerance threshold, akin to the mentally retarded portion of the normal distribution curve of additive genes for intelligence.

Note that diabetes is in essence a discontinuous trait. One either has diabetes or one does not. However, in this instance those who favor a polygenic basis are able to establish a distribution of measurements to which diabetes is related.

Carrying the matter a step farther, many discontinous traits that do not fit well the expectations based on one or two loci are also best explained by multifactorial inheritance *even though no metrical distribution associated with them can be established.* As in the case of hypertension and diabetes, the theory assumes that there is an underlying binomial distribution of genotypes for each trait of this type that is smoothed out (that is, caused to overlap and be improperly categorized) by environmental variables. The many genes, each with a relatively small effect, interact with the environment to determine whether the individual reaches a *threshold level* beyond which there is a risk that the trait will appear.

The inheritance of congenital cleft lip, with (Fig. 15–5) or without cleft palate, provides a particularly instructive illustration of such a trait. This condition, frequently abbreviated as CL(P), results from a failure of fusion, more or less complete, of the epithelia of median nasal and lateral nasal processes at the posterior end of the nasal pit of the embryo. Failure of the so-called secondary palate to fuse, cleft palate, accompanies cleft lip about 1-1/2 to 3 times as frequently as cleft lip occurs alone. Cleft palate may also appear alone, but this seems to be a different genetic entity than cleft lip (palate). Both conditions may be part of other genetic syndromes and both may accompany chromosomal aberrations (e.g., Fig. 3–9), and they may be produced by teratogenic factors such as hypervitaminosis A, rubella virus, and thalidomide acting at various stages of pregnancy, but these account for only a small proportion of cases.

Genetic factors are evident by the much higher frequencies of the trait in relatives of the affected than in the general population (Table 15–7). It is also evidenced

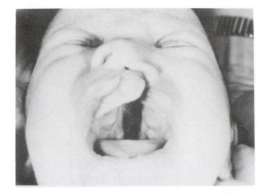

Fig. 15-5 Cleft lip with cleft palate. (Courtesy of D. M. Levy, M.D., Milwaukee, Wisconsin.)

by the higher incidence in both members of a pair of monozygotic twins (42 percent of the time) than in both dizygotic twins (7 percent).

The data fit no simple hypothesis of inheritance. If it were recessive, it should be much rarer in children of the affected than in their sibs, since the affected would almost never marry someone with the gene. The data show that sibs and children have it in about the same frequency (Table 15–7), about 35 times its frequency in the general population. This is the expectation for a dominant, but then second-degree relatives should be affected about half as often as those of the first degree; the data show they are affected about one-sixth as often. Neither hypothesis fits the observed difference between the rates of manifestation of sibs and monozygotic twins: If the monozygotic twin rate (aobut 40 percent) measures the degree of penetrance, about 20 percent of sibs (0.4 × 0.5) should be affected if the trait is dominant, about 10 percent (0.4 × 0.25) if recessive.

Clearly more complex heredity is involved, and it turns out that the data do fit very well the hypothesis of multifactorial inheritance. But how can one estimate

Table 15-7 The incidence of cleft lip with or without cleft palate in the general population and in relatives of 496 propositi in Utah and Arizona (Based on Woolf, 1971 and Woolf et al., 1964)

Classification	Number Observed	Number Affected	Frequency
General population		496	0.0012
(Cleft lip alone		161)	
(Cleft lip and palate		335)	
Sibs	1,574	63	0.0400
Children	3,734	171	0.0458
Parents	992	19	0.0192[a]
Uncles and aunts	4,747	41	0.0065
First cousins	11,698	42	0.0036

[a]This is about half of the expected figure based on sibs and children; it probably indicates a selective factor, social or natural.

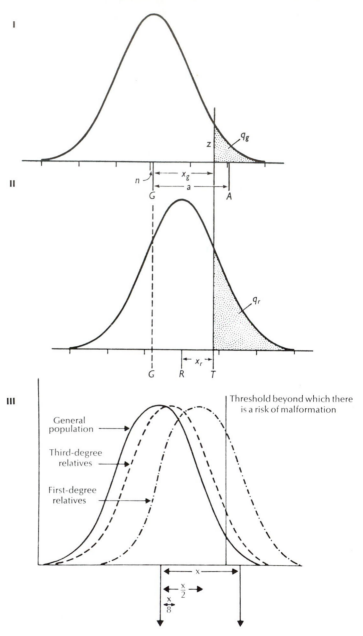

x: Deviation of mean of malformed individuals from the population mean

Fig. 15–6 Model distributions for multifactorial inheritance of discontinuous traits. The affected are those whose combination of genes puts them beyond a threshold (T). Parts I and II illustrate the parameters "A - G" and "R - G" needed to calculate the regression of relatives on propositi, as discussed in the text, when the only data available are the incidence of affected in the general population and in a population of their relatives. Part III illustrates the comparative displacement of the normal curve for different degrees of relationship. (Parts I and II modified from Falconer, 1965; courtesy of D. S. Falconer and the *Annals of Human Genetics*. Part III modified from Carter, 1969; courtesy of Churchill Livingstone, publishers of the *British Medical Bulletin*.)

the heritability when the only data available are relative incidences? How, in other words, can relative incidences be converted to regressions or correlations that can be substituted into the equation on page 344?

The solution stems largely from the brilliant work of D. S. Falconer, as an outgrowth of his work for the British Agricultural Research Council. If one assumes multifactorial inheritance is responsible, a normal curve would describe the distribution of the genes in the general population relating to the trait (Part I, or solid curve in Part III, of Fig. 15–6). The affected propositi are those members of this population whose complement of genes puts them beyond some point near the right tail of the curve. This point is the threshold. Using published tables for a curve with unit standard deviation, we can locate it by equating the incidence of the trait to the shaded area under the curve. For the general population of Table 15–7, for example, the threshold would be 3.04 standard deviations from the midpoint (mean) of the normal curve, because to the right of a vertical from this point 0.0012 (= the incidence) of the area is left under the curve.

Once we have the threshold deviate from the mean, shown as x_g on Part I of Fig. 15–6, we can calculate the mean (A) of the affected (shaded) section. It is obtained by dividing the ordinate of the normal curve (z) at the threshold by the frequency of the trait in the general population (q_g). For $CL(P)$ it is 0.00394 ÷ 0.0012, equal to 3.275 standard deviations from the mean. The difference between the general mean and the mean of the affected individuals, $A - G$, is often called the "selection differential," that is, the difference between the general population and the ones "selected" out of it by virtue of their manifesting the trait.

Falconer noted that the distribution of genotypes in a population of relatives of the affected of a given degree would again describe a normal curve (Part II of Fig. 15–6), with the same standard deviation, and, of course, the same threshold level. However, if heredity was involved, the affected would occupy a larger area, q_r, under the curve (another way of saying their incidence of the trait is higher). This curve is therefore displaced to the right of the curve for the general population, so that the mean of this curve, R, is closer to T than G is. In the above example, the threshold abscissa for sibs (incidence 0.04) would be only 1.70 standard deviations from R, as compared to 3.04 from G. The difference between the means of the two populations, $R - G$, that is, $(T - G) - (T - R)$, is often called the "response," by analogy to a selection experiment comparing the mean product of a general group and that of a sample selected to increase (or decrease) the number of product genes.

The higher the degree of relationship the more to the right the second curve would be displaced (Fig. 15–6, Part III). First-degree relatives would have a higher incidence than those of second degree, so that their threshold level would be farther to the left—and their whole curve moved farther to the right—in comparison with the curve for the general population. The curve for first cousins (third-degree relations) would be displaced less than the one for those of the second degree. For relatives more distant than third degree the curve becomes almost identical to that for the general population.

The degree of heritability also determines the degree to which the curve is dispaced. If heritability were zero (environment is all), the curve for even first-degree relatives would differ little, if any, from the curve for the general population. The more genetics plays a part in the trait the greater the likelihood that a close relative would also surpass the threshold.

In effect, the relative incidences of the trait in close relatives as compared to the general population become a reflection of the correlation between them of the number of genes they carry for the trait.

The ratio between the "response" $(R - G)$ and the "selection differential" $(A - G)$ measures the regression of relatives on the index affected, equal to b in the heritability equation on page 344. In the sib data above, $b = 1.34/3.275 = 0.39$; hence, $h^2 = 0.78$, or 78 percent.

The compiler of Table 12–7 calculated the heritability of $CL(P)$ as 0.67 from the second-degree data, and 0.78 from the cousins. The results from a comparable English study, 0.76 from first degree, 0.76 from second degree, and 0.67 from third-degree data, are quite close. They show that the genetic component for $CL(P)$ is substantial.

Table 15–8 summarizes heritability estimates by this method for a number of congenital abnormalities. They provide useful data for genetic counseling.

TWIN STUDIES

The basis of this classical method of analyzing the nature-nurture question has been noted already in Table 15–6: The coefficient of relationship of monozygotic twins is 1, whereas that of dizygotic twins is the same as that of ordinary sibs, 0.5. Hence, monozygotic (MZ) twins are commonly referred to as "identical" (though, as we shall see, they often are not), whereas dizygotic (DZ) twins are commonly spoken of as "fraternal."

Monozygotic twins are the result of separation of the daughter cells, produced by mitosis, of a zygote. Dizygotic twins, on the other hand, result from the nearly simultaneous fertilizations of separate eggs and sperm. Both forms of twinning

Table 15–8 Heritability estimates for some disorders that appear to involve multifactorial inheritance with threshold effects

Disorder	Heritability (in Percent)[b]	Source
Ankylosing spondylitis	80	Carter, 1969
Congenital dislocation of the hip	70	Carter, 1969
Cleft lip (palate)	67–78	See text.
Ischemic heart disease, early	60	Carter, 1969
Peptic ulcer	37 ± 6	Falconer, 1965
Pyloric stenosis, congenital	79 ± 5[a]	Falconer, 1965
Renal stone disease	46 ± 9	Falconer, 1965
Rheumatoid arthritis	70	Carter, 1969
Schizophrenia	70	Gottesman and Shields, 1982
Spina bifida cystica	60	Carter, 1969
Talipes equinovarus (clubfoot)	70 ± 8	Falconer, 1965

[a]Carter (1969) states the heritability is about 60 percent for males and 90 percent for females, so this may be a composite estimate.
[b]$\pm$ Standard error, where shown

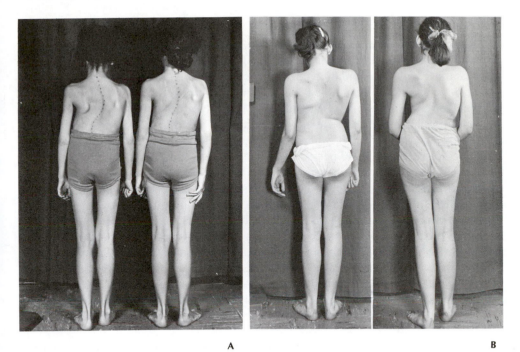

Fig. 15-7   A trait, idiopathic scoliosis, in which dizygotic (A) as well as monozygotic (B) twins tend to be concordant (Fisher and De George, 1967). This suggests that environmental factors are more important than genetic factors in its etiology, as is emphasized by the considerable variation often observed in the monozygotic pairs. Apparently intra-uterine maternal factors are involved (De George and Fisher, 1967. Osborne and De George, 1959). Courtesy of R. L. Fisher and *Clinical Orthopedics and Related Research.*)

involve sharing the intrauterine environment, though not usually to the same degree.

From these basic considerations, the fundamental tenet of twin studies has been that if a trait had no genetic component at all ("environment is all"), MZ twins would have no greater likelihood to both show the trait (be *concordant*) than DZ twins would (Fig. 15-7, for example). On the other hand, if a trait had no environmental component ("genetics is all"), MZ twins would always be concordant whereas DZ twins would be no more likely to be concordant than would siblings in general.

Many traits that do not show complete concordance in identical twins nevertheless show much greater concordance in them than in fraternals. Geneticists soon realized that this made twin studies valuable in studying the relative importance of genetics and environment, especially in multifactorial inheritance. If MZ's were much more concordant than that of DZ's, this meant that the genetic component was uppermost. If, on the other hand, the concordance of monozygotics was not significantly greater than that of dizygotics, that means the genetic component was a minor one.

Frequency of Multiple Births

Twins occur at the rate of about 1.4 percent of births of American Negroes and about 1.0 percent of American whites. The frequency of monozygotic twins is fairly constant for all the populations of the world, namely, 3 to 4 per 1000 (Table 15–9). There are, however, marked differences in the dizygotic rates. Apparently, fraternal twins are born more frequently to African Negroes than to persons of European ancestry, and least frequently to Asiatics. The dizygotic rate for whites generally is about 7 per 1000, whereas a rate of 20 per 1000 is common throughout Negro Africa, reaching 40 per 1000 at Ibadan, Nigeria, in a mainly Yoruba population. The rate among Negroes outside Africa is 12 to 13 per 1000 births. What makes these figures doubly impressive is the lower intrauterine survival rate expected among the American and African Negro twins. Furthermore, their higher rates extend to other forms of multiple births, triplets, quadruplets, and quintuplets, where the survival problems are even more severe.

In 1895, Dr. Hellin published an analysis in which he showed that twins occur about once in 89 births, triplets about once in $(89)^2$ births, quadruplets about once in $(89)^3$ births, quintuplets about once in $(89)^4$ births, and so on. Subsequent studies have shown Hellin's rule to be substantially sound. They may be disturbed, however, by a recent increase in multiple births resulting from widespread use of fertility medication described below.

The proportion of monozygotic twins may be predicted in any population by a method first suggested in 1902 by Wilhelm Weinberg, the remarkable German physician whose work we encountered also in Chapters 8 and 9. He noted that if the sex ratio is about 50:50, it is expected that there will be equal proportions of dizygotic twins of like and unlike sex. The chances being as in matching coins for heads and tails, 1 in 4 times there are expected to be paired boys, 1 in 4 times paired

Table 15–9 Incidence of twinning in various populations[a]

Population	Twin Pairs per 1000 Births		
	Monozygotic	Dizygotic	All
Spain (1951–1953)	3.2	5.9	9.1
U.S. Caucasians (1956–1958)	3.8	6.1	9.9
Norway (1946–1954)	3.8	8.3	12.1
Italy (1949–1955)	3.7	8.6	12.3
Denmark (1951–1955)	3.8	10.2	14.0
Australia (1947–1949)	3.8	7.7	11.5
Israel (1952–1957)	3.8	7.3	11.1
Japan (3 cities; 1949–1953)	3.8	2.7	6.5
Japan (country; 1956)	4.1	2.3	6.4
U.S. Negroes (1956–1958)	3.9	10.1	14.0
U.S. Negroes (1922–1954)[b]	3.9	11.8	15.7
Antigua, B.W.I. (1857–1951)	3.9	11.5	15.4
Johannesburg, S. Africa, Negroes	4.9	22.3[c]	27.2
Ibadan, Nigeria	5.0	39.9	44.9

[a]For references see Levitan and Montague (1977), p. 506.
[b]Standardized for age.
[c]Considered typical for African Negro populations

girls, and 2 in 4 times a paired boy and girl. Hence, the number of dizygotic twins of unlike sex should equal the number of dizygotic like-sexed twins in a randomly ascertained series, or to put it another way, doubling the number of known unlike-sexed twins gives us the total number of dizygotic twin pairs. The remainder of the twins, of like sex, would be the number of monozygous twin pairs. In the Unted States, for example, 31 percent of white twins are of unlike sex. Assuming that these are all dizygotic, as is true with only minor error, then it follows that another 31 percent are of like sex and dizygotic, while the remaining 38 percent are monozygotic.

In recent years the treatment of sterility in women by the administration of substances containing FSH and LH has resulted in a disproportionately large number of multiple births. (The Dionne quintuplets, however, were born prior to the introduction of these drugs.) Reduction of the dosage has resulted in fewer multiple births. These observations tend to confirm the role played by the pituitary in the production of multiple births.

In addition, statistics indicate that the chances of a multiple birth vary with the age of the mother (Fig. 15–8). The correlation is not linear, however. The older mothers tend to a greater frequency of fraternal twins. For example, if twins are born to a primigravid woman between 15 and 19 years old, the probability is more than half (0.58, to be exact) that they will be monozygotic; for a primigravid woman between 35 and 39, the probability that they will be monozygotic is only about one-third (0.34).

Whatever the maternal age the chances of having twins, especially dizygotic twins, rise with the number of previous pregnancies she has had. For the 15- to 19-year-old who bears twins in her third pregnancy, the probability that they are dizygotic is 0.59, as compared with 0.42 in her first pregnancy. The rate of increase in probability is not as great in older mothers [0.73 in pregnancy three as compared with the 0.66 mentioned above (1.00–0.34) for the 35- to 39-year-old], but it may be substantial if she has enough pregnancies.

That in some cases genetic factors are involved in the tendency to dizygotic twinning is suggested not only by the variations in various populations (Table 15–9) but also by the frequency in which such twinning tends to occur in certain families. For example, the sister of a woman who has borne dizygotic twins stands about twice the average chance of herself giving birth to twins. A woman who is herself one of a pair of twins also has a greater than average chance of having twins. The inheritance of twinning appears to be polygenic with a threshold effect, apparently limited to the mother's side. Twinning in the father's family seems to have little or no effect. However, the mother may inherit the twinning genes from *her* father.

Zygosity Diagnosis

A major criticism of twin studies is that errors have frequently been made in classifying the twins as monozygotic or dizygotic. All too often this was based on subjective criteria such as degree of resemblance. Usually this meant that dizygotics that looked very much alike were misclassified as monozygotics. The reverse also occurred, however, because monozygotics formed by a relatively late separation of

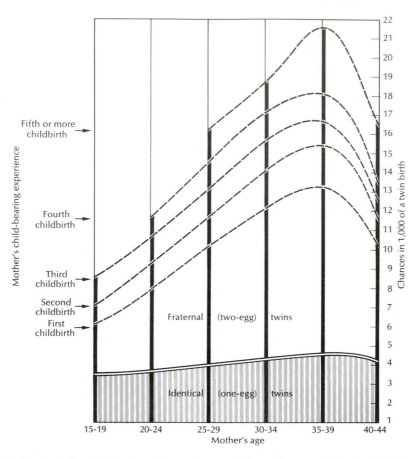

Fig. 15-8   A mother's twinning chances* . . . and how they are influenced by her age and previous childbirths. An expectant or prospective mother should note where the vertical line for her age group is cut by the dotted line for previous childbirths, then look across to the number at the right. The chances the twins will be identical are shown in the shaded lower part of the graph. (From Amram Scheinfeld, *Twins and Supertwins*, Philadelphia, J. B. Lippincott, Co., 1967. Courtesy of the author and publishers.)

the cells of the original zygote can exhibit mirror imaging in some characteristics. One may be right-handed and the other left-handed, for example, and various bilateral asymmetries may be reversed. In addition, chromosome abnormalities or mutations may develop in one MZ twin and not in the other, giving rise to phenotypic differences. In a few instances, it has even turned out that twins of unlike sex were really monozygotic, as one exhibited XO Turner's syndrome and the other was a normal male, or both were XY but only one showed testicular feminization.

*Figures given are for white mothers. Among American Negro mothers twinbearing chances are about one-third higher, and among Oriental mothers (Japanese, Chinese) about one-third lower than those of whites. The ethnic differences are mainly with respect to fraternal twins (Table 15–8).

Table 15-10   Types of placentas and membranes in twins (Based on Potter, 1963 and Cameron, 1968)

Type of Twin	Monochorionic		Dichorionic	
	Monoamnionic	Diamnionic	Single Placenta (By Secondary Fusion)	Two Placentas
MZ	Rare	~70	~15	~15
DZ	—	—	~50	~50

A more objective diagnosis of zygosity has been based on the type of placentation, but this, too, is fraught with possibilities of error. The developing zygote is enveloped by two membranes, the inner delicate *amnion* and the outer tougher *chorion* attached to the maternal tissue of the placenta. The most common arrangements of these membranes and the placentas in twins are indicated in Table 15-10 and Fig. 15-9.

Unequivocal diagnosis of zygosity is possible only when there is a monochorionic placenta (Fig. 15-9**B**), a condition that prevails in about 70 percent of monozygotic twins but in no dizygotics.

Dizygotics, on the other hand, are always dichorionic, because dizygotic twins always implant separately into the uterine epithelium and always develop their own membranes. They need not, however, present separate placentas of the type shown in Fig. 15-9A. In some 50 percent of dizygotic twins the two placentas are sufficiently close that they become secondarily fused (Fig. 15-9C). Such dizygotic twins of like sex are not infrequently misdiagnosed as monozygotic.

The clear demonstration of a double chorion does not prove that the twins are dizygotic, however, even if the placentas are also separate, because monozygotic twins may have two chorions and even two placentas. The dichorionic condition occurs in about 30 percent of monozygotic twin pairs. About half the time such monozygous twins have secondarily fused placentas (Fig. 15-9C), presumably because they implanted close together. The other half implant so far apart that they not only have separate chorions but also separate placentas (Fig. 15-9A).

Dichorionic twins of like sex, therefore, cannot be diagnosed by placentation methods. For statistical studies they can be subdivided by applying Weinberg's rule, but in individual cases other diagnostic methods must be used. Such ambiguous situations constitute about 45 percent of all twins. In a series of 668 pairs of twins about five-sixths of these ambiguous cases turned out to be dizygotic, about one-sixth monozygotic.

A more dependable method of diagnosing zygosity is by the skin graft test. A skin graft will almost always be accepted by a monozygous twin because of their identical tissue antigens (Chapter 16). Though often rejected by a dizygous twin, this is not certain, however. The method also poses many practical problems.

Most twin studies now base their diagnosis of zygosity on the similarity method, using Bayesian probabilities. One compares the twins for a series of simply inherited traits such as blood groups or RFLPs. A difference in one such trait establishes dizygosity. Resemblance in any given trait does not, on the other hand, prove monozygosity, since the offspring of the same parents are likely to resemble each other in many traits. However, the overall probability that dizygotic twins will be

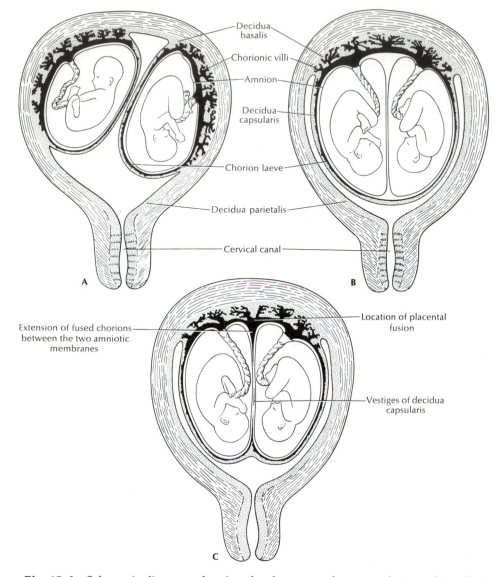

Decidua basalis

Chorionic villi

Amnion

Decidua capsularis

Chorion laeve

Decidua parietalis

Cervical canal

Extension of fused chorions between the two amniotic membranes

Location of placental fusion

Vestiges of decidua capsularis

A   B   C

Fig. 15-9 Schematic diagrams showing the three most frequent relations of the fetal membranes of twins. **A.** Twins with entirely separate placentas. **B.** Twins with a single chorion and separate amnions. **C.** Twins implanted close to each other with resultant secondary fusions of their membranes. **B** occurs only for monovular twins. **A** and **C** are more characteristic of diovular than of monovular twins, but they may be found with both types. The chorion *laeve* ("smooth chorion") is the portion devoid of villi because it is involved only minimally in the interchanges with the maternal placenta. The name *decidua* is given to various portions of the gravid uterine endometrium, the *basalis* being the major interchange area. (From *Human Embryology* by Bradley M. Patten, 3rd ed., 1968 © McGraw-Hill, Inc. Courtesy of B. M. Patten and McGraw-Hill Book Co. A similar figure may be found in subsequent editions, e.g., Corliss, 1976.)

alike in all of the traits studied is almost always much smaller than the corresponding probability for monozygotic twins. In other words, the similarity method is simply a method of arriving at degrees of probability as to the zygosity of a given pair of twins.

As an example, suppose like-sexed twins are born in a population where 35 percent of twins are of unlike sex. The mother of the twins is of blood types O, M, Lutheran (a−b+) and is positive for antigens Rh_0(D), rh'(C), hr'(c), and hr"(e). The father is of blood types A, MN, Lutheran (a−b+) and is positive for antigens Rh_0(D), rh'(C^w), hr'(c), and hr"(e). The twins have a brother who is type O and MN but otherwise resembles the mother for the listed traits, and a sister who is type O but otherwise resembles the father. (This family is patterned on the one analyzed by Race and Sanger, 1962, p. 369.) Both of the twins are type A but otherwise resemble their mother being type M, Lu(a−b+) and positive for the same Rh antigens. The analysis is as follows:

1. Since 35 percent of twins in this population are of unlike sex, by Weinberg's rule there are probably another 35 percent that are dizygous but like-sexed, leaving 30 percent monozygous. Thus as a first step the probability that these twins are monozygous is 0.30, that they are like-sexed and dizygous 0.35. These are the Bayesian initial probabilities.
2. The type O children indicate that the father is heterozygous, I^A/I^O (or, as clinicians often write it, AO). In that case given that one twin is type A, the probability that the second would also be type A is one-half if they are dizygous, one if they are monozygous.
3. Similarly, the probability that if one twin from an MN × M mating is MN, the other twin will also be MN is one-half if they are dizygous, one if monozygous.
4. For the Lutheran types, the probability of similarity of the twins is one whether they be monozygous or dizygous.
5. With the given Rh typing the probable genotype of the father is R^{1w}/r (C^wDe/cde) and that of the mother and the twins is R^1/r (CDe/cde). If one twin is R^1/r, the probability that the other has the same genotype is one-fourth if they are dizygotic, one if they are monozygotic.

Hence,

$$P \text{ (combination of traits if dizygotic)} = (0.35)(0.5)(0.5)(1)(0.25)$$
$$= 0.021875.$$
$$P \text{ (combination of traits if monozygotic)} = (0.30)(1)(1)(1)(1)$$
$$= 0.30.$$
$$\text{Probability (twins are monozygotic)} = \frac{0.30}{0.30 + 0.021875}$$
$$= 0.93.$$
$$\text{Probability (twins are dizygotic)} = \frac{0.021875}{0.30 + 0.021875}$$
$$= 0.07.$$
$$\text{Relative likelihood favoring monozygosity} = \frac{0.93}{0.07} = 13.3.$$

Many authors accept monozygosity if the relative likelihood favoring it is 19:1 or better. Attainment of these odds clearly depends on the number of traits for which information is available. Fortunately, for many polymorphic systems it is not necessary to know the phenotypes or genotypes of the parent. Estimates of relative probabilities for these traits can be calculated from population data by the methods described in Chapter 9. Indeed there are published tables and graphs that enable one to read off the pertinent probabilities at a glance.

Genetic Inference from Twin Studies

There have been many attempts to develop quantitative indices of heritability from twin studies. They have some historical interest, but most of them are not true measurements of heritability as defined earlier.

One of the earliest was simply to divide the frequency of monozygotic concordance by the frequency of dizygotic concordance. Such a statement of relative frequencies can be misleading, however. Under it the point on the scale indicating "no heritability" is not zero but one, that is, when dizygotics are just as likely to be concordant as monozygotics. Further confusion comes from the fact that the *bottom* of the scale is 100 percent.

One of the best improvements is Holzinger's formula. Under it

"Heritability" =

$$\frac{\text{Percent Monozygotic Concordance} - \text{Percent Dizygotic Concordance}}{100 - \text{Percent Dizygotic Concordance}}$$

or, in shorthand

$$"H" = \frac{C_{MZ} - C_{DZ}}{100 - C_{DZ}}$$

The theoretical maximum would occur if monozygotics were 100 percent concordant and dizygotics never, so that

$$"Heritability" = \frac{100 - 0}{100 - 0} = 1.$$

Similarly the minimum would come when concordances in both types were equal. If both were 30 percent concordant, for instance,

$$"Heritability" = \frac{30 - 30}{100 - 30} = 0.$$

Thus heritability could be scaled from zero to one.*

Unfortunately, Holzinger's formula would not be applicable to the majority of traits that, as has been noted above, need some such method as twin studies to elucidate their heritability component. When variation is continuous, difference in the genetic component does not take the form of all-or-none distinctions such as

---

*Negative values could ensue if dizygotics in a sample were more concordant than monozygotics, but this would have no more meaning than a coefficient of zero.

concordant or discordant. One cannot state, for instance, that concordance for intelligence means that both twins have *identical* IQ scores, any other result being labeled discordant. Clearly, a case in which twins have scores of 104 and 115 is less discordant than a case in which they have scores of 100 and 125.

The solution has been to modify Holzinger's formula so as to include measures of correlation of variables in each class of twins rather than the simple qualitative distinctions concordant or discordant. Holzinger himself modified his formula given above to use the correlation coefficient (r) as the measure of relative concordance and discordance; thus,

$$\text{``}H\text{''} = \frac{r_{MZ} - r_{DZ}}{1 - r_{DZ}}$$

A slight further modification of this formula, was the basic method of the classic study comparing monozygotic twins reared together (MZt) and similar twins reared apart (MZa) by Newman, Freeman, and Holzinger:

$$\text{``}H\text{''} = \frac{r_{MZt} - r_{MZa}}{1 - r_{MZa}}$$

Another frequently used form is:

$$\text{Heritability} = \frac{\text{Variance of dizygotics} - \text{Variance of monozygotics}}{\text{Variance of dizygotics}}$$

or,

$$\text{``}H\text{''} = \frac{\sigma_{DZ}^2 - \sigma_{MZ}^2}{\sigma_{DZ}^2}$$

If the monozygotics were always to present identical phenotypes their variance would be zero, and the heritability one, which is to say, heredity is all. If, on the other hand, the two types of twins vary to the same extent, the heritability is zero. In that case, all of the observed variability must be environmentally determined.

Problems of Twin Studies

In addition to questions concerning the reliability of zygosity diagnoses, twin studies have been subject to a number of other criticisms. One is that even if twin studies demonstrated that a trait is 100 percent inherited they would not show *how* it is inherited: Is it due to a single locus? Is there dominance? If it appears associated with another trait, is this due to linkage, and, if so, to what degree?

A more profound criticism has been concerned with the reliability of the variance of monozygotic twins as a measure of the environmental factor. It has been pointed out, for example, that both prenatally and postnatally the environmental differences of monozygotics tend to be minimized, with the result that true environmental contributions to the trait are underestimated and the heritability overestimated. Some of the postnatal biases are eliminated by comparing twins reared apart and those reared together, but even these do not achieve, as one critic has phrased it, the necessary "randomization ... over the range of environments obtainable in the population."

In addition, attempts to study specific traits in this way have encountered many obstacles of a technical nature. Many disagree, for example, on the propriety of using the typical IQ tests as measures of inherited intelligence, especially across class and cultural boundaries.

It is in the area of intelligence that some of the sharpest controversies have arisen over the use of the various techniques to study multifactorial inheritance in humans.

The theory that mental ability has a heritable component based on additive interaction of a large number of loci, each of which contributes a small amount to the phenotype, is in accord with many of the observations that can be made on this trait. It explains, for example, how it comes about that parents may have offspring ranging from very dull to very bright even though all of the children presumably partake to a large extent of the same environmental influences. It also explains why the inheritance of this trait is so imprecise, why very bright children can be born to relatively dull-minded parents, and vice versa.

When we attempt to go beyond plausibility and seek precise answers many difficulties, some already alluded to, set in. Many attempts have been made, for example, to obtain a quantitative estimate of heritability, by population measurements and by twin studies of various degrees of refinement, but there is very little agreement of the question. A commonly quoted figure is 50–60 percent, but many say that is too high; others that it is too low.

Even greater heat has been generated by attempts to determine whether various groups differ in intelligence. Over the years a somewhat acrimonious controversy has raged as to whether blacks are "inferior" because in some testing studies the mean of their normal distribution has been slightly below the mean of their white neighbors. Some writers (e.g., A. R. Jensen) go so far as to argue that these differences should determine social policy questions on such matters as public education.

Even if the differences were real, the proponents of these views often forget they are discussing widely overlapping normal distributions such as the close ones in Figure 15–6, part III. Such views ignore the injustice that would be done, on the one hand, by favoring the members of the apparent upper group merely because they happen to belong to the "upper" group even though they score below the mean of the so-called inferior group and, on the other hand, demeaning those who score above the mean of the apparent upper group merely because they have been labeled members of the "lower" group on the basis of physical resemblance. This is quite apart from the consideration that very often it is environment not heredity that determines whether one falls just below or just above the mean.

The conclusions of Jensen and others have been attacked as particularly inappropriate because, as one critic put it, we still know so little about how environments influence behavioral traits. In Lewontin's words:

> What is true for estimation of heritability "within" populations is doubly true for masking statements about genetic differences between races and socioeconomic classes. No design conceivable can randomize black and white children over family environments.

SUGGESTED EXERCISES

15–1. Discuss the terms "fraternal twins" and "identical twins." Why are certain other terms preferred?

15–2. In a certain population 1.2 percent of all births are twins. In a sample of 1000 twin births 352 consisted of two boys, 328 of two girls, and the rest of a boy and a girl. Assuming that these figures may be extrapolated, what percentage of births in this population are probably of:
   (a)   Monozygotic twins?
   (b)   Dizygotic twins?

15–3. Based on 1956–8 data in Table 15–3,
   (a)   How frequently are quadruplets expected to occur among U.S. Caucasians?
   (b)   Among U.S. Negroes?
   (c)   In the United States population as a whole, assuming Negroes comprise 10 percent of the population?

15–4. What can be said about the diagnosis of twinning in the following situations:
   (a)   One placenta, one chlorion, and one amnion.
   (b)   One placenta, one chorion, and two amnions.
   (c)   One placenta, two chorions and two amnions.
   (d)   Two placentas, two chorions, and two amnions.

15–5. A couple from a population in which about 30 percent of twins are mono-zygotic are both of blood types A and MN, and both are Gc2-1. Each had a type-O parent. They have twin girls who are likewise A, MN, and Gc2-1. What is the probability that the twins are monozygotic?

15–6. What can be said about the relative roles of heredity and environment in the following studies:

Subject	Monozygotic Twins		Dizygotic Twins		Authority
	No.	Concordant	No.	Concordant	
Tuberculosis	381	202	843	187	Diehl and Verschuer, 1936
Spina bifida	18	13	36	12	Gedda, 1951
Clubfoot	35	8	133	3	Gedda, 1951
Measles	189	180	146	127	Stern, 1973
Fingerprint ridge count	0.95[a]		0.49[a]		Holt, 1961

[a]Correlation coefficient.

15–7. Uchida and Rowe (1957) and Lamy et al. (1957) studied the incidence of congenital heart disease in twins. All 20 monozygous pairs had only one member affected, whereas in 22 dizygous pairs both twins were affected in one instance, only one twin in the other 21.

(a)   What can be said about the relative roles of heredity and environment?

(b)   What can be said about the similarity of the environment *in utero* in monozygous and dizygous twins?

The following five exercises are strictly theoretical and are not meant to imply that the disorder is actually produced in the manner outlined.

15–8. Suppose there were three loci D_1, D_2, and D_3 capable of producing diabetes and they operate in this way: An individual would manifest the disorder whenever he had no normal alleles at at least one of the loci. (At each locus, of course, the normal allele is dominant to the diabetes allele.) How many different diabetes genotypes would be possible? List them.

15–9. Under the system outlined in the previous exercise what proportion of diabetic children would be expected from the following marriages between diabetics:

(a) $\dfrac{D_1 \; d_2 \; D_3}{d_1 \; d_2 \; D_3} \times \dfrac{D_1 \; D_2 \; d_3}{d_1 \; d_2 \; d_3}$

(b) $\dfrac{D_1 \; D_2 \; d_3}{D_1 \; D_2 \; d_3} \times \dfrac{d_1 \; D_2 \; D_3}{d_1 \; d_2 \; D_3}$

(c) $\dfrac{d_1 \; D_2 \; D_3}{d_1 \; d_2 \; D_3} \times \dfrac{D_1 \; d_2 \; D_3}{D_1 \; d_2 \; D_3}$

15–10. What would be the answers to the previous exercise if the penetrance of any diabetes genotype (that is, any whole combination) were 40 percent?

Consider now a different theoretical hypothesis for the etiology of diabetes: That again three loci are involved and each has an uppercase allele and a lowercase allele. Each lowercase allele increases the glucose tolerance by 5 percent over the average for D_1/D_1 D_2/D_2 D_3/D_3 homozygotes, and every person with a glucose tolerance of 15 percent or more over this average is considered a diabetic. How many diabetes genotypes would be possible under this system? List them.

15–11. For each of the marriages in exercise 15–9, state whether the parents would be diabetic under *this* system and what would the expected proportion of diabetics be among the progeny.

15–12. If d_1, d_2, and d_3 each had a frequency of 10 percent in a certain panmictic population, what would be the frequency of diabetics with the least possible number of lowercase alleles under each hypothesis? A little thought will show that the arithmetic for the second system is not as formidable as it seems at first glance.

16

Immunogenetics

The immune system presents a number of contrasting aspects in medicine, and genetics plays a significant role in all of them. Foremost, of course, is the function of the system to protect the body against foreign substances, especially bacteria. The basic mechanism involves activation (sensitization) of the cells of the system on a first encounter with protein (or protein plus hapten) in the foreign body, which thus acts as an antigen. The activated T-cells of the immune system and the antibodies produced by the B-cells of the system are then mobilized to destroy or otherwise neutralize the foreign substance when it is encountered again. A major subdivision of immunogenetics is concerned with inherited disorders in which some aspect of this protective mechanism is defective.

The propensity of the immune system to destroy foreign proteins becomes a hindrance rather than a help when it is clinically *desirable* to introduce foreign tissues into the body, inasmuch as even members of the same kindred may present antigenic differences, particularly in the antigens of the cell surface, to which others may respond by producing antibodies. Such antigenic differences in the red blood cells are the basis of blood typing. It is particularly important in blood transfusion, whether premeditated (the usual case) or inadvertent (as in erythroblastosis fetalis).

Blood types, notably the ABO system, also play a role in organ transplants, but here the most important factors appear to be genetically determined tissue antigens, particularly those of the so-called Major Histocompatibility System. The discussion of this system and its relation to disease constitutes another major aspect of immunogenetics.

Closely related to these aspects are the Gm and Km systems, genetically determined antigenic differences in our antibodies, the immunoglobulins. Although not significant clinically, these systems are of great forensic and anthropological interest as well as possibly serving as helpful markers for linked medical disorders.

The final two major aspects of the immune system in medicine are allergy and autoimmunity. Although not usually considered as related and not usually treated by the same specialist, they have in common the fact that in each case the immune system *injures* rather than protects the individual.

We shall subdivide the material into four sections. First we shall consider red cell variation, that is, blood typing, because historically it was the first to be developed extensively. A second section will consider normal white cell and immunoglobulin variation. This will be followed by a discussion of associations, principally between diseases and red and white cell variants. The final section will discuss inherited disorders of the immune system, allergy, and autoimmunity.

RED BLOOD CELL VARIATION

The ABO Blood Group System

The left side of Table 16–1 reviews the ABO blood group genes, as discussed earlier. The biochemical basis of the resultant red cell surface antigens has also been discussed. The locus is on chromosome 9, closely linked to *AK-1* (adenylate kinase-1) and Np (nail-patella syndrome [Figs. 1–4, 1–5, 13–2, and 13–13]).

The ABO blood groups are unusual because, with rare exception, from some time between the third and sixth month after birth, everyone makes antibodies against ABO antigens that their blood cells do not possess. Thus the serum of a type O person almost always contains both anti-A (α) and anti-B (β), and so on (column 4 of Table 16–1). The result is that people have automatic incompatibilities when it comes to blood transfusion. If type A blood is given to a type O, for instance, there is an almost immediate antigen-antibody reaction between the donor red cells and the recipient's anti-A. Manifested as a clumping of the red cells (agglutination) on a slide or in a test tube, this becomes a lytic reaction (hemolysis), however, *in vivo,* because of the presence of complement, with serious or fatal consequences to the patient.

Fortunately ABO antibody molecules are usually of the immunoglobulin class (IgM, discussed later) that cannot cross the placental barrier. Otherwise, for instance, no type O mother could bear a type A child, since the fetus makes A and B antigens, if he has the requisite genes, very early. Some women do, however, produce antibodies, referred to as $\alpha\beta$ (last column of Table 16–1), which are IgG and can cross the placental barrier. These can often be demonstrated in the cord blood.

One consequence of such antibodies is some fetal loss. Marriages of type O women to type A men, for instance, have fewer type A children than the reciprocal cross (A × O). The difference is especially noticeable if the *A* is A_1. Many of the losses due to ABO incompatibility occur very early in pregnancy, sometimes even before implantation. More significant is the occasional birth of an ABO incompat-

Table 16-1   ABO genotypes and phenotypes, based on four alleles, with their expected erythrocyte antigens and serum isoagglutinins (Modified from Levene and Rosenfield, 1961)

Phenotypes	Genotypes	Erythrocyte Antigens	Constant Serum Agglutinins	Inconstant Agglutinins
O	OO	None	α and β	$\alpha\beta$
A_1	A^1A^1, A^1O, or A^1A^2	A_1, A	β	Anti-H
A_2	A^2A^2 or A^2O	A	β	α_1
B	BB or BO	B	α	Anti-H
A_1B	A^1B	A_1, A, B	None	Anti-H
A_2B	A^2B	A, B	None	α_1

ible child with symptoms resembling transfusion sickness. Here the effect occurs late in pregnancy, and it is termed "ABO-erythroblastosis." About 0.5 percent of newborn have clinical ABO disease, and about 40 percent of them seriously enough to need an exchange transfusion.

A transfusion is in effect a temporary graft (of blood cells). Surprisingly, ABO compatibility is a significant factor as to whether *any* tissue graft will be successful, ABO antigens being present on the surface of a wide variety of tissues. Hence, even for the transplant of a cadaveric kidney, the donor and recipient should be of the same ABO type.

The ABO system can also be very useful in forensic medicine. If a mother is type O and her child is type A, for example, ABO typing effectively eliminates type B men as putative fathers of this child. Indeed should the child be A_1, men who are A_2 or A_2B are also eliminated. Similar considerations apply to criminal cases. Thus bits of tissue found at the scene of a crime that contain A substance would vindicate an accused who does not produce this antigen (a type B or an O). Not all jurisdictions accept blood group evidence, however.

Additional rare alleles have been postulated to account for families with weaker than usual A or B antigens. They follow the rule indicated by the relation of A^2 to A^1: dominance to O and to any allele of the series with a higher superscript (as A^1 is to A^2); and codominance with B or A (e.g., in A_3B or A_1B_1).

The MNSs Blood Groups

As indicated earlier in the book, the basic system consists of two antigens, M and N, determined by codominant alleles on chromosome 4. Closely associated are two other common ones, S and s, which apparently result from codominants at a closely linked locus (Exercises 16–9 and 16–10). In addition to weaker forms of M or N, the system also includes a number of rarer associated antigens: Henshaw (He), Hunter (Hu), Vw, Miltenberg (Mi), Vr, Ridley (Ri), Stones (St), Martin (Mt), and Nyberg (Ny).

Medically, the system is interesting chiefly for its forensic aspects. Humans rarely produce antibodies against antigens of the system that they lack. Anti-S and anti-s sera are encountered more frequently than anti-M or anti-N, mostly the result of repeated transfusions with blood that is ABO compatible but of a different MNSs type than the recipient's. Thus the system rarely leads to transfusion reaction and even more rarely to erythroblastosis.

About 1 percent of American Negroes are both S− and s− and capable of forming anti-Ss (anti-U). They are said to be U negative, probably due to an amorph of the S locus (usually written S^u). They can make strong anti-U if transfused, leading to fatal hemolytic reactions.

The P Blood Groups

At first the P system, discovered by the same workers (Karl Landsteiner and Philip Levine), seemed even simpler than M-N: two alleles with dominance. It is now known, however, that there are three P-positive types, referred to as P_1, P_2, and p^k, and the system also includes another blood group, Jay. Jay is written "Tj" because

Table 16-2   Summary of the P blood group system

Type	Old Name	Reactions with Antibodies			Possible Antibodies	Approximate European Frequency
		Anti-P_1	Anti-P	Anti-Jay[a]		
P_1	P+	+	+	+	None	0.79
P_2		−	+	+	Anti-P_1	0.21
p^k	P−	−or+	−	+	Anti-P+P_1	Rare
p(pp)		−	−	−	Anti-Jay[a]	Rare

[a]Anti-Jay (anti-Tj^a) is commonly written "anti-P+P_1+p^k."

the finding of its original antibody in a Mrs. Jay was thought to be related to the fact that she was being operated on to remove a stomach tumor (hence the "T"). It turned out that Jay is negative only in persons, like Mrs. Jay, who are P-negative, and Tj-negative serum invariably contains antibodies against P-positive types.

The reactions of the system are shown in Table 16–2. The genes involved are, in order of dominance, $P_1 > P_2 > p^k > p$.

Beyond being an additional locus for forensic testing, the P system is of little medical importance, presumably because the antibodies are very weak.

The Rh System

In 1940 Landsteiner and Alexander Wiener reported that the red blood cells of about 85 percent of white persons were clumped by an antiserum prepared, first in rabbits and later in guinea pigs, against red blood cells of the Indian short-tailed rhesus monkey, *Macaca mulatta*. Apparently these human red blood cells contained an antigen that was similar, if not identical, to an antigen on the rhesus cells. They named it the Rh antigen. People whose blood was clumped by the anti-Rh serum were labeled *Rh-positive,* the 15 percent or so of whites (and somewhat lesser proportion of most other peoples) whose blood was not clumped were said to be *Rh-negative.*

Very soon two further findings established this as an epochmaking discovery for clinical genetics: (1) Wiener and his co-workers determined that most transfusion reactions unexpected on the basis of ABO typing were due to the fact that Rh-negative persons could develop antibodies against the Rh antigen; and (2) Philip Levine and collaborators proved that the new blood factor would explain most cases of a hemolytic disease of the newborn, erythroblastosis fetalis.

In a large percentage of cases of erythroblastosis the mother was found to be Rh-negative whereas her husband and the affected child were Rh-positive. The affected was rarely a first child; often it was their third or fourth Rh-positive child. Apparently the earlier pregnancies with Rh-positive children caused the mother to develop antibodies against the Rh antigen. When the concentration (titer) of antibody reached a high level in the later pregnancy, enough of these passed into the fetus's circulation (since anti-Rh are IgG) to attack its red blood cells.

Before the disease became better understood these conditions were very often responsible for the death of the baby before or shortly after birth. Many that survived were permanently affected with deafness or cerebral palsy related to intense neonatal jaundice and hypoxia. Once Rh incompatibility became established as the etiological basis of the disease, a number of measures, preventive and ameliorative, were instituted that have sharply decreased the toll of this once dreadful disease. A later discovery of Weiner's, that some anti-Rh do not agglutinate Rh-positive red cells but, instead, merely attach themselves to antigen receptors on their surfaces (that is, they "coat" these cells) has in recent years led to a particularly effective preventive measure against erythroblastosis fetalis. The injection of this so-called "incomplete" anti-Rh, often referred to as Rho Gam, into an Rh-negative woman within three days after giving birth to an Rh-positive child inhibits her capacity for the primary formation of Rh antibodies, apparently by blocking effectively the antigen on the red blood cells of the child that normally elicit the immune response of the mother in such a situation. The injected antibodies dissipate within a few months and present no danger to the mother or to her subsequent pregnancies. Even today, however, some 20 percent of affected but untreated fetuses are stillborn.

Its discoverers proved almost immediately that ability to produce the Rh antigen is inherited as a dominant trait, Rh-positive persons being R/R or R/r, and Rh-negatives, r/r. The locus is on chromosome 1.

Many additional antigens have been found to belong to the Rh family. Weiner named the original one Rh_0 and two of the new ones rh' and rh". A fourth that is present whenever rh' is absent he called hr', and one that is present whenever rh" is absent he called hr". Rh_0 has remained the most powerful antigen in eliciting antibody response in those who lack it, but the others have also been responsible for transfusion reactions and cases of erythroblastosis fetalis.

A controversy then developed as to the genetic basis for the additional Rh antigens. R. R. Race, a leading British worker in the field, and R. A. Fisher championed the idea of closely linked loci: one for Rh_0, called D in this nomenclature; a second for the alternatives rh' and hr', called here C and c, respectively; and third, with genes and antigens E and e, for rh" and hr". On the basis of the relative frequencies of various combinations of these genes, the postulated order is DCE. No anti-d has ever been demonstrated, however, so inclusion of "d" in a Fisher–Race combination merely denotes the absence of reaction to anti-D; d, in other words, is an amorph.

Wiener was more impressed by the inability to demonstrate proven cases of crossing over between the supposedly separate loci of the Fisher-Race theory. He believed, therefore, that the data are best explained by a single locus with multiple alleles, each of which is usually responsible for more than one antigenic specificity. Thus a person with the gene R^0 would react positively not only to anti-Rh[0] but also to anti-hr' and anti-hr". The first reaction would be inferred from the capitalization of the gene symbol, the last two from the absence of any indication of rh' or rh". Thus any allele written with a capital R indicates that the bearer is Rh positive in the original sense of the term. Conversely, alleles which are variants on a lowercase r show that a person who has only these genes, in any combination, is Rh-negative in the original sense. Superscripts indicate which of the "prime" factors is detected, the number 1 indicating rh', number 2, rh"; Z and y show that both rh' and rh" are produced.

Under either system a minimum of eight alleles or gene combinations are

Table 16-3 The eight original genes of the Rh series when we have the following five antisera: anti-Rh$_0$, anti-rh', anti-rh", anti-hr', and anti-hr"

	Gene	Antigenic Factor Produced					Fisher–Race Equivalent
		Rh$_0$	rh'	hr'	rh"	hr"	
	r	−	−	+	−	+	dce
	r'	−	+	−	−	+	dCe
	r''	−	−	+	+	−	dcE
	r^y	−	+	−	+	−	dCE
	R^0	+	−	+	−	+	Dce
	R^1	+	+	−	−	+	DCe
	R^2	+	−	+	+	−	DcE
Fisher–Race	R^z	+	+	−	+	−	DCE
Equivalent		D	C	c	E	e	

needed to account for the results of typing with the five antisera shown in Table 16–3. Table 16–4 shows the 18 phenotypes and 36 genotypes formed by these genes (or their equivalent combinations), and Table 16–5 shows some relative frequencies in a typical European-related population.

Table 16–5 shows two alleles not mentioned in Table 16–3. One of these, R^{1w}, is largely restricted to Caucasian populations (about 2 percent). As the name suggests, it is related to R^1 in that it determines factors Rh$_0$, rh', and hr"; however, it determines an additional factor named rh^w. A related allele, r'^w, is very rare. Its

Table 16-4 Eighteen phenotypes and 36 genotypes of the Rh-Hr system based on the five antisera and eight genes mentioned in Table 16–3. The reactions to the antisera are shown as for a binary code. Note how the reactions can be inferred from the type designations as well as from the possible genotypes (Modified from Wiener, 1967 and 1968)

Rh-Hr Type	Anti-Rh$_0$	Anti-rh'	Anti-rh"	Anti-hr'	Anti-hr"	Genotypes
rh	0	0	0	1	1	r/r
rh'rh'	0	1	0	0	1	r'/r'
rh'rh	0	1	0	1	1	r'/r
rh"rh"	0	0	1	0	1	r''/r''
rh"rh	0	0	1	1	1	r''/r
rh$_y$rh$_y$	0	1	1	0	0	r^y/r^y
rh$_y$rh'	0	1	1	0	1	r^y/r'
rh$_y$rh"	0	1	1	1	0	r^y/r''
rh$_y$rh	0	1	1	1	1	r^y/r; r'/r''^a
Rh$_0$	1	0	0	1	1	R^0/R^0; $R^0/r*$
Rh$_1$rh	1	1	0	1	1	R^0/R^1; R^0/r'; $R^1/r*$
Rh$_1$Rh$_1$	1	1	0	0	1	R^1/R^{1*}; R^1/r'
Rh$_2$rh	1	0	1	1	1	R^0/R^2; R^0/r'';$R^2/r*$
Rh^{2}Rh^2	1	0	1	1	0	R^2/R^{2*}; R^2/r''
Rh$_z$Rh$_z$	1	1	1	0	0	R^z/R^{za}; R^z/r^y
Rh$_z$Rh$_1$	1	1	1	0	1	R^1/R^{z*}; R^z/r';R^1/r^y
Rh$_2$Rh$_2$	1	1	1	1	0	R^2/R^{z*}; R^z/r'';R^2/r^y
Rh$_z$Rh$_0$	1	1	1	1	1	R^0/R^z; R^z/r; R^0/r^y; R^1/R^{2*}; R^1/r''; R^2/r'

[a]The most frequent genotype for this phenotype in a typical European or European-related population.

Table 16–5   Relative frequencies of 10 alleles of the Rh-Hr system and the most common phenotypes (types) in a representative sample of United States Caucasians.[a] The 10 alleles include the eight of Table 16–3 plus R^{1w} and r'^w (see text) (Based on Wiener and Wexler, 1958)

Gene	Frequency	Wiener Type	Fisher–Race Type[b]	Frequency
R^1	0.41	Rh_1rh	CDe/cde	0.334
r	0.38	Rh_1Rh_1	CDe/CDe	0.173
R^2	0.15	rh	cde/cde	0.144
R^0	0.027	Rh_1Rh_2 (or Rh_2Rh_0)	CDe/cDE	0.131
R^{1w}	0.02	Rh_2rh	cDe/cde	0.122
r'	0.006	Rh_2Rh_2	cDE/cDE	0.024
r''	0.005	Rh_0	cDe/cde	0.021
R^z	0.002	$Rh_1{}^wRh_1$	C^wDe/CDe	0.017
r^y	0.0001	$Rh_1{}^wrh$	C^wDe/cde	0.016
r'^w	0.00005	$Rh_1{}^wRh_2$	C^wDe/cDE	0.006
		$rh'rh$	Cde/cde	0.005
		All others (17 types)		0.007

[a]The Rh situation is more complex than this in Negroes, much less so in Orientals. In Negroes, gene R^0 is the most frequent (about 50 percent), followed by 25 percent r, 10 percent R^2, 5 percent R^1, and 2 percent r^n which is not on the list; the others are quite rare. Orientals have more R^1 and R^2 than Caucasians but are most notable for the relative scarcity of r (less than 10 percent in most populations).

[b]The Fisher–Race type is typically designated as shown by the most likely genotype, for example, CDe/cde for Rh_1rh. This could give the wrong impression, as the genotype could be, albeit less likely, Cde/cDe. The Wiener notation avoids this problem by using different symbols for phenotypes and genotypes (Table 16–4). Note also that C and D are typically stated in reverse of their postulated order.

possession determines all of the above except for Rh_0. A person who is R^{1w}/R^2 would be positive against at least six antisera, the five of Table 16–3 plus anti-rh^w.

If the Fisher–Race system is correct, the frequencies of the combinations would reflect an extreme linkage disequilibrium. One could calculate from Table 16–5 that the frequency of c is 0.562 in that population, D 0.609, and e 0.843. Given that crossing over occurs, one would expect the combination cDe (R^o) to have a frequency of 0.289. The actual frequency is less than one-tenth of that, 0.027.

Unfortuntely even the 10 genes shown in Table 16–5 do not exhaust the complexity of Rh, for over 30 antisera of the system have been described. A full discussion of them is beyond the scope of this text. One complexity is noted, however, in the footnote to Table 16–5.

Kell

The Kell complex resembles Rh in that there are three sets of antithetical factors which, according to the substitution principle, ought to be determined by alleles at separate loci. These factors had, unfortunately, received names before it was determined that they were part of the Kell system, and many continue to refer to them by these old names. One set consists of K (Kell) and k (Cellano) (Table 16–6). A second set comprises, Kp^a (Penney) and Kp^b (Rautenberg), and the third contains Js^a (Sutter) and Js^b (Matthews). Their relationship to Kell is based on population

Table 16-6   Reactions of Kell genotypes to anti-Kell (anti-K) and anti-Cellano (anti-k) sera. *f* refers to frequency (in percent) in a typical Caucasian population.

Rbc Genotype	*f*	Anti-Kell (anti-K)	Anti-Cellano (anti-k)
K/K	0.2	+	−
K/k	6.7	+	+
k/k	93.1	−	+

data. Although 14 to 20 percent of American blacks are Js(a+), for instance, only 8 percent of K(+) blacks are Js(a+). As in the case of Rh, however, it is not yet clear whether the relationship stems from three closely linked loci or from complex alleles at one locus.

After ABO and Rh, the Kell system is clinically the most important. Anti-K can be the cause of transfusion reactions and erythroblastosis. Indeed the system is named for a British family (whose name was Kellacher) in which a child with this condition was born and the mother was found to possess a new, non-Rh, serum antibody to which the red cells of the affected child, the husband, an older child, and about 7 percent of the population reacted positively. Anti-k is not only much weaker but also would affect many fewer persons (the K/K of Table 16–6). Of the other members of the system, only anti-Kp^b has been incriminated in erthyroblastosis and transfusion reactions, but people who can make the antibody, those who are Kp(b−), are very rare (0.02 percent). Erythroblastosis has also occurred because of an antibody that can develop in persons carrying a rare allele, K^0, which apparently suppresses all antigens of the system. Sutter-a (Js^a) is interesting anthropologically because it seems confined to blacks.

Lutheran

Basically this is a system of two antigens determined by codominant alleles, Lu^a and Lu^b, though there are indications of greater complexity in the literature. It is named for the blood donor, a Mr. Lutheran, whose red cells evoked production of anti-Lu^a in a transfused patient. However the only clinical problem, mild erythroblastosis, has been encountered because of anti-Lu^b, which only about 15 persons of 10,000 can make (the few persons who are Lu^a/Lu^a). Lu(a−b−) people, also very rare, carry a suppressor gene. Lutheran and secretor were the first two human autosomal loci proved to be linked (1954).

Duffy

Although antibodies of this system were first found in a multiply transfused patient named Duffy, its British discoverers chose the symbol "Fy" because "D" had been preempted by the Fisher-Race Rh notation.

There are two basic antigens, Fy^a and Fy^b. The substantial number of Fy(a−b−), particularly in blacks, Saudi Arabs, and Yemenite Jews, demands, however, that the locus has at least three alleles, Fy^a, Fy^b, and an amorph, Fy. As described in Chapter 6 Duffy became the first human autosomal locus assigned to a chromosome (number 1).

Although anti-Fy^a can cause erythroblastosis, this is not common. *Fy/Fy* appear to be unusually resistant to *P. vivax* malaria.

Kidd

First detected in a Boston family named Kidd, the antigen and gene symbols include the first initial, that is, Jk, because "K" was preempted. Like Kell, the system was first noted because of erythroblastosis that could not be explained by any known system, and, like Duffy, there appear to be three alleles, in this case *Jk^a* and *Jk^b*, which are of about equal frequency in Caucasoids, and a rarer amorph, *Jk*. The locus is probably on chromosome 7. It appears to cause more clinical problems than Duffy but fewer than Kell.

Diego

Two antigens are known, Di^a and Di^b, determined by codominant alleles. The first was discovered because of an otherwise unexplainable erythroblastosis. Its most noteworthy feature is its presence in polymorphic frequencies (>1 percent) only in Mongoloid peoples, chiefly Orientals and American Indians, though it is surprisingly rare or absent in Eskimos. As a cause of clinical problems it is probably on the same level as Duffy.

Other Blood Groups

The several additional blood groups known appear to have less significance for clinical medicine. One of these, Lewis, was discussed in Chapter 14, and others, such as Xg^a, Dombrock, Colton, and Scianna, occur in connection with their chromosomal localizations in Chapter 13 (Xg also in Chapters 7 and 9). Stoltzfus (Sf) is thus far known only among the Amish. A number of other red cell antigens are referred to as "public" because virtually 100 percent of tested individuals have them. These include I of the I-i system, Vel, Yt, Gerbich (Ge), Lan, and Sm. "Private" antigens, on the other hand, are so-called because they appear to be confined to a few people, often a single family. They include Levay, Jobbins, Becker, Ven, Cavaliere, Berrens, Wright, Batty, Romunde, Chr, Swann, Good, Bi, Tr, and Webb.

WBC AND IMMUNUNOGLOBULIN VARIATION

The Major Histocompatibility System

So-called "tissue antigens," the substances that are crucial in deciding whether a body will accept or reject transplanted tissue, are usually detected on a person's leukocytes (white blood cells), in particular on the lymphocytes. Although the leukocyte antigens of humans have been studied only since 1962, the area is one of the liveliest and most important in medical genetics. The responsible genes decide effectively whether transplanted tissue is *compatible* with the host's body; hence they are often referred to as histocompatibility (or, as some would have it, histo-*in*compatibility) loci.

Whether a transplant will be accepted or rejected is an immunologic problem. The body ordinarily reacts to the presence of foreign proteins (which act as antigens) in one, or both, of two ways: (1) the foreign antigen may stimulate certain lymphocytes to divide and transform to antibody-producing cells, mostly plasma cells. The resulting antibodies agglutinate the foreign materials or, in the presence of complement, lyse—that, is kill—it if it is cellular in nature; (2) the foreign antigen may stimulate certain other lymphocytes to proliferate and produce cells that attack the foreign material (particularly if it is a graft) and destroy it.

In the first way, involving humoral antibody production, the lymphocytes are generally referred to as B cells, named for the organ in which they were first localized, the bursa of Fabricius of birds. In mammals they are derived primarily from the bone marrow, so the B is still apt. The lymphocytes of the second, or cell-mediated, system are thymus-derived, so they are spoken of as T cells. It is now known that there are several kinds of T cells, variously referred to as helper, killer (lymphocytic), or suppressor T cells. Their actions and their interactions with the B cells form a fascinating chapter in the development of immunology. In addition to their role as antibodies, the immunoglobulins seem to act as antigen receptors on the surface of the lymphocytes, though much remains to be clarified about this aspect, particularly as to how they do so for the T cells. It is the T-cell system that is mainly involved in the rejection of transplants.

Suppressor T cells play a major role in the body's recognition of "self." This means that a person ordinarily cannot produce antibodies against his own proteins, and therefore not against the same protein when it is brought in by graft or transplant. It follows that two factors are uppermost in having a transplant accepted: (1) diminishing the body's ability to react immunologically; and/or (2) choosing a donor who does not differ—or who differs very little—in tissue antigens from the receptor.

Suppression of immune reaction may be accomplished by means of certain drugs and by radiation treatment of the bone marrow and other sources of antibody-containing white blood cells, but it runs the risk of simultaneously lowering the transplant receptor's resistance to bacterial infections, particularly pneumonia. Finding a compatible donor is safer, and this is why it is so important to understand the complex genetics of the histocompatibility genes.

The groundwork for our understanding of histocompatibility has come from especially extensive work in another mammal, the mouse. Although one must always be cautious in making transfers of information of this sort from one species to another, the situation is not radically different in human beings. There appear to be 15 or more mouse loci that can cause individual differences in tissue antigens. Several of these occur in a large number of allelic forms, and all the alleles are codominant to one another.

As a general rule a mouse will reject a skin graft or other transplant from a donor who has a tissue antigen which the recipient lacks. Grafts between genetically identical individuals are successful. Such transplants, often referred to as isografts, would be between (a) monozygotic twins, (b) animals belonging to the same highly inbred strain, and (c) F_1 from crosses between inbred strains.

The F_1 from crosses between inbred strains can usually also be successful recipients of transplants from both parents, but the reverse, grafts of F_1 tissue into the parents, usually fail. This is understandable, since the F_1 tissue will usually contain at least one different tissue antigen allele, from the other parent, that the recipient does not contain. Thus, if we denote one of the loci as the H_1 locus, one P_1 line being H_1^1/H_1^1 , the other H_1^2/H_1^2, the F_1 are H_1^1/H_1^2. Transplanting F_1 tissue into the H_1^1 parent will cause it to react immunologically against the antigen produced by the H_1^2 allele. Similarly, the H_1^2 parent would react to a transplant containing the antigens produced by the H_1^1 allele. By the same reasoning, grafts from F_2 or subsequent generations generally succeed in F_1 (since the recipients contain all of the histocompatibility genes of their descendants); however, reverse transplants, from F_1 into their descendants, often fail.

Some of the mouse tissue antigen loci are blood groups, and this has its counterpart in humans, where ABO compatibility is a significant factor in the acceptance of a transplant; the Lewis system probably also plays a role.

Just as many of the blood group antigens, even those produced by allelic genes, differ in the strength of the antibody which they can induce, so do the histocompatibility antigens of the mouse differ in strength. Some are 100 percent effective in causing graft rejection, whereas in others the responsible genes seem to exhibit incomplete penetrance in this respect. Even when two different histocompatibility genes (and their resultant antigens) are both successful in producing a rejection of the transplant, one often accomplishes this much quicker than the other. In one instance the median survival of the graft may be nine days, whereas in another median survival may be over four months. Quite often, however, alleles at different loci seem to determine antigens with similar ability, whether strong or weak, fast or slow, to elicit the immune response that spells rejection of the transplant. The antigens are depicted as major (strong) or minor (weak), depending on the strength and promptness of the immune response, and the loci responsible are referred to in the same way.

In humans, as in the mouse, a number of loci concerned with the strongest tissue antigens are grouped on a single chromosome. This is referred to as the Major Histocompatibility System. In both species this is closely linked to a number of other loci related to immunologic effects so as to form a "major histocompatibility complex." In the mouse it is part of the chromosome 17 linkage group. In humans it is on chromosome 6. Similar clusters of genes have been found in every well-studied mammal.

The major histocompatibility antigens of man are determined by four loci termed HLA-A, HLA-B, HLA-C, and HLA-D. "HLA" stands for "human leukocyte antigen." The first three are detected serologically, that is, by such immune reactions as cytotoxicity, agglutination, and complement fixation. Previously HLA-A was known as the first, LA, H-LA, or HL-A series, HLA-B as the second or FOUR series, and HLA-C as the third or AJ series. The antisera used to detect them are usually obtained, as in the case of Rh sera, from multitransfused patients or from women who have had a number of pregnancies. If the leukocytes being tested carry an antigen for which there is an antibody in the test serum, the cells will be killed in the presence of complement. Conversely, known antigen-bearing cells are continually being tested against new sera, so that new antisera and new antigens are found.

A recent compilation of the known antigenic specificities determined by the alleles of each series is shown in Table 16–7. As may be gathered from the last line of each column, additional specificities remain to be discovered, particularly in the HLA-C series. The workers in the field meet periodically in workshops that evaluate the validity of the claimed specificities and give the approved ones provisional names—the W items in the table. Later there is a further evaluation by a Nomenclature Committee under the auspices of the World Health Organization (WHO), and this gives the antigen its final HLA number.

The method of detecting HLA-D is indicated by its former name, the major mixed lymphocyte culture (MLC)—or mixed lymphocyte reaction (MLR)—locus. Mixing lymphocyte cultures from individuals with identical types at the other HLA loci occasionally stimulated them to grow, analogous to the way the presence of a foreign antigen stimulates the T- or B-cells of the host. On the other hand, the MLC

Table 16–7 The three segregant series of HLA antigens and the approximate frequencies of the corresponding genes in a Norwegian population. The "Blank" category means antigens yet to be discovered at the time the table was compiled. For further explanations see text (From Thorsby, 1974, WHO-Iuis Terminology Committee, 1975, and Thorsby, 1976)

HLA-A[a] (First, LA, series)		HLA-B[a] (Second, FOUR, series)		HLA-C (Third, AJ, series)	
-A1	0.16	-B5	0.04	-Cw1	0.03
-A2	0.34	-B7	0.16	-Cw2	0.05
-A3	0.17	-B8	0.13	-Cw3	0.20
-A9	0.10	-B12	0.16	-Cw4	0.10
-Aw23		-B13	0.01	-Cw5	0.04
-Aw24		-B14	0.01		
-A10	0.05	-B17	0.03		
-Aw25		-B18	0.02		
-Aw26		-B27	0.05		
-A11	0.05	-B15	0.10		
-A28	0.04	-B16	0.01		
-Aw19	0.07	-Bw38			
-A29	0.04	-Bw39			
		-Bw21	0.02		
-Aw30		-Bw22	0.02		
-Aw31	0.03	-Bw35	0.07		
-Aw32		-Bw37	<0.01		
-Aw33		-Bw40	0.11		
-Aw34		-Bw41	<0.01		
-Aw36					
-Aw43					
Blank	0.02	Blank	0.03	Blank	0.58

[a]Indented types will share with them the stated frequencies of -A9, -A10, -Aw19, and -Bw16.

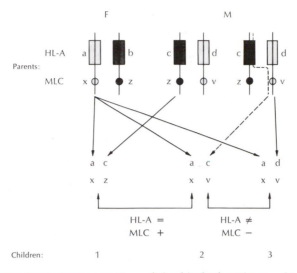

Fig. 16–1 Diagrammatic representation of the kind of evidence which demonstrates that the mixed lymphocyte culture (MLC) reaction is due to a different locus than those determining the serological HLA specificities. The critical progeny, exemplified by child 2, differ in these HLA specificities from some of their siblings, such as child 3; nevertheless a mixture of the lymphocytes of 2 and 3 do not show the MLC reaction. Postulating a separate, but closely linked, locus for MLC and assuming that child 2 represents a crossover would explain such results; this locus is known now as HLA-D. (From Thorsby, 1974; courtesy of E. Thorsby, Munksgaard International Publishers, Ltd., Copenhagen, Denmark, and *Transplantation Reviews.*)

reaction may be negative when the other HLA types are different. This indicates that the locus governing the MLC is different from those of the other three series, and the hypothesis is reinforced by the crossovers between them (Fig. 16–1).

The four HLA loci are very closely linked on 6p, with D apparently closest to the centromere and A farthest. Of the two in between, B is closest to D, and C is closer to B than to A (Fig. 16–2). Since the distance between even the farthest apart of the four is about 2 centimorgans, most of the time only two combinations of alleles (or antigen specificities) at the four loci are inherited from each parent. Each such combination is called a *haplotype*. Figure 16–3 illustrates the transmission of haplotypes in a family that was studied before HLA-D typing could be done. Many of the haplotypes represent combinations in linkage disequilibrium in the population.

A fifth series consists of MLR specificities that are present only in B-lymphocytes. These are designated as HLA-DR, that is, "D-related." (When they are only at the workshop stage of verification, these are called -DRw.) Recent evidence indicates that DR is one of four distinct sets of genes that make up a D complex: DP, DX, DQ, and DR. DR is the closest of the four to the HLA-B locus and DP the closest to the centromere.

The HLA-D genes of humans are thought to be analogous to the *I* subdivision

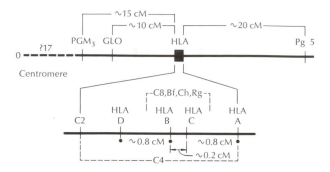

Fig. 16–2 Diagram of the apparent positions of localized genes on the short arm of chromosome 6. For an explanation of the symbols see text. (Courtesy of V. A. McKusick.)

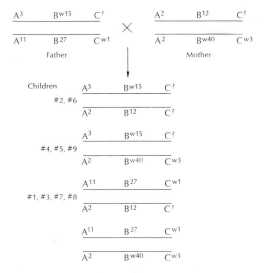

*Expected, among others, but not obtained in this family

Fig. 16–3 Diagram showing the transmission of the haplotypes of HLA-A, -B, and -C in a Norwegian family. C? means that the specificity determined by this allele had not yet been identified (part of "Blank" in Table 16–1). As indicated in Fig. 16–2, the correct order of the loci is ACB. (Based on data in Thorsby, 1974.)

of the major histocompatibility system of mice, which includes (1) immune response *(Ir)* genes that determine whether a mouse strain develops a strong or weak response to a given antigen, (2) "immune associated" (Ia) antigens on lymphocytes, and (3) susceptibility to viral oncogenesis, for example, whether a strain develops leukemia after injection of Friend virus. Whether these genes have similar effects in humans remains to be determined.

As indicated in Fig. 16–2, the complex also includes several loci concerned with components of complement: C2, C4, C8, Ch, and Rg, which are related to C4, and Bf, a gene for a glycoprotein proactivator of C3, as well as the loci of 21-hydroxylase.

Immunoglobulin Types: Km and Gm

The immunoglobulins, the molecules that carry our antibodies, can themselves act as antigens. As in the case of the blood groups, variations in these antigens are inherited, and several of the systems involve multiple alleles that attain polymorphic frequencies. In the jargon of the immunologist this is referred to as "allotype variation."

The immunoglobulins reside in the gamma globulin fraction of the serum proteins; indeed "gamma globulin" is often used as a synonym for immunoglobulin. Five major subdivisions are recognized. Their names and usual quantity in normal serum are shown in Table 16–8. The incomplete (coating) antibody mentioned in connection with Rho Gam consists of IgG, the most frequent type in normal serum and the one that has been best studied, whereas so-called complete antibody, such as noncoating anti-Rh, consists of the heaviest type, IgM.

Aided by the discovery that immunoglobulins (usually G, but sometimes A) in multiple myeloma are usually homogeneous—in fact, the IgG or IgA produced in excess by each patient is unique—G. M. Edelman and others have demonstrated that each immunoglobulin G molecule contains four polypeptide chains. Two of these, each 212 or 214 amino acids long, are termed light (L) chains, and two, each about twice as long, are heavy (H) chains. Although both types of chains vary, in any given molecule the two light chains are identical, as are probably the two heavy chains. The chains appear to be interconnected by disulfide (S-S) bonds, in the manner indicated in Fig. 16–4. This makes the total molecule a dimer, $(LH)_2$, of LH monomers. Actually, the immunoglobulin is a glycoprotein, because each heavy chain also has polysaccharide prosthetic groups (haptens) attached to it.

All the immonuglobulins contain light chains similar to those of IgG. As we shall see later, they differ in their heavy chains and certain accessory chains.

Bence–Jones proteins, which are found in excess in the urine of multiple myeloma patients and others, consist entirely of the light chains of their characteristic immunoglobulin. Hence it has been relatively easy to determine the amino acid sequences of IgG light chains. Those analyzed thus far fall into two categories, termed kappa (κ) and lambda (λ), respectively. In each category the carboxyter-

Table 16–8 The five major subdivisions of gamma globulin

Modern Name	Alternative Names or Terms	Normal Quantity in g/100 ml Serum
IgG	γG, γ_2	700–1780[a]
IgA	γA, γ_1	140–420[a]
IgM	γM, γ_3	50–190[a]
IgD	γD	0.3–30
IgE	γE, IgND	<0.1[b]

[a]These quantities are based on mean ± two standard deviations, after Kabat (1968).
[b]About 50–500 nanograms/ml, the equivalent of 5–50 micrograms/100 ml; but this gamma globulin is greatly increased in allergic persons and persons with parasitic infections.

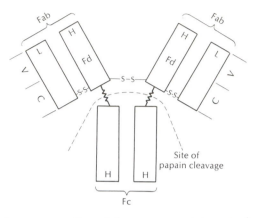

Fig. 16–4 Schematic representation of the structure of the IgG molecule. Cleavage by papain produces two fragments: a larger Fab, so-called because it includes the V portions and therefore the sites determining antibody production and the antigen-combining sites, and a smaller Fc, so named because it crystallizes, which determines placental passage, relation to complement, and other properties. In addition to the V regions of light and heavy chains, Fab fragments contain the C regions of the light chains and domain Cl of the heavy chains; the C2 and C3 domains are in Fc. All the C domains are thought to be homologous, derived by duplication from an originally single one. (Modified from Ellman and Bloch, 1968; courtesy of L. L. Ellman and the *New England Journal of Medicine*.)

minal half of the molecule is almost invariant, therefore referred to as the constant (C) region, whereas the aminoterminal region, residues 1 to 108, is not, and is therefore called the variable (V) region. It turns out that human κ and λ constant regions have only 40 residues in common. This accounts for some of the heterogeneity of the γ-globulin molecules.

Further analysis of Bence–Jones proteins has revealed that the locus determining the "constant" region of kappa light chains exhibits polymorphic variation in human populations. Formerly known as *Inv* genes, these codominant alleles are now referred to as *Km*, for "kappa marker." The three most common ones show single-step amino acid differences similar to most of the hemoglobin variants discussed in Chapter 5.

No polymorphic variation has been detected in the lambda light chains. However, normal individuals can produce λ chains with different amino acids at several C region positions because the genes for the lambda chain C regions are duplicated, probably in tandem fashion (see p. 99), much as the α- and γ-globin genes are (Figs. 14–9, 14–10).

Like the light chains, the heavy chains appear to be subdivided into a variable portion on their aminoterminal side and a so-called constant portion on the other side (Fig. 16–4). As we shall see below, from the point of view of antibody production the variable portions of the chains are the more interesting; moreover, they contain the antigen-combining sites. As in the light chains, however, the variation in the chains that gives them demonstrably different *antigenic* specificities resides in the constant portion. These are best known for the IgG molecules. Hence these antigenic differences are known as the *Gm* system.

The Gm allotypes are complicated by the expression of multiple specificities by the same individual, very much like the multiple specificities of the Rh system. Indeed some believed at first that these complexes could be explained by alleles of a single locus, comparable to the Wiener hypothesis for Rh. It is known now, however, that all individuals contain four different IgG H chains (so that there are four subtypes of IgG). The C regions of these four H chains, termed $\gamma 1$, $\gamma 2$, $\gamma 3$, and $\gamma 4$, are determined by very closely linked genes, and the Gm specificities are attributable to variations in at least three of them. Hence, part of the explanation for the multiplicity of specificities lies in the inheritance of haplotypes, similar to those of the HLA loci. Reading from 5' to 3', the order of these genes (which are interspersed with other heavy chain C sequences) is: γ_3, γ_1, γ_2, γ_4 (Fig. 16–6).

Naming of the Gm specificities has been a bit chaotic, especially since several independently discovered (and named) specificities have turned out to be identical. Table 16–9 is a recent summary suggested by a WHO committee.

The Gm system presents many features of genetic and anthropologic interest, and there are hints of others that could have medical overtones. A number of the complexes are racially specific, for example. Thus the complex G1m(3)G2m(23)G3m(5,13,14) has been found only in Caucasoids, whereas G1m(1,3)G2m(23)G3m(5,13,14) occurs only in Mongoloids, Micronesians, and Melanasians. As in the Rh, MNSs, and HLA series, many combinations of allotypes exist in linkage disequilibrium.

Table 16–9 Nomenclature of Gm Allotypes (Modified from Fudenberg et al., 1972)

WHO	Original	WHO	Original
Subtype known		Subtype unknown	
G1m(1)	a	Gm(7)	r
G1m(2)	x	Gm(8)	e
[a]G1m(3) or (4)	[a]f, b^w or b^2	Gm(9)	p
G1m(17)	z	Gm(12)	b$^\gamma$
		Gm(18)	Rouen (2)
G2m(23)	n	Gm(19)	Rouen (3)
		Gm(20)	z (S.F.)
G3m(5)	[a]b, b^1		
G3m(6)	[a]c^3, Gm-like		
G3m(10)	b^5, b$^\alpha$		
G3m(11)	b^0, b$^\beta$		
G3m(13)	b$_3$		
G3m(14)	b^4		
G3m(15)	s		
G3m(16)	t		
G3m(21)	g		
G3m(24)	c^5		
G3m(26)	u		
G3m(27)	v		

[a]Refer to the same antigenic determinant(s).

Antibody Diversity

A related problem is how to account for antibody diversity. It has been estimated that the immune system has the potential to produce up to 100 million different antibody specificities. Many thought this meant that there were thousands of different genes for the various chains of each immunoglobulin molecule, with the result that for each antigen there was a specific set of genes that responded to produce the specific antibody for it. Recent evidence has shown that this is not true, that there are a limited number of genes encoding for the parts of the immunoglobulin molecule. Antibody diversity stems from permutations of these genes as a result of recombination during differentiation of the immunoglobulin-producing cells, plus mutations and other chromosome modifications that occur during the process.

The genes involved are in several clusters, termed "multigene families." Unlike complexes such as the major histocompatibity complex (discussed above) and the alphalike and nonalpha globin complexes (Chapter 14), in which each part of the cluster acts independently to make its product, the units of each immunoglobulin chain complex must undergo pretranscriptional recombinations with one another and their products must undergo posttranslational combinations to form the final product, a light or a heavy chain of an immunoglobulin molecule. The cluster for kappa light chains is on chromosome 2, the cluster for lambda light chains on chromosome 22, and the largest cluster, for heavy chains, is on chromosome 14.

Each cluster for a light chain is composed of two parts, one for the variable region and one for the constant region, separated by 3 to 4 kilobases. The V portion is at the 5' side of the cluster, the C portion on the 3' side. The mature B cell variable portion of the cluster is further subdivided into three functional parts and a number of intervening sequences (Fig. 16–5). Reading from 5' to 3', the functional parts encode for: (1) a leader (L) segment, hydrophobic amino acids that form a signal peptide that is later spliced off in forming the definitive light chain; (2) a variable (V) segment, amino acids 1 to 95 of the chain; (3) a joining (J) segment, amino acids 96 to 108 of the chain.

In the stem cell leading to B cell differentiation (Fig. 16–5 "Germ Line"), each light chain complex contains 100 to 200 different V segment nucleotide sequences and five different J segment sequences. During differentiation one of the V sequences combines with one of the J sequences (plus an L and a C sequence) to form the active gene for the light chain that a given mature B cell will be capable of producing. In the kappa genome there is only one C sequence; for lambda there is a choice of six C sequences in the immature cell.

The various possible combinations of light chain V and J segments alone provide the potential to produce between 500 and 1000 different immunoglobulin molecules. (It will be recalled that the variable region is critical for antibody specificity because the antigen-antibody combining site is located there, probably in the vicinity of amino acid 96, that is, in or near the V-J splicing site.)

How does the V-J recombination come about? In the case of the kappa light chains, at least, it appears that there are two nucleotide sequences on each V segment that have complementary sequences on each J segment. One of these is, read-

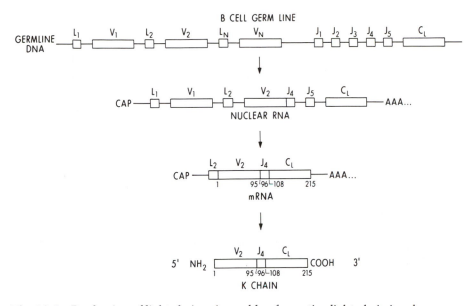

Fig. 16-5 Production of light chains. Assembly of an active light-chain involves recombinations that eventually join one of 100 to 200 different variable (V) regions, which encode amino acids 1 to 96, to one of five joining (J) regions for amino acids 96 to 108. Associated with a V region is a leader (L) segment encoding a signal peptide spliced off during light chain formation. The constant (C) region is encoded from a segment for amino acids 109 to 215 which follows a 3-4 kilobase noninformational sequence on the 3' side of the J. (There are additional noninformational sequences between each L and V.) The diagram relates particularly to kappa light chain formation. For lambda chains there is a choice of six C sequences in the germ line cell. (Adapted from Kindt and Capra, 1984; courtesy of J. D. Capra and Plenum Press.)

ing 5'–3', CACAGTG in the V segments and, in inverted sequence, GTGTCAC, in the J segments. The other, nearby, is ACATAAAC ("adenine-rich") in the V's and, complementarily, GTTTATGT, in the J's. The attractions between these sequences apparently provide the fulcrum ("stem structure") for the recombinations—and ensuing deletions of 99 to 199 V segments and four J segments—that lead to one V sequence combining with one J sequence in the maturation of the B cell.

Whatever the actual mechanism of these recombinations, it is fraught with possibilities for misalignment and resultant nonsense chain production: "wasted" recombinants. These errors determine a further source of diversity, namely, which light chain and which allelic gene for that light chain the B cell will use. Apparently the primordial cell first tries to form a functional kappa chain from the code on one chromosome 2. If the recombination in this sequence fails to produce a workable chain, the allelic kappa sequence tries to do so. Then if, and only if, both kappa genes fail, the lambda sequences (on chromosome 22) try. This explains why multiple myeloma Bence–Jones proteins contain only one kind of light chain.

Even if one disregarded the Km polymorphism and other C region differences, with at least 500 to 1000 possible V-region variations, one kappa C sequence, and six lambda C sequences, a minimum of 3500 to 7000 different light chains would be available for the immunoglobulins.

Even this figure is an understatement because additional variation comes from somatic point-mutational changes that are constantly occurring in the V region.

Further diversity in immunoglobulin production comes from analogous actions that lead to the structure, and kind, of the heavy chain produced. These are much more complicated than the light chain events. First, the heavy chain cluster of the stem cell contains constant chain sequences for every one of the eight possible heavy chains that different plasma cells will produce—10 if one counts the fact that the α C sequence is duplicated and there is a pseudo-ϵ sequence (Fig. 16–6). Each is thought to have an S ("switch") sequence on its 5′ side. Second, the variable side of the heavy chain contains a so-called D (diversity) sequence in addition to V and J sequences. In the germ line this part of the cluster contains six J sequences and a large number of V and D sequences. There is also a great deal of intervening DNA. The C-region alone is thought to be about 100 kb in length.

It appears that the same sort of recombinational events as were outlined for the light chains are responsible for the definitive heavy chain gene sequence of the mature B cell. As a result, each chromosome 14 of the mature B cell is thought to

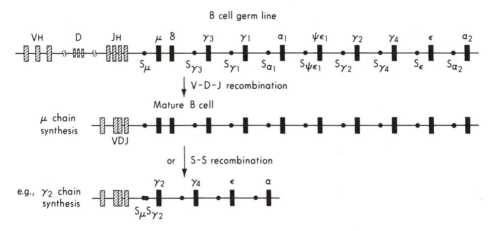

Fig. 16–6 Diagram of a heavy-chain gene cluster on chromosome 14 during B-cell differentiation. In the germ cell (top line) about 100 V segments, about 50 diversity (D) segments, and six J segments, on the 5′ side, are followed by a chain of various C segments (μ, δ, et cetera), each usually preceded by a switch (S) region. The cluster is also liberally interspersed with noninformational sequences (signified by plain lines between the named segments). After recombinational events have resulted in the presence of single V, D, and J sequence (line 2), synthesis of μ chains is by transcription of the code of the VDJ sequence plus the entire C region. Synthesis of δ chains (not shown) is controlled by an RNA splicing mechanism that deletes the μ sequence. Production of gamma, epsilon, or alpha chains involves a recombination event that switches the VDJ sequence to another site along the chromosome and deletes all C sequences on the 5′ side of the desired segment (as, for example, in line 3 for γ_2 chains). [Adapted from Kindt and Capra (1984), after Honjo (1982) and Gearhart (1982), and Leder (1983); courtesy of J. D. Capra and Plenum Press.]

contain one V sequence, one D sequence, one J sequence, and the entire constant region (as in Fig. 16–6, middle portion).

Differentiation of the B cell into a mature plasma cell involves determination of which heavy chain gene will be expressed. The first step is the appearance of μ heavy chains, followed by a light chain; these unite to form IgM, first cytoplasmic, then membrane-bound. Subsequent synthesis of cytoplasmic and membrane IgD qualifies the cell as a competent B-cell. After antigen encounter, membrane IgM and IgD disappear, and the cell begins to differentiate into a plasma cell. This either continues to produce IgM or undergoes heavy-chain switching to produce IgG, IgA, or IgE by deleting every unexpressed constant region sequence to the left (on the 5′ side) of the expressed one, but leaving intact those on the 3′ side (as in Fig. 16–6, lowest line).

If, estimating conservatively, there are 100 V sequences to choose from, 50 D sequences, and 6 J sequences, the heavy chain V region would allow for 30,000 differences in the heavy chains even before the choice of a constant region is made. Including the hypothesized variations of the light chains brings the possible variations for each kind of immunogloblin to between 210 and 420 million ($1-2 \times 10^3 \times 7 \times 3 \times 10^4$) before the additional variation due to somatic mutation.

Platelet Variation

Although platelets are not usually considered white blood cells, they are derived from macrophages; hence this is the appropriate place to note that there is inherited variation in these components of the blood, too.

Neonatal alloimmune thrombocytopenia is a bleeding disorder that is not due to absence of a clotting factor. It occurs because a few people (about 2 percent) lack the common KO or $P1^{A1}$ surface antigen on their platelets. A $P1^{A1}$-negative woman can produce antibodies against this antigen that cross the placenta and damage the fetal platelets. Analogous to erythroblastosis fetalis, it is usually less serious because platelet destruction tends to be less life-threatening than destruction of red blood cells. Like Rh disease it occurs, or achieves clinical notice, in far fewer cases than would seem to be susceptible, perhaps because of innate variation in ability to produce the requisite antibody.

ASSOCIATIONS OF MARKER GENES AND DISEASE

As we stressed in Chapters 12 and 13, even traits that appear together in *families* more often than expected on a random basis are not expected to show unusually coincident appearances in *populations*. When the loci involved are known to be linked, the coincidence is referred to as a linkage disequilibrium, and it demands an explanation. Sometimes, however, the linkage relations are unknown. In many cases, in fact, the genetic basis of only one of the coincident traits is known. There may even be strong grounds for doubting that the other trait is inherited. In such cases the purposefully vague term "association" is used to describe the coincident relationship. Despite the vagueness inherent in the term some associations are so strong that we must take cognizance of them and seek an explanation for them.

Trait Marker	T+	T−
G+	a	b
G−	c	d

Fig. 16-7   Distribution of individuals for a genetic marker (G) and another trait (T) for association analysis.

Associations are usually noted by finding the incidence or frequency of one of the traits (usually a common marker) in the portion of the population that expresses the other trait (usually a rare anomaly) and comparing this with its incidence or frequency in a control sample. If there is no association, the relative numbers with and without one of the trait should be the same in the sample with the anomaly as in the control. For example, if one in every 30 persons in prison for a violent crime turns out to have the chromosome constitution XYY whereas only one in 10,000 persons in a sample of XY people of comparable age and social background has a criminal record, this would be an indication of some sort of association between a tendency to commit a violent crime and the XYY karyotype. If there were no association, the frequency should be one in 30 or one in 10,000 for both samples.

Suppose we have a distribution of G+, G−, T+, and T− individuals as shown in Fig. 16-7. If there is *no* association,

$$\frac{\dfrac{a}{a+b}}{\dfrac{b}{a+b}} = \frac{\dfrac{c}{c+d}}{\dfrac{d}{c+d}}$$

or simply,

$$\frac{a}{b} = \frac{c}{d}.$$

It follows that

$$ad = bc$$

and

$$\frac{ad}{bc} = 1 \text{ when there is no association.}$$

The last expression, ad/bc, is the *relative incidence* of T in the G and non-G samples. It is also often referred to as the *odds ratio*.

An alternative sometimes used is the *relative risk*, formulated as

$$\frac{pd\,(1-pc)}{(1-pd)\,pc},$$

where pd = frequency in disease and pc = frequency in controls. It approximates the *relative incidence* when a/b and c/d are small.

In either case, when the ratio is quite a bit more than one, a significant association is probable. The real test comes from the chi-square with one degree of freedom testing whether the two samples are homogeneous. Chi-squares from a number of studies may be added even if the incidence of the marker and the anomaly are very different in the various studies, so that the overall x^2 tells us whether any apparent association is a general, widespread one with considerable meaning, or is a restricted one with much less meaning.

For example, 521 consecutive duodenal ulcer patients in the Liverpool, England, area and 680 random controls tested in the same area about the same time had the distribution of ABO types shown in Table 16–10. There are more O, and fewer A and B, among the ulcer patients than would be expected from the control series. The relative incidence of O as compared to A + B + AB in the two series is:

$$\frac{(284)(279 + 69 + 17)}{(315)(186 + 38 + 13)} = \frac{(284)(365)}{(315)(237)},$$
$$\text{Relative incidence} = 1.39.$$

This is somewhat lower than, but in the same direction as, the relative incidence, 1.53, that Clarke and his collaborators found in a larger sample in the same area several years before. To test the significance of the excess O, the contingency table for the 1959 data is:

	Type O		*Not O*		
	a	*e*	*a*	*e*	*Total*
Duodenal ulcer patients	284	259.8	237	261.2	521
Control series	315	399.2	365	340.8	680
Total	599		602		1201
Chi-square = 7.94 with 1 degree of freedom; P < 0.01.					

Apparently type O persons have a significantly greater chance to develop duodenal ulcers than do persons with other blood types. Similar results have been found in many countries (Table 16–11).

Table 16–10 ABO types of 521 duodenal ulcer patients and 680 controls from the Liverpool, England, area (Data from Clarke et al., 1959)

Blood Type	Control Series		Duodenal Ulcers	
	No.	%	No.	%
O	315	46.4	284	54.5
A	279	41.0	186	35.7
B	69	10.1	38	7.3
AB	17	2.5	13	2.5
Total	680	100.0	521	100.0

Table 16-11 Relative incidence of group O blood as compared with the others (A + B + AB) among persons with duodenal ulcer in various places (From Clarke, 1961, who lists the original references.) Each center x^2 has 1 d.f.

Center	Relative Incidence	$x_{(1)}^2$	P
1. London	1.54	39.83	$<10^{-10}$
2. Manchester	1.21	3.76	>0.05
3. Newcastle	1.57	22.75	$<10^{-5}$
4. Liverpool	1.53	44.26	$<10^{-10}$
5. Glasgow	1.17	7.51	<0.01
6. Copenhagen	1.48	25.06	$<10^{-6}$
7. Oslo	1.56	26.77	$<10^{-6}$
8. Vienna	1.22	9.95	<0.01
9. Iowa (whites)	1.37	26.49	$<10^{-6}$
10. Iowa (Negroes)	1.32	3.21	>0.05
11. Wilmington, Del.	1.22	2.82	>0.05
12. Tokyo	1.66	9.46	<0.01
Total		221.87	

The data from Japan are particularly interesting because the relative proportions of type O and the other blood groups are different from England and the United States, where most of the other studies were carried out. This discounts the criticism that the British and American associations occur because of stratification in the sample, that is, the population happens to be high in O and in susceptibility to duodenal ulcer without any causal relationship between them, just as northern Europeans tend to be both blue-eyed and blond-haired without the one being responsible for the other.

Not all type O samples, however, show an increased incidence of duodenal ulcer. Table 16–12 indicates that the significant association is with type O who are nonsecretors. This confirmed previous results from several laboratories. Apparently, the same gene that allows secretion of water-soluble ABH substances helps protect against peptic ulceration, especially in Group O persons, who are the most susceptible when they are not secretors.

Population surveys of this type have also disclosed strong associations between both carcinoma of the stomach and pernicious anemia with blood group A. Indeed nearly all significant associations of malignancies are with group A. Several studies found significant excesses of group A in patients with salivary gland tumors; one of these also found a small but significant excess of A in primary ovarian neoplasms and a much greater excess in secondary neoplasia of the same organ. Excesses of A have been reported also in cancers of the pancreas and of the esophagus, but not in those of the colon and rectum. Three studies of carcinoma of the cervix (uteri) also are consistent in showing relatively more A than O, but the excess of A is significant in only one of them.

With the development of widespread testing for histocompatability antigens, discussed above, a large number of associations have been discovered between such antigens and diseases (Table 16–13). Particularly consistent associations have been

Table 16–12 Division of the duodenal ulcer patients and controls of Table 16–10 when both ABO and secretor types are known (From Clarke et al., 1959)

Combination	Control Series		Duodenal Ulcer	
	No.	%	No.	%
O secretor	245	36.0	186	35.7
O nonsecretor	70	10.3	98	18.8
A secretor	204	30.0	124	23.8
A nonsecretor	75	11.0	62	11.9
B secretor	54	7.9	19	3.6
B nonsecretor	15	2.2	19	3.6
AB secretor	14	2.1	10	1.9
AB nonsecretor	3	0.4	3	0.6
Total	680	99.9	521	99.9

Chi-square testing ulcer vs. controls: 30.979 for 7 d.f.; $P \ll 0.01$.
Chi-square testing the two types of O nonsecretors vs. the rest: 17.750 for 1 d.f.; $P \ll 0.01$.

Table 16–13 A recent compilation of associations between diseases and HLA-B antigens. Additional associations and relations of some of these diseases and HLA-D and -DR are discussed in the text (Adapted from Bach and van Rood, 1976)

Disease	No. of Studies	HLA Antigen	Frequency in Patients (%)	Frequency in Controls (%)	Average Relative Risk	95% Limits
Ankylosing spondylitis	5	B27	90	7	141.0	80–249
Reiter's disease	3	B27	76	6	46.6	23–94
Acute anterior uveitis	2	B27	55	8	16.7	8–34
	6	B13	18	4	5.0	4–7
Psoriasis	6	B17	29	8	5.0	4–6
	4	B16	15	5	2.9	2–5
Graves's disease	1	B8	47	21	3.3	2–6
Celiac disease	6	B8	78	24	10.4	8–14
Dermatitis herpetiformis	3	B8	62	27	4.5	3–8
Myasthenia gravis	5	B8	52	24	4.6	3–6
Systemic lupus erythematosus	2	B15	33	8	5.1	2–11

found with ankylosing spondylitis (inflammation of the vertebrae with ossification of certain ligaments), with psoriasis (a skin disease), with certain types of arthritis, and with myasthenia gravis (a progressive syndrome of muscular fatigue and paralysis). As indicated in Table 16–13, the risk of developing ankylosing spondylitis is about 140 times greater in persons carrying the HLA antigen B27 than in the general population. The risk may not be this strong in black Americans.

Since alleles at the several loci of the major histocompatibility complex often are part of haplotype combinations in linkage disequilibrium, it is not surprising that the associations with disease often involve *several* HLA specificities. Multiple sclerosis (MS), for example, is associated with increased frequencies of both HLA-A3 and HLA-B7, with relative risks of 1.7 and 1.5, respectively. Even higher relative incidences have been reported for combinations of these two specificities and HLA-Dw2 in MS: 3.3 for -A3 and -Dw2, 2.9 for -B7 and -Dw2, and 2.7 for the combination of all 3 with MS.

Some diseases are associated with two or more antigenic specificities at the *same* HLA locus. In addition to several in Table 16–13 (uveitis—an eye inflammation—and psoriasis), this appears to be true for susceptibility to the virus-causing·hepatitis B, as manifested by the later presence of so-called Australia antigen in the blood. Here the associated HLA antigens are usually -Bw17 and -Bw35, and the relative incidence is greatest for those who are positive for both of these specificities (heterozygous additiveness). Presence of -B15, on the other hand, carries with it a negative association with hepatitis B antigenemia, that is, there is less risk than normal of susceptibility.

Associations of both types, multiple antigens of individual loci plus haplotypic combinations, between HLA and diabetes mellitus are playing a major role in clarifying the heredity of this disease. As suggested in Chapter 15, diabetes has been, in the words of one of its leading investigators, "a geneticist's nightmare." The major problem is its extensive heterogeneity: the likelihood that the disease has many forms with different etiologies.

Aside from several rare simply inherited forms and a clearly environmental, temporary form that appears often during pregnancy, so-called "gestational diabetes," the more common forms are frequently divided into (a) Type I: insulin-dependent, (IDDM), and (b) Type II: noninsulin-dependent (NIDDM). Type I is also sometimes referred to as "juvenile diabetes" or JDM, because of its typically early onset, whereas Type II, being generally of later onset, is frequently referred to as "adult diabetes." Since this distinction is not absolute, however, its proponents are forced to make additional categories, such as "juvenile noninsulin-dependent" that probably further confuse the picture. Of the two, type II is by far the most common.

This division is strongly reinforced by HLA typing. Maturity-onset diabetes is generally not associated significantly with any HLA types, whereas IDDM tends to be strongly associated with HLA. Significantly increased susceptibility to IDDM has been reported in persons positive for HLA-A1, -A2, -B8, -B15, -B18, -B40, -Cw3, -Dw3/DRw3, and -Dw4/DRw4, with particular emphasis on two haplotype complexes: (a) A1,B8,Cw3,Dw3/DRw3 and (b) A2,B15,Cw3, Dw4/DRw4. -B8 and -B15 seem to have additive effects on the relative risk of IDDM when together (heterozygotes), as do DRw3 and DRw4, but in no case do these have a dosage effect as homozygotes. HLA-A11, -B5, -B7, and Dw2/DRw2, on the other hand, appear associated with decreased susceptibility to IDDM, at least in Caucasians. No DRw2/DRw2 with IDDM, for instance, has ever been reported.

In a number of instances in which a disease is associated with specificities of several HLA loci the associaton is much stronger with one of them than with the others. Japanese workers have found, for example, that the development of acute glomerulonephritis after streptococcal infection has a relative risk of 2.1 for carriers of HLA-Aw19, 3.5 for -B12, and 9.0 for a specificity they refer to as -D En (that is, has no WHO number yet). The relative risk with -Aw19 is of borderline statistical significance, with the other two highly significant. The relative risk with -D En is, however, much greater than with -B12. Evidence exists, furthermore, of linkage disequilibrium between -B12 and -D En, so that removing those with both on the same haplotype from the affected with -B12 would probably place the association with this specificity below the level of statistical significance. The authors conclude, therefore, that the *primary association* of poststreptococcal acute glomerulone- phritis is with HLA-D En. The relationship with HLA-B12 (and possibly -Aw19) would then be termed a *secondary association.* Similarly the primary associaton of multiple sclerosis is with the HLA-D antigen (Dw2). For JDM, in the A1,B8,Cw3, Dw3/DRw3 grouping the primary association is with -Dw3/DRw3, and in the other grouping with increased risk it appears to be with -Dw4/DRw4 (though one group feels it is with -B15). And contrary to the earlier data quoted in Table 16– 13, the primary association of systemic lupus erythematosus appears to be with HLA-DRw3 (or -Dw3, which cannot be monitored in these cases), in some popu- lations also with -DRw2.

The Basis of Disease-Marker Associations

Since associations have been discovered, geneticists have sought an answer to the question of etiology: What is responsible? The two hypotheses that seem to have the largest following may be subsumed under (1) "common pathophysiology" and (2) "genetic linkage."

The first postulates that the substance or structure determined by the marker gene is somehow involved in the pathology, etiology, or development of the dis- ease. When HLA is involved, the hypothesis would suppose that some aspect of immunity is basic to the disease. In any case the disease need not be determined by a locus of its own, which is to say that it need not be inherited in the usual sense; if inherited, however, it need not be closely linked to the marker. This would fit well the involvement in associations of entities such as peptic ulcer, certain types of cancer, Reiter's disease, acute anterior uveitis, Grave's disease (thyrotoxicosis), celiac disease, myasthenia gravis, and systemic lupus erythematosus in which there either appears to be no genetic basis or the inheritance is on such weak grounds that there is widespread disagreement on its nature. Fitting well also is the fact that many of the conditions involve autoimmune pathology, as is especially evident for dermatitis herpetiformis, myasthenia gravis, and systemic lupus erythematosus; there is even some evidence for autoimmunity in juvenile diabetes. One could eas- ily imagine a scenario whereby tissue injury (in response in some cases to virus infection) and the lytic properties of B-lymphocytes would be related. It is therefore particularly interesting that the D/DR systems, in which the stimulating antigen is expressed on B cells, form so often the primary association when HLA is the marker. In addition to those mentioned earlier, these include such autoimmune diseases as rheumatoid arthritis (DRw4) and Hashimoto thyroiditis (DRw3). Cer- tain immune related genes may even make the person more (or less) susceptible to virus infection and thus set off (or block) the processes leading to the disease.

The second hypothesis implies that a gene critical to development of the dis- ease exists, and the association grows out of the close linkage of this gene and the marker locus. The association is seen as an expression of linkage disequilibrium between the disease-related gene and particular alleles of the marker locus. Sup- porting this hypothesis are recent findings that genes for a number of unrelated disorders that show HLA associations are closely linked to the MHC. These include genes for hemocromatosis (deposits of large amounts of iron in various tissues due to a metabolic error), congenital adrenal hyperplasia due to 21-hydroxylase deficiency, spinocerebellar ataxia, and a normotensive cardiomyopathy that can be detected by measurement of ventricular septal thickness. Further support comes from new findings of genetic involvement (e.g., increased susceptibility in monozygotic twins and other close relatives) for such HLA-associated diseases as juvenile diabetes, psoriasis, and multiple sclerosis. Indeed, many geneticists are coming to the conclusion that earlier hypotheses of autosomal recessive inheritance in diabetes may be correct for JDM. They postulate an IDDM locus close to the HLA-D and Bf loci of the MHC, an estimate of θ being 0.04 to HLA-D and slightly less to Bf.

Implicit to both the pathophysiological and linkage hypotheses that explain associations is the possibility that the real association may not be between the disease and the marker locus under study; it may be instead to another gene, perhaps an undiscovered one, linked to the marker locus. The association appears to involve the marker under study because it is in linkage disequilibrium with the actual interacting locus. We have seen instances of this disequilibrium when an association to HLA-A, -B, or -C alleles proved to be secondary to association with HLA-D or -DR. Even here one cannot be certain that this is the real primary association. Perhaps -D or -DR is only our present means of detecting another locus with which it is in strong linkage disequilibrium. Thus the Japanese workers who detected that poststreptococcal acute glomerulonephritis is associated with HLA-D En suspect strongly that the true association is with an as yet undiscovered immune response or immunosuppressive gene closely linked to the one for -D En. Note that one need not postulate a genetic basis for the disease, as indeed none is for the aforementioned glomerulonephritis, to include this possibility of linkage disequilibrium in the hypothesis. A more difficult task is to explain the rationale for linkage disequilibrium when a genetic basis of the disease *is* postulated.

DISORDERS OF THE IMMUNE SYSTEM

A number of disorders in the basic protective function of the immune system are known to be inherited. The nature of several of these are indicated by their names. The terms a- and hypo-gammaglobulinemia, for example, suggest deficiency of the serum protein that contains most of the antibodies. Others are simply referred to as immunodeficiencies. In many others, however, the name gives no clue that immune defect is a prominent feature; some examples are the Bloom syndrome, mannosidosis, ataxia telangiectasia, and metaphyseal chondroplasia. The last named, which includes T-cell deficiency among its symptoms, was termed "cartilage-hair hypoplasia" when described among the Amish by McKusick.

Perhaps the best known agammaglobulinemia is generally referred to by its eponymic, Bruton type, named for O. C. Bruton, an American pediatrician. It is also called infantile X-linked hypogammaglobulinemia. A "pure" B-cell disorder, it usually involves deficiency in all three major classes of gamma globulins, IgA, IgG, and IgM, and generally becomes manifest in the first year of life, as soon as transplacentally acquired maternal immunoglobulins are expended. Plasma cells are absent, but the thymus is normal, as are delayed hypersensitivity and the response of small lymphocytes to antigens or to such mitosis stimulators as phytohemagglutinin (PHA). Since the onset of antibiotic therapy, survival past the first decade is common.

Two other X-linked conditions involve both B-cell and T-cell systems. In the less severe of the two, the Aldrich (or Wiskott–Aldrich) syndrome, these systems are only partially deficient. Patients manifest eczema, proneness to infection, and thrombocytopenia (diminution of platelets, with resultant increased bleeding, e.g., bloody diarrhea). The primary defect appears to be in the "afferent" side of immunity, that is, in antigen recognition or processing. The more severe one is the X-linked form of Swiss type agammaglobulinemia (Fig. 16–8), known also as thymic epithelial hypoplasia or alymphocytosis. It differs from the Bruton type by the presence of lymphocytopenia, earlier age of death, vulnerability to viral and fungal as well as bacterial infections, lack of delayed hypersensitivity, and atrophy of the thymus.

Autosomal recessive Swiss type agammaglobulinemia is increasingly being referred to as SCID (Severe Combined Immunodeficiency Disease). As the name suggests, there are both B and T cell defects. A major advance has come with the recent demonstration that the patients are deficient in adenosine deaminase (ADA). On the basis of variant alleles, the structural locus of this enzyme appears to be on chromosome 20, but it remains to be determined if all cases of the associated immune deficiency involve mutation at the same locus, especially since a number of loci on other chromosomes affect production of this enzyme. Encouraging progress has been reported in treating this disorder by means of bone marrow transplants or by infusions of packed red blood cells (which release ADA).

Deficiency in nucleoside phosphorylase, the enzyme just prior to ADA in the same pathway, results in defective T cell immunity. Its structural locus appears to be on 14q. Another autosomal T-cell disorder, ataxic diplegia with defective cellular immunity, is associated with bone and cartilage defects. Some have therefore called it "achondroplasia with Swiss type agammaglobulinemia." T-cell hypoplasia is also the key feature of immune defect due to absence of the thymus.

Adult "acquired" hypogammaglobulinemia, a late onset disorder, was at first thought to be environmentally determined rather than genetic. Although the main pathology is a deficiency of serum immunoglobulins, this seems to stem in many cases to overproduction of a type of T cells that suppress Ig synthesis.

Less well understood immune disorders include intestinal lymphangiectasia, with lymphocytopenia and impaired allograft rejection; reticuloendotheliosis, with lymphadenopathy; and familial histocytic reticulosis, with hypergammaglobulinemia.

The heredity of several immune disorders commonly recognized by clinicians has not been fully established. One is the DiGeorge syndrome, also known as absence of thymus and parathyroids and as familial thymic aplasia, which may be a dominant. As its alternative names suggest, it involves T-cell deficiency. In reticular dysgenesis (congenital aleukia or aleukocytosis) the stem cells of all white blood cells fail to develop. It is extremely rare and invariably fatal in early infancy. Some call it "SCID with leukopenia."

A frequent by-product of deficient immunity is a greater than usual tendency

Incidence of Alymphocytosis in Three Families

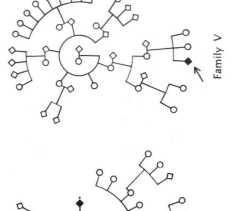

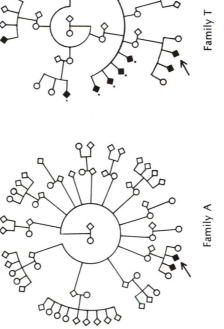

Family A

Family T

Family V

↗ = Propositus   ○ = Unaffected females

◆ = Affected males   ◆. = Presumably affected males

◇ = Unaffected males

Fig. 16-8 Swiss type agammaglobulinemia (alymphocytosis), an early lethal, in three families. (From Rosen et al., 1966. Courtesy of F. S. Rosen and the *New England Journal of Medicine*.)

to develop malignancies. Thus we shall encounter a number of the above-mentioned disorders in Chapter 17. Whether the immune deficiency is also related to the increased chromosomal breakage in some of these disorders, for example, ataxia-telangiectasia and the Bloom syndrome, is not known.

A number of disorders, while not clearly affecting B- or T-cell activity, involve defects in the ability of white blood cells to fight infection. Some of these are Chediak–Higashi disease, myeloperoxidase deficiency, G6PD deficiency, puretic syndrome, tuftsin deficiency, and several granulomatous diseases. Indeed, the list would include every hematologic disorder involving neutropenia. Similarly, most disorders involving failure to thrive, as is notably true of many of the enzyme deficiency disorders of infancy, also involve a proneness to infection; in many instances this is the direct cause of death.

Related to this is a question that is only beginning to be explored: What proportion of susceptibility to disease, whether constitutional or infective, is attributable to differences in the immune responses of individuals that are genetically determined? Recent evidence has demonstrated, for example, large inherited differences in production of antibody against a streptococcus antigen. In the Job syndrome there is defective local resistance to staphylococcal infection, and several loci are known that affect sensitivity to specific viruses. Elucidation of the fuller meaning of these relationships should prove to be one of the most exciting chapters in the human genetics of the future.

Allergy, or, more properly, "atopic hypersensitivity," is a collective term for one or more of the following: (a) coryza ("hay fever"); (b) asthma; (c) urticaria ("hives"); (d) atopic dermatitis ("eczema," Besnier prurigo); (e) angioneurotic edema; (f) vasomotor rhinitis; and (g) migraine. These conditions are notoriously heterogeneous, so that only a fraction of cases involve an immune reaction. When they do, the offending antigens are often referred to as allergens or atopens, and the antibodies as reagins. The latter are nonprecipitating, nonagglutinating, usually heat-labile, and are capable of causing a reddening or "sensitizing" reaction of the skin. They belong almost exclusively to the IgE class of immunoglobulins, the titer of which is usually increased manyfold in allergic individuals (also in many sufferers from parasitic infestation).

Despite the general impression of clinicians that susceptibility to allergies is familial and inherited, its hereditary basis remains ambiguous. Plagued by heterogeneity, as described above, and undoubtedly also by high rates of variable expressivity and incomplete penetrance, it has been described by various workers as a simple dominant (Fig. 16–9), a simple recessive with expression in some fraction of heterozygotes, a recessive at three different loci (one each for hay fever, atopic asthma, and atopic dermatitis), and as polygenic. However, a few syndromes with clear-cut inheritance include atopic symptoms, for example, eczema in the aforementioned Wiskott-Aldrich syndrome and the Dubowitz syndrome, a rare recessive; hereditary angioneurotic edema (Fig. 16–10), apparently due to C1 inhibitor deficiency; Netherton disease, a recessive with ichthyosiform erythroderma, almost completely confined to females; and the combination of urticaria, deafness, and amyloidosis, a dominant.

Recent work has centered around two major theses: (1) that the degree of IgE, and therefore of allergenic, response is inherited, and (2) that responses to atopens

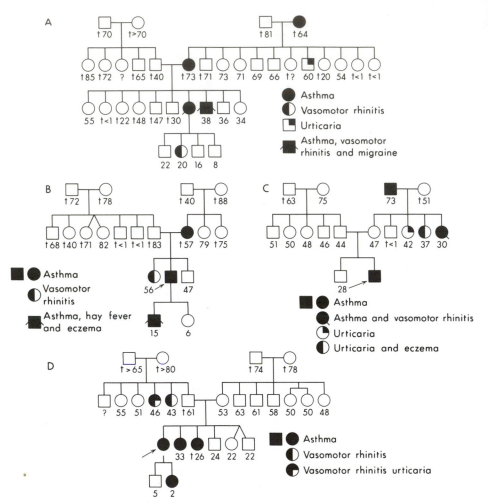

Fig. 16-9 Some typical pedigrees in the atopic hypersensitivity disorders. Note that members of a kindred often manifest different atopic conditions and that the same individual may be affected with more than one. The numbers indicate ages; † before such numbers indicates deceased. (From Levitan, 1973, after Schwartz, 1953.)

are associated with particular HLA types. Although suggestive, the data to date are rudimentary and, in some instances, contradictory.

Unlike allergy, in which the injurious antibody is produced in reaction to an external antigen, in autoimmunity the usual reluctance of the body to develop or to continue to circulate antibodies against its own tissue antigens somehow breaks down. This results in such disorders as myasthenia gravis, pernicious anemia, systemic lupus erythematosus, Hashimoto struma (thyroiditis), autoimmune thrombocytopenia, and some forms of rheumatoid arthritis. As noted earlier, there is the mounting evidence that juvenile-onset diabetes also originates as an autoimmune

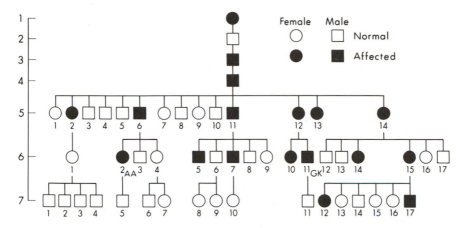

Fig. 16–10 Pedigree of a Swedish family with hereditary angioneurotic edema. (From Levitan, 1973, after Arnoldsson et al., 1967.)

reaction, and there is a long list of other diseases suspected as having an autoimmune basis.

Most often the critical factor in autoimmunity seems to be a defect in the structure or action of suppressor T-cells, which normally play a major role in the immune differentiation of self from nonself. It is very significant, therefore, that many of the autoimmune disorders exhibit associations with antigens of the HLA system, especially Dr3. Indeed, the converse is now true: any disorder showing such an association is suspect as being autoimmune in nature.

In autoimmunity, too, there have been many clinical impressions of hereditary tendencies, but again the situation is ambiguous, and for many of same reasons as for allergy. Some believe many of the observed familial aggregations may involve maternal antibodies, much like those responsible for erythroblastosis fetalis. The syndrome of lymphopenic hypergammaglobulinemia, antibody deficiency, autoimmune hemolytic anemia, and glomerulonephritis does appear to be a clear-cut recessive.

SUGGESTED EXERCISES

16–1. A man whose red blood cells react positively to anti-M, anti-S, and anti-s marries a woman who gives positive reactions to anti-M, anti-N, and anti-s. What MNSs phenotypes are expected in their progeny? (Remember that no answer is complete unless it also includes the relative proportion of each type.)

16–2. Although the M-N types are not significant for clinical problems, they are very useful in forensic medicine such as cases of disputed parentage. A woman who is type M has a type M child. She accuses a man who is type MN of being the father of her child. Her husband turns out to be type N. How would you advise the court?

16–3. What would have been your answer to exercise 16–2,
    (a)   if both husand and the accused man were type MN?
    (b)   if both were type M?
    (c)   if the accused were type M and the husband MN?

16–4. Draw up a table showing the six combinations of mother, child, and pur-ported father wherein a man who was accused unjustly of fathering a child could be exonerated on the basis of M-N typing. In a fourth column show the M-N types of men who would not be exonerated even if they were being accused unjustly. Hint: There should be 12 answers in column 4. What is interesting about type MN in this table?

16–5. A woman, her child, and the putative father are all type MN. The woman is positive against anti-S, but not anti-s, while the child and the putative father are positive for both.
    (a)   How would you advise the court? Why?
    (b)   Suppose the man's mother was also typed, and her cells were positive with anti-M and anti-s only. Would this cause you to change your advice to the court? Explain.

16–6. Gedde-Dahl et al. (1967) found a man and his wife both positive with all four common antisera of the MNSs system, as are seven of their 12 children. Two other children are positive only against anti-N and anti-s; two against anti-M and anti-S only; and one against anti-M, anti-N, and anti-S only. The presence of the rare dominant disorder epidermolysis bullosa (Fig. 1–3) in this family strengthens the likelihood from other evidence that all the children, especially the genetically troublesome one(s), are legitimate.
    (a)   Diagram the MNSs phenotypes and genotypes of the members of this family.
    (b)   Which do(es) not fit the usual inheritance of these traits?
    (c)   What are several possible explanations for the aberrant case(s)?

16–7. If a person's blood reacts positively with antisera against M, Jk^a, Fy^a, and Lu^a antigens whereas his mother's blood reacts negatively to the same four antisera, what can we conclude safely about the genes of his father for these loci?

16–8. Ten genotypes and six phenotypes (blood types) are possible on the basis of the 4 ABO alleles in Table 16–1. Name the six blood types and the possible geno-types of each.

16–9. Typical frequencies of the MNSs combinations in a white population are *MS* 0.25, *Ms* 0.28, *NS* 0.08, and *Ns* 0.39.
    (a)   Under equilibrium, what is the expected frequency of *NS* in this population?
    (b)   If the observed frequencies were based on a sample of 200 individuals, what would you conclude concerning the state of linkage equilibrium for these loci?

16–10. Calculate the frequecies of the coupling and repulsion double heterozygotes for the MNSs system in the population in Exercise 16–9 on the basis of the given combination frequencies.
    (a)   Are the two heterozygote frequencies equal?

(b)   Under what circumstances are they expected to be equal?

(c)   How does the answer to (a) affect your conclusion in Ex. 16–9 (b)?

16–11. On the basis of the frequencies of Rh genes in Table 16–5, calculate the expected frequency of the Fisher–Race combination *CDe* under linkage equilibrium? How does this compare with the actual frequency (shown in the table as R^1).

Assume that the recombination frequency between nail-patella and ABO is 10 percent.

16–12. A type O man who lacks the nail-patella syndrome marries a type A woman who has it. Her father and her husband have identical genotypes.

(a)   What are the probable genotypes of the persons named?

(b)   What is the probability that their first child, a girl, will resemble her mother in both respects?

(c)   What is the probability that one of their first two children will be a type O with nail-patella disorder and the other will be a type O without it?

A blood group incompatible marriage occurs when one spouse could not serve as a donor for the other. The incompatibility need not be reciprocal. Levine (1943) and others have noted that such incompatible marriages between type A and type O persons produce significantly fewer type A children when the mother is type O (A × O marriages) than when the father is type O (O × A marriages). Sometimes the type A child has ABO erythroblastosis. A detailed review of this subject is provided by Levene and Rosenfield (1961).

16–13. What proportion of the marriages in the population of exercise 9–3 would be expected to be of the following incompatible types:

(a) A × O?
(b) B × O?
(c) A × B?
(d) AB × B?

16–14. Of the children produced by marriages between type A and type O persons in the exercise 16–13 population:

(a)   What proportion would be expected to be type A?

(b)   What proportion would be expected to be incompatible with their mothers? (For this problem a type A child is considered incompatible with a type O mother, but a type O child is not incompatible with a type A mother).

Not only do A × O and B × O marriages show significant deficiencies of children incompatible with their mothers, but such marriages are more often completely sterile than their reciprocals. This is best shown by a deficiency of these marriages in compilations of marriages with live issue (Levene and Rosenfield, 1961).

16–15. If 4 percent of an Oriental population, 9 percent of a black population, and 16 percent of a Caucasian population were Rh-negative, what would be the expected frequency of erythroblastosis in each? Assume all erythroblastosis relates to anti-Rh_0 and that one-fortieth of the theoretically potential erythroblastotics actually manifest the disease.

16–16. Wiener (1950) tells of a couple who came to him in doubt as to whether the husband or another man was the probable father of her expected child. Following are the reactions of the child (after birth) and the adults to M-N and Rh-Hr antisera:

	Anti-M	Anti-N	Anti-Rh_0	Anti-rh′	Anti-rh″	Anti-hr′	Anti-hr″
Husband	+	−	+	+	+	+	+
Wife	+	+	−	−	−	+	+
Child	+	−	−	−	−	+	+
Other man	+	−	+	−	−	+	+

(a) How would you characterize the blood types of the four persons listed? (Use Table 16–4.)

(b) What are their possible genotypes?

(c) What can you conclude as to the paternity of the child?

16–17. The child in question in the previous exercise was the woman's third child, and it was certain that the husband was the father of the first two. The first two both gave the following reactions to the antisera.

anti-M anti-N anti-Rh_0 anti-rh′ anti-rh″ anti-hr′ anti-hr″

   +   +   +   −   +   +   +

(a) What are their blood types?

(b) What are their possible genotypes?

(c) Do these data throw any further light on the central question in the previous exercise?

16–18. If an Rhrh man is married to an Rh negative woman and they were to produce a child whose red blood cells were positive against anti-Rh_0, anti-rh′, and anti-hr″ but not anti-hr′, and chromosomal analysis revealed an apparent deficiency in one autosome, this would suggest that the Rh locus was located on that autosome.

(a) Explain the reasoning behind this statement.

(b) Can you think of other possible explanations for the aberrant blood typing?

17

Neoplastic Disease and Oncogenes

Hereditary factors have been prime suspects in the etiology of cancer, and there is probably no tumor that has not been reported to occur several times in the same family. Nevertheless, only about 70 well-established simply inherited disorders result, primarily or secondarily, in benign or malignant tumors (Table 17–1).

The reasons for the discrepancy are not hard to guess. For one thing, the rarity of most neoplasms makes it difficult to find a sufficient number of cohorts to firmly establish a particular hereditary pattern. In addition, many instances of these diseases are not recorded, either because of the notorious difficulties of detection or because, being frequently diseases of advanced age, the affected die of some other cause. If a theory which has many adherents is correct, that carcinogenesis demands two genetic changes, one in the original genome (usually a so-called germinal mutation) and a later one induced by or related to the environment of the cell that initiates the neoplasm (a so-called somatic mutation), it is easy to understand how often the condition would not appear even though the genomic predisposing gene had been transmitted according to Mendelian principles. Even if the second mutation is not needed, as suggested on page 408, environmental factors interacting with the one gene may bring considerable variable expressivity and lack of penetrance into the picture. Indeed, for a number of the more common cancers, the environmental variables make it difficult to determine whether the genetic basis is simple, but with a large penetrance factor, or multifactorial, with a heritability of 50 percent or less.

The vast majority of simply inherited neoplastic conditions are autosomal dominants. This suggests that the primary genetic factor in the genesis of these tumors is an error in synthesis of structural protein rather than an enzyme deficiency.

In contrast, most of those that are inherited as recessives are apparently not primarily neoplasms. In them tumor formation seems to be (a) part of a larger syndrome and (b) not specific for one kind of tissue or organ. These syndromes and the tumors associated with them are shown in Table 17–2. Particularly striking is the frequency of leukemia or lymphoma on this list. Noteworthy also is how often these syndromes include extensive chromosomal breakage, and how many of them appear among the immune deficiency disorders (Chapter 16).

Table 17-1   Loci and simply inherited disorders of interest in oncology (Based largely on McKusick, 1978[a] and Schimke, 1978)

10100	Acoustic neurinoma, bilateral
30100	Aldrich (Wiskott–Aldrich) syndrome, often with lymphoma or leukemia
20740	Antitrypsin deficiency of plasma, sometimes with hepatoma
20890	Ataxia-telangiectasia; see Table 17–2
10940	Basal cell nevus syndrome
21025	Beta-sitosterolemia, with xanthoma
21090	Bloom syndrome; see Table 17–2
11220	Blue rubber bleb nevus
11780	Cerumen variation: possible association of "wet" and breast cancer
21450	Chediak–Higashi syndrome; see Table 17–2
30500	Dyskeratosis congenita (Zinsser–Cole–Engman syndrome), often with cancer of pharynx, esophagus, lung, or cervix
12782	Dysplasia epiphysialis hemimelica with chondromas and osteochondromas
12920–50	Ectodermal dysplasia, at least two forms, sometimes with squamous cell carcinoma
13110	Endocrine adenomatosis, multiple (Wermer syndrome; multiple endocrine neoplasia, type I)
13170	Epidermolysis bullosa dystrophica, often with oral or esophageal cancer
13270	Epithelioma, hereditary multiple benign cystic (epithelioma adenoides cysticum of Brooke)
13280	Epithelioma (keratoacanthoma), self-healing squamous (of Ferguson–Smith)
22765	Fanconi pancytopenia; see Table 17–2
13500	Fibrocystic pulmonary displasia
22860	Fibromatosis, juvenile, often with tumors
30560	Focal dermal hypoplasia (Goltz syndrome), often with lip papillomas
13650	Focal facial dermal dysplasia (hereditary symmetrical aplastic nevi of temples)
23000	Fucosidosis, with angiokeratoma of skin
13800	Glomus tumors, multiple
23220,-50,-70	Glycogen storage disease I, IV, VI, sometimes with hepatoma
23370	Granulomatous disease, recessive form
30640	Granulomatous disease, X-linked form
14160	Hemochromatosis, sometimes with hepatoma
23520	Hemochromatosis, juvenile, sometimes with hepatoma
14415	Hyperkeratosis lenticularis persistans, sometimes with skin tumor
14500	Hyperparathyroidism, familial primary, often adenomatous
23920	Hyperparathyroidism, neonatal familial primary, often adenomatous
14598	Hypocalcinuric hypercalcemia, familial (FHH)
30824	Immunodeficiency, X-linked progressive combined variable (Duncan disease); see Table 17–2
14850	Keratosis palmaris et plantaris (tylosis) with esophageal cancer
15080	Leiomyomata, hereditary multiple, of skin (and uterus?)
15110	Leopard syndrome, often with nevi
24640	Letterer–Siwe disease; see Table 17–2
15190	Lipomatosis, multiple
15780	Milia, multiple eruptive
15835	Multiple hamartoma (Cowden) syndrome
16100	Naegeli syndrome, sometimes with pheochromocytoma
16220	Neurofibromatosis (von Recklinghausen disease)
16230	Neuromata, mucosal, with endocrine tumors (mucosal neuroma syndrome; multiple endocrine neoplasia, type III)

[a]*Note:* The number shown before each item is the one assigned to it in McKusick (1978). The first figure in the number is a "1" if the condition is considered an autosomal dominant, a "2" if it is an autosomal recessive, a "3" if it is X-linked. The rest of each number is based on alphabetical order within each of these categories. The catalog also gives a brief description and several references for each one.

Table 17-1   (*continued*)

16290–320	Nevus syndrome, at least three forms:
16290	Nevi (pigmented moles)
16300	Nevi flammei, familial multiple
16310	Nevus flammeus of the nape of the neck
	See also 10940, 11220, 19390
16670	Osteopoikilosis, with spotty nevi
25977	Osteoporosis pseudoglioma syndrome
16720	Pachyonychia congenita, may include steatocystoma, oropharyngeal cancer
16780	Pancreatitis, hereditary, may predispose to pancreatic carcinoma
16800	Paragangliomata
17130–40	Pheochromocytoma, two forms:
17130	Pheochromocytoma
17140	P and amyloid-producing medullary thyroid carcinoma (PTC syndrome; Sipple Syndrome; multiple endocrine neoplasia, type II)
	See also: 16100, 16230, 19330
17490–550	Polyposis, Intestinal, at least four forms:
17490	Polyposis coli, juvenile type
17510	Polyposis, intestinal, I (familial polyposis of the colon)
17520	Polyposis, intestinal, II (Peutz–Jeghers syndrome); see Table 17–3
17530	Polyposis, intestinal, III (Gardner syndrome); see Table 17–3
17645	Presacral teratoma
18020	Retinoblastoma
18160	Sclero-atrophic and keratotic dermatosis of limbs (sclerotylosis), often with skin and bowel cancer
18450	Steatocystoma multiplex (multiple sebaceous cysts)
18730	Telangiectasia, hereditary hemorrhagic, of Rendu, Osler, and Weber, sometimes with hepatoma
19110	Tuberous (or tuberose) sclerosis (epiloia; adenoma sebaceum)
27670	Tyrosinemia, often with hepatoma
19152	Upington disease (enchondromas and ecchondromas)
19330	von Hippel–Lindau syndrome, with retinal angiomata, cerebellar hemangioblastoma, sometimes pheochromocytoma
27770	Werner syndrome; see Table 17–2
19390	White spongy nevus of Cannon
27870–75	Xeroderma pigmentosum; see Table 17–2 and text
27880	Xerodermic idiocy of DeSanctis and Cacchione

A number of recessive neoplastic disorders are due to defects in DNA repair mechanisms. In xeroderma pigmentosum (Fig. 17–1) affected individuals exhibit unusually heavy freckling followed by ulcerations of the portions of the skin exposed to light, cancerous growth in these areas, and death, almost always before reproductive age. Their heterozygous siblings and parents are generally also quite heavily freckled. Apparently the freckling stems from their one dose of the abnormal allele; but rarely would they be distinguished from the many freckled persons who lack the gene, were it not for their severely affected relatives.

Cultured xeroderma pigmentosum cells are defective in their ability to repair DNA damaged by ultraviolet light (Fig. 5–7), probably because of deficiency in an endonuclease normally used to cut out the abnormal T-T linkages produced. These cells fall into at least six complementation types, suggesting there are at least six loci that can result in defective repair. Five involve excision repair. They vary in

Table 17-2   Recessive syndromes with neoplasms at various sites (Based largely on Schimke, 1978, after Swift, 1976)

McKusick No.	Syndrome	Sites of Primary Neoplasia[a]
20890	Ataxia–telangiectasia	Brain
		Hematopoietic tissue (leukemia)
		Lymphatic tissue
		Ovary
		Stomach
21090	Bloom syndrome	Hematopoietic tissue (leukemia)
		Tongue
21450	Chediak–Higashi syndrome	Lymphatic tissue (lymphoma)
		Various (Hodgkin's disease)
22765	Fanconi pancytopenia	Esophagus
		Hematopoietic tissue (leukemia)
		Liver
		Skin
24640	Letterer–Siwe disease	Liver
		Lymph nodes
		Spleen
27770	Werner syndrome	Biliary system
		Blood vessels
		Breast
		Hematopoietic tissue (leukemia)
		Larynx
		Liver
		Ovary
		Skin
		Thyroid
		Urinary bladder
27870–27875	Xeroderma pigmentosum	Hematopoietic tissue (leukemia)
		Skin
		Tongue
X-linked		
30100	Aldrich syndrome	Hematopoietic tissue (leukemia)
		Lymphatic tissue
30500	Dyskeratosis congenita	Cervix
		Esophagus
		Lung
		Oro- and nasopharynx
30824	Immunodeficiency, X-linked progressive combined variable (Duncan disease)	CNS
		Hematopoietic tissue (leukemia)
		Intestine
		Liver

[a]In alphabetical order, not necessarily in the order of frequency.

the amount of repair still possible, from less than 2 percent of normal to one where there may be 25 to 55 percent. In the sixth form the excision enzyme is normal, but there is a postreplication defect in the synthesis of the replacement segment. A similar defect in xerodermic idiocy of DeSanctis and Cacchione is complementary in such *in vitro* studies to the standard forms of xeroderma pigmentosum, so it is probably due to mutation at yet another locus.

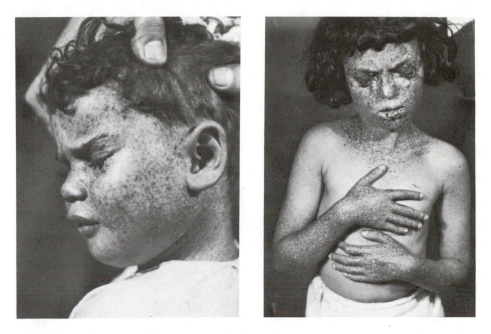

Fig. 17-1 Two cases of xeroderma pigmentosum. These individuals are probably homozygous for one of the responsible genes and therefore suffer from the severe, typically fatal disorder. The life expectancy of heterozygotes in the same kindred is not diminished, but they also are usually heavily freckled. (From El Hefnawi et al., 1965; courtesy of H. El Hefnawi and the *Annals of Human Genetics*.)

A DNA repair defect has also been implicated in Fanconi pancytopenia (also known as Fanconi's anemia or infantile panmyelopathy). In addition to the blood changes indicated by the name, there are again pigmentary changes in the skin and unusual susceptibility to malignancies, plus increased chromosomal breakage and malformations of the heart, kidneys, and extremities. The disturbance appears to be in a "joining" enzyme, or ligase (Fig. 5–7, part 5).

Deficiencies of repair enzymes, such as endo- and exo-nucleases and ligases, would fit well the recessive patterns of the disorders in Table 17–2. While this is closer to an understanding of etiology than we have for most diseases, the specific connection between these defects and an increased predisposition to cancer remains unexplained.

Occurrence of neoplasms in several different organs or tissues is also true of some of the dominants (Table 17–3). Although most of the tumors in each case seem to involve superficially similar tissue—endocrine glands, for example, in the three M.E.N. syndromes—no such unifying feature is fully correct in any item on the list. Even if most of the organs involved are endocrine glands, they often differ so much in embryonic origin and in the nature of the secretory product that it is hard to understand how the same locus could be responsible for oncogenesis in them. A good example of such an incongruity is the inclusion of both pancreatic

Table 17-3 Autosomal dominant syndromes with neoplasms at various sites

McKusick No.	Syndrome	Sites of Primary Neoplasm[a]
10940	Basal cell nevus syndrome	Cerebellum Iris Skin
11220	Blue rubber bleb nevus	Cerebellum Hematopoietic tissue Skin
12920	Ectodermal dysplasia	Cervix Tongue
13110	Endocrine adenomatosis, multiple (MEN I)	Adrenal cortex Pancreas Parathyroid Pituitary Skin Thyroid
13170	Epidermolysis bullata dystrophica	Esophagus Oral mucosa Tongue
16220	Neurofibromatosis	CNS Skin
16230	Neuromata, mucosal, with endocrine tumors (MEN III)	Adrenal medulla CNS Parathyroid Skin Thyroid

17140	Pheochromocytoma and
	  amyloid-producing medullary
	  thyroid carcinoma (MEN II)
		Adrenal medulla
		Parathyroid
		Thyroid

17520	Polyposis, intestinal, II (Peutz– Jeghers syndrome)	Bronchi Esophagus Intestines (especially jejunum) Kidney (pelvis) Nose Ovary Ureter Urinary bladder
17530	Polyposis, intestinal, III (Gardner syndrome)	Bone Colon Ovary Skin Small intestine Stomach Thyroid

18160	Sclero-atrophic and keratotic
	  dermatoses of limbs
	  (Sclerotylosis)
		Breast
		Tongue
		Uterus

19110	Tuberous sclerosis (Epiloia)	CNS Kidney Myocardium Skin
19330	von Hippel–Lindau syndrome	Adrenal medulla Cerebellum Retina

[a]In alphabetical order, not necessarily in the order of frequency.

islet cells and adrenal cortex among affected tissues in type I multiple endocrine neoplasia. (An association of thyroid, islets, and adrenal *medulla* is considered less fortuitous, since they are thought by some to belong to a unifying category: the so-called APUD—amine precursor uptake and decarboxylase—system.) Clearly much remains to be learned about these dominant syndromes.

Being dominants carries a redeeming feature, however: In many cases it becomes easier to utilize the family history to identify sibs, progeny, and other close relatives at risk and, by early detection of tumors or precancerous lesions, to practice in effect preventive medicine. This has been particularly successful for the several forms of multiple intestinal polyposis and the hereditary forms of retinoblastoma.

The pedigrees of the conditions listed in Table 17–3 often resemble closely those of so-called "cancer families." A particularly striking one is shown in Fig. 17–2. Hereditary of cancer in these families is not considered well-established, however, mainly because of the possibility that they represent chance (coincidental) aggregations. One is reminded of the occasional families with extreme sex ratios; there was always the temptation to postulate some genetic mechanism to account for them, until careful surveys demonstrated that their frequency was very close to the very small number of such unusual sex ratios expected by chance. Furthermore, as data about such families remain quite sparse, the possibility remains strong that the observed aggregations stem from some common environmental factor, such as

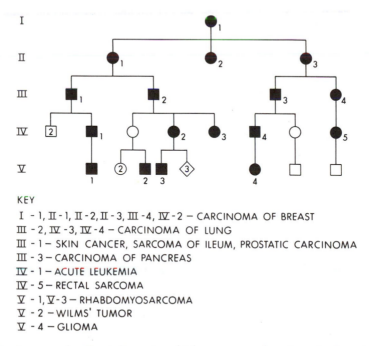

KEY

I - 1, II - 1, II - 2, II - 3, III - 4, IV - 2 — CARCINOMA OF BREAST
III - 2, IV - 3, IV - 4 — CARCINOMA OF LUNG
III - 1 — SKIN CANCER, SARCOMA OF ILEUM, PROSTATIC CARCINOMA
III - 3 — CARCINOMA OF PANCREAS
IV - 1 — ACUTE LEUKEMIA
IV - 5 — RECTAL SARCOMA
V - 1, V - 3 — RHABDOMYOSARCOMA
V - 2 — WILMS' TUMOR
V - 4 — GLIOMA

Fig. 17-2 A cancer family pedigree in which many members have had carcinomas of the breast or various soft-tissue sarcomas. (From Schimke, 1978, after Li and Fraumeni, 1969 and 1975; courtesy of R. N. Schimke and Churchill Livingstone.) Note that normal individuals are not numbered in this pedigree.

diet, chemicals, or virus infection. The physician encountering such an apparent cancer family would do well to study it carefully, however, particularly since the dominant pattern may hold promise for possible preventive measures. Reporting such families would probably increase considerably our understanding of the role of genetics in tumor formation.

A recent study of familial incidence of malignant melanoma illustrates the attempts to find a multifactorial explanation for data that do not fit well any simple Mendelian hypothesis. Among 1021 first degree relatives of melanoma patients, five also had melanoma. This is eight times the number expected from the incidence of melanoma in the general population. The parent–offspring and offspring–parent portion of these data are even more significant. The four cases observed, out of 623, are almost 13 times the number expected in a similar cohort of unrelated individuals. By methods similar to the threshold analysis of quantitative traits in Chapter 15, the estimated heritability of susceptibility to melanoma from these data is 0.49. This would mean that nearly half the observed variation in this trait is attributable to the additive effect of polygenes, slightly more than half to sunlight, hormones, contact with noxious chemicals, and other environmental variables.

This is a much higher estimate of heritability than was obtained in a smaller study of melanoma in Australia (0.11) and generally higher than the estimates of heritability obtained in similar studies of common cancers. (The increased incidence in *all* relatives for cancers of the stomach, breast, colon, uterus, and lung is about 2 to 4 times the incidence in the general population.) Undoubtedly some of the differences in the results of the melanoma studies stem from the small number of familial cases and from heterogeneity in the data (more than one type of melanoma may be involved).

Unfortunately, studies such as one cited cannot prove or disprove that quantitative inheritance is responsible for the observed data. They can only suggest this as a plausible explanation. Indeed, the authors show that almost all the observed incidence in their parent–offspring pairs could be attributed to the segregation of a simple recessive with $q = 0.005$, a gene frequency more than adequate to account for the observed frequency of this disease in the population. The pedigree data do not exist to confirm such a hypothesis, however.

One cannot leave the subject of genetics of cancer without noting again the intriguing—and ever-increasing—data concerning association of chromosomal aberrations and neoplasms. The strongest of these is the correlation of chronic myelocytic leukemia and the so-called "Philadelphia chromosome," usually via a 22:9 translocation (Chapter 4). A similar association exists between translocations involving 8q24 and lymphomas of the Burkitt type. Most of these are t(8q;14q), less often t(8q;2p) or t(8q;22q). Many of these lymphomas are being encountered in proven or presumed cases of AIDS (acquired immunodeficiency syndrome). We have noted also that some cases of retinoblastoma, Wilms tumor, and a urinary bladder cancer are associated with deletions, some not cytologically visible (Chapters 4 and 6). Noteworthy also, albeit with less consistency, is the association of meningioma with 22q− and some ovarian neoplasia with abnormalities of chromosome 1, particularly its heterochromatin. Possibly related also is the unusual susceptibility of trisomy-21 patients to leukemia.

The neoplastic cells of acute leukemias also often contain chromosomal abnormalities. These are diverse, involving nearly every chromosome, but as the reports are sorted out three chromosomes stand out as most commonly affected: numbers 7, 8, and 9, usually as trisomies or partial trisomies. Chromosomes 4, 12, 15, and 16, on the other hand, are only rarely abnormal in these conditions. It is possibly pertinent that two of the most affected chromosomes, 7 and 9, contain the preferential attachment sites of viruses that have been suspect in the etiology of malignant transformations, those of herpes and SV-40, respectively, and chromosome 9 (as well as number 1) contains attachment sites of adenovirus-12. Chromosomes 1 and 7 are also among the chromosomes with a significant excess of breaks in Fanconi pancytopenia, which, as noted in Table 17–2, has a predisposition to leukemia.

Another fascinating aspect of this story is the relationship of chromosomal abnormality to resistance to methotrexate, one of the most widely used antimetabolites in cancer chemotherapy. Very often cells exhibiting such resistance contain expanded homogeneously staining regions in elongated chromosomes (Fig. 17–3A) or multiple small bodies of extrachromosomal DNA known as "double minutes" (Fig. 17–3B). The "double minutes" are broken up enlarged homogeneously staining regions, and both phenomena apparently represent multiple copies ("amplification") of genes codings for dihydrofolate reductase, which decreases a cell's binding affinity to methotrexate. If the cells are in the "double minute" stage, sensitivity to the drug can be restored by temporarily withdrawing it. "Double minutes," lacking centromeres, are not passed on equally during cell division. Hence, in the absence of the drug, which favors them, the cells containing many are gradually replaced (a sort of natural selection) by cells containing few or none. The cells with enlarged regions divide normally, however, whether drug is present or not.

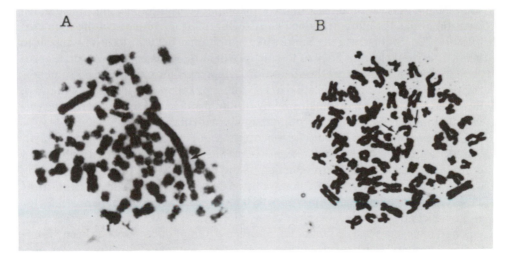

Fig. 17-3 Chromosomal aberrations in methotrexate resistance. **A.** Enlarged homogeneously staining region (HSR) in a human breast cancer cell line. **B.** Double Minutes (the small dotlike structures) in a human lung oat-cell carcinoma line. (From Jolivet et al., 1983, **B** after Curt et al., 1983; courtesy of G. A. Curt and *The New England Journal of Medicine*.)

Finally, there is the fascinating discovery recently of *oncogenes* on human chromosomes. These are DNA sequences in normal cells and in some, possibly all, tumor cells that are homologous to the "transforming" genes of certain oncogenic retroviruses (that is, RNA viruses that can use reverse transcriptase to make DNA). To distinguish between the cellular and the viral forms of these oncogenes, the prefix "c-" or "n-" (nuclear) is often added to the name of the former, whereas the latter receive the prefix "v-." It is remarkable that the same DNA sequences should be present in such diverse forms of life as viruses, on the one hand, and sponges, *Drosophila,* birds, and mammals, on the other; it is perhaps even more remarkable that under certain conditions they should have such a similar property: to be capable of "transforming" certain tissue culture cells, that is, causing them to grow in a multilayered jumble resembling the *in vitro* growth of cancer cells rather than the regular monolayer growth of normal cells.

The c-oncogene sequences are, as stated earlier, normal constituents of their chromosomes in which case they are often termed *protooncogenes,* becoming oncogenic under special circumstances that are not yet understood. The locus is named for the virus in which the homologous sequence occurs. One, for example, is called the c-*abl* homolog locus (CABL) because the sequence was first found in the Abelson murine sarcoma virus. In humans n-*abl* is located near the tip of 9q. At this writing, close to 50 oncogenes have been localized on human chromosomes, at least one on every chromosome except 4, 10, 16, and the Y. Chromosome 1 alone has ten such sites, and one form, *myc,* has sites on 3 different chromosomes.

Particularly interesting are oncogenes localized to chromosomal bands that are involved in the translocations or other aberrations associated with neoplasms. In several cases the aberrations bring these bands into new proximity to those containing the structural loci for parts of the immuglobulin molecules on chromosomes 2, 14, and 22. In the case of the Philadelphia chromosome, the typical translocation brings the aforementioned c-*abl* oncogene from 9q close to the Ig-related locus on 22q. Similarly in the Burkitt-like lymphomas the translocations appear to bring a *myc* oncogene at 8q24 to the vicinity of an Ig locus on 14q, 2p, or 22q. An attractive hypothesis is that the aberration derepresses the oncogene and somehow this causes increased multiplication of Ig-producing cells. It should be kept in mind, however, that each band contains many hundreds of genes, so one cannot be certain that these relationships are more than coincidental.

The products of a number of oncogene sequences have been identified. In some cases transforming ability seems to stem from production of an abnormal product, in others from overproduction of the usual product, the latter suggesting mutation in a regulatory gene. Some oncogenes produce substances identical or closely related to various human growth factors, such as epidermal growth factor and platelet growth factor. No clear connection exists, however, between these factors and oncogenesis. The product in another group of oncogenes has been identified as a protein kinase (phosphorylating enzyme), but how it functions in the normal and/or tumor cell is at this time not known. An oncogene from a human bladder cancer has been found to differ from its normal allele in a single codon, GCC (for glycine) being changed to GTC (for valine). This suggests that simple mutation, perhaps by a mutagenic chemical, is sufficient to set off the whole tumor-producing process. (This would also explain why so many mutagenic agents are also carcinogens.) While such a simplified view of oncogenesis is very attractive, it should be pointed out that, as mentioned earlier, carcinogenesis is generally recognized to be a multiphasic phenomenon.

Oncogenes are also proving to be useful diagnostic and prognostic aids. They can help to distinguish similar tumors with different degrees of disease severity. The extent of *myc* amplification in childhood neuroblastomas, for example, can be very meaningful in determining the kind of treatment to be applied.

As the bits and pieces of the puzzle come together, they appear to indicate that genetics plays an even more fundamental role in oncogenesis than had been realized.

18

Genetic Counseling: Prenatal Diagnosis and Empiric Risk

The deeply human problems of parents who have had a defective child have largely determined the nature of genetic counseling in the past. More than 90 percent of persons seeking genetic counseling fall into this category, and their problems will certainly continue to influence the development of the discipline.

Such parents want to know whether or not they should have any more children. They want to know what the risks are, and it should at once be made clear that the genetic counselor is often unable to offer clear-cut, unequivocal answers. No rule-of-thumb judgments, of course, can be made since every case will almost certainly be unique, owing to the complexity of the variables involved. Troubled patients need a dispassionate and balanced statement, drawn from the history they have provided, of probable risks in any subsequent births. Such a statement should not include advice for or against further childbearing. This is a decision which those who have been responsible enough to seek genetic counseling must make for themselves. It is the responsibility of the genetic counselor to supply all relevant available information and to dispel ignorance, factual error, and superstition. It is a common experience that the mere statement of facts can reduce anxiety and alleviate the discord that may have arisen between parents who blame each other for the birth of a defective child.

Still, the genetic findings in individual cases can be very disturbing. Presented with them, parents and society are confronted with the problem of choosing the best course of action under the circumstances. Genetic counseling must be conceived as something a great deal more than the simple presentation of risk facts and figures. Its aim must be that of medicine in general: the prevention and cure of disease, the relief of pain, and the maintenance of health. The quality of human life, emotional health, individual and family integrity, compassion, and an understanding of the tragic element in life are some of the factors that must be borne in mind by the counselor. Guilt feelings must be assuaged, recrimination between spouses obviated or dispelled. Irrational behavior and emotional behavior can be met and made manageable by a rational and authoritative exposition of the causes and nature of the disorder that is of concern.

410

PREVENTIVE GENETICS

With prophylactic counseling or preventive genetics a great many incipient conditions could be recognized and prevented from further damaging development. For example, even under present conditions, when an individual is found to have a heritable disorder, examination of other members of the extended family may turn up individuals in whom the disorder is not yet expressed, and who may be advised, by taking the proper measures, say as in glaucoma, to head off the damaging effects that could result from failure to recognize the condition early enough. Philosophers are not yet kings, and geneticists do not know the answers to many of the questions they are asked, but one thing is certain: Tragedies could have been avoided for numberless human beings had heredity counseling been available to them.

As illustrative of what can be done by way of general preventive genetics, in some communities with a high frequency of certain deleterious genes that in double dose result in fatal hereditary disorders, preventative genetic programs have already been successfully instituted, and as a consequence there has been a significant decrease in the occurrence of these disorders. For example, in some of the townships in the district of Ferrara, Italy a beta-thalassemia gene is present in one out of five persons. In the homozygous state these genes may lead to the development of a fatal thalassemia major (Cooley's anemia). A rigorous system of testing, especially of schoolchildren, makes it possible to determine the heterozygotes displaying the less serious form of the disorder, thalassemia minor, and hence to warn all such individuals against the danger of marrying anyone with the same condition. Since thalassemia genes are widely distributed throughout the Mediterranean, the Middle East, India, and the Orient, and are present in moderate frequency in Canada, the United States, and in certain parts of England, they pose a very real problem, the more especially because it is easily mistaken for iron deficiency anemia.

A developing and valuable arm of preventive genetics is carrier detection. It is now possible, in many cases, to detect the carriers of deleterious recessives in the heterozygous condition by biochemical and other means, and every year such tests are being developed for more and more disorders.

Another development in preventive genetics is the increasing use of techniques for examination of the genetic status of the fetus *in utero*. Most frequently this is done by sampling of the contents of the amniotic fluid from the uterus, usually by transabdominal *amniocentesis* (Fig. 18–1). Although possible at any stage of pregnancy, the quantity of fluid available and the increased risk to the fetus makes it impractical to use this procedure before the twelfth week of gestation. Likewise, the general reluctance to perform an abortion, were one to be desired, that late in gestation usually makes it impractical to do after the eighteenth week.

The cumulative experience of prenatal detection centers summarized in Table 18–1 has been that early amniocentesis entails minimal risks and complications. About 5 percent of the time amniotic fluid is not obtained at the first attempt. When fluid is obtained, about 1 to 2 percent of the time the cells in it fail to grow. Spontaneous abortion followed early amniocentesis in 149 of the 10,754 patients in Table 18–1 (1.4 percent). The authors of the table believe this reflects "serious

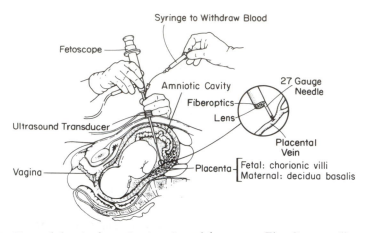

Fig. 18-1 Transabdominal amniocentesis and fetoscopy. The diagram illustrates fetoscopy, which involves introduction of a fiberoptic needlescope in a cannula that is 2.7
mm in its largest dimension. It is equipped with a fiberoptic lens for viewing the fetus
and a 26- or 27-gauge needle that goes through a sidearm in the cannula. The needle is
connected to a syringe for drawing the blood (as little as 10 to 50 microliters is usually
sufficient) from the placental vein located by the fiberoptic lens. Ultrasound is used to
localize the placenta and to grossly guide the procedure. In ordinary amniocentesis a
much smaller cannula can be used as one needs only to introduce a needle into the
amniotic sac to withdraw some amniotic fluid. (Modified from Alter, 1979, after Nadler,
1975; courtesy of B. P. Alter, H. L. Nadler, and the *Journal of Pediatrics*.)

underreporting," since this is lower than the well-documented spontaneous abortion rate of 2 to 3 percent between the weeks 14 and 18 of gestation. They state that
in a long-range NIH study on safety and accuracy the age-adjusted fetal loss rate
was 3.3 percent in women who had undergone amniocentesis and 3.4 percent in
controls.

Table 18-1 gives insight also into the indications that warrant using amniocentesis. Most of the cases relate to the possibility of chromosomal aberration. The
test is used either to check on possible recurrence or as a preventive measure in
cases of increased risk, such as advanced age of the mother or knowledge that one
of the parents is the carrier of a translocation. Another large group concerns the
recessive X-linked disorders. Here it may not even be necessary to be able to identify the specific malady. It may be sufficient to know whether the fetus is a male
who, therefore, has a 50 percent risk when the mother is known to be heterozygous.

In an increasing number of patients the test is able to detect the presence of
specific metabolic disorders (Table 18-2). Some are detectable by the absence or
low activity of an enzyme in the amniotic fluid or in the suspended cells. In most
cases, however, the analysis is made on a cell culture derived from the specimen.

At first the number of conditions detectable in this way seemed restricted to
those in which the pertinent enzyme was present in the fluid or in the amniotic
cells, and this number has been growing steadily. Recent developments in molecular biology that enable geneticists to analyze directly portions of the DNA (Chapters 6 and 13) have greatly increased the scope of amniocentesis. These methods

permit detection, for example, of the deletion thalassemias (Chapter 14). Also, genes that normally do not function in the culturable amniotic cells (usually fibroblasts) can often be induced to function following hybridization of these cells with certain tumor cells (hybridomas). Further increases in the number and kinds of cases diagnosable prenatally have come from increasing skills of obstetricians and other in obtaining blood samples and skin samples of the fetus by fetoscopy (Fig. 18–1), although, as we noted before, the new molecular techniques obviate most of the earlier needs for these riskier procedures.

Amniocentesis and associated procedures are greatly aided by increasing use of ultrasound (Fig. 18–2) and other advancing techniques in multidimensional imaging that enable the clinician to localize the placenta and many fetal structures. These techniques can themselves be the agents of prenatal diagnosis for such conditions as neural tube defects. The most common conditions covered by this rubric are spina bifida and anencephaly (Fig. 18–2), but it includes also hydrocephaly, myelomeningocele, meningocystocele, and similar abnormalities. Note that these account for over 15 percent of the indications for amniocentesis (Table 18–1), usually because of a previous occurrence of one of these conditions in the family. Often the first indication of a problem is an elevated alpha-fetoprotein level in the mother's serum. Amniocentesis can then determine the level of this substance in the fetus. There is a high frequency of false positives, but ultrasound can in many cases determine not only whether a problem exists but how serious it might be. This is very important because infants born with relatively mild lesions, and even some with extensive spina bifida, can grow up to lead useful lives after surgical closure.

Table 18-1   A compilation of the cumulative experience of prenatal detection centers in diagnosing fetal abnormalities (From Epstein and Golbus, 1977)

Indication	Pregnancies Studied	Affected Fetuses Found[a]
Chromosomal		
Translocation carriers	290	29 (10.0%)
Maternal age ≤35 years	3,012	79 (2.6%)
>40 years	864	36 (4.2%)
35–39 years	979	16 (1.6%)
Previous trisomy 21	1,887	23 (1.2%)
Miscellaneous	1,284	26 (2.0%)
X-linked diseases	429	199[b] (46.4%)
Biochemical defects	438	106 (24.2%)
Neural-tube defects	1,571[c]	86[d] (5.6%)
Total	10,754	610 (5.7%)

[a]For X-linked diseases, all males, whether actually known to be affected or not, are listed as affected.

[b]One trisomy 21 fetus is included.

[c]Since individuals from a family with a history of neural-tube defects are at a 4–5% risk of having children with such a defect, they are the ones referred for prenatal diagnosis.

[d]Another 10 fetuses with neural-tube defects found when amniocentesis was performed for other genetic indications are not included.

Table 18–2   Some enzymes that may be detected by antenatal procedures (Based largely on Nadler, 1972a and Milunsky et al., 1970, which should be consulted for references; see also Milunsky, 1976)

Enzyme	Associated Disorder
N-acetyl-a-acetylglucosaminidase	Sanfilippo syndrome B
β-D-N-acetylglucosaminidase	Sanfilippo syndrome C
Acid lipase	Wolman disease
Acid phosphatase	Acid phosphatase deficiency
Adenosine deaminase	Agammaglublinemia, complete
Adenylate pyrophosphate phosphoribosyl transferase	Congenital hyperuricemia
Aldolase	Hereditary fructose intolerance
Alkaline phosphatase	Hypophosphatasia (some types)
Amylo-1,6-glucosidase	Glycogen storage III
Arginase	Argininemia
Argininosuccinase (ASAase)	Argininosuccinicaciduria
Argininosuccinic acid synthetase	Citrollinemia
Arylsulfatase A	Metachromatic leukodystrophy
Arylsulfatase B	Maroteaux–Lamy syndrome
Branched-chain ketoacid decarboxylase	Maple sugar urine disease
Brancher enzyme	Glycogen storage IV
Ceramide trihexosidase	Fabry's disease
Cystathionine synthase	Homocystinuria
DNA repair enzyme (UV endonuclease)	Xeroderma pigmentosum
α-Fucosidase	Fucosidosis
Galactocerebroside-β-galactosidase	Krabbe's disease
α-Galactosidase	See ceramide trihexosidase
β-Galactosidase	Generalized gangliosidosis
Galactokinase	Galactokinase deficiency
Galactose-1-PO$_4$ uridyl transferase	Galactosemia
Glucocerebrosidase	Gaucher's disease, prenatal
Glucose-6-phosphate dehydrogenase	G6PD deficiency (favism, etc)
α-1,4-Glucosidase	Glycogen storage II
β-Glucosidase	Gaucher's disease, adult
β-Glucuronidase	Mucopolysaccharidosis VII
Heparan sulfate sulfatase	Sanfilippo syndrome A
Hexosaminidase A	Tay–Sachs disease
Hexosaminidase A and B	Sandhoff disease
C21-hydroxylase	Adrenocortical hyperplasia III
Hypoxanthine guanine phosphoribosyl transferase	Lesch–Nyhan syndrome
α-L-Iduronidase	Hurler (mucopolysacch. I)
α-L-iduronic acid-2-sulfatase	Hunter (mucopolysacch. II)
Lysozymal enzymes, multiple	I-cell disease
α-Mannosidase	Mannosidosis
Methylmalonyl-coA isomerase	Methylmalonic aciduria
Ornithine transcarbamylase	Hyperammonemia II
Ornithine-α-ketoacid transaminase	O-α-ka-t deficiency
Orotidylic pyrophosphorylase and decarboxylase	Orotic aciduria
Phytanic acid α-hydroxylase	Refsum's disease
Placental sulfatase	Placental sulfatase deficiency

Table 18-21 (*continued*)

Enzyme	Associated Disorder
Propionyl coA carboxylase	Ketotic hyperglycinemia
Pyrurate decarboxylase	Intermittent ataxia
Sphingomyelinase	Niemann–Pick disease
Sufatide sulfatase	Mucopolysaccharidosis III?
Uroporphyrinogen I synthetase	Acute intermittent porphyria
Valine transaminase	Valinemia

Although they are not frequent, the diagnostic errors that occur in amniocentesis merit some discussion. Occasionally it turns out that the cultured cells were maternal, rather than fetal, in origin. More serious are misdiagnoses leading to the therapeutic abortion of normal fetuses. There were six such instances (0.06 percent) in the Table 18–1 material. In addition, there were seven errors (0.07 percent) in which a fetus was diagnosed as being unaffected but after delivery was found to be abnormal. Most of the errors occurred very early in the cumulative experience and can be avoided with current methodology. However, even if technological errors are eliminated completely, problems of interpretation will remain. In the most difficult to resolve cases the same fluid produces both a chromosomally normal population and an abnormal one. In some instances the fetus is indeed a mosaic of both normal and abnormal cells, but in others it is not, the abnormal cells being artifactual in origin.

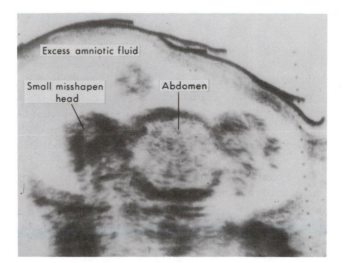

Fig. 18-2 Example of ultrasound scanning or sonography, a technique similar to radar, using the reflection of sound waves to measure distances and density. In this sonogram of an anencephalic fetus *in utero* the head is seen to be small and misformed and there is a compensatory excess of amniotic fluid. Normally the head and abdominal diameters are approximately equal. (From Epstein and Golbus, 1977; courtesy of M. S. Golbus and *American Scientist*.)

One of the greatest problems attendant on amniocentesis is the emotional strain on the parents and the rest of the family when there is a positive finding. The incidence of depression and other psychological sequelae of selective abortion is greater than that usually associated with elective abortion for psychosocial reasons or with delivery of a stillborn. Nevertheless, most of the families in one such study indicated that they would repeat their course of action and considered selective abortion preferable to the birth of a defective child.

Chorionic Villus Sampling

Chorionic villus sampling is a new antenatal procedure that produces results earlier than amniocentesis. It can be done between the 8th and 12th week of pregnancy and its results can be known soon after that. Because the chorion consists entirely of embryonic tissue, the cells should reflect the genetic makeup of the fetus. The villus sample may be obtained from the developing placenta transabdominally, as in amniocentesis, or transcervically, via the vagina, by means of a biopsy forceps or a flexible catheter, assisted by sonography. These routes may be visualized from Figs. 18–1 and 15–9, the aim being to reach the placenta after passing through the decidua basalis. The procedure is not without problems, however. Fetal loss and inaccuracies due to presence of maternal (decidual) cells seem to be more common than in amniocentesis. In addition it cannot be used to measure alpha-fetoprotein or other chemicals found in amniotic fluid. The technique gives promise, nevertheless, of becoming an important adjunct or alternative to amniocentesis.

EMPIRIC RISK FIGURES

In Chapter 15 we mentioned that in a certain number of disorders the combination of probable multifactorial inheritance and environmental factors (which include embryologic mishaps) plays such a large role, that no clear-cut statement of Mendelian expectation can be made. Unfortunately, this is particularly true of, some of the most frequent disorders in which heredity plays a part, such as hydrocephalus, diabetes, cleft lip, cleft palate, congenital dislocation of the hip, and many others. In these situations, empiric risk figures substitute for genetic ratios in counseling.

Empiric risk figures are derived from the study of family histories for a particular condition. For example, in a study of congenital dislocation of the hip, 320 affected individuals of normal parents have 666 siblings of whom 25 exhibit the condition. The empiric risk of the condition being repeated among the siblings of an affected individual is therefore 3.8 percent.

In the use of empiric risk figures it is necessary to bear in mind that factors such as age of mother, parity, age of father, and complications of pregnancy are in some cases capable of affecting these figures. Furthermore, empiric risk figures are based on samplings obtained from particular geographic populations. Each of these is comprised of individuals with high, low, and intermediate risks, and the relative proportions of these classes of risk in the population is unknown. Hence, empiric risk figures have been described as a measure of our ignorance. There are, however, degrees of ignorance, and refinement of our empiric risk figures is gradually and progressively occurring.

Empiric risk figures represent a useful aid in genetic counseling, but it must be clearly understood that in most cases they represent very rough approximations of the likelihood that under particular circumstances a certain condition is likely to occur in a particular individual. Empiric risk figures can never be a substitute for accurate etiologic diagnosis, since risks are based only on the knowledge of the outcome of cases involving similarly affected families and not on the knowledge of the genetic or environmental mechanisms that are operating. In particular there may be great variation in the incidence and relative risks among national, racial, or ethnic groups.

Empiric risk figures available for several conditions are presented in Table 18–3. For want of better data, the overall incidence of a trait is usually considered the risk figure when no one in the kindred is known to have been affected. The figure is obviously too high for most families because it is weighted by the few families of unusually high risk. When there is an affected individual in the kindred, the risk figure is more properly termed an estimate of recurrence risk, though some would limit that term to the likelihood of another birth with the trait in the same sibship.

Several important characteristics of multifactorially inherited traits should be kept in mind during counseling for conditions such as those in Table 18–3.

1. The rarer the trait in the population, the greater the risk to relatives. Rarity of the trait means that the particular set of genes needed to express the trait do not come together very often, but when they do it stands to reason that they would be more likely to come together again in a relative of the affected person than in an outsider. In addition, the pertinent environmental variables are more likely to recur in members of the same kindred, who tend to share food habits, marital customs, climatic factors, etc., including perhaps susceptibility to virus infections.

Almost all of the other points may be considered corollaries of at least the genetic aspects of the first one. They are:

2. The rarer the trait in the population, the greater the difference in risk between first- and second-degree relatives and between second- and third-degree relatives.

3. The more severe the malformation in the proband, the greater the risk to relatives. Note the difference in Hirschsprung's disease when a long segment is involved (severe) and when a short segment is involved.

4. If there is a sex difference in frequency of the trait, risks will be higher to relatives of affected members of the less frequently affected sex—because it takes a much greater concentration of the genes to affect the sex in which the trait is rarer. This is most clearly seen in the statistics for congenital pyloric stenosis (Table 18–3). The trait appears about five times more often in males than in females, but the relatives of the affected females are at greater risk than those of the affected males. Note, however, that it is in either event the *male* relatives that are at greatest risk, since it takes ostensibly fewer of the genes to go over the threshold in the male. The opposite situation would occur in congenital dislocation of the hip, but the data are not as extensive.

5. The risk to relatives of the proband are higher if other members of the

Table 18-3 Empiric risk figures (in percent) for some conditions in which there is probably a substantial multifactorial inheritance component. A = affected; M = male; F = female; Par = parent; x° = relative of xth degree affected

Condition	Risk to	Sex Ratio M:1F	Incidence[a] (0 Relat. A)	1 Sib A — M	1 Sib A — F	1 Par A — M	1 Par A — F	All 1° A — M	All 1° A — F	2° A — M	2° A — F	3° A — M	3° A — F	2 Par A
Anencephaly (see neural tube defects)														
Cleft lip (± cleft palate)			0.1	4.0		4.0								
Cleft palate			0.04	2.0		6.0								
Clubfoot	All	1.8	0.12	3.9		1.4		3.1		0.61		0.2		
	M			3.5				2.4	0					
	F			6.1	5.9			6.2	2.5					
Congenital dislocation of the hip	All	0.27	0.1	3.75		4.85		3.90		1.77		.50		
	M		0.02	23.5	0.9									
	F		0.08	5.6	4.6									
Congenital heart defects														
Atrial septal defect	All		0.5	3		3		3						
Pat. Duct. arteriosus	All		0.05	1.52		1.68								
Diabetes	All		1.3	4.7		11.4								16.0
Hirschsprung disease	All		0.01											
Short segment		4.7	0.008	3.1				3.1		0.26		0		
Long segment		1.5	0.002	12.7				12.7		0.4?		1.5		
Hydrocephalus			0.2	1.6										
Manic-depressive psychosis		0.9	0.4	9–12		12–16								
Neural tube defects (mainly spina bifida and anencephaly)[b]	All	0.55	0.29	4.45						1.67		0.54		
	M		0.21	2.3	3.9					2.1	4.1	0.9	0.7	
	F		0.38	4.9	6.3					0.4	0	0.2	0.3	
Pyloric stenosis	All	5.	0.30	4.3		6.1								
	M		0.50	3.8	9.2	5.5	18.9							
	F		0.10	2.7	3.8	2.4	7.0							
Spina bifida (see neural tube defects)														
Schizophrenia (by age 55)	All	~1	1.	9.70		7.2				3.28				46.3

[a]Figures are complicated by substantial age effects which are not shown here. Also many of the "All" data here and in other columns are composites of data that are heterogenous; shown here for heuristic purposes.

[b]Many forms can now be diagnosed prenatally by the elevation of alpha-fetoprotein, en embryonic α_1-globulin, in the amniotic fluid (Seller, 1974).

kindred are known to be affected. This is another way of saying that the combination of genes is more definitely clustered here.

The violation of some of these points in the data on schizophrenia and manic-depressive psychoses (especially the greater risk in parent affected vs. sib affected) is partially responsible for the claims that major epistatic loci are more important in the genetic portion of their etiologies than are polygenes.

It is important to communicate empiric risk figures in such a manner to clients that they clearly understand the meaning of them. Many people have, for example, heard that maternal age is associated with the incidence of "mongolism" and that the incidence rises with the age of the mother. They have taken this to mean that the older mother is more likely to have a "mongoloid" child than she is to have a normal one. Actually, Down's syndrome happens to be in the very low risk class no matter how old the mother is, and this should be emphasized with unequivocal clarity. Even if a mother is over 45 years of age, her chance of giving birth to a Down's child in the absence of a translocated number 21 is about 1 in 45, or less than 3 percent. Such figures, however, need more positive statement. In other words, when the figures for risk per pregnancy (which may be considered the percent recurrence risk in the absence of translocation of number 21) have been given, these should be completed by the more positive statement that the chance of a normal baby being born to a mother in that age group is more than 97 percent.

SUGGESTED EXERCISES

18-1. In the family reported by Schrott et. al. (1973) the proband was a 21-year-old woman who presented to a medical genetics clinic in the thirteenth week of her second pregnancy inquiring whether there was any chance that her children might develop muscular dystrophy. The family history revealed that three maternal uncles and four maternal cousins suffered from Steinert's disease. Her mother was diagnosed as having the condition only after the discovery of an advanced state of this disorder in her son, the proband's brother. Physical examination revealed that the proband herself is affected, but her husband and father are normal. The proband's mother is a nonsecretor, the proband and her father secretors, of ABH substances. The husband, too, is a secretor. His parents could not be tested, but two of his half-sisters (same mother) are nonsecretors. The proband agreed to amniocentesis. The Se and Steinert's loci are linked, with θ = about four percent.

(a) What were the *a priori* risks in this case, that is, without considering the linkage?

(b) If the amniocentesis had found that the fetus was a nonsecretor, what would you have told the proband as to relative odds for dystrophy?

(c) It turned out that the fetus was strongly secretor positive in the amniotic fluid. What would you say to the parents in the light of this result? (State maximum and minimum likelihood of dystrophy.)

(d) Comment on the value of amniocentesis in this case.

The following four exercises are paraphrased with a few modifications from material in Neel and Schull (1954).

18–2. A man, whose wife has just given birth to their first child, a son, has two older sisters, each of whom gave birth to a son with Tay–Sachs disease. Everyone else in the family is normal, including the two other children of one of the sisters. The sisters' husbands and the man's wife were not related to the family nor to each other, but his father and mother are first cousins. How would you answer the following questions?

    (a) If the sister who already has three children were to have a fourth, what are the chances that it would be normal?

    (b) What is the probability that his recently born child will develop the disease, knowing that the entire kindred consists of Ashkenazi Jews? Assume that the incidence of T–S in this group is 14.4×10^{-5} and that only one of the man's parents had the gene.

    (c) How would the answer to (b) change if both of the man's parents carried the gene?

    (d) In line with the data in (b), if the man's son proves normal and also marries an unrelated woman of Ashkenazi extraction, what would be the chances of *his* having a child with the disorder?

18–3. A six-month-old girl is up for adoption. Her mother has schizophrenia, but there is no other history of the disease in the family as far as can be determined. However, the maternal grandfather, two maternal aunts and a half-brother (by the same mother) of the child are known to suffer from a nerve-type deafness that is inherited as a dominant with 50 percent penetrance.

    (a) What is the probability that the child will develop schizophrenia?

    (b) What is the probability that she will develop the deafness?

    (c) What is the probability that the child will be normal in both respects?

18–4. Both children of a certain couple had died at an early age, the first of an atrial septal defect, a form of congenital heart disease, the second of cystic fibrosis. During the second pregnancy it was found that the wife was Rh negative and the husband's probable Rh genotype was R^1/r, and the wife developed a considerable titer of anti-Rh; however, the baby did not develop erythroblastosis fetalis, though it is nearly 100 percent certain in this case that any subsequent Rh positive child would.

Assuming that no prophylactic measures are instituted to guard against the recurrence of erythroblastosis, what is the probability that the couple's next child will be normal in all respects, including not having erythroblastosis?

18–5. A couple's first child, born when the mother was 25, appears normal. Their second child, born the next year, has Down's syndrome, the first case of the sort on either side of the family as far as is known. The couple had anticipated having a large family, but they are disturbed by the birth of the second child. They come to you for advice.

    (a) What would you advise them?

    (b) Could an appropriate risk figure be given at some point? Explain, being specific.

    (c) Their pediatrician has advised a "rest period" of three or four years before their having another child, with the implication that the birth of the Down's child was related to "maternal reproductive exhaustion." What do you think of such advice in this situation? Explain.

18–6. Suppose you were investigating a pedigree of multiple polyposis of the colon (see exercise 8–1). In one sibship a widow free of the disease has six progeny, all apparently normal with respect to this trait. Shortly after the birth of the sixth child her husband, whose mother had been affected with the disease, had died. Two of his three siblings were known to be affected, the other one normal. Prior to his death he had passed some blood per rectum but refused to get medical treatment. How would you evaluate his position in the pedigree?

References*

Aguilar, L., R. Lisker, and G. G. Ramos. 1978. Unusual inheritance of Becker muscular dystrophy. *J. Med. Genet.,* 15:116–118.

Alter B. P. 1979. Prenatal diagnosis of hemoglobinopathies and other hematologic diseases. *J. Pediat.,* 95:501–513.

Alter, M. 1966. Dermatoglyphic analysis as a diagnostic tool. *Medicine,* 46:35–56.

Arnoldsson, H., L. Bellin, L. Hallberg, E. Helander, B. Lindholm, and H. Westling. 1967. Hereditary periodic oedema. *Acta Med. Scand.,* 181:115–124.

Bach, F. H., and J. J. van Rood. 1976. The major histocompatibility complex–genetics and biology. *New Engl. J. Med.,* 295:927–936.

Baglioni, C. 1962. The fusion of two peptide chains in hemoglobin Lepore and its interpretation as a gene deletion. *Proc. Natl. Acad. Sci.* (U.S.), 48:1880–1886.

Bailey, N.T.J. 1951. The estimation of the frequencies of recessives with incomplete multiple selection. *Ann. Eugen.,* 16:215–222.

Bannerman, R. M., and J. H. Renwick, 1962. The hereditary elliptocytoses: clinical and linkage data. *Ann. Hum. Genet.,* 26:23–38.

Barr, M. L. 1957. Cytologic tests of chromosomal sex. *Prog. Gynecol.,* 3:131–141.

Barr, M. L. 1960. Sexual dimorphism in interphase nuclei. *Am. J. Hum. Genet.,* 12:118–127.

Barr, M. L. 1966. The sex chromosomes in evolution and in medicine. *Can. Med. Assn. J.,* 95:1137–1148.

Bell, J. 1926. Colour-blindness. Eugenics Laboratory Memoirs, 23. *The Treasury of Human Inheritance* (U. of London: Frances Galton Lab. Natl. Eugenics), 2(2):125–167.

Bemiss, S. M. 1958. Report on influence of marriages of consanguinity upon offspring. *Trans. Am. Med. Assn.,* 11:319–425.

Beyer, W. H., ed. 1966. *C.R.C. Handbook of Tables for Probability and Statistics.* Cleveland, Ohio: Chemical Rubber Company.

Bloom, A. D., A. A. Awa, S. Neriishi, T. Honda, and P. G. Archer. 1967. Chromosome aberrations in leucocytes of older survivors of the atomic bombings of Hiroshima and Nagasaki. *Lancet,* 2:802–805.

Blumberg, B. S., L. Melartin, R. A. Guinto, and B. Werner. 1966. Family studies of a human serum isoantigen system (Australia antigen). *Am. J. Hum. Genet.,* 18:594–608.

*This reference list includes articles and books referred to in exercises, figure legends, and tables. Also included are the sources of new text items that mention their discoverers. More extensive references may be found in Levitan and Montagu (1977).

Boehm, C., and H. H. Kazazian, Jr. 1985. Prenatal diagnosis of hemaglobinopathies by DNA analysis. *CRC Crit. Rev. Oncol. Hematol.,* 4:155–167.

Boyer, S. H., ed. 1963. *Papers on Human Genetics.* Englewood Cliffs, N.J.: Prentice-Hall.

Bowen, P., C.N.S. Lee, C. J. Migeon, N. M. Kaplan, P. J. Whalley, V. A. McKusick, and E. C. Reifenstein. 1965. Hereditary male pseudohermaphroditism with hypogonadism, hypospadias, and gynecomastia (Reifenstein's Syndrome). *Ann. Int. Med.,* 62:252–270.

Bradley, T. B., Jr., S. H. Boyer, and F. H. Allen, Jr. 1961. Hopkins-2 hemoglobin: a revised pedigree with data on blood and serum groups. *Bull. Johns Hopkins Hosp.,* 108:75–79.

Brooks, W.D.W., M. A. Heasman, and R.R.H. Lovell. 1949. Retinitis pigmentosa associated with cystinuria: two uncommon inherited conditions occurring in a family. Lancet, 1:1096–1098.

Brown, M. S., and J. L. Goldstein. 1986. A receptor-mediated pathway for cholesterol hemeostasis. *Science,* 232:34–47. (Also in *Nobel Lectures* [Amsterdam and New York: Elsevier]).

Bunn, H. F., and B. G. Forget. 1986. *Hemoglobin: Molecular, Genetic, and Clinical Aspects.* Philadelphia: Saunders.

Burt, C. 1963. Is intelligence normally distributed? *Br. J. Stat. Psych.,* 16:175–190.

Cameron, A. H. 1968. The Birmingham twin survey. *Proc. Roy. Soc. Med.,* 61:229–234.

Carr, D. H., M. L. Barr, and E. R. Plunkett. 1961. An XXXX sex chromosome complex in two mentally defective females. *Can. Med. Assn. J.,* 84:131–137.

Carter, C. O. 1969. Genetics of common disorders. *Br. Med. Bull.,* 25:52–57.

Castel, Y., R. Masse, J. Roche, and J. Mollaret. 1967. Sur un cas de poïkilodermie congénitale de Thomson. *Ouest-Médical,* 20:890–896.

Caspersson, T., S. Farber, G. E. Foley, J. Kudynowski, E. J. Modest, E. Simonsson, U. Wagh, and L. Zech. 1968. Chemical differentiation along metaphase chromosomes. *Exptl. Cell Res.,* 49:219–222.

Chicago Conference. 1966. Standardization in human cytogenetics. *Birth Defects, Orig. Art. Ser.,* 2(2):3–9.

Childs, B., W. Zinkham, E. A. Brown, E. L. Kimbro, and J. V. Torbert. 1958. A genetic study of a defect in glutathione metabolism of the erythrocyte. *Bull. Johns Hopkins Hosp.,* 102:21–37.

Clarke, C. A. 1961. Blood groups and disease. *Prog. Med. Genet.,* 1:81–119.

Clarke, C. A., D. A. Price Evans, R. B. McConnell, and P. M. Sheppard, 1959. Secretion of blood group antigens and peptic ulcer. *Br. Med. J.,* 1:603–607.

Cook, P. J. L. 1975. The genetics of α_1-antitrypsin: a family study in England and Scotland. *Ann. Hum. Genet.,* 38:275–287.

Cooley, T. B., and P. Lee. 1925. A series of cases of splenomegaly in children, with anemia and peculiar bone changes. *Trans. Am. Pediat. Soc.,* 37:29–30.

Corliss, C. E. 1976. *Patten's Human Embryology: Elements of Clinical Development.* New York: McGraw-Hill.

Crow, J. F. 1983. *Genetics Notes.* 8th ed. Minneapolis: Burgess Publishing.

Crow, J. F., and J. V. Neel, eds. 1967. *Proceedings of the Third Int'l Congress of Human Genetics* (Chicago, Ill., Sept. 5–10, 1966). Baltimore: Johns Hopkins Press.

Curt, G. A., D. N. Carney, K. H. Cowan, J. Jolivet, B. D. Bailey, J. C. Drake, C. S. Kao-Shan, J. D. Minna, and B. A. Chabner. 1983. Unstable methotrexate resistance in human small-cell carcinoma associated with double minute chromosomes. *New Engl. J. Med.,* 308:199–202.

Dahlberg, G. 1929. Inbreeding in man. *Genetics,* 14:421–454.

Dahr, P. 1942. Ueber die bisher im Kölner Hygienishen Institut gewonnenen Untersuchungsergebnisse über das Blutmerkmal P. *Ztschr. Immunitätsforsch. Exp. Therapie,* 101:346–355.

Davenport, C. B., and A. G. Love, 1921. *The Medical Department of the U.S. Army in the World War. vol. 15: Statistics. Part I: Army anthropology.* Washington, D.C.: Government Printing Office.

De George, F. V., and R. L. Fisher, 1967. Idiopathic scoliosis: genetic and environmental aspects. *J. Med. Genet.,* 4:251–257.

Dewey, W. J., I. Barrai, N. E. Morton, and M. P. Mi. 1965. Recessive genes in severe mental defect. *Am. J. Hum. Genet.,* 17:237–256.

Didisheim, P., and J. H. Lewis. 1958. Congenital disorders of the mechanism for coagulation of blood. *Pediat.,* 22:478–493.

Diehl, K., and O. von Verschuer. 1936. *Erbeneinfluss bei der Tuberkulose.* Jena: G. Fischer. (quoted by Lenz, 1963).

Donahue, R. P., W. B. Bias, J. H. Renwick, and V. A. McKusick, 1968. Probable assignment of the Duffy blood group locus to chromosome 1 in man. *Proc. Natl. Acad. Sci. (U.S.),* 61:949–955.

Dronamraju, K. R. 1965. The function of the Y-chromosome in man, animals, and plants. *Adv. Genet.,* 13:227–310.

El-Hefnawi, H., S. M. Smith, and L. S. Penrose. 1965. Xeroderma pigmentosum—its inheritance and relationships to the ABO blood-group system. *Ann. Hum. Genet.,* 28:273–290.

Ellman, L. I., and K. J. Bloch. 1968. Heavy chain disease. Report of a seventh case. *New Engl. J. Med.,* 278:1195–1201.

Epstein, C. J., and M. S. Golbus. 1977. Prenatal diagnosis of genetic diseases. *Am. Scientist,* 65:703–711.

Epstein, C. J., and A. G. Motulsky. 1965. Evolutionary origins of human proteins. *Prog. Med. Genet.,* 4:85–127.

Evans, D. A. Price, K. A., Manley, C. F., Merryman, M. A. Ferguson-Smith, and V. A. McKusick. 1959. Isoniazid inactivation—a genetically determined phenomenon. Program and Abstracts, *Am. Soc. Hum. Genet.* (Penn State U., Penn., Aug. 30–Sept. 3): 12 only.

Evans, D. A. Price, K. A. Manley, and V. A. McKusick, 1960. Genetic control of isoniazid metabolism in man. *Br. Med. J.,* 2:485–491.

Falconer, D. S. 1965. The incidence of liability to certain diseases, estimated from the incidence among relatives. *Ann. Hum. Genet.,* 29:51–71.

Ferguson-Smith, M. A. 1967. Clinical cytogenetics. In Crow and Neel (1967):69–71.

Ferguson-Smith, M. A., M. E. Ferguson-Smith, P. M. Ellis, and M. Dickson. 1962. The sites and relative frequencies of secondary constrictions in human somatic chromosomes. *Cytogenet.,* 1:325–343.

Fogh-Anderson, P. 1942. Inheritance of harelip and cleft palate. *Opera ex Domo Biologiae Hereditariae Humanae Universitatis Hafniensis,* 4:83.

de Fontenay, O. E. 1881. Results of examinations for colour-blindness in Denmark. *Arch. Ophthalmol.,* 10:8–19.

Ford, C. E., K. W. Jones, O. J. Miller, U. Mittwoch, L. S. Penrose, M. Ridler, and A. Shapiro. 1959a. The chromosomes in a patient showing both mongolism and the Klinefelter syndrome. *Lancet,* 1:709–710.

Ford, C. E., K. W. Jones, P. E. Polani, J. C. de Almeida, and J. H. Briggs. 1959b. A sex-chromosome anomaly in a case of gonadal dysgenesis (Turner's syndrome). *Lancet,* 1:711–713.

Forget, B. G. 1983. Normal and abnormal human globin genes. In Goldwasser, E., ed., *Regulation of Hemoglobin Biosynthesis* (New York: Elsevier-North Holland):27–40.

Fraccaro, M., H. P. Klinger, and W. Schutt. 1962. A male with XXXXY sex chromosomes. *Cytogenet.,* 1:52–64.

Fialkow, P. J., E. R. Giblett, and A. G. Motulsky. 1967. Measurable linkage between ocular albinism and Xg. *Am. J. Hum. Genet.,* 19:63–69.

Fisher, R. A. 1925. *Statistical Methods for Research Workers.* Edinburgh: Oliver and Boyd. Also later editions, the last being 1948.

Fisher, R. A., and F. Yates, 1949. *Statistical Tables for Biological, Agricultural and Medical Research.* Edinburgh: Oliver and Boyd, and New York: Hafner.

Freire-Maia, N. 1957a. Inbreeding levels in different countries. *Eugenical News (Eugen. Quart.),* 4:127–138.

Freire-Maia, N. 1957b. Inbreeding in Brazil. *Am. J. Hum. Genet.,* 9:284–298.

Fudenberg, H. H., J.R.L. Pink, D. P. Stites, and A.-C. Wang. 1972. *Basic Immunogenetics.* New York: Oxford U. Press.

Gall, J. C., G. J. Brewer, and R. J. Dern. 1965. Studies of glucose-6-phosphate dehydrogenase activity of individual erythrocytes: the methemoglobin-elution test for identification of females heterozygous for G6-PD deficiency. *Am. J. Hum. Genet.,* 17:359–368.

Gates, R. R. 1946. *Human Genetics.* 2 vols. New York: Macmillan.

Gearhart, P. J. 1982. Generation of immunoglobulin variable gene diversity. *Immunol. Today,* 3:107–112.

Gedda, L. 1951. *Studio dei Gemelli.* Rome: Edizioni Orizzonte Medico.

Gedde–Dahl, T., Jr. 1969. *Epidermolysis bullosa. A Clinical, Genetic, and Epidemiological Study.* Thesis. U. of Oslo. Also, Baltimore: Johns Hopkins Press (1971).

Gedde-Dahl, T., Jr., A. L. Grimstad, A. Gunderson, and E. Vogt. 1967. A probable crossover or mutation in the MNSs blood group system. *Acta Genet. Stat. Med.,* 17:193–210.

German, J. L., A. P. De Mayo, and A. G. Bearn. 1962. Inheritance of an abnormal chromosome in Down's syndrome (mongolism) with leukemia. *Am. J. Hum. Genet.,* 14:31–43.

Gershowitz, H., and J. V. Neel. 1965. The blood groups and secretor types in five potentially fatal diseases of Caucasian children. *Acta Genet. Stat. Med.,* 15:261–308.

Gilles, H. M., K. A. Fletcher, R. G. Hendrickse, R. Lindner, S. Reddy, and N. Allan. 1967. Glucose-6-phosphate-dehydrogenase deficiency, sickling, and malaria in African children in southwestern Nigeria. *Lancet,* 1:138–140.

Goodall, H. B., W. Guthrie, and N.R.M. Buist. 1965. Familial haemaphagocytic reticulosis. *Scot. Med. J.,* 10:425–438.

Gottesman, I. I., and J. Shields. 1982. *Schizophrenia, the Epigenetic Puzzle.* Cambridge and New York: Cambridge U. Press.

Graham, J. B., and R. W. Winters. 1961. Familial hypophosphatemia: an inherited demand for increased vitamin D. *Ann. N.Y. Acad. Sci.,* 91:667–673.

Gram, H. C. 1932. The heredity of oxalic urinary calculi. *Acta Med. Scand.,* 78:268–281.

Gripenberg, U. 1967. The cytological behavior of a human ring-chromosome. *Chromosoma,* 20:284–289.

Gusella, J. F., N. S. Wexler, P. M. Conneally, S. L. Naylor, M. A. Anderson, R. E. Tanzi, P. C. Watkins, K. Ottina, M. R. Wallace, A. Y. Sakaguchi, A. B. Young, I. Shoulson, E. Bonilla, and J. B. Martin. 1983. A polymorphic DNA marker genetically linked to Huntington's disease. *Nature,* 306:234–238.

Hamilton, J. B. 1951. Patterned loss of hair in man: types and incidence. *Ann. N.Y. Acad. Sci.,* 53:708–728.

Hamilton, M., G. W. Pickering, J. A. Fraser Roberts, and G.S.C. Sowry. 1954. The aetiology of essential hypertension. 2. Scores for arterial pressures adjusted for differences in age and sex. *Clin. Sci.,* 13:37–49.

Hansen, R. G., R. K. Bretthauer, J. Mayes, J. H. Nordin. 1964. Estimation of frequency of occurrence of galactosemia in the population. *Proc. Soc. Exp. Biol. Med.,* 115:560–563.

Harper, P. S., S. Youngman, M. A. Anderson, M. Sarfarazi, O. Quarrell, R. Tanzi, D. Shaw, P. Wallace, P. M. Conneally, and J. F. Gusella. 1985. Genetic linkage between Huntington's disease and the DNA polymorphism G8 in South Wales families. *J. Med. Genet.,* 22:447–450.

Harris, H., ed. 1963a. *Garrod's Inborn Errors in Metabolism.* London: Oxford U. Press.

Harris, H. 1963b. The "Inborn Errors" today. In Harris (1963a):120–197.

Harris, H. 1966. Enzyme polymorphisms in man. *Proc. Roy. Soc.* (London), B, 164:298–310.

Harris, H., and D. A. Hopkinson. 1972. Average heterozygosity per locus in man: an estimate based on the incidence of human polymorphisms. *Ann. Hum. Genet.,* 36:9–20.

Hemet, J., D. Lamachere, J. Forthomme, and J. Ensel. 1967. Trisomie 13 par aberration de structure. *Ann. d'Anat. Path. (Paris),* 12:101–104.

Herskowitz, I. H. 1973. *Principles of Genetics.* New York: Macmillan.

Holt, S. B. 1961. Inheritance of dermal ridge patterns. In Penrose (1961):101–119.

Holt, S. B. 1968. *The Genetics of Dermal Ridges.* Springfield, Ill.: C. C. Thomas.

Hongell, K. 1974. Chromosome investigations in 480 mentally retarded persons. *Hereditas,* 78:317 (Abstr.).

Honjo, T. 1982. The molecular mechanisms of the immunoglobulin class switch. *Immunol. Today,* 3:214–217.

Hsia, D.Y.-Y. 1966. *Inborn Errors of Metabolism.* 2nd ed. 2 vols. Chicago: Yearbook Med. Publs.

Hsia, D.Y.-Y., I. Huang, and S. G. Driscoll. 1958. The heterozygous carrier in galactosemia. *Nature,* 182:1389–1390.

Hsu, T. C. 1948. Tongue upfolding. A newly reported heritable character in man. *J. Hered.,* 39:187–188.

Huisman, T. H. 1972. Normal and abnormal human hemoglobins. *Adv. Clin. Chem.,* 15:149–253.

Hulten, M. J., J. Lindsten, P. L. Ming, and M. Fraccaro. 1966. The XY bivalent in human male meiosis. *Ann. Hum. Genet.,* 30:119–123.

Ikin, E. W., A. M. Prior, R. R. Race, and G. L. Taylor. 1939. The distributions in the A_1A_2BO blood group in England. *Ann. Eugen.,* 9:409–411.

Imamura, T. 1966. Hemoglobin Kagoshima: an example of hemoglobin Norfolk in a Japanese family. *Am. J. Hum. Genet.,* 18:584–593.

Ingram, V. 1963. *The Hemoglobins in Genetics and Evolution.* New York: Columbia U. Press.

Jacobs, P. A., A. G. Baikie, W. M. Court Brown, D. N. MacGregor, M. MacLean, and D. G. Harnden. 1959a. Evidence for the existence of the human "super-female." *Lancet,* 2:423–425.

Jacobs, P. A., A. G. Baikie, W. M. Court Brown, H. Forrest, J. R. Roy, J.S.S. Stewart, and B. Lennox. 1959b. Chromosomal sex in the syndrome of testicular feminization. *Lancet,* 2:591–592.

Jacobs, P. A., M. Brunton, M. M. Melville, R. P. Brittain, and W. F. McClemont. 1965.

Aggressive behavior, mental sub-normality and the XYY male. *Nature,* 208:1351–1352.

Jameson, R. J., S. D. Lawler, and J. H. Renwick. 1956. Nail-patella syndrome: clinical and linkage data on Family G. *Ann. Hum. Genet.,* 20:348–360.

Jolivet, J., K. H. Cowan, G. A. Curt, N. J. Clendeninn, and B. A. Chabner. 1983. The pharmacology and clinical use of methotrexate. *New Engl. J. Med.,* 308:1094–1102.

Kan, Y. W., and A. M. Dozy. 1978. Antenatal diagnosis of sickle-cell anaemia by DNA analysis of amniotic-fluid cells. *Lancet,* 2:910–912.

Kendall, M. G. 1947. *The Advanced Theory of Statistics.* 3rd ed. vol. 1. London: Griffin and Co.

Kerr, C. B. 1965. Genetics of human blood coagulation. *J. Med. Genet.,* 2:254–303.

Khachadurian, A., and K. Abu Feisal. 1958. Alkaptonuria. Report of a family with seven cases appearing in four successive generations, with metabolic studies in one patient. *J. Chronic Dis.,* 7:455–465.

Kindt, T. J., and J. D. Capra. 1984. *The Antibody Enigma.* New York and London: Plenum Press.

King, R. C. 1965. *Genetics.* 2nd ed. New York: Oxford U. Press.

Klinefelter, H. F., Jr., E. C. Reifenstein, Jr., and F. Albright. 1942. Syndrome characterized by gynecomastia, aspermatogenesis with a-Leydigism, and increased excretion of follicle-stimulating hormone. *J. Clin. Endocr.,* 2:615–627.

Knight, R. A., M. J. Selin, and H. W. Harris. 1959. Genetic factors influencing isoniazid blood levels in humans. *Trans. Conf. Chemotherapy Tuberculosis* (Washington, D.C.: U.S. Veterans Administration), 18:52–60.

Knox, W. E., and E. C. Messinger. 1958. The detection in the heterozygote of the metabolic defect of the recessive gene for phenylketonuria. *Am. J. Hum. Genet.,* 10:53–60.

Kohn, G., B. H. Mayall, M. E. Miller, and W. J. Mellman. 1967. Tetraploid-diploid mosaicism in a surviving infant. *Pediat. Res.,* 1:461–469.

Komai, T. 1934. *Pedigrees of Hereditary Diseases and Abnormalities in the Japanese Race.* Kyoto, Japan: Maruzen.

Lamy, M., J. Frézal, J. de Grouchy, and J. Kelley. 1957. Le nombre de dermatoglyphes dans un échantillon de jumeaux. *Ann. Hum. Genet.,* 21:374–396.

Lawler, S. D., J. H. Renwick, and L. S. Wildervanck. 1957. Further families showing linkage between the ABO and nail-patella loci, with no evidence of heterogeneity. *Ann. Hum. Genet.,* 21:410–419.

Leder, P. 1983. Genetic control of immunoglobulin production. *Hosp. Practice,* 18:73–82.

Lejeune, J., M. Gautier, and R. Turpin. 1959. Étude des chromosomes somatiques de neuf enfants mongoliens. *C. R. Acad. Sci. (Paris),* 248:1721–1722. Reprinted in Boyer (1963):238–240.

Lenz, W. 1963. *Medical Genetics.* Chicago: U. of Chicago Press.

Levene, H., and R. E. Rosenfield. 1961. ABO incompatibility. *Prog. Med. Genet.,* 1:120–157.

Levine, P. 1943. Serological factors as possible causes in spontaneous abortions. *J. Heredity,* 34:71–80.

Levine, P., E. Robinson, M. Celano, O. Briggs, and L. Falkinburg. 1955. Gene interaction resulting in suppression of blood group substance B. *Blood,* 10:1100–1108.

Levitan, M. 1964. The first thousand aberrations induced by a maternal factor: a progress report. *Genetics,* 50:265–266.

Levitan, M. 1973. Allergy. In Sorsby, A., ed., *Clinical Genetics,* 2nd ed. (London, But-terworths):560–567.

Levitan, M., and A. Montagu. 1971. *Textbook of Human Genetics.* New York: Oxford U. Press.

Levitan, M., and A. Montagu. 1977. *Textbook of Human Genetics.* 2nd ed. rev. by M. Levitan, New York: Oxford U. Press.

Li, F. P., and J. F. Fraumeni, Jr. 1969. Soft-tissue sarcomas, breast cancer and other neoplasms. *Ann. Int. Med.,* 71:747–752.

Li, F. P., and J. F. Fraumeni, Jr. 1975. Familial breast cancer, soft-tissue sarcomas and other neoplasms. *Ann. Int. Med.,* 83:833–834.

Lindsten, M. Fraccaro, D. Ikkos, K. Kaijser, H. P. Klinger, and R. Luft. 1963. Pre-sumptive iso-chromosomes for the long arm of X in man. Analysis of five fam-ilies. *Ann. Hum. Genet.,* 26:383–406.

Lundin, P. M., and I. Olow. 1961. Polycystic kidneys in newborns, infants, and chil-dren. *Acta Paed.,* 50:185–200.

Maroteaux, P., B. Levêque, J. Marie, and M. Lamy. 1963. Une nouvelle dysostose avec élimination urinaire de chondroitine-sulfate B. *Presse Médicale,* 71:1849–1852.

Marsh, D. G., D. A. Meyers, and W. B. Bias. 1981. The epidemiology and genetics of atopic allergy. *New Engl. J. Med.,* 305:1551–1559.

Marshall, J. S., R. P. Levy, and A. G. Steinberg. 1966. Human thyroxine-binding glob-ulin deficiency. A genetic study. *New Engl. J. Med.,* 274:1469–1473.

Marshall, R. C., C. T. Caskey, and M. Nirenberg. 1967. Fine structures of RNA code-words recognized by bacterial, amphibian, and mammalian transfer RNA. *Sci-ence,* 155:820–825.

Mason, M. K., D. A. Spencer, and A. Rutter. 1975. A case of partial (9p) trisomy in a family with a balanced translocation 46,XX,t(1p+9q−). *J. Med. Genet.,* 12:310–314.

McIntosh, R., K. K. Merritt, M. R. Richards, M. H. Samuels, and M. T. Bellows. 1954. The incidence of congenital malformations: a study of 5,694 pregnancies. *Pediat.,* 7:505–521.

McKusick, V. A. 1964. Approaches and methods in human genetics. *Am. J. Obstet. Gynecol.,* 90:1014–1023.

McKusick, V. 1972. *Heritable Disorders of Connective Tissue.* 4th ed. St. Louis: Mosby.

McKusick, V. A. 1978. *Mendelian Inheritance in Man: Catalogs of Autosomal Domi-nant, Autosomal Recessive, and X-Linked Phenotypes.* 5th ed. Baltimore: Johns Hopkins U. Press.

McKusick, V. A. 1983. *Mendelian Inheritance in Man: Catalogs of Autosomal Domi-nant, Autosomal Recessive, and X-Linked Phenotypes.* 6th ed. Baltimore: Johns Hopkins U. Press.

McKusick, V. A. 1986. The human gene map. *Clin. Sci.,* 29:545–588.

McKusick, V. A., R. A. Norum, H. J. Farkas, P. W. Brunt, and M. Mahloudji. 1967. The Riley-Day syndrome—observations on genetics and survivorship. *Israel J. Med. Sci.,* 3:372–379.

McNiel, J. R. 1967. Family studies of thalassemia in Arabia. *Am. J. Hum. Genet.,* 19:100–111.

Mendel, G. 1865 (published in 1866). Versuche über Pflanzen-hybriden. *Verh. Naturf. Verein Brünn,* 4:3–47. Royal Hort. Soc. (1901) translation reprinted by Harvard U. Press (1948); also in Peters (1959):2–20. New translation appears in Stern and Sherwood (1966).

Merz, B. 1985. Markers for disease genes open new era in diagnostic screening. *J. Am. Med. Assn.*, 254:3153–3159.

Miller, D. A., O. J. Miller, V. G. Dev, S. Hashmi, and R. Tantravahi. 1974. Human chromosome 19 carries a poliovirus receptor gene. *Cell,* 1:167–173.

Miller, O. J., P. W. Allderdice, D. A. Miller, W. R. Breg, and B. R. Migeon. 1971. Human thymidine kinase gene locus: Assignment to chromosome 17 in a hybrid of man and mouse cells. *Science,* 173:244–245.

Milunsky, A. 1976. Current concepts in genetics: Prenatal diagnosis of genetic disorders. *New Engl. J. Med.,* 295:377–380.

Milunsky, A., J. W. Littlefield, J. N. Kanfer, E. H. Kolodny, V. E. Shih, and L. Atkins. 1970. Prenatal genetic diagnosis. *New Engl. J. Med.,* 283:1370–1381, 1441–1447, 1498–1504.

Moore, K. L., and M. L. Barr. 1955. Smears from the oral mucosa in the detection of chromosomal sex. *Lancet,* 2:57–58.

Moorhead, P. S., and E. Saksela. 1963. Non-random chromosomal aberrations in SV_{40}-transformed human cells. *J. Cell. Comp. Physiol.,* 62:57–83.

Morris, J. M. 1953. The syndrome of testicular feminization in male pseudohermaphrodites. *Am. J. Obstet. Gynecol.,* 65:1192–1211.

Morse, J. O., M. D. Lebowitz, R. J. Knudson, and B. Burrows. 1975. A community study of the relation of α_1-antitrypsin levels to obstructive lung diseases. *New Eng. J. Med.,* 292:278–281.

Morton, N. E. 1958a. Segregation analysis in human genetics. *Science,* 127:79–80.

Morton, N. E. 1958b. Empirical risks in consanguineous marriages. Birth weight, gestation time, and measurement of infants. *Am. J. Hum. Genet.,* 10:344–349.

Morton, N. E. 1959. Genetic tests under incomplete ascertainment. *Am. J. Hum. Genet.,* 11:1–16.

Morton, N. E. 1961. Morbidity of children from consanguineous marriages. *Prog. Med. Genet.,* 1:261–291.

Morton, N. E. 1962. Segregation and linkage. In W. J. Burdette, ed., *Methodology in Human Genetics* (New York: Holden-Day, Inc.), 17–52.

Muller, H. J. 1962. *Studies in Genetics: The Selected Papers of H. J. Muller.* Bloomington: Indiana U. Press.

Nadler, H. L. 1972. Prenatal detection of genetic disorders. *Adv. Hum. Genet.,* 3:1–37.

Nadler, H. L. 1975. Prenatal detection of inborn defects: A status report. *Hosp. Practice,* 10:41–51.

Neel, J. V., and W. J. Schull. 1954. *Human Heredity.* Chicago: U. of Chicago Press.

Neel, J. V., M. Kodani, R. Brewer, and R. C. Anderson. 1949. The incidence of consanguineous matings in Japan. With remarks on the estimation of comparative gene frequencies and the expected rate of appearance of induced recessive mutations. *Am. J. Hum. Genet.,* 1:156–178.

Nettleship, E. 1914. A pedigree of colour-blindness including two colour-blind females. *Roy. London Ophth. Hosp. Rep.,* 19:319–327.

Nienhuis, A. W., and E. J. Benz, Jr. 1977. Regulation of hemoglobin synthesis during the development of the red cell. *New Engl. J. Med.,* 297:1318–1328.

Nowell, P. C., and D. A. Hungerford. 1961. Chromosome studies in human leukemia. II. Chronic granulocytic leukemia. *J. Natl. Cancer Inst.,* 27:1013–1035.

Osborne, R. H., and F. V. DeGeorge. 1959. *The Genetic Basis of Morphological Variation.* Cambridge: Mass.: Harvard University Press.

Paris Conference (1971). Standardization in human cytogenetics. *Birth Defects, Orig. Art. Ser.,* 8(7), 1972.

Pearson, P. 1972. The use of new staining techniques for human chromosome identification. *J. Med. Genet.,* 9:264–275.

Penrose, L. S. 1951. Measurement of pleiotropic effects in phenylketonuria. *Ann. Eugen.,* 16:134–141.

Penrose, L. S. 1961. *Recent Advances in Human Genetics.* Boston: Little, Brown.

Penrose, L. S. 1965. Mongolism as a problem in human biology. In Park, W. W., ed., *The Early Conceptus, Normal and Abnormal: Papers and Discussions Presented at a Symposium Held at Queens College, Dundee, Sept. 17–19, 1964* (Dundee, Scotland: D. C. Thomson for U. of St. Andrew):94–97.

Penrose, L. S., and G. F. Smith. 1966. *Down's Anomaly.* Boston: Little Brown.

Peters, J. A. 1959. *Classic Papers in Genetics.* Englewood Cliffs, N.J.: Prentice-Hall.

Pola, V., and J. Svojitka. 1958. Klassische Hämophilie bei Frauen. *Folia Haematologica* (Leipzig), 75:43–51.

Potter, E. L. 1963. Twin zygosity and placental form in relation to the outcome of pregnancy. *Am. J. Obstet. Gynecol.,* 87:566–577.

Povey, S., D. M. Swallow, M. Bobrow, I. Craig, and V. van Heyningen. 1974. Probable assignment of the locus determining human red cell acid phosphatase ACP_1 to chromosome 2 using somatic hybrids. *Ann. Hum. Genet.,* 38:1–5.

Prochownik, E. V., S. Antonarakis, K. A. Bauer, R. D. Rosenberg, E. R. Fearon, and S. H. Orkin. 1983. Molecular heterogeneity of inherited antithrombin III deficiency. *New Engl. J. Med.,* 308:1549–1552.

Pyeritz, R. E., and V. A. McKusick. 1979. The Marfan syndrome: diagnosis and management. *New Engl. J. Med.,* 300:772–777.

Race, R. R. 1944. An "incomplete" antibody in human serum. *Nature,* 153:771–772.

Race, R. R., and R. Sanger. 1950. *Blood Groups in Man.* Oxford: Blackwell Scientific Publications.

Race, R. R., and R. Sanger. 1962. *Blood Groups in Man.* 4th ed. Oxford: Blackwell Scientific Publications.

Reitalu, J. 1968. Chromosome studies in connection with sex chromosomal deviations in man. *Hereditas,* 59:1–48.

Rhoades, M. M. 1950. Meiosis in maize. *J. Hered.,* 41:58–67.

Roberts, J. A. Fraser. 1967. *An Introduction to Medical Genetics.* 4th ed. New York: Oxford U. Press.

Rohwedder, H. J. 1953. Ein Beitrag zur Frage des Erbganges der Osteogenesis imperfecta Vrolik. *Arch. Kinderheilk.,* 147:256–262.

Rosen, F. S., S. P. Gotoff, J. M. Craig, J. Ritchie, and C. A. Janeway. 1966. Further observations on the Swiss type of agammaglobulinemia (alymphocytosis). The effect of synergic bone-marrow cells. *New Engl. J. Med.,* 274:18–21.

Rothwell, N. V. 1976. *Understanding Genetics.* 2nd ed. Baltimore: Williams and Wilkins.

Rothwell, N. V. 1982. *Understanding Genetics.* 3rd ed. New York: Oxford U. Press.

Rowley, J. D. 1973. A new consistent chromosomal anomaly in chronic myelogenous leukaemia identified by quinacrine fluorescence and Giemsa staining. *Nature,* 243:290–293.

Sandberg, A. A., G. F. Koepf, T. Ishihara, and T. S. Hauscka. 1961. An XYY human male. *Lancet,* 2:488–489.

Sanders, J. 1938. Die Heredität des Albinismus. *Genetica,* 20:97–120.

Schiotz, I. 1922. Rotgrünblindheit als Erbeigenschaft. *Klin. Monatsbl. Augenheilk.,* 68:498–526.

Schimke, R. N. 1978. *Genetics and Cancer in Man.* Edinburgh: Churchill Livingstone.

Schrott, H. G., L. Karp, and G. S. Omenn. 1973. Prenatal detection in myotonic dystrophy: guidelines for genetic counseling. *Clin. Genet.,* 4:38–45.

Schuh, B. E., B. R. Korf, and M. J. Salwen. 1974. A 21/21 tandem translocation with satellites on both long and short arms. *J. Med. Genet.,* 11:297–299.

Schull, W. J., and J. V. Neel, 1958. Empirical risks in consanguineous marriages: sex ratio, malformation, and viability. *Am. J. Hum. Genet.,* 10:294–343.

Schwartz, M. 1953. Allergy. In Sorsby, A., *Clinical Genetics* (London: Butterworths):551–557.

Scott, E. M. 1960. The relation of diaphorase of human erythrocytes to inheritance of methemoglobinemia. *J. Clin. Invest.,* 53:1194–1196.

Scott, J. 1778. An account of a remarkable imperfection in sight. In a letter from J. Scott to the Rev. Mr. Whisson of Trinity College, Cambridge. Communicated by the Rev. Michael Lort. B. D., F.R.S. *Phil. Trans. Royal Soc. London,* 68:611–614.

Seller, M. J. 1974. Alpha-fetoprotein and the prenatal diagnosis of neural tube defects. *Devel. Med. Child Neurol.,* 16:369–371.

Slatis, H. M., R. H. Reis, and R. E. Hoene. 1958. Consanguineous marriages in the Chicago region. *Am. J. Hum. Genet.,* 10:446–464.

Smith, D. W. 1966. Dysmorphology (teratology). *J. Pediat.,* 69:1150–1169.

Smith, E. W., and J. V. Torbert. 1958. Study of two abnormal hemoglobins with evidence for a new genetic locus for hemoglobin formation. *Bull. Johns Hopkins Hosp.,* 102:38–45.

Smits, M., and J. Huizinga. 1961. Familial occurrence of phaeochromocytoma. *Acta Genet. Stat. Med.,* 11:137–153.

Sohar, E., M. Pras, J. Heller, and H. Heller. 1961. Genetics of familial Mediterranean fever (FMF). A disorder with recessive inheritance in non-Ashkenazi Jews and Armenians. *Arch. Int. Med.,* 107:529–538.

Sohar, E., J. Gafni, M. Pras, and H. Heller. 1967. Familial Mediterranean fever: a survey of 470 cases and review of the literature. *Am. J. Med.,* 43:227–253.

Southern, E. M. 1975. Detection of specific sequences among DNA fragments separated by gel electrophoresis. *J. Mol. Biol.,* 98:503–517.

Spritz, R. A., and B. G. Forget. 1983. The thalassemias: molecular mechanisms of human genetic disease. *Am. J. Hum. Genetics,* 35:333–361.

Stern, C. 1953. Model estimates of the frequency of white and near-white segregants in the American Negro. *Acta Genet. Stat. Med.,* 4:281–298.

Stern, C. 1960. *Principles of Human Genetics.* 2nd ed. San Francisco: W. H. Freeman.

Stern, C. 1973. *Principles of Human Genetics.* 3rd ed. San Francisco: W. H. Freeman.

Stern, C., and E. R. Sherwood. 1966. *The Origin of Genetics: a Mendel Source Book.* New York and London: W. H. Freeman.

Stevens, W. L. 1938. Estimation of blood-group gene frequencies. *Ann. Eugen.,* 8:362–375.

Stevenson, A. C., and E. A. Cheeseman. 1956. Hereditary deafmutism, with particular reference to Northern Ireland. *Ann. Hum. Genet.,* 20:177–231.

Strong, L. C., V. M. Riccardi, R. E. Ferrell, R. S. Sparkes. 1981. Familial retinoblastoma and chromosome 13 deletion transmitted via an insertional translocation. *Science,* 213:1501–1503.

Sutter, J., and L. Tabah. 1958. *Recherches Sur les Effets de la Consanguité chez L'Homme.* Lons-le-Saunier: Declume Press.

Swift, M. 1976. Malignant disease in heterozygous carriers. *Birth Defects, Orig. Art. Ser.,* 12:133–144.

Taillard, W., and A. Prader. 1957. Étude génétique du syndrome de féminisation testiculaire totale et partielle. *J. Génét. Hum.,* 6:13–32.

Tanaka, K. R., W. N. Valentine, and S. Miwa. 1962. Pyruvate kinase (PK) deficiency hereditary hemolytic anemia. *Blood,* 19:267–295.

Taylor, K., and R. Briggs. 1957. A mildly affected female hemophiliac. *Br. Med. J.,* 1:1494–1496.

Thorsby, E. 1974. The human major histocompatibility system. *Transpl. Rev.,* 18:51–129.

Thorsby, E. 1976. Personal communication to the author.

Tips, R. L. 1954. A study of the inheritance of atopic sensitivity in man. *Am. J. Hum. Genet.,* 6:328–343.

Tjio, J. H., and A. Levan. 1956. The chromosome number of man. *Hereditas,* 42:1–6.

Turner, H. H. 1938. A syndrome of infantilism, congenital webbed neck, and cubitus valgus. *Endocrinol.,* 23:566–574.

Valentine, W. N., A. S. Schneider, M. A. Baughan, D. W. Paglia, and H. L. Heins, Jr. 1966. Hereditary hemolytic anemia with triosephosphate isomerase deficiency; studies in kindreds with coexistent sickle cell trait and erythrocyte glucose-6-phosphate dehydrogenase deficiency. *Am. J. Med.,* 41:27–47.

Valls, A. 1967. Consanguineous marriages in a Spanish population. *Acta Genet. Stat. Med.,* 17:112–119.

Watson, J. D. and D.H.C. Crick. 1953. Molecular structure of nucleic acids. A structure for deoxyribosenucleic acid. *Nature,* 171:737–738.

Weinberg, W. 1920. Methodologische Gesichtpunkte für die statistiche Untersuchung der Vererbung bei Dementia praecox. *Ztschr. ges. Neurologie Psychiat.,* 59:39–50.

Westerveld, A., and P. Meera Khan. 1972. Evidence for linkage between human loci for 6-phosphogluconate dehydrogenase and phosphoglucomutase$_1$ in man-Chinese hamster somatic cell hybrids. *Nature,* 236:30–32.

WHO-Iuis Terminology Committee. 1975. Nomenclature for factors of the HLA system. *Histocompatibility Testing 1975:*5–11.

Wiener, A. S. 1950. Heredity of the Rh blood types. IX. Observations in a series of 526 cases of disputed paternity. *Am. J. Hum. Genet.,* 2:177–197.

Wiener, A. S. 1967. Elements of blood group nomenclature with special reference to the Rh-Hr blood types. *J. Am. Med. Assn.,* 199:985–989.

Wiener, A. S. 1968. Modern blood group nomenclature. *J. Am. Med. Technol.,* 30:174–179.

Wiener, A. S., and I. B. Wexler. 1958. *Heredity of the Blood Groups.* New York: Grune and Stratton.

Wiener, A. S., E. B. Gordon, and J. P. Wexler. 1963. The M-N types, with special reference to the mating MN × MN. *Exp. Med. Surg.,* 21:89–100.

Wildervanck, L. S. 1950a. Hereditary congenital anomalies of bones and nails in five generations. Luxation of the capitulum radii, luxation or absence, resp. hypoplasia of the patella, crooked little fingers and dystrophy or absence of the nails and abnormal lunulae. *Genetica,* 25:1–28.

Wildervanck, L. S. 1950b. Hereditary congenital abnormalities of the elbows, knees and nails in five generations. *Acta Radiol.,* 33:41–48.

Wolf, C. B., A. Peterson, G. A. Logrippo, and L. Weiss. 1967. Ring 1 chromosome and dwarfism—a possible syndrome. *J. Pediat.,* 71:719–722.

Woolf, C. M. 1971. Congenital cleft lip: a genetic study of 496 propositi. *J. Med. Genet.,* 8:65–83.

Woolf, C. M., F. E. Stephens, D. D. Muliak, and R. E. Gilbert. 1956. An investigation of the frequency of consanguineous marriages among the Mormons and their relatives in the United States. *Am. J. Hum. Genet.,* 8:236–252.

Woolf, C. M., R. M. Woolf, and T. R. Broadbent. 1964. Cleft lip and heredity. *Plast. Reconstruct. Surg.,* 34:11–14.

Wright, S. 1931. Evolution in Mendelian populations. *Genetics,* 16:97–159.

Yunis, J. J. 1976. High resolution of human chromosomes. *Science* 191:1268–1270.

Zinkham, W. H., A. Blanco, and L. Kupchyk. 1966. Isozymes: biological and clinical significance. *Pediat.,* 37:120–131.

Zourlas, P. A., and H. W. Jones, Jr. 1965. Clinical, histologic and cytogenetic findings in male hermaphroditism. II. Male hermaphrodites with feminine external genitalia (testicular feminization). *Obstet. Gynecol.,* 25:768–778.

Zuelzer, W. W., J. V. Neel, and A. R. Robinson. 1956. Abnormal hemoglobins. *Prog. Hematol.,* 1:91–137.

Index

Particularly common terms, such as DNA, gene, gamete, protein, polypeptide, are indexed only selectively. Many compounds are indexed under the more unusual portion of the name. With the exception of the list of names on page 247 (which is not indexed), names of persons are indexed if they appear in the narrative but not in connection with a reference. Italic indicates a figure or its legend.